PERSPECTIVES IN RESOURCE MANAGEMENT IN DEVELOPING COUNTRIES

VOLUME- 1
Resource Management: Theory and Techniques

Perspectives in Resource Management in Developing Countries

About the Editor

Professor B. Thakur, Vice-Chancellor of L. N. Mithila University, Darbhanga holds substantive position in the Department of Geography, Delhi School of Economics, University of Delhi. He is also the President-Elect of National Association of Geographers, India. His 38 years of experience include interests in resource management, natural hazards and urban development at the Universities of Ranchi, Patna, Waterloo, Akron, Delhi and Mithila. He was a Commonwealth Scholar at the University of Waterloo (Canada) and Fulbright Visiting Professor at the University of Akron (USA). He has successfully supervised 13 Ph.D. Theses, 30 M.Phil and 50 M.A. dissertations. He has authored a book on *Urban Settlements in Eastern India: Entropy Changes and Pattern Analysis* (Concept, 1979) and edited volumes on *Geographic and Planning Research Themes for the New Millennium* (with Noble, Mukerji and Costa, Vikas, 2000); *Recent Advances in Geomorphology, Quaternary Geology and Environmental Geosciences: Indian Case Studies, Felicitation Volume in Honour of Professor V.K. Verma* (with S. K. Tandon, Manisha, 2002). *Geography in Delhi: Research Themes and Perspectives* (Manisha, 2003) and *Perspectives in Resource Management in Developing Countries* in 14 Volumes (Concept, 2003, in Press) and has published 60 research papers in journals of India and abroad. Professor Thakur has shouldered many responsibilities, such as Secretary General of National Association of Geographers, India; Recorder and President of Earth System Sciences of Indian Science Congress Association; Editor and President of Association for Geographical Studies, Delhi University; and Chairman of the Commission on Natural Hazards and Resource Management of NAGI.

Concept's International Series in Geography— 5

PERSPECTIVES IN RESOURCE MANAGEMENT IN DEVELOPING COUNTRIES

VOLUME- 1

Resource Management: Theory and Techniques

Edited by
BALESHWAR THAKUR
Professor of Geography
Department of Geography
Delhi University, Delhi

Currently, Vice-Chancellor
L.N. Mithila University
Darbhanga

CONCEPT PUBLISHING COMPANY, NEW DELHI-110059

ISBN 81-8069-037-7 (Vol. 1)
ISBN 81-8069-036-9 (Series)

First Published 2003

Published and Printed by
Ashok Kumar Mittal
Concept Publishing Company
A/15-16, Commercial Block, Mohan Garden
New Delhi-110059 (INDIA)

Phones : 25351460, 25351794
Fax : 091-11-25357103
Email : publishing@conceptpub.com

Dedicated to
My Wife
Chanda Thakur

Preface

Thinking minds in the developing world today are deeply concerned at the massive quantitative expansion in the population size and the concomitant pressure on natural resources. This population pressure has often exceeded the carrying capacity of the land as traditionally used. It has resulted in loss of cultivated lands, disappearance of forests, soil erosion, energy crisis, ecological imbalances, pollution hazards, environmental harassment, regional water shortage and deterioration of water quality. Little wonder that we cannot maintain a growing population at a high standard of living without adequate natural resources. Thus, natural resource studies have become a subject of great importance in the perpetuation and enrichment of civilized human existence and, ultimately, even our biological survival.

The purpose of this multi-volume series is, therefore, to contribute to and provide scientific knowledge on natural resources in developing countries for their rational and sustainable development. It creates an understanding of the critical and decisive role that resource development and management play in today's society by an intelligent garnering of natural resources, restocking of forests and the achievement of a long-term rotational agro-forestry, arresting of soil erosion and depletion, prudent management of range and preservation of fish reserves and mammals.

Identifying current issues and responses of renewable and non-renewable resources, it suggests scientific techniques to permit greater flexibility and sophistication in the assessment of alternative management schemes, and demonstrates the role of new technological developments in their inventory and appraisal. Assessing the impact of natural hazards in resource management, it develops a scientific basis for integrated resource management and probes deeply into the questions of future resource supply as well as adequacy.

B. THAKUR

Acknowledgements

More than a decade has elapsed since the multi-volume project was launched by Concept Publishing Company. During this journey many geographers have contributed advice, comments and ideas in preparation of this work. Particularly, I have greatly benefited from the interaction with Professor (Mrs.) Savitri G. Burman, Professor R. Ramachandran, Professor R.P., Misra, Professor P. Dayal and Professor V.K. Verma. I would like to thank particularly Mrs. Preeti Joshi, Dr. P.K. Parihar and Dr. Ramashray Prasad who offered helpful comments in reviewing the articles.

Some already published materials have also been reproduced, because these still have great relevance. I would like to offer my thanks to these authors and publishers who have allowed the use of copyrighted materials.

I express my deepest gratitude to Shri Ashok K. Mittal of Concept Publishing Company for his full dedication, encouragement, support and suggestions in creating a special working environment. The 'computer age' made this endeavour more efficient and expedient. I am thankful to Shri Bachi Ram, Cartographer, for his cartographic assistance.

I must thank my wonderful wife, Chanda, who gave me so much support, inspiration and practical help. I would specially like to thank my sons Sudhir and Rajiv, and daughter-in-law Raj Rani and Madhuri, who took on onerous task of checking the completeness of the references for every chapter of the book.

I hope this book will stimulate and generate an new thinking on natural resource management in general and developing countries in particular and would be popular among the students and teachers of natural resource management, planners, administrators and policy makers.

B. THAKUR
Vice-Chancellor
L.N.M.U., Darbhanga

Publisher's Note

Concept Publishing Company has successfully launched its multi-volume series entitled "Concept's International Series in Geography." Till date four multi-volume series have already been published and well received among the academic world. The details of the series are as follows:

1) Perspectives in Agricultural Geography, edited by *Dr. Noor Mohammad* (In 4 volumes)
2) Perspectives in Urban Geography, edited by *Dr. C.S. Yadav* (In 16 volumes)
3) Perspectives in Geomorphology by *Dr. H.S. Sharma* (In 4 volumes)
4) New Dimensions in Agricultural Geography, edited by *Dr. Noor Mohammad* (In 8 volumes)

The present series was initiated about more than a decade ago. We have received an encouraging response from the scholars around the world. Although it took long time to see the light of the day, the problems in utilization and management of Natural Resources are still the same and a great concern for the sustainable development in the developing countries.

This series is planned in fourteen volumes. Each volume covers one particular natural resource, in detail.

Ashok K. Mittal
Publisher

Contents

SUSTAINABLE RESOURCE DEVELOPMENT

TECHNOLOGY AND RESOURCES

List of Contributors

Agunbiade, Boye, Ph.D. Nigerian Institute of Social and Economic Research P.M.B.5, U.I. Post Office, Ibadan, Nigeria.

Armstrong, Patrick, Department of Geography, University of Western Australia, Nedlands, Western Australia, 6009

Bansal, Manju, Sarwar, Nikhat and **Mukerji, K.G.**, Applied Mycology Laboratory, Department of Botany, University of Delhi, Delhi-110007

Batisse Michel, Senior Environmental Adviser United Nations Educational Scientific and Cultural Organisation (UNESCO) 7, Place de Fontency, 75352 Paris 07 SP France.

Bilsborrow, Richard E. and **DeLargy, Pamela F.**, Caroline Population Centre, The University of North Caroline at Chapel Hill, University Square, CB=8120 123 West Franklin Street Chapel Hill, NC 27516-3997 (U.S.A.)

Burman, G. Savitri is Retd. Professor and Head, Department of Geography, Delhi School of Economics, University of Delhi, Delhi.

Conacher, A.J., Department of Geography, The University of Western Australia, Nedlands, WA 6009, Australia.

Coppock, J.T., is Ogilvie Professor of Geography, University of Edinburgh.

Dasgupta, Partha, Professor, University of Cambridge, Faculty of Economics and Politics, Austin Robinson Building, Sidgwick Avenue, Cambridge CB3 9DD (U.K.)

De Gregori, Thomas R., Department of Economics, college of Social Sciences, University of Houston, Houston, Texas 77204-5882, U.S.A.

Derrick Sewell, W.R. Departments of Economics and Geography, University of Victoria, Victoria, British Columbia, Canada.

Jeroen, C.J.M. van den Bergh and **Nijkamp, Peter**, Faculty of Economics, Free University, P.O. Box 7161, 1007 MC Amsterdam, The Netherlands.

Jodha, N.S., International Centre for Integrated Mountain Development, P.O. Box 3226, Kathmandu, Nepal.

Kumar, S. Suresh, Scientist-Coordinator, Planning and Incharge, Polytechnology Transfer Centre, Regional Research Laboratory, Thruvananthapuram-695019

Mitchell, Bruce, Department of Geography, University of Waterloo, Waterloo, Ontario, Canada N2L 3GI.

Mukerji, K.G., Applied Mycology Laboratory, Department of Botany, University of Delhi, Delhi-110007

Muthoo, M.K., engaged in a research project at the Commonwealth Forestry Institute, University of Oxford, England.

Pimentel, D., Department of Entomology, Cornell University, Ithaca, NY 14853, USA.

Prasad, Maheshwari, Professor of Geography, Ranchi University, Ranchi, Bihar.

Rampal, K.K., Professor, Department of Civil Engg. Indian Institute of Technology, Kanpur (UP) 208016

Raza, Moonis, Former Professor Emeritus, Jawaharlal Nehru University, Vice-Chancellor, University of Delhi.

Redclift, Michael, Wye College, University of London, Wye, Ashford, Kent TN25 5AH, U.K.

Shariff, Ismail, Professor/Chair Economics, University of Wisconsin-Green Bay, 2420 Nicolet Drive, Green Bay, Wisconsin 54311-7001 (U.S.A.)

Simon, David, D.Phil. (Oxon.) Centre for Developing Areas Research, Department of Geography, Royal Holloway and Bedford New College, University of London, Egham Hill, Egham TW 20 0EX, England, U.K.

Singh, C.P., Professor of Geography, Delhi School of Economics, University of Delhi, Delhi-110007

Singh, R.B. and **Khan, A.R.,** Department of Geography, Delhi School of Economics, University of Delhi, Delhi-110007

Srivastava, V.K., Assistant Professor, Department of Applied Geophysics, Indian School of Mines, Dhanbad-826004

Thakur, Baleshwar, Professor of Geography, Delhi School of Economics, Delhi University, Delhi , currently Vice-Chancellor L.N. Mithila University, Darbhanga.

Tisdell, Clem, Professor of Economics, Department of Economics, The University of Queensland, Brisbane Qld 4072, Australia.

Introduction

BALESHWAR THAKUR

This volume provides the practitioner access to the most practical and recent thinking on the subject of natural resource management including models, theories and paradigms. This will, therefore, be an essential reading for those concerned with the resource management process as it operates both in developed and developing countries. It elaborates the concepts of renewal and non-renewable resources, ecological, economic, behavioural and integrated approaches and emphasizes an approach to sustainable development of resources. It also demonstrates the use of Geographic Information Systems and Remote Sensing Techniques in inventory and appraisal of natural resources, to improve the quality of decision-making as well as in monitoring and evaluation of public policy.

Resource managers and developers in the developing world today are deeply concerned at the massive quantitative expansion in population size and the concomitant pressure on natural resources. This population pressure has often exceeded the carrying capacity of land as traditionally used. It has resulted in loss of cultivated lands, disappearance of forests, soil erosion, energy crisis, ecological imbalances, pollution hazards, environmental harassment, regional water shortage and deterioration of water quality. Little wonder that we cannot maintain a growing population at a high standard of living without adequate natural resources. Thus, natural resource studies have become a subject of great importance in the perpetuation and enrichment of human existence in the Third World and, ultimately, even our biological survival. The volume leads to an understanding of the critical and decisive role that resource development and management play in today's society by an intelligent garnering of natural resources, restocking of forests and the achievement of a long-term rotational agro-forestry, arresting of soil erosion and depletion, prudent management of range and preservation of fish reserve and mammals. Such studies also identify current issues and responses of renewable and non-renewable resources, suggest scientific techniques to permit greater flexibility and sophistication in the assessment of alternative management schemes, demonstrate the role of new technological developments in their inventory and appraisal, assess the impact of natural hazards in resource management, develop a scientific basis for integrated resource management, and probe deeply into the questions of future resource supply and adequacy.

All living and non-living elements of tropical regions including deserts, oceans, the atmosphere and the interior of the earth have become valuable resources for raising the standard of living of the growing numbers. In reality, improved natural resource utilization without excessive environmental damage is necessary to provide an acceptable quality of life for current and future generations. In the past, in the absence of accepted methodologies and criteria, resource evaluation was a highly subjective process based on experience and trial and error, beset with incomplete information at the regional level. At present our management decisions concerning resource utilization must not be based on fantasy or a simplistic slogan: they require the understanding of the parts of the physical, biological and socio-economic systems involved in any region. This understanding is based on accurate resource inventory, but goes much further to consider the linkages and interactions between the different parts of the systems. Hence, one of the important functions of geography and related disciplines, involved more specifically with research and planning of natural resources, is to seek the means of improving the ways in which natural resources in the regional framework may be surveyed, assessed and utilized scientifically and managed efficiently to meet our growing needs in the developing countries in the future.

Geographers have played a major role in promoting resource management as a serious area of academic study. Indeed, resource management has probably proven to be a major integrating point for physical and human geographers. It is, therefore, not surprising that geographers should be at the forefront in detailing the complexity of the social-physical resource interface and the institutional arrangements which surround biological and physical resource development.

Concept

In this sub-field a considerable confusion exits amongst students, resource managers and environmental practitioners between the concepts of resource management and environmental management. Conacher in his article on "Resources and Environmental Management: Some Fundamental Concepts and Definitions" briefly considers the difference between them. The standard and widely accepted definition of Zimmermann (1951) is preferred. Resources are a cultural concept and are socially defined and are, therefore, products of society. The characteristics of resources and of environment, the means used to measure them, and the goals of the two managements are quite distinct. The environment has been defined in a systems conceptual sense as being the environments of resource systems. Resource management goals are usually more specific, more immediate and more clearly defined than those of environmental management. Goals of resource management are often single-purpose, whereas those of environmental management are invariably multi-purpose. This is because the former focuses on its resource system, while the latter with resource system and their environments. Resource management seeks single solutions to problems within the resource system only often in engineering and economic terms, whereas environmental management is concerned with the adaptability of complex environments. Resource managers are environmentally aware, whereas environmental problems turn out to be a conflict between two or more competing resource systems. This means environmental management focuses on the functional links between resource systems and their environments, and to attain desirable environmental system states. The focus is on quality in response to community values and aspirations; whereas that of the resource manager is on quantity, always in material and in monetary terms. Thus, the goals, methodologies, expertise and attitudes of the two managerial groups are seen to be totally different according to Conacher.

Muthoo in his paper on "Concept of Renewable Resources" has critically assessed the different resource classification schemes proposed by Ciriacy-Wantrup (1942), Hammar (1942), Heady (1950), Crawford (1952) and Allen and Leonard (1966); and expressed dissatisfaction at exhaustible and inexhaustible, and stock and flow resources classification having no accord with economic significance between economic concept and physical quantities of resources. He formulated a conceptual frame within which a rational classification of resources becomes possible as well as meaningful in the perspective of resource development and management strategy. To bring out the distinction between renewable and non-renewable resources, Muthoo's illustration is useful. The former could be used and yet he renewed subject to the limitations set by the frame of nature and technological availability, whereas the latter are depleted as when used up. One of the author's main objectives is on the renewability criterion applied for the resource classification as this concept automatically takes care of the relation of an exploitation strategy on resources. It is with the help of the renewability concept that a region can save itself from the grim consequences of absolute physical scarcity, depletion of resources and finally, catastrophic collapse of the society. This essay briefly points out that the renewable resource systems are eco-systems and attempts to infuse ecological thinking into resource functions. It explains how their survival depends on mutual harmony between them and the human activity. To bring out the essential role of man in the renewable resource system, Muthoo's illustration with the help of a biotic pyramid array of natural resources is useful. The entire system is conceived as a conglomerate of the mutual interactions between man and the resources and the system depicted embodies interdependent and interacting physical and biological features of the environment. In his view, the systems analysis calls for an ecological way of looking at nature so as to combine together the diverse fields of environmental sciences involved in the use of resources. Perhaps, therefore, Muthoo suggests, that a careful coordination between environmental science (understanding of the biosphere) and the environmental technology (manipulation skills of man) could provide the basis for the sustainable use of natural resources. However, Rees (1991, 8) suggests conventional typology of renewable (flows) and non-renewable (stocks) as misleading because it has limited value in the debate over future resource availability. Instead, she suggests of resource 'continuum' rather than of stocks and flows.

The problem of exhaustible mineral resources is considered from an economists viewpoint by Dasgupta in his essay on "Exhaustible Resources". Man has been exhausting the earth's resources ever since he climbed down from the trees and minerals and the fuel resources are the hardest hit. Mineral demands are increasing exponentially not only with population increase but also with rising living standards. Therefore, many mineral economists including Dasgupta foresee an impending critical increase of the need for several ores. This will lead to an even greater reliance by industrial nations on imports, and to possible scarcity and increasing costs of several minerals that today are in adequate supply. Phosphates, some trace elements and especially fossil fuels are likely to run out in the foreseeable future. Heavy use of such resources cannot be sustained indefinitely and scarcity will ultimately occur. The problem must lie in far-sighted research and the development of new technology. According to Dasgupta recycling has been seen as a palliative to expand the resource base. He also adds to the view that our society will settle into a steady-state of substitution, which we may call the age of substitutability. Resource substitutability is thus regarded as a key to understanding the economics of exhaustible resources. But, is this age of substitutability merely a dream or is it a real possibility?

The non-renewable resources, consisting of non-living things especially fuels and metals, are being depleted at a rate which is fast increasing. They have taken millions of years to form and so from a human perspective are now fixed in supply (Rees, 1985). Their physical quantity does not increase significantly with time. It is an urgent task for all of us concerned to ensure an adequate supply of non-renewable resources for coming generations; but it is full of uncertainties. The determination of the future prospects of these resources is complicated and fraught with both measurement and conceptual problems (Berry, Conkling and Ray, 1993). There are conflicting views on the measurement of its quantity. The environmentalist view, according to Berry, Conkling and Ray (1993) is "that the world has a fixed upper carrying capacity of population that it can support and of resources that it can supply. Technology can raise current levels toward, but not beyond, the full potential of the world's productive capacity. The environmentalist focus is long-term. Its concern is with the results of the next doubling of the world's population and the impact of that doubling on environmental pollution and on demands for resources". The economists view is quite contrary to the environmentalist view. According to Berry, Conkling and Ray (1993), "resources are not fixed in amount but created in response to needs, through market mechanisms. If a resource becomes scarce, its price rises and the quantity consumed drops. The price increase stimulates an increase in the supply of the product and a search for substitute products." Thus it is quite clear from both the viewpoints that the environmentalist's view is appealing and pragmatic, and has widespread recognition.

With all those problems and resource management issues, resource geographers and others in related disciplines practice in many different resource fields and with various perspectives: for example, resource appraisal, institutional arrangements, perceptions and attitudes, policy and decision-making processes, environmental and socio-economic impact assessments, public involvement, hazard and risk assessment, resource planning etc. The field is interdisciplinary and highly fragmented with strong empirical and policy-oriented emphasis. Still, these broad components have been the focus of the construction and development of many conceptual models. Mitchell in his paper on "Models of Resource Management" describes the role and application of models in both resource analysis and resource management. These models are grouped as biophysical, economic, cultural and integrative and are evaluated using Bunge's four standards (clarity, simplicity, generality and accuracy) and Kuhn's three categories of research (determination of significant fact, establishment of relationship, and articulation of theory). Mitchell notes that such models "have yet to lead to the generation of a geographical theory of natural resources" or of a more limited theory applicable to a specific open problem in resource management.

Approaches

Resource management field is inter-disciplinary in nature in which varieties of approaches have been developed to provide a framework for the rational use and management of natural resources. They are gleaned from a very large and varied literature and are well searched viewpoint. The approaches have been developed to protect/safeguard natural resources against their reckless exploitation and misuse by human and animal population. Also they draw attention to the consequences of his perverse or inadvertent interference with their intricate workings of the natural systems. Currently, it has been seen that the world's most pressing social, economic and political problems are valid topics are resource management analysis (O'Riordan, 1971). According to him, the major focus of attention for the geographer interested in resource management should be to clarify the various issues involved in order to provide a clearer basis for public judgment and social action (O'Riordan, 1971). As geographers, we believe it is vital to emphasize that some of the most significant problems in resource management can be examined only in their appropriate local settings: that is, we must never lose sight of the undeniable authenticity, the uniqueness of the economic, political and physical milieu of each region (Powell, 1980, 7). There are at present five major approaches to resource management which influence the questions that the practitioners ask and the methods that they employ. They are ecological, economic, behavioural integrated and policy making.

Ecological

This approach is also called as physical science (Ferguson and Alley, 1984, 37) which focuses upon natural sciences, the good earth and the empirical method. These are shared by geomorphologists, climatologists, hydrologists and biogeographers who attempt to find solutions to problems of resource management in the measurement of physical attributes. This approach stresses upon nature and limits of resource but is silent about the human implications. Our ecological environment, although infinitely complex and varied, is a dynamic and organic whole. It is in a constant state of flux and is characterized by the dynamics of a certain number of interacting elements. We must understand these mechanisms, take them into account to make better use of the environment. Every intervention modifies this dynamics and affects the interactions and so does every development. Perhaps more significant is the fact that in order to attain the required goal, resource development should take full account of these dynamics and interdependencies. According to Tricart and Kiewietde Jonge (1992), a rational management of the environment can be understood only through a knowledge of its dynamics. The study of the interrelationships that exist between organisms and their environment is known as ecology. Odum (1971) has commented that "conservation in the broadest sense is probably the most important application of ecology." Over the last two decades (1970s and 1980s) the conservation lobby has become more vocal and effective in creating a popular awareness and scientific interest in environmental damage. And also it was becoming increasingly unacceptable because this damage could have serious repercussions for mankind. As a consequence, resource developers have increasingly begun to recognise that some kind of understanding of ecological processes is necessary before major resource development schemes are implemented (O'Riordan, 1979). Ramade (1981, 1) has drawn attention to the fact that since ecosphere is the origin of all natural resources except solar energy, it is easy to appreciate the importance of ecological science to the understanding of problems caused by the exploitation and consumption of such resources in our present technological civilization.

The systems approach has been incorporated in the analysis and management of environmental systems which not only includes the physical components solely, but economic and social considerations as well. To quote Quade (1968), "systems analysis involves a systematic approach to helping a decision-maker choose a course of action by investigating his full problem, searching out objectives and alternatives and comparing them in the light of their consequences, using an appropriate framework—in so far as possible analytic—to bring expert judgment and interaction to bear on the problem". There has thus been the advent of systems techniques which have been increasingly applied to environmental problems and have also proved to be promising in the analysis and management of resources. Arising from this system perspective is the ecosystem theory which has an interesting repute in its own contributions. This theory came to formally exist after a pioneering paper authored by Tansley (1935) who suggested the concept of an ecosystem. He used it to express an older body of ideas that populations of plants and animals interact with each other and their non-living environment in a systematic way. The ecosystem could be defined as "any unit—that includes all of the organisms in a given area interacting with the physical environment, so that a flow of energy leads to clearly defined tropic structure, biotic diversity and material cycles within the system (Odum, 1971). The ecosystem is the basic functional unit in ecology (Evans, 1956), since it includes both organisms and the abiotic environment, each influencing the properties of the other and both necessary for the maintenance of life on the earth.

A natural resource ecosystem forms integrated system, an element of which is a product which is of direct or indirect significance to man. The product may be biological or physical, the former including forests, ranges, agricultural products, wildlife, marine life etc., while the latter ones would include water, air, land and soil. Every natural resource ecosystem involves man directly in the complex set of ecological interactions. As management involves the manipulation of the ecosystem by man, beneficial management would involve manipulation to maximize returns, while exploitation would lead to a reduction of the productivity of the ecosystem over a long period of time. The efficient management of renewable resources depends on a knowledge of the interrelationships of the organisms of various levels of activity and their relations to abiotic subsystems. This knowledge of relationship among parts of the system has been applied to the management of systems in which such pairs of components exit, assuming that significant relationships for each system have been studied. Resource management involves similar goals of output maximization and cost reduction, along with protecting the producing capital of resources for the future use. It, therefore, assumes paramount importance in the decision-making of utilizing any kind of resource, because no matter what type of resource man manages, the sole objective is to optimize the harvest, i.e., to obtain maximum production. As outlined by Bennett and Chorley (1978) the more complex the segment of the real world, the greater the likelihood that it will be modelled like a synthetic system, and the ecosystem provides a prime example of systems synthesis, but the application is questionable, mainly because of the cross cuttings of the diverse information systems which may alter or disrupt the analysis of the system under study. It is in this context that Chorley (1973) has outlined that the ecological model may fail to encompass the activities of an important and rapidly expanding portion of social and economic life styles. To overcome these problems we need to develop more complex method of systems interfacing between physico-ecological and socio-economic systems. Resource management and analysis has become a highly integrated science, which needs the cooperation of a number of environmental specialists. The synthesizing of the geographer in such a field has been evidenced by the contribution of geographers like Burton and Kates (1965), Mitchell (1989), O'Riordan (1971) and Simmons (1974).

For rational use of natural resources in biosphere all efforts must depend on basic ecological principles and models proposed by many ecologists over a decade. Bansal, Sarwar and Mukerji in their essay on "Application of Ecological Principles in Conservation of Natural Resources" dwell upon five such fundamental ecological variables determining these principles. They are energy, space, matter, time and diversity. It is stressed that the priorities for resource conservation should be: (i) maintenance of essential ecological processes and life support system (i.e., regulation and protection of soils, maintenance of food webs, major energy and nutrient cycles, purification of water etc.); (ii) the preservation of genetic diversity on which most of these processes depend for their function; and (iii) ensuring long-term exploitation of ecosystems and species. Working on these priorities and taking care of all fundamental ecological principles, the various renewable and non-renewable resources can be conserved for future generation.

Contrary to common belief, environmental degradation or degradation of a natural resource is not the result of a single activity but results from the combined effects of all the economic activities in the locality and its neighbouring regions as well as the physical character, capabilities, and interlinkages of the locality itself. The article by Burman on "Ecological Interlinkages in Resource Management and Development" draws attention to the interlinkages between different physical parameters of the ecosystem which are utilised as natural resources either directly, as land, minerals, biotic etc. or indirectly, in the processing and production of economic goods like energy, air, water etc. It also throws light on the connection between the physical system, the natural resources and the human usages of these resources. The paper analyses methodologies adopted by some of the traditional systems of agriculture like grazing systems and utilisation of long slopes by adapting the village structure in the Himalayas; to utilise the natural system to their optimum level. The outstanding character of these traditional systems is the adaptation of the humans to get the most out of each situation in terms of locality, product, time and available technology. The paper notes that the concept of development began to change drastically in the 20th century, especially in the latter half, and in the countries freed from colonial rule and which were termed 'under-developed'. The latter word implying that their natural resources had not been harnessed to the fullest extent. The overall policy of all these nations, which largely lie in the tropics has been formed with the objective of developing their natural resources as fast as possible with the help of latest technology. The technology, unfortunately, being imported from the temperate region or the 'advanced nations', coupled with lack of knowledge of the basic interlinkages and processe in the ecosystems of the tropical regions have brought about many environmental and linked social problems. A few of these problems are analysed in this article. It also suggests very briefly some strategies suitable for sustainable development, including the efficacy of using watershed as a unit for sustainable development.

Probably the most significant influence of ecology on resource management has been the concept of biosphere reserve developed within the framework of UNESCO's MAB programme as a multifunctional tool to protect biodiversity, promote sustainable landscape resources development and ensure local people's participation. This programme has been unusually strong, seeing national parks and other protected areas as part of a cooperative network of institutions and mechanisms working for better scientific understanding of the environment and better protection and use of it (Nelson, 1987, 293). The IUCN (1985) has provided the following descriptions of biosphere reserve: "It is intended to consume representative natural areas throughout the world through creation of global and national networks of reserves. It includes representative natural biomes, or communities, species of unique interest, examples of harmonious landscapes resulting from traditional uses, and modified or degraded landscapes capable of restoration to more natural conditions. Biosphere reserves provide benchmarks for monitoring environmental change and areas for science, education and training." Batisse's article on "Developing and Focusing the Biosphere Reserve Concept" deals with the evolution, present content and formulation of the biosphere reserve concept. This concept has emerged from UNESCO's Man and the Biosphere Programme (MAB). The idea originated from the 1968 Conference on the Rational Use and Conservation of the Resources of the Biosphere as an international and interdisciplinary research programme with objective to provide the scientific knowledge for sound and sustainable management of land resources. It aimed at the conservation of ecosystems by preserving representative samples of significant ecosystems, original habitats of domesticated plants and animals, and remnant populations of rare and endangered species. More dimensions were added to this emerging concept in 1969 through identifying a coordinated worldwide network of national parks, biological reserves and other protected areas. However, its first official reference was made in 1970. As a tool of environmental management, biosphere reserves has been used in three ways, namely: (1) as a conservation role to maintain biological diversity, (2) as a logistic rule by setting up international network of areas for field research and monitoring activities, and (3) as a development role by associating environmental protection and land resources development as a governing principle for research and education. By 1992, 311 biosphere reserves were located in eighty-one countries. Batisse calls it a hasty blossoming. A special task-force was convened in Paris in 1974 jointly by UNESCO an UNEP and drew up a set of objectives and stressed the multiple functions of biosphere reserves. It proposed a generalized zoning pattern for biosphere reserves: core area (strictly protected), buffer zone (strictly delineated, and transition area (undelineated). The concept was given impetus at the First International Biosphere Reserve Congress, held in

Minsk (USSR) in 1983 and drew up a 'World Action Plan for Biosphere Reserves'. The author has proposed a schematic spatial distribution pattern of biosphere reserve functions as follows: (1) each biosphere reserve includes one or several core areas that are strictly protected and should be representative of the surrounding ecosystems; (2) the size and shape of the core areas depend on the type landscape in which they are located; (3) core areas may correspond to 'strict nature reserves', to wilderness area or to other types of strictly protected areas; (4) the core areas are normally surrounded by a buffer zone; (5) the buffer zone must have a clearly established legal or administrative status; (6) the core areas and the buffer zone are surrounded by a transition area and this area corresponds more to biogeographic than to administrative units. The transition area extends into a larger and open area where attempts are made to bring out cooperative activities between researchers, managers and the local population; and management of this area is commonly the responsibility of a variety of authorities; (7) partly within the buffer zone or outside, a biosphere reserve may include many types of associated areas to develop knowledge and skills for ecosystem use and management; (8) cluster biosphere reserve combining a number of non-contiguous areas serving the same or different functions. Finally, it is suggested that the real success lies when all possible functions of the biosphere reserve are fully operational and properly coordinated through an overall management plan, taking the transition area into account.

In another scintillating paper on "Development and Implementation of the Biosphere Reserve Concept", Batisse has presented a critical view of three main roles of a biosphere reserve, that is, development, logistic and conservation in the light of present experience in implementing the programme. Batisse raises fundamental questions. It is argued that this concept was developed by terrestrial ecologists, thus the functional zonation patterns which were drawn for its practical implementation apply best to terrestrial environments. It also emphasizes that there is a worldwide heterogeneity in its implementation—from a densely population region to sparsely populated region. The cultural and social characteristics of such populations and their relationships with the national authorities are also important. He is of the opinion that conservation in biosphere reserves should stress maintenance of ecological processes and features rather than protection of individual species of biota. Most of biosphere reserves do have some research or observation facilities—some highly sophisticated, some very limited—but there is hardly any correlation between them. There is also little common understanding on what type of research or monitoring has to be conducted. He is also of the view that in many developing countries, and probably in some developed ones, protection of ecosystems and species has little future unless the human populations in the area see some direct benefit for themselves deriving from the conservation measures involved. Thus, according to Batisse, biosphere reserve concept requires considerable flexibility in its implementation to accommodate the great ecological, economic and social complexity of our world; and the conservation concern can be translated in zonation patterns for coastal areas also because there is conspicuous absence of coastal biosphere reserves in almost all areas of the world.

In the current debate on ecology and development that is raging in the world, geography brings a vitally important input. Moonis Raza in his paper on "Ecology and Development with Particular Reference to the Management of Water Resources" stresses the interactive relationship between ecology and development. He is of the view that man as an element of the ecosystem cannot conquer non-human nature but must learn to live in harmony with it within a system of interdependencies. It is suggested that regional development should be viewed as the articulation of qualitative charges in the geo-bio-techno-social complex of interdependent phenomena in such a manner that the quality of human life improves within the framework of the integrity of the ecosystem. This is termed as eco-development and the basic premise of this is the unity in diversity through the mechanism of interaction between social man and nature. Since the naturalization of man and the humanization of nature proceed simultaneously through man's interaction with nature, the two constitute a differentiated unity. The author points out that man interacts with nature through labour, transforms it and himself gets transformed in the process. This man is the focus of eco-development. In the eco-development context, the ecology-development contradiction is a false one. It is also pointed out that development through proper resource utilization comes from those nations who are themselves the major culprits of eco-destruction through the dysfunctional monopoly of natural resources in an international system of inequalities, where 20 percent of world population is misusing 80 percent of its resources. Therefore, our concern with ecology within the framework of an eco-systemic approach is directed to optimizing development so as to extricate the Third World people from the vicious stronghold of hunger and poverty for the Third World, hunger continues to be a most potent pollutant—an eco-destructive force of tremendous magnitude for it destroys man, the crucial component of the contemporary ecosystem. The author offers a four-way classification scheme of prioritisation in resource use arranged vertically from higher to lower in terms of their degree of expandability: (1) inexhaustible like solar energy; (2) cyclic like water in the hydrological cycle; (3) renewable like natural vegetation; and (4) non-renewable like fossil fuels. Then, problems and management of water resources are discussed.

In contrast to the above concepts, which focus on ecosystem management and ecology and development, numerous scholars from diverse academic and institutional backgrounds have investigated the interaction between environmental and political forces in parts of Asia, Africa and Latin America (Bassett, 1988; Bell and Roberts, 1991; Black, 1990; Blaikie and Brookfield, 1987; Grossman, 1993; Schmink and Wood, 1987; Stonich, 1993; Thrupp, 1993). In most of these studies, the objective is the integration of political and environmental understanding in diverse settings. This approach has been termed as Third World political ecology and it was only in 1980s, this emerged as a research agenda (Bryant, 1992). The term political ecology is broadly defined as the attempt to understand the political sources, conditions and ramifications of environmental change (Bryant, 1992, 13). In particular, resource problems are approached by examining the social order in dynamic relationship with environment (Emel and Peet, 1989). This agenda addresses more complex questions. Two new developments stand out. The first is awareness that both social order and environment are not static as with other approaches. The second is a search for broader theoretical explanation of resource management and political ecology. Both of these developments are reflected in ambitious new research that are likely to play important roles in shaping knowledge on political ecology and unity of environment and development. Research on this field has been enriched with work by Blaikie and Brookfield (1987), who have first proposed the phrase 'regional political ecology' in their book *Land Degradation and Society*. Political ecology is used to denote the theoretical basis of an approach to land degradation in which relationships between farmers and the physical environment are considered in their historical, political and economic context. In dealing with ecological issues, it emphasizes institutions and political structures that set a matrix of limits, constraints, and possibilities for resource management. The focus is upon three basic issues: (1) it calls for an integration of human and physical approaches to land degradation, combining the concerns of ecology with those of political economy; (2) it emphasizes regionally-based accounts of land degradation; (3) it is concerned with political economy as to how structures external to rural society leads to land degradation, that is focusing on the role of international capitalism and the state on land. The political ecology currently forms a centre of intellectual activity in resource and environmental management and the subfield can be expected to continue to evolve and mature over the next decade or two.

In this context Singh in his article on "Perspectives in Resource Management and Political Energy" provides a broad canvas on the changing complex nature-man relationships in which political ideology, attitude of man towards nature and application of science and technology are thought to be instrumental. He describes the global variability of ecological processes and the importance of politics under the three heads: (1) historical perspective, (2) catastrophic trajectory, and (3) disastrous impact. He believes that the beginning of the present social, economic and ecological problems, and the exploitation of nature and man started crystallizing in the 16th century Europe due to the impact of scientific method. This method gave increased power to technologically advanced countries through which they understood laws of nature, subjugated countries and started transforming human civilization. However, with regard to the exploitation of nature and man, there is no difference between capitalism and communism; but the difference is in the ownership of resources. In the former, the individual initiative and drive were considered as the vehicle for development, while in the latter, the State was given this role with egalitarian objectives. In practice, both exploited man and nature recklessly; and both the systems were aggressive and exploitative. The developed countries consume more natural resources, disturb the ecology more and cause more pollution than the developing countries. The underlying contention of this paper is that the present trend of industrialism as well as consumerism should be reversed for global human survival.

Economic

The most comprehensive and fundamental approach to resource management is a theory of resource allocation developed by economists

(Barnett and Morse, 1963; Krutilla and Eckstein, 1958). This theory attempts to express the relationship between willingness to pay to satisfy wants via the willingness to sacrifice other wants, and in so doing has developed an important body of theory as to the manner and timing of resource allocation. This theory rests upon the assumptions of efficiency and the concept of maximization of net returns (O'Riordan, 1971). Net returns are maximized when the marginal value of goods and services consumed just equals the marginal costs involved in producing them (O'Riordan, 1971). Economists have been involved in resource allocation research and have made important contributions in understanding the processes operating to produce current resource and welfare allocations; in evaluating the resulting outcomes; in analyzing who has the power to determine the distributive patterns; and in assessing the role and efficacy of public policy measures to affect significant change in the allocative system (Rees, 1985). The overall aim of this theory is the allocation of the wealth or welfare derived from the resource base and the distribution of the costs of resource conservation.

The term political economy has often been used synonymously to indicate the area of resource allocation and the determination of aggregate economic activity. This has appeared frequently in recent studies of contemporary economies, politics, international relations and resource management. It has a long history and numerous interpretations. This is mainly associated with the works of Smith, Ricardo, Malthus, Mill and Marx. It studies the interaction of democratic political processes and the market determined economic relations (Bottomore, 1983, 375). The forms of political economy constitute those theories that maintain either the political domination of economies or the economic determination of politics (Barry Jones, 1988, 2). Political economy has made a gratuitous appearance in the field of resource management because it illuminates key social factors that shape people's action and that cannot be explained by ecology alone. This approach emphasizes the recursiveness of the relation among social-structural formations, economic forces, and political-power relations that generally underlie and determine resource exploitation and development processes (Blaikie, 1985); Hecht and Cockburn, 1989; Milliken, 1992; Redclift, 1987; Rees, 1985; Thrupp, 1993; Watts, 1983). This term does not imply geography as a type of economies, rather economy is understood as social economy or way of life founded in production (Peet and Thrift, 1989, 3). This initially took its direction from Marxist political economy and geographers began to develop a fruitful dialogue with political economists and sociologists. It led to the belief and appraisal that social production is viewed not as a neutral act by neutral agents but as a political act carried out by members of classes and other social groupings (Peet and Thrift, 1989, 3). To this end, Marx's work has been used by geographers to provide insights on the particular problem being analyzed. For example, in trying to understand the causes of soil erosion in a region, it is not adequate to examine only physical processes, i.e. erosivity of rain, credibility of soil, or the tillage methods or cropping patterns, but to systematically analyze other societal factors that influence the farmers' practices. Thus, this approach takes into view the historical-structural stance incorporating within its framework its structural-institutional forces and individual or household responses to such factors in the wider political economy. However, this approach has rarely been applied to Third World settings, Blaikie's (1985) study being one exception on the political economy of soil erosion in developing countries. In a colonial model of soil conservation, the problem of soil erosion is seen as environmental, rather than socio-economic. The model lays the blame on irrational and ignorant land-users and overpopulation. But, in particular, the solution is found in the involvement of cultivators and pastoralists in market economies. More significantly, Blaikie's emphasis lies on the social element—that is, why certain land uses take place in terms of the political-economic context in which land users find themselves. Repeatedly, erosion occurs in a number of social contexts: peasants and pastoral groups employing family labour; peasant and pastoral groups working underexploitative class relations; centrally planned economies and advanced capitalist economies. Marxism has far long provided the fulcrum of opposition to conventional theory in geography. Hence, the social relations of production under which land is used are key elements in the explanation of soil erosion. However, the existence of soil erosion is contingent on an enormous variety of physiographic and human variables; it is probably impossible to attempt a single theory of soil erosion and Blaikie, therefore, attempts to theorize substructures in a theory of soil erosion. Another example of such work is the comprehensive examination of the social, economic and political dimensions of global natural resource use (Rees, 1985). She stressed that it is naive to believe that reordering social relations automatically can or will solve resource scarcity problems. The problem is not just a question of reordering society to respond to the demands of the population, but of deciding which demands have priority over what time scale. Central to Rees analysis is a critique of the neoclassical economic view and also that the resource problems are complex and cannot be explained by blaming the capitalist system in general. In many regards, this work can be viewed as an effort to capitalize on the theoretical insights and methodological strengths of essentially neoclassical economic theories of resource allocation.

Behavioural

Perhaps the most rapidly growing approach to resource management is the behavioural aspects of the human use of the environment resources. This focuses upon the human dimensions of resource management. It includes of lay public, technical experts, private managers and public managers (Burton, 1971, 3). This approach emphasizes on behaviour and on processes relating to the human actors of resource system (Golledge, Brown and Williamson, 1972, 59). Behavioural geographers argue that farmers' knowledge of soils and weather conditions constitute what is termed as perceptual knowledge which may be invariant with knowledge of soils and weather derived from other sources, i.e. from the soil survey or from the meteorology department, and farmers decisions about land uses are conditioned not much by the real environment as by the perceived environment. This approach involves a consideration of three basic aspects: environment, choices or alternatives and goals, each of which is imperfectly perceived by man, and which eventually lead to decisions. As alluded to earlier, recent research in behavioural geography has tended: (1) an assessment of the perceived knowledge of the environment, (2) perception of alternate land uses available to the farmer, and (3) perception of the goals sought by farmer, whether this is concerned with subsistence, profit maximization, and so on. This would then lead to examination of the decision framework—whether this is conscious or habitual. Decision theory provides the means of understanding the bases of perception and behavioural geographers tend to view the decision process in the context of uncertainty. There has been developing a vast gamut of research literature on the role of perceptions and attitudes in decision-making, and these studies provide an input into the planning process and to serve as a vehicle for public participation in decision-making (Burton, 1971,1). Indeed, studies on perception and attitudes present insights about resource management strategies (Mitchell, 1989). Perception is the ability of mind to apprehend objects through the senses of sight, hearing, smell and touch. As Wood (1969, 129) has observed, "the explanation and understanding of the vast range of material which human geographers study, from continental patterns of migration to the behaviour of farmers in areas of climatic hazard, can be greatly increased by consideration of the individual's perception of his environment. Attitude refers to belief or preference held by a person with respect to an object (White, 1966, 224). A highly acclaimed geographical contribution to the resource management field is the work on natural hazards undertaken under the guidance of White (1945) at Chicago. He made a series of investigations into the human response to natural hazards guided by theories of decision-making influenced by methods of psychology and sociology. His work examined the extent of occupancy of hazardous areas and the range of possible adjustments to hazard that people could conceivably make, how this range has been perceived and what adjustments have been made. During the 1960s and 1970s a large number of studies appeared adopting perceptual and attitudinal variables focusing on flood plain resource decision (Kates, 1962), drought hazard (Saarinen, 1966), energy conservation (Jackson, 1980), water conservation (Baumann, 1983), soil erosion (Mather, 1982) and recycling (O'Riordan and Turner, 1979). Through these studies it has been determined the way in which individuals perceive resource management problems and issues and also to examine the range of strategies. Perception and attitude studies contribute significantly to resource management problems and studies. Mitchell (1989, 122) offered pragmatic reasons for citizen involvement: (1) surveys of public viewpoints provide basic information which the managers can consider when making decisions, and (2) managers can better judge the transferability of experiences from one region to another. Thus, a recurring theme in this approach is that experts are not the best judges as to what is desirable or necessary in a region. It is the citizen participation and public involvement in resource decisions which is of direct interest to most state and local resource management agencies.

The task of evaluation in resource management decision-making is becoming increasingly complex. No longer is it merely a matter of estimating the costs of construction and operation, and weighing these against anticipated revenues. Nor is it a matter of assessing only the local on-site impacts. More and more it is becoming necessary to consider proposals for resource development in terms of their broad social, environmental and institutional consequences, as well as their economic and financial effects. Increasingly, the region or the local area is the appropriate areal unit for evaluation. With the aid of a descriptive model of policy-making process, the paper by Derrick Sewell on "Broadening the Approach to Evaluation in Resources Management Decision-Making" examines the extent to which present procedures for evaluation are able to provide the data that decision-makers require at various stages of that process. It shows that while considerable progress has been made in the past decade in developing tools for evaluation, there remain important weaknesses in this connection. These weaknesses stem in part from the incapacity to identify and measure certain effects, notably aesthetics, other intangibles, and future values, and in part from institutional biases towards some strategies rather than others. The author suggests that many of these weaknesses might be overcome through the acceleration of social science research in the resources management field, and particularly in the following five areas: (1) the identification of the nature and magnitude of resources problems and of the demands for resource-related goods and services; (2) the delineation of alternative strategies for dealing with resource problems; (3) highlight reviews of projects and policies; (4) examination of alternative ways of identifying public views; and (5) development of more sophisticated techniques for taking account of multiple objectives, multiple strategies, and a wide range of values. The article concludes with a list of specific type studies that might be undertaken in connection with each of these areas.

Integrated

A striking trend in recent years has been the approach called integrated resource management. This approach has attracted the geographer and geography is the best possible disciplinary background for practicing it because integration is possible through a spatial approach, showing not only overall relationships between supply and demand of resources, but also locating where they can be on the ground. Consonant with ecological tradition of geography, the themes stressed in this approach centre upon the integration of natural resources. Historically, the use of land, water, forest and other natural resources has often been viewed as separate resource issues; but now, research has resulted in an increased awareness that they are integrated. The dictionary meaning of the term integration is to unite parts or elements so as to form a harmonious whole and to coordinate diverse elements. According to Mitchel (1986, 13-14), integrated resource management incorporates four elements: (1) a multiplicity "of purposes, means and participant strategies, (2) a blending of various resource sectors, (3) the use of resource management as a mechanism for social and economic change, and (4) a striving for accommodation and compromise. As a concept, integration is well established in the management field which leads to cooperation and coordination, and, in turn, leads to improved effectiveness. The search for integration can occur at normative, strategic or operational levels. A normative level considers a reconsideration of the value premises underlying decisions, the definition of desired ends and ideals, and decisions that determine what ought to be done. A strategic level includes analysis and evaluation of alternative goals and objectives, the selection and design of means to attain desired goals, and decisions that determine what can be done. And lastly, an operational level takes into account plan implementation, purposeful actions/interventions to affect change, and decisions that determine what will be done.

Water plays very critical role in all kinds of developmental activities and in the maintenance of ecological balance within the watershed of the river basin. Integrated resource management implies the orderly marshalling of water resources of river basins for multiple purposes to promote human welfare. This concept has evolved as a sub-paradigm in the comprehensive development and planning of river basin to maintain its ecological unity and integrity. The river basin forms a biogeographical system which is generally called process-response system and it is dynamic in nature. Thus, a river basin is selected as a unit for development and management of resources, the presumption being that its physical unity makes in general a suitable multi-purpose economic region (Teclaff, 1967). In modern times, approaches to the planning for the development of water resources have progressed from single-purpose use of water of river basin, such as irrigation, flood control and the generation of hydroelectricity to multipurpose uses due to the development of engineering techniques. The terms "total catchment management", "integrated catchment management", "integrated resource management" and "river basin management" are used interchangeably (Mitchell and Pigram, 1989). Integrated catchment management is a process or tool which allows consideration of diverse elements and values (Mitchell and Pigram,

1989). It is desirable wherever there are conflicting or competing land and water uses and multiple institutional responsibilities. Further, according to Mitchell (1986), "integration involves relating resource management to management of other societal concerns ranging from job opportunities to housing and regional transportation; and resources are viewed as but one of societies legitimate concerns and as a tool to achieve broader and more fundamental societal goals". This idea took shape into an operational one when the Tennessee Valley Authority was created for the first time in U.S. in 1933. The second great event took place in India when the Damodar Valley Corporation was created by the Act of Parliament in 1948. These two events have virtually become landmarks in the history of the integrated resource management. It was followed by the Gal Oya Development Board, a government corporation on the Gal Oya river in Sri Lanka created by Act of Parliament in 1949; the Comissado do Vale do Sao Francisco in Brazil in 1949; Corporacion Autonoma Regional del Causa in Columbia in 1954; Volga in the old USSR; and Snowy Mountain Scheme of Australia. By the 1970s the integrated river development approach underwent further modification (White, 1977, 3): (1) increased attention was given to the variety of ways in which natural resources might be developed by employing both engineering and social modes of management; (2) much greater recognition was given to the consequences for the biological and physical environment of the construction and management of engineering projects; (3) problems of water quality; and (4) water management within metropolitan regions. However, Lang (1986, 2) has observed that "this concept misses an appropriate conceptual framework, a body of guiding principles and a set of tested methods that are ready for use and that enable the lessons of practice to transcend the limitations of their unique contexts."

Policy Making

Behavioural and perceptual research has a bearing on a wide range of issues relating to policy making approach. This approach is assuming growing importance in resource development and management decision-making. It focuses in identifying problems, specifying strategies as well as formulating, implementing and evaluating policy (Derrick Sewell and Mitchell, 1984). Policy research generally concentrates upon conscious choice processes as opposed to habitual or unconscious/trivial choices (Kates, 1962, 17) and policy making provides the broad guidelines for the decision-making. A decision is a conclusion or termination of a process. Resource management decision-making is a process that selects a problem for decision and produces a limited number of alternatives. In other words, resource management decision-making is conceived of as evolving the search for both problems and alternative programmes at local, state or national levels. These tasks are performed as decision-makers, as internal advisers or as consultants or critics (Coppock and Sewell, 1976). Thus, the term policy making is frequently used synonymously which involves choices and collectivity of intersecting decisions. The developers of this approach have never been happy with the descriptive limits of the behavioural school, and they have a considerable faith in the analytical techniques of policy and project appraisal (Ferguson and Alley, 1984). Many topologies of policy models have been develoged. Mitchell (1989) identifies and differentiates the comparative role of prescriptive and descriptive policy models and their implications for resource management. Prescriptive models establish an ideal or standard against which actual policy processes are assessed. They provide insight and also indicate areas which are not being handled adequately so that further improvement is made in the allocation process. By contrast, descriptive models indicate the nature of the actual process of resource allocation. Several studies show how a process could be made more effective by appreciating the reality of policy processes (Mitchell, 1989). With patience, a bit of specialized skill, and some imagination, policy models yield unparalleled insights and enable the analyst to predict more accurately future decisions or policies. Even more powerful is the awareness of policy and decision processes, which Mitchell (1989, 284) believes should make the investigator more sensitive to the opportunities for and barriers against incorporating public input.

In this context Coppock and Sewell in their paper on "Resource Management and Public Policy: The Changing role of Geographical Research" have indicated a long tradition of geographical research in the field of resource management and public policy specially in North America and the U.K. at different scales. This includes development of abstract models of resource systems, construction of models of decision-making process in resource management, studies of policies, and development and application of techniques of analysis. Research on work of public agencies and policy formulation has become an area of renewed activity in recent years and several geographers have contributed to this effort apart from playing more direct role as advisers or members of committees.

Sustainable Resource Development

The 1970s and 1980s have been decades of profound social, political and economic changes in the developing countries and studies have focused upon the "food crisis", the "debt crisis", the "environmental crisis", the "population crisis", and the "energy crisis". Thus, a deep concern has heightened over the connection between environment and development (Adams, 1990; Brundtland, 1987; Manning, 1990; McCormick, 1989; Mukherjee and Agnihotri, 1993; Pierce, 1992; Raza, 1992 and Turner, 1993) in the developing countries. Geographers, economists and environmental planners have noted dramatic changes to the quantity and quality of the earth's resources and evidence of increasing inequality in human welfare (Pierce, 1992, 306). This difference is the result of comparative advantage, colonialism, economic geography, access to capital and a number of social, cultural and political factors (Pierce, 1992, 313). Sustainable development has been proposed as a possible solution to this problem which is a powerful alternative to the traditional model of development as well as a new prescription for economic development. This solution permits and encourages development as long as this development builds on the strengths of the environment as a resource base, and does not violate natural constraints (Manning, 1990, 291). The concept has been borrowed from both natural and social sciences and it means different things to different people. It contains short history with complex pedigree. The United Nations Conference on the Human Environment, held in Stockholm in 1972, reflected this theme and stimulated discussion on environmental issues. Subsequently, a number of authors (Eckholm, 1982; Glaeser, 1984; Riddell, 1981; Sachs, 1980) and international agencies such as the United Nations Environment Programme (UNEP) and the International Union for Conservation of Nature and Natural Resources (IUCN) have also talked about sustainable development. It was the central concept in the World Conservation Strategy published in 1980 where it became the linchpin of IUCN. The concept of sustainable utilisation of resources received a more formal airing in the World Conservation Strategy which identified three vital ingredients (O'Riordan, 1993, 49-50): (i) the maintenance of essential ecological processes, of oxygen, carbon, sulphur and nitrogen fluxes governed or strongly moderated by ecosystems, and providing the primary bases for food production, health and other aspects of human survival; (2) the preservation of genetic diversity, both in the species varieties of local food production as well as for species in the wild to act as insurance against disease or climatic stress, and an investment for future food varieties and genetically modified organisms; (3) the sustainable development of species and ecosystems, particularly fisheries and other wild species which are cropped, forests and timber resources, and grazing land. The term sustainable development achieved prominence in the Brundtland Commission Report (1987). It was defined as: "development that meets the needs of the present without compromising the ability of the future generations to meet their own needs." This definition, published in the World Commission on Environment and Development (WCED), placed the emphasis on human needs of the poor. It argued that "sustainable development is a process in which the exploitation of resources, the direction of investments, the orientation of technological development and institutional change are all in harmony, and enhance both current and future potential to meet human needs and aspirations (Brundtland, 1987, 46). The publication of the Brundtland Report put this issue more firmly on the international political agenda making it geopolitically significant. Thus, the basic implication of the concept of sustainable development, as embraced by this report and others, is that we should leave to the next generation a stock of quality of life assets no less than those we have inherited (Pierce, Markandya and Barbier, 1989).

The preceding discussion on the evolution of the concept of sustainable development has highlighted different perspectives on it. It is a broad goal with a highly desirable end-point of development aspirations. It is an overarching and optimistic concept which implies that through concerted efforts and wise decisions, there can be a satisfactory solution to the massive problems which currently beset the human occupancy of the planet (Manning, 1990, 291). Due to greater human-generated environmental pressure than ever before, massive problems are emerging associated with pollution, the depletion of non-renewable resources, the loss of genetic diversity, deforestation, erosion-provoking agricultural and livestock-raising practices, and the essentially permanent loss of farmland and wilderness to urban development and infrastructure provision. In this regard, therefore, sustainable development is an anthropocentric approach to the globe because it relates to the human use of the biosphere. The powerful idea underlying the concept is that of inter-generational equity; what follows is that development that does not meet the intergenerational equity criterion simply must be had development (Holmberg and Sandbrook, 1992, 23). This suggests and regards sustainable development as a policy objective, rather than a methodology (Redclift, 1991, 37). Of significance, however, is the common theme of integration of different biophysical and socio-economic information and geography have the unique opportunity to play a significant role in integration. The most effective way to pursue integration is through spatial approach, showing not only overall relationships between supply of and demand for environmental functions but also locating where they can be matched on the ground (Manning, 1990, 291). The essential principles of sustainable development, according to Daly (1991), are as follows: (1) it implies a stationary population, (2) it does not imply constant technology, (3) it must deal with sufficiency as well as efficiency, (4) technological progress for sustainable development should be efficiency-increasing rather than throughput increasing, (5) renewable resources should be exploited on a sustained-yield basis, and (6) non-renewable resources should be exploited at a rate equal to the creation of renewable substitutes.

The six papers in this section of the book deal with a selection of perspectives on sustainable development focusing on sustainable resource use in developing countries, poor people's use of sustainability in seeking livelihoods from resource-poor areas of the South, methodologies for assessment of sustainability, economic concepts and criteria of sustainability and modelling integrated ecological-economic systems for sustainable development. These papers present variety of views on developing policies for sustainable resource use in developing countries, review current thinking on sustainable development, pinpoint problems of their operationalisation, consider dimensions of sustainability and place sustainable economic development in three-dimensional context of time, space and substance.

Tisdell in his paper on "World Conservation Strategy, Economic Policies and Sustainable Resource—Use in Developing Countries" states that the World Conservation Strategy (WCS) proposed by international bodies stems from the fear that world economic activity, growth and development may prove unsustainable because it is damaging the biosphere and decision-makers are not making adequate allowance for this. The biosphere provides ecosystems supporting all life, including human life, and damage to it, especially if permanent, can at the very least be expected to reduce economic productivity. He reiterates that population growth, rising consumption levels, inadequate environmental planning and lack of forethought may be so damaging ecologically that economic growth cannot be sustained and, indeed, affluence may give way to poverty. However, WCS claims that if basic ecological guidelines are followed sustainable economic development is possible and it points to particular measures that need to be taken in developing countries. Different types of sustainable resource use are possible and these are discussed in this paper. It is argued that policies for sustained resource use may be of more importance to less developed countries. Policies for promoting environmentally sound use of resources are discussed together with obstacles to their implementation.

Redclift in his paper on "The Multiple Dimensions of Sustainable Development" aims to portray the vagueness of the appeal of this concept and points to a number of significant areas of both convergence and divergence. He has critically evaluated definitions put forward by Barbier (1989), Bartelmus (1987), Brundtland Report (1987), Chambers (1988), Conway and Barbier (1988) and Pearce *et al.* (1987) and has sought to extend his own definition by enlarging the compass of debate and considering the economic, political and epistemological dimensions of sustainability. He has raised the question about the needs to be sustained and levels of sustainability. He argues what makes development unsustainable at the global level are the patterns of consumption in the rich countries, while most efforts to tackle development problems are essentially production-oriented. Redclift, then, defines sustainable development as meeting human needs, or maintaining economic growth or conserving natural capital or all three. He is critical of an assessment of environmental and economic trade-off and rightly asserts the necessity of addressing the political and economic forces behind unsustainable practices. Indeed, he cites this as a principal shortcoming of ecocentric philosophies and ecodevelopment approaches as well as of World Conservation Strategy which probably did more than any other document to popularize the concept of sustainability. Thus, his broad-based concept focuses attention on poor people's use of sustainability in seeking livelihoods from the resource-poor areas of the South Asia.

Emerging from the review of both conceptual and empirical aspects of Barbier's paper (1987), the World Commission on Environment and Development Report (1987) and Redclift book (1987) are some critical issues that are challenging this approach today and are shaping the direction that sustainable development paradigm will take in the future. These issues are discussed and debated in Simon's cogently written paper on "Sustainable Development: Theoretical Construct or Attainable Goal ?". By integrating these approaches, a systematic and coherent approach embracing both theory and praxis is developed. An historically sensitive political perspective is proposed as appropriate for embracing not only the more traditional ecological and economic aspects but also the crucial political factors underlying uneven development and underdevelopment in the age of an increasingly integrated global economic system. While, according to Simon, sustainable development is or has to become an attainable goal, appropriate methodologies and techniques for translating this into practice are still required. The paper concludes that a blend of 'top down' and 'bottom up' approaches would give greatest flexibility, and suggests how the assessment of sustainability at the level of individual agro-ecological systems might be advanced.

It is clear that no consensus exists about sustainable development due to differences in disciplinary biases and ideological disputes of the practitioners. Tisdell in his paper "Environmental and Resource Economics: Its Role in Planning Sustainable Development Abstract" claims that ERE provides a complete conceptualization of the interdependency of the economy and the environment and their implications for planning because economic discussions of the relationships between humans and their surroundings are the main focus of this subfield. The view taken is that natural resources are held by current generations on trust for future generations. Depletion of natural resources by current generations can reduce the ability of future generations to meet their needs. Therefore, economists like Pearce, Markandya and Barbier (1989) suggest as a general principle that "future generation should be compensated for reductions in the endowment of resources brought about by the actions of present generations". They also suggest that man-made capital, generated through economic activity, through human ingenuity and technological change—the produced means of production—might be used to compensate future generations. On the other hand, natural capital consists of three major components: (1) non-renewable resources, (2) renewable resources, and (3) environmental services. such as maintenance of the quality of the atmosphere, climate, operation of the hydrological cycle including flood controls and drinking water supply, waste assimilation, recycling of nutrients, generation of soils, pollination of crops, provision of food from the sea, and the maintenance of a vast genetic library (Berkes and Folke, 1994, 129). But the question is how adequate is man-made capital as a substitute for natural capital or as compensation for a reduction in natural resource stocks ? Also, to what extent is this substitution possible without endangering the ability of future generations to sustain income levels in an equitable manner? There are, however, some potential challenges in ensuring rising standards of living for future generations by continuing to substitute man-made capital for natural resource stock. There is an awful distance between hopes and realities. If environmental economists are able to invent and support devices that systematically encourage cumulative improvement, the status of their field will improve.

Shariff in his paper on "Towards a Sustainable Development: An Economic Policy Perspective" justifies the world heading towards a variety of environmental and human disasters and pinpoints that environmental problems are inseparable from those of the human welfare and from the process of economic development. The author is of the view that sustainable development may arrest the depletion of our resources while provide a decent survival means for the future and also prudent resource management without diminishing the consumption possibilities of future generations. It is suggested that economic policy for sustainable development is focused on true income, that which is available for consumption in the current period without diminishing the value of capital and natural resources. Appropriate policies and management strategies cannot be developed from a biological perspective; instead, he highlights environmental aspect as the core concept of sustainable development focusing on externalities, property rights, optimum rates of depletion and option values.

Bergh and Nijkamp in their paper on "Ecologically Sustainable Economic Development: Concepts and Model Implications" take an integrated ecological-economic system point of view for modelling sustainable development. This sub-field is going through a period of intellectual exploration as it centres on search for model building at both theoretical and operational levels. Ecologically sustainable concept is recognized as the "continued existence of the environment, which acts as a basis for human welfare as it provides living conditions and environmental amenities, and acts also as a productive basis".

The ecologically sustainable economic development is defined as "the development of economic activities, human preferences and human population, such that an acceptable standard of life for every human being is fulfilled and all aspects of this development can be sustained in the long run by natural resource availability, ecosystems and life support systems. The authors place sustainable economic development in three-dimensional context of time, space and substance. They explore the central components of sustainable development paying due attention to: (1) intergenerational trade-off, (2) interregional aspects, (3) multiple use of resources, and (4) risk and uncertainty, and consider their implications for model building.

Thus, one is struck by the robustness of this universal paradigm and particularly by its multifaceted nature. However, there are many criticisms against this, such as, what needs to be sustained, whether for present or future populations, whether intergenerational or intragenerational. The concept is also labelled as highly ethnocentric and a North-biased view, and it fails to consider seriously the integrity of other cultures. According to Manning (1990), successful transition to sustainability requires knowledge of natural environment and human condition; data on demographic and socio-economic factors including attitudes and expectations; data on biophysical characteristics which determine the ability of the environment to supply the functions; base data on both supply and demand, particularly that are comparable over time; data central to understanding of changing stresses on the environment; and data allowing decision-makers to realize the range of demands being placed on our ecosystems. Berkes and Folke (1994, 146) are of the view that "sustainable development is a continuous process and not a state; it is never achieved once and for all, but only approached. As such, it can only be reinforced, not attained. Sustainable development calls for maintenance of the dynamic capacity to respond adaptively, which is a property of all successful species and societies. It is not meaningful to measure the absolute sustainability of a society at any point in time."

Technology and Resources

The topics of technology and resources are important ones within conservation and management of resources because each region is actively pursuing economic development by attempting to enhance its technological level.

There is nothing new in intimate connection between technology and natural resources. People have been inventing better ways of exploring, assessing and using resources ever since they climbed down from the trees. Technology is the means by which man extends his power over his surroundings and our knowledge of the ways of doing this constitute the rules of technology (Hamilton, 1973). Technology has been described as an inexhaustible resource, but it is not technology that is inexhaustible—rather it is man's ingenuity and inventiveness (Kates and Burton, 1965, 443). It appears, then, that technological change is very much associated with knowledge industry. It is also evident that changes in technology mean changes in resource uses and in a sense competition among resources for given uses. Technology is supported and propelled by modern science. Recent advances in science and technology are strongly influencing the production and use of natural resources and will have in the future also. Technology provides immense benefits to society. It can sustain men in space and the ocean depths; it can harness the immense surge of the tides and modify the weather; at the same time, it can blast whole cities to ruins with atomic explosion, and yet control the same enormous power to yield plentiful supplies of electricity (Hamilton, 1973). The available stock of a resource depends upon technology, costs, and social constraints. Aluminium contained in ores other than bauxite was not a useful resource until recovery technology was developed in the 1970s. The production of many minerals from seawater is technologically feasible but in most cases is currently ruled out by high costs.

It is essential, therefore, to arouse interest to foster the kind of understanding that is needed between technology and resources. Historically, the technologies have differed conspicuously among themselves. Contribution to inventory and appraisal of resources is many-sided and wide-ranging. It is done by ground survey, geophysical and geochemical explorations, geobotanical method, aerial photographs, remote sensing and G.I.S. Perhaps the most significant appraisal is done by space technology which has brought revolution in this field. It is a dynamic, multidisciplinary technology used by geographers and geologists to obtain detailed spatial information about the earth and human activities. It has proved to be a powerful tool in providing the means to achieve an improved understanding of humanity's relationship to planet Earth.

Ground survey is the traditional method of resource studies. It includes recording of direct observations in the field primarily on maps and makes use of notes and photographs to supplement the map. A series of traverses across an area provides a complete coverage of recording nature and extent of resource distribution. Another fruitful method of collecting information on resources is through interviews of citizens, experts and officials. Both types of information are statistically and cartographically analyzed to arrive at sound and meaningful conclusions. The period since 1950 has been one in which geophysical exploration techniques experienced steady growth. These techniques depend on the measurement of various physical characteristics such as electrically/magnetic parameters and the recognition of abnormal values which may be due to the presence of mineral deposit. Geochemical exploration is based on the premise that materials of the earth around a mineral deposit—rocks, soils, stream, lake water, vegetation and the air—may be expected to differ in chemical composition from similar materials where there is no mineral deposit present (Smith, 1977, Ch. 2). It is, therefore, concerned with location of economic deposits by means of chemical analysis of samples and they can be rock, soil, water and plants. Geobotany refers to the science of plant of the past; in technical terms it is also known as Paleo-botany. One of the applications of Paleo-botany based on the presence or absence of specific type of pollen-grain is in the exploration of petroleum deposits in the earth's crust.

Aerial survey has proved a fruitful source of information in resource studies. The reasons are not far to seek. Aerial photographs normally show a complete record of the physical and cultural landscapes and they are a unique means of grasping the landscape ecological conditions prevailing in areas covered by them (Gupta, 1971). They offer the quickest and complete resource inventory of an area for a great variety of purposes; for the inventory of forest resources, soils, underlying geology, identification of mineral outcrops, land use and water. The study of aerial photographs detects the interrelations between the geological, geomorphological, pedological, hydrological, vegetational and other resources of the land which are very difficult to observe by traditional methods. Aerial photographs also provide an instantaneous view of the resources of large areas of land surface in a shorter time and in a comprehensive manner than was possible by ground survey methods (Gupta, 1971). However, early photographic experiments and aerial photography were developed before 1909, but during 1920-1960 a number of airborne systems, sophisticated in design and use expanded at an increasing rate. During this time many earth scientists especially geographers became acquainted with analytical tool. Consequently, they were used as substitutes for maps. The relative low cost of aerial surveys, accurate results of investigation, three-dimensional view of the landscape features and suitability for any terrain in unknown areas particularly in selection of sampling sites and boundary demarcation made them very useful in resource research. Despite its impressiveness and dramatic increase in demand, its importance started declining as aerial photographs were affected by darkness, cloud cover or rains. The humid tropics and regions of polar nights were difficult to be photographed.

Space technology has now come to the aid of resource and environmental scientists. While grand traditional ground survey and aerial photography continues, satellite imageries in the recent past have made the task of geographer easier and better. Almost over two decades now the development of satellites has provided a new dimension of airborne surveillance. The term remote sensing means reconnaissance at a distance and this term was coined in the early 1960s by geographers at the Office of Naval Research to describe the process of obtaining data by use of both photographic and non-photographic instruments (Simonett, Reeves, Estes, Bertke and Sailer, 1983). It involves the use of surface, airborne or spacecraft instrumentation capable of scanning large areas of the earth, its atmosphere, its oceans to provide high resolution data. These data are of immense significance and useful for resource and environmental planning. According to Curran (1987), remote sensing is defined as "the measurement of some property of an object of interest by a sensor that is not in direct physical contact with the object." Sensors play very important role in the remote sensing system as they direct energy at an object on the earth's surface and measure the rebounded energy as radiowaves. The remotely sensed data, in the form of electrical signals and converted into digital numbers, are recorded on magnetic tape, memorized, and periodically transmitted by radio to ground stations, where they are prepared for processing and use (Tricart and Kiewietde Jonge, 1992, 144). Haggett (1979, 556) explains two advantages of radar images over conventional photographic images for mapping purposes: (1) radar imagery is independent of solar illumination and is unaffected by darkness, cloud cover or rain, that means, any part of the globe can be scanned including the zones especially difficult to photograph by conventional methods; and (2) radar imagery gives greater detail of the terrain. The U.S.A. Russia, Japan, Canada, West European countries, India are actively participating in space exploration programme and there has been an exponential increase in expenditure on space exploration. The high level of technical ability in space exploration programme has been demonstrated by NASA organization (1958), European Space Research Organization (1964) later combined since 1975 to form European Space Agency (ESA), space research programme in Russia and Indian Space Programme (1962). In 1969, the Indian Space Research Organization (ISRO) was set up and is responsible for the planning, programming and management of research and development activities in the country in space science technology. Among its many thrusts, resource surveys and management, and environmental monitoring and meteorological survices are quite important. From resource and environmental point of view, the most important development in remote sensing technology was the launch of the First Earth Resource Technology Satellite (ERTS) in July 1972 from the U.S.A. In 1975, this satellite was named LANDSAT. It makes 14 revolutions a day around the earth, its sensors covering a series of 160 Km. wide strips, so that the whole surface of the earth is covered once in every 18 days (Haggett, 1979, 558). This began almost uninterrupted recordings of most of the earth by a multispectral scanner. The satellite height is approximately 920 Km., always well above the terrestrial atmosphere and the typical coverage of a satellite photograph is 180 × 180 Km. The merit of remote sensing in resource and environmental studies is quite considerable. Haack (1982, 899-909) lists the following 11 landsat data characteristics making it a valuable tool for resource inventory and analysis: (1) worldwide coverage, (2) repetitive coverage, (3) synoptic view, (4) uniformity over time, (5) uniformity over large areas, (6) multispectral, (7) digital, (8) planimetric, (9) readily available, (10) easily usable, and (11) inexpensive. Resource managers increasingly use remotely sensed data for land classification and development, rock, soils and vegetation resources, extracting land use/ cover information, groundwater exploration, delineating water bearing formation and estimating their hydrological characteristics, mapping water quality and water surface temperatures, reservoir sedimentation monitoring lakes and reservoir levels, snow-cover mapping, run-off prediction, locating ore bodies, watershed-run-off characteristics, bathymetric mapping and coastal geomorphology. Research continues to yield basic new knowledge about the Earth and to expand our understanding of the applications of remote sensing. The publications of scientific and technical results on theory, experiments, and systems design in remote sensing technology and applications are available in journals (International Journal of Remote Sensing, Photogrammetric Engineering and Remote Sensing, Remote Sensing of the Environment, Photonirvachak, IEEE Transactions on Geoscience and Remote Sensing, Geocarto International: A Multidisciplinary Journal of Remote Sensing, Canadian Journal of Remote Sensing, Photogrammetric Record) and books (Barrett and Curtis, 1982; Campbell, 1987; Colwell, 1983; Curran, 1985; Jensen, 1986; Lo, 1986; and Townshend, 1981). However, remote sensing studies are also reported to encounter problems (Barrett and Curtis, 1976; and Gupta 1971): (1) one of the most severe problems is that of obtaining repetitive data over a given area at suitable intervals of time; (2) some millions of bits of data can be gathered in a second by sophisticated sensors, and the task of processing, digesting and acting upon such a massive information flow is beyond the present capabilities of many potential users; and (3) there lies the problem of understanding the nature of simple relations between sensor and surface object. Still, much of it remains to be prospected.

Thus, remote sensing is unique in obtaining spatial information about the Earth and human activities and those data can be transformed into information by using analogue or digital image-processing techniques (Jensen *et al.*, 1989, 746). But, conversely, other techniques such as cartography, geographic information systems and statistics rely on data that are already available. The challenges created by global environmental change and resource depletion and degradation demand research approaches that are worldwide in scope and interdisciplinary in application. The rapidly growing tool of geographical information systems (GIS) provides a collaboration of scientific disciplines and information in order to understand earth processes and the interrelationships of the terrestrial atmospheric, hydrologic and biotic systems (Walsh, 1988, 17). Apart from geographers being quite prominent in developing this tool, a number of other disciplines such as computer science, surveying engineering, landscape architecture, remote sensing, soil science, forestry and environmental studies are also involved. Thus, GIS is a computer-based system which allows the input, management, retrieval, analysis, manipulation and presentation of geoinformation. Also, GIS is a multidisciplinary enquiry into the nature of such systems and the role that such systems play in scientific modelling involving geo-referenced information.

Geographical data describe both natural and human resources.

The spatial distribution of such data is usually shown graphically on maps, charts or images. Alternatively, the data may be in the form of list of variables that are grouped by location and related to places on maps. Computer-based systems designed to store and analyze data have existed for more than thirty years. But, the advent of GIS technology has made possible for the first time the efficient integration, management, and analysis of the varied types of geographical information such as imagery, text and maps (King, 1991, 66-67). It provides an integrated package containing a high resolution data base, characterized by digital-based technologies, where information is electronically encoded as binary numbers (King, 1991, 66). It represents a new frontier in technical innovation where maps are put into computers, and shapes and images are converted into numbers. These numbers are used by the available digital computers. This process is called as digital information revolution in geography and GIS is at the forefront (King, 1991, 66). To Abler (1988, 137), "GIS are simultaneously the telescope, the microscope, the computer, and the xerox machine of regional analysis and synthesis", and it can be "viewed as a set of processes and procedures that approach the heart of modern geography." Since GIS promises to be a very effective tool for geographers and earth scientists for analyzing spatial data, there is likelihood of it becoming a fundamental research instrument for solving spatial problems. And since digital geographical information systems are computer-based and extremely technical in nature, and the potential users are not trained in this sophisticated technology, it is imperative to acquire this tool for the input, storage, manipulation, analysis and output of spatial information. The theory and practice of GIS can be found in many publications which include the American Cartographer, Photogrammetric Engineering and Remote Sensing, the International Journal of Geographic Information Systems and the Professional Geographer. There are several books on geographical information systems (Burrough, 1986; Chrisman, 1989; Estes and Starr, 1989; Green, 1994; Marble, Calkins and Peuquet, 1984; Martin, 1991; Peuquet and Marble, 1994; Taylor, 1991; Worboys, 1994) which provide up-to-date information for users, vendors and researchers. They offer a wide range of reading from different backgrounds covering developments in GIS, catering for the novice to the specialist, and from the small scale to the large scale user.

The six papers in this section of the book deal with technology and resources focusing on sustainable development as a product of a changed perspective on social and technological development, improved technologies in resource management, theory and applications of aerial photo interpretation, remote sensing and geographic information systems as a consequence of the ongoing electronic revolution.

Suresh Kumar in his paper on "Technology and Natural Resources: An Ecological Model for Agriculture and Industry" suggests that regenerative practices in agriculture and environmental supportive modes of industrial organization are required to ensure parts of sustainable development. The simplistic models of economic growth based on physical and monetary flows have to yield to ecological models which take into account the externalities also. The consequences of resource depletion, social anomie and environmental degradation are not just externalities any more. The costs due to them are to be internalised to realise appropriate social benefits which is the essence of sustainable growth. In this paper the important premises for an ecological model and the major parameters for sustainable development particularly with reference to the agricultural and industrial practices are highlighted.

The next paper by Pimentel on "Technology and Natural Resources" progresses to efficient use of resources and limits to efficiency with concerns to support human numbers with a high standard of living. Throughout the world, new technologies have enabled humans to use land, water, energy and biological resources to improve the standards of living. The author points out that for economic development it is vital to have both resources and technology. Technology without resources makes development impossible. Resources are limited in the world because of a growing demand by the world population, limits of availability, and problems of rapid degradation and/or consumption. Although some technologies can improve the efficient use of resources, limits exist to efficiency. Pimentel shows, therefore, that these technologies arid resources can only support 10-15 billion humans living at or near poverty, or support approximately one billion humans with a relatively high standard of living.

De Gregori in his paper on "Resources Are Not, They Become: An Institutional Theory" De Gregori argues that the creative process of fashioning the material and non-material stuff of our environment in a form usable and serviceable to human beings is determined by science and technology. Following the tradition of Zimmermann and Ayers, De Gregori affirms that: it is the sum total of human knowledge and capability that is the prime resource and the one that defines all others. Accordingly, all references to "natural resources", "natural endowments", "given resources", and "fixed and finite resources" in the neoclassicist literature are outmoded. De Gregori continues: "Resources, then, are not stuff or materials; they are a set of capabilities. These capabilities use the stuff of the material and non-material universe in a life-sustaining manner. These capabilities define a functional relationship that we call resources." Given the prior existence of humans and materials, it is people as active, discretionary agents employing ideas who create resources. The process of resource creation is one of dynamic interaction and reinforcing feedback mechanisms reflected in the "human generation of ideas, their embodiment in the process of technology, and in the creation of resources." De Gregori refines meanings, critiques alternate views, and demonstrates the cogency and credibility of this theory of resource creation. Consideration is given to resource dependency, entropy-based pessimisms, and resource renewability. Two extended applications of this theory of the technological determination of resources are the world-wide availability of minerals and the provision of food stuffs. He concludes the essay with the suggestion that technology as ideas and as the creator of resources is liberating in several respects: it opens new and optimistic avenues for consideration of the sustainability of human life; it offers some intellectual escape from the heavy orthodox dependency on the construct of scarcity; it provides a process of choosing that actually expands the range of choices. The process of resource creation is one of emergent evolution. It requires that people must choose their future and this essay suggests that instrumental valuing is the credible way of determining the character of that future.

Resource managers and developers should understand the fundamentals of aerial photos, remote sensing and other monitoring technologies and advances arising from the electronic revolution in order to use them properly in their scientific investigations. The papers by Rampal, Prudhvi Raju, Srivastava and Singh deal with them. The paper by Singh on "Geographic Information System in Natural Resources Management" discusses various components and principles of GIS. Resource management requires to analyze phenomena, processes and their interaction throughout space and time. The resource information system, therefore, has to be considered as multi-dimensional, that is, attribute dimension, spatial dimension and temporal dimension. Geographic Information System (GIS) offers such capabilities as they integrate multi-sector, multi-level and multi-period data base. Of course, internationally, the research on GIS started in the early sixties, however, in India it is the recent phenomenon. Sometimes, it is also known as Land Information System (LIS) or Environment Information System (EIS). The preparatory stage of GIS (1978-1980) began with the theoretical approach followed by software development, setting up research groups and organising some regional experimental researches and training programmes. The National Natural Resources Management System (NNRMS) project was started in 1988 by the Department of Space to adopt a holistic approach for rational management of natural resources of the country. The Department of Science and Technology launched a comprehensive programme in 1982 on the development of Natural Resources Data Management System by setting up computerised data bases at micro level taking district as the unit. Thus, with this multidisciplinary conception, an integrated approach to the utilisation, monitoring and conservation of the environment is essential. Coping with global and regional environmental change scenarios, Singh argues that GIS as a tool serves a number of applications including land and forest cover change, water and air quality assessment, soil erosion risk analysis, natural hazard monitoring, selection of afforestation areas, land capability and suitability analysis and data directory study. The author is also of the view that remote sensing and GIS can be very effective tools for resource management when carefully evaluated and applied within an appropriate conceptual framework, and the new age of micro-computers and increased potential for information exchange may aid in assembling new programmes in developing countries.

BALESHWAR THAKUR

REFERENCES

Abler, R.F. (1988). "Awards, Rewards and Excellence: Keeping Geography Alive and Well", *Professional Geographer*, 40, 135-40.

Adams, W.M. (1990). *Green Development: Environment and Sustainability in the Third World*, London and New York: Routledge.

Allen, S.W. and Leonard, J.W. (1966). *Conserving Natural Resources*, New York: McGraw-Hill Book Co.

Barbier, E.B. (1987). "The Concept of Sustainable Economic Development", *Environmental Conservation*, 14(2), 101-10.

Barbier, E.B. (1989). *Economics, Natural Resource Scarcity and Development*, London: Earthscan.

Barnett, H.J. and Morse, C. (1963). *Scarcity and Growth: The Economics of Natural Resource Availability*, Baltimore: Johns Hopkins University Press.

Barrett, E.G. and Curtis, L.F. (1982). *Introduction to Environmental Remote Sensing*, 2nd Edition, New York: Halsted Press.

Barry Jones, R.J. (1988). "Political Economy: Contending Perspectives on a Changing World", in R.J. Barry Jones (ed.) *The Worlds of Political Economy*, London and New York: Printer and Publishers, 1-26.

Bartelmus, P. (1987). *Environment and Development*, London: Allen and Unwin.

Bassett, T. (1988). "The Political Ecology of Peasant-Horder Conflicts in the Northern Ivory Coast", *Annals of the Association of American Geographers*, 78, 453-72.

Baumann, D.D. (1983). "Social Acceptance of Water Reuse", *Applied Geography*, 3, 79-84.

Bell, M. and Roberts, N. (1991). "The Political Ecology of Dambo Soil and Water Resources in Zimbabwe", *Transactions of the Institute of British Geographers*, N.S. 16, 301-318.

Bennett, R.J. and Chorley, R.J. (1978). *Environmental Systems: Philosophy, Analysis and Control*, London: Methuen.

Berkes, F. and Folke, C. (1994). "Investing in Cultural Capital for Sustainable Use of Natural Capital", in A. Jansson, M. Hammer, C. Folke and R. Costanza (eds.) *Investing in Natural Capital: The Ecological Economics Approach to Sustainability*, Washington, D.C.: Island Press, 128-48.

Berry, B.J.L. Conkling, E.C. and Ray, D.M. (1993). *The Global Economy: Resource Use, Locational Choice and International Trade*, Englewood Cliffs, N.J.: Prentice Hall.

Black, R. (1990). "Regional Political Ecology in Theory and Practice: A Case Study from Northern Portugal", *Transactions of the Institute of British Geographers*, N.S. 15, 35-47.

Blaikie, P. (1985). *The Political Economy of Soil Erosion in Developing Countries*, New York: Longman.

Blaikie, P. and Brookfield, H. (1987). *Land Degradation and Society*, London: Methuen.

Bottomore, T. (ed.) (1983). *A Dictionary of Marxist Thought*, Delhi: Oxford University Press.

Brundtland Commission (1987). *World Commission on Environment and Development: Our Common Future*, Oxford: Oxford University Press.

Bryant, R.L. (1992). "Political Ecology: An Emerging Research Agenda in Third World Studies", *Political Geography*, 11(1), 12-36.

Burrough, P. (1986). *Principles of Geographical Information Systems for Land Resource Assessment*, Oxford: Clarendon Press.

Burton, I. (1971). "The Social Role of Attitude and Perception Studies", in W.R.D. Sewell and I. Burton (eds.) *Perceptions and Attitudes in Resources Management*, Ottawa: Information Canada, 1-6.

Burton, I. and Kates, R.W. (eds.) (1965). *Readings in Resource Management and Conservation*, Chicago: The University of Chicago Press.

Campbell, J.B. (1987). *Introduction to Remote Sensing*, New York: Guilford Press.

Chambers, R. (1988). "Sustainable Rural Livelihoods: A Strategy for People, Environment and Development", *Institute of Development Studies*, University of Sussex.

Chorley, R.J. (1973). "Geography as Human Ecology", in RJ. Chorley (ed.), *Directions in Geography*, London: Methuen, 155-69.

Chrisman, N.R., Cowen, D.J., Fisher, P.P., Goodchild, M.F. and Mark, D.M. (1989). "Geographic Information Systems", in G. L. Gaile and C.J. Willmott (eds.) *Geography in America*, Columbus: Merrill Publishing Company, 776-96.

Ciriacy-Wantrup, S.V. (1942). "Private Enterprise and Conservation", *Journal of Farm Economics*, 24(1), 75-96.

Colwell, R.N. (ed.) (1983). *Manual of Remote Sensing*, 2nd edition, Falls Church, V.A.: American Society for Photogrammetry and Remote Sensing.

Conway, G. and Barbier, E. (1988). "After the Green Revolution: Sustainable and Equitable Agricultural Development", in D. Pearce and M. Redclift (eds.), *Futures*, 20(6), 651-78.

Coppock, J.T. and Sewell, W.R.D. (eds.) (1976). *Spatial Dimensions of Public Policy*, Oxford: Pergamon Press.

Crawford, J.G. (1952). *The Economics of Conservation*, Canberra: Bureau of Agricultural Economics, Department of Commerce and Agriculture.

Curran, P.J. (1985). *Principles of Remote Sensing*, New York: Longman.

Curran, P.J. (1987). "Remote Sensing Methodologies and Geography", *International Journal of Remote Sensing*, 8, 1255-75.

Daly, H.E. (1991). "Sustainable Development: From Concept and Theory to Operational Principles" in K. Davis and M.S. Bernstam (eds.), *Resources, Environment and Population: Present Knowledge, Future Options*, New York: Oxford University Press, 25-43.

Eckholm, E.P. (1982). *Down to Earth: Environment and Human Needs*, London; Earthscan.

Emel, J. and Peet, R. (1989). "Resource Management and Natural Hazards", in R. Peet and N. Thrift (eds.) *New Models in Geography: The Political Economy Perspective*, Vol. 2, London: Unwin Hyman, 49-76.

Estes, J.E. and Starr, J.L. (1989). *Geographic Information Systems*, Englewood Cliffs, N.J.: Prentice Hall.

Evans, F.C. (1956). "Ecosystem as the Basic Unit in Ecology", *Science*, 123, 1127-28.

Ferguson. A. and Alley. J. (1984). "Resource Geography: Is There a Shape to the Terrain ?" *The Operational Geographer*, No. 5, 36-38.

Glaeser, B. (ed.) (1984). *Ecodevelopment: Concepts, Projects, Strategies*, Oxford: Pergamon Press.

Golledge, R.G., Brown, L.A., and Williamson, F. (1972). "Behavioural Approaches in Geography: An Overview", *The Australian Geographer*,

12, 59-79.

Green, D., Rix, D. and Cadoux-Hudson, J. (eds.) (1994). *Geographic Information 1994: The Sourcebook for GIS*, Basingstoke, Hampshire: Taylor and Francis.

Grossman, L.S. (1993). "The Political Ecology of Banana Exports and Local Food Production in St. Vincent, Eastern Caribbean", *Annals of the Association of American Geographers*, 83, 347-67.

Gupta, R.A. (1971). *Planning Natural Resources*, New Delhi: Nab Traders.

Haack, B.N. (1982). "LANDSAT: A Tool for Development", *World Development*, 10, 899-909.

Haggett, P. (1979). *Geography: A Modern Synthesis*, New York: Harper and Row Publishers.

Hamilton, D. (1973). *Technology, Man and the Environment*, London: Faber and Faber Ltd.

Hammar, C.H. (1942). "Society and Conservation", *Journal of Farm Economics*, 24(1), 109-23.

Heady, E.O. (1950). "Some Fundamentals of Conservation Economics and Policy", *Journal of Farm Economics*, 32(4), 1182-95.

Hecht, S. and Cockburn. A. (1989). *The Fate of the Forest: Developers, Destroyers and Defenders of the Amazon*, New York: Verso.

Holmberg, J. and Sandbrook, R. (1992). "Sustainable Development: What is to be Done ?" in J. Holmberg (ed.) *Policies for a Small Plane: From the International Institute for Environment and Development*, London: Earthscan, 19-38.

IUCN (1985). *The World Conservation Strategy, Geneva: International Union for Conservation of Nature and Natural Resources.*

Jackson, E.L. (1980). "Perceptions of Energy Problems and the Adoption of Conservation Practices in Edmonton and Calgary", *Canadian Geographer*, 24, 114-30.

Jensen, J.R. (1986). *Introductory Digital Image Processing: A Remote Sensing Perspective*, Englewood Cliffs, N.J.: Prentice Hall.

Jensen, J.R., Campbell, J., Dozier, J., Estes, J., Hodgson, M., Lo. C.P., Lulla, K., Merchant, J., Smith, R., Stow, D., Strahler, A. and Welch, R. (1989). "Remote Sensing", in G.L. Gaile and C. J. Willmott (eds.), *Geography in America*, Columbus: Merrill Publishing Company, 746-75.

Kates, R.W. (1962). *Hazard and Choice Perception in Flood Plain Management*, Research Paper No. 78, Department of Geography, University of Chicago, Chicago.

King, G.Q. (1991). "Geography and GIS Technology", *Journal of Geography*, 90, 66-72.

Krutilla, J.V. and Eckstein, O. (1958). *Multiple Purpose River Development*, Baltimore: Johns Hopkins University Press.

Lang, R. (ed.) (1986). *Integrated Approaches to Resource Planning and Management*, Calgary: University of Calgary Press.

Lo, C.P. (1986). *Applied Remote Sensing*, New York: Longman Scientific and Technical.

Manning, E.W. (1990). "Sustainable Development: The Challenge", *Canadian Geographer*, 34, 290-302.

Marble, D.F., Calkins, D.F. and Peuquet, D.J. (eds.) (1984). *Basic Readings in Geographic Information Systems*, Buffalo, N.Y.: Spad Systems.

Martin, D. (1991). *GIS and Their Socio-Economic Applications*, London: Routledge.

Mather, A.S. (1982). "The Changing Perception of Soil Erosion in New Zealand", *Geographical Journal*, 148, 207-18.

McCormick, J. (1984). *The Global Environmental Movement: Reclaiming Paradise*, London: Belhaven Press.

Milliken, B. (1992). "Tropical Deforestation, Land Degradation and Society: Lessons from Rondonia, Brazil", *Latin American Perspectives*, 19(1), 45-72.

Mitchell, B. (1986). "The Evolution of Integrated Resource Management", in R. Lang (ed.) *Integrated Approaches to Resource Planning and Management*, Calgary: University of Calgary Press, 13-26.

Mitchell, B. (1989). *Geography and Resource Analysis*, 2nd. edition, Harlow, Essex: Longman Scientific and Technical.

Mitchell, B. and Pigram, J.J. (1989). "Integrated Resource Management and the Hunter Valley Conservation Trust, NSW, Australia", *Applied Geography*, 9, 196-211.

Mukherjee, A. and Agnihotri, V.K. (eds.) (1993). *Environment and Development: Views from the East and the West*, New Delhi: Concept Publishing Company.

Nelson, J.G. (1987). "National Parks and Protected Areas, National Conservation Strategies and Sustainable Development", *Geoforum*, 18(3), 291-319.

Odum, E.P. (1971). Fundamentals of Ecology, Philadelphia: W.B. Saunders Co.

O'Riordan, T. (1971). Perspectives on Resource Management, London: Pion.

O'Riordan, T. (1979). "Ecological Studies and Political Decisions", Environment and Planning, 11A, 805-13.

O'Riordan, T. (1993). "The Politics of Sustainability", in R. Kerry Turner (ed.). Sustainable Environment Economics and Management: Principles and Practice, London and New York: Belhaven Press, 37-69

O'Riordan, T. and Turner, R.K. (1979). "Recycling and Households Attitudes: A Survey of Norwich", Resources Policy, 5(1), 42-50.

Peet, R. and Thrift, N. (1989). "Political Economy and Human Geography", in R. Peet and N. Thrift (eds.). *New Models in Geography: The Political-Economy Perspective*, Volume I, London: Unwin Hyman, 3-29.

Peuquet, D. and Marble, D. (1994). (eds.) Introductory Reading in Geographic Information Systems, Basing Stoke, Hampshire: Taylor and Francis.

Pearce, D., Barbier, E. and Markandya, A. (1987). "Sustainable Development and Cost-Benefit Analysis", London Environmental Economics Center, Paper 88-01.

Pearce, D., Markandya, A. and Barbier, E. (1989). Blueprint for a Green Economy, London: Earthscan.

Pierce, J.T. (1992). "Progress and the Biosphere: The Dialectics of Sustainable Development", *Canadian Geographer*, 36(4), 306-20.

Powell, J.M. (1980). *Approaches to Resource Management: An Introduction for Australian Students*, Malvern: Sorrett Publishing.

Ranade, F. (1981). *Ecology of Natural Resources*, Chichester: John Wiley and Sons.

Raza, Mehdi (ed.) (1992). *Development and Ecology: Essays in Honour of Professor M. Shafi,* Jaipur: Rawat Publications.

Redclift, M. (1987). *Sustainable Development: Exploring the Contradictions*, London: Methuen.

Redclift, M. (1991). "The Multiple Dimensions of Sustainable Development", *Geography*, 76, 36-42.

Rees, J. (1985). *Natural Resources: Allocation, Economics and Policy*, London and New York: Routledge.

Rees, J. (1991). "Resources and the Environment: Scarcity and Sustainability", in R. Bennett and R. Estall (eds.) *Global Change and Challenge: Geography for the 1990's,* London: Routledge, 5-26.

Riddell, R. (1981). *Ecodevelopment: Economics, Ecology and Development: An Alternative to Growth Imperative Models*, Aldershot: Gower Publishing.

Saarinen, T.F. (1966). Perception of the Drought Hazard on the Great Plains, Research Paper No. 106, Department of Geography, University of Chicago, Chicago.

Sachs, I. (1980). *Strategies de ecodevelopment*, Paris: Les Editions Ouvrieres.

Schmink, M. and Wood, C. (1987). "The Political Ecology of Amazonia" in P.D. Little and M.M Horowitz (eds.) *Lands at Risk: Local Level Perspectives*, London: West View Press, 38-57.

Sewell, W.R.D. and Mitchell, B. (1984). "Geographers, The Policy Process and Education", *The Operational Geographer*, 5, 23-28.

Simmons, I.G. (1974). The Ecology of Natural Resources, London: Edward Arnold.

Simonett, D.S, Reeves, R.G., Estes, J.E., Bertke, S.E. and Sailer, C. (1983). "Development and Principles of Remote Sensing", in R.N. Colwell (ed.). *Manual of Remote Sensing, Falls Church*, V.A.: American Society for Photogrammetry and Remote Sensing, 1-35.

Stonich, S.C. (1993). *I am Destroying the Land: The Political Ecology of Poverty and Environmental Destruction in Honduras*, Boulder: Westview Press.

Taylor, D.R.F. (ed) (1991). *GIS: The Microcomputer and Modern Cartography*, Oxford: Pergamon Press.

Teclaff, L.A. (1967). *The River Basin in History and Law*, The Hague; Martinus Nijjhaff.

Tansley, A.G. (1935). "The Use and Abuse of Vegetational Concepts and Terms", *Ecology*, 16, 284-307.

Thrupp, L.A. (1993). "Political Ecology of Sustainable Rural Development: Dynamics of Social and Natural Resource Degradation", in P. Allen (ed.) *Food For the Future: Conditions and Contradictions of Sustainability*, New York: John Wiley and Sons, 47-73.

Townshend, R.G. (ed.) (1981). *Terrain Analysis and Remote Sensing*, London: Allen and Unwin

Tricart, J. and Kiewietde Jonge, C. (1992). Ecogeography and Rural Management: A Contribution to the International Geosphere-Biosphere Programme, Harlow, Essex: Longman Scientific and Technical.

Turner, R.K. (1993). "Sustainability: Principles and Practice", in R.K. Tuner (ed.). *Sustainable Environmental Economics and Management: Principles and Practice*, London and New York: Belhaven Press, 3-36.

Walsh, S.J. (1988). "Geographic Information Systems: An Instructional Tool for Earth Science Educators", *Journal of Geography*, 87(1), 17-25.

Watts, M. (1983). *Silent Violence: Food, Famine and Peasantry in Northern Nigeria, Berkeley*: University of California Press.

White, G.F. (1945). Human Adjustment to Floods, University of Chicago, Department of Geography, Research Paper No. 29, Chicago.

White, G.F. (1966). "Formation and Role of Public Attitudes" in H. Jarrett (ed.). *Environmental Quality in a Growing Economy, Baltimore*: Johns Hopkins University Press, 105-27.

White, G.F. (1977). (ed.) *Environmental Effects of Complex River Development: International Experience*, Boulder: Westview Press.

Walsh, S.J. (1988). "Geographic Information Systems: An Instructional Tool for Earth Science Educators", *Journal of Geography*, 87(1), 17-25.

Watts, M. (1983). *Silent Violence: Food, Famine and Peasantry in Northern Nigeria*, Berkeley: University of California Press.

White, G.F. (1945). *Human Adjustment to Floods*, University of Chicago, Department of Geography, Research Paper No. 29, Chicago.

White, G.F. (1966). "Formation and Role of Public Attitudes" in H. Jarrett (ed.) *Environmental Quality in a Growing Economy*, Baltimore: Johns Hopkins University Press, 105-27.

White, G.F. (1977). (ed.) *Environmental Effects of Complex River Development: International Experience*, Boulder: Westview Press.

Wood, L.J. (1970). "Perception Studies in Geography", *Transactions of the Institute of British Geographers*, 50, 129-42.

Worboys, M.F. (1994). *GIS: A Computer Science Perspective*, Basingstoke, Hampshire: Taylor and Francis.

Worboys, M.F. (ed.) (1994). *Innovations in GIS*, Basingstoke, Hampshire: Taylor and Francis.

Zimmermann, E.W. (1933, 1951 revised). *World/Resources and Industries*, New York: Harper and Brothers.

CONCEPT

1

Resources and Environmental Management: Some Fundamental Concepts and Definitions

A.J. CONACHER

In practice, in teaching and in research in the fields of resources and environmental management, the author has repeatedly found a lack of clarification and definition of fundamental concepts and terms in the literature. Personal experience has shown that this lack of clarification produces difficulties amongst students, resource managers and environmental practitioners, who often confuse or treat as synonymous the terms 'resource management' and 'environmental management'. This leads to difficulties in setting operational goals in theoretical and applied work in environmental studies.

Whilst there appears to be some consensus as to what is meant by 'resource' and 'resource management', the terms 'environment' and 'environmental management' are less well served. For example O'Riordan (1971a), who devotes an entire chapter to environmental management in his excellent book on *Perspectives in Resource Management*, does not define the term: and Powell (1976), in his pioneering work *Environmental Management in Australia 1788-1914*, uses 'resources management' and 'environmental management' interchangeably. Since environmental problems are nearly always related to the use of resources (whether human or physical), the fields of resources management and environmental management need to be considered together; but, as will be argued, their respective goals, techniques and managers are not (and should not be) the same.

This chapter first briefly considers 'resource': what it is, what its characteristics are, how it is measured and how it is managed; and then turns to 'environment', which is defined in relation to 'resource'.

The concept and definition of 'environmental management' is based on the discussion which precedes it. The clear distinction which emerges between resources management and environmental management has important implications for the political decision-makers. Good decision-making in an adversary situation demands that both sides receive every opportunity to present their cases. Further, the decision-makers also need to re-assess their own attitudes which, it is suggested, have for too long been influenced predominantly by the outmoded arguments and attitudes of the resource managers.

Resource

A definition may be of several kinds; by analogy, example, or by attempting to define the essence of the concept. The last approach is preferably since specific examples may then be matched against the concept, whereas a definition by analogy or example will almost certainly be incomplete.

With regard to resource, a preferred definition would include a functional statement (in that an object is not a resource until it is used), and be couched in terms of human needs (by necessity the definition must be anthropomorphic) within a socio-economic-technological context. Uranium is a resource to highly developed technological societies but not to a Papuan hill tribe. From a number of possibilities, the standard and widely accepted definition of Zimmerman (in Hunker, 1964) is preferred: '*a resource is a response to man's appraisal and perception of his environment in a want-satisfying capacity, satisfying individual, group and social objectives. It involves an appraisal as to whether the environment provides, supports or serves the supply of desirable goods or services (food, shelter and comfort)*'.

The fundamental operational concept in this definition is that an object does not become a resource until it is used. Hoggett (1972) has more recently summarised the useful associated concept of 'stock'. 'The sum total of all the material components of the environment, including both mass and energy, physical and biological, can be described as the *total stock*. ... In spite of its abundance, the vast proportion of the earth's total stock is of very little interest to man. Either it is wholly inaccessible under existing technology... or (it) represents substances that man has not learned to use. Resources are therefore a cultural concept. A stock becomes a resource when it can be of some utility to man in meeting his needs for food, shelter, warmth, transportation, and so on'. Haggett also makes the point that the transformation from stock to resource can work in reverse since, with changing technology, a resource may lose its utility.

Characteristics of Resources

Resources may be physical or human. Human attributes of numbers, intelligence and educational attainment are just as fundamental a resource as are coal deposits, land or water.

The traditional way of classifying resources is exemplified in O'Riordan (1971a), and this is arguably still the most appropriate. The basic subdivision is into non-renewable and renewable categories, with the latter further subdivided according to the degree to which the resource may be depleted, sustained, or increased according to the degree of human use or misuse.

Measurement of Resources

Measurement techniques will clearly vary according to the nature of the resource; basically they are attempts to delimit quantity, flow, renewability and quality. However, a characteristic common to all kinds of resources measurement is that they are narrowly assessed in terms of utility, and a monetary parameter is often applied.

Exceptions do occur, in which case the motivation is most frequently political. In both cases the intention is supposedly to satisfy the utilitarian needs and wants of man.

Resource Management

The goal of resources management can now be seen to relate to the definition of resource; that is, to satisfy man's utilitarian needs and wants through the use of some object or set of objects. The idea of exploitation has been clearly associated with resources management objectives of maximising profits and efficiency (Edwards and Tversky, 1967). Thus *resources management may be defined as the set of technical, economic and managerial practices by which stocks are converted to resources for the purpose of satisfying man's utilitarian needs and wants under prevailing socio-economic and technological conditions*. Extraction, manufacturing, marketing, waste disposal and recycling are all included under this definition, where appropriate. Since the idea of 'use' is included in the definition of 'resource', the two terms together are superfluous. Hence it is preferable to use the term 'resource system' (rather than 'resource use') to incorporate all the technical, economic and managerial activities associated with the conversion of stocks to resources, and as defined above by 'resource management'.

As human needs are often seen by resource managers in monetary terms, the goals are *in practice* narrowly conceived (although *theoretically* they need not be). It follows that resources management operates within circumscribed limits. It is precisely this characteristic of (traditional) resources management that has given rise to environmental problems. But the distinction between resources management and environmental management goes further than this. The resources managers or operators (mining companies, farmers, water engineers, entrepreneurs) are also of necessity specialised by training and hence in outlook. The narrow conception of resources management is hence perpetuated. Further, it would be very difficult (and unfair) to expect a company, producing a product to sell competitively on the open market, to give equal consideration in its endeavours to other (environmental) goals which may conflict with the company's prime function, or at least not enhance it. This does not imply that the company has *carte blanche* to behave irresponsibly but, seen in this light, the goals and nature of resources management are quite distinct from those of environmental management.

Environment

A conceptual and functional definition of 'environment' is again preferred to definitions by example or analogy. In general terms, 'environment' has been defined by Hall and Fagen in their classic paper on general systems theory: '*A system's environment is the set of all objects whose behaviour is influenced by the behaviour of the primary system, and those objects whose behaviour influences the behaviour of the primary system*' (Hall and Fagen, 1956). As previously stated, most if not all environmental problems (air and water pollution, soil erosion, deterioration of rural and urban habitats, and social, economic, cultural and political disorder) relate to resources use or resource systems, as previously defined. Paraphrasing Hall and Fagen, therefore, the environment of a resource system can be defined as: *The set of all objects whose behaviour is influenced by the behaviour of the resource system, and those objects whose behaviour influences the behaviour of the resource system.*

This conceptual definition is particularly appropriate; it focuses attention not only on the 'objects' of the environment, but on the links between the resource system and its environment, stated in functional (behavioural) terms (see also Emery and Trist, 1965). Clearly a resource system's environment, so defined, is extremely comprehensive and complex. In practical terms, once the resource system of interest to the analyst has been established and its environment defined and identified, attention is then directed to those environmental aspects which have the more significant links with the resource system. At the outset, it should be clearly recognised that the environment of one resource system will include other resource systems.

Characteristics of Environment

A resource system's environment can be conventionally classified into categories, such as physical, biological, social, economic, political, cultural, and other resource systems. More importantly and usefully, in an operational sense, a resource system's environment can also be characterised by the nature of the definitive linkages with the resource system: the direction of the link (whether from the environment to the resource system or *vice versa*, or both); whether the link is direct or indirect (operating through some other sub-system); whether the relationship is positive (beneficial) or negative (harmful); and the strength of the link. Again, such a classification or characterisation stresses the functional relationship between the behaviour of the two sets of objects; resource systems and their environments are dynamically interrelated.

The existence of dynamic relationships amongst resource systems and their environments leads to consideration of a further environmental characteristic; that is, its stability. Natural systems exhibit a tendency to attain or to fluctuate around a steady state; the activities incorporated within resource systems may, through their links with their environments, lead to a breakdown of the equilibrium condition and produce a tendency to attain a different steady state or, alternatively, a disequilibrium state. The degree to which an environmental system can adapt to future uncertainties is, therefore, an important characteristic.

Measurement of Environment

Although environment as conventionally classified (above) can be measured by various traditional parameters, such measurements say little directly about the dynamic interaction between environment and resource system which is so fundamental to the concept and definition of environment. Nevertheless, such measurements (evaluation) may be necessary at some stage, and here it is noteworthy that, unlike the measurement of resources, environmental measurement is rarely carried out in economic terms. Rather, the measurements are usually statements about 'quality' in relation to some established or arbitrarily selected standard; as for noise, air and water pollution, and occasionally, aesthetics. Similar work and setting of standards for economic, social, political and cultural attributes of environment appear to be lagging by comparison.

More useful and functional approaches are those which attempt to measure the linkages between resource systems and their environments. Here there appears to be three groups of widely used techniques. First are those statistical approaches associated with simple and multiple correlation and regression analysis, which attempt to measure statistically the degree and nature of the relationships amongst two or more phenomena. In this way the strength, direction and nature of the links can be assessed. Examples of this approach are given in Chorley and Kennedy (1971: see especially Chapter 8).

Secondly, there is the environmental impact matrix approach pioneered by Leopold *et al.* (1971). Here are an essentially subjective attempt is made to quantify the magnitude and importance of the effects of resource system activities on a set of environmental attributes, and to characterise them as beneficial (positive) or damaging (negative). Various writers have made useful modifications to this approach in an attempt to reduce subjectivity (for example Dee *et al.*, 1972: in Munn, 1975, pp. 63-67); but it is still essentially the perception or perceptions of the links by an evaluator or evaluators which is involved.

The third approach, which may be regarded as an offshoot of the second, is the use of sample interviews of populations to assess the reaction and perception of a much larger and, if possible, representative community group, to the activities or behaviour of a resource system (example: O'Riordan, 1971b and other chapters in the same volume). Various gaming-simulation techniques may also be included in this third category (example: Open University, 1973).

All of these measuring techniques are important, but they do not permit identification of changes through time. Here the application of time-series analysis (for example, Chorley and Kennedy, 1971, Ch. 7), although undeveloped in the present context, may be a useful means of assessing the stability or degree of adaptability of environmental systems.

The possibility of change of an environmental system from one state to another is not, in itself, undesirable. 'Desirability' or otherwise can only be assessed by the community, in relation to its system and scale of values. Such an assessment is especially (but not solely) important when dealing with environmental systems which are in the realm of common 'ownership' (oceans, rivers, groundwater, air, state forests, and the condition or state of the community itself). Knowledge and awareness by the community of the direction of change, and of the likely future state of the environmental system, is essential if meaningful value judgements of desirability are to be made; hence the importance of measurement and of communication of the results.

Environmental Management

It is now possible to propose a definition of environmental management based on the preceding discussion. First, it follows logically that an important goal of environmental management is to enhance positive links and minimise negative links amongst resource systems and their environments. Since these beneficial and adverse links can only be so categorised anthropomorphically, the goals of environmental management must be couched in terms of community perceptions and desires. Another goal of environmental management is to attain environmental system states which accord with those deemed by the community to be desirable. Such a goal could be to return a disturbed system to its original equilibrium state (for example, the revegetation of a mined site), or to change the system to a new and different equilibrium state (for example, to convert a mined site not to its previous condition but into a recreational lake). It is conceivable, but unlikely, that a community may consider it desirable to have an environmental system in a state of continuous disequilibrium.

Thus, *environmental management may be defined as those activities which enhance beneficial links and minimise adverse links amongst resource systems and their environments, and which seek to attain desirable environmental system states, in response to community perceptions and desires, under prevailing socio-economic and technological conditions.*

Although human needs and wants are incorporated in the definitions of both resources and environmental management, the first is usually narrowly focused and the second much more broadly conceived the idea of community becomes more important in environmental management. Further, the characteristics of resources and of environment, the means used to measure them, and the goals of the two managements, are quite distinct. Frequently, there is a clash of wants and needs between the goals of the two management groups.

In addition, since resource management goals are usually more specific, more immediate and more clearly defined than those of environmental management, the latter tend to be neglected.

In particular, the goals of resources management are often single-purpose whereas those of environmental management are invariably multi-purpose. This is because resources management focuses on its resource system whilst environmental management must deal with both resource system and their environments. Environmental management is connected with the adaptability of complex environments to future uncertainties, whereas resources management seeks single solutions to problems within the resource system only, often in engineering and economic terms. Moreover, since community desires and value are fundamental to environmental management goal-setting, and since unanimity of such desires and values within heterogeneous communities is highly unlikely, multiple-purpose goals are inevitable. In contrast, resources managers consider community desires only if they impinge upon or threaten their specific resource system objectives of survival and the need to make a profit.

The Environment Managers

It follows from what has been said that, although resource managers should be environmentally aware, resources management and environmental management cannot and should not be carried out by the same group of people. This is particularly the case when, as so often happens, the 'environmental problem' turns out to be a conflict between two or more competing resource systems. Here it should be noted that, for example, a conservation reserve is just as much a resource system, as defined, as is an operating coal mine. Further, the nature of the skills and expertise required by the two groups are not the same. The point is easily demonstrated by comparing the personnel in an alumina refinery with those working for an environmental protection agency. The question arises whether one group should be set over the other; and the answer must be that both groups should have equal standing, accessibility to and influence on political decision-makers and legislators. A most crucial point, however, is that the community and the decision-makers should be equally well informed, and the community's views widely canvassed, since decisions for *both* managerial groups rest on 'human wants and needs', different and conflicting though they may be.

There is, however, a group of organisation which is not so easily categorised as 'resource managers' or 'environmental managers', whose goals and functions overlap between the two — which may well be a root cause of a great deal of public dissatisfaction. This group of organisation include statutory *ad hoc* authorities and government departments. In Western Australia such organisation include, for example, the Public Works Department, responsible for water resources management amongst other functions; the Forests Department; and various town planning authorities.

Such bodies tend to behave more like 'resource managers' than 'environmental managers' and operate within constraints imposed by outmoded legislation. One consequence is their tendency to respond to events in an incremental fashion rather than anticipating or projecting within a wider environmental context. This incremental process is what Lindblom (1959) called 'the science of muddling through'. Moreover, since they are government or semi-government bureaucracies operating under Public Service Regulations, their decisions are almost impossible to reverse or modify since they usually have ministerial approval by the time the community gets to hear about them (example: Conacher, 1975). The resultant controversy can cause considerably frustration, loss of time and money of all sides, and a resentful and cynical electorate.

A clearer conceptualisation of what is meant by resources and environmental management, enabling the goals and functions of various organisations to be more clearly identified and defined, would at least clarify the issues in environmental conflict situations and lead to improved decision-making. Moreover, where bureaucratic activities impinge upon the realm of common ownership and where they involve manipulation of the environment as defined there — as they are invariably must — then the explicit incorporation of community desires and values is essential if sound, multiple-purpose management goals are to be identified and attained.

Conclusion

Personal experience has shown that there is considerable confusion in the community, and by resource managers and environmental agencies, as to what is meant by 'environment' and hence 'environmental management'. Too often 'the environment' is conceived as being a vaguely defined grouping of physical phenomena — air, soil, water, vegetation and, perhaps, landscape aesthetics. Yet these phenomena, together with the elements of the social, economic and political 'environment', are also undoubtedly resources. Clearly a distinction between resources and environment cannot be based on the nature of the constituent objects themselves.

By taking a system conceptual viewpoint it can be seen that 'environment' cannot be conceived as an abstract entity: it must be the environment of something. Often it is thought of as being the environment of man. But it is only when man acts that responses, and hence problems occur.

This chapter has taken the viewpoint that it is the range of man's actions in connection with manipulation of resources — comprising what has been termed here the 'resource system' — that is the prime cause of what are commonly thought of as being environmental problems; degradation of nature, various kinds of pollution, social breakdown. 'The environment' has therefore been defined in a systems conceptual sense as being the environments of resource systems. Operationally, this means that the focus of attention of environmental managers is on the functional links between resource systems and their environments, and on the stability of the environment systems; and their goals are to minimise adverse links and to maximise beneficial links between resource systems and their environments, and to attain desirable environmental system states. The focus is on *quality*, in response to community values and aspirations; whereas that of the resource managers is on *quantity*, always in material and often in monetary terms, in relation to perceived demands for food, shelter and consumer goods. The goals, methodologies, expertise and attitudes of the two managerial groups are hence seen to be totally different.

In particular, resources managers see management as a rational process carried out by 'economic men' operating under conditions of certainty, complete knowledge and predictability. Their objectives are, firstly, to maximise profits and to minimise costs, and secondly, to maximise the efficiency of the means of production, distribution and exchange. This nineteenth-century viewpoint is becoming increasingly recognised as being wholly unrealistic, but there is a clear tendency for resources managers to operate as though these conditions can be fulfilled and as though the objectives are still valid. In contrast, environmental managers operate under conditions of uncertainty, incomplete knowledge and unpredictability. Their mode of operation is not couched in economic terms and they seek multiple objectives, which must also retain flexibility so as to allow for future uncertainties, in order to satisfy (not maximise) heterogeneous community ideals, values and desires.

It follows that resolution of conflict goals between these groups must be carried out at a higher level. In a democratic society this is done by parliament; but it cannot be stressed too strongly that, if this is the case, then the two managerial groups must have equal representation and carry equal weight before the political decision-makers — who ought to make their decisions on the basis of the needs and aspirations of the whole community. Needless to say, all too often this does not happen. The lone environmental representative in Cabinet is not only outnumbered but his utterances are frequently indistinguishable from those of his colleagues who, mistakenly, perceive their responsibilities to the community as being confined to maximising the development of resource systems.

REFERENCES

Chorley, R.J. and Kennedy, B.A. (1971). *Physical Geography: A Systems Approach,* Prentice-Hall, London.

Conacher, A.J. (1975). *Environment-Industry Conflict: The Manjimup Woodchip Industry Proposal, Southwestern Australia,* Geowest, Working Papers of the Department of Geography, University of Western Australia, No. 4.

Edwards, W. and Tversky, A. (Eds.) (1967). *Decision Making,* Penguin.

Emery, F.E. and Trist, E.L. (1965). The causal texture of organisational environments. *Human Relations,* 18, 21-32.

Haggett, P. (1972). *Geography: A Modern Synthesis,* Harper an Row, New York, 180-81.

Hall, A.D. and Fagen, R.E. (1956). Definition of system. *General Systems,* 1, 18-28.

Hunker, H.L. (ed.) (1964). *Zimmerman, Erich Walter: Introduction to World Resources,* Harper and Row, New York.

Leopold, L.B., Clarke, F.E., Hanshaw, B.B. and Balsley, J.R. (1971). A procedure for evaluating environmental impact. *US Geol. Surv. Circular,* 645.

Lindblom, C.E. (1959). The science of 'muddling through'. *Public Administration Rev.,* 19, 79-88.

Munn, R.E. (Ed.) (1975). *Environmental Impact Assessment: Principles and Procedures,* International Council of Scientific Unions, Scientific Committee on Problems of the Environment (SCOPE), Report 5, Toronto.

Open University (1973). *A Local Government System — A Case Study of the Brighton Corporation and Brighton Marina,* Systems Behaviour: Module 4, Open University Press, Milton Keynes.

O'Riordan, T. (1971a). *Perspectives on Resource Management,* Pion Ltd., London

O'Riordan, T. (1971b). Towards a strategy of public involvement, in W.R.D. Sewell and I. Burton (Eds.), *Perceptions and Attitudes in Resource Management,* Policy Research and Coordination Branch, Dept. of Energy, Mines and Resources, Ottawa, 99-110.

Powell, J.M. (1976). *Environmental Management in Australia 1788-1914,* Oxford University Press, Melbourne.

2

The Concept of Renewable Resources

M.K. MUTHOO

"Land is an element of nature, inextricably interwoven with man's institutions"
—Polyani (1957)

Natural Resources

It is inadequate to consider natural resources as those 'existing in, or formed by, nature' (Oxford English Dictionary, 1933). According to such definition, only one of the five types of forests identified by Poole (1968) would be considered as natural resources, viz., 'those established by natural regeneration without deliberate assistance from man'. But, natural forests managed and perpetuated by man may be more important for human welfare, for otherwise they would not be managed. This illustrates that a rigid definition is not useful and that natural resources need to be viewed in relation to man. Nature and natural resources influence human welfare in many ways. They yield materials for production, such as petroleum, and psychic goods for consumption, such as enjoyable landscape. Nature causes distress to man, such as through floods and bush fires. It may act as a barrier to development, such as through distance in the space resource and rugged terrain.

All kinds of wealth can be sources of human prosperity. To treat natural resources differently because they are nature's gifts is not rational, if the end is human welfare. The origin of a resource is immaterial; natural as well as non-natural resources are the constituents of social capital. That a resource may have been created naturally

Reprinted with permission from '*The Geographer*', Aligarh Muslim University, Aligarh.

instead of by the 'coagulation' of past labour inputs is irrelevant to present and future use of resources. For being harnessed,[1] natural resources require to be combined with other economic factors, such as labour. They constitute economic resources, depending upon demand and accessibility; lack of demand or inaccessibility to factors and markets leaves them economically unimportant to society.

In the process of harnessing natural resources, their occurrence in Nature is altered. Nevertheless, they retain the character of natural resources in so far as these are the vehicles by which mankind draws upon Nature's physical power for production and regulation. They differ from purely man-made capital, like machines, in that their role in human welfare is constrained by environmental factors. They occur in a natural flux, amenable to working within the framework of geosphere, of which man is but one of the elements. It is realistic to group natural resources as a separate form of capital, subject to natural changes in addition to the wear and tear engineered by man.

Natural resources may, as such, be defined as the features and products of Nature[2] amenable to use as factors of production and consumption goods. Originating in Nature, they are subject to manipulations depending upon the amenability to such process on the one hand, and the objectives, skills and complementary resources at Society's command on the other. The main natural resource types may be listed as hereinbelow[3]:

1. Land (including site and soil),
2. Vegetation,
3. Animal Life,
4. Water (in cycle),
5. Atmosphere, and
6. Minerals and Fuels.

Renewable Resources

Allen and Leonard (1966) arrange natural resources into three 'groupings', of which the first comprise the 'inexhaustible resources'. Hammar (1942) too makes the 'foremost' distinction between 'exhaustible' and 'inexhaustible' resources, including 'water power sources, the elements of soil fertility, brick clay' in the latter group. Such classifications seem to be so motivated that services required by mankind, whenever obtainable from 'inexhaustible' as well as 'exhaustible' resources may be secured from the former. If it is so, they are in the same category of importance as the statement that if labour does all the work, there need be no depletion of energy resources. Another consideration in such classifications is the physical availabilities of resources. Even assuming a static state of arts, it is arbitrary to distinguish resources as exhaustible and inexhaustible on the basis of such availability. The 'availability' depends on the relative proportions required for use, accessibility and demand. It varies by additions through discovery and other changes. It is not possible to identify objectively an amount that demarcates the line of exhaustibility and inexhaustibility of a resource.

The above classification is static in concept. The role of resources varies from time to time and place to place. The degree and manner of resource use depend upon society's development. Forests may have appeared as an inexhaustible resource to Amer-Indians just as brick clay appears to Hammar. Similarly, water power sources are not necessarily inexhaustible when considered in the three dimensions of resource, time and space. Examples are not wanting whence sources at a particular place do not hold the same potential as in the not-too-distant past. Changes manifest in the drying up of rivers, like Saraswati in India, and the accelerated run-off and sedimentation have reduced the water power sources of many areas. Such *exhaustibility* is a feature of immense economic significance by warranting expenditure on water conservation and allied measures. *Indeed all resources are capable of exhaustion and it is a misnomer to call any resource as inexhaustible* (Darling, 1969).

Hammar (*op. cit.*) may be right that the elements of soil fertility are 'inexhaustible', if considered in terms of geological time spans or the basic components of a resource. But peering into either the remote future of the elements of resources neither identifies nor changes the relationship of resources to man at present and in the relevant future. Such a view renders all resources 'homogeneous' in being basically 'inexhaustible', because the *elements* of no resource are exhaustible. A classification so based is tantamount to no classification. In practice, spatial changes take place even in elements, say through rivers flowing to seas and winds blowing across deserts. That apart, even if the elements of soil fertility are 'inexhaustible', soil fertility in many circumstances runs down and gets exhausted. Soil fertility is exhaustible. For soil as a natural resource, it is the liability to exhaustion and not the so-called inexhaustibility of soil fertility elements that matters. Soil fertility elements, if divorced from soil, are not exhaustible, because they may be technically perpetuated by manufacturing and applying fertilisers. But soil fertility elements that can be captured from soil, through the medium of which these are available for man's use, are exhaustible. It is this feature that necessitates fertilisation and other measures for maintaining soil productivity, so that the exhaustibility and not the inexhaustibility is of practical importance.

Ciriacy-Wantrup (1942) defines resources as *'flow resources if different units of a resource become available at different units of time... (and) as stock resources if the total quantity of resource available either does not vary significantly or decreases with time'* Kelso (1961) comments that being a 'stock' or a 'flow' resource influences the functioning of a related industry. Crawford (1952) too separates 'flow resources' of 'land, forests and water' from what he calls 'fund resources like coal and iron.' Heady (1950) distinguishes 'stock-derived products' from 'flow-derived products', for being with and without scope for substitution between time periods, respectively.

Since such distinctions focus attention on the composite supply of 'stock and flow resources', the objective is shifted to the substitution of 'stock resource' services in the current periods by 'flow resource' services in order that the former might be 'conserved'. In this respect, this classification is not different in theme from that of 'exhaustibles and inexhaustibles'. It would serve as a sequel to a policy for 'conservation' of 'stock' resources. Such classification is applicable only when the conservation of 'stock resources' is decided *ad lib* and not from an objective assessment of the spatial as well as temporal desirability of substitution and relative conservation needs for human welfare.

It is inapt to distinguish resources as being inherently either 'stocks' or 'flows'. *These are economic terms. The interpretation of 'stock and flow resources' is not in accord with the economic significance, causing confusion between economic concept and physical quantities of resources. Additional conceptual difficulty arises in making categories of resources into 'stock' or 'flow' resources.* A forest can be both a stock and a flow resource. At a particular time the quantity of wood is the stock. The amount of wood added through growth increment to (and/or reduced through decay or removal from) the original quantity of the stock is the flow from the date of the last inventory. One and the same tree holds a stock and a flow; it is a stock resource in static sense and a flow resource in dynamic sense. Considered through time dimension, minerals too exhibit flows. Kelso's (*op. cit.*) classification of ground water as a 'stock resource' in contrast to other water sources regarded as 'flow' resource is ambiguous. Ground water need not be of 'limited life span' (Davis, 1960), if a balance is struck between the rates of pumping and recharge. Parallel considerations are warranted for 'flow' water sources. Water drawn from a lake has to be balanced by inflow as otherwise it will dry up; a river cannot sustain an irrigation system larger than its discharge pattern and hence the real-world inter-state river basin problems.

Scott (1955) recognises the 'two classes' of 'stock resources' and 'renewable resources'—the former 'are lying ready for further processing...(and) are the subject of decision about depleting by employing current factors' and the latter 'are the subject of decision about employing... factors of production'. But the 'stock' resources need not always be the subject of depletion. They may actually be added to existing reserves such as by importing. The other objection is the conceptual incompatibility in interpreting 'stocks', as discussed earlier.

The concepts of 'stock' and 'renewable' resources are simultaneously applicable to most resources; the distinction is blurred for an objective analysis. Soil resource, for instance, may be depleted or mined 'by employing current factors' without investing for maintaining its present state and/or fertility. Contrariwise, it may be actually built up or, what is tantamount to that, improved from its existing state by proper husbanding that involves employing 'factors of production'. An example of the former is the practice of destructive, shifting cultivation in the tropics. Soils are used up or devastated and the erstwhile good soil resources stand depleted like a 'stock' resource (Jacks and Whyte, 1939). An opposite example is strikingly presented by Ladakh where lamas actually 'create' soil by meticulously gathering it from all over and spreading it on fields protected against erosion by building stone walls. Price (1954) records a similar practice in Malta where 'hard rock (was) slowly reduced to small pebbles and then covered with scraps of soil collected laboriously from cracks and crevices'. Another example is the floating fields in Kashmir's Dal Lake, built up by weaving mats of reeds and spreading weeds, soil and debris collected from the lake. Terracing for paddy cultivation in the East is another kind of example where soil gets treated as a 'renewable' resource by employing the 'available factors of production'.

A particular young tree can be regarded as a 'stock' which might be cut down. At the same time, it can be an object of further expenditure for producing more wood thirty years later. In such cases, the two categories blend together. Scott (*op. cit.*) dismisses the paradox by saying that 'there is no need to create further categories'. The problem, however, is not of having more than two categories but of classifying less ambiguously and more appropriately.

The primary consideration in classification should be the relationship of resources to man, i.e. their amenability to use and the influence of man's actions on resources. The objective in resource use should be to economise on scarce means of production and enjoyment, not on human welfare for the sake of the 'welfare' of resources. There is no inherent distinction between one or the other resource except for the relative scarcity and the scope for their renewal through use. No resource is intrinsically more valuable than others. The value depends upon the demand for resources and the ease with which they can be made available for use. Given an endowment of resources, an indifference between the inherent merits of different resources allows objective decision-making by society that relies on them as economic factors. A distinction for the prospects of renewability permits society to avoid the consequences of scarcity and depletion, i.e. by reducing the chances of rising prices for more supplies.

The distinction between renewable and non-renewable resources[4] *is that the former could be used and yet be renewed subject to the limitations set by the frame of Nature and available technology.* Of the six main types of resources listed earlier, all but the minerals and fuels may be considered renewable, i.e. *capable of renewal.* These resources may not be depleted, exhausted or destroyed while consuming or employing them for production in combination with other factors. This is possible for soils by using their content only to the extent of new additions through soil formation and other processes, including conservation farming; for animal life by restricting the manner and size of catch so that communities continue reproducing; for vegetation by not exceeding its removal in excess of regrowth; for underground water by tapping in accord with the rate of recharge; for water in rivers and lakes by using watersheds for logging, grazing, recreation and other purposes without damaging water production; and for atmosphere by using it in consonance with natural recycling and purification capability. Thus renewable resources could be maintained in quantity and even increased or altered for what may be considered an improvement in their quality during the process of use. There is no such scope for non-renewable resources which are depleted as and to the extent these are used up.

The above distinction of resources on the basis of their nature in use relates their consumption and renewal through time with technology. It does not presuppose a given or immutable economic policy and can be operated for varying economic structures. In addition to bringing out the scope of different resources in the overall context, it enables the adoption of a planning strategy most suitable for each of them separately too. In contrast, the earlier classifications are oriented mainly to the treatment of resources in a composite manner so that one kind could substitute the other. The latter approach fails to take notice of the problem beset in renewable resource planning and management, which is greater than that for non-renewable resources. This is so because renewable resources may have to be operated upon with the twin objectives of use and renewal, with mutual effects. With non-renewable resources, only the rate of use of a resource to meet demand requires to be determined from time to time. The distinction made is thus useful not only in providing an objective exposition of the relationship between resources and man but also in use planning under different economic conditions.

The classification into renewable and non-renewable natural resources does not involve any arbitrary limit of the quantities of a resource nor does it anticipate policies such as conservation of a particular resource. It avoids ambiguity between the natural resource classes and conflict in the use of terminology does not arise. It takes the relationship between man and resources into consideration through technology. But it does not presume any particular aspects of the relationship as being less or more important, for the role to resources is assigned from what they are used for and how they are usable. It is simple: all it stresses is the amenability or otherwise of resources through use (or misuse). It does not anticipate that use of renewable resources should substitute that of non-renewable resources in order to extend the quantity (and/or quality) of the latter over time; such decisions would vary from economy to economy and from time to time.

Renewable Resource System

Air, land and water together comprise an ecological whole, characterised by growth, decay and transformation of matter and energy. Change is perpetual and the ecosystem is ever developing like any living organism. Renewable resources include living things and occur in an ecological flux. Their study and use should consider the aspects of living nature, so that the constituent parts, including the human society, operate in mutual harmony and adaptation.

Organic nature, furnishing renewable resources, constitutes a complex dynamic system of interacting components. They are equilibrated and interrelated in such mutual dependency that change in one component entails changes in the rest of the system. Such systems can have no truly isolated parts. Technological measures considering the ecological requirements can improve upon conditions found in raw nature, in the sense of increasing 'yield' and reducing waste. But they will fail in a compartmentalised approach, because of the disregard of the cohesiveness of the total network of interrelations. The treatment of such multifactorial and multivariant systems requires suitable new methodologies. This author (1970) analysed the nature of the renewable resource problem. Instead of confining attention to limited aspects, he proposed systems analysis which can cope with the interrelatedness and interdependence of the factors involved, including man's objectives and attitudes. Suffice it to say here that the singling out for study individual components of a complex network is artificial, because component members do not actually exist in isolation.

The survival of an ecological system depends on the coexistence of interdependent mixtures of components and environmental conditions in requisite proportions. Their relative significance cannot be judged from statistics on bulk or averages. Therefore, an essential prerequisite for ecologically sound management of renewable resources is a quantitative as well as qualitative inventory and the study of the present use pattern for both absolute totals and spatial distribution.[5] However, existing equilibria are not necessarily optimal. By alterations of the mixture of components, on a scale short of endangering the integrity of the whole system, improved combinations could be discovered which come closer to maximising the total 'yield'.

Optimising the *total* should become an objective at par with the current general practice of maximising a specific *partial* result at the sacrifice of their interrelated parts. This requires the introduction into the total perspective of the system a sense of proportions. For instance, one need investigate not only how to eradicate a given pest or wastage, but also the lower limit to which such reduction could be carried and still remain harmless for the continued thriving of the afflicted system. A certain minimum of 'pollutants' or admixtures of organisms and inorganic items is often not only compatible with, but essential for, optimum results.[6] One-sided preoccupation with standards of purity is not only utopian but also undesirable.

Because of the net-like character of the renewable resource system, the prevailing concept of cause-to-effect chains of natural events is organically unreal. Accordingly, the conclusion that any deviation of a link along such chain irrevocably leads to a deviant result in untenable. By contrast, the network type of causal relations in an integrated system with re-anastomosing lines of interdependencies ensures equilibrating adjustments and development of the system as a whole. This establishes a multiplicity of alternative routes towards a given end, viz., optimisation. Only that, in view of the living nature of the ecological systems, matching combinations of steps for groups of components will be harmonious than isolated steps for individual components. Nevertheless, the idea is that equivalent improvements, i.e. same degree of optimisation of the *total* result, can be achieved by a variety of combinations of steps involving different parts of the system. The management's task, therefore, should be to unravel the opportunities for potential major progress by trying a much wider variety of heretofore untried novel combinations. The scientific task is to circumscribe the degrees of re-combinative freedom and to define the margins of tolerable adaptive flexibility within a given ecosystem.

The optimisation of renewable resource system cannot be achieved by fragmentary and sporadic attention to isolated parts of the problem. It requires a systematic process of investigation and evaluation in reference to total perspective. What by itself might be an insignificant contribution to total resource structure might, by its position in the total network, assume strategic significance beyond its independent quantitative rating.[7] Or, small component improvements may contribute to a large sum total. Conversely a big single improvement may negate the effectiveness of other components, so that the net result is insignificant. It is important to trace the linkages in a system and the interrelatedness of different courses of action at various points in the system.

Man and Renewable Resources

The present human environment, i.e. the earth, may be conceived as a spaceship (Boulding, 1966). In this, the throughput is not the desideratum, but the nature, extent, quality and complexity of total resources, including the state of human bodies and minds. Successfully manipulating the environment for the continuing benefit of man depends on the degree to which the whole environment is considered. Actions considering only the benefits to a part of the landscape or the lack of understanding of the chain of events that follow a large-scale manipulation are unhelpful. The zealous application of DDT affecting beyond threshold levels (Bloomfield, 1969) exemplifies the ignorance about cycling in systems. One-problem-one-solution approach fails to consider the side-effects, which in totality may result in more loss than gain to human welfare. Instead, some form of systems analysis which considers man as part of, not apart from, the environment is required.

Land, the first of the natural resource types listed earlier, occupies a unique position in the renewable resource system. An area of 'land expresses all the various natural factors existing in the area' (Graham, 1967). It can be captured as a resource through its attributes and not by itself, i.e. land represents the fundamental resource to which other natural resources are related and are a part of. Ely and Wehrwein (1964) conceive land as 'nature, space and property'. A more complete concept is that it is 'the sum total of the natural and man-made resources over which possession of the earth's surface gives control' (Barlowe, 1961). Land is the area unit on which human enterprises are conducted. But it is within the frame of renewable resource system that land as a factor of production is amenable to continued use by man. Besides minerals and the non-renewable role of rocks as the substratum, land provides the renewable resource of soil. Formed and developed, *inter alia*, under the influences of atmosphere and water, soil sustains the biotic resources of vegetation and animal life. Of the last named, human resources conventionally comprise the separate economic factor of labour and enterprise. All these resources are inextricably linked with each other. Man, circumscribed by other economic, political, socio-cultural, technological and physical conditions, plays a key role in the renewable resource system. The entire system may be conceived as a conglomerate of the mutual interactions between man and the resources. Such a biotic pyramid of which man is the apex and a dependent on all that is below him is illustrated in Fig. 2.1.

From the attributes of land as soil, landform and site flow the resources of vegetation, water in place, and animal life. Their amenability as factors of production or consumption goods depends upon the nature of these attributes within the framework of environment, including man and climate. The complex is represented by the form of watershed and landscape. A watershed or landscape may include

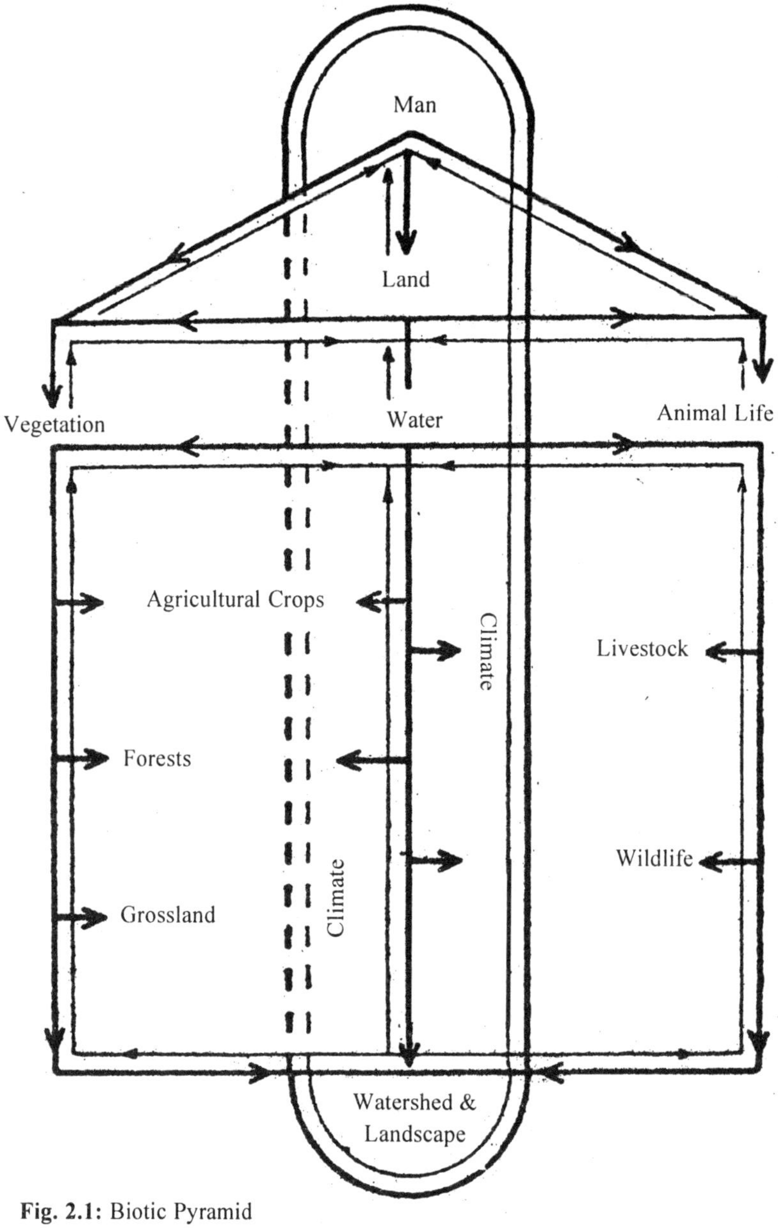

Fig. 2.1: Biotic Pyramid

agricultural, forest and grasslands, and, besides man, may carry livestock and wild life. All these are renewable resources.

The system depicted above embodies interdependent physical and biological features of the environment. The system may be defined as a biological organisation comprising the organisms in a given area i.e. the 'community interacting with the physical environment'. The systems analysis calls for an 'ecological way of looking at nature' (Cain, 1968) so as to weld together the diverse sciences involved in the use of resources. Since man is the pivotal agent in directing the use and the end is his welfare through harmony with the environment, biological and physical analyses alone are inadequate. The economic, political and social parameters also require to be incorporated. However, conflicts may arise due to such diversity. As Odum (1969) says, "the natural strategy of 'maximum protection' (i.e. trying to achieve maximum support of complex biomass structure to buffer physical environment) often conflicts with man's goal of 'maximum production' (trying to obtain the highest possible yield)". Such conflicts stem from the contrasting characteristics of different ecosystem types, as abstracted below:

Characteristics of Ecosystems

Young	*Old*
Production	Protection
Growth	Stability
Quantity	Quality

The burning of chirpine forests and of grasslands in Himalayas by nomadic graziers is an example of the practice to maintain vegetation at an early development stage. The young type is favoured to achieve high rates of production of readily available harvestable products with little standing crop left on the landscape, i.e. high production/biomass efficiency. On the other hand, nature's strategy is directed towards a high biomass/production ratio, which is attained by mature-type ecosystems said to be in a natural balance (Lotka, 1956). Since the environment is our living space as well as a supply source for food and fibre, its gas exchange, waste purification, climatic effects, and recreational and aesthetic capabilities are no less important than the throughput. Many of these 'protective' or 'living-space' functions are better served by the mature-type ecosystems. Therefore, we need to have a balance between 'productive' and 'protective' landscape; a system analysis would be incomplete if protective watershed resource use is not considered, as is often the case.

The above conflict between man's and nature's strategy is germane to renewable resource management strategy. Nothing is redundant among the contrasting aspects of production-protection, growth-stability, and quantity-quality. All the six characteristics are desirable. The dilemma is: can we have the cake as well as eat it? From the foregoing two paragraphs, we can think of any species to be harvested as subject to a 'technological' law of growth governed by the ecological characteristics of the biosystem in which it resides.[8] Commercial exploitation, say fishing and logging, is equivalent to the entry of man as a predator. Smith (1968) illustrates that in such a scheme, the commercial production from a renewable resource:

> 'need not in time destroy the resource. Exploitation by man *may* disrupt a delicate balance which destroys a resource. But the existence of external diseconomies does provide a built-in mechanism tending to resist annihilation of the resource: harvesting depletes the stock, costs rise and, *ceteris paribus*, discourages harvesting with the possibility if not a guarantee of an equilibrium.'

The crucial point is the recognition of external diseconomies, which does not always happen resulting in exhaustion of a species like the whooping crane. Renewable resources do exhibit production externalities, but these are not significant to the industry if the resource is unappropriated. Then the resource becomes a free for all good, like the early treatment meted out to supposedly limitless forests and soils in North America, which gave rise to 'grapes of wrath'. The externalities are usually ignored by entrepreneurs, for the aim is maximisation of their objectives (viz. profits). This results in the generally uncompensated social costs of private enterprise (Kapp, 1950), such as the exhaustion of fish in a lake or river by the effluents discharged by woodpulp industry. Thus, if perpetual resource use, to which renewable resources are amenable, is desired to be maintained, producers need to recognise externalities so that production is not pushed to exhaustion. Among other measures, the objective can be facilitated by unifying resource management. This may be done through corporate or public ownership or by social control over the use of resources, so that externalities of one component felt elsewhere in the system are captured by the management.

The conflict between prevalent practices adopted by man and the nature's strategy can be resolved by renewable resource usages which respects the contrasting aspects of ecosystem types. From a strictly "technical and scientific point of view, quantity and quality do not necessarily constitute alternative, or even complementary, attributes of the resources of nature" (Lepawsky, 1967). Instead, they are intertwined in decision-making and the management strategy should be aimed at the optimisation of the system, as conceived in the last section. Since the *extremes* of production-protection, or quantity-quality, cannot be had at the same time and place on the landscape, the optimisations should consider averting conflicts and effecting compromises which enhance human welfare. The multiple-resource use concept is relevant to this (Muthoo, 1968). It is the deliberate and carefully planned integration of various uses, so as to interfere with each other as little as possible. It may involve no use of some resources, e.g. protective watershed forest, for the optimisation of the total benefits from the renewable resource system. It does not imply that every acre of the landscape should produce multiple benefits, i.e. a little of protection, of production, of quantity. Instead, it implies that since people's needs are variegated and should be met as best as possible from the limited resources, each landscape type needs to be used in the manner which is compatible with its characteristics and the socio-economic climate.

Conclusion

In the use of renewable resources, Nature has put constraints on the manipulative ability of man. Though their use is for human welfare just as is of any other resource, the influence of natural 'laws' in their use gives them a class of their own. In the natural ecosystems, or the biosphere, solar radiation, moisture and soil nutrients are absorbed and processed in a complex, interwoven chain for the growth of plants, on which animals and man 'feed'. The economy also uses water and biological products through complex technological media, substituting natural processes and products, for meeting man's demand. The difference is that while the biosphere is a self-contained system organised to provide all its own needs and to breakdown, disseminate and re-use its waste materials, 'the technosphere is dependent on the biosphere not only for much of its input but also for important outlets at the far end of the production chain' (Nicholson, 1970). The co-ordination of environmental science (i.e. the understanding of the biosphere) and the environmental technology (i.e. man's manipulative skills) can lead to optimisation in more satisfactory manner if larger systems are considered. Then there will be scope to adapt different resource areas to what they are suited for rather than if optimisation is sought over smaller parcels of a forest or agricultural land. The integration of ecological and socio-economic systems is a challenge to those desirous of improving the environment and increasing the benefits to mankind from the renewable resource endowment. The implementation of landscape designs based on such analyses require co-operation from resource users and the will of society to enforce integrated use.

NOTES

1. For providing the material or consumption benefits, for controlling their harmful effects and for overcoming their influence as impediments to development.
2. Nature operates as the creative and regulative physical power; it includes the environmental phenomenon which occur unhindered or unaided by human agency, such as climatic changes, geological upheavals and evolution of species.
3. These do not include resources which arise as attributes of the basic resource types. One or more of them may form an 'integrated resource', e.g. amenity, recreation, from and space utility.
4. Barlowe (1961) uses the 'relative renewability' as the basic criterion but distinguishes between 'fund resources, flow resources, and a composite group of resources that have some characteristics of both fund and flow resources'. This concept involves the same inherent weaknesses as in those aiming to distinguish between stock and flow resources. The 'composite group comprises the biological and soil resources akin to renewable resource class, but discrepancy arises by the inclusion of non-natural resources of man-made capital such as 'houses, office buildings, farm service buildings, highways' (*Ibid.*).
5. This enables the assessment of use-possibility of a resource endowment, required for optimisation discussed hereinafter.
6. While in the interests of suitable environment the exhaustion of the renewable natural reservoirs of dilation and assimilative capacity needs to be prevented, the deleterious side effects (or externalities) associated with residual discharge may appear only at certain threshold values. The values 'are relevant only at some stage of economic development and

industrial and population concentrations' (Ayres and Kneese, 1969). It is for such reasons, besides their resource poverty, that the implications of 'conservation' in developing as distinct from industrial countries are different (Muthoo, 1969).

7. The far-reaching role of the earthworm in soil fertility or of cowdung if used as manure are some of the examples.
8. That is, the *mass* growth will depend upon certain biological characteristics of the species and on its environment, i.e. the abundance of nutrients, and the existence and efficiency of other species which have predator or symbiotic relationships with the given species.

REFERENCES

Alen, S.W., and J.W. Leonard, (1966). *Conserving Natural Resources*. McGraw-Hill Book Co., New York, 3rd ed., pp. 432

Ayres, R.U., and A.V. Kneese, (1969). Production, Consumption and Externalities. *Amer. Econ. Rev.*, 59 (3) pp. 282-297.

Barlowe, R. *Land Resource Economics*. Prentice-Hall, Inc., Englewood Cliffs, N.J. 585 pp. (3rd Ptg.).

Bloomfield, H., (1969). Slow Death for DDT? *Am. Forests*, 75 (11) 16-61.

Boulding K.E., (1966). The Economics of the Coming Spaceship Earth. *In* H. Jarret (Ed.), *Environmental Quality in a Growing Economy*. – Resources for the Future Inc. Washington D.C., pp. 3-14.

Ciriacy-Wantrup, S.V., (1942). Private Enterprise and Conservation. *Journ. Farm Economics*, 24(1). pp. 75-96.

Crawford, J.G., (1952). *The Economics of Conservation*. Bureau of Agricultural Economics, Department of Commerce and Agriculture, Canberra, A.C.T., pp. 59.

Davis, Jr. I.F., (1960). *Colorado's Ground Water Problems. Bull.* 506 S — The Economic Picture, Colorado State University Experimental Station, Fort Collins.

Darling, F.F., (1969). The Impact of Man on his Environment. *The Listener*, 82 (2121) 693-696.

Ely, R.T., and G.S. Wehrwein, (1964). *Land Economics*. The University of Wisconsin Press, Madison, pp. 24-112.

Graham, E.H., (1967). Land-Use Principles and Needs. *In* C.H. Collison (Ed.) *America's Natural Resources*. The Ronald Press Co., New York. Revd. Ptg., pp. 170-186.

Hammar, C.H., (1942). Society and Conservation. *Journ. Farm Economics*, 24(1), 109-123.

Heady, E.O., (1950). Some Fundamentals of Conservation Economics and Policy. *Jour. Farm. Economics*. 32(4), pp. 1182-1195.

Jacks, G.V. and R.O. Whyte, 1939. *The Rape of the Earth*. Faber and Faber Ltd., London. pp. 313.

Kapp, K.W., (1950). *The Social Costs of Private Enterprise*. Harvard University Press, Cambridge, Mass. pp. 287.

Kelso, M.M., (1961). The Stock Resource Value of Water. *Jour. Farm Economics* 43(4) pp. 1112-1129.

Lepawsky, A. (1967). The Quest for Quality in the Administration of Resources. *in* S.V. Ciriacy-Wantrup and J.J. Parsons (Eds.). *Natural Resources: Quality and Quantity*. Univ. of California Press, Berkeley, pp. 162-175.

Lotka, A.J. (1956). *Elements of Mathematical Biology*, New York, p. 28.

Muthoo, M.K. (1968). Forestry as a Major Land Use. *Proceedings*, Fourth Forestry Symposium – *Forestry in a Changing Society* – Oxford University, pp. 1-10.

——, (1969). Conservation Policy and Renewable Resource Planning in Developing Countries. *Jour. Oxford Forest Soc.* 6th Srs. (4), pp. 25-29.

——, (1970). The Renewable Resource Planning Problem. *Socio-Economic Planning Sciences*.

Nicholson, M., (1970). *The Environmental Revolution, A Guide for the New Masters of the Earth*. Hodder and Stoughton, London, pp. 366.

Odum, E.P., (1969). The Strategy of Ecosystem Development. *Science* 164 (3877) pp. 262-270.

3

Exhaustible Resources

PARTHA DASGUPTA

Introduction

All human activities are ultimately based on resources found in nature. Whether it is consumption, production, or exchange, the commodities which are involved can always be traced to constituents provided by nature.

A tractor requires for its manufacture iron and steel, rubber, plastics, non-ferrous metals, labour of various skills, factory-machinery, water, and so on. Of these, to take an example, the steel requires for its production iron ore, coal, furnaces, water, labour, and so forth. The furnaces in turn require for their manufacture, among other things, iron ore, brickworks, and labour. One can thus break down any produced good into the inputs involved in its manufacture and one can, if one has sufficient patience, trace them ultimately to a combination of labour and natural resources. Of course, labour too is produced and sustained by natural resources. So ultimately all commodities and services can be traced to natural resources.

My purpose in reminding you of the morphology of produced goods and services is not to prepare a chapter on the resource-theory of value. Like Marx's labour theory, such a construct quickly runs into analytical difficulties. My purpose, rather, is to set a materialistic tone so that one may in an unhampered way view natural resources in the light of their *use* to us in running our lives. I am not suggesting that this is the

Reprinted with permissions from L. Friday and R. Laskey (eds.) (1989) The Fragile Environment: Darwin College Lectures, Cambridge University Press.

only defendable perspective; I am merely indicating that this is the attitude I shall strike in this chapter. I need to declare my position at the outset, because if you scratch a resource economist you are likely to find a nature-worshipper trying to get out. I am going to suppress this urge and concentrate instead on the *instrumental* value of natural resources.

It is usual, and convenient, to divide natural resources into two classes: *exhaustible* (such as coal, oil and natural gas) and *renewable* (such as fisheries, aquifers, forests and woodlands, and soil quality). On the face of it, the classification is misleading, because even renewable natural resources are in danger of exhaustion if they are harvested at too fast a rate. But the idea behind the distinction is clear enough. Resources such as fossil fuels enjoy growth rates which operate only over geological time. Thus, their stock cannot increase. It can only decrease, or if none is mined for a while, stay constant. Improvement in technology — for example, learning to drill offshore — can increase the *usable* stock; but this is a different matter. Then again, discoveries of new deposits increase the *known* available stock. That, too, is a different matter. Now, what I have said about fossil fuels is true also of recyclable material such as metals. The redoubtable Second Law of Thermodynamics ensures that we will never recover an entire ton of secondary copper from a ton of primary copper in use, or an entire ton of tertiary copper from a ton of secondary copper in use. There is leakage at every round, and a simple formula, based on compound-decay, tells us how much copper can be used from the initial stock once you know the recovery, or recycling, ratio. Since the formula is easy to derive I am presenting it in Table 3.1. In Table 3.1, I assume that 100 tons of an ore are initially put to use, and that recycling occurs at the beginning of every period. Now, the recycling ratio is in fact subject to choice, the higher the ratio sought the greater is the cost of recycling. The key point though is that the ratio can never be unity. For simplicity of exposition I avoid all the complications that such choice introduces and assume merely that the recycling ratio is a fixed fraction, 0.8. Thus, in the second period only 80 tons remains in use, in the third period $0.8 \times 80 = 64$ tons, and so on. Adding all these figures yields an effective initial stock of 500 tons, five times greater than the nominal stock of 100 tons. But even 500 is finite. It is as though we are given 100 tons to use in the first period, 80 tons in the second period, 64 tons in the third, and so on, going down to vanishingly small figures in the long run. So metals and ores are also exhaustible resources.

Table 3.1: Expansion of resource base through recycling

Assume that there are 100 tons of the ore, which are recycled each 'year' at a recycling ratio of 80 per cent. Then total effective stock is:

$$100 + 0.8 \times 100 + 0.8 \times 0.8 \times 100 + 0.8 \times 0.8 \times 0.8 \times 100 + \ldots$$
$$= 100 \{1 + 0.8 + (0.8)^2 + (0.8)^3 + \ldots)$$
$$= 100/ (1 - 0.8) = 100/0.2 = 500 \text{ tons}$$

History

Fear of the impending exhaustion of natural resources would seem to be a periodic state of mind — and not always prompted by good reasons. The worldwide concern over the availability of fossil fuels in late 1973 was in great part occasioned by the four-fold price increase in Gulf oil. But this increase ought not to have been seen as a signal for increased resource scarcity. Worldwide reserves had not suddenly shrunk. Nor had demand jumped all at once without notice. The rise in price was, rather, the exercise by OPEC as a cartel of its market power. The consequences to the world economy have been enormous, as Michael Bruno of the Bank of Israel and Jeffrey Sachs of Harvard University, have recently documented (see Bruno and Sachs, 1985). But it had nothing to do with resource exhaustion. You can see this vividly in the fact that, with the weakening in cohesion among OPEC members, energy scarcity has fallen from the agenda of public anxiety.

This is not to suggest that societies have not faced resource scarcities in the past, nor that they have not done something about it. Man has been exhausting the earth's resources ever since he began walking around and making fires and he will be doing so for a long while yet. Indeed, if one is in that sort of mood one can look at history as a relentless pursuit of new, substitute, resource bases for existing, vanishing ones. These substitute resources are sometimes present in ready-made form. Sometimes they are not. In either case it is a matter of devising ways of *using* them, and by this I mean *economically* feasible ways of using them. This is the hard part. It involves research and development: R&D. The point I am trying to highlight is the banal fact that the basic ingredients of all present and future commodities and services are present today. It is only when we learn to make use of them, or when we start expecting to make use of them, that they attain some economic value. Then we take an interest in them. To put it in the words of E.W. Zimmerman: 'Resources are not, they become'.

To cite a concrete episode, a number of historians have seen the Industrial Revolution as a response to a concern with the supply of raw materials, especially sources of energy. Preindustrial societies were dependent upon wind, water and animal power. Above all, they were dependent upon *wood*, not only as a building material, as an industrial raw material and as a source of chemical inputs, but also as a source of *fuel*. The need for finding substitutes for wood-fuel was being signalled in England as early as the Elizabethan period. The signal was a secular increase in fuel prices, which, as it happens, rose during this period three times as fast as prices generally. The Industrial Revolution in Britain involved a substitution of cheap coal for wood as a source of fuel and power and an abundant source of iron for vanishing timber resources. The process was slow, because this substitution was fraught with technical difficulties, but it happened.

An extreme version of this viewpoint was expressed by the economic historian Brinley Thomas some years ago:

> In the second half [of the eighteenth century] Britain experienced an energy crisis ... there was a growing general shortage of timber and especially charcoal, whereas coal was relatively plentiful ... [the problem] could only be resolved by switching the energy base from wood to coal ... but this could not be done until a fundamental innovation had been made. ... At the beginning of the 1780s Britain was in trouble, a special kind of trouble which no other country faced at that time ... she was in a severe energy crisis, dangerously dependent on wood fuel ... In the previous twenty-five years as many as thirteen inventors had attempted to overcome the technical difficulties. It was not until 1784 that the problem of refining pig iron with coal or coke was finally solved by Henry Cort's process ... the Industrial Revolution occurred in Britain at the end of the eighteenth century not because Britain was 'well-endowed' in various respects, but because she was 'ill-endowed' in one fundamental respect — she was running out of energy and had to do something about it. France had no such problem.
>
> (Thomas, 1980)

The point of view is single-minded, but the thesis is at the very least suggestive.

In the United States, where resource endowments were quite different, the temporal pattern of resource-use was also different. In the early part of the nineteenth century, wood in America constituted an abundant and cheap fuel. Consequently, its use continued long after England had ceased to rely on it and had adopted coal. In 1850, mineral fuels supplied less than 10 per cent of all fuel-based energy in the United States, whereas wood supplied 90 per cent. By 1915 wood had declined to less than 10 per cent, whereas coal accounted for 75 per cent. The story since the end of the First World War has largely been one of a move away from coal to oil and natural gas as sources of energy (see Chapter 14 of Rosenberg, 1976, for an elaboration of this).

Resource Substitution as the Key Process

This example of alternative energy sources and the reasons underlying a move from one source to another with the passage of time is indicative of an elementary but important truth. Demand for minerals is for the most part derived demand; that is, it is derived from our demand for final goods and services. Now, it is not the minerals *per se* which are necessary for the production of the final goods and services; it is certain key *properties*, or *characteristics* that are required, and it is these we seek in minerals. The properties I have in mind are familiar; for example, tensile strength, conductivity — or lack of it — durability, porosity, texture, specific gravity — high or low — colour, magnetism, and so forth. To take an example discussed by Anthony Scott (1962) in a most interesting article on resource substitution in the past no one cares for the metal 'tin' as such. One *does* care for certain of its properties. It makes copper harder and iron resistant to corrosion. It is also durable, light and malleable, and this makes it a convenient constituent of containers for food. Each of these functions can now be performed by other means. Tin's hardening of copper can be achieved by other metals. Glass jars have replaced tin cans as food-containers in many circumstances. The basic constituent for glass is sand, available in vast quantities, and glass requires for its manufacture less expenditure of energy than does the extraction of tin, when the latter is sought in low-grade deposits containing minute quantities of the stuff. This is precisely why glass jars are replacing tin cans. Lead and mercury are being replaced in a similar way. And one could go on.

What are the innovative mechanisms, the characteristics of technological change, which bring forth such resource substitution as I have been discussing? They would appear to be seven in number, often overlapping, and often simultaneously occurring.

There is, firstly, the sort of innovation which enables a given resource to be used for a given purpose, that is, to use Zimmerman's aphorism once again, the kind of innovation which enables a resource 'to become'. The development of techniques for using coal in the refining of pig iron is a classic example of this. Research and development aimed at the control of nuclear fusion is designed to bring forth this sort of innovation. There is, secondly, the development of new materials, such as synthetic fibres. Thirdly, there are technological developments which increase the productivity of extraction processes; or in other words, make extraction of certain minerals cheaper. In the early part of this century the manufacture of large earth-moving equipment made the strip-mining of very low-grade ore deposits possible. Fourthly, there are scientific and technological discoveries which make exploratory activities cheaper. Developments in aerial photography and seismology have been crucial here. Fifthly, there are technological developments which increase efficiency in the use of resources. To give an example, during the period 1900 to the 1960s, the quantity of coal required to generate a kilowatt-hour of electricity fell from nearly seven pounds to less than one pound, a more than seven-fold reduction. Sixthly, there are developments of techniques which enable one to exploit low-grade, but abundantly available, deposits. For example, the discovery of the technique of froth floatation allowed low-grade sulphide ores to be concentrated in an economical manner. Seventhly, there are constant developments in techniques of recycling, increasing the recycling ratio at a lower cost, thereby raising the effective stock in the manner I indicated earlier, in Table 3.1.

There is in fact an eight mechanism, much more prosaic, and unconnected with any *new* technological development. It consists simply of the substitution of lower-grade resources for vanishing high-grade deposits, where the move involves a more costly extraction process, one which has been available all along. In early years, when the high-grade deposits are amply available there is no need to exploit lower-grade ores. But, being exhaustible, the superior deposits eventually get depleted. This is then the time to move on to inferior deposits, for which extraction and refining costs are higher Examples of this abound.

(I should add parenthetically that economic theorists have also explored a ninth possible mechanism, the substitution of fixed, produced capital, e.g. factories, for vanishing resource use. However, substitution possibilities along this route are severely limited, so I shall not consider them further here.)

All this looks like pure taxonomy, and taxonomy induces boredom. Fortunately, there is a single organising idea behind all these substitution mechanisms, and this enables one to study the economic process of resource exhaustion and substitution within a single analytical framework.

It can be shown that all the first seven mechanisms can be understood in terms of the eighth. There is thus a single analytical framework which encompasses all the eight mechanisms I have listed above. In particular, the eighth mechanism is a special case of each of the first seven. This is comforting, because even at first sight the eighth mechanism is the simplest to understand: it alone does not involve the production and use of new knowledge.

As it happens, the economic analysis of the eighth mechanism had been presented, and presented to all intents and purposes in a complete form, in a 1931 article by a great statistician-economist, the late Harold Hotelling. His classic article, which reads as though it was written last week, went pretty much unread, presumably because the timing was wrong — the beginning of the Great Depression. In any event, no progress in the analytical economics of exhaustible resources was made for over 40 years subsequent to the publication of Hotelling's classic.

Now, this reductionism — the reduction of the first seven economic mechanisms to the eighth — may appear to be a sleight of hand. New knowledge as required by the first seven economic mechanisms must by definition be unpredictable in some sense, and in extreme cases one may not even have a language to discuss it prior to its acquisition. So then how can one analyse and plan for resource exhaustion and substitution on the basis of the first seven-fold taxonomy? The answer is that in discussing the means of resource substitution we are not required to concern ourselves with the *exact* nature of future discoveries. If we needed to we would be caught in the sort of dilemma the Greeks found irresistible: to know now something we will only know in the future. So of course we do not try to do that. What we try to do instead is to identify the economic characteristics of *possible* discoveries. Thus, for example, we may not now possess the technology for mining deep-sea nodules from the middle of the Pacific, but technologists may have good reasons to be sanguine that if so much research attention is given to the problem, within 20 years' time there is a good chance that economically viable techniques will have been developed. The key term here is 'economically viable' and one can easily see that the characteristics of certain operations are the relevant things, to wit: finding cheap ways of operating equipment several miles below the ocean's surface over vast tracts of the occan floor and bringing up the nodules. Technologists may be able to predict with fair accuracy the time and effort needed to bring this about despite the fact that they do not know how to do it today. The point is that all researches are goal-oriented. Productivity increases occur not only through expenditure on research and development. It increases also through the process of resource-use, what one would call learning-by-doing, or learning-by-using. Getting children to learn their multiplication tables are proto-typical learning-by-doing: repeated use, in this case the arithmetic operation, teaches one to operate more efficiently. Past experience is often a reliable guide to the extent of future learning through doing, or through using.

We thus see that there is, to put it metaphorically, a constant tension between forces which *raise* extraction and refining costs — as high-grade deposits are depleted — and those which *reduce* such costs — as newer and newer technological processes are discovered. It is the balance between these two forces that determines the evolution of extraction and refining costs. Both are influenced by policies affecting extraction rates and R&D expenditure. As we will see shortly, unit costs of extraction and refinement of exhaustible resources, in the aggregate, fell steadily over the first 40 years of this century. But there are reasons for thinking that they have been rising slowly during the past few decades. We will study the implications of this.

Technological improvements and their influence on resource substitutability are a key to understanding the economics of exhaustible resources. One can, therefore, see why it is often suggested that future generations need increased knowledge and capital equipment to exploit currently *unusable* resources rather than just vast quantities of currently usable resources. But for technological discoveries to occur there needs to be a motive and thence an incentive. If serendipity is the drug which includes new discoveries, potential profits provide the far more reliable carrot and stick. These profits can be private or social, depending on the agency instituting the research — the lone inventor, the giant corporation, the private consortium, the government, or whatever. As we may infer from our seven-fold list of discoveries, these profits may be generated by the discovery of new deposits or from discovering ways of using existing deposits more efficiently. In short, there are profits to be had from expanding the resource base. As we are all painfully aware, research and development involves the expenditure of resources; not only by way of equipment but also in the form of salaries. In order to strike the appropriate balance in scientific and technological research the expected costs of research and development must be compared with the expected benefits (or profits) to be enjoyed from it. It is in the estimation of expected benefits that one needs to know the resource base and its economic characteristics.

It is essential to realise that it is the size of the existing usable stock and not the current resource price which influences the expected profitability of a new technological discovery. As we noted earlier, the four-fold price increase of Arab crude oil in late 1973 was not a signal for impending resource depletion. It was a message that a cartel was exercising its market power. Nevertheless, one might think that as a resource gets depleted its price rises, signalling growing scarcity. Thus, one might think that, ignoring such exceptions as resource cartels coalescing effectively, price increases are the signals the market provides for benefit-seeking inventors, firms and governments. It transpires that this is not quite precise enough. The matter is not unduly difficult to fathom, but it is a good deal deeper. So I now turn to the behaviour of market prices of exhaustible natural resources, to see *which* price we ought to be monitoring, and why.

Analysis of Resource Prices

A pool of oil, or a vein of iron or a deposit of coal in the ground is a capital asset to society — and to its owner if the deposit is owned by an individual agency. The deposit draws its value, say a market value, from the prospect of extraction and sale. In the meanwhile, as a distinguished economist aptly remarked, the resource owner is looking down at his mine and asking, 'What have you done for me lately?' There are two ways an asset can yield a return to its owner: by appreciating in value — capital gains — and by earning a dividend. Most assets offer a combination of both. (Of course, assets are all too often known to depreciate in value — capital losses — but this is merely the negative of appreciation and so fall in the same category.) The fundamental point about an exhaustible resource deposit lying untapped is that the only way it can earn a return for its owner is by appreciating in value. It cannot earn any dividend, by definition. We must not ask by how much the deposit should appreciate in value over time in order that investors are willing to hold a mixed portfolio consisting of shares in this deposit and shares of other market assets. This is easy to answer. In order for people to wish to hold a mixed portfolio of assets — inclusive of the resource deposit — the expected capital gains on the resource deposit must equal the expected rate of return on other capital assets in the same risk class. This is the fundamental principle of the economics of exhaustible resources and is today referred to by economists as the Hotelling Rule, in honour of the man who first deduced it in a rigorous manner while analysing the eighth mechanism in my earlier list.

Now, the capital gains I have been talking about are the rates of appreciation in the value of the resource deposit underground, the rate of capital gains on the value of the mine. They are thus the rate of appreciation of the *ground rent*, or *royalty*, on the mine. The Hotelling Rule states that the expected rate of capital gains on the mine will — under equilibrium conditions — grow in a compound manner at a rate r given by the expected rate of return on any other capital asset belonging to the same risk class. The royalty is *not* the final sales price of the extracted and refine ore. It is less, sometimes far less, because extraction and refinement, not to mention transportation, all involve costs. The final sales price of the extracted, refined and transported resource must be approximately the *sum* of its ground rent — or royalty — and its extraction, refinement and transportation cost.

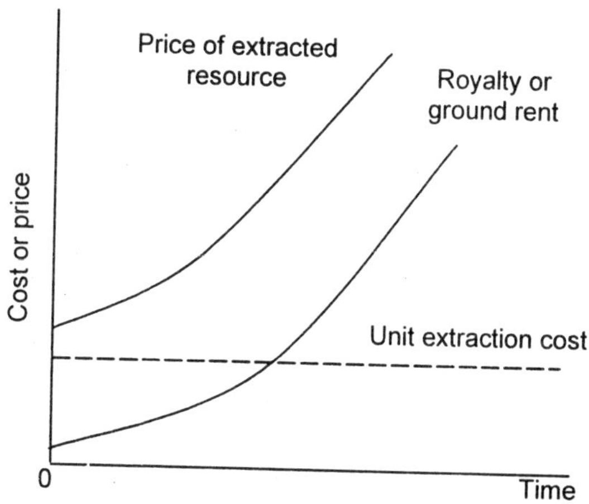

Fig. 3.1: Competitive price path of exhaustible resource: Constant unit extraction cost.

The simplest general case to study is one where the cost of extraction of a unit of the ore is constant over time. The final sales price of the extracted ore is then a constant amount in excess of the royalty, which as we have seen, grows at a compound rate, *r*, equal to the rate of return on other assets. The final sales price of the refined ore in this case grows at a rate *less* than *r*. Figure 3.1 displays the price trajectories of such a resource. Now, one would not expect extraction costs to remain constant, for reasons we have already discussed. If unit costs of extraction are expected to grow because society will be forced to mine more and more inferior grades, the final sales price will rise, for two reasons now, rather than the single reason prevailing if unit extraction costs remain constant. But if technological advances lower extraction costs at a sharp enough rate the final sales price would indeed fall. But it cannot fall forever, because extraction costs have a floor to them, namely, zero. Eventually the final sales price must rise, and rise at nearly a compound rate, for the ground rent term will eventually come to dominate (see Fig. 3.2). The key word here is 'eventually' and I shall come back to it.

If the existing, usable, deposit is large, the ground rent will initially be very low relative to extraction costs, but as the deposit eventually gets depleted the ground rent comes to dominate (Fig. 3.1).

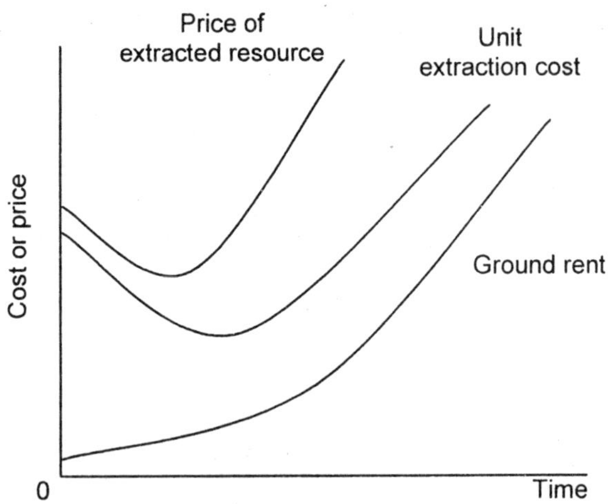

Fig. 3.2: Competitive price path of exhaustible resource: Variable unit extraction cost.

This conclusion holds even if new deposits are continually being discovered through the process of search. It is an easy matter to check that the argument emanating from the fact that an untapped deposit cannot yield a dividend continues to hold even when new deposits are being discovered in a predictable way. The Hotelling's Rule is thus robust against this form of generalisation.

Matters are different if there is uncertainty in the discovery process. In this case, prices that are expected arc not necessarily realised. If discoveries over a period happen to be systematically larger than anticipated, the realised ground rent will decline over the period (see Dasgupta and Heal, 1975, 1979, and Arrow and Chang, 1980). Nevertheless, even in the face of uncertain discoveries, a modified version of Hotelling's Rule holds, the rule now pertaining to the ground rent which in some sense is *expected* to prevail, not to that which is ultimately realised.

Royalties as a Measure of Resource Scarcity

Now, data on grounds rents, or what one may call royalties, are hard to come by. However, there have been several analyses of time series of extraction costs and final sales prices of exhaustible resources. In their pioneering work titled *Scarcity and Growth*, Barnett and Morse (1963) argued that with the exception of timber, both extraction costs and final prices of natural resources displayed a secular decline during the first half of this century. If true, this must have been due to a combination of our first seven mechanisms. Barnett and Morse concluded from this that resources were not getting scarcer. On the contrary, they were getting less scarce.

Now this is an incorrect conclusion to draw. We have noted that if extraction costs fall fast enough the final sales price will fall for a while even if there were a single deposit and no discoveries in sight. We would scarcely say that the resource was in this case getting less scarce. So then which price signals growing scarcity? The ground rent of course: its 'expected' value grows at a compound rate, signalling the expected growing value of the resource. Thus ground rents, as a fraction of extraction costs, say, are a true index of resource scarcity. If the deposits are initially very large the ground rent is tiny and it is many years before the rent rises to appreciable figures. Even at 5 per cent per annum — a generous figure for the real interest rate — a penny takes about 120 years to become a five-pound note. Compound interest is no doubt remorseless, but it can at the beginning be very slow if what is compounded is very small to start with.

In any case time series of resource prices are not unambiguous. Estimates of the behaviour of resource prices tend to vary from study to study. In a careful study Brown and Field (1979) assess different estimates and show that the prices of a selected group of key minerals did not display a secular decline during the first half of this century. Indeed, for one set of data (See Table 3.2) given for three selected years, prices display a U-shaped path.

Table 3.2: Real price of selected minerals using the price of capital as a numeraire, selected years, 1920-50

	1920	*1940*	*1950*
Coal	340	195	413
Copper	170	125	129
Iron	216	149	146
Phosphorus	—	141	170
Molybdenum	—	—	186
Lead	292	211	298
Zinc	301	281	335
Sulphur	—	—	281
Aluminium	647	297	217
Gold	—	615	337
Crude petroleum	547	205	278

Source: G. Brown and B. Field, 'The adequacy of measures for signalling the scarcity of natural resources. In V. Kerry Smith, *Scarcity and Growth Revisited*, Johns Hopkins University Press (Baltimore), 1979.

Transition from Exhaustible to Durable Resource Base

It should now be clear what I am leading up to. I began by suggesting that it is not specific resources we care for, it is certain characteristics we seek, certain services we need and desire. A wide variety of resources may offer the same set of services. This is precisely why *substitution* is the key concept in resource economics. Timber, coal, oil and natural gas are all sources of energy. So is uranium 238 a source of energy today, although it was not so 50 years ago. Moreover, if at some future date nuclear fusion comes to be controlled at an acceptable risk, or if solar energy comes to be tapped in large amounts at reasonable cost, we will have at our disposal vast new deposits of energy, so vast that to all intents and purposes we will have a renewable source, which is to say that the royalty on such sources, when they become technologically and economically viable for exploitation, will be tiny for a long while. But the economic availability of such renewable sources is at the moment conjectural. Provided resources are diverted towards research and development of these alternative sources we may expect to develop them at some time in the future, and the greater the R&D effort the earlier the expected date of success. Meanwhile we have to rely on finite resources. What then will be the price trajectory of the service provided by such resources? In Fig. 3.3, I present the competitive price path of a service, such as, say, energy, when it has to be obtained from a finite deposit initially and where it is expected that a renewable source will become available at a date, T, somewhat far away in the future. (For simplicity of exposition I assume away uncertainty once again, so that expectations are realised. See Dasgupta and Heal (1975) for an analysis of the case where T is uncertain.) Clearly, the expected date of completion of the R&D programme on the alternative energy source influences the current and future resource price. Clearly also, the size of the existing deposits of fossil fuels will, and should, influence the rate of R&D effort and thus the expected date of completion. These mutual relationships can be analysed, and there is now a substantial body of literature which does precisely this, having taken into account such obvious extensions as uncertainty in research completion times and in the cost of energy obtainable from these future technologies (see Dasgupta, Heal and Majumdar, 1977, and Dasgupta, 1982).

Fig. 3.3, describing a possible time profile of energy price, is stylised to indicate the crucial features. The *transition* from the exhaustible, fossil fuel base to the more durable, renewable, nuclear or solar base will not be dramatic, unlike that shown in Fig. 3.3. If and when such renewable sources are put into operation alternate sources will co-exist, possibly for quite some time, as indeed they do now. Prices will not display the discontinuity suggested in Fig. 3.3 because the diagram has not allowed for the facts that new technologies inevitably suffer from teething trouble, that production costs go down as experience grows, and that plants take time to build. In short, transition from an exhaustible resource base to a durable, renewable, resource base can always be expected to be gradual.

The nagging question remains: isn't all this too fanciful? We began by discussing exhaustible resources and we are now making the mental transition to durable resource bases. Is this the right conceptual framework? The fact that economic theorists have analysed the implications of such possibilities provides no reason why this is the right way of going about thinking on the matter. In any case, I have been concentrating so far on energy resources. Why should we think this is the only biting constraint, the most important issue to discuss?

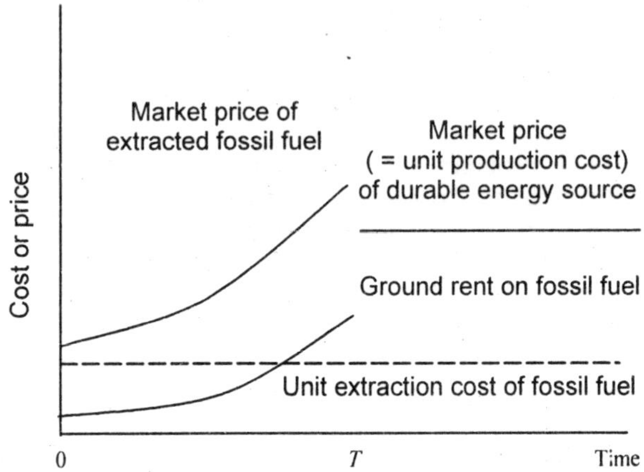

Fig. 3.3: *T* shows time of substitution of renewable energy source for non-renewable resources.

Prospects for Transition to the Age of Substitutability

Such questions as these can only be broached by physical scientists, and as it happens two such people, H.E. Goeller and A.M. Weinberg of the Oak Ridge National Laboratory and the Institute for Energy Analysis at Oak Ridge, Tennessee, respectively, addressed precisely this class of questions in a bold and highly original article entitled 'The age of substitutability' (1976). To the best of my knowledge theirs is the first empirical attempt at this question. I will be surprised if their estimates, which I will present below, are not controversial. I will also argue that their estimates must not be taken literally, for they are cavalier in their treatment of some fundamental issues. Nevertheless, the spirit of their exercise is just right. For a first step this is what matters most.

Goeller and Weinberg went through the periodic table, examining all the elements and then some important compounds, such as hydrocarbons, noted their worldwide use in the year 1968—the author's base year — and estimated the global presence for each item, having leant on an extremely generous definition of potential resource deposits.

The deposits included the atmosphere, the oceans and a mile-thick crust of the earth. Their attitude towards what constitutes a resource is light-years away from the attitude I have taken in this chapter: they make only cursory reference to costs of resource extraction and they concern themselves mainly with their physical *presence,* not with their economic *availability*. For example, a given quantity of a resource may be thinly distributed over the earth's crust, in which case extraction costs will be very high. Alternatively, the same amount may be present in highly concentrated forms, in which case extraction costs will be low. This, as we have noted, can make an enormous difference. (To illustrate the point I am driving at consider the fact that soil erosion — that is, loss of top soil — is today a major form of environmental degradation, a serious loss in world-wide agricultural output. The quantity of soil in the atmosphere, the seas and a mile-thick crust of the earth remains pretty much the same. But the soil has got 'relocated', it has got 'blown away', and this matters greatly). Nevertheless, Goeller and Weinberg's treatment is just the kind of preliminary analysis one needs to complement the analysis that economists have provided, or if one feels more comfortable seeing it the other way, the economists' analysis is precisely the kind one needs to complement theirs.

I want first to give some idea of our current use of exhaustible materials. In Table 3.3 world demands in 1974 of the major non-renewable materials are presented. In terms of quantity, far and away the most important are sand, stone and related products (accounting for nearly 60 per cent), and this is followed by fossil fuels (nearly 37 per cent). These materials, plus iron, aluminium and magnesium, and eight of the other most widely used elements constitute more than 99.5 per cent of all non-renewable materials currently used by society. If one includes prices and computes their relative importance in value terms, fossil fuels leap to first place, accounting for nearly 55 per cent (right-hand column), building materials plummet to a rock-bottom place, accounting for under 5 per cent, and iron, aluminium and magnesium jump to a second place at nearly 27 per cent. In value terms these principal materials account for over 90 per cent of all non-renewable materials currently used by society.

I now come to the Goeller-Weinberg estimates. In Table 3.4 data on the hydrocarbons and a few of the more notable elements are provided. The most revealing column is the last one. It presents, for each resource, the total stock in the atmosphere, the oceans and a mile-thick crust of the earth, divided by the 1968 world demand for it. In other words, it presents the number of years each resource can be expected to last at the 1968 rate of world use. (The underlying assumption is that recycling is not possible.) Now, demand must surely be expected to grow, though not necessarily at the same rate for all resources, as incomes rise and population grows, and I will come back to the adjustments that will be required to account for such changes. But note first that the only causes for worry are the phosphates — a mere 1300 years' supply; fossil fuels, labelled CH_x — some 2500 years; and manganese — about 13000 years. The rest are available for more than a million years, which is pretty much like being inexhaustible.

Table 3.3: World demand for non-renewable materials, 1974

Material	*World total demand*	
	% of total quantity	*% of total value*
Fossil fuels (CH_x)		
Coal and peat	17.02	11.37
Petroleum	14.56	40.41
Natural gas	4.87	2.75
Sub-total	36.45	54.53
Sand and gravel (SiO_2)	32.28	1.98
Crushed stone ($CaCO_3$)	23.58	1.95
Clay, gypsum, pumice	2.94	0.75
Sub-total	58.80	4.68
Iron	2.63	24.44
Aluminium and magnesium	0.08	2.31
Sub-total	2.71	26.75
Other major		
Chlorine	0.14	0.66
Sodium	0.36	0.49
Nitrogen	0.37	1.91
Sulphur	0.26	0.27
Oxygen	0.26	0.16
Hydrogen	0.10	0.98
Potassium	0.10	0.23
(Phosphorus)	0.07	0.24
Sub-total	1.66	4.94
All other	0.38	9.10

Source: H.E. Goeller, 'The age of substitutability: a scientific appraisal of natural resource adequacy'. In *Scarcity and Growth Reconsidered*, V. Kerry Smith (ed.), 1979.

At a more specific level Goeller and Weinberg argue that on the basis of geological and technological data, the essential raw materials are effectively in infinite supply, with the exception of phosphorus, fossil fuels and some trace elements needed for agriculture, notably zinc and copper. They argue that as the world exhausts its non-renewable raw materials it can move to lower-grade inexhaustible resources. The increase in the energy required to extract and process these low-grade materials is not huge. Goeller and Weinberg present crude estimates of the ratio of the energy required to extract a ton of some of these low-grade abundant metal ores to that required to extract a ton from high-grade ores. In none of these cases does the ratio exceed two (See Table 3.5). One should note though that these *are* crude estimates and, as I mentioned earlier, not much attention has been given to the concentration in which the raw materials are found in the earth's crust.)

Table 3.4: Present or future nearly inexhaustible resources for the most extensively used elements. The last column gives R/D, the resource-to-demand ratio in 1968

Element	*Resource*	*World resource (tons)*	*R/D (years)*
CH_x (extractable)	Coal, oil gas	1×10^{13}	2500
C (oxidised)	Limestone	2×10^{15}	4×10^{6}
Si	Sand, sandstone	1.2×10^{16}	5×10^{6}
Ca	Limestone	5×10^{15}	4×10^{6}
H	Water	1.7×10^{17}	$\sim 10^{10}$
Fe	Basalt, laterite	1.8×10^{15}	4.5×10^{6}
N	Air	4.5×10^{15}	1×10^{8}
Na	Rock salt, seawater	1.6×10^{16}	3×10^{8}
O	Air	1.1×10^{15}	3.5×10^{7}
S	Gypsum, seawater	1.1×10^{15}	3×10^{7}
Cl	Rock salt, seawater	2.9×10^{16}	4×10^{8}
P	Phosphate rock	1.6×10^{10}	1300
K	Sylvite, seawater	5.7×10^{14}	4×10^{7}
Al	Clay (kaolin)	1.7×10^{15}	2×10^{8}
Mg	Seawater	2×10^{15}	4×10^{8}
Mn	Sea floor nodules	1×10^{11}	13000
Ar	Air	5×10^{13}	2×10^{8}
Br	Seawater	1×10^{14}	6×10^{8}
Ni	Peridotite	6×10^{11}	1.4×10^{6}

Source: H.E. Goeller and A.M. Weinberg. 'The age of substitutability', *Science*, 20 February, 1976.

Table 3.5: Energy requirements for the production of abundant metals and copper. Gross energy is estimated at 40 per cent thermal efficiency for generation of electricity. The last column gives the ratio of the energy required to extract a ton of metal for low-grade (E_L) compared to high-grade (E_H) ores

Metal	*Source*	*Gross energy (kilowatt-hours per ton of metal)*	E_L/E_H
Magnesium ingot	Seawater	100 000	1
Aluminium ingot	Bauxite	56 000	1
	Clay	72 600	1.28
Raw steel	Magnetic taconites	10 100	1
	Iron laterites	11 900	1.17 (with carbon) ~2 (with electrolytic hydrogen)
Titanium ingot	Rutile	138 900	1
	Ilmenite	164 700	1.18
	Titanium-rich soils	227 000	1.63
Refined copper	Porphyry ore, 1% Cu	14 000	1
	Porphyry ore, 0.3% Cu	27 300	1.95

Source: E.H. Goeller and A.M. Weinberg, 'The age of substitutability', *Science*, 20 February 1976.

Thus the problematic resources are phosphorus, some trace elements needed for agriculture and fossil fuels. The solution for phosphorus and the trace elements must then lie in recycling. Indeed, H.G. Wells, in his book *The World Set Free*, had already suggested that phosphorus is in limited supply and that we may need to recycle it as fertiliser by crushing bones! The supply of hydrocarbons, adjusting for population growth, which Goeller and Weinberg take as 10 billion in the long run, will last only a few hundred years, a good deal less than the 2500 years estimated on the basis of 1968 demand. This then is the fly in the ointment, the bottleneck, the binding resource: limited hydrocarbons, currently the main source of energy. In a sense we are back, full circle, to where we began in this chapter, the exhaustibility of energy resources. Here Goeller and Weinberg have an interesting suggestion. They observe that both carbon and hydrogen are abundant in oxidised form, specifically, in the form of carbon dioxide and water respectively. They also note that there are a number of known technical processes which allow one to reduce carbon dioxide and water to hydrocarbons needed for transport and energy. The only trouble is, these processes in turn require a good deal of energy! So there we are, back to the 'ultimate' resource: cheap and non-risky sources of usable energy. In an interesting work *The Next Million Years*, C.G. Darwin, grandson of the man round whose works this Lecture series revolves, saw only one possible source of unlimited energy: nuclear fusion. Today we conceive of other inexhaustible sources, solar, geothermal and clean nuclear breeder reactors.

Goeller and Weinberg see the pattern of future resource-use as consisting of three stages. The first, lasting for another 30-40 years at least, would be a continuation of present patterns of use of exhaustible resources. The second, lasting several hundred years, would be one where society depends mainly on coal — there would be little oil and natural gas left — and less reliance would be placed on non-ferrous metals, more on alloy steels, aluminium, magnesium and titanium. Beyond that is the third stage, the Age of Substitutability, by which time fossil fuels will have been pretty much exhausted. In this final age economic activities will be based almost exclusively on materials that are virtually inexhaustible, with relatively little loss in living standards. Goeller and Weinberg speculate that the Age of Substitutability will be based largely on glass, plastics, wood, cement, iron, aluminium and magnesium.

Such a situation may be difficult to imagine perhaps, but then, eighteenth-century society would have found it difficult to imagine us today, certainly they would be astonished at the resource base upon which modern economic activity rests. But for me the importance of the Goeller-Weinberg study lies in that they asked the right questions and they attempted to chart the right avenue for locating answers to these questions. As a start, one must try and account for what resources are around us and what technological processes are currently known or are in the offing. It is only against such a background that one can begin to discuss policy options, such as, for example, the relative merits of different research and development programmes. The details of the Goeller-Weinberg speculations are not of great importance, nor would they, I imagine, wish to emphasise them. The merit of their work, in contrast to the far more well-known and well-packaged World Models of Jay Forrester, Dennis Meadows and their collaborators, is that Goeller and Weinberg have attempted only to get things approximately right, not accurately wrong.

And yet, talk of controlled nuclear fusion and clean breeder reactors smacks of futurology, wishful thinking. If such technological possibilities appear to be remote now, and this remoteness a cause for anxiety about the future, we should remember that even in the second half of the *nineteenth* century thoughtful people worried about declining energy sources and saw no way out. In a famous chapter on possible substitutes for coal, the economist W.S. Jevons, in his book *The Coal Question*, published in 1865, expressed deep concern about the future of British industry. And he wrote:

> I draw the conclusion that I think anyone would draw, that we cannot long maintain our present rate of increase of consumption; that we can never advance to the higher amounts of consumption supposed ... the check to our progress must become perceptible considerably within a century from the present time; that the cost of fuel must rise, perhaps within a lifetime, to a rate threatening our commercial and manufacturing supremacy; and the conclusion is inevitable, that our happy progressive condition is a thing of limited duration.

That Britain's commercial and manufacturing supremacy was under threat cannot be doubted, since the supremacy did not last. But the price of fuel had nothing to do with it.

Well, I can almost *hear* the reader thinking, trust an economist to goof so badly. But before economists are judged to be systematically worse at this sort of thing than others I will quote a passage from an editorial comment in the September 1876 issue of the *Scientific American*:

> A recent lecture was given by Professor Carey Foster, F.R.S., at South Kensington on 'Electricity as a Mode of Power'. Dr. Siemens, F.R.S., took the chair. Professor Foster first showed with a number of experiments that by very simple arrangements light bodies can be moved by electricity ... Although we cannot say what remains to be invented, we can

> say that there seems no reason to believe that electricity will be used as a practical mode of power. There is always power lost by the inverse current. Work of some kind must be done to produce electricity, and this can more economically be done by employing that power directly.

The moral is banal. We are all given to myopia.

FURTHER READING

There is a large historical literature on resource substitution. The sample below is an interesting as any I know:

Rosenberg, N. (1976). *Perspectives on Technology*, Cambridge University Press. Chapters 13 and 14.

Rosenberg, N. (1980). Technology, natural resources and economic growth. In Bliss, C.J. & Boserup, M. (eds.). *Economic Growth and Resources*, Vol. 3: *Natural Resources*. London: Macmillan.

Scott, A. (1962). The development of extractive industries, *Canadian Journal of Economics*, 28, 70-87.

Thomas, B. (1980). Towards an Energy Interpretation of the Industrial Revolution, *Atlantic Economic Review*, 8, 1-15.

The decade of the 1970s saw vigorous activity in the economics of exhaustible resources, both analytical and empirical. The earliest mathematical treatment of the subject is:

Hotelling, H. (1931). The Economics of Exhaustible Resources, *Journal of Political Economy*, 39, 137-75.

A characteristically lucid treatment of Hotelling's analysis and its extensions completed by 1973 can be found in:

Solow, R.M. (1974). The economics of resources, or the resources of economics, *American Economic Review*, 64 (Papers and Proceedings), 1-21.

The development of a unified framework for analysing various resource substitution mechanisms was undertaken in a series of articles by a number of economists:

Arrow, K.J. & Chang, S. (1980). Optimal pricing, use, and exploration of uncertain natural resource stocks. In Liu, P.T. (ed.), *Dynamic Optimisation and Mathematical Economics*. New York: Plenum Press.

Dasgupta, P. & Heal, G. (1975). The optimal depletion of exhaustible resources. *Review of Economic Studies*. Symposium Issue, pp. 1-23.

Dasgupta, P., Heal, G. & Majumdar, M. (1977). Resource depletion and research and development. In M. Intriligator (ed.), *Frontiers of Quantitative Economics*. Vol. III. Amsterdam: North Holland.

Dasgupta, P., Gilbert, R., & Stiglitz, J. (1982). Invention and innovation under alternative market structures: the case of natural resources, *Review of Economic Studies*, 49, 567-82.

Dasgupta, P., Gilbert, R., & Stiglitz, J. (1983). Strategic considerations in invention and innovation: the case of natural resources, *Econometrica*, 51, 1439-48.

Dasgupta, P. & Stiglitz, J. (1981). Resource depletion under technological uncertainty, *Econometrica*, 49, 85-104.

Gallini, N., Lewis, T. & Ware, R. (1983). Strategic timing and pricing of a substitute in a cartelised resource market, *Canadian Journal of Economics*, 16, 429-46.

Hoel, M. (1978). Resource extraction, substitute production and monopoly, *Journal of Economic Theory*, 19, 28-37.

Semi-technical presentations of this literature can be found in:

Dasgupta, P. (1981). Resource pricing and technological innovations under oligopoly: a theoretical exploration, *Scandinavian Journal of Economics*, 83, 289-318.

Dasgupta, P. (1982). Resource depletion, research and development and the social rate of return. In R. Lind (ed.), *Discounting for Time and Risk in Energy Policy*. Baltimore: Johns Hopkins University Press.

An outstanding introductory text on the economics of natural resources is:

Hartwick, J.M. & Oleweiler, N.D. (1986). *The Economics of Natural Resource Use:* New York: Harper and Row.

For an advanced treatise on the subject, see:

Dasgupta, P. & Heal, G. (1979). *Economic Theory and Exhaustible Resources*. Cambridge University Press.

Estimates of the world's resource deposits, the behaviour of resource prices and discussions of measures of resource scarcity can be found in:

Barnett, H.J. & Morse, C. (1963). *Scarcity and Growth: The Economics of Natural Resource Scarcity*. Baltimore: Johns Hopkins University Press.

Brown, G. & Field, B. (1979). The adequacy of measures for signalling the scarcity of natural resources. In Kerry Smith, V. (ed.), *Scarcity and Growth Revisited*. Baltimore: Johns Hopkins University Press.

Goeller, H.E. (1979). The age of substitutability: a scientific appraisal of natural resource scarcity. In Kerry Smith, V. (ed.), *Scarcity and Growth Reconsidered*. Baltimore: Johns Hopkins University Press.

Goeller, H.E. & Weinberg, A.M. (1976). The age of substitutability, *Science*, 191 (February 20), 683-89.

Harris, D.P. & Skinner, B.J. (1982). The assessment of long-term supplies of minerals. In Kerry Smith, V. & Krutilla, J.V. (eds.), *Explorations in Natural Resource Economics*. Baltimore: Johns Hopkins University Press.

Zimmerman, E.W. (1964). *Introduction to World Resources*. New York: Harper and Row.

Debrajan, S. & Fisher, A.C. (1982). Measures of natural resource scarcity under uncertainty. In Kerry Smith, V. & Krutilla, J.V. (eds.), *Explorations in Natural Resource Economics*. Baltimore: Johns Hopkins University Press.

Slade, M.E. (1982). Trends in natural-resource commodity prices: an analysis of the time domain. *Journal of Environmental Economics and Management*, 9, 122-37.

For a study of, among other things, the effect of recent increases in the price of oil on the world's economy see:

Bruno, M. & Sachs, J. (1985). *The Economics of Worldwide Stagflation*. Oxford: Basil Blackwell.

An outstanding treatment of the transition problem, that is, the transition from exhaustible to inexhaustible resource bases, in which both analytic and numerical issues are highlighted, can be found in:

Koopmans, T.C. (1980). The transition from exhaustible to renewable or inexhaustible resources. In Bliss C. & Boserup, M. (eds.), *Economic Growth and Resources. Vol. 3: Natural Resources*. London: Macmillan.

For a treatment which highlights the substitution of fixed capital for vanishing resource-use in production, see:

Stiglitz, J. (1979). A neoclassical analysis of the economics of natural resources. In Kerry Smith, V. (ed.), *Scarcity and Growth Reconsidered*. Baltimore: Johns Hopkins University Press.

4

Models of Resource Management

BRUCE MITCHELL

Resource management has attracted the interest of geographers for many years (Whitaker, 1954; White, 1963). Numerous reviews have discussed the general characteristics, strengths, weaknesses and opportunities in this field (Sewell and Burton, 1967; Wise, 1969; O'Riordan, 1971a; Birch, 1973; Gregory, 1974; Mikesell, 1974; Coppock and Sewell, 1975; Mitchell, 1979). The focus of this chapter is upon the progress achieved and obstacles encountered in developing models for resource management in a variety of problem areas. While most of the studies covered here were completed by geographers, enquiries conducted in other disciplines are included.

The nature and characteristics of models are well known (Haggett and Chorley, 1965, 361; 1967, 22). They are highly selective regarding information and omit details in order to focus upon basic variables, relationships and processes. While representative of real world conditions, they often are not realistic. As a result, they require constant re-examination to determine whether modifications would lead to improvement. In evaluating models for resource management, Bunge's (1962, 2-3) four standards (*clarity, simplicity, generality* and *accuracy*) and Kuhn's (1962) three categories of research (determination of significant fact, establishment of relationships, and articulation of theory) will be used to gauge accomplishments and progress.

For the purpose of this chapter, the concept of resource management is broken into two components: *analysis* and *management*. If 'analysis'

Reprinted with Permission from *Progress in Human Geography* 4; 32-56.

implies the examination of phenomena to determine their essential features, then as a resource analyst the geographer seeks to understand the basic characteristics of natural resources and the processes through which they are allocated and utilised (Mitchell, 1979, 2-3). In contrast, 'management' suggests *control, handling or direction*. Following this meaning, *resource management* represents actual decisions concerning policy or practice regarding how resources are allocated and under what conditions resources may be developed (Mitchell, 1979, 3-4). This chapter considers the role of models in both resource analysis and resource management.

MODELS OF RESOURCE MANAGEMENT

For organisational convenience, the derivation and application of models are discussed under the headings of 'biophysical', 'economic', 'cultural', and 'integrative'. As these categories are not always mutually exclusive, individual studies were allocated to one or the other on the basis of the main emphasis in the investigation. The coverage is selective, although an effort has been made to include experience from a range of world regions.

Biophysical Models

In this section, attention is directed to ecological and geomorphological models. Studies emphasizing hydrology and climatology are not covered systematically (More, 1967; Barry, 1967). However, these latter aspects are touched upon elsewhere, such as when considering natural hazards research in the section on 'integrative' models.

Numerous models have their roots in biogeography and ecology (Watt, 1968; Sochava, 1971; Simmons, 1974). A basic concern has been to model the exchanges of mass and energy within the biosphere. These exchanges occur between plants, animals, air, soil, water and space and involve energy, oxygen, carbon dioxide, water, nitrogen, and various mineral nutrients (Hewitt and Hare, 1973, 24). Such fundamental research is highly pertinent for resource management if the consequences of human intervention in natural ecosystems is to be anticipated. In this sense, ecological models are essential for the accurate prediction of environmental impacts arising from the development of natural resources.

Russian geographers have been prominent in the derivation of energy exchange models which have potential for application to resource management problems (Bazilevich and Rodin, 1971; Bazilevich *et al.*, 1971; Sobolev, 1971). However, one of the most promising geographically oriented models for resource management has been developed by Dansereau (1971; 1973). Discussion of his model highlights the way in which ecological models can contribute to the resolution of complex resource management problems.

In Dansereau's model, *resources* are cycled by *agents* through *processes* typical of each *trophic regime*. *Products* are the outcome of agents' action upon resources. These components lead to a conceptual model which outlines the structure of an ecosystem on the basis of its *resources* and the dynamics of predominant *trophic regimes* (Fig. 4.1).

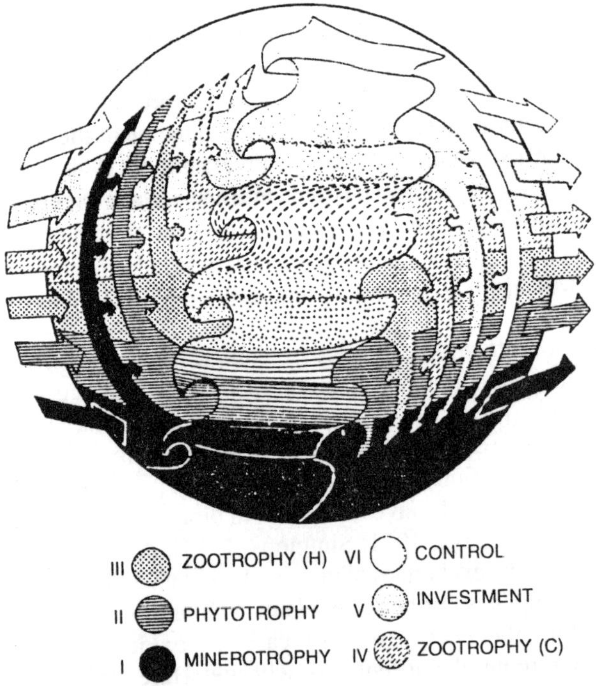

Fig. 4.1: Dansereau's ecosystem model. A scheme showing a projection on the six trophic levels of the mainstream flow of energy (central part), the supply of resources (left part), and the reinvestments (right part), as well as the import (left margin) and export (right margin) *Dansereau (1971).*

This model can be applied to any ecosystem (a pond, a forest, an orchard, a suburb, a city core). Dansereau argued that the model can guide studies concerned with understanding basic process or the potential impact of human intervention in an ecosystem. To either end, he maintained that it is essential to make an inventory of the quantity, quality and availability of *resources* at each trophic level, the number, variety, and identity of *agents* capable of exploiting them, and the quantity, quality and movement of *products* resulting from the processes occurring at each level. Such work would identify losses to or gains from other ecosystems, and the relative efficiency of production at each trophic level. Furthermore, application of the model would highlight three critical sets of problems: the detection of *broken chains* in ecosystems, the question of how to evaluate *fitness*, and the consequences of *man's developing power*.

This model has been used to guide an interdisciplinary enquiry into the environmental impact of a major international airport (Dansereau, 1976). In 1969, the Canadian government decided to construct a new international airport northwest of Montreal. Some 38,850 hectares were expropriated, of which 7000 were required for the airport itself. Dansereau directed a team which applied the trophic model to the expropriated area. The research focused upon the various trophic levels identified in Figure 4.1 and demonstrates that ecological models for resource management need to take a catholic interpretation of ecosystem and ecology. In this sense, the trophic model sets a high standard. At the same time, Dansereau recognised that it is but one of many models, and that 'further comparative studies will be necessary before judgement can be passed on it' (Dansereau, 1976, 24).

Geomorphologists have also demonstrated the relevance of their concepts for resource management (Flawn, 1970; Coates, 1971; Cooke and Doornkamp, 1974). As with ecological research, that in geomorphology has illustrated the importance of the resource manager appreciating basic processes. Indeed, it has been noted that man has often encountered serious difficulties when developing resources without understanding natural processes. As Price (1972, 1) remarked:

> An understanding of these processes is vital to rational development ... the entire history of man's exploitation of marginal environments—tropical rainforests, deserts, and Tundra—has been to apply middle latitude technology and approaches to land utilisation. The infamous British groundnut

> scheme in East Africa is an outstanding example of mid-latitude technology applied to a tropical problem.

Problems of a similar nature have been encountered in established urban areas through ignoring basic processes and relationships (Schmid, 1974; Kitchen, 1976). To demonstrate the significance of geomorphological research, the following discussion focuses upon work in one of Price's marginal environments—the Tundra. This type of environment has attracted the interest of geomorphologists in the United States (Lachenbruch and Marshall, 1969; Péwé, 1969), Canada (Harwood, 1969; Brown, 1970), the Soviet Union (Gorbunov, 1978), and the Scandinavian countries (Dylik, 1967; Washburn, 1970). This research illustrated by Mackay's enquiries in the Canadian Arctic, also indicates how work initiated as 'pure' enquiry can later become socially 'relevant'.

During the early 1950s, Mackay (1962; 1966) initiated a research programme concerned with classifying or modelling different types of underground ice, mapping their distribution, and analysing associated landforms. Such work, pursued in the spirit of intellectual curiosity, concentrated upon basic processes and required a long-term commitment due to the slow rate of energy exchange in the Tundra environment. There seemed no immediate prospect that such work would contribute to the resolution of resource management problems in high-latitude regions. Nevertheless, with the discovery of oil off the coast of Alaska in 1968, Mackay's 'pure' research suddenly became 'applied' and 'relevant' as decisions had to be made about constructing roads and pipelines establishing communities, and siting utilities. As Mackay (1972, 12) explained the situation:

> Not much more than three years ago research on underground ice was viewed by many as a scientific luxury, interesting, but of little concern to the affairs of modern man. It is an instructive commentary on our rapidly changing attitudes to note that it took only the successful completion of two oil wells at Prudhoe Bay in 1968, and the present energy situation, to completely change the scene. As industry began its painful discovery of the existence of underground ice, and government has been faced with the responsibility for environmental protection, it has gradually become clearer and clearer to all that the real impediment to much northern development has

> long been misidentified. The principal villain is not a hostile Arctic climate, nor permafrost itself but underground ice.

The geomorphological work by Mackay and others in the Tundra environment stresses that long-term research programmes and analysis of fundamental natural processes are frequently a prerequisite to resolving practical problems. Models keyed to these aspects often involve considerable frustration, disappointment and setbacks, yet such work must be conducted if resource management is to be improved. Geographers too often have focused upon the short-term and the immediately 'relevant' issues in resource management without having a fund of accumulated knowledge about basic processes to support their recommendations. This tendency is unfortunate, for as Bernard and Pelto (1972, 5) have noted 'concern is no substitute for knowledge and competence'.

It is hoped that more geographers will address themselves to deriving models of natural or social processes. Until such basic work is completed, the opportunities for providing constructive input to resource management decisions will be reduced. At the same time, it should be recognised that such models often will, and should, cut across boundaries of subfields and disciplines. Encouraging progress has been made by the International Geographical Union Commission on High Altitude Geoecology (Plesnil, 1978; Uhlig, 1978). The Commission has combined geomorphological and ecological concerns in analysing processes and problems in high-altitude regions.

Economic Models

Models have been created to understand the patterns and processes associated with the production, distribution and consumption of resource-based commodities, products and services. Some models, with close ties to those developed by cultural geographers, have incorporated the concept of *spatial interaction* and have considered the actual or potential flow of goods, people, services and ideas between places. Other models have been concerned with *spatial organisation*, or the pattern and distribution of resource-based activity. In both situations, geographers have been concerned with what is, what could be, and what should be.

Spatial interaction research is represented here by commodity flow and gravity models whereas diffusion research is discussed in the section on cultural models. Commodity flow analysis has been of interest to geographers for many years (Ullman, 1957; Smith 1970). It has been applied to a variety of resource management problems. Wilson (1967) compared the theoretical market area of coal mines in New South Wales and Queensland against actual commodity movements. The use and distribution patterns verified an assumption of rational economic man regarding location of production centres. At a similar regional scale, Mercer (1970) analysed urban recreational hinterlands defined by travel behaviour. In such work, the concept of *distance-decay* has stimulated research. Thus, Trotter (1965) and Cole and Mitchell (1969) applied this concept to movement of people among parks. Such research could help to establish distance thresholds between individual parks in a regional or national network.

At an international scale, Williams and Zelinsky (1970) studied the movement of tourists among 14 countries. Their objective was to model the dynamics of tourist flows, as well as to explore the implications for other population movements and the question of knowledge diffusion. They developed a flow assignment model which facilitated comparison of actual and expected flows for each pair of countries.

The model served as a heuristic device, as it generated a set of hypotheses to account for movement which was patterned rather than random. The hypotheses included the ideas that flows were influenced by (1) spatial distance and the resulting inequalities in travel time and distance; (2) the existence of significant commercial and other business dealings, extensive labour commuting, political linkages, and military relationships; (3) the general touristic appeal of one country for another; (4) the role of intervening opportunities; (5) the staging of specific events (Olympics, World Fairs); (6) the possible effect of the national character of the source country, and (7) the mental image of target areas held by potential visitors. While Williams and Zelinsky did not systematically assemble evidence to test these hypotheses, their model served a useful role by focusing attention upon possibly important variables.

Gravity models also have been applied to commodity flow problems, especially those involving recreation (Ullman and Volk, 1962; Crevo, 1963; Bell, 1977). An early study by Ellis and Van Doren (1966) illustrates the characteristics of such research. They developed a model to replicate flows of campers among the parks in the Michigan state system. As with most work with gravity models, considerable effort was devoted to determining the value of the exponent in the formula. Numerous exponents derived from regression analysis were tried before one was selected, and that exponent still resulted in a standard deviation of prediction of 44 per cent.

The results from the gravity model were compared with those from a system theory model, the latter being an electrical analogue model. While the systems theory model produced more accurate results, Ellis and Van Doren (1966, 67) concluded that the gravity model was still useful. They noted that the electrical analogue model required skills and facilities that many resource management agencies did not have whereas the gravity model was relatively simple to understand and apply.

This distinction concerning accuracy and sophistication is one to which more researchers should pay heed. A danger exists that in searching for increased explanatory or predictive power geographers will create models having little practical value for resource managers. Thus, geographers should recognise the need for trade-offs regarding accuracy and sophistication, and could usefully spend more time discussing their research with potential users of the models. Otherwise, as Andreski (1972, 116) has noted, the geographer 'obsessed with frameworks, jargon and techniques resembles a carpenter who becomes so worried about keeping his tools clean that he has no time to cut the wood'.

Models of spatial organisations may be quantitative or qualitative. Several studies indicate the attributes of each type. Aldskogius' (1967; 1977) research on vacation house settlement patterns and recreational day-trip behaviour illustrates the value of multivariate models for resource management. Aldskogius (1967) wanted to account for vacation house patterns in the Siljan region of Sweden, northwest of Stockholm. He designated the dependent variable as 'recreational place utility', a concept operationalised by using the real estate values of vacation homes. His independent variables reflected concern with the concepts of site (landforms, vegetation, land use) and situation (accessibility, proximity to amenities and service facilities). A notable feature of Aldskogius' work was the care taken to satisfy the assumptions of regression, especially that of normality. All variables were checked and, if necessary, appropriate transformations were applied. In this sense, his study is a refreshing change from the usually over-casual attention given to technique assumptions by most geographers applying inferential statistics to resource management problems.

Through stepwise multiple regression, Aldskogius developed four models which accounted for 51 to 70 per cent of the variation in the dependent variable. Open land, presence of partially used settlements (seter settlement), and length of shoreline were statistically significant in all of the models. Mapping of residuals suggested areas for possible improvement in the model. However, Aldskogius cautioned that his regression model had excluded the time element and therefore provided little insight into the process of vacation house growth. To resolve this weakness, he suggested that a diffusion model should be developed.

Another type of quantitative model has involved the application of linear programming to what has been called the *transportation problem* (Scott, 1971). The purpose is to develop a model which minimises the total cost of transportation within a system. In the United States, Cox (1965) used linear programming to analyse inter-state movement of aluminium, and King *et al.* (1971) applied the same technique to the movement of coal in the Great Lakes region. For the Soviet Union, Barr (1970) investigated the role of transportation costs in determining the location and flow patterns of the wood-processing industry. He found that actual transportation costs exceeded optimal costs by 12 per cent, and were accounted for by assumptions made to operationalise the model, motivations other than those of economic man, and trade-offs among transportation and other costs. Nevertheless, the linear programming model pinpointed areas where transportation costs might be reduced and indicated areas required research.

Models of a more qualitative nature have also proved useful in studies of spatial organisation. A good example is the work on the forest industry in New York state by Dinsdale (1965). She related changing spatial patterns to stages in the Industrial Revolution, and adopted Lewis Mumford's (1934) model which described three stages—eotechnic, palaeotechnic, neotechnic—in the evolution of European and North American society. For each stage, Dinsdale modelled the appropriate spatial structure of the forest industry and contrasted that pattern against what actually happened. She discovered that historical inertia in the New York state forestry industry and other variables inhibited the adoption of the new technology associated with successive stages in Mumford's framework.

Spatial interaction and organisation have provided the conceptual foundation for many of the economic models applied to resource management problems. Investigators have used a mix of qualitative and quantitative models, and have shown awareness of the importance of change over time even when their models have not explicitly incorporated the temporal dimension. Since human motivations regarding resource development may vary, it has been the cultural models which have been more sensitive to the temporal dimension.

Cultural Models

For resource analysis or resource management, the cultural or social variable is usually important, since motivation, values, and preferences often shape management decisions. In this context, several models offer considerable potential, although their application to resource management problems has been limited.

The first, developed by a political geographer, is based on the unified field theory of Jones (1954). This theory consists of an idea-area chain incorporating the following links: political idea-decision-movement-circulation field-political area. Jones contended that his unified field theory provided a means of integrating historical, political and geographical data and that an investigator could start an enquiry at either end of the chain.

A study of national parks in Kenya illustrates the value of Jones' unified field theory (de Blij and Capone, 1969). The *idea* of nature reserves for Africa developed during the 1890s in Britain and Germany. The intent was not to preserve representative ecosystems but to raise revenue through controlled hunting. The *decision* to establish nature preserves was taken at a London conference attended by the colonial powers. In British East Africa this led to the establishment of several game reserves by 1906. However, rights to traditional hunting grounds and ancient nomadic migration routes were ignored in delimiting boundaries. The space requirements of a viable ecological unit were overlooked and wildlife movement was affected. This lack of understanding of existing *movements* and *circulation fields* resulted in disruption of established patterns.

Gradual recognition of problems associated with the new *areas* lead to the concept of a hierarchy of conservation preserves. Six levels of protection and control were identified. It proved difficult to implement all of the levels, and by the late 1960s these areas had been reduced to three—national parks, game reserves, and game-controlled areas.

In addition to affecting existing movements and circulation fields, the decision to establish parks generated new patterns. Administrative control affected people whose involvement with the central government had been minimal. Areas that might not have receive roads for years or decades were scheduled for road construction which brought the local people into contact with new people, ideas and technologies. The tourist industry was particularly significant. Non-Kenyan hotel owners and outside touring parties affected the aspirations of local people.

De Blij and Capone (1969) illustrated that the idea-area chain, if not a theory, certainly served as a useful organisational framework to analyse the evolution of an idea and associated events. For their analysis it provided the three things envisioned by Jones (1945, 111): a compact description, a clue to explanation, and a tool for better work. Further application of the idea-area chain in resource management might provide greater insight into allocation processes. Used in conjunction with simulation models, the concept could help studies move from description to explanation.

Jones' unified field theory stressed the activity generated by an idea. Diffusion models have been developed as a quantitative means to describe and predict the spread of an innovation in a region and thus have the same conceptual roots as Jones' model. The research is based on the pioneering work of Hägerstrand (1952; 1967) who used probability models to analyse the diffusion of ideas, goods or services by focusing upon communication networks in rural areas in Sweden. In the field of resource management, diffusion models have been applied to topics as diverse as fluoridation (Crain, 1966) and agricultural practices (Polgar *et al.*, 1963).

A study of the spread of pump irrigation on the northern high plains of Colorado shows the value of diffusion models in resource management. Bowden (1965) sought to replicate the diffusion of the 410 irrigation wells established between 1948 and 1962 in the northern high plains. His simulated total fell within ten per cent of the actual number and followed the spatial pattern. Subsequently, he used the 1962 pattern as a base and simulated future development to 1975 and 1990. In this manner, he believed that he could explore the physical, legal, economic and social implications of the rapid expansion of irrigation activity. Colorado resource managers subsequently used his study to determine a maximum limit on the number of wells per township and a minimum distance between wells.

A third model illustrates the way in which explicit consideration of behavioural variables can assist studies in determining not only *what* occurred but also *how* or *why* events occurred as they did.

Variables including communication skills, interpersonal relationships, personalities, and values, possibly significant in accounting for the success or otherwise of resource management decisions, are incorporated in this model.

Draper (1977) has vividly shown the significance of such variables, and has introduced an anthropological model which deserves greater attention by geographers. Her study involved an evaluation of the establishment of an Indian cooperative fish processing plant on a remote part of the northwestern British Columbia coast. Draper adapted an anthropological model to account for the communication network which largely determined the problems at the processing plant (Paine, 1971).

She suggested that in public resource management situations, a *patron-middleman-client relationship* may exist. The patron and the client enter into an association to benefit from their transactions. However, due to different backgrounds, values and beliefs, these two groups find communication difficult. Their association requires a middleman (one or more persons or groups) who serves as an intermediary. Where the patron and client's messages are handled honestly, the middleman serves as a *go-between*. Where the messages are manipulated to the advantage of the middleman, the role becomes one of a *broker*. Draper argued that often one or more brokers are involved in resource management decisions involving public funds. Identifying such brokers may be crucial for determining the relative success of policies, programmes or projects.

The models discussed here illustrate that geographers have many opportunities in resource management research. Jones' unified field theory and Hägerstrand's diffusion model represent models developed within geography but still needing application and testing against a range of resource problems. How many models in other areas of the discipline remain untapped by those in resource management? One suspects that there are many, including central-place theory (Kreutzwiser, 1973). Simultaneously, cognate disciplines offer opportunities. While behavioural geographers have drawn heavily upon the ideas of psychology and sociology, models from anthropology have been relatively neglected. Draper's adoption of the *patron-middleman-client* model suggests that this oversight has been unfortunate.

Integrative Models

The models in the preceding sections tend to stress either biophysical economic or cultural considerations. In this section, examples of models which integrate these different aspects are presented. The models focus upon cultural ecology, carrying capacity, natural hazards, and policy-making.

In the field of resource management, Nelson has made significant contributions through his melding of concepts from cultural ecology, history and geomorphology to both basic and policy-oriented research. In his words, the work can be described as studies in 'land-use history and landscape change' (Nelson, 1973, 348) and has been applied to national parks, coastal areas and northern environments.

As his work on ecosystems, landscapes and land use evolved, Nelson felt a need for an organisational framework or model which would pull together the maze of possible relevant theories, methods and techniques from a range of disciplines. He wanted a model that would be 'broad and integrative, useful to administrators, academics, and others. It should be flexible and capable of use at different levels of generalisation' (Nelson, 1973, 349). The four-part model which he developed contained the following components: *ecology; strategies and institutional arrangements; perceptions, attitudes and values; technology*.

Nelson has demonstrated that this general model may be applied in several ways. It can function as an organisational device when reviewing the state of the art for a selected problem in resource management (Nelson, 1973). The model may also serve as a framework for collaborative studies. Working through the International Geographical Union Committee on Man and the Environment, Nelson distributed a description of his model to potential investigators during the IGU meeting in 1972. at the 1976 IGU meeting in Moscow, collaborators from around the world met to exchange their findings based on application of the model to analysis of park management in Europe, North and South America, Africa, Asia and the Soviet Union (Nelson *et al.*, 1978). The four-part model provided common terms of references and thereby facilitated comparability of findings.

A second integrative model relates to carrying capacity research. Setting aside the operational difficulty of defining carrying capacity, this concept has attracted substantial research effort by geographers. Stankey's (1972) model clearly identifies the questions being attacked relative to recreation management decisions (Fig. 4.2).

Ecological carrying capacity relates to changes in the biophysical environment through both natural processes (erosion, siltation) and

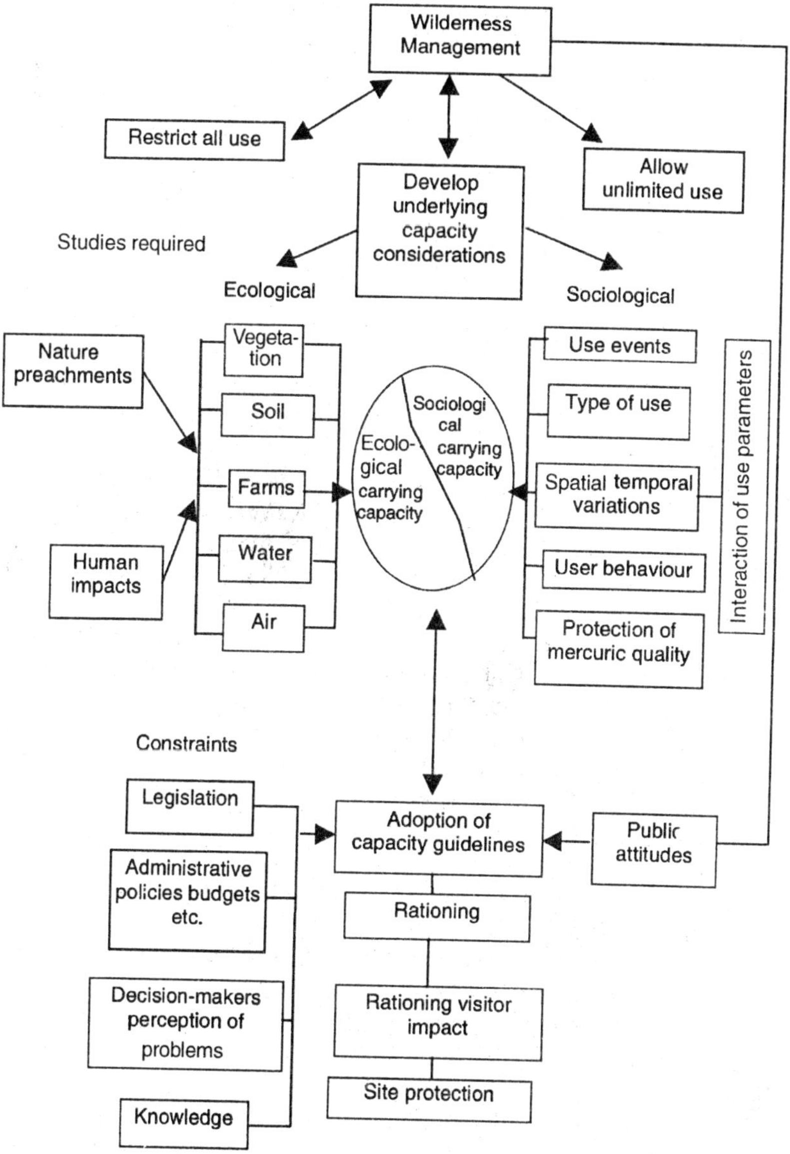

Fig. 4.2: Stankey's model for carrying capacity in the wilderness. Stankey (1972).

human activity (walking, camping). The research task becomes to determine critical thresholds beyond which vegetation, soil, water and wildlife are unable to maintain themselves. Nelson's notion of ecology becomes critical in this regard, as the investigator has to differentiate between natural evolution in the environment (plant succession) and change resulting from human intervention.

A benchmark study regarding the effect of trampling on vegetation was conducted by Bates (1935) on footpaths in England. Following the principles of experimental design, Bates initially used existing footpaths as treatment groups and adjacent areas as a control. These observations were supplemented by establishing experimental plots on which different grasses were grown and on which walking systematically varied. To achieve a greater degree of control, Wagar (1961) extended this work in Michigan by using a mechanical tamp to simulate the action of walking. This procedure allowed him to regulate the intensity of trampling on the treatment plots. The basic procedure of using an experimental research design and either actual or simulated walking has been applied by Willard and Marr (1970; 1971) on a hiking trail in Colorado, Bell and Bliss (1973) in a national park in Washington state, Ward and Berg (1973) in a Michigan state park, and Dale and Weaver (1974) on trails in Teton and Yellowstone National Park. In Britain, similar work has been done by Watson *et al.* (1970), Streeter (1971), Chappell *et al.* (1971) as well as by Liddle and Greig-Smith (1975). The main finding has been that most of the damage to vegetation and soil occurs relatively quickly as a result of human use and that recovery time normally is relatively long. These results have significant managerial implications, as they suggest that closing trails or camp sites after overuse may be misguided, as the recovery time may be longer than a closure period based on a seasonal rotational system.

Sociological or behavioural carrying capacity is concerned with the thresholds beyond which user satisfaction declines. Its determination requires data on types, levels and distributions of use as well as the user's perception of what constitutes a quality experience. Research has indicated that 'social crowding' often is correlated inversely with user satisfaction. This finding has led to a search for the critical number of encounters beyond which enjoyment declines. The practical implications of such work are substantial. For example, Lucas (1964) found that different users in the Boundary Waters Canoe Area in Minnesota had different tolerance levels concerning the number and type of groups which could be encountered and still maintain a 'wilderness experience'. Based upon his findings about the variables influencing satisfaction and those contributing to crowding and congestion, he proposed a system of spatial zoning to reduce conflicts among different types of users. O'Riordan (1969) studied variables affecting satisfaction of boaters in the fenlands of northeast Norfolk, and offered similar zoning provisions to reduce conflict. The work on social carrying capacity subsequently evolved to analysis of quota and permit systems to ration use in popular wilderness areas (Hendee and Lucas, 1973). A Markhov model has been developed and applied to establish visitor distribution programmes for several parks in North America (Hulbert and Higgins, 1977; Peterson, 1977; de Bettencourt *et al.*, 1978).

A third integrative model has evolved from the work on natural hazards by White and others. Set in the context of Barrows' (1923) interpretation of geography as the science of human ecology, this research has addressed a general problem defined by White (1973, 1974) in the following words: 'How does man adjust to risk and uncertainty in natural systems, and what does understanding of that process imply for public policy'. A relatively simple but widely applied paradigm has guided the hazards research. Its five objectives include: (1) estimating the extent of human occupance in areas subject to extreme events in nature; (2) determining the range of possible adjustments by social groups to those extreme events; (3) examining how people perceive the extreme events; (4) examining the process of choice among damage-reducing adjustments; and (5) estimating the effects of varying policy to broaden the range of adjustments. These concerns have guided studies of natural and man-made hazards by collaborating investigators around the world (White, 1974; Burton *et al.*, 1978).

The approach to hazards research emphasizes the interaction of man and nature based upon responses in the human system and changes in the natural system. Kates (1971) has made the most substantive contribution towards modelling the interaction of these systems. His model and linked hypotheses indicate the sources of variation in human behaviour relative to specific hazards, stages of techno-social development, as well as to specific types of decisions and decision-makers (Fig. 4.3).

Investigations of policy and decision processes tend to pull together many of the considerations in resource management and represent another type of integrative modelling. As O'Riordan (1971a, 109) observed, 'resource management in the final analysis is a decision-making process ...'. It is not surprising, therefore, that numerous geographers have attempted to model these processes. In this work, geographers have concentrated upon what Sewell (1974, 241) has called 'strategic' rather than 'routine' management issues. A distinction has also been made between prescriptive or normative models which demonstrate how the process *should* occur and descriptive models which indicate how the process *does* occur. Occasionally, both types of model are used in a study. The prescriptive ones establish an ideal to be sought while the descriptive models indicate the nature of the existing process.

Geographers have used prescriptive models as standards against which to judge actual management practices. Hamill (1968) and Sewell (1973) have both provided outlines about the nature of the ideal process relative to resource management. The ideal process begins with a statement of desirable goals and identification of problems. Subsequent steps include consideration of constraints, delineation of potential solutions, formulation of alternative strategies, appraisal of alternatives, selection of a solution, and review after implementation.

However, the ideal is rarely obtained. Often, the resource manager is not confronted with a well-defined problem but rather with a host of causes and effects. This situation frequently results in symptoms rather than basic causes being addressed. Societal goals may not be known, or else may be vague, ambiguous or conflicting (Mitchell, 1976). Information required to identify and compare alternatives may be incomplete or lacking, and attaining additional data may necessitate an exorbitant expenditure of time and effort. In political science, these conditions have contributed to the generation of alternative models which focus upon the actual rather than the ideal process (Lindblom, 1968; Etzioni, 1967, 1968; Lowi, 1964, 1970, 1972). Geographers too have sought to develop descriptive models which have direct applicability to resource management.

White (1961, 1963) outlined a basic model which has influenced many other subsequent geographical policy models. He was concerned with describing the *actual choices* in resource management and contrasting them with the *theoretical range of choice*. The purpose was to see in what way, if at all, man could make better use of the natural environment. White's model has five components which include:

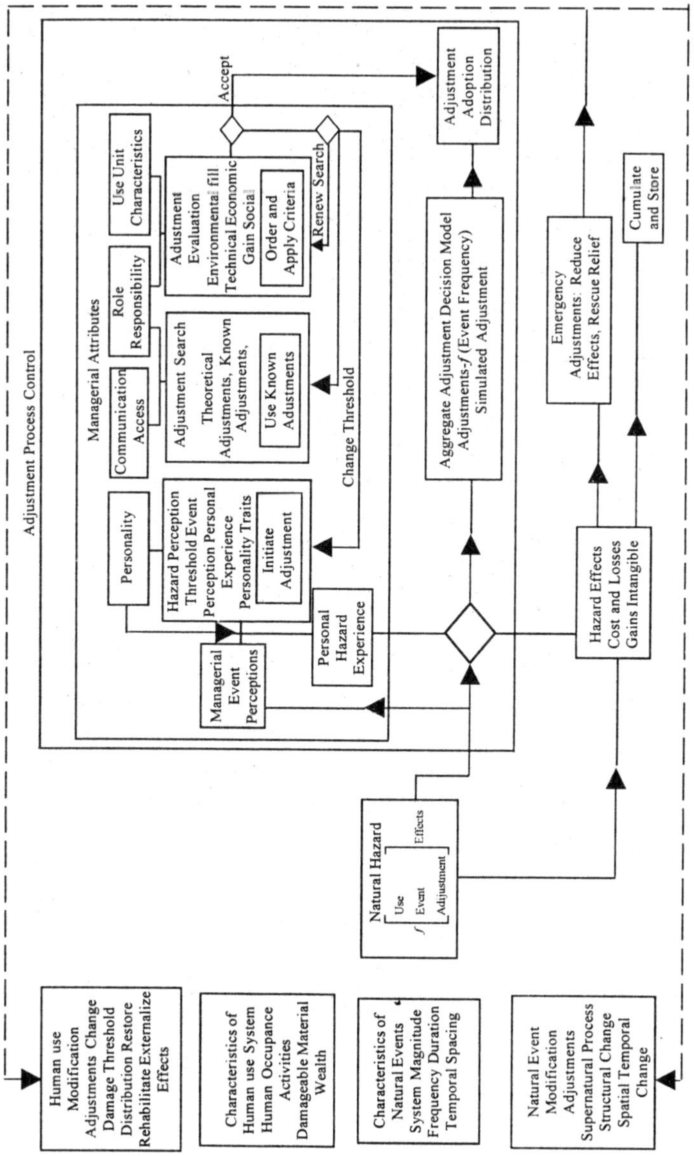

Fig. 4.3: Kate's model of human adjustment to natural hazards. *After Kates (1971).*

1. *Perceived range of choice*—the range of resource use recognised by the resource manager;
2. *Resource estimates*—judgements about the quantity and quality of the physical resource available;
3. *Technology*—as it affected future demand, production and actual use of resources;
4. *Spatial linkages*—the relationship of a given use to other resource uses in contiguous or functionally related areas; and
5. *Social guides*—the customs, attitudes, education and organisations of a society that influence (1) to (4) above.

This model served as a departure for Kate's (1962) study of the urban flood hazard, Wong's (1968) investigation of industrial water management, Baumann's (1969) enquiry into recreational practices on water-supply reservoirs, and MacIver's (1970) analysis of water supply alternatives. White (1969) also applied the model when assessing water management strategies which have evolved in the United States.

Based upon the ideas of White, and of Easton (1957), Kasperson (1969a; 1969b) developed a 'stress' model for resource management (Fig. 4.4). His model suggests that, at any time, a resource manager faces a range of stresses or problems. Managerial perception of the stress is influenced by the way in which the problem is articulated, giving a significant role to interest groups and the media. The manager seeks adaptive strategies which are rational to his limited understanding of the stress and compatible with other stress in the system. The manager thus functions as Simon's (1957) 'administrative man' rather than the 'economic man' of the prescriptive models.

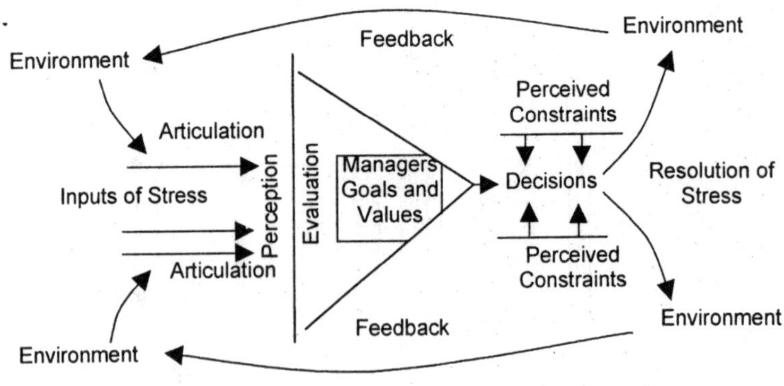

Fig. 4.4: Kasperson's model for stress management. *Kasperson (1969, 485).*

In applying this model to the stress created by drought during the early 1960s in a Massachusetts community, Kasperson demonstrated that the lack of attention and slow response to drought-induced stress was partially due to preoccupation with other stresses (school programmes, sewage treatment, transportation, urban renewal) in the municipal system. He concluded that understanding the characteristics of a political system and the behavioural characteristics of participants was basic to appreciating the resource management process. The importance of these variables was confirmed in another study by Wood (1976) which illustrated the multitude of stresses bombarding the resource manager.

The concept of stress is also basic to a decision model developed by O'Riordan (1971b; 1971c; 1972). Drawing upon the ideas of Kasperson, and of Wengert (1955), O'Riordan's model postulates a management process underlain by group struggle and conflict. Interest groups respond to a perceived shortage or deterioration of resources, and pass their concern to an elected official or public agency. Technical advice is sought and other interests are consulted before a decision is taken. However, since the decision confers differential benefits and costs to societal groups, its implementation generates new stresses and problems which p)mpt subsequent group reaction and pressure on decision-makers. This situation leads to a second decision which in turn leads to a third and so on. Through this procedure, the management process is seen as one of group bargaining. The public interest becomes a residual of conflict rather than a positive expression of conscious choice. This model clearly indicates that the actual process does not evolve in the comprehensive, rational and detached manner suggested by the prescriptive models.

Numerous other policy and decision models for resource management have been prepared, and draw upon basic ideas from political science. These are reviewed in detail by Mitchell (1979). At this point, it is sufficient to emphasize that modelling of policy and decision processes has focused upon both prescriptive and descriptive aspects.

IMPLICATIONS

The purpose of models is to simplify the complexity of the real world to facilitate our understanding of it. The strengths of models are their identification of potentially important features or relationships, their generation of research questions, and their applicability to a range of situations or problems. These strengths imply some weaknesses, especially the deliberate elimination of detail or information and the relevance to only a limited range of reality.

In resource analysis, models serve as a vehicle to improve understanding of basic variables and processes associated with resource systems or the procedures through which resources are allocated. For resource management, models may aid in anticipating the consequences of mankind's adjustment to or modification of the environment. In either situation, models have contributed towards identification of significant facts and establishment of relations (Kuhn, 1962). However, to date, models have yet to lead to the generation of a 'geographical theory of natural resources' or of a more limited theory applicable to a specific open problem in resource management (e.g. carrying capacity, natural hazards, environmental impact).

As representative of the types of models developed or applied by geographers in resource management, those reviewed here have several characteristics which help to account for this situation. Using Bunge's (1962) four standards, the models would be ranked highly for their *simplicity*. However, given our poor understanding of natural and human systems, it is not always clear that the variables incorporated into the models are necessarily the correct ones. In other words, the *accuracy* and *clarity* of most models have not been validated. The main reason is the lack of comparative studies using the same model. The natural hazards model, White's descriptive decision model, and Nelson's cultural ecology model are partial exceptions to this statement. For those models, concerted research effort has been based on a common framework.

The lack of comparative and cumulative research in resource management also means that the *generality* of most models has not been established. Indeed, if 'progress in research requires the continual discarding of outdated models, and subsequent remodelling' (Haggett and Chorley, 1967, 27), geographic modelling for resource management is in its infancy. Geographic models are mainly first-generation in vintage. In this regard, Dansereau's comment about his model is applicable to all (In Sub-head Biophyical Model). Each model is but one of many which requires verification through comparative studies before its ultimate value can be determined.

The potential of most of the models has been identified and discussed by their developers, but few have been tested rigorously by investigation other than the individual who generated them. External testing and verification of available models is an important task requiring attention. To date, there has been a tendency for new models to be created before existing ones have been tested for their clarity, simplicity, generality and accuracy. In this regard, geography is out-of-step with the way in which most disciplines achieve progress through model-building.

REFERENCES

Aldskogius, H. (1967). Vacation house settlement in the Siljan region. *Geografiska Annaler* 49B, 69-95.

Aldskogius, H. (1977). A conceptual framework and a Swedish case study of recreational behaviour and environmental cognition. *Economic Geography* 53, 163-83.

Andreski, S. (1972). *Social Sciences as Sorcery*. Harmondsworth: Penguin.

Barr, B.M. (1970). *The Soviet Wood-Processing Industry: A linear Programming Analysis of the Role of Transportation Costs in Location and Flow Patterns*. Toronto: University of Toronto, Department of Geography.

Barrows, H.H. (1923). Geography as human ecology. *Annals of the Association American Geographers* 13, 1-14.

Barry, R.G. (1967). Models in meteorology and climatology. In Chorley, R.J. and Haggett, P., editors, *Models in Geography*, London: Methuen, 97-144.

Bates, G.H. (1935). The vegetation of footpaths, sidewalls, carttracks, and gateways. *Journal of Ecology* 23, 470-87.

Baumann, D. (1969). *The Recreational use of Domestic Water Supply Reservoirs: Perception and Choice*. Chicago: University of Chicago, Department of Geography, Research Paper 121.

Bazilevich, N.I. and Rodin, L.Y. (1971). Geographical regularities in productivity and the circulation of chemical elements in the earth's main vegetation types. *Soviet Geography* 12, 24-53.

Bazilevich, N.I., Rodin, L.Y. and Rozov, N.N. (1971). Geographical aspects of biological productivity. *Soviet Geography* 12, 292-317.

Bell, K.L. and Bliss, L.C. (1973). Alpine disturbance studies: Olympic National Park, USA. *Biological Conservation* 5, 25-32.

Bell, M. (1977). The spatial distribution of second hornest a modified gravity model. *Journal of Leisure Research* 9, 225-3.

Bernard, H.R. and Pelto, P.J. (1972).: Introduction. In Bernard, H.R. and Pelto, P.J., editors, *Technology and Social Change*, New York: Macmillan, 1-8.

Birch, J.W. (1973): Geography and resource management. *Journal of Environmental Management* 1, 3-12.

Bowden, L.W. (1965). *Diffusion of the Decision to Irrigated Simulation of the Spread of a New Resource Management Practice in the Colorado Northern High Plains*. Chicago: University of Chicago Press, Department of Geography, Research Paper 97.

Brown, R. (1970). *Permafrost in Canada.* Toronto: University of Toronto Press.

Bunge, W. (1962). *Theoretical Geography, Lund Studies in Geography, Series C, General and Mathematical Geography* 1, Lund: Gleerup.

Burton, I., Kates, R.W. and White, G.F. (1978). *The Environment as Hazard.* New York: Oxford University Press.

Chappell, H.G. *et al.* (1971). The effects of trampling in a chalk grassland ecosystem. *Journal of Applied Ecology* 8, 869-92.

Coates, D.R. (1971). *Environmental Geomorphology.* Binghampton: State University of New York.

Cole, R.L.S. and Mitchell, L.S. (1969). Attendance as a negative function of distance, Great Smoky Mountains National Park Campgrounds. *Southeastern Geographer* 9, 13-24.

Cooke, R.U. and Doornkamp, J.C. (1974). *Geomorphology in Environmental Management.* Oxford: Clarendon Press.

Coppock, J.T. and Sewell, W.R.D. (1975). Resource management and public policy: the changing role of geographical research. *Scottish Geographical Magazine* 9, 11.

Cox, K.R. (1965). The application of linear programming to geographic problems. *Tijdschrift voer Economische en Sociale Geografie* 56, 228-36.

Crain, R.L. (1966). Fluoridation: the diffusion of an innovation among cities. *Social Forces* 44, 467-76.

Crevo, C.C. (1963). Characteristics of summer weekend recreational travel. *Highway Research Record* 44, 57-60.

Dale, D. and Weaver, T. (1974). Trampling effects on vegetation of the trail corridors of North Rocky Mountain forests. *Journal of Applied Ecology* 11, 767-72.

Dansereau, P. (1971). Dimensions of environmental quality. *Sarracenia* 14. (109 pp.).

Dansereau, P. (1973). *Inscape and landscape*. Toronto: Canadian Broadcasting Corporation.

Dansereau, P. (1976). *EZAIM: ecologie de la zone de l'aeroport international de Montreal: le cadre d'une recherché ecologique interdisciplinaire.* Montréal: Les Presses de l'Université de Montréal (393 pp.).

De Bettencourt, J.S., Peterson, G.L. and Wang, P.K. (1978). Managing wilderness travel: a Markhov-based linear programming model. *Environment and Planning* A 10, 71-9.

De Blij, H.J. and Capone, D.L. (1969). Wildlife conservation areas in East Africa: an application of field theory in political geography. *Southeastern Geographer* 9, 94-107.

Dinsdale, E.M. (1965). Spatial patterns of technological change: the lumber industry of northern New York. *Economic Geography* 41, 252-74.

Draper, D.L. (1977). *Resources Management, Socio-Economic Development, and the Pacific North Coast Native Cooperative: A Case Study.* University of Waterloo, unpublished Ph. D. dissertation.

Dylik, J. (1967). Solifuxion, congelifluxion and related slope processes. *Geografica Annaler* 49A, 167-77.

Easton, D. (1957). An approach to the analysis of political systems: *World Politics*, 383-400.

Ellis, J.B. and Van Doren, C.S. (1966). A comparative evaluation of gravity and system theory models for state-wide recreational traffic flow. *Journal of Regional Science* 6, 57-70.

Etzioni, A. (1967). Mixed-scanning: a 'third' approach to decision-making. *Public Administration Review* 27, 385-92.

Etzioni, A. (1968). *The Active Society.* New York: Free Press.

Flawn, P.T. (1970). *Environmental Geology: Conservation, Land-Use Planning, and Resource Management.* New York: Harper and Row.

Gorbunov, A.P. (1978). Permafrost investigations in high-mountain regions. *Arctic and Alpine Research* 10, 283-94.

Gregory, S. (1974). The geographer and natural resources research. *South African Geographer* 4, 371-82.

Hāgerstrand, T. (1952). *The Propagation of Innovation Wares.* Lund: University of Lund, Department of Geography.

Hāgerstrand (1967). *Innovation Diffusion as a Spatial Process.* Chicago: University of Chicago Press.

Haggett, P. and Chorley, R.J. (1965). Frontier movements and the geographical tradition. In Chorley, R.J. and Haggett, P., editors, *Frontiers in Geographical Teaching*, London: Methuen, 385-78.

Haggett, P. and Chorley, R. J. (1967). Models, paradigms and the new geography. In Haggett, P. and Chorley, R.J., editors, *Models in Geography*, London: Methuen, 19-41.

Hamill, L. (1968). Process of making good decisions about the use of the environment of man. *Natural Resources Journal* 8, 279-301.

Harwood, T.A. (1969). Some possible problems with pipelines in permafrost regions. In Brown, R.J.E., editor, *Proceedings of the Third Canadian Conference on Permafrost*, Ottawa: National Research Council.

Hendee, J. C. and Lucas, R. C. (1973). Mandatory wilderness permits: a neccessary management tool. *Journal of Forestry* 71, 206-209.

Hewitt, K and Hare, F. K. (1973). *Man and Environment: Conceptual Frameworks*, Washington DC: Association of American Geographers.

Hulbert, J. and Higgins, J. (1977). BWCA visitor distribution system. *Journal of Forestry* 75, 338-40.

Jones, S.B. (1954). A unified field theory of political geography. *Annals of the Association of American Geographers* 44, 111-23.

Kasperson, R.E. (1969a). Environmental stress and the municipal political system. In Kasperson, R.E. and Minghi, J.V., editors, *The Structure of Political Geography*, Chicago: Aldine 481-96.

Kasperson, R. E. (1969b). Political behaviour and the decision-making process in the allocation of water resources between recreational and municipal uses. *Natural Resources Journal* 9, 176-211.

Kates, R.W. (1962). *Hazard and Choice Perception in Flood Plain Management*. Chicago: University of Chicago, Department of Geography, Research Paper 78.

Kates, R. W. (1971). Natural hazard in human ecological perspective hypotheses and models. *Economic Geography* 47, 438-51.

King, L.J., Casetti, E., Odland, J. and Semple, K. (1971). Optimal transportation patterns of coal in the Great Lakes Region. *Economic Geography* 47, 401-413.

Kitchen, C.M. (1976). Ecology and urban development: the theory and practice of ecoplanning in Canada. In McBoyle, G.R. and Sommerville, E., editors, *Canada's Natural Environment: Essays in Applied Geography*, Toronto: Methuen, 217-40.

Kreutzwiser, R. (1973). *A Methodology for Estimating Tourist Spending in Ontario Counties*. University of Waterloo, unpublished MA thesis.

Kuhn, T.S. (1962). *The Structure of Scientific Revolutions*. Chicago: University of Chicago Press.

Lachenbruch, A.H. and Marshall, B.V. (1969). Heat flow in the Arctic. *Arctic* 22, 300-311.

Liddle, M.J. and Greig-Smith, P. (1975). A survey of tracks and paths in a sand dune ecosystem. I: soils, II: vegetation. *Journal of Applied Ecology* 12, 893-930.

Lindblom, C.E. (1968). *The Policy-making Process*. Englewood Cliffs, New Jersey: Prentice-Hall.

Lowi, T. (1964). American business, public policies, case studies and political theory. *World Politics* 16, 677-715.

Lowi, T. (1970). Decision making vs. policy making: toward an antidote for technocracy. *Public Administration Review* 30, 314-25.

Lowi, T. (1972). Four systems of policy, politics and choice. *Public Administration Review* 32, 298-310.

Lucas, R.C. (1964). Wilderness perception and use: the example of the Boundary Waters Canoe Area. *Natural Resources Journal* 3, 394-411.

MacIver, I. (1970). *Urban Water Supply Alternatives: Perception and Choice in the Grand Basin, Ontario*. Chicago: University of Chicago, Department of Geography, Research Paper 126.

Mackay, J.R. (1962). Pingos of the Pleistocene Mackenzie delta area. *Geographical Bulletin* 18, 21-63.

Mackay, J. R. (1966). Segregated epigenetic ice and slumps in permafrost, Mackenzie delta area, NWT. *Geographical Bulletin* 18, 59-80.

Mackay, J. R. (1972). The world of underground ice. *Annals of the Association of American Geographers* 62, 1-22.

Mercer, D.C. (1970). Urban recreational hinterlands: a review and example. *Professional Geographer* 22, 74-8.

Mikesell, M.W. (1974). Geography as the study of environment: an assessment of some old and new commitments. In Manners, I.R. and Mikesell, M.W., editors, *Perspectives on Environment*, Washington, DC: Association of American Geographers, 1-23.

Mitchell, B. (1976). Decision-making and consultation in resource management: the BC salmon fishery. *Journal of Environmental Management* 4, 211-23.

Mitchell, B. (1979). *Geography and Resource Analysis*. Harlow, Essex: Longman.

More, R.J. (1967). Hydrological models in geography. In Chorley, R.J. and Haggett, P., editors, *Models in Geography*, London: Methuen, 145-85.

Mumford, L. (1934). *Technics and Civilisation*. New York: Harcourt Brace.

Nelson, J.G. (1973). Canadian national parks and related reserves: research needs and management. In Nelson, J.G., Scace, J.C. and Kouri, R., edition *Canadian Public Land use in Perspective*, Ottawa: Social Science Research Council, 348-79.

Nelson, J.G., Needham, R.D. and Mann, D.L., (eds.), (1978). *International Experience with National Parks and Related Reserves*. Waterloo, Ontario: University of Waterloo, Department of Geography, Publication 12.

O'Riordan, T. (1969). Planning to improve environmental capacity: a case study is Broadland, *Town Planning Review* 40, 39-58.

O'Riordan, T. (1971a). *Perspectives on Resource Management*. London: Pion.

O'Riordan, T. (1971b). Public opinion and environmental quality: a reappraisal. *Environment and Behaviour* 3, 191-214.

O'Riordan, T. (1971c). Towards a strategy of public involvement. In Sewell, W.R.D. and Burton, I., editors, *Perceptions and Attitudes in Resources Management*, Ottawa: Information, Canada, 99-110.

O'Riordan, T. (1972). Decision-making and environmental quality: an analysis of a water quality issue in the Shuswap and Okanagan Valleys, British Columbia. *Okanagan Water Decisions, Western Geographical Series* 4, Victoria, BC: University of Victoria, 1-111.

Paine, R. (ed.), (1971). *Patrons and Brokers in the East Arctic*. Toronto: University of Toronto Press.

Peterson, G.L. (1977). The computer takes a canoe trip. *Naturalist* 28, 9-11.

Pewe, T.L. (1969). *The Periglacial Environment*. Montreal: McGill-Queen's University Press.

Plesnik, P. (1978). Man's influence on the timberline in the West Carpathian Mountains, Czechoslovakia. *Arctic and Alpine Research* 10, 491-504.

Polgar, S., Dunphy, H. and Cox, B. (1963). Diffusion and farming advice: a test of some current notions. *Social Forces* 42, 104-111.

Price, L.W. (1972). *The Periglacial Environment, Permafrost, and Man*. Washington DC: Association of American Geographers.

Schmid, J.A. (1974). The environmental impact of urbanisation. In Manners, I. R. and Mikesell, M.W., editors, *Perspective on Environment*, Washington DC: Association of American Geographers, 213-51.

Scott, A.J. (1971). *An Introduction to Spatial Allocation Analysis.* Washington DC: Association of American Geographers.

Sewell, W.R.D. and Burton, I. (1967). Recent innovations in resource development policy. *Canadian Geographer* II, 327-40.

Sewell, W.R.D. (1973). Broadening the approach to evaluation in resources management decision-making. *Journal of Environmental Management* 1, 33-60.

Sewell, W.R.D. (1974). Perceptions, attitudes and public participation in countryside management in Scotland. *Journal of Environmental Management* 2, 235-57.

Simmons, I.G. (1974). *The Ecology of Natural Resources.* London: Edward Arnold.

Simon, H.A. (1957). *Administrative Behaviour.* New York: Macmillan.

Smith, R.H.T. (1970). Concepts and methods in commodity flow analysis. *Economic Geography* 46, 404-416.

Sobolev, L.N. (1971). The relationship between the productivity of plants, plant communities and their geographical systems and the factors of the environment (three levels of research). *Soviet Geography* 12, 61-66.

Sochava, V.B. (1971). Geography and ecology. *Soviet Geography* 12, 277-93.

Stankey, G.H. (1972). A strategy for the definition and management of wilderness quality. In Krutilla, J.V., editor, *Natural Environments: Studies in Theoretical and Applied analysis*, Baltimore: Johns Hopkins University Press, 88-114.

Streeter, D.T. (1971). The effect of public pressure on the vegetation of chalk downland at Box Hill, Surrey. In Duffey, E. and Watt, A.S., editors, *The Scientific Management of Animal and Plant Communities for Consideration*, Oxford: Blackwell, 459-68.

Trotter, J.E. (1965). Some factors influencing attendance at Illinois State Parks. *Journal of Geography* 64, 23-31.

Uhlig, H. (1978). Geoecological controls on high-altitude rice cultivation in the Himalayas and mountain regions of southeast Asia. *Arctic and Alpine Research* 10, 519-29.

Ullman, E.L. (1957). *American Commodity Flow.* Seattle: University of Washington Press.

Ullman, E.L. and Volk, D.J. (1962). An operational model for predicting reservoir attendance and benefits: implications of a location approach to water recreation. *Papers of the Michigan Academy of Science, Arts and Letters* 47, 473-84.

Wagar, J.A. (1961). *The Carrying Capacity of Wildlands for Recreation.* University of Michigan, unpublished Ph.D. dissertation.

Ward, R.M. and Berg, R.C. (1973). Soil compaction and recreational use. *Professional Geographer* 25, 369-72.

Washburn, A.L. (1970). An approach to a genetic classification of patterned ground. *Acta Geographica Lodziensia* 24, 437-46.

Watson, A., Bayfield, N. and Moyes, S. (1970), Research on human pressures on Scottish mountain tundra, soils and animals. In Fuller, W.J. and Kevan, P.G., editors, *Productivity and Conservation in Northern Circumpolar Lands,* Morges: IUCN.

Watt, K.E.F. (1968). *Ecology and Resource Management.* New York: McGraw-Hill.

Wengert, N. (1955). *Natural Resources and the Political Struggle.* New York: Doubleday.

Whitaker, J.R. (1954). *The geography: Inventory and Prospect,* Syracuse: University of Syracuse Press, 226-39.

White, G.F. (1961). The choice of use in resource management. *Natural Resources Journal* 1, 23-40.

White, G.F. (1963). Contributions of geographical analysis to river basin development. *Geographical Journal* 129, 412-36.

White, G.F. (1969). *Strategies of American Water Management.* Ann Arbor: University of Michigan Press.

White, G.F. (1973). Natural hazards research. In Chorley, R.J., editor, *Directions in Geography,* London: Methuen, 193-216.

White, G.F., (Ed.), (1974). *Natural Hazards: Local, National, Global.* New York: Oxford University Press.

Willard, B. and Marr, J. (1970). Effects of human activities on alpine Tundra ecosystems in Rocky Mountain National Park, Colorado. *Biological Conservation* 2, 257-65.

Willard, B. and Marr, J. (1971). Recovery of alpine tundra under protection after damage by human activity in the Rocky Mountains of Colorado. *Biological Conservation* 3, 181-90.

Williams, A.V. and Zelinsky, W. (1970). On some patterns in international tourist flows. *Economic Geography* 46, 549-67.

Wilson, M.G.A. (1967). The coal traffic of Eastern Australia. *Economic Geography* 43, 128-42.

Wise, M.J. (1969). On the utilisation of resources. *Geography* 54, 257-70.

Wong, S.T. (1968). *Perception of Choice and Factors Affecting Industrial Water Supply Decisions in Northeastern Illinois.* Chicago: University of Chicago, Department of Geography, Research Paper 117.

Wood, C.J.B. (1976). Conflict in resource management and the use of threat: the Goldstream controversy. *Natural Resources Journal* 16, 137-58.

5

Application of Ecological Principles in Conservation of Natural Resources

MANJU BANSAL, NIKHAT SARWAR & K.G. MUKERJI

Introduction

A resource can be simply defined as a form of energy and/or matter which is and essential for the functioning of organisms, populations and ecosystems. All resources are subdivided into 2 groups. Non-renewable are those dependent on a finite stock and is non-reproducible, e.g. fossil fuels, or raw materials whose usage involves dispersal (e.g. Phosphate fertilisers). Renewable resources are those that are reproducible, i.e. are obtained from the biomass of living organisms. The current environmental crisis mainly is concerned with non-renewable resources. The five fundamental ecological variables included among the natural resources are — energy, matter, space, time and diversity. Thus, all theories concerning the use of natural resources must depend on the laws which govern variations in these five quantities.

ECOLOGICAL PRINCIPLES GOVERNING THE USE OF NATURAL RESOURCES

Certain ecological principles must be followed if the resources of the biosphere are to be protected and used rationally (Woodbury, 1984; May, 1976). These ecological principles involve phenomena occurring at the various levels of organisation, viz. population, community, ecosystem and finally the entire biosphere.

Principles Concerning Energy

(a) The production of biomass in a given ecosystem, and thus the availability of plant and animal resources is governed by solar radiation (Hammond, 1971). The potential biological productivity in every ecosystem is determined mainly by the mean intensity of solar radiation. In the final analysis, the whole of the energy flow in a given community depends on the amount of solar energy captured per unit area per unit time by the leaf systems and stem of green plants.

(b) Energy is transformed in food webs from one form to another but is neither created nor destroyed, in accordance with the first law of thermodynamics. Both in primary producers and in animal consumers (= secondary producers), part of the energy available is stored in the biomass, with the remainder being used up in metabolic processes. Thus in autotrophic plants, only a fraction of the incident solar radiation is converted into biochemical energy through photosynthesis. After that, immediate photorespiration and other forms of respiration will reutilise a large proportion of the solar radiation already converted into biochemical substances. The efficiency of energy conversion in ecosystem is always low and it can never approach 100 per cent. This is a consequence of the second law of thermodynamics which shows that all transformation of energy is accompanied by a loss of quality in some of the initial amount present. Thus, at all stages in food webs or food chains, there will be a loss of useful energy, reflecting what is observed during typical metabolic processes in each individual. Out of the total solar radiation incident on the earth of about 10^8 Kcal per day, about 10^6 Kcal per day is taken up by producers, around 10^4 Kcal per day passes to herbivores and only 10^3 Kcal per day goes to carnivores of the first order. This is an excellent example of Lindemann's law and it illustrates why food chains can't be of unlimited length. In terrestrial environments, the longest chains are generally of the type:

Trophic level :

I	II	III	IV
Plant →	herbivore →	carnivore 1 →	carnivore

2

Most common is grass → cattle → humans.
In an aquatic environment, we can have :
phytoplankton → zooplankton → microphagous fish →
predator fish → superpredator fish.

Principles Concerning Matter

(a) No natural resource whether it is mineral or biological can exist in unlimited quantities. The availability of a resource is in practice restricted by various abiotic and/or biotic factors. Such factors as the spatial distribution of a mineral element or biogenic molecule (e.g. H_2O), the difficulties of transference from the lithosphere (e.g. P) or from the atmosphere (e.g. N_2); and many others, may combine in such a way that many chemical elements and mineral molecules which are abundant on the earth's surface become limiting factors for primary and secondary production because of their unavailability. In the case of biological resources, even those whose biomass in a given ecosystem appears considerable, but the fact is that their true availability depends on the energy flow in that ecosystem, i.e. on the productivity. No proportional relation exists between total biomass and productivity. In particular, environments like tropical rain forests or animal species like whales, all with considerable biomass, do not exhibit a distinctly greater primary or secondary productivity than more modest ecosystems or species.

(b) A second principle that concerns matter is a generalisation of Liebig's law and it takes the following form: both the scarcity (or even just a relative lack of availability) of a mineral element and its excess through natural or human agency (pollution) can act as factors limiting the take-up of other natural resources. The principle is well illustrated by the case of water in semi-arid climates and by that of phosphorus in land-based or aquatic environments. In the latter, e.g., for instance, the concentration of phosphates in soils or H_2O is a basic factor that determines the productivity of continental or oceanic ecosystems. This can be illustrated by fresh-water environments : a relative deficiency of phosphorus is responsible for the low productivity of oligotrophic lakes, while at the other extreme, an excess of P stimulates so much primary productivity that it is the main cause of dystrophic lakes — in which salmon and trout breeding can be ruined because of the lowered secondary productivity.

(c) A third principle concerning matter is the law of the optimum. This states that an increase in the availability of a nutrient, whether a mineral element or an organic molecule, does not produce an unlimited increase in productivity : there is always either an asymptote or a maximum beyond which the productivity decreases.

A good illustration of this principle is provided by the law of diminishing yield. According to this, the yield from cultivated land never increases in proportion to the supply of fertiliser. Instead, when the latter grows in a geometric progression, the yield increases roughly in arithmetic progression — although this cannot be exact because as the fertiliser supply tends to infinity, the yield tends to an asymptotic limits.

In cases where the law of diminishing yield applies, the increase in availability of resources in the ecosystem is a non-stimulatory effect. At the other extreme, resources may induce stimulatory effects. Here, in an initial phase, an increase in the availability of a resource produces a growth in productivity (or other biological processes) that is more than merely proportional. Gradually, however, further increases in availability will produce limiting factors that slow down the growth.

There are two different ways in which the availability of a resource can affect ecological processes like productivity. In the first category are resources which produce a stimulatory effect, where the relationship is expressed by logistic or sigmoid curves. After the initial rise, the effects eventually tend to an asymptotic limit as the availability tends to infinity. This type of response is observed for resources coming under the category of 'matter' as well as 'energy'.

In the second category are resources for which an increase in availability produces a growth in the effects up to a maximum, beyond which they begin to decrease. Here, excessive concentration of an element will have harmful effects and will become toxic or pollutant.

This type of relationship between effect and concentration is observed with a large number of mineral and organic substances which are said to have hermetic properties. They are materials, which are indispensable to living organisms in small doses, but which become toxic beyond certain concentrations, e.g. fluorine, cobalt, and some vitamins.

Principle Concerning Space

(a) The space available to each biological entity, whether an individual, a species or a community, is always restricted because the area it occupies is smaller than that covered by the complete ecosystem to which it belongs. This is true for humans as well as for other species, e.g. the amount of land capable of being cultivated in any country is always smaller than the total area because of the poor structure of some of the soils, or for bioclimatic reasons (Pimentel *et al.*, 1976).

(b) The area available for ensuring that each individual is fed decreases more rapidly than the population density increases.

Principles Concerning Diversity

Of all the fundamental ecological variables, diversity is the one that best characterises the biotic component of ecosystems.

(a) The first principle concerns the relationship between diversity and the stability of ecological factors. The greater this stability, the greater the diversity of the ecosystem.

(b) A second principle relates to the effects of another resource, time, on the species diversity, effects which are manifested as a fundamental ecological phenomenon called succession. The diversity of an ecosystem increases as a function of time from an initial state where it has a minimum to one where it has a maximum value, when the ecosystem is called a climax community.

(c) The biomass/productivity ratio of an ecosystem is proportional to its diversity. The diversity is a measure of the degree of organisational complexity in ecosystems. It is linked to the amount of energy stored in the biomass and to the flow of energy per unit time. The time taken for a quantity of energy to traverse an ecosystem will be greater with greater diversity. Diversity is a measure of the complexity of food webs. The path of the energy from the producers through to the super carnivores and the detritivores will take longer in a food web comprising a large number of steps than in a short linear chain of the type producer $\rightarrow$ herbivore.

(d) The most diversified ecosystems are the most stable. The capacity of a community for homeostasis will grow with its diversity.

(e) Diversified ecosystems exploit less diversified ecosystems. In general, mature systems (Climax communities) are observed to remove energy, matter and diversity from immature or less diversified systems that surround them. A classic example is provided by forest — savanna contact in tropical regions (Lamotte, 1975). Forest animals mostly seek their food in the neighbouring open ground where grass is the predominant ground cover. By doing that, they prevent the savanna from evolving to a more diversified stage : the removal of seeds by birds, and the crushing of young trees, prevent the more advanced stages of succession from developing. The transition to tree-covered land is thus blocked by the exploitation and the savanna remains in a state of immaturity.

A similar example is observed in a marine environment at the meeting zone between blue tropical waters and the immature ecosystem of the colder waters. Predators in the tropical zone seek their food in the cold waters of high productivity and maintain the latter ecosystem in a less advanced successional stage.

Principles Concerning Populations

The growth and regulation of natural populations are governed by a number of laws. Knowledge of these is essential for the rational exploitation of the resources in the biosphere (Pereira, 1973).

APPLICATION IN RESOURCE CONSERVATION

Ecological models for proper management of earth's surface and rational utilisation of biosphere has been put forward by various ecologists over a decade (Allen, 1980). All ecological models and principles are based on five fundamental resources, viz., energy, matter, space, time and diversity. Based on these ecological variables, or resources IUCN on behalf of United Nations organisation proposed a programme or strategy stating that main resources indispensable to humanity must be conserved (Lucas and Synge, 1978). Followings should be the priorities for resource conservation :

(a) The maintenance of essential ecological process and life support system, e.g. the regulation and protection of soils, the recycling of soils and inorganic nutrients, the natural purification of water.
(b) The preservation of genetic diversity on which most of these processes and systems depend for their functioning.
(c) Supervision and control of the long term exploitation of ecosystem and species.

Agricultural Ecosystems

Global food production has increased substantially over last two decades, but the factors such as population pressure and environmental degradation are undermining the agriculture conditions and future prospects. Long ago in 1798 Malthus in the famous *Essay on the Principle of Populations* was insisting on the fact that possibilities for growth in human population are infinitely greater than those of soil for production of the necessary food.

Agricultural ecosystem is in stress in both developing and developed countries (Hopper, 1976). Farmers in developing world try to increase production by increasing irrigated area and fertilisers input, both of which carries substantial environmental risk. Farmers in industrial world faces a different set of pressures. They are increasingly aware of the environmental toll taken by conventional agricultural practices which can rapidly erode farm soils and wash fertilisers and pesticides into surfaces. Such environmental degradation, soil erosion for example, costs farmer money by reducing future production. When such losses are quantified, resources conservation practices can be both economically and environmentally superior to conventional practices.

Besides the various demographic policies that may be followed by developing nations there are various ecological factors which determine whether and by what amount increase in the world food production can be achieved (Wortman, 1976).

Synecology shows that the productivity of agricultural ecosystems depends essentially on three of ecological variables : energy, matter (in the form of inorganic nutrients available) and the species that make up total population (that is the nature of plant species and varieties chosen for cultivation plus the breeds of animal chosen for secondary productivity). Finally, the primary and secondary productions and agricultural ecosystem depend on space; that is the total area of cultivated land that is available.

The Agricultural Energy Budget

Any increase in agricultural yield per unit area depends on three factors:

(a) The energy supplied, since a greater productivity automatically implies an increase in energy flow through ecosystem.
(b) Matter, in the form of water supplies and nutrients (organic and inorganic fertilisers).
(c) The use of cultivated varieties (cultivars) of crops and breeds of livestock that are highly productive equivalent in a way to an increase in the species diversity in world agricultural ecosystem.

The productivity of the biosphere is directly governed by the flow of energy through it. This means that the amount of food available per individual depends primarily upon the production of energy input to each ecosystem that can be diverted towards satisfying the food requirement of human beings (Lieth, 1975). From the beginning of agriculture in the Neolithic age, increase in yield have been achieved by a continuous growth in energy flow through the ecosystem (Ehrlich *et al.*, 1977). Also the dramatic increase in productivity during the last few decades is a result of a greater input of artificial energy ultimately provided by fossil fuels. A detailed analysis of the energy budget in primary production (growing of crops) and secondary production (rearing of stock) shows that energy content of foodstuffs produced owes nearly as much as fuel as photosynthetic conversion (Hulter, 1976) or in some cases more. As H.T. Odum (1971) says "Human beings no longer at potatoes produced only by photosynthesis — that we eat today are partly made up from oil".

Choice of species of crops or breeds of livestock that are particularly well adapted to human diets is a sort of technological process designed divert a greater proportion of incident solar radiation to our benefit through its conversion into primary energy by autotrophic producers. Looked at in that way agriculture can be assimilated into the overall food web with human consumption at the summit of the pyramid (Woodwell, 1970). Depending upon circumstances, humans can occupy the second trophic level (herbivore) or the third (carnivore) and sometimes even a level between third and fourth.

Cultivated and Potentially Cultivable Area

The primary factor governing world agricultural production is the soil and with it the amount of land with soil suitable for cultivation. The estimate quoted recently (World resources 1992-93) reveal the distribution of land as shown below:

Total land area (in hectares)	13,128,841
Crop land area	1,477,877
Permanent pastures	3,322,943
Forest and woodland	4,095,317
Other land	4,232,737

One of the principles concerning space states that the amount of arable land available not only decreases as population increases but does so at a greater rate than mere inverse proportionality. Besides rapid urbanisation of land (Friedman, 1977), various physico-chemical changes cause soils to deteriorate when they are cultivated or when their natural plant cover is destroyed through human activity. Various phenomenon responsible for deterioration of arable soil are :

(i) *Salinization* : Refers to accumulation of a white efflorescence over soil, due to accumulation of sodium chloride and sodium sulphate.

(ii) *Laterization*: Formation of lateritic soils, i.e. acidic with a low concentration of silica and a high concentration of iron and aluminium oxides that gives this yellow colour (McNeil, 1964).

(iii) *Soil Erosion*: Refers to catastrophic erosion of surface layers of soils because of deforestation and to unsuitable cultivation practices.

Thus for conservation of agriculture ecosystem and to ensure flow of supplies, the approach should be to ensure enough land available, for less intensive agriculture and to make inexhaustible cheap energy source.

Forest Resources

The term forest covers ecosystems that very widely in their tree species, in their biological productivity and in their potential as resources of timber. Forests play a major part in the conservation and regeneration of soils and by protecting areas of high relief against erosion, saving drainage basins both from flooding and from becoming badly silted up. They also smooth our climatic fluctuation and increase rainfall. Finally, they act as genetic reservoir not only for all existing tree species, but for whole community of living organisms that inhabit them (Maldague, 1984). Four principal causes for destruction of these forests are : excessive felling of trees for timber; over-grazing; fire and clearance of land for cultivation and for pastures. Forests and woodlands are renewable resources important to the human race in many ways. If they are managed rationally, taking into account of all basic ecological factors involved they should provide all wood needed for the purposes, where it is indispensable.

Broadly speaking there are two ways of exploiting such resources : conservatively or destructively. The conservative method observes certain safeguards in the use of forests and does not significantly change the structure or the productivity of the biocoenoses or biotopes concerned.

The silvicultural management here is based on selective felling of trees, a moderate cropping of animal life by hunting, some recreative and tourist use and a certain amount of grazing of the undergrowth (Spurr, 1979). The creation of nature reserve, or the use of woodland to counteract soil erosion in the areas of high relief or to provide water supplies for a drainage basin all clearly represent conservative measure as well.

The destructive forms of exploitation on the other hand can often be observed. An example is the felling of trees of timber by the practice of clear cutting in forests growing on lands with high relief of fragile soil structure (Likens *et al.*, 1970). Over-grazing also leads to an irreversible degradation through the removal of young plants in such quantities as to prevent any eventual regeneration.

The methods are particularly suitable for natural or semi-natural woodlands where trees covering a range of species, ages and sizes all co-exist. Selective mature trees are felled and a particular care is taken during this operation not to damage the younger ones left standing. An excellent example of the way the selection system allows the resources and structure of a clarion forest to be preserved is provided by mixed plantation of beech and fir.

The shelter wood system is practiced in circumstances where there is a need to reduce competition between individual trees belonging to the same or to different dominant species. The idea is to encourage the growth of the best specimens and for this purpose harvesting is carried out on two or more occasions are spaced out over several years. One cutting removes most of the young trees but leaves the more mature specimens to provide seeds for further seedlings and to provide shelter to enable the remaining young trees to become established. A second cutting then removes the mature trees at an appropriate time. This type of silviculture has also been used to regenerate forests where excessive exploitation to provide firewood has caused them to regress to mere coppices with low productivity.

Tree populations containing a single species all of the same age make a mockery of ecological principles. The complete lack of diversity in these so-called forests makes them particularly vulnerable to attack by pests; that is by pathogenic insects and fungi (Charas, 1980), e.g. frantic planting of conifers provide a perfect illustration of the harmful consequences of anti-ecological practice (Noirfalise, 1964). The disadvantage or negative effects include accumulation of more humus and fulvic acid that encourage podozolisation. This results in reduction in porosity of upper soil horizons, making them impermeable (Duchaufour, 1979). The water cycle is modified; there is a two-fold or three-fold increase in run-off and loss by evaporation increases because fine needles retain a large amount of rainwater. This affects soil fauna. Diversity of arthropod populations in general is reduced. Decomposers are also greatly affected and a marked reduction in bacteria occurs, particularly in the micro-organisms involved in the nitrogen cycle.

The final disadvantage of uniform conifer plantation and by no means an insignificant one, is their high susceptibility to fire. Taking all these factors into account, the current practice of reforestation with conifers in temperate and even in tropical regions would seem to constitute an astonishing perseverance with mistaken methods on the part of the authorities responsible for forests in the various countries involved.

Energy and Mineral Resources

Sources of energy and supplies of minerals occupy a special place among the various natural resources exploited by humans (Hubbert, 1969; 1971). They are both essentially non-renewable even where they have a biological origin; as in case of fossil fuel or of certain metal bearing deposits. They thus form a stock which is undergoing rapid exhaustion according to the size of the various geological deposits and the speed with which contemporary technological civilisation is exploiting them.

Balance in energy production and use are vital to sustainable developments and environments of all countries. Burning of fossil fuels for example contributes to global warming. An analysis of the way ecosystem functions shows that flow of energy and cycle of energy and matter cannot be dissociated from each other. Ecological models are used to analyse the manner in which the energy and the matter are transported through anthropoecosystems.

Comparison of flow of energy and the cycle of matter in two types of ecosystems are dominated by agriculture and other dominated by industrial process reveal about the deteriorating state of energy resources of earth. The premature rural civilisation man could be said to have lived on the interest from their energy stock produced from cultivated plants and forests. This interest trapped by photosynthesis and consumed by humans through primary productivity represented only a small fraction of total incident solar radiation. In complete contrast, today's technological societies are living on their energy capital, which is bound to exhaust after certain period. In fact the apparent prosperity of industrial countries in large measure is artificial if the plundering scarce and non-renewable rational resources are taken into account.

The Atmosphere and Climates

The ecological principles governing energy and matter emphasize the occurrence of various geochemical cycles. This is true also, as for any system to continue there must always be a movement of materials in a cyclic manner. The mineral elements taken up from the environment (soil as well as atmosphere) by green plants — the producers are again returned to the environment. In this taking and returning process as of minerals, there are involved a number of organisms as well as some physico-chemical phenomenon that make together an orderly operating cycle. The chemical composition of the atmosphere is being modified by the mixing into it of particles gases and volatile substances, all more or less toxic to living organisms. This hinders the renewal of certain natural resources, upsets the normal functioning of atmosphere and runs the risk of inducing irreversible ecological changes on a world-wide scale. These changes in ecological balance of atmosphere at local level cause serious public health problems and it is causing grave danger to existence of various forests and plants.

The atmosphere protect us from sun's most harmful rays, provide a moderate and stable climate, and renew and cleanse itself to provide fresh air to breathe. At the level of entire ecosphere, it is upsetting the principal biogeochemical cycles and producing climatic effect of certain magnitude. The cyclic occurrence of various biogeochemical cycles is of primary importance for existence of human being.

Our industrial civilisation has already disturbed the carbon and sulphur cycles quite considerably. Also it has significantly altered the occurrence of nitrogen cycle and ozone cycle.

Perturbation of C-cycle

Carbon cycle and energy as given by Ramade, 1978a is

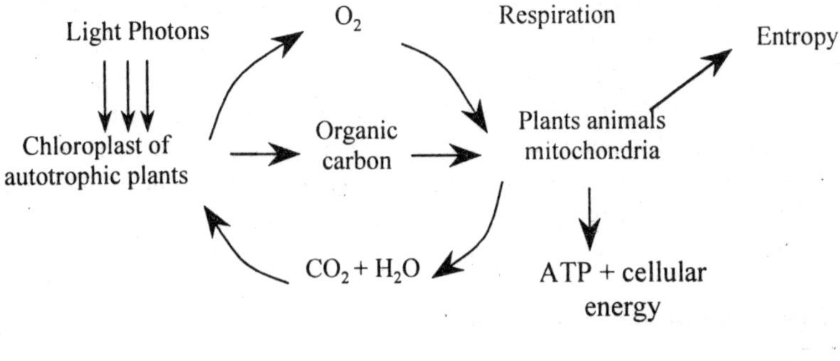

Fig. 5.1: Carbon Cycle and Energy as given by Rama de, 1978a

The C-cycle serve as is fundamental since it is main vehicle of transfer between atmosphere, hydrosphere and various biocoenoses. Concentration of CO_2 in atmosphere is increasing because of various anthropogenic activities (Bramryd, 1979). The release of CO_2 into the atmosphere from consumption of fossil fuels is undoubtedly a basic cause of perturbation in C-cycle (Woodwell, 1978). Deforestation, another factor of human origin is also responsible for alteration in carbon cycle (Broecker, 1975; Adams *et al.*, 1977).

If the land after deforestation is put to agricultural use after clearing it, then the resulting oxidation of the forest humus stored in it will release a further 2×10^9 tonnes of carbon per year. This excess of CO_2 can be accumulated in two sections of biosphere — the biomass and the oceans. Increase in photosynthesis by an increase in atmospheric concentration of CO_2, is far less from being capable of compensating for this increase. The only way of increasing the storage of C in the biomass and reabsorbing a significant proportion of excess CO_2 is by putting an immediate stop to the destruction of forests accompanied by intensive reforestation on a continental scale.

Perturbation of the Ozone Cycle

Ozone is an important part of oxygen cycle. Ozone is formed from molecular oxygen which is dissociated by UV (100-245 nm)

$$O_2 + UV \longrightarrow 2O \; (100 - 245 \text{ nm})$$
$$2O + O_2 \longrightarrow 2O_3 + 2.2 \text{ ev}$$
$$NO_2 + hr \longrightarrow NO + O$$
$$(< 400 \text{ n or } 3.1 \text{ ev})$$
$$NO_2 + O \longrightarrow NO + O_2$$
$$NO + O_3 \longrightarrow NO_2 + O_2$$
$$H_2O \longrightarrow OH^- + H^2$$
$$2H^+ + O_3 \longrightarrow H_2O + O_2$$

In absence of human intervention the dynamic equilibrium of atmospheric ozone is maintained. The various processes that are capable of interfering with ozone cycle are explosion of nuclear devices, combustion which produces oxides of nitrogen, use of fluorocarbon gas propellants in aerosol sprays (Rasool and Schneider, 1971; Maugh, 1979).

Perturbation in Sulphur Cycle

Fossil fuel combustion has had a marked effect on the sulphur cycle. The SO_2 comes into contact with atmospheric oxygen and water vapour and is transformed into sulphuric acid and then to sulphates, both of which are taken back to earth's surface by rain, snow etc. (Granat *et al*., 1976). The increased SO_2 in atmosphere is related to combustion of greater and greater quantities of sulphur risk oil and coil.

Ecological consequences of disturbing sulphur cycle are many. Among the immediate and most noticeable are the toxic effects on plant and animal physiology of the atmospheric pollution. No plant can grow in air that permanently contain more than 100 p.p.b. of SO_2 and great damage is done by chronic SO_2 pollution.

Conclusion

The various principles that have been put forward and discussed show a strong degree of interdependence for, e.g. the utilisation of energy, both at the level of populations and ecosystems, conditions the differentiation of ecological niches, the diversity, the productivity, the stability of populations, their spatial distribution and so on.

Two main factors are the root cause of the current environmental crisis : population explosion and the other is the wasteful consumption of energy and other natural resources by the developed countries of the world. The extent of the present environmental crisis, and its disastrous consequences indicates the need for urgent implementation of a world strategy for conservation. The IUCN has evolved a programme on behalf of the United Nations Organisation. This programme brings together the work of more than 700 specialists in general and applied ecology, in environmental planning and in related disciplines. Ecological models for the proper management of the earth's surface and the rational utilisation of the biosphere have been put forward by various ecologists for over a decade. By applying these ecological models, new so-called post-industrial, type of civilisation be conceived, which will be free from the present difficulties. It is with this aim in mind that IUCN evolved its strategy, and proposed that the main resources indispensable to humanity should be conserved through the application of the ecological principles.

It is essential that this programme should be implemented with the greatest urgency and objectives are achieved without delay.

REFERENCES

Adams, J.A.S. (1977). Wood *versus* fossil fuels as a source of excess carbon dioxide in the atmosphere : a preliminary report, *Science*, 196, no. 4285, pp. 54-56.

Allen, R.A. (1980). *How to Save the World? Strategy for World Conservation*, Kagan Paul, London, pp. 150.

Bradmryd, T. (1979). The effects of man on the biogeochemical cycle of carbon in terrestrial ecosystems. In : *The Global Carbon Cycle*. Ed. Bolin *et al*., Wiley, pp. 183-218.

Broecker, W.S. (1975). Climatic changes : are we on the brink of a pronounced global warming ? *Science*, 189, No. 4145, pp. 13-16.

Granat, L., Rodhe, H. and Hallberg, R.O. (1976). The global sulphur cycle. In Svensson and Soderlund, N, P and S - Global Cycles, *Ecological Bulletin* No. 22, pp. 89-122.

Harmmond, A.L. (1971). Solar energy : a feasible source of power? *Science*, 172, pp. 660.

Hopper, W.D. (1976). The development of agriculture in developing countries, *Scient. Amer*., 235, No. 3, pp. 196-205.

Hubbert, M.K. (1969). Energy resources, In : *Resources, and Man, US Nat. Acad. Sci., Freeman*, pp. 157-242.

Hubbert, M.K. (1971). Energy resources, In : *Environment, Resources, Pollution and Society*, Sinauer, pp. 89-116.

IUCN, (1975). *The Red Data Book*, IUCN, Gland, Switzerland.

IUCN, (1980). *World Conservation Strategy*, undertaken with the support of UNEP and WWF, Gland, Switzerland.

Lamotte, M. (1975). *The Structure and Function of a Tropical Savannah Ecosystem*, Springer-Verlag, pp. 179-222.

Lieth, H. (1975). Primary production of the major vegetation units of the world. In : *Primary Productivity of the Biosphere*, (Eds.) H. Lieth and R.H. Whittaker, Springer-Verlag, pp. 203-215.

Likens, G.E., Bormann, F.H., Johnson, N.M. (1970). Effects of forest cutting and herbicide treatment on nutrient budgets in the Hubbard Brook Watershed Ecosystem, *Ecol. Monographs*, 40, pp. 23-47.

Lucas, G. and Synge, H. (1978). *The IUCN Plant Red Data Book*, IUCN, Gland, Switzerland.

McNeil, M. (1964). Lateritic Soils, *Scient. Amer*., 211, Nov., pp. 97-102.

Maldague, M. (1984). The biosphere reserve concept : its implementation and potential as a tool for integrated development. In : *Ecology in Practice, Part 1 : Ecosystem Management*, (Eds.) F.Di Castri, F.W.G. Baker and M. Hadley. Tycooley, Dublin and Unesco, pp. 375-401.

Maugh, T.H. (1979). The threat to ozone is real, increasing. *Science*, 206, pp. 1167-1168.

May, R.M. (1976). *Theoretical Ecology, Principles and Applications*, Blackwell Scientific Publications, pp. 317.

Odum, E.P. (1977). The emergence of ecology as a new integrative discipline. *Science*, 195, No. 4284, March, pp. 1289-1293.

Pereira, H.C. (1973). *Land Use and Water Resources in Temperate and Tropical Climates*, Cambridge University Press.

Pimentel, D., Terhune, E.C., Dysar-Hudson, R. (1976). Land degradation : effects on food and energy resources, *Science*, 194, 8 October, pp. 149-155.

Rasool, S.L., and Schneider, S.H. (1971). Atmospheric CO_2 and aerosols : effects of large increases on global climate, *Science*, 173, pp. 138-141.

Spurr, S.H. (1979). Silviculture, *Scient. Amer.*, 240, No. 2, pp. 62-75.

Woodbury, A.M. (1954). *Principles of General Ecology*. New York : McGraw Hill Book Co.

Woodwell, G.M. (1970). The energy cycle of the biosphere, *Scient. Amer.*, September, pp. 26-36.

Woodwell, G.M. (1978). The carbon dioxide question, *Scient. Amer.*, 238, January, pp. 34-43.

Wortman, S. (1976). Food and Agriculture, *Scient. Amer.*, 235, No. 3, pp. 31-39.

6

Ecological Interlinkages in Resource Management and Development

SAVITRI G. BURMAN

In the World of today there is tremendous clamour about the degradation of the environment and exhaustion of resources on the one hand and increasing demand on each of the natural resources on the other. This is not only to satisfy the increasing number of people but also to fulfil the rising expectations of the individuals to raise their standard of living, which is defined in terms of per capita consumption. Majority of the articles of consumption are derived from the natural resources of the Earth, either directly or indirectly. Even the processes of manufacturing require the presence of natural resources like energy, water and air, and even land as space, in addition to the raw materials, derived largely from rocks, soils and biota. In today's World man's dependence on them is overwhelming. Production of economic goods both in variety and numbers in spite of advancing technology does not reduce man's dependence on natural resources but actually enhances it both for those that are used as raw materials as well as those that act as catalysts or whose presence is required in all chemical, physical and biological reactions.

As we reach the end of the 20th century, and take stock of our natural resource assets, we find that among our worldwide concerns are resource exhaustion and depletion. Maladies like poor productiveness or the total break up of the resource system in terms of their physical regeneration are evident in large parts of the World, especially the underdeveloped ones. This situation is both the cause and consequence of overall environment degradation.

As long as human beings led a life of subsistence, there was no need to manage the environment, it managed itself. Humans took out only what they required for their basic needs and processed resources with the help of nature or according to natural laws. If and when these resources were depleted because of a catastrophe or over population, the human either moved away or they were decimated. It was only with the advance of technology and industrial revolution and increase in trade and commerce and the consequent historico-political factors that pressure on some basic natural resources increased, resulting in large scale depletion of those resources and degradation of the interlinked ones. This is particularly evident in the depletion of plant and animal resources and consequent degradation of soils and water in the area. This situation is particularly pronounced in the underdeveloped countries, where the above said exploitation took place first under colonial rule and later in the 'race for modernisation'. Currently, this faster rate of degradation results not only from overuse of a resource but also from lack of understanding of the basic ecological processes connected with them. In a country like India, the first twenty years of economic planning laid stress only on harnessing the natural resources without even recognising their ecological character, which was done only around late 1960s. Even then the economic plans continued to be made without any concern with ecological situations. It was only in 1987, in the Seventh Plan document that there was a clear statement that 'a judicious blend of economic and environmental concerns should inform all our developmental programmes in the future'.

Resource Interlinkages

Natural resources in use, directly or indirectly, are interlinked in a well defined system, generally known as an Ecosystem or Ecological system in which the physical and organic parameters are not only interlinked and in a state of balance but where changes in one parameter leads to chain reactions in all the others till a new balance is reached. This complex natural system is composed of a variety of living organisms, dead organic matter as well as the inorganic components like energy, air, water, soils, rocks and minerals and land space. All components of the system are interlinked by complicated processes and are dependent on each other.

Energy, both light and heat, which in nature is derived largely from the Sun, pervades through the entire ecosystem changing in strength and form, while passing from one parameter to the other. It lies in storage for varying periods of time especially in plant bodies and in water and is capable of being re-used after release. Energy is the driving force for all physical, chemical and biological processes. The power 'generated' and utilised by human kind is basically the natural energy either trapped directly or generated by natural forces, or that which is stored in fossil fuels.

Air is another essential as well as an all pervading component of the ecosystem. Very few chemical or biological processes are possible without the presence of air. Not only all living beings require to breathe air, but all chemical processes whether in nature or the laboratory or factory require the presence of air. The quality or composition of the air is just as important, for its major components are utilised directly either by plants or by animals and increase of one or the other is detrimental to one or the other living community. Much of the nitrogen of the air is the source of nitrates on the earth's surface. All other components of the air are a part of chains of actions and reactions that go on in the other parameters of the system. Many of the natural cycles like carbon and nitrogen cycles that are a part and parcel of the break up of complex materials into simple ones involve a gaseous phase, which is contained in the air envelope. One of the most important transient phases of a resource that is held by air is water vapour. Several fine particles of solids like salt and others are held by air and transported from place to place. Vertical and horizontal transportation of heat by air currents is one of the major basis of climatic phenomena.

Water, just like energy and air, is also all pervading in its different forms — gas, liquid and solid, especially the first two. It is in these different forms that water is a part and parcel of the entire litho-bio-atmospheric system; the system from which we derive all our natural resources. The water cycle involves the formation (of a phase), movement, and storage of the different phases of water and is directly connected with energy, particularly heat. Solar energy is the main force driving this cycle. In the gaseous form or the water vapour form it is largely held in the air envelope. In its hygroscopic form it is attached as a film to inorganic materials like minerals, rocks, etc. The liquid form may be in storage, as lakes on land surface, or underground filling the pores of rocks or soil, or in oceans and seas; or running downslope in rivulets and streams. In its solid form i.e. ice, it is in storage in ice sheets, snow caps and glaciers, which enhance both the liquid supply and the gaseous form from time to time. The movement of the ice form of water is directly connected with the slope of land and changing temperature. Water is most intimately connected with heat energy for all its transformation and movements are a result of absorption and release of heat energy.

Like air, very few chemical and biological processes are possible without water either in nature or a factory. Human economy especially in terms of agriculture is almost totally geared to water both in quantity and quality as well as seasonality. As water has back and forth linkages with all the parameters of the ecosystem as well as with the economic system, its loss or rather change to unusable forms brings disaster to both the natural and human systems. This is more so in the human system as it is much less adaptable as compared to the natural system. Increase or decrease of the water supply in a soil is immediately followed by the germination of the corresponding seeds that are awaiting in the soil for such a situation.

Water has the most intimate relationship with the climate. The climate of any area or locality is a direct result of the interplay of energy, water and air, with water playing the major role. This interplay is determined by the area's location — latitudinal and altitudinal, landforms and their alignments regards the sun and wind systems as well as the vegetation cover. The wind system itself is a result of differential heating of the air masses. Wind speed, temperature regimes and atmospheric humidity beneath a forest are remarkably different from a nearby grassland, a barren area, or a 'built up' area with tarmac and concrete; for each of these habitats have varying rates of absorption and reflection of solar energy which to a large extent are determined by the amount of water present in any form. Holding capacity of water and other chemical reactions also vary in each of these habitats. Climate exercises a very strict and sometimes a direct control on the life cycles and distribution of plants, animals and soils, and through them the humans that are directly linked to them. All species have a specific range of moisture and heat requirements.

Land, which has myriads of facets and functions, is often termed the Primary Resource. All other natural resources are anchored on, above or below it. All human activities are also carried on, on this space. Each parcel of land has distinct physical character in terms of location — latitudinal, altitudinal and vicinal, slope, aspect regards the sun, rock character and surface cover which collectively determine its receipt of insolation and precipitation. It is the overall land character that determines the distribution, availability and economies of usage of all natural resources. The mineral components of the land system in the form of rocks or loose materials are structured as well as pulverised by the processes of chemical and mechanical action guided by heat and pressure of energy, water and air. The area encompassing this system is not only the surface of the earth but also the substrata and the lower atmosphere.

Minerals which form the very base of our industrial economy especially in the form of metals and fossil fuels, attained their inherent character in the very depths of the Earth, some of them very deep down. They have formed over long periods of time, sometimes millions of years. The formation of each group and type being different from the other. They are all formed by natural processes, be they geologic, involving chemical actions like in the case of many metals and others, formed under heat and pressure; geomorphic processes, as in the case of sedimentary rocks, like shales and limestones or iron ores formed from laterites. It is the biological processes which are responsible for the formation of coal and petroleum. Man's use of them are infinitely faster than their rate of production, hence they are termed exhaustible, non-regenerative or fund resources.

Soils of varying structures, textures and thicknesses in different parts of the globe are also a result of the interaction of several parameters of the ecosystem. Its formation and qualities are dependent both on weathered rock material or the parent material, decaying organic matter and microbial life in the presence of water, heat and air. In other words, it is a laboratory/factory where organic matter is decomposed and mixed with mineral matter derived from pulverised rock and made ready for absorption by plants. This task is carried on by armies of worms, insects and bacteria. Soils are a true synthesis of biotic and abiotic components. Not only soils supply the plants their nutrients dissolved in water but they also form an anchor for them. The root length of any given plant is also related to the soil depth. The relationship between the plants and soils is the most direct for neither of them can exist nor form, without the other.

Biota or the plants and animals associated with them are the product and reflection of the entire environment of that particular niche or habitat in which they are found. Their association and dependence on each other, as well as other components of the system are so intimate and direct that there is a change in species and plant types, every few inches or feet. This is specially so in mountain environments where the character of the physical system is highly variable. The plants ability to utilise different combinations of heat and water are most conspicuous in areas of diametrically opposed seasons like the contrast between lush green vegetation, and dry, dusty, skimpy vegetation in different seasons of the monsoon lands; or a desert area abloom with flowers after a sharp shower and to return to being a desert after a few days.

Vegetation not only controls the absorption, storage and release of energy, minerals and water, but also the distribution of animals most rigorously; for there is often a symbiotic relationship between the different species of plants and animals. Each species of animal life is not only dependent on plant species for their food but also form an important link in their life cycles like pollination, dispersal of seeds, and even supplies of nitrogen, as in the case of nitrogen fixing bacteria living on the roots of plants of the leguminaceae family (peas, beans etc.). Quite often a plant species also disappears with the extinction of an insect species. What is more dangerous however is the 'release' of insects, bacteria and viruses that lived in a symbiotic relationship with disappearing plants and animals. They move on to other biota causing diseases in cultivated plants, livestock, and even humans. Vegetation and fauna also have reciprocal relationship with soil and landforms, each contributing to the other.

Ecosystems differ greatly in their ability to maintain their equilibrium or stability over long periods. The more complex or complete a system, the more stable it is. For example, the humid tropical ecosystems are most stable, while the arctic and higher mountain systems are the least. In the tropical world, each environmental zone has an abundance of species and each niche has many competitors because of the abundance of energy and water availability as well as a fast turnover of organic matter and nutrients. Here after any disturbance, a rapid repair job is done without the whole system going into a trauma, though some of the original species may be lost. It is the opposite in those systems where the growth rate is slow and diversity less because of less heat and low water availability like in the polar regions and the high mountain reaches. Here restoration of the system is exceedingly slow and hence they are referred to as 'fragile'.

The examples cited in the above pages clearly bring out the interlinkages and interdependence of one resource on the other by means of varied and complicated processes. Energy fixed from the atmosphere, nutrients absorbed from the soil are manufactured into organic compounds and stored in the plant bodies and are passed on to animal bodies via the food chain, where they are converted back into energy. Dead and decaying organic matter in turn releases both energy and nutrients into the soil, water and air. Each of the components and processes of formation and decay have their individual cycles, but are interdependent on each other. The carbon cycle, the nitrogen cycle and even the cycles of erosion and deposition are dependent on the water cycle and the energy cycle. These cycles bring a dynamism to the whole, striving towards a balance of stability.

Human beings, both in body and occupations, are bound by the same principles as other animals — intake of air, water and food as well as output of 'waste' materials. Man's socio-economic realm is also an essential part of this system, no matter how sophisticated his economy or technology is. Human beings have, over centuries, utilised the environmental niches according to their needs and technologies. Over a period of time they had adapted both their technologies and themselves to the different environment parameters around them.

Traditional Technologies

Examples of linkages between social and economic systems and the ecosystems are many in the areas which have been settled for centuries. As there is a great deal of symbiotic relationship between the people and the natural systems, in these areas, practically all traditional systems of social and economic functioning show up in these interlinkages. An example of grazing systems in the Himalayan watersheds explained below illustrates the ecological arrangements between man and nature. Animals form a very important component not only in the overall economy here, for their products and labour, but also a very important link between natural vegetation and agriculture by providing manure to the poor, thin soils. As transport is a major constraint, because of the mountainous terrain, be it for fodder or for manure, it is the animals that are moved around. Although there is a great deal of variation in the grazing systems depending upon the locality, the general pattern is that all animals with the exception of milch cattle are taken to long distances and for varying periods of time in the summer season. This practice generally known as transhumance, not only manages to utilise natural vegetation at different altitudes for animal food, but also manages to manure the fields in the vicinity, where they are folded at night. After the crops are set, the animals are taken to higher slopes to avoid the young crops being trampled or demolished and to utilise the fresh grasses in the upper pastures. In the Kumaon hills the village cattle may be taken up and brought back 4-5 times in the spring and summer months to synchronise with the requirements of labour and to utilise fresh growth of grass. While on the move, generally young males, of the family engage in other activities like making of agricultural implements from nearby forests and the manufacture of butter and 'ghee'. Long distance transhumance like those of the Bhotias, Gaddis etc. are even more synchronised with not only the natural systems, traversing the entire length from the alpine pastures to the foothills and terai; but also with socio-economic systems as well in the realm of trade, religion, and processing of animal products.

The outstanding character of the traditional system of agriculture is the adaptation of the humans to get the most out of each situation in terms of locality, product, time and available technology. Here, cropping, livestock raising and other economic practices are closely intermeshed; with economy and society being interwoven into the physical dependencies. For example, village structures in mid-slope areas conform to the utilising of different parts of the slope in different seasons. Quite often a single village is made up of 2-3 hamlets located on different parts of the slope, with each area being utilised for different crops and for animal grazing according to the seasons. Only some members of the family move up and down these hamlets.

Modern Technologies, Commercialisation and their Adverse Effect

The concept of development in the latter half of the 20th century, especially in countries freed from colonial rule is to harness their natural resources as fast as possible in order to provide the nation with overall economic development in the modern sense, hence the connotation of 'underdeveloped' countries. These natural resources are also being utilised to generate revenue to meet the industrial requirements as well as to rapidly arrive at parity with the developed world, in total disregard to the natural character of the resources themselves. The methodologies, technologies and equipment utilised for this processes has largely been imported, which very often has not been a success in an alien system, both physical and social. Development has been largely sectoral and is generally viewed in the national context or at the most in the context of political division like the state, with no thought to the physical region or locality. The stress so far has been on exploitation of forest and mineral resources, horticulture and commercial agriculture without adequate infrastructural facilities to support them. The combination of the focus on sectoral development, macro regions, foreign technology and 'outside' parties to execute these development plans have bypassed the local people as well as the local ecology. This methodology of development has led to considerable strain both on the society and the physical systems of the locality. This is specially conspicuous in ecologically fragile area like mountains, hills, semi-deserts and mangroves.

A few examples cited particularly from the agricultural and horticultural sector in a fragile ecosystem like the Himalayas, illustrates what is said above. A case of unrealistic planning, in the agricultural sector is the advocacy of the jersey cow in the Himalayas. The sole advantage of the jersey cow is milk production, against which a high input of food, water and labour — each of them being highly scarce in the area. As the fodder is scarce, or has to be brought from long distances, the jersey's milk production reduces to the level of the local cow in a matter of a few years. Unlike the local cow and buffalo, it cannot fend for itself against wild animals and cannot go up the mountain trails. The local people's requirements is not milk, but dung for manure and the animal for ploughing operations; and for both of these purposes, the animals are moved to the site which is often some distance from the settlement. However, wherever extra milk is produced for income, a buffalo does the job better, for it can fend for itself.

Cultivation methodologies unsuited to the local environment of several commercial crops on steep slopes like maize and potatoes are leading to accelerated erosion. It is estimated that the up and down cultivation of maize, even on an 8° slope, in some mountain areas have concurred a soil loss of 28.5 tons per hectare. Loosening of the soil by root crops like potatoes, which are harvested in the autumn, leads to removal of tons of finer soil particles by daily mountain winds, making them steadily coarser and vulnerable to being washed away. Removal of this top soil by wind and water leads to heavy loss of nutrients.

The use of chemical fertilisers in order to coax more yields are also leading to damaged soils by making them more compact and dry. This in turn inhibits the growth of life in these soils and the compactness leads to greater runoff of water. In time soil erosion is the result. It is also said that the use of chemical fertilisers in the paddy fields reduces the yield of wheat which very often follows the rice crop. The chemicals that flow out in the adjoining water bodies lead to greater weed proliferation and consequent loss of water in transpiration. Both the Dal lake in Kashmir and Naini Tal lake in U.P. are already showing eutrophication.

Encouragement of the production of single product without making provisions for its ancillary requirements and ignoring the adverse effects on other natural resources is a common phenomenon. The classical example in this area is that of apples and packing cases in Kashmir. To encourage the export of apples from the valley, government subsidies to the tune of 50% were provided on packing cases, which in turn has led to devastation of vast areas of forests. In 1981, 23.5 million boxes of apples were exported from the Kashmir valley, utilising 14.1 million cft of wood at the rate of 0.6 cft per box, half of which came from the coniferous fir forests. Some studies indicate that for packing the produce of one acre of apples, 10 acres of forests are devastated.

The high pressure on land for local food production in many parts of the Himalayas is now tremendous, resulting from increasing population, not only local but incoming as well including tourists. This pressure also results from loss of land to use for commercial products, as well as increasing degradation. One of the disastrous fallouts is the formation of a 'degradation syndrome'. As the land looses its productive capacity, it leads to cultivation of unsuitable lands generally on the higher margins with larger number of animals, leading to the same result. In the process, both the natural vegetation support area and the water supply are affected. This leads to working males migrating to the plains in search of earning cash, leaving children, females and old people behind. The entire burden of agriculture then falls on the females, who because of their inability to carry on heavy manual work such as repair of terraces, unconsciously pave the way for soil wash. This situation also triggers off increase in animals, who are left to graze on these abandoned agricultural terraces, as pastures are also lacking. This action leads to further erosion, till rill and gully erosion start, when the agricultural land is finally abandoned and landslides start the debris flowing downslope. Then the sequence starts all over again in still more unsuitable lands.

Sustainable Development Strategies

The fallout from the current development strategies, some of which are listed above shows that there is an urgent need for finding alternatives for sound economic development. One such strategy that is now being talked of increasingly in recent years is 'sustainable development', which implies a development that can sustain over a long period without degrading or exhausting the natural resources.

Such a development is only possible if planned and executed according to the inherent capability of the resource to the point where its regeneration is left intact; and the ecological system in which it is placed. It may even mean, the orientation of human demands in tune with the ecosystem, both in quantity and quality. For sound development of a nation's resources, it must not be based on short term gains; rather development has to be long range and sustainable. This is only possible if there is a rational use of basic resources, like land and water, for optimum production and not maximum production, with a minimum of changes to the natural system. Very often havoc is created, when an ecosystem is disturbed but no effort is made to restore it because of economic reasons the effect of limestone quarrying in the Musoorie hills is a famous example. The developmental schemes have to be holistic in nature and not sectoral for an ecosystem is such a region where the physical and biotic parameters are so closely linked that unless taken care of disruption of one parameter leads to chain reactions in the entire system.

Watershed river basins as a unit for development implies an overall development of a natural areal unit in a holistic fashion. A watershed, large or small is a well defined ecosystem. It can be defined as an area of land which drains into a common outlet. The area is generally bounded by a watershed divide, which represents the highest altitudinal strip along the watershed parameter. Rain or snow falling in the Watershed will ultimately find their way towards the major stream draining the area. The other parameters of micro-climate, vegetation, soils, topography and gravitational flows follow the characteristics of the watershed and interact very closely. Here, the output of water and sediments in the streams are governed by intermediate processes like percolation, evaporation and runoff. These in turn are the result of structure, slope, vegetation cover, and intensity of land use. Strictly speaking, a watershed is the upper part of a river system, where a major amount of its water is collected. It lies in a higher altitude zone compared to the rest of its flow area and is very often the upper hilly or mountainous part of the river system. A large watershed is a compendium of several micro-watersheds being drained by its tributaries, each of which is a unit by itself. A river basin is a larger unit, with its watershed lying in the hilly and mountainous part, a middle part formed of flat plain area and a lower part, often delta, formed by deposition of materials.

Human beings settled in the watershed or basin is an integral part of the system and cannot be treated as separate entities. Trying to manage a watershed in small patches areally or based on individual resources has been the biggest drawback of current development strategies. The yearly spate of increased floods in the North Indian plains results from the faulty management in the upper parts of the watersheds and catchment areas in the Himalayas. There are a myriad of linkages in different parts of a watershed or a river basin; specially the lower parts in relation to the upper, whether it be ridge crest or ridge slope; plains part *versus* the mountain part; or the delta section in relation to the upper and middle parts. Ignoring such interlinkages has either negated the development efforts or has caused serious injury to the system as a whole, in both its physical and human components.

It is clear from the above discussion that rational resource management is not desirable in unlinked sectors in any area because all natural resources are closely interlinked and enmeshed with each other. It is erroneous to think that resource utilisation and environmental management are two different spheres and can be dealt with separately. They go hand in hand at all times and under all conditions. Therefore sound resource utilisation is sound environmental management. The 'butterfly effect' as put out by meteorologists — "the slight stirring of the air caused by a butterfly's wings in Manila today may determine whether a thunder storm strikes Miami three weeks from now" is quite applicable in the realm of development and management of natural resources as well.

REFERENCES

Burman, Savitri G. and N.D. Jayal (1989). "Watershed as a unit for Environmental Management", *South Asia Journal*, Vol. 3: Nos. 1 and 2, pp. 63-68.

Burman, Savitri G., N.D. Jayal, J.S. Lall and B.G. Verghese (1989). "Regional Cooperation for the Protection of Mountain Resource Management in South Asia", *South Asia Journal*, Vol. 3, No. 5, pp. 121-128.

Burman, Savitri G. (1991). "Environmental Degradation of the Himalayan Resources Resulting from Development Strategies in Agriculture", paper presented to the workshop on SAARC Scenarios, Kathmandu.

Burman, Savitri G. (1992). "Himalayan Agriculture and Its Impact on the Environment", in N. Mohammad (ed.) *New Dimensions in Agricultural Geography*, Vol. 5 : Spatial Dimensions of Agriculture, New Delhi : Concept Publishing Company, pp. 37-67.

Burman, Savitri G. (1993), "Watershed — An Ecosystem", *Janata — A Journal of Democratic Socialism*, Vol. 48 : No. 5, pp. 9-11.

Hillary, E. "Ecology 2000".

Singh, J.S. and O.P. Chaturvedi (1981), "Ecology, Environment and Development", in J.S. Singh *et al.* (ed.) *Science and Rural Development in Mountains*, Gyanodya Prakashan, Nainital.

7

Developing and Focusing the Biosphere Reserve Concept

MICHEL BATISSE

The term 'biosphere reserve', which has become fairly common in environmental and conservation literature, was born some fifteen years ago. The first biosphere reserves were designated in 1976, and since then the international network which they constitute has reached 261 biosphere reserves located in 70 countries all over the world. During this period, and particularly in the last two years, considerable debate has been devoted to the characteristics and value of this new concept, which has been refined and clarified in the light of practical experience. In this context, it appears useful to formulate the common understanding that has emerged from this process, with a view to offer some guidance for improving and strengthening the international network. The time has obviously not yet come to write the history of biosphere reserves. History deals with things of the past and, by their very nature, biosphere reserves should have a long and prosperous future ahead of them. But a clarification of the concept requires an understanding of its evolution — in other words some insight into its history. This appears all the more important in that much of the confusion that has sometimes been associated with the real meaning of biosphere reserves stems from this very evolution.

The Beginnings of an Idea

The concept of biosphere reserve has emerged from UNESCO's Man

Reprinted with permission from *Nature and Resources*, Vol. XXII, No. 3, July-September, 1986.

and the Biosphere Programme (MAB) of which it constitutes an essential part. MAB itself originated from the 1968 Conference on the Rational Use and Conservation of the Resources of the Biosphere, as an international and interdisciplinary research programme whose major objective is to provide the scientific knowledge and trained personnel needed for sound and sustainable management of land resources. One of the recommendations of that conference dealt with the 'utilization and preservation of genetic resources' and proposed to make specific efforts to preserve representative samples of significant ecosystems, original habitats of domesticated plants and animals, and remnant populations of rare and endangered species. Another recommendation dealt with the 'preservation of natural areas and endangered species', inspired in particular by the inventory work undertaken on terrestrial conservation under the International Biological Programme. There was, however, no reference to 'biosphere reserves' at the time of the conference.

In 1969, when intensive scientific consultations were being held to formulate the elements of the MAB programme, the idea emerged of 'a co-ordinated worldwide network of national parks, biological reserves and other protected areas' serving conservation as well as research and education needs. Because these multifunctional biological reserves were to be set up in the framework of the programme on Man and the Biosphere, those involved in its preparation began to refer to them occasionally as 'biosphere reserves' without, however, giving a precise meaning to this term. And the mention of a network had no specific implication besides that of ensuring the best possible world coverage.

At the same time, we felt that it would be desirable for the emerging MAB programme to benefit from some clearly identified territorial and logistic base for its activities in the various countries. Such an approach had been successfully followed for the International Hydrological Decade, where multipurpose 'decade stations' had helped greatly to focus interest and efforts in this earlier inter-governmental scientific venture. In a parallel way, biosphere reserves could play this very important role for MAB.

From these early beginnings, it appears that three different concerns were already present behind the introduction of the biosphere reserve scheme, namely: (a) the need for reinforcing the conservation of genetic resources and ecosystems and the maintenance of biological diversity (*conservation role*); (b) the need for setting up a well identified international network of areas directly related to MAB field research and monitoring activities, including the accompanying training and information exchange (*logistic role*); and (c) the need to associate concretely environmental protection and land resources development as a governing principle for research and education activities of the new programme (*development role*).

These three concerns and these three roles had to converge towards the establishment of biosphere reserves as shown in Fig. 7.1. They were, however, not clearly expressed, nor properly integrated in the early stages of the project, thus unavoidably leading to some misunderstandings or to some distortions in its implementation.

The first official reference to biosphere reserves was made in 1970 in the plan submitted to the General Conference of UNESCO for the launching of the MAB programme (UNESCO, 1970). It is noteworthy that this reference appears under the 'basic operations and facilities for the execution of the international scientific programme', rather than under the 'scientific content' of this programme. Thus it stressed what we call the logistic role of biosphere reserves, primarily for research and monitoring purposes, rather than their conservation or development roles.

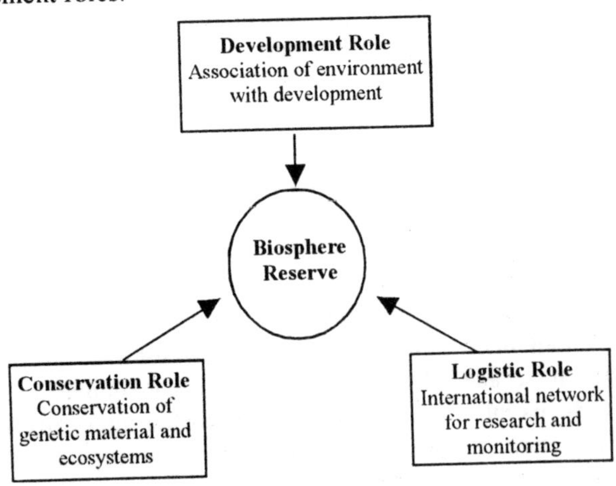

Fig. 7.1: Three Roles of Biosphere Reserve

When the MAB International Coordinating Council met in 1971 at its first session, the programme was focused around a number of research themes, with theme No. 8 identified as 'Conservation of natural areas and of the genetic material they contain' and spelling out the idea of a worldwide network of protected areas (UNESCO, 1971). Biosphere reserves were mentioned under this theme (and under this theme only) and were at the same time proposed 'as basic logistic resources for research where experiments can be repeated in the same places over periods of time, as areas for education and training, and as essential components for the study of many projects under the Programme'. Emphasis was thus placed on both the conservation and logistic roles, with the development role left rather undefined. The idea and the term of 'biosphere reserves' were officially launched, but in a somewhat hazy manner, without much clarity about their exact role and nature.

The Emergence of a Concept

During the early 1970s all the research themes identified as components of the MAB programme had to be elaborated and translated into operational guidelines for national and international implementation. This was done for theme No. 8 in two stages. A first panel meeting held at IUCN headquarters in 1973 concentrated on the scientific content of the theme, making only a passing reference to biosphere reserves and referring only to their conservation role. In fact, developing the concept of biosphere reserve within theme 8, which was devoted strictly to conservation, was automatically leading to such a bias. This bias was to be partly mitigated in 1974 thanks to a special 'task force' convened jointly by UNESCO and UNEP in Paris, which for the first time drew up a set of objectives and a set of characteristics for biosphere reserves (UNESCO, 1974). By and large these are still valid today. They define and stress the multiple functions of biosphere reserves, covering the three basic needs indicated in Fig. 7.1. The characteristics listed can, however, be interpreted in many different ways: they cover a wide variety of situations but are given without any hierarchy and provide no priorities for selection. These characteristics were obviously drawn up from a theoretical standpoint at a time when the practical implementation of the project had not yet started. It is all the more to the credit of the task force that much of its work remains relevant today. In particular it proposed a simple generalized zoning pattern for biosphere reserves combining a core area, a delineated 'inner buffer zone' and an undelineated 'outer buffer zone'. This zonation of the buffer zone passed unfortunately unnoticed at the time but is of great

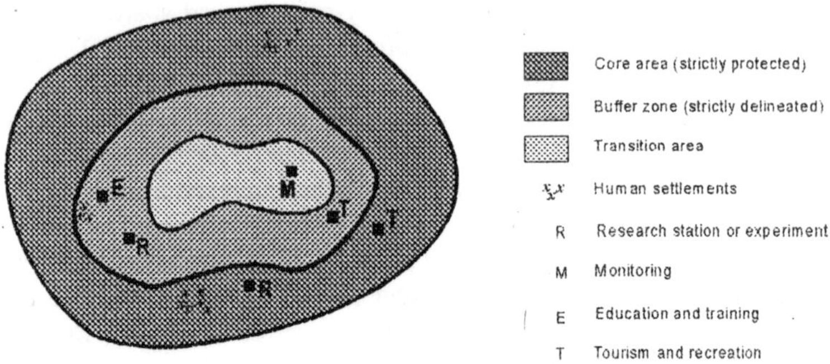

Fig. 7.2: Schematic zionation of a biosphere reserve, [In this zonation, already proposed in 1974 the core area is strictly protected: The buffer zone (formerly called 'inner buffer zone') can be used for regulated non-destructive activities and is strictly delineated. A national park normally corresponds to a core area together with a buffer zone of this type. The transition area (which was originally called 'outer buffer zone') covers other functions of the 'biosphere reserve including experimental research, traditional use, rehabilitation, etc., and it extends to form the area of co-operation of the biosphere reserve.]

importance, as will be shown later, with this 'outer buffer zone' corresponding to what is now known as the 'transition area'. Fig. 7.2 presents an updated schema illustrating this generalized zoning pattern.

On the basis of the task-force report, but mainly following their own interpretation of the new concept for their local needs, countries began to propose areas for designation as biosphere reserves. The procedure for actual designation had, however, not been defined and the MAB Co-ordinating Council, overwhelmed with proposals, felt that it was too delicate a matter to be handled in a large and open forum. At its fourth session in 1975 it delegated this task to its six-member Bureau. Meanwhile, discussions in the council continued to emphasize the conservation role of biosphere reserves and the references made to an international network were primarily meant only to ensure a more systematic coverage of protected areas around the world. The association of the biosphere reserve concept with MAB theme No. 8 had blurred their development and logistic roles.

A Hasty Blossoming

In this context, it is not surprising that when the MAB Bureau designated a first batch of fifty-seven biosphere reserves in mid-1976, the main criterion used for their selection was their conservation role. The same thing happened in early 1977 when a second batch of sixty-one biosphere reserves were designated. In fact, the Bureau adopted a very flexible approach considering it sufficient when the areas proposed by the MAB National Committees for designation appeared interesting for the conservation of ecosystems, had appropriate legal protection and were the object of a reasonable amount of research work. The process was launched and was to continue over the following years, but at a slower pace. By 1981, 208 biosphere reserves had been designated in fifty-eight countries.

What was the situation after this rapid blossoming? In a compilation published in 1981 (UNESCO, 1981), it is stated, "Biosphere reserves form an international network of protected areas in which an integrated concept of conservation is being developed, combining the preservation of ecological and genetic diversity with research, environmental monitoring, education and training. Biosphere reserves are selected as representative examples of the world's ecosystems."

In other words, in this first phase of implementation of the programme, the conservation role had been kept prominent, and the logistic and development roles largely forgotten. Almost all designated biosphere reserves were areas already protected, such as national parks or nature reserves, and in most cases the designation was not adding new land, new regulations or even new functions. Research work was conducted in these protected areas, but the research was in many cases of a rather academic character, not clearly related to ecosystem and resource management, and not addressing explicitly the relationship between environment and development. Moreover, the linkages between biosphere reserves and the exchanges of information on this research remained largely formal and did not constitute a true international network. A proper balance between the three concerns shown in Fig. 7.1 had not been reached.

Admittedly this situation did not prevail in all cases and a number of bright spots could be identified. Some biosphere reserves were created *ex nihilo*, adding not only new areas under protection but endeavouring to demonstrate the multiple functions of the new concept, including its development role. The case of Mapimi in Mexico has been often quoted in this respect (Halffter, 1981) but is by no means unique: a good number of biosphere reserves for instance were using an existing national park as a starting-point but adding new functions to it (which usually implies co-ordination between separate administrative units). The example of Waterton Biosphere Reserve, centred on Waterton Lake National Park in Canada, can be given in this respect.

An important step was the introduction of the very useful idea of 'clustering' developed at a joint USA-USSR Symposium on Biosphere Reserves and endorsed by the MAB International Co-ordinating Council as early as 1977. This idea aims at accommodating the many situations where all the functions of biosphere reserves cannot be performed in contiguous areas and where a regrouping and co-ordination of activities between several discrete areas is required. This is often the case when conservation in core areas has to be associated with integrated research and manipulative experimentation in other areas, as illustrated in Fig. 7.3. A well-known example of this approach is developing around Great Smoky Mountains National Park in the United States.

Another important development was the linking of a biosphere reserve with a MAB-integrated pilot project for research, training and demonstration. Such linking was obviously establishing a better balance and combination between the three concerns of Fig. 7.1 and was achieved in a number of cases. This includes quite a few examples in the tropical forest biome (such as Omo in Nigeria) or in the arid zone (such as Mount Kulal in Kenya).

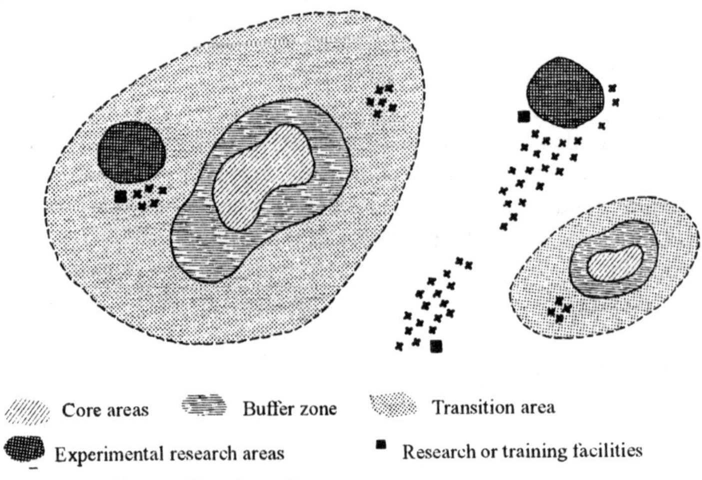

Fig. 7.3: Cluster Biosphere Reserve

By and large, however, the actual international list of designated biosphere reserves did not properly convey the innovative multifunctional approach embodied in the concept.

Some voices could thus hold the view that, as a category of protected areas, biosphere reserves were not adding much to other existing categories and indeed were rather creating confusion. Other voices considered that the project had to begin in some manner and stressed that the concept was a highly imaginative and valuable one, which had to be developed and applied in a more and more systematic manner, not only to supplement current efforts in nature conservation, but to build up the multiple functions of biosphere reserves [for instance: Batisse (1982); di Castri and Robertson (1982); Miller (1983)].

Evaluation and Review

When the 'Ecology in Action' conference was organized in 1981 to mark the tenth anniversary of the launching of MAB, it whole-heartedly confirmed the value of the biosphere reserve scheme and expressed its satisfaction for what it had achieved. At the same time it recognized the existence of some confusion between biosphere reserves and other protected areas. It noted that the term 'biosphere reserve' was occasionally perceived as designating a cultural 'reservation', or more often as conveying the idea of a static and closed area for nature conservation only. In an attempt to clarify matters, it decided to add the expression 'representative ecological area' as a subtitle. The new expression was meant to imply a more dynamic and open approach but was not clearly defined and little used later. Contributions and debates in the 1981 conference showed also the complexity of implementing the biosphere reserve project in relation to the very diverse situations and concerns occurring in various parts of the world [for instance: Maldague (1984); Gregg and Goigel (1984)]. All this illustrated the need for a fresh look and impetus for the project.

The fresh look and the impetus were to come in the autumn of 1983 from the first International Biosphere Reserve Congress held in Minsk, Byelorussia, USSR, jointly organized by UNESCO and UNEP in co-operation with FAO and IUCN. On the basis of the very diverse experience gained in many countries, the congress was able to review the overall situation and to lay down general guidelines for the future. It confirmed and underlined the multiple functions that characterize biosphere reserves. It explored how the network could really function as such through complementarity and exchange of information. It developed proposals for research, monitoring, training, education and local participation (UNESCO-UNEP, 1984).

On the basis of the work of the Minsk Congress, it became possible to draw up a world 'Action Plan for Biosphere Reserves', which, after considerable consultation, was adopted by the MAB Co-ordinated Council in December 1984 and formally endorsed subsequently by UNEP, UNESCO and IUCN (UNESCO, 1984). One of the recommendations of the Action Plan was to establish a 'Scientific Advisory Panel for Biosphere Reserves', a very sensible step that perhaps should have been taken earlier. The first meeting of this panel was held in Cancūn (Mexico) in September 1985 and undertook an in-depth critical examination of the situation and of the obstacles to be surmounted for the implementation of the Action Plan. It recognized that some of these obstacles were of a conceptual nature and devoted a good deal of time to analyse what is meant to be unique about biosphere reserves. The second meeting took place in La Paz (Bolivia) in August 1986 and has come to concrete formulations that should help improve the current network and ensure that new biosphere reserves meet all necessary requirements.

The main results of this conceptual soul-searching can be expressed in a very simple way: any biosphere reserve, no matter where it is located in the world, must to some extent address itself to the three basic concerns of Fig. 7.1 and to their combination. In particular, it must have one or several protected core areas to ensure its 'conservation role', which must always be present. It must obviously participate in the international network and thus have a 'logistic role', supporting a certain amount of research work of international significance and taking part in the corresponding exchange of information. And it must fulfil as far as possible the 'development role' through problem-oriented research, demonstration, education and local participation. The relative importance of these three roles will vary from one biosphere reserve to the other, but it is their combined presence which is characteristic of the project. In other words, a biosphere reserve that does not have a protected core area is not a true biosphere reserve. A national park that has no concern for the sustainable development of the surrounding area is not a true biosphere reserve either. An area that combines conservation with research and education for ecosystem development can only become a proper biosphere reserve if it joins the international network of research, monitoring and information exchange.

By this simple yardstick, it is clear that there are serious weaknesses in the present list of biosphere reserves and that very few of them, if any, fully meet this combination of criteria. But it appears at the same time that it would be readily possible to improve the functioning of many of these existing reserves by some administrative or managerial arrangements that would enhance their suitability in the network.

A Generalized Functional Pattern

In order to help move in this direction and provide some guidance for tightening up the network, we believe that a schematic spatial distribution pattern of biosphere reserve functions can be proposed at this stage. This is attempted in Fig. 7.4 and rests upon the following considerations, which derive from the Action Plan, from the discussions in the Scientific Panel and from a quick survey of actual situations encountered on a worldwide basis.

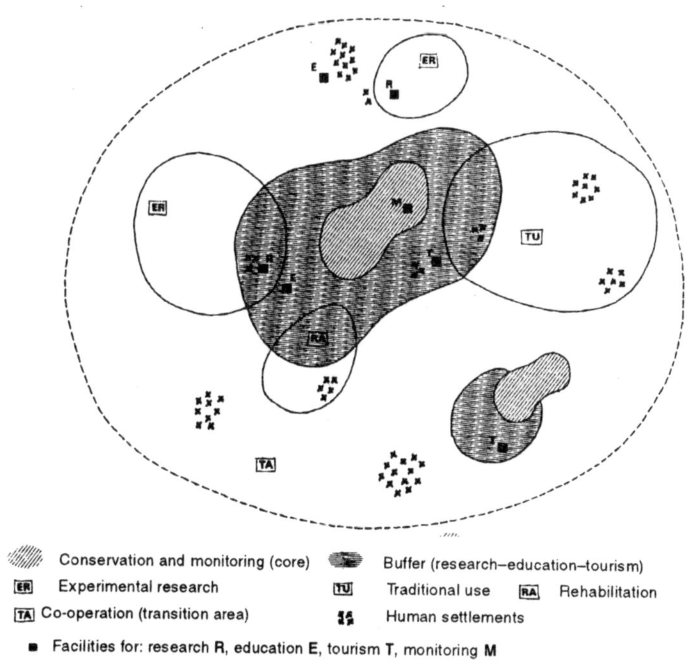

Fig. 7.4: Schematic Distribution of Biosphere Reserve Functions.

1. Each biosphere reserve includes one or several core areas that are strictly protected according to well-defined conservation objectives and consist of typical samples of natural or minimally disturbed ecosystems. Collectively these core areas should be large enough to be effective as *in situ* conservation units and, whenever possible, have value as benchmarks for measurements of long-term changes in the biosphere and in the ecosystems they represent. Normally, the core area, or some of the core areas, should be representative of the surrounding ecosystems where sustainable development is to be promoted.
2. The size and the shape of the core areas depend on the type of landscape in which they are located and on the conservation objectives they are intended to meet. They can obviously be much larger in low population density regions than in regions with heavier human pressure and less available land.
3. Core areas may correspond to 'strict nature reserves', to 'wilderness area' of national parks, or to other types of strictly protected areas. Strict protection of core areas does not necessarily mean 'non-intervention': they can be submitted to different types of protective management, depending on their specific conservation objectives and on the character and history of the landscape. Strict protection also does not necessarily entail strict delineation where, for instance, inaccessibility effectively prevents human interference. Thus, in such cases, a core area may remain undelineated within a delineated buffer zone. The protection against any action that could endanger the conservation role assigned to the core area must, however, be fully ensured. Core areas naturally exclude the presence of significant human settlements. Besides non-destructive research, one activity of growing importance that typically can take place in the core area of biosphere reserves is environmental observation and monitoring (M).
4. The core areas are normally surrounded by a buffer zone corresponding to the inner buffer zone in Fig. 7.2 which must be strictly delineated and very often corresponds, together with the core areas, to a single and autonomous administrative unit. Thus, a number of national parks that have been designated

as biosphere reserves are constituted in fact by core areas namely the strictly protected areas or the 'wilderness areas' of the national park — surrounded by a delineated buffer zone corresponding to the boundaries of the park. In some national parks where very limited human activity takes place, the core area may, in fact, be very large relative to the buffer zone.

5. This buffer zone must have a clearly established legal or administrative status even when several administrative authorities are involved in its management. Only activities compatible with the protection of the core areas may take place. This includes in particular research (R), environmental education and training (E), as well as tourism and recreation (T) or other uses carried out in accordance with the management requirements and regulations. Besides its other functions the buffer zone may well serve to protect areas of land that could be used to meet future needs for experimental research.
6. The core areas and the buffer zone are surrounded by a transition area that may also constitute a protective buffer, corresponding to the 'outer buffer zone' in Fig. 7.2 and which serves several characteristic functions of the biosphere reserve, particularly its developmental role. Usually, the transition area as a whole is not strictly delineated and corresponds more to biogeographic than to administrative limits. It normally extends into a larger and open area where efforts are made to develop co-operative activities between researchers, managers and the local population, with a view to ensure appropriate physical planning and sustainable resources development in the region while maintaining the greatest possible harmony with the purposes of the biosphere-reserve. This broad and open multiple-use area constitutes an 'area of co-operation' of the biosphere reserve where one of the main goals, the association of environment and development, is actively pursued. The management of the transition area is usually the responsibility of a variety of authorities and therefore requires appropriate co-ordination arrangements.
7. Partly within the buffer zone or entirely outside, a biosphere reserve may include anyone or some combination of the following types of associated areas, used to develop knowledge

and skills for ecosystem use and management: (a) Areas suitable for experimental manipulation to develop, assess and demonstrate methods for sustainable development [experimental research areas (ER)], (b) Examples of harmonious landscape resulting from traditional patterns of land use [traditional use areas (TU)]; and (c) examples of modified or degraded ecosystems that are suitable for restoration to more natural conditions [rehabilitation areas (RA)].

8. Experimental research areas (ER), where manipulative research on managed ecosystems is performed, are normally delineated by the research organization concerned and may be entirely located outside the buffer zone. The latter situation corresponds to a type of 'cluster biosphere reserve'. This cluster concept refers more generally to a combination of a number of non-contiguous areas — and possibly of research and education centres or laboratories — serving the same or different functions of biosphere reserves. These areas and centres are not usually administered by the same entity and hence the overall management of a cluster biosphere reserve calls for co-ordinating mechanisms through which the various administrative authorities concerned — as well as the local population — will cooperate.

Figure 7.4 attempts to show how the different functions of a biosphere reserve can be distributed on the ground. It may appear rather complex because it represents a cluster biosphere reserve where all functions and variety of possible situations are presented. It does not correspond to any particular existing biosphere reserve but endeavours to present a conceptual generalized pattern that could apply to most of them. It does not necessarily cover the entire range of possible situations that may exist. In particular, it would require some adjustments to meet the case of azonal ecosystems or of coastal biosphere reserves. But it shows how the multiple functions of biosphere reserves can be articulated and illustrates the originality of the concept.

A Road for Progress

At a time when so many biosphere reserves have already been designated, it might seem futile to further elaborate on this concept and more sensible to concentrate efforts on getting these biosphere reserves to function satisfactorily. But precisely to this end, it is useful to compare the pattern proposed in Fig. 7.4 with the actual patterns occurring in existing or planned biosphere reserves. This will help in identifying the strengths and the weaknesses of their configuration and possibly suggest some ways to enhance or complete their functions.

A small-scale illustration of such a comparison is given in Fig. 7.5, which relates to the Cévennes Biosphere Reserve in southern France. It shows that the 'central part' of the previously existing national park corresponds to the buffer zone of the biosphere reserve and that the transition area of the latter, defined on a biogeographical basis, does not correspond exactly with the administrative delimitation of the 'peripheral part' of the national park. It illustrates schematically how the different functions are distributed in this biosphere reserve, located in a region having a long history of human use. The core areas that have various conservation objectives are relatively small. Particular emphasis is placed on applied research and on the 'development role' in co-operation with the local population.

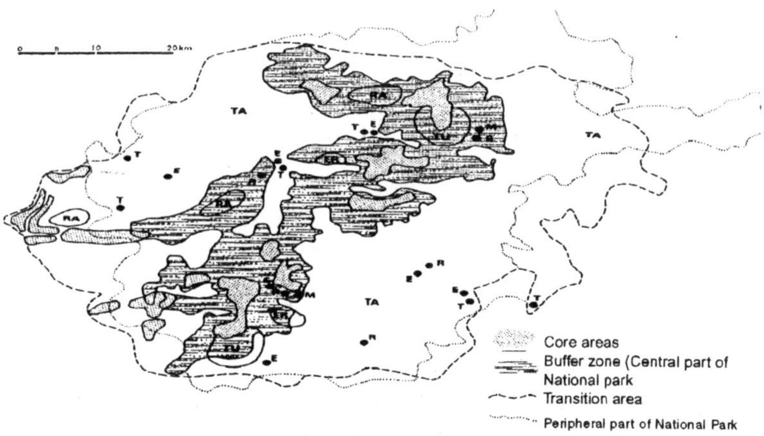

ER =	Experiment Research;	TU =	Traditional use;
RA =	Rehabilitation;	TU =	Cooperation (Transition Area)
R =	Research;	E =	Education;
T =	Tourism;	M =	Monitoring

Fig. 7.5: Schematic Distribution of Functions in the Cévennes Biosphere Reserve.

This comparison exercise between any particular biosphere reserve and the generalized pattern will often show that little attention has been paid to the transition area where many of the activities relating to the 'development role' can best take place. One major reason for this neglect lies in the open, undelineated character of the transition zone. Whereas administrative responsibility for the core areas and the delineated buffer zone is usually very clearly established — and in a majority of cases rests upon a single authority — the administration of the transition area is almost inevitably split among a variety of public and private bodies, with little or no attempt having been made to organize co-ordination and co-operation among them. This situation is demonstrated by the relatively large number of designated biosphere reserves which have no real transition area, which are in fact limited to a core area, surrounded or not by some kind of buffer zone, and which often merely bear the name of an already existing national park or conservation area.

In order to improve this situation, the first step appears to be to convince the various administrative authorities having responsibilities in the proposed transition area to co-operate in the establishment of a fully functional biosphere reserve. Whereas the conservation role and the logistic role will be obviously enhanced by the interest and support of these authorities, they have to see how the biosphere reserve can fit in with their own objectives and how it will bring a variety of benefits to local people, particularly through its 'development role'. A simple move at this stage would be to flag the open character of the biosphere reserve by giving it a name which does not refer to a strictly delineated area, and which would relate more to an ecological, biogeographical or ethnological denomination. The next step will be to set up some simple co-ordinating group where those in charge of the core areas, of the buffer zone and of the experimental research areas, would meet with representatives of the local people and of the administrative authorities of the transition area. This requires some administrative imagination consistent with local customs.

The real step forward, however, will be reached when all possible functions of the biosphere reserve are fully operational and properly co-ordinated through an overall management plan, taking the transition area into account. This would in particular help enlist the continuing support and co-operation of the local people, without which long-term sustainable conservation of species or ecosystems is seriously open to question in many countries. It would indeed demonstrate to them the benefits and value of the efforts being made in their own environment and in their own interest through the biosphere reserve for conservation of genetic material, for practical and problem-oriented research, for general environmental education, for specialized training, and more generally for land use planning and sustainable resources development of their own region.

This co-operative process in the transition area could take considerable importance in the future. For instance, it appears clearly that the changes in agricultural and forestry production techniques, combined with the world market constraints, will lead to abandoning lands of marginal value in certain regions. This is already happening in Europe. The establishment of biosphere reserves and the extension of their transition areas could be one of the means of responding to such an evolution through providing certain viable alternative uses for these lands and their inhabitants.

While comparison with the generalized pattern should provide useful hints for improvement, it could probably be said that no two biosphere reserves will ever present exactly the same configuration, face the same problems, and require the same management measures since each one of them deals with a specific geographical, historical, human and socio-economic situation. From the icy wastes of Greenland or from the Sahara deserts to the patched human-made landscapes of Central Europe or South Asia, it is not easy to define common yardsticks. The sharp distinctions between core areas, buffer zone, experimental research areas, transition area, etc., have to be qualified in certain concrete cases depending on the objectives pursued and the local realities. The key word for the implementation of the Action Plan for Biosphere Reserves remains therefore 'flexibility'.

This flexibility particularly applies when dealing with different regions of the world having very different histories and intensities of human impact. What is appropriate in one region may be unacceptable elsewhere. This will have direct consequences on the size of biosphere reserves, on their number, and on the relative importance of the various functions they serve. In this respect, the requirements of a fully operational global network may be somewhat different from those of a regional or sub-regional network where some specific objectives are sought. And at the national level the need might well be felt to establish certain biosphere reserves that correspond to biogeographic regions and biological communities well covered elsewhere and do not appear essential at the international level.

This pragmatic flexibility, however, should not hide the originality and specificity of the biosphere reserve concept, as it has developed over the past years and as the above remarks and diagrams have attempted to define it. While the early formulation and implementation of this new concept has been somewhat erratic, it has now reached stability and cruising speed for what will be — we hope — a very long journey into the future. The problem now is not so much to further refine the concept, but to actually apply it as far as practicable to many existing biosphere reserves that require improvements as well as to all the new ones, so that their participation in the network be fully effective and meaningful. To this end, all countries concerned must fulfil their national and global responsibilities as outlined in the Action Plan. Biosphere reserves come under their sovereignty and are proposed for designation upon their own initiative. Their satisfactory management and functioning are of vital importance to the world and to our common future. All countries, in co-operation with the appropriate international organizations, must therefore provide the means — administrative, technical, personnel and financial — necessary to give all present and future biosphere reserves their full operational and multi-dimensional character.

ADDENDUM

Since the publication of this paper in 1986, the Biosphere Reserves project has developed considerably. At present, there are 311 Biosphere Reserves in the international network, located in 81 countries. The value of the concept has been universally recognized, including in cases where formal designation of the areas concerned has not yet taken place. A number of countries are reviewing their national system of Biosphere Reserves to ensure that they fulfil to a broader extent their multiple functions. Concrete efforts are made to apply the concept to coastal areas (Batisse, 1990). The World Congress on National Parks and Protected Areas, held in Caracas, Venezuela, in 1992, has adopted a specific recommendation to support the development of the international network. The General Conference of UNESCO has set up an International Advisory Committee on Biosphere Reserves which held its first session in April 1992 (UNESCO, 1992). The Co-ordinating Council of the Man and the Biosphere (MAB) Programme, at its recent meeting in Paris (January 1993) has given a central role to Biosphere Reserves in the further development of the MAB programme as a flexible and multifunctional tool to protect biodiversity, promote sustainable landscape resources development and ensure local people's participation. Biosphere reserves thus constitute a major element in the response of UNESCO to the challenge of UNCED.

REFERENCES

Batisse, M. (1990). Development and implementation of the Biosphere Reserve concept and its applicability to coastal regions. *Environmental Conservation*, Vol. 17, No. 2, pp. 111-116.

Batisse, M. (1982), The Biosphere Reserve: A Tool for Environmental Conservation and Management. *Environmental Conservation*, 9 (2), pp. 101-11.

Di Castri, E. Robertson, J. (1982). The Biosphere Reserve Concept: 10 Years After. *Parks*, 6(4), pp. 1-6.

Gregg, W., Goigel, M. (1984). Putting the Biosphere Reserve Concept into Practice: The U.S. Experience. In: *Ecology in Practice*, Part I. pp. 460—84. Paris, UNESCO and Dublin, Tycooly International Publ. Ltd.

Halffter, G. (1981). The Mapimi Biosphere Reserve: Local Participation in Conservation and Development, *Ambio*, 10(2-3), pp. 93-96.

Maldague, M. (1984). The Biosphere Reserve Concept: Its Implementation and Its Potential as a Tool for Integrated Development. In: *Ecology in Practice*, Part 1. pp. 367-401. Paris, UNESCO and Dublin, Tycooly International Publ. Ltd.

Miller, K. (1983). Biosphere Reserves in Concept and in Practice. In: *Towards the Biosphere Reserve: Exploring Relationships between Parks and Adjacent Lands*. Denver, Colo., National Park Service, Rocky Mountain Region.

UNESCO (1970). *Plan for a Long Term Intergovernmental and Interdisciplinary Programme on Man and the Biosphere*. General Conference, sixteenth session. 31 pp. (Document 16C/78).

UNESCO (1971). *International Co-ordinating Council for the Programme on Man and the Biosphere*, first session. 65 pp. (MAB Re port Series, No. 2.)

UNESCO (1974). *Task Force on Criteria and Guidelines for the Choice and Establishment of Biosphere Reserves*. 61 pp. (MAB Report Series, No. 2.)

UNESCO (1981). *MAB Information System: Biosphere Reserves*. Compilation No. 2. 313 pp.

UNESCO-UNEP (1984). *Conservation, Science and Society*. UNESCO, Paris, 2 vols. 612 pp. + annexes (Natural Resources Research Series, No. 27).

UNESCO (1992). Report of the first meeting of the Advisory Committee for Biosphere Reserves. Doc. SC/92/CONF 502/6, 29 p.

8

Development and Implementation of the Biosphere Reserve Concept and its Applicability to Coastal Regions

MICHEL BATISSE

Origin and Development of a Concept

The Biosphere Reserve Concept originated some fifteen years ago within the Man and the Biosphere Programme (MAB), which itself can be considered as an offshoot at the intergovernmental and interdisciplinary level, of the earlier International Biological Programme (IBP). The origin and development of these two programmes have been reported in a number of publications: *see* for instance, Worthington (1983), and Batisse (1980). Under IBP, the need for conservation of ecosystems was particularly stressed. When MAP was formulated, the concept of Biosphere Reserve responded simply, at the beginning, to this need to preserve more systematically genetic resources within representative ecosystems. For those more directly involved in the organisation of the MAB Programme, it was also meant to provide a network of identified areas for basic operations as well as research facilities, which were required for such an international scientific effort. And, while this was not emphasized in the first place, the inclusion of Biosphere Reserves in a programme whose main objective was the rational utilisation of natural resources by Mankind, necessarily implied that the imperatives of resource management and

Reprinted with permission from *Environmental Conservation*, Vol. 17, No. 2, Summer 1990.

development would not be ignored in their design. Thus, although in a somewhat 'fuzzy' or hidden way, the three fundamental concerns of Biosphere Reserves were present from the beginning, and were bound to emerge more forcefully as implementation of the project moved on.

The three roles responding to these concerns can be briefly presented as follows (Batisse, 1986): (i) a 'conservation role' (providing protection of genetic resources, species, and ecosystems, on a world-wide basis), (ii) a 'logistic role' (providing interconnected facilities for research and monitoring in the framework of an internationally coordinated scientific programme), and (iii) a 'development role' (searching for rational and sustainable use of ecosystem resources and hence for close cooperation with the human populations concerned). Many areas in the world have been performing one or two of these functions for a long time, but few can claim to perform them all.

The very idea and distinctive feature of Biosphere Reserves is that each one of them must — at least to some extent — address itself to all three basic concerns and to their synergistic combination, as illustrated very simply in Fig. 8.1. Naturally, the relative importance of the three roles will vary considerably from case to case, depending on the great diversity of situations the world over; but it is the combined presence of these three roles which characterises the Biosphere Reserve concept. In other words, a 'Biosphere Reserve' that does not have a protected core area is not a true Biosphere Reserve. A National Park that does not care for the sustainable development of the surrounding regions and for the basic needs of their population, is not a true Biosphere Reserve either. While *conservation* has been, and should remain, the first concern of Biosphere Reserves, in no way should any of them simply be considered as a 'Nature reserve' or other conventional form of 'protected area'.

Clearly the concept of Biosphere Reserve was developed by terrestrial ecologists, so that the functional zonation patterns which were drawn for its practical implementation apply best to terrestrial environments. The well-known simplest pattern (Fig. 8.2) consists in a *core area*, devoted to strict protection, surrounded by a delineated *buffer zone* where only activities compatible with the conservation objectives can take place, itself surrounded by a more or less defined *transition area* where cooperation with the population and sustainable resource management practices can be developed. In reality the zonation of a Biosphere Reserve is bound to be more complex, as illustrated in Fig. 8.3; but basically the three main types of area should remain, namely core areas, buffer zones and transition area.

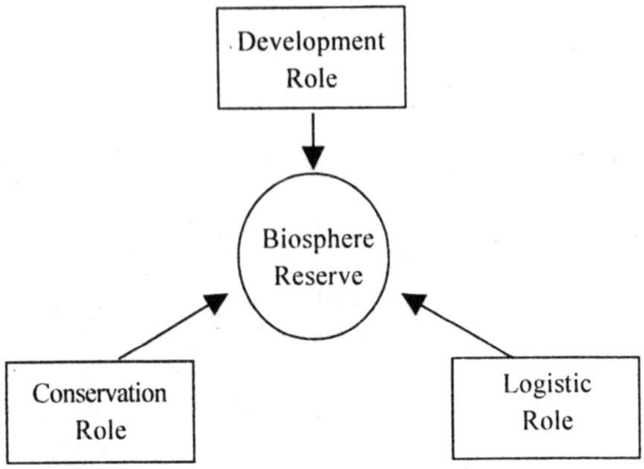

The Three Concerns and The Three Roles of a Biosphere Reserve

— Association of Environment with Development

— Conservation of Genetic Material and Ecosystems

— International Network for Research and Monitoring

Fig. 8.1: The three basic concerns and the three main roles of a Biosphere Reserve: Development, Conservation and Logistics

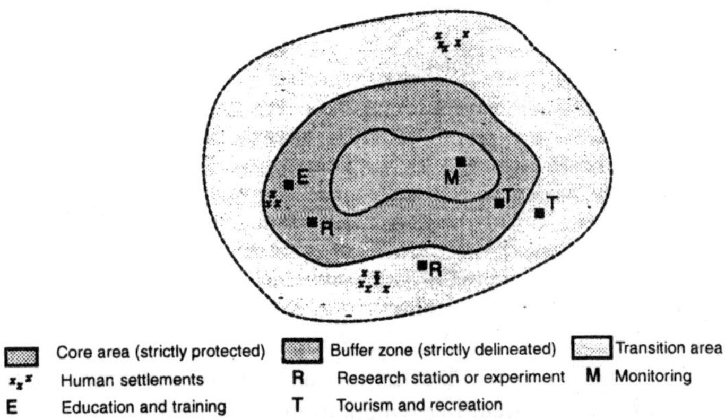

Fig. 8.2: Schematic zonation of a Biosphere Reserve. The Core Area is devoted to strict protection. The Transition Area is not necessarily delimited, but implies involvement of local population.

It is interesting to note that, in the very early stages of the programme, the particular importance of coastal areas was underlined, and that sketches of possible configurations of coastal Biosphere reserves were given in the first MAB report on 'Criteria and Guidelines for the Choice and Establishment of Biosphere Reserves' (UNESCO, 1974). Those sketches, drawn by Professor G. Carleton Ray, related to a river estuary with a reef complex, to a continental lagoon with a barrier beach, and to a partly-inhabited tropical atoll.

It should be admitted, however, that — even in the case of terrestrial areas — the concept of Biosphere Reserves was somewhat loosely described in the early years of its implementation (including in the above-mentioned report), and that it has been understood in rather different ways by various people or in various parts of the world.

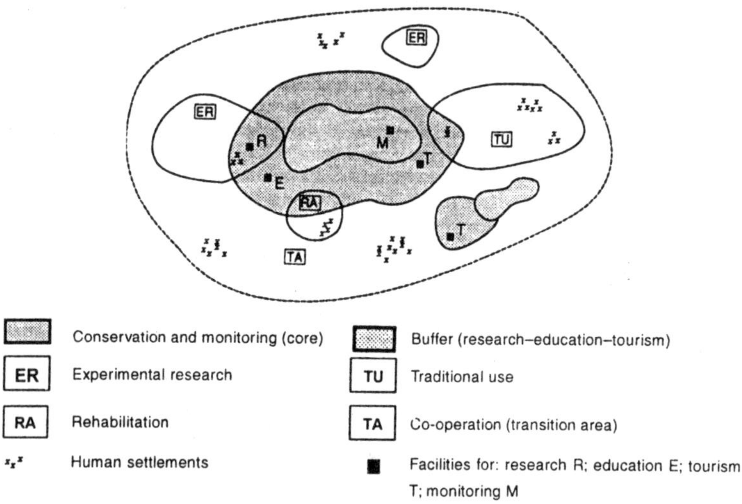

Fig. 8.3: Schematic distribution of Biosphere Reserve Functions: Inevitably complex but with the three main types of areas remaining, namely Core Areas, Buffer Zones and Transition Area.

Implementation of the Project

In the initial phase of implementation of the project — roughly from 1976 (when the first batch of Biosphere Reserves were designated) to 1981 (when their total number went over 200), the conservation role was kept prominent and the logistic and development roles were largely forgotten. In fact almost all Biosphere Reserves then designated were areas already under protection, such as national parks, and in most cases the designation did not add any new land, new regulations, or even new functions. The designation was mainly seen as a quality label for some existing protected areas, and the basic combination of concerns shown in Fig. 8.1 was hardly achieved anywhere. This evolution indeed is not surprising — not only because of the initial lack of clarity in the formulation of the new concept, but also because of its very novelty and of the practical difficulties in implementing it adequately and on a world-wide basis.

World-wide Heterogeneity

The world-wide approach was seen as a major yardstick for implementation in the MAB framework, and the land surface of the globe was classified in terms of 'biomes' and biogeographic provinces with the idea that a representative network of Biosphere Reserves would include at least one of them in each terrestrial biogeographic unit (Udvardy, 1975). This approach is naturally commendable but may lead to neglect of some other basic aspects of the real situation. For instance, the establishment of a protected area presents very different problems when one is dealing with a densely populated region having a long history of human occupation — such as in many parts of Europe, the Middle East, or Southern and Eastern Asia — as opposed to a sparsely populated region having received relatively little human impact, such as much of Africa and the Americas.

The presence or quasi-absence of local population around the buffer zone, makes a considerable difference in terms of management and in the very significance of the development role. The cultural and social characteristics of such populations, and their relationships with the national authorities, are also important, and so are some other aspects. Accordingly it should come as no surprise to find considerable heterogeneity in the current list of designated Biosphere Reserves — altogether 285 in 72 countries, and ranging from previously established national parks in Africa, the USA, and the USSR, to small biological reserves in Europe. They also include field research stations with some land around, or rural landscapes with traditional human settlements but little 'Nature' to conserve. This heterogeneity is inevitable and should in no way be harmful to the programme. I reflect the complexity of land systems in relation to human presence and the reality of the world, which some Nature conservationists would like sometimes to ignore.

Uneven Fulfilment of Roles

What is much less satisfactory — and should progressively be corrected — is that many 'Biosphere Reserves' on the official list do not perform in a true manner the three roles indicated in Fig. 8.1, and are not therefore proper Biosphere Reserves. For a better assessment of this problem we should reflect briefly upon the actual significance of these three roles in the light of present experience in implementing the programme.

1. As regards the *conservation role*, which was initially taken for granted, the question may be asked: conservation of what and for what? Some Biosphere Reserves encompass, for instance, a large piece of tropical forest, and one tends to consider that this is a good thing *per se* as long as nobody questions it. When traditional or new human pressures develop in the area, the justification for conserving land without any development disturbance has, however, to be made convincingly. When the area has been already the subject of past or continuing serious anthropic impacts, the exact purpose of conservation has to be clarified. It is not sufficient to say that in a Biosphere Reserve the core area, or core areas, should be 'strictly' protected — an objective which in many cases is in fact impossible to achieve when one thinks of possible interferences as diverse as long-range air or water pollution, poaching, or fire. What is necessary is to define precise conservation objectives — which can be more or less ambitious — and to ensure that management of the Biosphere Reserve (including, of course, its core areas) is fully compatible with these conservation objectives. Some people, for instance, find it hard to understand that maintenance of sheep-grazing may be compatible with conservation of important grassland ecosystems in Europe. Generally speaking, conservation in Biosphere Reserves should stress maintenance of ecological processes and features rather than protection of individual species of biota.
2. The *logistic role* of Biosphere Reserves is also a multifaceted one. Its primary purpose is supposed to be to provide research and monitoring facilities for participation in an international

network. However, such a network is still in its infancy from an operational viewpoint, and much has to be done to give it life and value. Most Biosphere Reserves do have some research or observation facilities — some highly sophisticated, some very limited — but there is hardly any correlation between them. There is also little common understanding on what type of research or monitoring has to be conducted. As time goes on, Biosphere Reserves will have to participate in some cooperative programmes either of global character, such as the International Geosphere-Biosphere Programme, or of a regional or interregional character, to study specific problems such as tropical forest-soil fertility. But at any rate, Biosphere Reserves have their own individual research requirements for which some facilities are required. This type of local research naturally relates to the improvement of knowledge regarding the Biosphere Reserve itself — inventories, and functioning of ecosystems, etc.; but, as the case may be, basic and applied local research must also be oriented towards the development needs of the surrounding population, and look for sustainable use of resources and appropriate technologies that are compatible with the conservation objectives of the core areas. Incidentally, the presence of permanent research facilities and personnel is an additional guarantee of protection of these core areas.

3. The *development role* of a Biosphere Reserve obviously depends very much on the socio-cultural context within its more or less extended transition area. It is certainly the most difficult and the most innovative role for Biosphere Reserves to fulfil, and it is only natural that it was blurred through the first stages of the programme. Yet, two points should be stressed. The first is that in many developing countries, and probably in some developed ones, protection of ecosystems and species has little future unless the human populations in the area, who often have legitimate claims on the land and the waters, see some direct benefit for themselves deriving from the conservation measures involved. The second — and related — point is that, in many areas of the world which are of great interest for conservation but of marginal agricultural

value, there are people living for whom some satisfactory form of rural development should be sought. Wherever this applies, conservation of a given ecosystem could proceed hand-in-hand with compatible forms of development of the same ecosystem under the Biosphere Reserve approach, where such conservation and such development are engineered through participation of, and cooperation with, the people concerned. In this respect, the Biosphere Reserve should be seen as a tool for environmental management (Batisse, 1982).

Flexibility Required

It will appear obvious from the preceding remarks that the Biosphere Reserve concept requires considerable flexibility in its implementation to accommodate the great ecological, economic, and social, complexity of our world, but that it provides a consistent backbone and unifying link for a new unconventional approach to conservation. The major obstacles in the proper establishment and functioning of Biosphere Reserves are not conceptual or technical — we know fairly well, in each particular situation, what would be desirable — but, rather, managerial and institutional. Here we do not know exactly how to act, and in particular how to organise cooperation between the different partners involved.

The flexibility in implementing the Biosphere Reserve concept is naturally reflected in the zonation patterns which are adopted for each one of them, and through which its multiple functions can be distributed and carried out. In sparsely-inhabited regions, for instance, the core areas will tend to be large, with less-extended buffer zones where most human activities would be prohibited, and the transition area may have low significance. Conversely, in areas with high human pressure, the reverse situation would tend to occur, and certain human activities would be permissible in the buffer zone and even in core areas, depending on local conditions and objectives.

The schematic zonation patterns which we have considered so far apply easily when the Biosphere Reserve is located within a region with some ecological and geographical unity — a forest and forest climax ecosystem, for instance. The zonation is more intricate when such unity does not exist, for instance in the case of an oasis in a desert or an isolated mountain. In fact, in all cases where the area of interest includes an ecotone — an interface or zone of tension between very different ecosystems — zonation presents a real problem, and in particular the distribution of the three roles of the Biosphere Reserve illustrated in Fig. 8.1 is easier to apply to each side of the interface than to the interface itself.

We probably encounter here one of the main reasons why so few coastal Biosphere Reserves have been created. Not more than ten on the current list can claim this qualification, and only three or four really deserve it. At the opening of the 1983 International Biosphere Reserve Congress in Minsk (UNESCO-UNEP, 1984), we had to note that 'the conspicuous absence of coastal biosphere reserves in almost all areas of the world is a matter of concern'. Yet, the ensuing 'Action Plan for Biosphere Reserves' adopted later on (UNESCO, 1984) was almost silent about what should be done about the matter, apart from calling for a 'classification of representative ecological areas covering intertidal and marine habitats in coastal areas'. Such a classification was worked out (Hayden *et al.*, 1984) and provides a useful supplement to the former terrestrial classification, but naturally it constitutes only a supporting measure for encouraging the establishment of coastal Biosphere Reserves.

Applicability to Coastal Regions

It would seem today that there should be no semantic ambiguity about the meaning of the word 'coastal'. 'The coastal zone is the band of dry land and adjacent ocean space (water and submerged land) in which land ecology and use directly affect ocean-space ecology, and *vice versa*. The coastal zone is a band of variable width which borders the continent... Geographically, the landward boundary of the coastal zone is necessarily vague... The seaward boundary has been defined as the extent to which man's land-based activities have a measurable influence on the chemistry of the water or on the ecology of marine life' (Ketchum, 1972).

In other words it should be well established in all languages that the 'coastal zone' is both land and sea, and that its boundary extends rather widely on each side of the coastline interface. However, most terrestrial ecologists tend to forget the marine part of the coastal zone, and most oceanographers seem to consider that it stops at the hightide mark. This forceful split between scientific disciplines and scientific institutions is aggravated in practically all countries of the world by an equal split between responsible administrations, the jurisdiction of land authorities stopping somewhere between high- and low-tide marks, and the maritime authorities denying any competence to anyone else over any part of the sea realm.

The above outdated and narrow-minded conflict between disciplines is scarcely conducive to building up a solid scientific front for protection of coastal environments! Similarly, the multiplicity of centres of decision that attempt to preserve, often very jealously, their sectoral authority, is not conducive to the rational management of coastal areas. Yet everyone knows that these areas contain very special, very important, very fragile, and very threatened, ecosystems and biota, on both sides of the coastline, which interplay in a highly complex fashion. When considering the concentration of human population, and of economic activities in coastal regions defined in a broad way, they constitute in fact about the most important sub-division of the planet (Ray & McCormick-Ray, 1987), and should receive priority attention for adequate planning and rational development, including through the Biosphere Reserve Programme. The results of the future studies of the Blue Plan, concerning the Mediterranean Basis, are particularly revealing as regards the crucial importance of coastal regions and of their proper management for both developed and developing countries (Grenon & Batisse, 1989).

The Coastal Conservation Concern

Assuming that the political will exists for their establishment, coastal Biosphere Reserves should respond in the first place to the widespread and increasing conservation concern for coastal ecosystems.

Considering, first, conservation on the land side, the application of the concept in a coastal area has of course to embody the general principles recalled earlier, including delineation of a buffer zone and protection of a core area. A major obstacle to conservation in terrestrial coastal areas arising all over the world, and particularly in those with dense human populations and long histories, is the high economic value of coastal land, where a large variety of very profitable human activities tend to concentrate, including urbanisation, industry, energy, tourism, and all forms of transport. It is well known for instance that protection of inland lagoons and other coastal wetlands, which are all-too-often considered as areas for discharging waste or for covering with concrete, is a formidable challenge.

The problem is aggravated by the need to protect the marine side of a Coastal Biosphere Reserve from what takes place on land, as river discharge and effluents come from there and as human activities which disturb marine ecosystems are largely land-based. Proper delineation of a coastal conservation area demands protection of the marine part from what comes from the land. This imperative has been too-often forgotten in the establishment of marine parks and of some Biosphere Reserves (such as Miramare in Italy or Malindi-Watamu in Kenya, the latter of which is shown in Fig. 8.4). This implies, in particular, adequate consideration of what takes place in whose watersheds, though admittedly it is difficult to control sediment and pollution reaching the sea from large-scale watersheds.

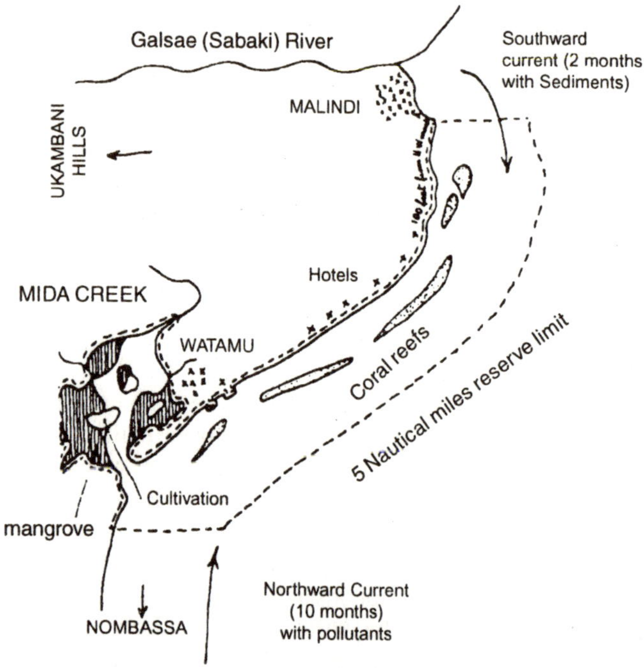

Fig. 8.4: Sketch-map of Malindi-Watamu Biosphere Reserve Kenya (coastal length approximately 30 km.)

When we come to conservation on the marine side of the coastline as such, we are confronted with a dynamic system having two major interacting components, the water-column and the sea-bottom. With the exception of traditional rights of fishermen and similar groups, jurisdiction over the sea-bottom and definition of authority or 'ownership' is not fully clear. It would appear, however, that delineation of core areas or buffer zones on the sea-bottom could be made by the national authority concerned, in order to ensure some degree of conservation of benthic life. One approach could consist of deciding of a certain depth for delineation of a buffer zone. The definition of core areas within the buffer zone could in theory follow, although these core areas may have to be modified with time because of geomorphological changes and as actual enforcement of protection may raise serious difficulties. (In the case of the Iroise Biosphere Reserve in France, marine core areas exist in fact only because the extremely rough sea, the chaotic rocky bottom, and the strong currents, prevent any human approach in a fairly large part of the Biosphere Reserve).

Delineation of the sea-bottom has, however, no effect on the water column, which is not a fixed element and is subject to external influences from currents, tides and other movements. This would make it hard to define meaningful core areas and buffer zones protecting pelagic life. The situation is comparable to some extent with what happens in a terrestrial area where atmospheric or river-borne pollutants cannot be prevented from entering a reserve. Nevertheless, from the point of view of properly controlled fishing activities, the idea of a transition area on the sea-ward side, which would be somewhat analogous in purpose to a terrestrial transition area, may have real value.

It appears in conclusion that the conservation concern of Biosphere Reserves can be translated in zonation patterns for coastal areas provided zonation is extended both on land and on the sea-bottom, the water column being subject to minimal disturbing influences of human origin. At the same time, however, the protection of the interface demands spatial continuity at some point between terrestrial and marine core areas — a criterion which in our view should be given very high importance for establishment and evaluation of coastal Biosphere Reserves.

The Coastal Development Concern

There is no need for long discussion on the logistic role of a coastal Biosphere Reserve, as it corresponds closely to the terrestrial situation with the obvious addition of facilities for marine studies. Research and monitoring activities will be essential, both as regards land and sea, and moreover as regards local studies and participation in cooperative programmes and networking.

Conversely, the development concern in coastal Biosphere Reserves will be marked by the specific features of coastal regions. These relate broadly to three major types of human occupation and use, which can be characterised as follows:

(a) The continuing presence in many parts of the world — particularly, but not exclusively, in developing countries — of traditional coastal cultures making use of marine resources for their daily life (fish, molluscs, corals, mangroves, seaweeds, local navigation, etc.);

(b) The rapid development of international and/or domestic coastal tourism (beaches, hotels, marinas, second homes, scuba diving, sport fishing, high demand for freshwater and imported products, etc.); and

(c) The increasing concentration of population in many coastal areas of developed and developing countries alike, accompanied by rapid urbanisation (often unplanned) and development of agriculture, industry, trade, and transport — all competing for land-use on limited linear-shaped coastal space.

Obviously, Biosphere Reserves cannot be established in or very close to areas that are characterised by the latter type of dense human occupation — which unfortunately tends to spread along practically all the coastlines of the world — and would contribute little to the economic life of these areas. But where their access is not too difficult, they can provide much-needed educational and recreational facilities for such urban populations.

Coastal Biosphere Reserves will, naturally, have to be established where there is still something to protect or where restoration can take place, and they will have to play their development role as well as their conservation role for this purpose. Their main development role will thus be directed towards meeting the traditional needs of the coastal populations which were mentioned under the first type of human occupation. This implies protection and sustainable management of both their terrestrial and their marine resource base — particularly traditional fishing. It also relates to the role and impact of tourism, the second type of human occupation which was referred to above. The coastal Biosphere Reserve has to promote forms of tourism which benefit concretely the local population, and which are compatible with the maintenance of their cultural identity as well of course as with the conservation objectives that have been established and that in particular do not disturb the dynamics of the coastline.

Conclusion and Summary

Generally speaking, the fragile and highly-coveted coastal regions of the world badly need integrated land and water-use planning to reconcile their multiple functions, including that of terrestrial and marine conservation. Properly designed and managed, coastal Biosphere Reserves could constitute a most useful tool for this purpose. Ideally, they would pay equal attention to conservation requirements on the land side and on the marine side, keeping particularly in mind the impact of land-based activities on the marine side. On the land side, consideration should be given not only to the type of eco-systems to be included, but also to land-use in coastal plains and to coastal landscapes. On the marine side the precise place of traditional activities, such as various forms of fishing, will have to be appreciated. Fig. 8.5 suggests a very idealised zonation pattern for a hypothetical Biosphere Reserve where the above considerations have been kept in mind.

A number of existing Biosphere Reserves, which have a coastline or consist of islands, could easily be extended so as to cover the marine part to a given depth. Some existing Biosphere Reserves, centred on the marine side, should be extended on the land side through purchase of land, and arrangements should be made with authorities or the owners concerned to help to make them effective from the viewpoint of marine conservation.

As far as the deeper ocean is concerned, where the water column plays the major role, it would seem that the concept of Biosphere Reserves could only be used where it could be clearly linked in realistic operational terms with the adjacent terrestrial area. The seaward extension of a Biosphere Reserve to reach the Exclusive Economic Zone or the continental shelf, could be conceivable as a buffer zone or transition area as long as it could be handled and remained meaningful in relation to the basic concept.

When considering the international list of Biosphere Reserves, we feel that the first priority is not so much to add new ones on the

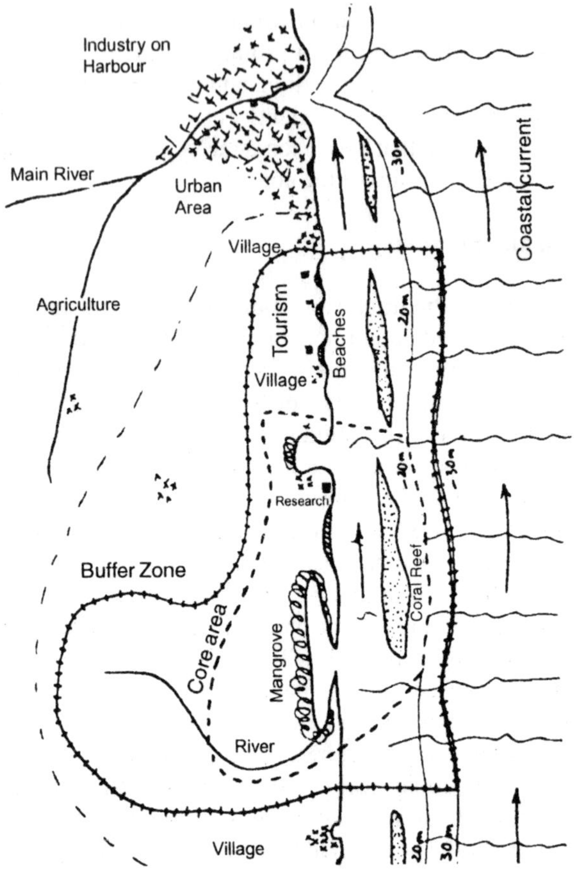

Fig. 8.5: Zonation pattern of an ideal coastal Biosphere Reserve (hypothetical).

terrestrial realm, but rather to improve the structure and functioning of existing ones and to establish operational research, monitoring, and information exchange, networks between them. But an equal priority is, definitely, to set up, all over the world, a substantial number of fully functional coastal (*i.e.* both terrestrial and marine) Biosphere Reserves as a major contribution to the rational use and conservation of these most threatened and most precious areas of Planet Earth. Even more than for strictly terrestrial ones, the key to successful coastal Biosphere Reserves will be the proper design and operation of their management, and therefore the continued will and cooperation of all specialists, authorities, and people, concerned. When there is a will there is a way. Biosphere Reserves could, and should, contribute significantly to the objective, stated by IUCN, of protecting effectively at least one-third of the coastlines and coastal landscapes and seascapes of the world.

Acknowledgements

This paper is based upon a presentation made at the UNESCO-IUCN Workshop on the application of the Biosphere Reserve Concept to Coastal Systems, hosted by the US National Ocean and Atmosphere Administration in San Francisco, California, from 14 to 20 August 1989. Thanks are due to Mary T. Agardy (Woods Hole Oceanographic Institution), Daniel Elder (IUCN), G. Carleton Ray (University of Virginia), and Jane Robertson (UNESCO), for their helpful comments. It is expected that in due course UNESCO and IUCN will issue guidelines on the subject.

REFERENCES

Batisse, M. (1980). The relevance of MAB. *Environmental Conservation*, 7(3), pp. 179-84.

Batisse, M. (1982). The Biosphere Reserve: A tool for environmental conservation and management. *Environmental Conservation*. 9(2), pp. 101-11, 8 figs.

Batisse, M. (1986). Developing and focusing the Biosphere Reserve Concept. *Nature and Resources*, XXII(3), pp. 2-11.

Grenon, M. & Batisse, M. (Eds.) (1989). *Futures for the Mediterranean Basin: the Blue Plan*. Oxford University Press. Walton Street, Oxford OX2 6DP, England UK: xxi + 279 pp., 69 figs. 67 tables.

Hayden, B.P., Ray, G.C. & Dolan, R. (1984). Classification of coastal and marine environments. *Environmental Conservation*. 11(3), pp. 199-207.

Ketchum, B.H. (1972) (Ed.). *The Water's Edge: Critical Problems of the Coastal Zone*. The MIT Press, Cambridge, Massachusetts, USA.

Ray, G.C. & McCormick-Ray, M.G. (1987). Coastal and Marine Biosphere Reserves. Pp. 68-78 in *Symposium on Biosphere Reserves. Fourth World Wilderness Congress*. US National Parks Service.

Udvardy, M.D.F. (1975). A classification of the Biogeographical Provinces of the World, IUCN Occasional Papers No. 18, IUCN, Morges, Switzerland, 49 pp.

UNESCO (1974). *Programme on Man and the Biosphere (MAB) Task Force on: Criteria and Guidelines for the Choice and Establishment of Biosphere Reserves*. MAB Report Series No. 22, UNESCO, Paris, France: 61 pp., illustr.

UNESCO (1984). Action Plan for Biosphere Reserves. *Nature and Resources*. XX(4), pp. 11-22.

UNESCO-UNEP (1984). *Conservation, Science and Society.* (Natural Resources Research Series XXI.) UNESCO, Paris, France: pp. 13-6.

Worthington, E.B. (1983). *The Ecological Century: A Personal Appraisal*. Clarendon Press, Oxford, England, 266 pp.

9

Ecology and Development with Particular Reference to the Management of Water Resources

MOONIS RAZA

Meaningful probes into the complexities along the ecology development interface call for the generation of an adequate degree of clarity on these concepts themselves by clearing some of the ideological cobwebs, theoretical inabilities and methodological inconsistencies which have accumulated around them during the last half a century or so.

The most effective constraint in the received conceptualisation of this interactive relationship, which clutters clear thinking, pertains to the inability of current thought structures to break from the Cartesian dichotomies and assimilate as well as transcend the dualism between matter and energy, wave and particle, quantum and field, living and non-living, plant and animal or material and spiritual. The assertion of the monist view and a holistic approach should, however, not be mistaken, as Bookchim points out, 'for a spectral openness that yields cosmic dissolution in structureless *nirvana*'. The wholeness is not a bleak undifferentiated 'universality' that involves the reduction of a phenomenon to what it has in common with everything else. Nor it is a celestial, omni-present 'energy' that replaces the vast material differentia of which the natural and social realms are composed. To the contrary, wholeness comprises the variegated structures, the articulations, and the mediations that impart to the whole a rich variety of forms and thereby add unique qualitative properties to what a strictly analytic mind often reduces to 'innumerable' and 'random' details.

Taking up the concept of development in its regional context, the starting point of our Odyssey of learning must be the categorical assertion that regional development is not a substitute for but the most effective form of and instrumentability for development. Its definitional attributes, therefore, flow from the universality of the noun which is the set and the specificity of the governing adjective, which distinguishes it from the universality of the noun which is the set and the specificity of the governing adjective, which distinguishes it from other sub-sets of the set. It is important to state this elementary position because some ideologues of the developed world have explicitly or implicitly taken the position that regional development is of *particular* relevance for developing societies to ensure the availability of the 'basic minimum needs' with the help of 'appropriate technologies' for the hewers of wood and drawers of water of the impoverished Third World. Such a distorted view needs to be categorically rejected.

Regional development, as an integrated system of ideas, practices, methodologies and approaches is definitionally global. It is an expression of the contemporary realisation that man as an element of the ecosystem, cannot conquer non-human nature but must learn to live in harmony with it within a system of interdependencies. Regional development should, therefore, be viewed as the articulation of qualitative changes in the geo-biotechno-social complex of interdependent phenomena in such a manner that the quality of human life improves within the framework of the integrity of the eco-system. Regional development, in this vital and fundamental sense, is eco-development.

The basic premise of eco-development is the unity in diversity of all that objective exists. It not only rejects the segmentation of the human condition for analytical purposes and consequently the fragmentation of the social sciences but proceeds much further along the line and denies the validity of a taxonomy of knowledge, wherein the categories of the first order are the natural and the social sciences.

To the extent that a body of knowledge qualifies to be a science at all, it is both natural and social; for it studies the cause-effect complexes which transcend these distinctions. Such is the nature of matter in motion through space and time. Objectively, it is certainty so; it is geography alone among the sciences which recognises it to be so. Such a recognition *is the raison d'etre* of the discipline. 'The separation of the whole into man and his environment', said Herbertson, 'is a murderous act ... The living whole ... is no longer the living whole when it is so dissected, but something dead and incomplete.'

A proper understanding of eco-development — both

epistemologically as a model of transformation and methodologically as an analytical tool, has to contend with the continuing rigidities of the fragmented hierarchies in knowledge. While the social sciences have moved towards a certain degree of internal cohesion, the world of non-human nature is still alien to it, at best producing unnecessary noise in their sophisticated computer programmes. The agricultural economist would rather not dirty his hands with the soil, this nauseating residual in his regression model, which cannot be whisked away. The incapacity of the natural sciences to go beyond the rigid limits of their sub-system is no less alarming. The internal integration of the natural sciences has at best produced the science of ecology. In their just concern with the autotrophs and the hetrotrophs, the ecologists, tend to forget that the *homo sapien* constitute a category qualitatively different from the other hetrotrophs, that their explanatory system is incapable of accounting for the behaviour of social man; that they are asking only limited questions and can, therefore, get only inadequate and partial answers. At best, they recognise man as an element in the man and nature syndrome and have shown a unique incapacity to recognise the reality of man in nature. They fail to see that the rationality of man is as much natural as the irrationality of the monsoon wind, the chernozem or the xerophyte. The unifying concept of the eco-development has arisen to break the constraints imposed by the complementary inadequacies of the social and the natural sciences. While the former cannot come to terms with the animality of man, the latter cannot come to terms with his humanity. It is in the background of such a serious crisis in knowledge that the geographical science has a modest but a significant role to play. Though deeply rooted in nature, the discipline has manifested a unique capacity to come to terms with man. This enables geography to bring a vitally important input in the current debate on ecology and development that is raging in the world, particularly in its third segment.

The concept of eco-development is based on the unity of the system of interdependencies through the mechanism of interactions between social man and nature. The essentiality of man and nature is based on 'man as a natural being and nature as a human reality'. Since the naturalisation of man and the humanisation of nature proceed simultaneously through man's interaction with nature, human history may be viewed as a continuation of, and a qualitative new stage in natural history — the two constituting a differentiated unity. It is no doubt true that primeval nature is prior to man and continues to exist without him everywhere except on the micro-dot of a planet in the vastness of the universe. This non-humanised nature which has not naturalised man is of only marginal interest directly in the development process. Nature comes within the orbit of development primarily as a constituent element of social practice. Man interacts with nature through labour, transforms it and himself gets transformed in the process. This man, who makes himself in remarking nature, is the focus of eco-development.

In the process of transforming nature and himself, social man moves from the realm of necessity to that of freedom in the sense in which Spinoza conceived the latter: 'recognised necessity'. To the extent that man does not understand the processes of nature through social practice, to that extent he is in the realm of blind, unrecognised necessity; to that extent he is unfree — a slave crouching in awe and supplication before the rising sun or the mighty mountains. Also as long as he fails to perceive how absolute is the necessity of maintaining the integrity of his habitat, he would crouch in awe before the eco-disruptive products and processes of an entirely *erstaz* civilisation, and be a willing slave to the God of consumerism.

The realm of freedom defined as cognised necessity is the noosphere, the sphere of the planet earth which has been 'humanized' by rational human activity. The traditional division of the planet into the lithosphere, hydrosphere, atmosphere and the bio-sphere would interest the geologist, the hydrologist, the meteorologist and the biologist, and they would engage themselves in the study of each independently. However, when the alluvial fan in the Himalayan valley gets transformed into a system of terraces, when the mighty torrents are tamed to fertilise the thirsty earth, when a new crop rotation system is evolved to take advantage of a short growing season, when a wrong grazing practice leads to deforestation — then the segments of the lithosphere, the hydrosphere, the atmosphere and the biosphere get synthesised and transformed into the noosphere — the realm of cognised necessity. This is the realm of eco-development.

The Noosphere — the sphere of man-nature interaction may be viewed as a triangle of forces. Nature provides the base, lays down the limits of freedom and indicates the direction along which optimum appropriation through social labour is possible in the long run. Technology aids natural processes, bends them to human (and humane) purposes, modifies them and thus extends the range of freedom. Institutions are either conducive to or restrictive on man-nature interaction. The trajectory of eco-development moves through this triangle of forces.

With such a conceptualisation of eco-development it is possible to steer clear of two erroneous strategies — first, the strategy of 'development' at all costs leading to eco-destruction; and second, the strategy of rejecting development in the name of ecology. In the eco-developmental context, the ecology-development contradiction is a false one. The laws of nature not only impose constraints on but also point to the direction of optimal development. Unless this dual relationship between the ecological correlates and the development process is fully recognised, one tends to get neck-deep in the morass of 'hippie' ecology, the spurious environmental concerns of the 'flower people' for whom nature is a virgin which should not be violated through human intervention. The latter view, under different colours and hues is being assiduously sold by some of the ideologues of the developed world to the developing countries. The situation is rather ironical. The advice not to proceed along the path of development through proper resource utilisation comes from those nations who are themselves the major culprits of eco-destruction through the dysfunctional monopoly of natural resources in an international system of inequalities, wherein 20 per cent of the world population is permitted to misuse 80 per cent of its resources, and wherein the city of Chicago alone is allowed to consume more oil than the second most populous country in the world. There appears to be considerable weight in the assessment of some scholars of both the developed and the developing world to the effect that the anti-development injunctions, being issued for the benefit of the innocents of the Third World by the prophets of doom of the Club of Rome, or the dons of MIT and/or Sussex, are really intended to widen the North-South gap and perpetuate the poverty and misery of the bulk of humanity. Our concern with ecology within the framework of an eco-systemic approach is directed to optimising (and not maximising) development so as to extricate our people from the vicious stranglehold of hunger and poverty; for, in the Third World hunger continues to be a most potent pollutant — an eco-destructive force of tremendous magnitude for it destroys man, the crucial component of the contemporary eco-systems. Those who rightly lose their night's sleep over the fate of a blighted tree or a faded flower should sometimes also look at the bloated bellies, sunken eyes and the skinny arms of hungry children.

It is heartening to note that in the case of India as early as in the

Fourth Five Year Plan, a fairly clear understanding about relationship between ecology and development was discernible. It was stated therein: "The physical environment is a dynamic, complex and inter-connected system in which any action in one part affects others ... Planning for harmonious development recognises this unity of nature and man. Such planning possible only on the basis of a comprehensive appraisal of issues — particularly economic and ecological ... It is necessary, therefore, to introduce the environmental aspects into our planning and development. Along with effective conservation and rational use of natural resources, protection and improvement of human environment is vital well-being. It is particularly important that long term basic considerations should prevail over short term commercial considerations, that the social costs and benefits be used as the yardstick rather than private gains and losses".

In the perspective of eco-development, it should be possibly to develop a scheme of prioritisation in resource use, flowing from the *degree of expandability* of the resource. It is being suggested that the two-way classification of natural resources into the replenishable and the non-replenishable is inadequate to catch the full extent of their differentiated spectrum. A four-way classification may be far more appropriate from the point of view of eco-development. These four classes of natural resources may be arranged vertically from higher to lower in terms of their degree or expandability as follows:

(i) inexhaustible like solar energy;
(ii) cyclic like water in the hydrological cycle;
(iii) renewable like natural vegetation; and
(iv) non-renewable like fossil fuels.

A sound resource use policy should be based on the principle that one moves to a lower order in the scale only after the possibility of utilising the higher order resource has been carefully examined and found to be impossible. Taking the example of energy use, for example, attempts should be made to use solar energy as far as possible; failing which one should move down one step to hydro-electric power. If that is also not found to be feasible one may move down a step further to bio-mass energy. Only in case all these have been ruled out, coal may be used as a last resort.

The significance of water as a natural resource lies in the fact that it is high up in the scheme of prioritisation in the use of natural resources presented above. Water, as a necessary element of the biosphere, is neither good nor bad, neither positive nor negative in itself. It is a *natural resource*, which may be either optimally utilised or partially utilised or misutilised by the homo sapien in the development process.

The importance of water flows from the fact that the hydrological cycle is an intrinsic component of the biosphere. Life, having originated in relation to water, the cycle cannot be destroyed except with the biosphere. It follows from the above that the optimal utilisation of water as a natural resource can and should be based on a scientific understanding of the nature of the hydrological cycle. Water occupies a prime position in the scheme of resource use due to its cyclic character and consequently its indestructibility. Though the cycle cannot be destroyed it can, however, be

(i) distorted as in the case of excessive flooding in the lower reaches due to deforestation in the upper reaches;
(ii) delayed as in the case of blockage of percolation by large concrete surfaces in metropoles; and
(iii) polluted as in the case of acid rain or oil spills.

The *problematic* of water utilisation for development relates to the fixing of the limits of tolerance in the biosphere to the distortions, delays and pollution of and within the hydrological cycle.

The chemical compound made up of two atoms of hydrogen and one of oxygen has, in its many existential form, inspired love and reverence among the people all over the world since the dawn of proto-history. It is deeply rooted in the primevalpsyche of the human race and is repeatedly expressed in ancient human, medieval ballads and contemporary folklore. It was not accidental that the transition from the food gathering to the food producing societies took place in locations of rain fed plant growth and the emergence of the earliest civilisations of mankind were intrinsically linked with perennial river systems of the old world. Water is deeply etched into the mythological idiom of traditional societies. The Nordic sagas sang of the seas and the *Rigveda* of the rivers of the Sapta Sindhu. The Ganga emerging from the tresses of Shiva, has become the symbol of motherhood — as the Ganga *mayya* — or the teaming millions of this vast subcontinent. The *malhar* and the *kajari* catch the notes of the monsoon drops falling on the parched, thirsty earth. Olman River of the Negro spiritual, the tilting notes of the Vltava in the Smetana's Ma Vlast touch the deepest chords in the inner being of sensitive men and women all over the world. The stray references mentioned above bring out the deep involvement of water in the human condition and its crucial role of water in the evolution and development of the homosapien as biological species.

Biosphere in its natural state is an important source for the economy of collection. The biomass living in and/or on water-marine, river and lake surfaces — plays an important role in the sustenance of human life. There is need for conserving as well as augmenting these natural resources for social use and of putting checks on and controlling human intervention which is destructive of such organisms. It may also be noted that natural vegetation and wild animals living therein — both being sustained by the availability of water in variable quantities — are an important natural resource. The conservation of such habitats is crucially important not only for them but also for human life. It may be noted in this connection that there is a correspondence between precipitation zones on the one hand and vegetation zones on the other and disrupting this relation beyond the limit of tolerance would be counter productive. The dangers inherent in transforming the basic character of vegetation zones, e.g. of deserts into forests, must be fully appreciated before interfering in these systems.

While surface flow plays an important role as a source of energy and provides a medium of transport of passengers and commodities and while water bodies are a continuing source of aesthetic recreation and sports, it is water biomass relationship in primary production which occupies the centre stage particularly in India and other developing countries.

In a country as vast as India, there are several regional dimensions pertaining to water as a natural resource which need to be studied in depth. For example, there is an intricate net of channels in the Bengal delta on one hand and a complete absence of surface flow in the Thar on the other... One of the heaviest rainfall areas are found in Meghalaya and the scantiest exist in the western most parts of Rajasthan. This, coupled with the types of soils, human skills, technology and other parameters, offers a large variety of cropping patterns. But while some crops can grow with minimum water inputs, others flourish on heavy waterings. In this whole process, though it is generally agreed that crop-management and water-management go hand in hand, the former is resources, and the latter, where the degree of this control is higher. A judicious combination of these, therefore, can be operative both in the water abundant and in the water scarce regions. Farmers favour water-intensive crops in areas which abound in rainfall and where better irrigational facilities are available, while in others, which are frequented by dry spells, more hardly crops are grown. In between, there is a whole canvas of the partially dry and partially wet areas which segregates them from each other by the extent of irrigation provided to them. These variegated shades get reflected in the mix of crops that are grown in these regions over the seasons. Needless to say that there is an overwhelming depçndence of the agrarian economy on rainfall in the dry regions. It is not only the quantum but also an even spread of rainfall during the relevant seasons, which is important, particularly in areas which are susceptible to intermittent or long dry spells. In such areas, therefore, adjustment by man manifests itself in the form of crop-management. As the facility of water improves, an acreage shift is noticed from the low-water base cereal crops to the relatively low-water requiring cash crops and then to the superior cereals needing more waterings.

Studies carried out in the Centre for the Study of Regional development, Jawaharlal Nehru University, do suggest that as the arid conditions intensify, rainfall becomes the single most crucial factor determining crop yields. In the Indian desert, where water is usually very scarce, it was seen that in years of good rainfall, there was an acreage shift from Bajra to pulses, Sesamum and Gowar though admittedly, not all variations in yield could be explained by variations in rainfall only. But there is a critical limit, beyond which, with an increase in the level of rainfall, its correlation co-efficient with the hectarage under a dry land crop like Bajra becomes negative. However, similar relationships pertaining to crop management are propounded between the low irrigated-rain dependent regions on one hand and the relatively better irrigated areas on the other. In another study of irrigation levels for semi-arid crops like pulses, it has been shown that in regions with irrigated area above 30 per cent of the cropped area, there is a negative association between the share of irrigated area and the share of acreage under these crops because with better availability of irrigational facilities, it is beneficial for farmers to switch over to other lucrative crops. This has particularly happened in the wheat belt where due to an access to the high-yielding technology of wheat, hectarage under rabi pulses declined significantly. Regions where less than 20 per cent of the cropped area was irrigated, showed an increase in the hectarage of these crops along with positive variations in the level of irrigation. In those areas where these levels ranged between

20 to 30 per cent, it was the level of rainfall which determined the watershed.

An intertwining relationship between the roles of water and new agricultural technology is established in explaining agricultural productivity differentials in a study conducted for Punjab State in 1978. At low levels of agricultural technology, water played a dominant role in influencing productivity, and thereafter, new agricultural technology, having the support of assured water supply became important. With a gradual stabilisation of this technology, the intensity of water use, coupled with intensive use of complementary inputs assumed a prominent role.

Underwater management, not only its various sources such as rainfall and other artificial means of irrigation need to be emphasised, it is equally important to take into view point the number of waterings and the quantum of each watering which is to be supplied to a group of crops. Therefore, this does not call for an even and an equal distribution of water over space, over seasons and among crops, but a distribution which maximises returns per unit of water in a given region during the agricultural seasons, where one or more sources may be combined.

A district-wise analysis of the eastern region in 1980-82 confined to the states of East U.P., Bihar, Orissa and West Bengal, showed that variations in agricultural productivity of the districts falling in the uplands and highlands of Chota Nagpur plateau, the Central Tableland and the Eastern Ghat were explained by rainfall upto an extent of 8 per cent, while this coupled with irrigation through canals explained these variations upto 22 per cent. In the meso-region of plains of the above mentioned states, the role of rainfall in explaining productivity variations was negligible but when canal and tubewell irrigated areas were taken into consideration, the extent of explanation with each added step was 6 per cent and 9 per cent respectively. This does not mean that water has a less important role to play in the plains but only that the variations in productivity across space are more influenced by other technological and infrastructural facilities whose use was more limited in the less developed meso-region of the uplands.

In yet another study carried out for Uttar Pradesh relationships between Agricultural Water Use (AWU) and agricultural productivity for 1954-57, 1964-67 and 1974-77 trienniums revealed that productivity increased by Rs. 47, Rs. 121 and Rs. 185 per hectare (at constant harvest prices of 1974-77) with an additional supply of 100 mm of water during the three periods. This increase in productivity over time is mainly due to the efficiency achieved in the use of water and of other inputs arising due to improved management of these resources.

Dhawan and Satyasai[1] a recent study, measuring output impact per gross irrigated hectare in rice equivalent units in Andhra Pradesh, Gujarat and Uttar Pradesh, taking various sources and combinations of sources of irrigation, show that while private tubewells gave the highest output in Andhra Pradesh, purchase of water from pumpset owners ranked the highest in Gujarat; ownership of a pumpset to lift water from other sources was top-ranking in Uttar Pradesh. The same was true even in terms of per unit of watering per hectare except that it was the highest under private dugwells equipped with pumpsets in Uttar Pradesh. This does generally show that a source where the availability of water is either combined with ownership or with some control over the newer techniques of lifting water compared to other traditional sources, is more output efficient and hence it is noticed that in agriculturally advanced pockets of a region or among the relatively prosperous peasant households in water scarce regions, there is a higher degree of not only privatisation of irrigation sources but also popularisation of those sources which combine more control with improved technology.

On the whole, India has made significant progress in exploiting the irrigation potential in the last three and a half decades. The gross irrigated area in the country during 1950-51 was only 22.6 million hectares which increased to 52.0 million hectares in 1982-83 representing an almost two and a half times increase over the base year. Though the growth of irrigation is impressive over time, the irrigated hectarage represents less than one-half of the ultimate irrigation potential in the country which is estimated at 113 million hectares. Not only this, the efficiency of irrigation management is low which is reflected in an under-utilisation of the created irrigation potential. Among the agricultural holdings in the country, only about 48 per cent of them were wholly irrigated in 1976-77 while the rest of them were only partially irrigated. To the latter, the contribution of the large-sized holdings was the maximum. Even as late as 1983-84, only 30.5 per cent of the cropped area in the country was irrigated and whereas near one-third proportion of both rice and wheat crops were irrigated, most of the other crops had less than 5 per cent of their sown hectarage under irrigated condition. No spectacular change is envisaged for 1990s though area under irrigation will continue to increase each year. Therefore, with limited availability of irrigational facilities on one hand and with an increased performance for superior crops especially those using the package of new technological inputs requiring an assured water supply on the other, water management along with crop management should be the slogan for the coming decade. In a country where nearly three-quarters of the net sown area, contributing 45 per cent to the country's grain production is dependent upon rainfall, it is as significant to harness water in regions, sub-regions and in small pockets, where it is found in abundance or which are frequented by floods as it is to release it for areas where it is scarce, which are under long dry spells or are drought prone. This calls not only for area specific planning for water resources but also for season-specific, crop-specific and source-specific management.

REFERENCE

1. B.D. Dhawan and K.J.S. Satyasai, 'Productivity of Irrigated Farming: Survey Evidence from three States', *Journal of Indian Water Resources Society*, Vol. 7, No. 3, July, 1987.

10

Perspectives in Resource Management and Political Ecology

C.P. SINGH

Till the beginning of the 1960s environment and ecology were not so significant "issues". But within the past 30 years they have become the most significant issues of the 20th century. They are considered as important and threatening as the nuclear issue. Scientific studies in different parts of the world have found that what was expected to happen in the first quarter of the next century may actually happen in the closing years of the present century. For instance, the depletion of the ozone layer over the northern hemisphere, particularly in the temperate latitudes of the USA, Canada, Europe and Russia, has taken place at a much faster rate than estimated earlier. This prompted the US President to announce the end of chlorofluorocarbons (CFC) production by 1995, five years ahead of the target date. Environment is making headlines all over the world in news media. The United Nations Conference on Environment and Development (UNCED), termed as the Earth Summit, in Rio de Janeiro in the first fortnight of June 1992, has also added to the heightened awareness regarding the environmental and ecological crisis on the planet earth. The green movements in the West, or the Advanced Developed Countries (ADC), have concerned themselves beyond the popular preoccupation of the ozone layer, increase in greenhouse gases, industrial pollution, caring for furry animals like the panda, or protection of certain wild animals and presentation of cruelty to animals in general. They have extended their concern to all the living and non-living, something that has been part of the Indian culture since the ancient times, and they have called for a shift from an anthropocentric attitude to all-life centric attitude. For this they have argued for a radical restructuring of the whole of political, social and economic life of man on the earth. Whether such a radical view is going to be acceptable to the people, will there be any compromises, what policies will be formulated and what will be their likely consequences, and what sacrifices people are prepared to make, especially those who have attained a very high standards of living and have luxurious lifestyles, are some of the questions which constitute the aspects of the convergence of the fields of politics, ecology and geography.

To avoid any confusion, distinction between the terms "environment" and "ecology" is necessary at this stage. Environment is the habitat of living species comprising the atmosphere, *terra firma*, the ocean, sea, river and lake systems and the built environment for human societies. The word ecology, in its biological context, deals with the mutual relationship between organisms and their environment, and sociologically, with the spatial distribution of populations in relation to materials and to social cause and effect, while the relationship between living species and their habitats represent ecology and its basis as a biological science. In geographical studies, ecology is taken as the interrelationship between the four main physical zones of the Earth's system: biosphere, atmospheres, hydrosphere and lithosphere (Simpson, 1990, 11). For the economists, ecology studies the flow of energy and the cycles of materials in ecosystems (Martinez-Alier, 1987). Thus ecology is a much wider term than environment, though the two are closely interrelated.

For its existence and survival, life in all forms utilises materials from its surroundings for the metabolism of the body. The materials are both living and non-living. These allow the growth and renewal of tissue and provide energy for chemical processes such as movement. The energy is transformed from chemical energy to heat and given off to the atmosphere, from whence it can be reclaimed. As a result of energy consumption and metabolic processes, excretory matter is produced, which contains mineral substances which could be of value to other plants and bacteria, setting the chain of interaction of living organisms with their abiotic environments. An area within which the web of networks of the living and the non-living, the ecological system, develops has natural limits to the total amount of living matter that can be supported in it. These limits may be set by the amount of solar energy and moisture available in that part of the earth, the terrain, and the supply of nutrients like nitrogen and phosphorus (Simmons,

1987, 4). This intricate web of ecological relationships in which transactions of matter and energy take place in numerous forms is vital for all the members of the system. It is in this symbiotic relationship of all the living and non-living that each species is living in its given environment on the planet earth. Elimination or extinction of anyone of the species from the ecological system will affect all the surviving species. Theoretically, new ecological relationships will develop with the extinction of various species that could survive or the new ones that may come into existence. But in an ecological disaster there is no guarantee that human species would survive. It is in the interest of humankind to maintain and protect the existing ecological balance, because it is in this particular set of ecological relationships that man has become dominant among all the species and attained mastery over the nature, to the extent that he has acquired the power to destroy the earth, not once or twice but several thousand times.

Historical Perspective

How did man come to acquire such powers, how far are the prophets of gloom and doom regarding the threat to his existence on the mother earth right, are there any courses open to him to avoid the ecological disaster are some of the questions which require a brief overview of human development on the earth and man's relations with all animate and inanimate beings during different times.

Life on the earth began more than 2,000 million years ago as a chemical event of absolutely overwhelming improbability. Like the unity in the structure of matter in the universe, from minute atoms to the distant and large heavenly bodies, the evolution of living matter, which covers the earth, manifests a single gigantic organism, taking different forms. In this elemental drama all life is revealed as one. The processes of cell division is common to all earthly life; neither man nor amoeba, the giant squid nor the simple yeast cell can long exist without carrying on this process (Rachel Carson, 1965, quoted in Mackenzie, 1979, 26). To make scientific sense, it can be said that life began with certain big molecules of specifiable chemical composition, and matter existed, as mass energy, even before that. What existed before matter is still a matter of conjecture. Matter and life appear to be externally different, as matter is dead and unchanging whereas life creates continually what is radically new. But recent knowledge of genetic engineering has shown that matter and life are closely interconnected with each other. Both are governed by the laws of physics and chemistry together. This unity of the living and the non-living, which is reflected in their delicate balance of ecological relationships, is the basis of their right to equal existence.

In the evolution of ecological complexity three major transitions, or break of continuity, have been discerned: transition from matter to life; transition from animal to man; and transition from man the wandering scavenger to man the master and destroyer of nature (Mackenzie, 1979, 22 and 35). The present species of man, homo sapiens, with a big brain is no more than 100,000 years old, which is indeed no time in the history of the earth. Man had several advantages over other species: a highly developed brain, an erect body, and the faculty of speech. The human brain is capable of reason and abstraction. It can visualise, conceptualise and imagine. His erect body facilitated his movements and activities, while the power of speech allowed communication with members of his species. Man also had the capacity to eliminate those lives which disagreed with him, or which threatened his own life. This is something that is not known to other living beings. The number of human beings killed by man in his entire history has no parallel among other species. He is his own biggest enemy. Armed with nuclear weapons and other means of warfare today he is most dangerous to all the species, including himself.

The march of man from the wandering scavenger in what has been termed as the Stone Age to the modern age of hydrogen bombs, instantaneous global communication, interplanetary probes, sprawling cities and large industrial centres, global economy and culture has been rather quick. The Nilotic Revolution when man first domesticated animal and produced food crops and he became a farmer instead of a nomad or a gatherer took place not more than 10,000 years ago. This is equivalent to the lifecycle of nuclear waste from nuclear reactors of today. Given the pace of scientific and technological developments, and the momentum that they are gaining each passing day, it is impossible to visualise what our planet, its inhabitants and their interrelationships will be like 10,000 years from today.

The mastery of nature by man is of very recent origin. It started with modern science and the crystallization of the scientific method in the 16th century Europe. But the roots of this can be found in the developments in mathematics, astrology, medicine, and others in the Chinese, Hindu and Islamic civilisations nearly 6,000 years ago in several river valleys in Asia and Northern Africa. Their objective, however, was not to place man in the most dominating position among all the species. On the contrary, as in the case of the old Hindu civilisation, man was required to live in perfect harmony with all the living and non-living. It went even beyond that in recognising the need of man in harmony with himself as much as with the outside world. The happiness from the total harmony could be obtained by compassion towards all living beings and nature. The essence of the philosophy has been captured by Mahatma Gandhi in the following words in his *The Story of My Experiments with Truth:*

> "To see the universal and all-pervading Spirit of Truth face to face one must be able to *love the meanest of creation as oneself*... I must *reduce myself to zero.* So long as a man does not of his own free will *put himself last among his fellow creatures*, there is no salvation for him. Ahimsa (non-violence or non-aggression) is the farthest limit of humility." (emphasis mine)

Killing even of smallest creatures pricks the conscience of many Indians to this day. India still has the largest vegetarian population in the world. The terms like "environment friendly" and "green", which came into vogue in the past two decades in the West, are superfluous in the Indian context. The idea of non-aggression towards all living and non-living beings is part of the culture of India, which has been passed on from one generation to another for at least the past two and a half millennia. A very important aspect of these practices was that it was voluntary and self-motivated. The voluntary abstinence or renunciation of physical comforts or power was not uncommon. It was natural for a Buddha, a Mahavir or a Gandhi to be born in such a culture, which has deeply influenced the thinking of Western thinkers like Schumacher, the originator of *Small is Beautiful*, who believed that economic well-being should be accompanied with ecological and spiritual well-being. In fact, there have been innumerable people in India who have renounced riches and their materialistic possessions voluntarily. If applied at the international level today, it can lead to denuclearisation and equitable distribution of wealth and welfare of all living beings on the earth, which sounds like the "green" manifesto. But the colonialists in their arrogance of power deride this philosophy as something of an Oriental mysticism. It should also be pointed out here that scientific knowledge attained by Hindu, Islamic or Chinese civilisations was not used as a means of subduing nature and for exploitation of resources. In contrast to these civilisations, Europe, with its "witch-burning popes, appears retrograde and barbaric, sunk in the gloom of Dark Ages" (Hoodbhoy, 1991, 1) just 600 years ago.

The Catastrophic Trajectory

The beginning of the environmental and ecological catastrophy can be seen in the nature of Western science and ideology. It is true that modern science has ameliorated the life of man and saved him from its day-to-day drudgeries. It has given his medicines that have increased his longevity. It has also given him means of entertainment which did not exist earlier. It has liberated him from superstition. But it is argued that it is not so much the nature of modern science and its associated technology that are responsible for many of the problems that man and all living beings are facing today. It is the attitude with which science and technology were employed by the western man in the past four hundred years that is responsible for the present situation. There are, of course, those who insist that scientific epistemology — the very nature of scientific knowledge and its mode of inquiry — itself is fatally flawed. But our concern here is not a discussion of an alternative science. The burden of the argument here is that it was the particular ideology, general prevailing attitude of man towards nature and application of science and technology, and subsequently the control of science and technology by a few who had developed a vested interest in it, that is at the root of the present global crisis.

The crystallisation of the scientific method occurred in the 16th century Europe. Experimentation, quantification, prediction, and control became the paradigm of a new culture. "Modern science sought, by means of a clearly defined methodology, a rational comprehension of the physical universe ... This methodology derived from a coherent set of rules and criteria independent of the hierarchies of power and wealth certainly could now be interpretable on the basis of facts that anyone could check... A mysterious and capricious universe could now, for the first time in human history, be understood as mechanical and orderly ... To its possessors, the scientific method gave undreamed of power. In part this power was used to understand the laws of nature, and subsequently to create new technologies. *But, in part, science became the weapon with which less technologically developed peoples around the world were to be systematically subjugated and colonised.*" (emphasis mine) (Hoodbhoy, 1991, 3).

So long as science was a means of satisfying man's curiosity about the world he lived in it was an innocuous experience in the pursuit of knowledge. But once it was taken to be a source of power in the hands of the State, or the capitalist, it began transforming the entire human civilisation irreversibly. The attitudes of Enlightenment in the 18th century Europe that man to a great extent was the master of his own destiny; that God was a mathematician whose calculations, although infinite in their subtle complexities, were accessible to man's intelligence; and that "universal reason" was preferable to "local habit" principally because it helps to drive out superstition, contributed significantly to the arrogance and aggression of Western man on the rest of the humanity and nature (Dobson, 1990, 35-38). Besides, Baconian science itself proclaimed that nature was there to be conquered. While the conquest of man was seen to be a dubious undertaking, the conquest of nature was seen as a noble aspiration (Bacon quoted in Atkinson, 1991, 135). The fatal deception in Bacon's thinking — and one which has been carefully maintained by the West to this day — concerns the notion that science can and will be used for the benefit of all mankind (Atkinson, 1991, 135). But science was from the beginning a tool with which to advance interests of certain individuals, classes and nations, and continues without any deception in the emerging international economic order (Sethi, 1990). Military strength, political power and economic prosperity have become contingent upon the ability of modern nations to understand, control and create modern science (Hoodbhoy, 1991, 2). From this point of view what we call as Man's power over Nature turns out to be power exercised by some men over other men with Nature as its instrument. The much acclaimed scientific project of the West became the means to subjugate mankind and Nature in pursuit of the interests of a few men both in Europe and its colonies.

New modes of industrial production from new raw materials leaving the individuals free in their enterprises, buttressed by the philosophy of *laissez faire*, sent hordes of Europeans in search of new lands to be colonised. The scramble for Africa, Asia, Australia and the Americas set them fighting with each other in those lands. In colonising these lands the colonialists trampled upon the existing environmental and cultural values that man had evolved over several thousand years in some cases. But in his arrogance of the newfound power of science and technology, and wealth, some of which was acquired from the resources of the colonies, they were blinded by greed, and encouraged by the Enlightenment attitudes of "liberating" the natives from superstition, set upon themselves the task of "civilising" them. The plight of the long existent cultures under the onslaught of colonialists has been vividly captured by Hoodbhoy (1991, 3) in the case of Islam in the following words:

> "Faced with the brutal onslaught of 18th century mercantile imperialism, traditional Muslim society stood defenceless. Almost all of the Muslim world, ranging from West Africa to East Asia, was rapidly colonised. But the defeat was not in military terms alone, although that was humiliating enough for a civilisation hitherto accustomed to conquer. This first contact with modern imperialism — whose strength derived not from numbers but from the analytical methods of modern science — left the Muslims numbed, disoriented, and unsure of themselves. It was an unequal contest. Imperialism was a complex system — an intricate and well-oiled machine whose parts seemed to move with clockwork precision. Modern rifles and cannons — as at the battle of Plassey in 1757 — were certainly the most visible manifestations of its strength. But it was the telegraph, steamship, machine-produced goods, and modern organisational methods, which were the backbone of the new colossus. These elements were alien to an agrarian and pastoral civilisation. Large local armies, untutored in military techniques, fought valiantly but were decimated by disciplined British and French regiments a tenth of their size. ... In the confrontation of an industrial and capitalist West with a traditional and pre-capitalist society, there could be little doubt of the outcome. Bringing untold miseries in the process, modern imperialism set out on its mission to 'civilise' the 'natives' by destroying their culture."

Echoes of similar experiences can be found in the literature on colonialism from other parts of the world. The production systems and cultural practices evolved before the arrival of the Western man armed with the newfound science and technology, weaponry and the attitude of subduing Nature and man everywhere, could not cope with this kind of aggression. Those who came in contact with the imperialists were so overawed by their power, lifestyles and methods of exploitation of resources that they developed a sense of inferiority towards their own cultures. The colonial structures, like roads, railways, ports, shipping, telegraph and later telephone lines, postal system, trading and commercial systems, were erected to exploit the resources in new lands, which were now owned and controlled by the Europeans. Similarly, the surveys of land, forests, minerals, fisheries, etc., were not done for altruistic objectives but for the unsatiable greed of the capitalists. *Laissez faire* was advocated to keep the State out of economic exploitation of the colonies. In fact, the State was called upon to protect the exploiters in the colonies and police the routes through which trading was done. At home, the State was supposed to create conditions in which the capitalist system could function unhindered and creation of more and more wealth could be done. This was the beginning of the present social, economic and ecological problems that man is facing at the end of the 20th century. The flowering of Western civilisation, created out of the scientific project and ideological baggage devised for the exploitation of resources of the world, made heavy demands on the planet earth. The depletion of forests, heavy concentration of industries, pollution of air, water and earth, migration of people from rural to urban centres all began to make heavy demands on nature. Billions of men all over the world were marshalled, willingly or unwillingly, in ever-increasing exploitation of soils, forests, mines, animals, fisheries, or others which became of any value to men who owned technology to process them and convert them into items of human use. There was no possibility of compassion towards these living and non-living objects of nature. Everything was being gobbled up for making profits. The yardstick for development and growth came to be how much of the earth's resources were used up and how much value addition was done to them. In this enterprise, the exploiters of nature and man encouraged and controlled science and technology by employing best scientists in their laboratories and registering and patenting new inventions in their own names to have continued profits from such research. Some of the enterprising and independent scientists who patented their inventions in their own names deservingly made big fortunes for themselves. For instance, Alfred Bernhard Nobel, a Swedish chemist and engineer who invented dynamite and other high explosives and a number of machines, made so much money that he bequeathed what are known as Nobel Prizes to the scientific community, considered to be the highest honour scientists could aspire for today.

With regard to the exploitation of nature and man there was no difference between capitalism and communism. The yardstick of progress under both the systems was the same. The difference was in ownership of resources. In the former the individual initiative and drive were considered as the vehicle for growth and development, while in the latter the State was given this role with egalitarian objectives. The exploitation of man and nature by the individual in the capitalist system was as tyrannical as the control of the State apparatus in communism by a small coterie of people. In practice, both exploited man and nature recklessly, basically by and for a small number of people in whose hands wealth and power got concentrated.

Disastrous Impact

The impact of armed robbery of resources from different parts of the world by the colonialists, legitimised and couched under the philosophy of capitalism, and aided by modern science and technology towards extraction of resources, increasing navigational skills and increasing military efficiency (Merton, 1970, 137-198) was disastrous for both man and nature. It produced a vast spiral of consumption which is sucking everything on the earth — man, materials, living beings, the land, the air, the water, the sky. As it gains momentum through improvements in technology, particularly in communication technology, it is becoming self-perpetuating. What took months once upon a time is happening in seconds today. The period of communication for trade transactions has been curtailed and deals between national and international buyers and sellers are executed within the shortest possible time. If the goods are ready they can be despatched and received very quickly by fastest means of transport. The electronic media is being used to generate unnecessary demand through advertisement and publicity. This is accelerating production and consumption. Consequently, the spiral is gaining momentum and is generating a force of its own to sustain itself. The speed of which it is moving over the planet is no less than a hurricane or tornado at the micro level. Its aftermath will be even more devastating. The only difference is that it cannot be seen by the common man if he does not have the perceptive eye.

The centre of the spiral lies in the Advanced Developed Countries (ADCs), also called the North. The speed of the spiral is very fast at the centre, but it is slower on the outer margins where the Developing Countries (DCs) and the Least Developed Countries (LDCs), also termed as the South, are located. The ADCs have become integrated with each other, despite their differences, to a considerable extent to form an integrated whole. They will come even closer with the European Community finding full roots. If the outer margins constituting the LDCs cannot keep pace with the speed of the centre, which is quite unlikely, then under the tremendous centrifugal force they are likely to get fractured from the spiral. They will in that event not be part of the global system, or the New World Order, that is being put in place today by the ADCs (see also Sethi, 1990). Such countries either manage to exist and survive on their own, or just get perished altogether. The new dictum for the world at the end of the 20th century is, either keep pace with the centre or get perished. There is no question of interdependence between the centre and the periphery. There is only dependence of the periphery on the centre, in a relationship that is detrimental to the former. The periphery means very little to the centre, which having reached the stage of becoming self-propellent does not need it, not even for its resources any more because the centre is capable of finding substitutes with the help of most recent scientific and technological knowledge that only the ADCs have. There is enough evidence of the growing arrogance among the ADCs for owning knowledge, wealth and power. They have started dictating terms to the LDCs, through denial of entry into their economic system, deceptively called as global system, or through just plain coercion ignoring even the pretensions of respect for the sovereignty of the DCs and LDCs. That more than three-fourths of the nearly six billion strong humanity on the earth today do not matter in the new global order in itself is alarming enough.

These developments do not portend well both for the man and the nature, in the centre as well as on the periphery. The alienation of man from nature in the ADCs and his dehumanisation in the LDCs will leave mankind worse off than ever before. The exploitation of man by man in his quest for quantitative increase in income and profit, accumulation of wealth and concentration of coercive power in the hands of a few cannot bring happiness even to those who are their proud possessors. Man does not live by bread alone. This has been proved by the collapse of communism in Eastern Europe and the USSR, which promised to provide the basic minimum necessities of life. But for this the price to be paid was the freedom of the individual. Similarly, capitalism promises to provide the luxuries of life, but only to those who can succeed in fierce competition, which actually means being deceitful, manipulative and opportunistic to undercut the competitors.

The fierce jealousies to come up on top and remain there is no different than the laws of the jungle. That is why under both the major ideologies all human beings could not get the happiness that the two systems promised. The existence of poor people in the midst of excessive affluence in the ADCs and the yearning of people to throw away the oppressive communist system in many countries of Europe recently have proved the inadequacy of both the ideologies. However, both resemble each other with regard to the exploitation of man and nature for consumerism, high productivity for economic growth, and possession of weapons of mass destruction. Under capitalism this is done by a few who have control over wealth and power attained through open competition and democratic manner; while in the communist countries it is the small coterie of people who have the stranglehold over the people and the economy by capturing power in the name of State through a stage-managed democratic system. But in the ultimate analysis, both the systems are aggressive and exploitative of man and nature.

The consequences of this began appearing all over the world in the 1960s. Pollution, extinction of some species of animals, birds and plants, nuclear radiation and climatic changes were some of the visible symptoms of the mankind moving towards a possible ecological disaster. Environmental problems, conservation and effects of population explosion were widely discussed with genuine concern about them. But they were not regarded as symptoms of the suicidal trajectory that human civilisation had taken, though persons like Gandhi visualised it long before their appearance. Rachel Carson's *Silent Spring* (1963) aroused considerable scientific and public consciousness of the effects of uncontrolled application of insecticides, herbicides and fungicides containing highly toxic chlorinated hydrocarbons upon human health, and of the threat of ecological imbalance brought about through the destruction of wildlife. The active agitations by anti-nuclear power groups brought nuclear threat in the forefront, which led to the Kennedy-Khrushchev decision in 1963, inspired by Jawaharlal Nehru's appeal in 1955, to adopt ban on atmospheric nuclear testing and take steps to dispose of nuclear wastes. The effects of population growth and the transformation of ecosystems to meet exponentially rising demands for energy, food, shelter, transport, etc. were brought to the focus of the public and governments. Family planning was extensively promoted on an international scale. Several international programmes encouraging scientific study on a range of conservation and biological issues and population problems were promoted nationally and internationally. The management of arid zones, biological productivity and careful use of natural resources became the focus of such programmes. But these were at best cosmetic exercises. The main problem was much bigger and lay under the surface: excessive consumerism and the will to dominate others by acquisitions of wealth, technology and instruments of violence.

The high consumption of industrial and consumer goods, increasing in quantity and value in each succeeding year, led to high consumption of the earth's resources, environmental pollution, extinction of several species, depletion of the ozone layer (first detected over the Antarctica and recently over the northern hemisphere), increase in greenhouse gases, etc. This high consumption, throw-away society, a way of life that has been termed as "industrialism", is the product of the vast and violently strong spiral mentioned earlier. The affluent in the ADCs, along with the elite of the DCs and LDCs, constitute the core of industrialism. They are the largest consumers of the earth's resources and biggest polluters of environment. The poor in the ADCs, DCs, and LDCs, who constitute the outer margins of the spiral, are contributing to the degradation of environment by making heavy demands on the earth's resources for basic human needs of their large and fast-increasing populations.

The DCs and LDCs, particularly the latter, are losing out in several other ways in which the global system works against them. The elite in these countries have common interests with the rich in the ADCs and the two cooperate with each other in transferring technical personnel, resources and capital to the ADCs. The technical personnel, trained at high cost by the LDCs and DCs, migrate to the ADCs in search of better opportunities of life. The so-called aid programme of international organisations and governments of the ADCs work negatively for the LDCs, as a large portion of the aid is squandered away and expropriated by the elite, much of it is transferred to the ADCs through clandestine channels. It is not even a zero sum game for the LDCs; it is a negative sum game for them. They also find industrialism as a model to be emulated, and if they can have their way they would also be as exploitative of nature as well as man as their counterparts in the ADCs.

The reversal of this trend of industrialism, and the change in the course of the suicidal trajectory, is necessary for human survival. Change in social habits and practices in the ADCs and control of population growth in others are immediately required. It is not a plea for generalised poverty all over the world. But the element of human greed as the basis of production and consumption should be altered. If there are limits to growth, as few thinkers have recently argued, there are limits to consumption also. The present trend of high consumption increasing every year, encouraged to maintain the economic growth rate, is impossible because of the finite productive limits imposed by the Earth. If, for the sake of argument we imagine that the present nearly 6 billion population is able to achieve even one-third the present level of consumption of the rich in the ADCs, it seems impossible to attain even this level of production and consumption without seriously disturbing the existing ecological balance. An ecological catastrophe may not destroy and erase the earth from the universe. But it can largely or totally wipe out man and numerous species which exist in their present ecological relationships. Scientists have proved that with a small rise in the temperature certain grases, plants, insects, even animals may be squeezed out by the growth of new species which may seize this opportunity to grow and multiply. Or should a nuclear calamity take place in which man and all life from the earth may be exterminated completely, it may be the beginning of a new ecology from which man may be missed out.

The grand scientific project of the West started about 400 years ago to serve the mankind has been expropriated by a few, who control and use it for self-aggrandizement. They have brought the extinction of homo sapiens, man the wise, closer. These were the dangers of which Gandhi had warned the world before the middle of the present century. He had raised the basic question whether technology would remain controlled and in service of man to reduce his drudgery and to help solve man's material problems, or whether man would become so subservient to technology that he would be forced to sell his soul to "Mephistophelian materialism" and become alienated both from his fellow beings and nature by plundering it (Sethi, 1978, 49). A non-violent economic society and the replacement of demand-oriented production by need-oriented production are two principles out of the many which he puts forward. Note that he argued not for de-industrialisation and demechanisation completely, but for a need-oriented production, needs that would be limited and controlled voluntarily. There has to be a radical change in the outlook and lifestyle in the ADCs to move from artificially-generated demand-oriented society to a society where minimum needs of all are satisfied and man can live in harmony with fellow human and non-human beings on this planet. Modern science should be the heritage and property of the whole mankind, and not of a few in the ADCs. Afterall the trunk of modern science lies in the earlier civilisations of Asia and Africa. It is also time that due recognition is given to those cultural values from these civilisations which inculcated love and respect for all the living and non-living on the Earth. These values had become part of daily life at a time when environmental pollution and threat to ecological balance were thousands of years away.

In the light of the above discussion, the so-called Earth Summit in Brazil in June 1992, has fallen short of expectations. It is unfortunate that global politics of environment and ecology was played in the true spirit of politics — self-interest of nation-states. Even before the Summit a clear North-South divide on the Earth Charter that was expected to be produced in the Conference had resulted in a deadlock. The charter was being negotiated on the basis of a draft proposed by the LDCs (1977) countries, which raised the basic issues of environmental and economic justice. The North, however, wanted to avoid any serious environment or development issues raised in the Earth Charter. A major block in the North-South negotiations was the "White Man's burden" — the assumption of the West that they have privileged enlightenment and have to raise the non-West out of its state of ignorance (Shiva, 1992). Yet it was not just cultural arrogance but also material opportunism which created blocks in the dialogue on the Earth Charter. The North wanted to have a clean environment for itself, but not for the planet as a whole. It wanted to protect its wasteful lifestyles by exporting the environmental burden to the South and it wanted to increase its political leverage by environmental conditionalities on the South. The other contentious issue between the North and the South was the demand of the latter to include in the Charter reference to the use of weapons of mass destruction to be treated as a crime against both humanity and environment.

The North, however, wanted to avoid any reference to these real threats to the planet and was not prepared to commit itself to financial resources for the LDCs to make the transition to sustainable development. The USA especially did not want to discuss "consumption". With regard to the issue of biosafety and the hazards of genetic engineering the USA got all references to the issues of risks and health and environmental costs deleted. The general attitude of the North at the Earth Summit was that environmental movement was obstructive to economic growth and that it would have a catastrophic impact on the world economy, on jobs, on standard of living and even on health care, and that a tax on fossil fuels could be accompanied by a painful transition period in which the ADCs as well as the LDCs would risk several years of economic stagnation and high unemployment.

The centre of the spiral, as referred to above, therefore, is not willing to make sacrifices, does not want to reduce the speed, and does not want to change the lifestyles it has achieved. As noted earlier, it does not care for the rest of the humanity and is willing to dump some of the negative externalities of its present culture to the rest of the world. This is because changing the course of the trajectory will not make good politics internally within and among the LDCs. The stand taken at the Earth Summit would have a direct political fallout in the USA, where the process of Presidential election is already under way. The politicians in France, Italy and the United Kingdom, where elections have already been completed, could afford to take a slightly different line of action. Their fortunes would not be affected by the fallout of the Earth Summit. That is why President Bush was in a dilemma to attend or not to attend the Summit.

It is not the politicians of the ADCs only who used such an event as the Earth Summit for furthering their political cause but politicians in the DCs and LDCs equally exploited the opportunity to promote their personal and national interests. The LDCs, especially where relatively stronger governments exist as in India, wanted to make their negotiation positions at the international level stronger by talking in terms of State sovereignty over natural resources, and in terms of people's sovereignty, which goes against the spirit of democracy at the global level (Shiva, 1992). That countries, depending upon their level of economic development, jockied for a position where they could be better placed to satisfy their national and personal political interests falls much short of reversing the trend of high consumption and high production, which are at the root of the crisis that homo sapien are heading to. The greatest contribution of the Earth Summit, nevertheless, has been a heightened consciousness about the environment and ecology all over the world, and it can be hoped that it would lead to another Summit in the not too distant a future to attack at the root cause.

REFERENCES

Atkinson, Adrian, (1991). *Principles of Political Ecology*, London: Belhaven Press.

Bryant, Ronald L., (1992). "Political Ecology: An Emerging Research Agenda in Third World Studies", *Political Geography*, 11(1), 12-36.

Dobson, Andrew, (1990) *Green Political Thought*, London: Unwin Hyman.

Hoodbhoy, Pervez, (1991) *Islam and Science*, London: Zed Books Ltd.

Hurst, P., (1990). *Rainforest Political Ecological Destruction in South East Asia*, London: Zed Books Ltd.

Johnston, R.J., (1989). *Environmental Problems: Nature, Economy and State*, London: Belhaven Press.

Mackenzie, W.J.M., (1979). *Biological Ideas in Politics*, Manchester: Manchester University Press.

Martinez-Alier, J., (1987). *Ecological Economics: Energy Environment and Society*, Oxford, Basil Blackwell.

Merton Robert K., (1970). *Science, Technology and Society in Seventeenth Century England*, New York: Howard Fertig.

Saldanha, I.M., (1990). "The Political Ecology of the Traditional Farming Practices in Thana District, Maharashtra (India)", *Journal of Peasant Studies*, 17, 433-443.

Sethi, J.D., (1978). *Gandhi Today*, New Delhi: Vikas.

Sethi, J.D., (1990). *International Economic Disorder and a Gandhian Approach*, Simla: Indian Institute of Advanced Studies.

Shiva, Vandana, (1992). "Why South Greens See Red", *Sunday Times of India*, April 26.

Simmons, I.G., (1987). *The Ecology of Natural Resources*, London: Edward Arnold.

Simpson, Struan, (1990). *Guide to the Environment*, London: Times Books.

11

Decision-Making in Resource Management: Perceptions, Attitudes and Public Participation

BALESHWAR THAKUR

One of the most significant advances in the area of resource management in recent decades has seen in decision-making as it provides insights into resource management strategies and an input into the planning process. This approach is based on how individuals perceive resource management problems and issues, and has developed as a vital research agenda based on years of systematic research. It has a well recognised public policy component. Its importance lies in the recognition that: (a) it provides understanding of the manner in which resources are allocated, (b) the variables that shape policy, and (c) in improving the effectiveness of citizen involvement (Mitchell, 1989, 262). It is also noteworthy that proper decision-making improves the efficiency and productivity of resource use but also clarifies the understanding of the man-environment interaction (O'Riordon, 1971, 109). There is, therefore, a need for an understanding of decision-making process, the behavioural base of the people. The task of resource management decision-making has become ever more complex and multi-dimensional. Perception and attitude contribute significantly to resource management problems. Decision makers collect and process information on the basis of their perceptions of the environment and the available options (Kunreuther and Slovic, 1986, 153). In fact, there has been developing a growing body of research literature on the role of perceptions and attitudes in decision-making (Burton, 1971, 3). Moreover, behavioural geographies tend to view the decision process in the context of uncertainty because environment is imperfectly perceived by man and understanding the attitudes and reactions of the managers and interpreting their responses are the most difficult. Perception studies have been criticised, therefore, for not offering empirical evidence to link individual perceptions of risk to overt behaviour (Mitchell, 1984). However, recently, resource managers have also made breakthrough in trying values and emotions as valid inputs in resource management decisions.

The vast majority of recent studies have focused upon individuals, groups of lay public, technical experts, private and public managers and their responses to resource management problems and issues (Burton, 1971, 3). The value of such studies, of course, is twofold: (1) who has the real decision-making power over the allocation of natural resources? and (2) experts are not the best judges as what is desirable and acceptable option. However, an effort to date has been put forward by resource managers advocating greater citizen participation and public involvement in resource decisions. Moore (1975, 13) noted that no accepted schema, paradigm or model has emerged in the specific area of resources management. But, during the last 20 years, a few descriptive as well as prescriptive models have been developed which have lent considerable insights into the subtleties of decision-making processes. Attitudes and values, both in the developed and developing countries, are changing and becoming more diverse. Similarly, a wide spectrum of information gathered from a large number of diverse sources from digital revolution and satellite technology appears to be available to the decision makers. Faced with such information load, decision makers must take decisions and form judgements carefully. Given this background on the importance of decision-making in resource management, it is worthwhile to: (1) present an overview of decision theory and decision support system, (2) examine the roles perceptions, attitudes, values and emotions play in resource management decision-making, (3) evaluate the nature and limitations of individual and public decision-making in resource allocation and utilization decisions, and (4) assess and evaluate models of decision-making in resource management.

Overview of Decision Theory

Decision theory deals with these variables which influence choices (Edwards and Tversky, 1967). A choice is defined as a search among alternatives and decision made by individuals are governed by the utility, values or attractiveness assigned to spatially located alternatives.

It implies that an individual is characterised as an active decision-maker who processes available information, evaluates it against criteria, compares a sit of alternatives and ultimately selects one which gives the greatest satisfaction. From this point of view, decision theory is viewed as the relative probabilities of choosing among several competing alternatives where a decision-maker selects a problem for decision and produces a number of alternatives (*International Encyclopaedia of the Social Sciences*, 1968, 62-66). In pursuing this goal, the objective is to provide rationale for making wise decisions under conditions of risk and uncertainty. Decisions under uncertainty are typically represented by a payoff matrix, in which the rows correspond to alternative acts that the decision-maker can select and the columns correspond to possible states of nature (Slovie, Kunreuther and White, 1974, 188). The term policy-making is frequently used synonymously which involves choice and collectively for intersecting decisions (Mitchell, 1989). Thus, decision theory focuses upon the individual and the group and postulates a dynamic relationship between people, places and environment by striving towards an interdisciplinary understanding of this interface. This theory draws heavily on the work of economists, psychologists, sociologists, political scientists and mathematicians and currently dominated by the research of geographers (Golledge and Stimson, 1987; Cowlard, 1990; Timmermans and Golledge, 1990). Utility and probability provide the conceptual underpinnings of this theory: utility being concerned with preferences among alternatives, and probability with the likelihood of these preferences being realized (Moore, 1975, 3). A major advance in decision theory came when von Neumann and Mergenstern (1947) developed a formal justification for the expected utility criteria. They showed that, if an individual's preferences satisfied certain basic axioms of rational behaviour, then his decisions could be described as the maximisation of expected utility.

During the past 40 years there has been a profound change in the decision concept from rationality to satisfying and to information processing. In the social sciences man has been variously characterised as : (1) optimiser or rational man or economic man, (2) Freudian or psychological man, and (3) the satisficer or man of bounded rationality. The first two represent two extreme view points. The economic man is considered to have complete knowledge of means (alternates) and ends (goals) and is able to make consistent decisions no matter how complex the situation is. Rational man is seen as model and according to Audley

(1967) is a good basis for the examination of real decisions. As opposed to this is the psychological man who is non-rational and whose behaviour is not predictable. In the real world people are neither completely rational nor completely non-rational, but given imperfect knowledge about reality people make decisions which are nevertheless satisfactory. Applied decision theory assumes that the rational decision-maker wishes to select an action that is logically consistent with his basic preferences for outcomes and his feelings about the likelihoods of the events (Slovic, Kunreuther and White, 1974, 188). In geography, this assumption would mean that farmers have complete knowledge about their environment and choice of crops and cropping practices, even those that are possible only in theory. This has been known as maximization (rationality) hypothesis, where man seeks to reach only one objective—the maximization of utility. This is a normative theory of decision making which is concerned with how a rational decision-maker would act in a given situation. It seeks to discover rules for making decisions which are 'best' (Ilbery, 1978, 451). The best example of a normative theory of decision making is game theory which is concerned with situations which involve choice for two or more players, where the outcome is the joint result of choices made independently by different players (Gould, 1963). But the leading critic of utility maximization has been Simon (1959) who states that the idea of profit maximization is unrealistic because the acquisition of complete knowledge is impossible. According to Simon (1959, 272), "the classical theory is a theory of a man choosing among fixed and known alternatives, to each of which is attached known consequences. But when perception and cognition intervene between the decision-maker and his objective environment, this model no longer proves adequate. We need a description of the choice process that recognizes that alternatives are that given but must be sought; and a description that takes into account the arduous task of determining what consequences will follow on each alternative." Thus, the concept of bounded rationality developed by Simon formed the basis for behavioural approaches to individual decision-making under conditions of uncertainty. This theory postulates that decision-makers do not think probabilistically and that they try to avoid the necessity of facing uncertainty directly (Slovic, Kunreuther and White, 1974, 190). It is also reflected that the goal of the decision-maker is assumed to be the achievement of a satisfactory, rather than a maximum outcome; because he is constrained by limitations of perception and intelligence, the boundedly rational decision-maker is forced to proceed by trial and error (Slovic, Kunreuther and White, 1974, 190). The theory suggests that the aspiration levels tend to adjust to the attainable, and to levels achieved by other individuals with whom he compares himself (Wolpert, 1964, 545). Most recently, Blundon (1977) has enriched the satisficer concept by recognizing the limitations of a decision-maker whose attitudes will be constrained by age, education, experience, socio-economic background, personal traits, personal ambitions, attitudes, belief and interests, as well as the realities of the world in which he exists. During the 1970s, the psychological man's assumptions were also questioned. For example, Tversky and Kahneman (1974) advocated that the majority of individuals have rather limited information processing capabilities and because of these limitations were unlikely to make decisions according to some *a priori* computed optional function.

It is to the decision-making processes that we now turn. Process refers to the sum of particular techniques, methods, procedures and strategies—conscious and unconscious—by which a given decision is made (Robinson and Majok, 1967, 179). Properly speaking, process comprises of how making a decision. Decision-makers collect and process information on the basis of their perceptions of the environment and the available options (Kunreuther and Slovic, 1986, 153). However, their final choice reflects numerous constraints imposed by their limited ability to collect and process information. Kunreuther and Slovic (1986) emphasize three interesting factors that jointly determine the optional choice: (1) the shape of the utility curve, (2) the estimate of probabilities of different states of nature, and (3) the estimates of the consequences associated with each alternative. The term decision support system implies the use of computers to assist managers in their decision processes. The computer plays a key role in facilitating data analysis and standardizing the data bases so that costs and benefits of different programmes are made.

Geographers have also advocated that a decision can be made in a number of different ways, and in this sense it is misleading to talk of the decision process (Moore, 1975, 41). Thus, it is more useful to identify elements of variation in ways of making decisions, moving in the direction of a typology of decision processes. This section presents two meaningful typologies of the major aspects of the decision-making process. First, Thorton (1962) has produced a threefold typology: objectives, context of the decision and methods employed. The goals and objectives of a decision-maker is believed to be important in decision-making as it influences choice and a decision-maker has a complex set of goals which are related to many aspects of his life. A knowledge of these goals is vital to the understanding of the formulation of objectives (Ilbery, 1978, 450). The context of decision-making is based on decision-makers perceived view of reality, which is possibly linked and shaped by his past experiences. In particular, the selectivity of the memory process and emotional associations are also linked. And, finally, a decision-maker searches for a plan of action within its appropriate natural and human environmental context. Robinson and Majok (1967) also identify three types of decision sub-process: intellectual, social and quasi-mechanical. The intellectual part of the process is the analytic aspect of decision-making, which is performed largely by individual and group thought processes (Robinson and Majok, 1967, 180). Increased use of available information with regard to any particular decision is its central objective. The rational optimizing models of economics and the satisficing model of Simon are basic and fundamental intellectual decision processes. The social processes operating in a decision have been particularly important and have received the most widespread attention in decision-making, essentially an effort to bring interaction amongst groups in the decision organisation towards the making of the decision. Moore (1975, 41) identifies a theoretically and practically meaningful concept of cooperation, coalition formation, interest group interaction and interest aggregation as the elements of the social processes. Moore (1975, 41), drawing heavily on Deutsch (1963) has described the flow of information between individuals and groups quite essential in the making of a group decision. The quasi-mechanical processes, of which the best example is the market and price system, are those which are "built into" the system, and are closely related to the decision organisation. Much administrative decision-making is quasi-mechanical. However, it should be stressed that these three types of process do not operate in isolation. As Robinson and Majok (1967, 184) emphasize that "in the final analysis decision-making cannot be understood adequately, or decision outcomes predicted without taking into account all three process types. It is the interaction of these processes, and their cumulative effects, that best explain decision outcomes."

Perceptions and Attitudes in Decision-Making

Perceptions and attitudes provide the means of understanding the bases of decision-making process including risks and biases under uncertain conditions. They play a significant role in decision-making by providing a humanistic outlook and they have emerged as an important component in decision-making since 1960. Behaviouralists dwell upon the perceptions and attitudes among and between resource users and resource managers. The emphasis is upon distinguishing mental maps of problem definition and problem response (Ferguson and Alley, 1984, 37). Therefore, they have become a focus of research in resource management decision-making. The concept of perception and attitude and its relevance to decision-making is not new to geography, and indeed many significant contributions have been made from the standpoint of a number of disciplines (Allport, 1955; Craik, 1968; Lowenthal, 1961; Lynch, 1960; Parsons, 1949; and Sommer, 1969). Geographers have used the term in the sense of how things are seen by people especially with respect to perception of resources or hazards (Burton, 1972; Burton and Kates, 1964; and Saarinen, 1966). Perception is a psychological process. However, psychologists have tended to treat perception as a sub-set of cognition and an inferential process in which a person plays a maximal role in interpreting, categorizing and transforming the stimulus input (Golledge and Stienson 1987, 36). The real world is complex and sends out millions of information signals associated with environment and all aspects of life. An individual receives these signals through his senses of sight, hearing, smell, taste and touch which are of concern to him. In this case, perception can be defined as the ability of the mind to apprehend objects and the processes by which man abstracts and identifies components in his realm of awareness. perception is not simply a function of immediate sensory stimulus, but is the product of the cultural milieu of the sensor, his previous experiences and training, his motivations and social circumstances in which he acts (O'Riordan, 1971, 92-93). Therefore, perception is a highly subjective and fluctuating phenomenon and is influenced by attitudes of the decision-maker.

Attitude is a key variable emphasizing the uniqueness of the individual and his feelings towards and beliefs about an object. Schiff (1971, 8-9) defined an attitude as an organized set of feelings and beliefs which will influence an individual's behaviour towards a given situation. It brings together the internal mental life of man (his cognition, motivations and emotions) and his overt behavioural responses within one framework (Gold, 1980-23). A more comprehensive literature review is available in Golledge and Stempson (1987, 35-51) where it has been focused that attitude are evolutionary through the learning process. O'Riordan (1973) suggests that even if attitudes are changed there is not necessarily going to follow a change in behaviour because there is a gap between stated attitudes and actual behaviour. Schiff (1971, 8) reports the agreements of psychologists that attitudes may be broken into affective, cognitive and behavioural components. The affective component consists of an individual's feelings of liking and disliking the object motivated by desires and values. The cognitive component involves perceiving, knowing and thinking processes by which the individual knows his environment. The behavioural component involves acting, doing and striving relative to the object. Mitchell (1989, 102) noted that individuals organize their affective and cognitive components into an attitudinal system which lead to a predisposition to respond to an object consistent with that system. Therefore, geographers (O'Riordan, 1971) have strongly advocated the attitudinal-based framework within which environmental stimuli are evaluated and acted upon. Attitudes help to guide norms against which judgements can be made and the concern of action set. They are now incorporated routinely along with perception into public policy decision-making. However, attitudes are partly posed and conditioned by values that underlies the various issues and choices.

Values are significant throughout the decision-making process because they strongly influence the objectives that individuals pursue and the means they select for achieving these objectives (Henning and Mangun, 1989, 53). Many executives are strongly attached and devoted to their beliefs or values (Donaldson and Lorch, 1983, 111), "values are individuals or collective conceptions about what in important or desirable with emotional judgmental and symbolic components. Values are formed by groups of attitudes that represent a behavioural predisposition towards a given environmental object. Values encompass goals, beliefs, attitudes and traditions that have significant influence on human interactions and the exercise of power" (Henning and Mangun, 1989, 51-52). Since decision-making is an ongoing, dynamic process and few decisions are of a final nature, values are also constantly changing. In this area, researchers have developed a set of empirical statements that: (a) in most real life situations some values would have to be sacrificed for the sake of others, (b) no one can assume a value-free role in environmental problem solving, (c) old values may be changed or strengthened while few ones are learned, and (d) decision-making occurs against a background of conflicting, personal and organisational pressures (Henning and Mangun, 1989, 53-54). It is also useful to consider attitudes to be linked to emotions which encompasses a wide range of both physiological and mental conditions.

Emotions are a state of excitement that is characterized by strong feeling and usually with both mental and physical manifestations. It is considered as a valid input to decision-making process because it contributes to the ways people reason. Vining and Schroeder (1987), drawing on recent theories of psychology, hold that emotions connected to rational arguments are ignored at a time in which natural resource policy processes are increasingly subjected to intense scrutiny by diverse interest groups. They state that preference data are more easily obtained and interpreted than emotional and provide useful pointers to the relations between emotions and decision-making. It would also appear that public emotional responses to environmental problems are important but poorly understood, interpreted and under-utilized by professional managers. Sometimes, it is difficult to trace and verbalize emotional statements. Conversely, professional managers do not have emotional responses to environmental problems because decisions are made in the legal and scientific milieu (Vining and Schroeder, 1987, 182-83). Their decisions are logical, objective and unemotional; and are highly traceable, justifiable and verbalized. In this context, it should not be forgotten that managers obtain advice from planning staffs which are composed predominantly of technicians and scientists whose professional standards are objective and logical. As a consequence, this process may increase the gap of understanding between professional decision-makers who must rationally justify their decisions and members of the general public who may be emotional in their decisions (Vining and Shroeder, 1987, 182-83). Resource managers and planners, therefore, need to design research in an appropriate manner, so that emotional processes arising in natural resource decision problems can also be understood and linked to decision-making. This is a major task which has not been completed so far.

The Contributions of 'BKW' and 'MOSS' to Resource Management Decision-Making

The geographic work on the role of perception to natural hazards and resource management, one of the most intellectually challenging and socially relevant branches, has its genesis in the study of flood plains and flood problems in the American Middle West by Gilbert White and his students, Ian Burton and Robert Kates (BKW) at the University of Chicago. These people formed the focus of the Natural Hazards Research Group, which became established at the University of Chicago and have made significant additions to its growing literature. The seminal work and massive output of these three scholars provides a benchmark for this field as a whole and much of the theoretical and conceptual background for resource management decision-making derives from their interactions and the inspirations they have provided to the other scholars.

A systematic and policy-oriented research into hazard assessment and hazard reduction began with the work of White (1945), who was the first to recognise that previous heavy expenditures on flood protection—mainly in the form of structural engineering works—had not curbed flood problems. His work on human adjustment to floods views the human response to hazards from a systems perspective and focuses on the interaction between human use of the environment and natural events within the environment (Walmsley and Lewis, 1984, 109). Such works are of immense and enduring value to resource managers in hazard-prone environments in so far as it seeks to emphasize and evaluate adjustment decision strategies in order to arrive at policy recommendations as to the cost-effectiveness of alternative hazard prevention and mitigation techniques (Kates, 1971). The fundamental question asked is: how does man adjust to risk and uncertainty in environments and what does understanding of that process imply for planning? White began by investigating the factors affecting human adjustment to flood plains and applied the theoretical concept of adjustment to the analysis of human responses to hazard. In this research area, adjustments were regarded as actions taken by man to ameliorate or offset the effects of floods. These studies reveal that for individuals choice of adjustments to hazards is a function of perception of the hazard, perception of choice open to them, the command over technology and perceived linkages with other people. Variations from place to place of hazard perception are the result of physical characteristics of the hazard, recency and severity of personal experience with the hazard and personality traits, such as risk taking propensity. Thus, his research activity was concerned primarily with: (1) explanations of why people occupied hazardous areas and how they adjusted to flooding (White, 1945), discussions concerning the extent of development in flood plains (White *et al.*, 1958) and (3) the examinations of the choice processes that flood plain residents and managers undergo in coping with the hazard (White, 1964).

Gilbert White approached the study of perception from the need to understand the management choices that were having a significant impact on natural resources (Whyte, 1986, 240). In fact, the ultimate objective of its study is to provide a better basis for individual and collective choice (White, 1958). It was after the seeming conflicts between the myriad choices of individuals and public policy decisions that he sought to bring to the attention of governments (Whyte, 1986, 240). In discussing certain aspects of resource management, he suggested a distinction between a theoretical range of choices open to any resource user and a more limited range of practical choices (Wood, 1970, 132). The latter partly results from the lack of total awareness by the dwellers. Thus, White moved beyond utilitarian analysis to the boundaries of psychology and economics, contributing geographic field study and experience to the rapidly developing, interdisciplinary study of decision processes (Kates and Burton, 1986, XII). Thus, his intellectual output can be clearly summed as: the concept of human adjustment, its broad theoretical and practical range, and the role of perception and decision-making in resource management (Kates and Burton, 1986, XII). As well as giving an interdisciplinary framework with which to link geography, economics, psychology, geophysics and engineering, his broad-ranging intellect has focused upon decision-making, managers and the goal of human adjustment. A closer examination of his work reveals that over time the scale of his research expanded from the local and the particular natural extremes in the United States to the national and the worldwide range of natural hazards (White, 1974). Burton and Kates (1986, 15) succinctly summarise his research, teaching and leadership: "Through half a century of scientific research and teaching, White has organized detailed studies that exemplify an understated philosophy of cautious 'empirical stewardship'. He has eschewed grand theorizing and polemics for painstaking empirical research, guided by a deep concern for the well-being of people and nature. Much of his effort has gone into distillation and synthesis of findings in a way that can be appreciated and used by those who make policy as well as those who live and work with hazards and resources, demonstrating that such research beginning at the local level can change the world."

Gilbert White, Ian Burton and Robert Kates continued to research alternative strategies for flood hazards until, in 1967, a collaborative study of cross-cultural adjustment to natural hazards was mounted at the University of Chicago (later transferred to the University of Colorado), University of Toronto and Clark University. Innovative hazard research units throughout North America are the Natural Hazards Research and Application Centre, University of Colorado; the International Federation of Institutes of Advanced Study, Toronto; the Centre of Technology, Environment and Development, Clark University and the World Hunger Centre, Brown University. Much valuable research has emanated from these institutions, and since 1970s, the volume of literature in this field has grown rapidly. Early work employed rational theories of individual decision-making and emphasized opportunities for broadening the range of choice; but later studies took more explicit account of the cognitive and behavioural factors that modify decisions about hazards (Mitchell, 1984).

Ian Burton and Robert Kates are probably among the few greatest American contributors to the theory and practice of resource management decision-making. They have emphasized the importance of interdisciplinary work and an effective blend of academic and practical experience. They have linked fruitfully their scholarship with major public-policy issues. They have massively extended the work of White and have shown a strong propensity to rethink his ideas and to change concepts on various occasions. Farmer's perceptions of flood risk in the US and the impact on land use decisions were studied by Burton (1962) and the perception of hazard and choice in flood plain management by urban residents and businessman by Kates (1962). Both applied the theoretical concept of adjustment to the analysis of human responses to hazard. Kates paid particular attention to the ways in which individuals viewed risks and how they reached decisions to reside flood-prone areas. He rejected the frequently used model of economic man and preferred Simon's concept of satisficing notion of bounded rational behaviour. He has also provided a useful summary of this concept in solving complex problems. Kates was among the first to recognise the influence of managerial perception on adjustment decisions. His study highlighted the behavioural basis for decision-making and indicated that the past knowledge and experience is related to the perceived probability distribution of floods. He broke decision processes into three categories—conscious, habitual and unconscious or trivial to explore how individual's approached the risk in an uncertain environment. Burton and Kates (1964) have advanced a set of hypothesis that have since been substantiated on many natural hazards, like variations in hazard perception were explained in terms of the relation of the hazard to the dominant resource use, and the frequency of occurrence of the hazard and variations in degree of personal experience is directly related to resource use. It has been revealed that differences in the physical characteristics of extreme natural events can strongly influence the perception of hazard. Burton and Kates (1964) have indicated that hazard perception is related to the frequency of such events and it is an important factor affecting resource manager decisions. Although the importance of perception is widely acknowledged, comparatively little is known about other factors which influence the process of adjustment. Burton, Kates and White (1968) have suggested that age, education, socio-economic status and experience exert little influence on adoption decisions.

Another notable direction in the evolution of hazard perception studies was the extension of the work done on flood plains to coastal storms and hurricane hazards along the shores of the coastal megalopolis of the north-eastern United States (Burton, Kates and Snead, 1969). It has been confirmed that persons with greater experience of floods and droughts tend to perceive and adopt more adjustments (Burton, 1962; Kates, 1962; Burton, Kates and Snead, 1969). Kates (1971) summarised various elements and relationships involve in adjustment to natural hazards in the form of a general system model. This model depicts three initial inputs: the physical environment, the human use system and the characteristics of those people deemed to be managers of the environment at some decision-making level. These interact to produce three processes: the hazard, the perception of hazard and adjustment. This approach demonstrates continuation of White's earlier work on identifying the range of theoretical and actual adjustment in the human occupancy of flood plains. It is a descriptive model of how information about hazard is processed from the point of view of resource management. Another development in hazard perception was to study "all hazards-at-a-place" instead of considering each hazard in isolation and the choice of adjustment to it. This study was done in London, Ontario (Hewitt and Burton, 1971).

A major emphasis is the importance of the co-existence in time and space of a natural event and a human use domain as the basis for an ecological approach to hazards study. Thus, in the search for better hazard management policies, formulation of human ecological models of hazard, identification of opportunities for intervention, assessment of alternative courses of action, and expansion of the range of choice that is available to decision-makers have become important features of subsequent research on a wide variety of hazards at regional, national and international levels (Burton, Kates and White, 1978; Kates, Hohenemser and Kasperson, 1984; White, 1974; White and Haas, 1975). Recently, several researchers have extended the research paradigm to analyze global environmental change (Burton, 1987; Kates, 1987; Kates, Ausubel and Berberian, 1985); unfortunately, the role of human agency has been largely neglected, and little attempt has been made to address the task of providing information that might be useful for managing the risks of long-term global change (Mitchell, 1989; 410-421).

The 'MOSS' group of resource managers includes Bruce Mitchell, University of Waterloo (Canada), Timothy O'Riordan, University of East Anglia (U.K.), Thomas F. Saarinen, University of Arizona (U.S.A.) and W.R. Derrick Sewell, University of Victoria (Canada). A striking common features of the careers of all four is that they have emphasized perceptions and attitudes in resource decision-making, behavioural and institutional analyses, and resource management model building and theory development for three decades of their careers. In all cases, however, as nature scholars they have paid increasing attention to the context within which policy is formulated and implemented and to the identification of basic research issues and natural resource policy concerns. Complex theoretical, methodological and policy questions raised by them have stimulated a significant degree of interdisciplinary liaison between geographers, psychologists, economists, engineers and planners. As a student at the University of Chicago and as White's intellectual heir, Saarinen shared the same spirit for perception as a factor in resource management and hazard studies. Saarinen's (1966) study on drought hazard perception in the Great Plains of the United States marked an important deviation from the BKW group of work although it came from the same Chicago School of Geography, Saarrinen studied drought, not floods, focusing on the other end of the spectrum of evapo-transpiration. This study is based on a large questionnaire and a Thematic Apperception Test (TAT).

(TAT). He adopted an explicitly psychological explanatory mode—that of the individual farmer's personality in relation to his age and drought experience (Whyte, 1986, 242). He has confirmed that perception of drought varies with degree of aridity and perception is important in the decision-making process to extent that it influences the learning processes whereby the images of the decision environment are determined (Saarinen, 1969). He not only presents an excellent review of environment perception studies to 70, but also discusses the design of a standard questionnaire, the basic tool in attitude and perception studies (Saarinen, 1971). Darrick Sewell carved his world-wide reputation in the resource management field through his work in water resources and perception and attitude studies. Sewell's (1965) study of water management in the Fraser River basin is a pioneering work in hazard perception and choice. He suggests that for any given hazard, a large number of adjustments are theoretically possible but, in practice, only a few are usually known to individual managers. His emphasis on the appropriate role of various participants in the decision-making process, and specifically, how their views are brought to hear in that process is valuable (Sewell, 1971). Sewell's writings were not confined to North American waters, however, he made a significant contribution to the development and management of the Mekong River. He also wrote extensively about issues of water management and planning both in Canada and abroad (Windsor, 1993, 227-277). Equally important in establishing his credentials as one of the foremost specialists in resource management are his study of conflict resolution and jurisdictional disputes of the assessment of social values (Dearden, 1989). O'Riordan is the active practitioner of resource management, as he laid the groundwork for interdisciplinary focus by emphasizing: first on the problems of resource allocation and particularly the 'question of identifying and measuring the important extra-market effects of resource decisions; and secondly, the decision-making process whereby resources are evaluated and allocated both by the professional resource manager and by the individual citizen (O'Riordan, 1971). This takes place according to the needs, aspirations, and desires of man over space and time within the framework of his technological inventiveness, his political and social institutions, and his legal and administrative arrangements (O'Riordan, 1971, 19). Evaluation and efficiency are his watchwords and the process of decision making is the unit of study emphasizing managerial information, perception, attitudes and behaviour. In the same book, O'Riordan presents a strategy for public involvement based on incremental decision-making through constant interaction between public interest groups and administrators yet, beyond this important work, one of the most significant advances has been the development of a model to describe the manner in which stress is handled by resource managers (O'Riordan, 1971a).

The most substantial contribution to the thematic research focusing on the behavioural theme in resource management has been by Mitchell (1989). Institutional arrangements, policy and decision-making processes, perceptions and attitudes and public involvement are catchwords in his innovative approaches to resource management problems. In a review of this research area, Mitchell (1980) noted that models have yet to lead to the generation of a geographical theory of natural resources management. He suggested that the basic weakness in resource analysis research is lack of understanding of basic processes and relationships. O'Riordan (1981) also observed that little progress has been realized in developing a theory which interrelates demands with collective necessities. The research is piecemeal and lacks in either a theoretical or policy-oriented framework. Mitchell (1989, 294) suggested to focus upon the understanding of the crucial variables associated with biophysical and social processes linked to resource management. Another criticism of behavioural resource geography approach is that its contributors neglect to ask about the sources of values and beliefs affecting behaviour or the processes through which belief systems are maintained (Emel and Roberts, 1989).

Other Recent Work

In addition to the areas included about several general studies can be singled out in this broader context. Decision-making in land use and land management is an extremely complex process. Use of land reflect human decisions, and an understanding of land use patterns requires an understanding of these decisions. Ilbery (1978) suggested that land uses may be unaware of the bases of their decisions, being unknowingly influenced by factors they have never recognised. Since decision-making process in agriculture has a spatial dimension, many of the factors affecting decision behaviour may be expected to differ spatially. Increasingly, geographers have demonstrated two kinds of management decisions: policy-making or large-term decisions, and organisational or day-to-day decisions (Morgan and Munton, 1971). They are of the view that land use patterns are mainly affected by long-term decisions, as major agricultural decisions have to be made by particular dates and seasons. Fortunately, research has resulted in an increased awareness that the role of risk and uncertainty in decision-making is more important for the peasant family farm than for modern industrial farm in developed countries (Low, 1974; Wiens, 1977).

McIver (1970) uses a modified version of White's model of resource management decision-making as its analytical framework to find out how much people know about their community water supply and what factors influence their preference in choosing among future alternatives in south-western Ontario. Again, following White of examining how people make their choices in managing water, Kroman and White (1984) have developed a rich empirical data base on preferences for adjustments to reduce depletion of the High Plains Aquifer among populations of the High Plains States. Research has confirmed that the perception and behaviour characteristics of floodplain users in Britain are similar to those in the United States (Smith and Tobin, 1979); but the links between perception research results and policy development in Britain have been tenuous and less than originally expected (Parker and Penning-Rowsell, 1983).

Borrowing behavioural concepts and methods previously used in the analysis of environmental hazards, geographers have helped explain the choices people make that affect their consumption of residential energy. Attitudes, beliefs, values, personality, habit and information flows all have been shown to be significant predictors of home energy conservation behaviour (Macey and Brown, 1983). Jackson (1980) has argued that the success of energy conservation programmes ultimately depends upon the responsiveness of consumers to government incentives as well as on public perception of energy problems.

The study of perception in taking on increasing importance in recreational resource management. As elsewhere in the field, this is occurring because the role of communications, values information available to the individual, and other factors are clearly of importance in influencing the kinds of recreational decisions made. Perception studies by recreation resource managers are many. Ewing and Kulka (1979) investigated ski-resort attractiveness and provided an in-depth analysis of a specific type of facility. Jackson and Schinkel (1981) considered different perceptions of activity preferences between resident and tourist campus in a specific area. Recreation planners and managers are unlikely to make optional decisions unless they are aware of recreationists perceptions, needs and preferences. Recreational choices reflect an underlying set of preferences and perceptions which enter into recreational decision-making in a variety of ways (Jackson, 1989, 131). Recreational use of domestic water supply reservoirs, scenic areas and forest has received increasing attention and constitutes important themes in recreation research and management which previously had not been included in management strategy. Thus, the recent upsurge of interest in water-based recreation has created an interesting pattern of user and institutional conflict over the protection or development of public water supply reservoirs in the United States and Australia (Baumann, 1969, Dunn, 1993).

Brookfield (1969) explored the potential of perception studies to understand resource utilization, the role of new information, decision-making and change in a traditional society. However, perception studies have been criticized for not offering empirical evidence to link individual perceptions of risk to overt behaviour (Mitchell, 1984). A recent review by Fischhoff, Svenson and Slovic (1987) links this problem to a lack of theoretical cohesion for a plethora of piecemeal empirical studies. Yet, perception and behaviour elements are now regularly incorporated into natural hazards research, water management, land management and outdoor recreation and public policy decision-making.

Public Participation

The basic question as to who makes decisions and pays greater attention to more comprehensive resource and environmental management has received considerable attention (Erickson, 1980; Mitchell, 1989; Nelson, 1982; Sadler, 1981; Smith, 1982). In this respect the distinction between individual resource managers and the public is relevant. Essentially, individual decisions are governmental political decisions made by politicians, judges, bureaucrats or experts who are acting as leaders, representatives or employees of all the people in the territory in which their authority is applicable (Moore, 1975, 5). On the other hand, public or citizen decisions are made by groups or individuals in attempting to maximise their utility functions. A group decision represents same synthesis of a set of individual decisions. According to Whyte (1986, 263) the contribution of ordinary people's perceptions and knowledge to better decision-making and public policy has been the enduring theme in environmental perception research. Public participation is generally defined as that part of the decision-making process which provides opportunity and encouragement for the public to express its view (Henning and Mangun, 1989, 61). The public actively shares and participates in the decisions that experts or government makes in resource utilization and allocation; but their useful participation is contingent upon the supply of non-technical information and opportunities to use that information. Furthermore, surveys of public viewpoints can provide basic information which the managers and experts can consider when making decisions (Mitchell, 1989, 122). Participation typically includes suggestions, question, information, views and critiques. They are made through both formal and informal participatory processes and may be solicited or unsolicited (Henning and Mangun, 1989, 61). The EPA has suggested that public participation should: (1) promote the public's understanding and involvement in planning and implementing programmes and proposed actions with emphasis on the non-technical aspects; (2) keep the public informed about significant issues, problems, and changes in programmes or proposed subjects, including associated values and alternatives; (3) make sure that government and personnel understand public concerns and values and that they are responsive to them; (4) demonstrate that the agency consults with interested or affected segments of the public and takes public viewpoints and values into consideration when decisions are made; (5) foster public involvement and activities that focus on identifying problems, laying out and exploring all of the alternatives to resolving the problems, and setting forth a preferred alternative; (6) foster a spirit of mutual trust, support and openness between government, personnel and the public through a variety of informal and formal contacts for public participation (Henning and Mangun, 1989, 61-62). Even more interesting are five basic functions needed to ensure effective public participation: identification, outreach, dialogue, assimilation, and feedback (Henning and Mangun, 1989, 62-63). Behavioural analyses are increasingly important in studying participation. Combined with that is a realization that public participation permits a wide variety of values to be articulated and analyzed, including people's perceptions and attitudes. However, it must be stressed that the degree of public participation depends upon both the general attitudes of the government and the interests of the public.

Another resource manager has recently explored and provided ways and guidelines for the development of an effective public participation programme (Mitchell, 1989, 117-20). Impetus for this effort largely can be attributed to the emergence of more effective and equitable resource allocation process. Attempts at participation programme have proceeded in six ways: (1) What degree of public involvement is desirable and feasible? (2) which segments of the public should be consulted? (3) at which points in the planning and policy processes should public input be sought? (4) What are the components of a good public participation programme? (5) which public participation mechanism are most effective in given situations? and (6) how the time needed for public participation programmes can be balanced against the desire to reduce the time and cost to make decision?

The last four decades have seen much fieldwork in perception and perception studies as a part of development strategy. The studies have articulated for the silent majority as well as for illiterate peasants, their local knowledge and their preferences (Whyte, 1986, 263). However, according to Sewell (1971) neither public participation nor perception and attitude studies represent a panacea for resource management problems. He is also of the view that there is possibility of introducing bias into responses, the variations in meanings of various terms to different people, the tendency of information to quickly get out of date, the impact of continuous sampling of a given population on responses, and the scarcity of competent personnel to conduct studies. These issues have emerged recently, and they have to be overcome if perception and attitude studies are to be useful to resource managers (Mitchell, 1989, 122). Saarinen (1976, 157) suggests that some managers are both to involve the general public because they fear it would make decision-making cumbersome, inefficient, or perhaps even impossible. It must also be emphasized that the making of a public decision or citizen involvement represents a redistribution of power from the managers to the public, while in developing countries this may not happen because power is concentrated in the hands of a few bureaucrats. O'Riordan (1971) suggests that "public attitudes and actions towards resource management problems are after divergent, decision-makers are reluctant to include public perceptions in their plans." He is also of the opinion that "public attitudes are dependent upon external stimuli, among which is the amount of relevant information available to the public, but does not examine how such information is received, interpreted and assessed by the public. Thus, the inclusion of public values the resource management strategy is absolutely critical.

Development of Models in Decision-Making

Models in resource management decision-making fall into two broad classes. The first category may be called descriptive, and the second prescriptive. The descriptive model is concerned with the making of decisions as to how decisions are made? or, how do people go about making choices. This model attempts to understand how the process actually works. On the other hand, the prescription or normative model seeks to demonstrate how policy making should occur relative to pre-established standards (Mitchell, 1989, 264). This model is comprehensive, rational, detached and unemotional. The main feature of descriptive models is that they reject the concept of economic man and favour Simon's (1959) idea of the boundedly rational person who satisfies rather than maximizes. As Mitchell (1989, 265) explains, in descriptive model, alternatives are not fixed and known goals may be vague and inconsistent, and information may be incomplete or lacking.

To this effect, a significant initial framework was White's (1961, 1966) hazard perception model. Rather than contribute by theorizing about how decisions ought to be made, White has sought to formulate a model of how actual decisions are made in resource management. In this context, the descriptive model on the range of choice was produced by White. White has identified six components of decision-making: (1) perceived range of choice, (2) resource estimates, (3) available technology, (4) economic efficiency, (5) spatial linkages, and (6) social guides. The strength of White's model is its focus on how decisions were reached in terms of perceived range of choice, estimate nature of resource and constraints based upon economic, technological, spatial and social considerations (Mitchell, 1989, 273). Thus, White emphasized the role of the decision-makers perception of the range of possible choices, and the impact this has upon the final decision. White (1966, 108-109) further defined this range of choices in terms of attitudes, "attitudes enter into decisions in three ways: first there are the personal attitudes of the people sharing in the decision; second, are their opinions as to what others prefer; third, are their opinions as to what others should prefer". Within this context, his model has been used as a benchmark upon which a number of stress models were developed. Kasperson (1969) dealt with the perceptions and attitudes of politicians in making resource management decisions. He developed a descriptive model of municipal stress management to explore the role of various groups in the policy and decision processes towards drought occurrence in Massachusetts. The model describes the process through which municipal managers evaluate and respond to stresses. The strength of this model is its focus on the managers perception and evaluation of the stress, understanding the characteristics of the municipal political system and the behavioural characteristics of the participants with an effort to appraise the resource management process. This model was also adopted by McIver (1970) in his study of the choice of alternative sources of water supply in the Grand River basin. O'Riordan (1971) also stresses the role of the decision-makers perception in his "deliberately simple and descriptive" model of decision-making in resource management which focuses mainly upon four principal stages: information strategy, decision and evaluation. Each of them is interconnected by feedback loops. It is demonstrated that decision-making is an on-going process, where decisions of the past are usually reflected in decisions of the present, and where the outcomes of any present decision affect the basis for any future choice (O'Riordan, 1971, 113-14).

Prescriptive models establish an ideal against which actual policy processes may be assessed. They help to draw the attention of those areas which are not covered sufficiently, and thereby specify where the resource manager should focus to ameliorate the allocation process. A study of water transfers in England and Wales illustrates how a prescriptive model may be used in evaluating resource policy (Mitchell, 1971). He has provided the most notable contributions to our understanding of the policy and decision-making processes. As Mitchell (1971, 2-3) explained the process, "before deciding upon a plan, it is necessary that objectives should be determined on the basis of criteria and constraints under which the decision-maker must operate. Having determined a set of objectives, the decision-maker then must consider the various methods or strategies with which objectives should be gained...... After establishing the problem, objectives, criteria, constraints, alternative strategies and programmes of action, the decision-maker must estimate the possible consequences of any course of action before choosing a plan which appears to best meet the given circumstances. This plan will subsequently be implemented, and then the decision-maker must observe the outcome in case it is necessary to make adjustments to overcome unforeseen results". Sewell (1973) has presented a model involving a series of interconnected steps among which there is continuous feedback. The model envisages progressive levels of responsibility in decision-making including identification of problems, consideration of constraints, delineation of potential solutions, formulation of alternative strategies, appraisal of alternatives, selection of a solution and hindsight review following implementation. Sewell's main purpose in outlining the model is to provide a framework in which to discuss various evaluation techniques and the way in which these may be improved, thereby making the decision-making process more efficient. He suggests that one of the major reasons the hindsight reviews are not undertaken by the agencies "may be rooted in a fear that the findings of such evaluations might result in criticism of the management agency or its personnel. Apart from those models of the decision-making process discussed above, a few other models (Aldskogius, 1977) on recreational decision-making merit attention.

Conclusions

The following conclusions are derived from the above review. *First*, the emphasis on the decision-maker has been a key factor in studies of resource management, therefore, it becomes essential to find out who they are and what their attitudes are towards the resources. *Secondly*, it is clear that perceptions and attitudes studies are how incorporated into public policy decision-making, but, the precise role of values and emotions are not worked out. *Thirdly*, it has been generally agreed that public should participate more in resource management decisions, though they are generally unspecific as to the precise role the public should play, apart from providing information in the form of public opinion polls. *Fourthly*, its contributors have ignored to ask about the sources of attitudes and beliefs affecting behaviour or the processes through which belief systems are maintained. *Fifthly*, although in recent years geographic studies have added considerably to our knowledge in the subfield of locational, consumer and residential decision-making and have increased our understanding of the decision-making process, such model-building in resource management decision-making is poorly developed. The decision-making models in resource management lack rigorous theoretical framework and are still in the early stages of development and verification. Since the decision-making is highly complex and is affected by a large number of behavioural variables, it appears appropriate to identify individually all pertinent variables. The number of variables is great and the number of possible relationships between them is astronomical, as is the possibility of variations in these relationships. *Sixthly*, this review concludes that here lies a vast and relatively uncharted area of research for Third World resource developers and managers in the testing and modification of their models.

REFERENCES

Aitken, S.C., Catter, S.L. Foote, K.E. and Sell, J.L. (1989). "Environmental Perception and Behavioural Geography", in G.L. Gaile and C.J. Willmott (eds.) *Geography in America*, Columbus: Merrill Publishing Company, 218-38.

Aldskogius, H. (1977). "A Conceptual Framework and a Swedish case study of Recreational Behaviour and Environmental Cognition", *Economic Geography*, 53 : 163-83.

Allport, F.H. (1955). *Theories of Perception and the Concept of Structure*, New York: John Wiley.

Alston, R.M. and Freeman, D.M. (1975). "The Natural Resources Decision Maker and Political and Economic Man: Towards a Synthesis", *Journal of Environmental Management*, 3 : 167-83.

Audley, R.J. (1967). *Decision-Making*, London: BBC.

Ayoade, J.O. and Akintola, F.O. (1980). "Public Perception of Flood Hazard in Two Nigerian Cities", *Environment International*, 4 : 277-80.

Baumann, D. (1969). The Recreational Use of Domestic Water Supply Reservoirs: Perception and Choice. Research Paper No. 121, Department of Geography, University of Chicago, Chicago.

Blunden, J. (1977). Rural Land Use in Fundamentals of Human Geography, Section II, Spatial Analysis, D204 Open University, Milton Keynes.

Borton, T.E. and Warner, K.P. (1971). "Involving citizens in Water Resources Planning : the Communication-Participation Experiment in the Susquehanna River Basin", *Environment and Behaviour*, 3 : 284-306.

Bradley, M.D. (1973). "Decision-making for Environmental Resource Management", *Journal of Environmental Management*, 1 : 289-302.

Brookfield, H.C. (1969). "On the Environment as Perceived", *Progress in Geography*, 1 : 51-80.

Burton, I. (1962). Types of Agricultural Occupance of Flood Plains in the U.S., Research Paper No. 75, Department of Geography, University of Chicago, Chicago.

Burton, I. (1971). "The Social Role of Attitude and Perception Studies", in W.R.D. Sewell and I. Burton (eds.) *Perceptions and Attitudes in Resources Management*, Ottawa : Information Canada, 1-6.

Burton, I. (1972). "Cultural and Personality Variables in the Perception of Natural Hazards", in J.F. Wohlwill and M. Carson (ed.) *Environment and the Social Sciences: Perspectives and Applications*, Washington, D.C.

Burton, I. (1987). "Our Common Future: The World Commission on Environment and Development", *Environment*, 29 : 25-29.

Burton, I. and Kates, R.W. (1964). "The Perception of Natural Hazards in Resource Management", *Natural Resources Journal*, 3(2) : 412-41.

Burton, I., Kates, R.W. and White, G.F. (1968). The Human Ecology of Extreme Geophysical Events, Natural Hazard Research Working Paper No. 1, Department of Geography, University of Toronto, Toronto.

Burton, I., Kates, R.W. and Snead, R.E. (1969). The Human Ecology of Coastal Flood Hazard in Megalopolis, Research Paper No. 115, Department of Geography, University of Chicago, Chicago.

Burton, I., Kates, R.W. and White, G.F. (1978). The Environment as Hazard. New York: Oxford University Press.

Burton, I. and Kates, R.W. (1986). "Introduction" in R.W. Kates and I. Burton (eds.) Geography, Resources and Environment: Vol. II Themes from the Work of G.F. White, Chicago: University of Chicago Press, 1-16.

Churchill, R.A. and Hutchinson, D.M. (1984). "Flood Hazard in Ratnapura, Sri Lanka: Individual Attitudes vs. Collective Action", *Geoforum*, 15 : 517-24.

Cowlard, K. (1990). *Decision-Making in Geography : A Manual of Method and Practice*. London : Edward Arnold.

Craik, K.H. (1968). "The Comprehension of the Everyday Physical Environment", *Journal of the American Institute of Planners*, 34 : 29-37.

Davis, R.K. (1968). *The Range of Choice in Water Management*. Baltimore : Johns Hopkins University Press.

Dearden, P. (1989). "W. R. Derrick Sewell and Wilderness". *Natural Resources Journal*, 29 : 1-8.

Deutsch, K.W. (1963). *The Nerves of Government: Models of Political Communication and Control*. New York : Free Press.

Dolman, A.J. (ed.) (1980). *Global Planning and Resource Management: Towards International Decision-Making in a Divided World*. New York: Pergamon.

Donaldson, G. and Lorch, J.W. (1983). *Decision-Making at the Top*. New York: Basic Books.

Dunn, J. (1993). "Decision-Making Concerning the Recreational Use of New South Wales Domestic Water Supply Reservoirs", in H.D. Foster (ed.), *Advances in Resource Management : Tributes to W.R. Derrick Sewell*. London : Belhaven Press, 335-46.

Edwards, W. and Tversky, A. (1967). *Decision-Making Harmondsworth*. Penguin.

Emel, J. and Roberts, R.(1989). "Ideologies of Property : Property Rights in Texas and New Mexico Groundwater Resources", *Economic Geography*, 65.

Emel, J. and Peet, R. (1989). "Resource Management and Natural Hazards", in R. Peet and N. Thrift (eds.). *New Models in Geography : The Political Economy Perspective*. London : Unwin Hyman, 49-76.

Erickson, D.L. (1980). "Public Involvement in Resource Agency Decision-Making", *Journal of Soil and Water Conservation*, 35 : 224-9.

Ewing, G.D. and Kulka, T. (1979). "Revealed and stated Preference Analysis of Ski-Resort Attractiveness", *Leisure Sciences*, 2 : 249-75.

Ferguson, A. and Alley, J. (1984). "Resource Geography : Is There a Shape to the Terrain?" *The Operational Geographer*, 5 : 36-38.

Fischhoff, B., Svenson, O., and Slovic, P. (1987). "Active Responses to Environmental Hazards : Perceptions and Decision-Making", in D. Stokols and I. Altman (eds.) *Handbook of Environmental Psychology*, Vol. 2. New York : John Wiley, 1089-1133.

Freeman, A.M. (1969). "Advocacy and Resource Allocation Decisions in the Public Sector", *Natural Resources Journal*, 9 : 166-75.

Gardner, J.E. (1989). "Decision-Making for Sustainable Development : Selected Approaches to Environmental Assessment and Management", *EIA Review*, 9 : 337-66.

Goveling, T. and Golledge, R. (1988). "Environmental Perception and Cognition", in E. Zube and G. Moore (eds.), *Advances in Environmental Behaviour and Design*, Vol. 2, New York : Plenum Press, 203-38.

Gold, J.R. (1980). *An Introduction to Behavioural Geography*. Oxford : Oxford University Press.

Golledge, R.G. and Steinson, R.J. (1987). *Analytical Behavioural Geography*. London : Croom Helm.

Gould, P.R. (1963). "Man against his Environment : A Game Theoretic Framework", *Annals of the Association of American Geographers*, 53 : 290-7.

Grima, A.P. (1972). *Residential Water Demand : Alternative Choices for Management*. Toronto : University of Toronto Press.

Hendee, J.C., Clark, R.N. and Stankey, G.H. (1974). "A Framework for Agency use of Public Input in Resource Decision-Making", *Journal of Soil and Water Conservation*, 29 : 60-66.

Henning, D.H. and Mangun, W.R. (1989). *Managing the Environmental Crisis: Incorporating Competing Values in Natural Resource Administration*. Durham: Duke University Press.

Hewitt, K. and Burton, I. (1971). *The Hazardousness of a Place : A Regional Ecology of Damaging Events*. Toronto: University of Toronto Press.

Ilbery, B.W. (1978). "Agricultural Decision-Making: A Behavioural Perspective", *Progress in Human Geography*, 2 : 448-66.

Ilbery, B.W. Foster, I.D.L. and Donoghune, P.J. (1982). "Perception and Water Quality : A Geographical Perspective", *Progress in Physical Geography*, 6 : 524-40.

International Encyclopaedia of the Social Sciences (1968), Vol. 4, in D.L. Sills (ed.) *Decision-Making*. New York : Growell-Collier and Macmillan.

Jackson, E.L. (1980). "Perceptions of Energy Problems and the Adoption of Conservation Practices in Edmonton and Calgary", *Canadian Geographer*, 24 : 114-30.

Jackson, E.L. (1989). "Perceptions and Decisions", in G. Wall (ed.) *Outdoor Recreation in Canada*. Toronto : John Wiley and Sons, 75-132.

Jackson, E.L. and Schinkel, D.R. (1981). "Recreational Activity Preferences of Resident and Tourist Campers in the Yellow Knife Region", *Canadian Geographer*, 25 : 350-64.

Johnson, J.F. (1972). Attitudes Toward Renovated Waste Water as an Alternative Source for Municipal Water Supply, Research Paper, Department of Geography, University of Chicago, Chicago.

Juvick, S.P. (1986). The Role of the State in Resource Use Decision-Making: The Case of the Moomba-Sydney Gas Pipeline", *Australian Geographical Studies*, 24 : 57-71.

Kasperson, R.E. (1990a). "Environmental Stress and the Municipal Political System", in R.E. Kasperson and J.V. Minghi (eds.), *The Structure of Political Geography*. Chicago : Aldine, 481-96.

Kasperson, R.E. (1969a). "Political Behaviour and the Decision-Making Process in the Allocation of Water Resources between Recreational and Municipal Uses", *Natural Resources Journal*, 9 : 176-211.

Kates, R.W. (1962). Hazard and Choice Perception in Flood Plain Mnagement, Research Paper No. 78, Department of Geography, University of Chicago, Chicago.

Kates. R.W. (1967). "The Perception of Storm Hazard on the shares of the Megalopolis", in D. Lowenthal (ed.), *Environmental Perception and Behaviour*, Research Paper No. 109, Department of Geography, University of Chicago, Chicago, 60-74.

Kates, R.W. (1971). "Natural Hazards in Human Ecological Perspective: Hypotheses and Models", *Economic Geography*, 47 : 438-45.

Kates, R.W. (1987). "The Human Environment: The Road Not Taken, the Road Still Beckoning", *Annals of the Association of American Geographers*, 77 : 525-34.

Kates, R.W., Hohenemser, C. and Kasperson, J.X. (1984). *Perilous Progress: Technology as Hazard*. Boulder, Co. : Westview Press.

Kates, R.W., Ausubel, J.H., and Berberian, M. (eds.) (1985). Climate Impact Assessment, Scope Report No. 27, New York: John Wiley.

Kates, R.W., and Burton, I. (1986). "The Great Climacteric, 1798-2048: The Transition to a Just and Sustainable Human Environment", in R.W. Kates and I. Burton (eds.), *Geography, Resources and Environment*, Vol. 2, Chicago : University of Chicago Press, 339-60.

Kromm, D.E. and White, S.E. (1984). "Adjustment Preferences to Groundwater Depletion in the American High Plains", *Geoforum* 15 : 271-84.

Kunreuther, H. and Slovic, P. (1986). "Decision-Making in Hazard and Resource Management", in R.W. Kates and I. Burton (eds.), *Geography, Resources and Environment*, Vol. 2. Chicago: University of Chicago Press, 153-187.

Lord, W.B. and Warner, M.L. (1973). "Aggregates and External Information Needs for Public Natural Resource Decision-Making", *Natural Resources Journal*, 13 : 106-17.

Low, A.R. (1974). "Decision-Making under Uncertainty : A Linear Programming Model of Peasant Farmer Behaviour", *Journal of Agricultural Economics*, 25 : 311-21.

Lowenthal, D. (1961). "Geography, Experience and Imagination: Towards a Geographical Epistemology", *Annals of the Association of American Geographies*, 51 : 241-60.

Lynch, K. (1960). *The Image of the City*. Cambridge, Mass : MIT Press.

Macey, S.M. and Brown, M.A. (1983). "Residential Energy Conservation : The Role of Past Experience in Repetitive Household Behaviour", *Environment and Behaviour*, 15 : 123-42.

McIver, I. (1970). Urban Water Supply Alternatives : Perception and Choice in the Grand Basin, Ontario, Research Paper No. 126, Department of Geography, University of Chicago, Chicago.

Mercer, D.C. (1971). "The Role of Perception in the Recreational Experience: A Review and Discussion", *Journal of Leisure Research*, 3 : 261-76.

Mercer, D.C. (1974). "Perception in Outdoor Recreation", in P. Lavery (ed.), *Recreational Geography*. Devon : David and Charles, 51-69.

Mitchell, B. (1971). "A Famework for Decision-Making in Water Management: A Review and Commentary", Geographical Inter-University Resource Management Seminar No. 3, Department of Geography, Waterloo Lutheran University, Waterloo.

Mitchell, B. (1976). "Decision-Making and Consultation in Resource Management : The B.C. Salmon Fishery", *Journal of Environmental Management*, 4 : 211-23.

Mitchell, B. (1980). "Models of Resource Management", *Progress in Human Geography*, 4(1) : 32-52.

Mitchell, B. (1989). *Geography and Resource Analysis*, 2nd Edition, Harlow : Longman.

Mitchell, J.K. (1974). Community Response to Coastal Erosion : Individual and Collective Adjustments Hazard on the Atlantic Shore, Research Paper No. 156, Department of Geography, University of Chicago, Chicago.

Mitchell, J.K. (1974). "Natural Hazards Research", in I.R. Manners and M.W. Mikesell (eds.), *Perspectives on Environment*, Commission on College Geography, Publication No. 13, Association of American Geographers, Washington, D.C. 311-41.

Mitchell, J.K. (1984). "Hazard Perception Studies: Covergent Concerns and Divergent Approaches during the Past Decade", in T.F. Saarinen, D. Seamon and J.L. Sell (eds.) *Environmental Perception and Behaviour: An Inventory and Prospect*, Research Paper No. 209, Department of Geography, University of Chicago, Chicago, 33-59.

Mitchell, J.K. (1989). "Hazards Research", in G.L. Gaile and C.J. Willmott (eds.), *Geography in America*, Columbus : Merrill Publishing Company, 410-24.

Mohai, P. (1987). "Public Participation and National Decision Making", *Natural Resources Journal*, 27 : 123-55.

Moore, P.W. (1975). "Public Decision-Making and Resource Management : A Review", Discussion Paper Series No. 17, Department of Geography, University of Toronto, Toronto.

Morgon, W.B. and Munton, R.J.C. (1971). *Agricultural Geography*. London : Methuen.

Murphy, P.E. (1980). "Perceptions and Preferences of Decision-Making Groups in Tourist Centres: A Guide to Planning Strategy? In *Tourism Planning and Development Issues*. Washington: George Washington University Press.

Nelson, J.G. (1982). "Public Participation in Comprehensive Resource and Environmental Management", *Science and Public Policy*, 9 : 240-50.

O'Riordan, T. (1971a). *Perspectives on Resource Management*. London : Pion.

O'Riordan, T. (1971b). "Public Opinion and Environmental Quality: A Reappraisal", *Environment and Behaviour*, 3 : 191-214:

O'Riordan, T. (1972). "Decision-Making and Environmental Quality: An Analysis of a Water Quality Issue in the Shuswap and Okanagan Valleys, British Columbia", in *Okanagan Water Decisions*, Western Geographical Series, Vol. 4, Department of Geography, University of Victoria, Victoria, I-III.

O'Riordan, T. (1976). "Attitudes, Behaviour and Environmental Policy Issues", in I. Altman and J.F. Wohlwill (eds.), *Human Behaviour and Environment*, New York : Plenum, 1-36.

O'Riordan, T. (1981). *Environmentalism*. London : Pion.

Ortolano, L. (1984). *Environmental Planning and Decision-Making*, New York: John Wiley and Sons.

Parker, D.J. and Penning-Rowsell, E.C. (1983). "Flood Hazard Research in Britain", *Progress in Human Geography*, 7 : 182-202.

Parsons, T. (1949). *The Structure of Social Action*, Glencoe: The Free Press.

Robinson, J.A. and Majok, R.R. (1967). "The Theory of Decision-Making", In J.C. Charlesworth (ed.) *Contemporary Political Analysis*, New York, 175-88.

Saarinen, T.F. (1966). Perception of the Drought Hazard on the Great Plains, Research Paper No. 106, Department of Geography, University of Chicago, Chicago.

Saarinen, T.F. (1969). Perception of the Environment, Resource Paper No. 5, Commission On College Geography, Association of American Geographies, Washington, D.C.

Saarinen, T.F. (1971). "Research Approaches and Questionnaire Design", in W.R.D. Sewell and I. Burton (eds.) *Perceptions and Attitudes in Resources Management*. Ottawa: Information Canada, 13-25.

Saarinen, T.F. (1976). *Environment Planning : Perception and Behaviour*. Boston: Houghton Mifflin.

Sadler, B. (ed.) (1981). *Public Participation in Environmental Decision-Making*. Edmonton : Environment Council of Alberta.

Schiff, M.R. (1971). "The Definition of Perceptions and Attitudes", in W.R.D. Sewell and I. Burton (eds.), *Perceptions and Attitudes in Resources Management*. Ottawa : Information Canada, 7-12.

Sewell, W.R.D. (1965). Water Management and Floods in the Fraser River Basin, Research Paper No. 100, Department of Geography, University of Chicago, Chicago.

Sewell, W.R.D. (1971a). "Environmental Perceptions and Attitudes of Engineers and Public Health Officials", *Environment and Behaviour*, 3 : 23-59.

Sewell, W.R.D. (1971b). "Integrating Public Views in Planning and Policy Making", in W.R.D. Sewell and I. Burton (eds.), *Perceptions and Attitudes in Resources Management*. Ottawa: Information Canada, 125-31.

Sewell, W.R.D. (1973). "Broadening the Approach to Evaluation in Resources Management Decision-Making", *Journal of Environmental Management*, 1 : 33-60.

Sewell, W.R.D. (1974). "Perceptions, Attitudes and Public Participation in Countryside Management in Scotland", *Journal of Environmental Management*, 2 : 235-57.

Sewell, W.R.D. and Phillips, S.D. (1979). "Models for the Evaluation of Public Participation Programmes", *Natural Resources Journal*, 19 : 337-58.

Sewell, W.R.D. Dearden, P. and Dumbrell, J. (1989). "Wilderness Decision-Making and the Role of Environmental Inter-groups: A comparison of the Franklin Dam, Tasmania and South Moresley, British Columbia Cases", *Natural Resources Journal*, 29 : 147-69.

Simon, H.A. (1959). "Theories of Decision-Making in Economic and Behavioural Science" *American Economic Review*, 49: 253-83.

Slovic, P. Kunreuther, H. and White, G.F. (1974). "Decision Processes, Rationality and Adjustment to Natural Hazards", in G.F. White (ed.), *Natural Hazards: Local, National and Global*, New York: Oxford University Press, 187-205.

Smith, L.G. (1982). "Mechanisms for Public Participation at a Normative Planning Level in Canada", *Canadian Public Policy*, 8 : 561-72.

Smith, L.G. (1983). "The Evaluation of Public Participation in Water Resources Management : A Canadian Perspective", in J.W. Frazier, B.J. Epstein, M. Bardecki and H. Jacobs (eds.). *Papers and Proceedings of Applied Geography Conferences*, Vol. 6. Department of Geography, Ryerson Polytechnical Institute, Toronto, 253-44.

Smith, K. and Tobin, G.A. (1979). *Human Adjustment to the Flood Hazard*, London: Longman.

Sommer, R. (1969). *Personal Space: The Behavioural Basis of Design*, Englewood Cliffs : Prentice Hall.

Stankey, G.H. (1972). "The Use of Content Analysis in Resource Decision-Making", *Journal of Forestry*, 70 : 148-51.

Thomas, W.A. (1976). "Attitudes of Professionals in Water Management towards the use of Water Quality Indices", *Journal of Environmental Management*, 4 : 325-38.

Thornton, D.S. (1962). "The Study of Decision-Making and its Relevance to the Study of Farm Management", *Farm Economist*, 10 : 40-56.

Timmermans, H. and Van der Heijden, R. (1987). "Uncovering Spatial Decision-Making Processes : A Decision Net Approach Applied to Recreational Choice Behaviour", *Tijdschrift voor Economische en Sociale Geografie*, 78 : 297-304.

Timmermans, H. and Golledge, R.G. (1990). "Application of Behavioural Research on Spatial Problems II : Preference and Choice", *Progress in Human Geography*, 14 : 311-54.

Tversky, A. and Kahneman, D. (1974). "Judgment Under Uncertainty: Heuristics and Biases", *Science*, 185 : 1124-31.

Vining, J. and Schroeder, H.W. (1987). "Emotions in Environmental Decision-Making : Rational Planning versus the Passionate Public", in M.L. Miller, R.P. Gale and P.J. Brown (eds.), *Social Science in Natural Resource Management Systems*, Colorado: Westview Press, 181-92.

Von Neumann, J. and Morgenstem, O. (1947). *Theory of Games and Economic Behaviour*. Princeton, N.J. : Princeton University Press.

Walmsley, D.J. and Lewis, G.J. (1984). *Human Geography : Behavioural Approaches*, London : Longman.

Wengert, N. (1971). "Public Participation in Water Planning: A Critique of Theory, Doctrine and Practice", *Water Resources Bulletin*, 7 : 26-32.

Wescoat, J.L. (1986). "Expanding the Range of Choice in Water Management : An Evaluation of Policy Approaches", *Natural Resources Forum*, 10 : 239-54.

Wescoat, J.L. (1987). "The Practical Range of Choice in Water Resources Geography", *Progress in Human Geography*, 11 : 41-59.

White, G.F. (1945). Human Adjustment to Floods : A Geographical Approach to the Flood Problem in the United States, Research Paper No. 29, Department of Geography, University of Chicago, Chicago.

White, G.F. (1958). "Broader Bases for Choice : The Next Key Move", in H. Jarett (ed.) *Perspective on Conservation*, Baltimore: Johns Hopkins University Press, 205-26.

White, G.F. (1961). "The Choice of Use in Resource Management", *Natural Resources Journal*, 1 : 23-40.

White, G.F. (1964). Choice of Adjustments to Floods, Research Paper No. 93, Department of Geography, University of Chicago, Chicago.

White, G.F. (1966). "Formation and Role of Public Attitudes", in H. Jarrett (ed.), *Environmental Quality in a Growing Economy*. Baltimore : Johns Hopkins University Press, 105-27.

White, G.F, (ed.) (1974). *Natural Hazards : Local, National and Global*. New York : Oxford University Press.

White, G.F. *et al*. (1958). Changes in Urban Occupance of Flood Plains in the United States, Research Paper 57, Department of Geography, University of Chicago, Chicago.

White, G.F. and Haas, J.E. (1975). *Assessment of Research on Natural Hazards*. Cambridge : MIT Press.

Whyte, A.V.T. (1986). "From Hazard Perception to Human Ecology", in R.W. Kates and I. Burton (eds.) *Geography, Resources and Environment*, Vol. II: Themes from the Work of Gilbert F. White, Chicago : University of Chicago Press, 240-71.

Wiens, T.B. (1977). "Uncertainty and Factor Allocation in a Peasant Economy", *Oxford Economic Papers*, 29 : 48-60.

Windsor, J.E. (1993). "Water Diversions and Export : Threat or Opportunity?" in H.D. Foster (ed.), *Advances in Resource Management: Tributes to W.R.D.* Sewall. London : Belhaven Press, 227-77.

Walpert, J. (1964). "The Decision Process in Spatial Context", *Annals of the Association of American Geographers*, 54 : 537-58.

Wong, S.T. (1968). "Perception of Choice and Factors Affecting Industrial Water Supply Decisions in North-eastern Illinois", Research Paper No. 117, Department of Geography, University of Chicago, Chicago.

Wood, L.J. (1970). "Perception Studies in Geography", *Transactions of the Institute of British Geographers*, 50 : 129-42.

12

Broadening the Approach to Evaluation in Resources Management Decision-Making*

W.R. DERRICK SEWELL

The task of evaluation in resource management decision-making is becoming increasingly complex. No longer is it merely a matter of estimating the costs of construction and operation, and weighing these against anticipated revenues. Nor is it a matter of assessing only the local on-site impacts. More and more it is becoming necessary to consider proposals for resource development in terms of their broad social, environmental and institutional consequences, as well as their economic and financial effects. Increasingly, the region or the nation rather than the local area in the appropriate areal unit for evaluation.

With the aid of a descriptive model of the policy-making process, this article examines the extent to which present procedures for evaluation are able to provide the data that decision-makers require at various stages of that process. It shows that while considerable progress has been made in the past decade in developing tools for evaluation, there remain important weaknesses in this connection. These weaknesses stem in part from the incapacity to identify and measure certain effects, notably aesthetics, other intangibles, and future values, and in part from institutional biases towards some strategies rather than others. The author suggests that many of these weaknesses might be overcome through the acceleration of social science research in the resources management field, and particularly in the following five areas: the identification of the nature and magnitude of resource problems

---

Reprinted with permission from *Journal* of *Environmental Management* (1973),1, p. 33-60.

and of the demands for resource-related goods and services; the delineation of alternative strategies for dealing with resource problems; hindsight reviews of projects and policies; examination of alternative ways of identifying public views; and development of more sophisticated techniques for taking account of multiple objectives, multiple strategies, and a wide range of values. The article concludes with a list of specific types of studies that might be undertaken in connection with each of these areas.

INTRODUCTION

In May 1968, the British government appointed a Royal Commission, charged with the responsibility to recommend a location for a third London airport. After what was probably the most extensive analysis of a public project ever undertaken in the U.K., the Commission concluded that the most advantageous site was at Cublington in Buckinghamshire (Adams, 1971). The government, however, has decided to build the airport at Foulness in the Thames estuary, at a cost of almost £200 million more than that estimated for Cublington.

In British Columbia, following a disastrous flood on the Fraser River in 1948, an engineering board was established to study the problem and recommend solutions. In its Final Report, published in 1963, the Fraser River Board stressed the urgency of taking immediate action. It noted that the existing drinking system was inadequate, and recommended the construction of a multiple purpose scheme of upstream storage (Fraser River Board, 1963). Today, some nine years later, little action has been taken, other than the repair of some of the existing dykes. The flood threat remains.

The foregoing experiences raise some important questions about the role of evaluations in the decision-making process, and about the ability of such studies to provide the data that are required for sound decisions. A cynical reaction to the experience relating to the Roskill Commission report and the recommendations concerning flood control on the Fraser River might be that the outcomes of such enquiries have little influence on decisions and therefore the former are a waste of time. The evidence is, however, that decision-makers usually attach considerable importance to the findings of these investigations, even though they may choose not to accept all the recommendations that are based upon them.

The more serious problem is the nature and adequacy of the

information which the evaluation provide. The abandonment of the Spading expressway in Toronto after some $65 million had been spent on it (Newland and Newland, 1970), the costly delay in the Nelson River Diversion Scheme in Manitoba (Schramm, 1970), and the failure of the South Saskatchewan River Development Scheme to yield the benefits claimed for it by the promoters (Canada Hansard, 1959) suggest that some important questions may not have been asked. Had they been posed and satisfactorily answered the decision-makers would have been able to detect, for example, changes in the public's views about the desirability of the projects, shifts in values placed upon the preservation of certain environmental attributes, or preferences for one way of life (such as dry farming) versus other ways of life (such as irrigation farming).

The task of evaluation in resources management decision-making is clearly becoming increasingly complex. No longer is it a simple matter of estimating costs of construction and weighing them against anticipated revenues. No longer is it a matter of assessing only the local, on-site impacts. More and more it is becoming necessary to consider proposals for resource development in terms of their broad social, environmental and institutional consequences, as well as their economic and financial effects. More and more the region or the nation rather than the local area is the appropriate areal unit for evaluation.

Given this change in focus, it is pertinent to ask if present procedures for evaluation are adequate to meet the challenge, and, if they are not, in what ways they need to be improved? More specifically, in what ways might geographical and other social science research assist in improving them? The answers to these questions might best be found through an examination of the decision-making process on the one hand, and of techniques of evaluation on the other.

THE DECISION-MAKING PROCESS

The decision-making process may be thought of as a series of interconnected elements or steps, leading from the recognition of a problem and the identification of potential solutions to the selection and adoption of an appropriate strategy. Ideally, the various steps follow in sequence, and there is feedback amongst particular elements. Sometimes only one person, or a single group of people, is involved in the various steps. More often, however, different groups play particular roles at various stages in the process.

Fig. 12.1 describes the basic elements in an idealised planning and policy-making process. The process begins with a statement of the goals sought and is followed by the identification of the specific problems to be solved, and the delineation of the planning or policy-making context in which the analysis is to be undertaken. It continues with a delineation of potential solutions, formulation or alternative sets of strategies, and the evaluation of each of these sets. It reaches a final stage with the selection of an optimal solution or set of strategies. Hindsight reviews of experience with the selected solutions provide an input into future planning and policy-making processes.

Statement of Goals

Goals might include one or more of the following broad social objectives: (a) increasing national or regional income, (b) redistributing income among regions, (c) redistributing income among social groups, (d) improving environmental quality.

Sometimes goals are set out in a formal statement of government policy. An illustration of this is Senate Document 97 which prescribes the broad national objectives of water and related land resource development in the United States (U.S. President's Water Resources Council, 1962). More often, however, goals are implicit rather than explicit, and even when they are stated they are more expression of *means* than of *ends*. For example, typical objectives stated in water resources plans in North America are "increasing irrigated acreage", "providing hydro-electric power", or "furnishing low cost water transport". Satisfactory appraisal of such plans, of course, is possible only if it is known *for what purpose* such goods and services are to be provided. Is it to facilitate an increase in national income, or a transfer of income from the rich to the poor? Is it to stimulate the growth of a lagging region? Only with answers to these questions would it be possible to determine whether a given plan represented the best means of attaining a given end or purpose.

Ideally, goals should be formulated through extensive, rational discussion between the various groups involved in decision-making, as well as with those who are likely to be affected by the decisions. Generally, however, it seems that goals evolve not from logical debate but from an admixture of historical precedent, political opportunism, and assumptions about public attitudes (O'Riordan, 1971). Usually there is little or no attempt to discover what the public wants or would like to have. Politicians and their technical advisers, it seems, tend to

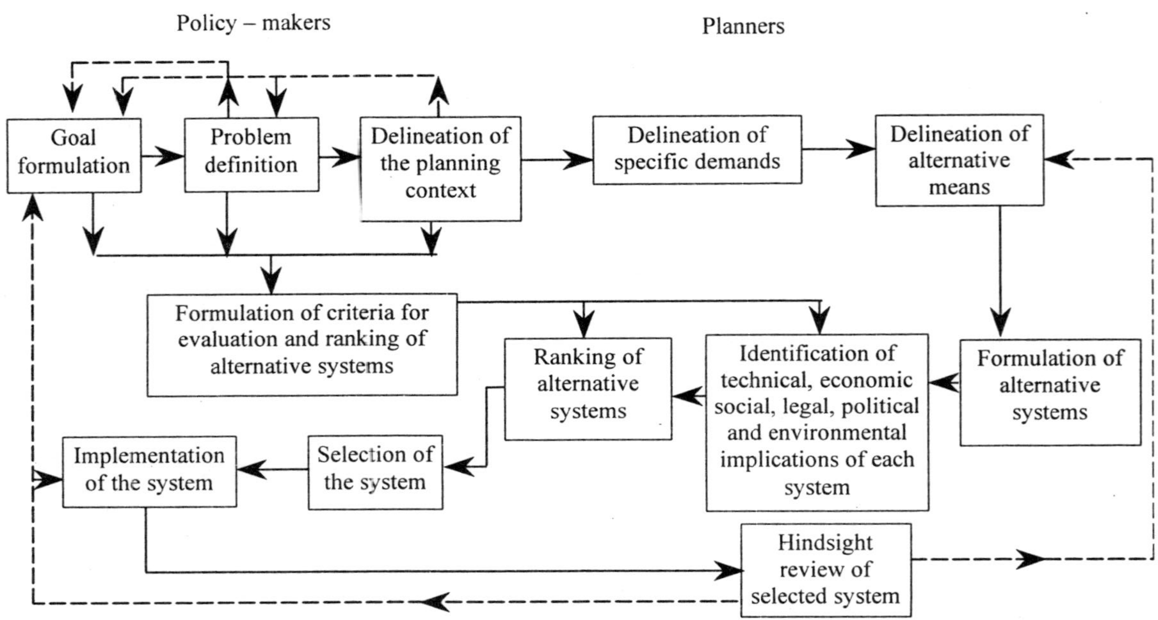

Fig. 12.1: Schematic representation of the planning and policy-making process.

Note: The planning and policy-making process is a continuous one involving constant iteration and frequent policy decisions. Only the major feedbacks and policy check points are shown here.

rely mainly on their own judgements as to the latter rather than canvassing public opinion in a systematic way (White, 1966). A possible consequence may be that decision-makers will misperceive the goals which the public expects them to pursue. Another may be that decision-makers will fail to detect shifts in the relative importance attached to particular goals. Experience relating to the South Saskatchewan project seems to suggest that the promoters of the scheme misperceived the goals of the people in the Prairie region. The costly delays in the construction of electric power projects in various parts of North America may be a result of a general shift in the relative importance attached to continuous economic growth as compared with attempts to improve the quality of the environment.

A pre-requisite in evaluation of resources management projects or policies is then a clear statement of the goals to be pursued, and an indication of the extent to which that statement reflects the relative importance which the public currently attaches to particular aims and objectives.

Identification of Problems and Need

The next step in the planning and policy-making process is the identification of specific resources management problems to be solved, and the estimation of demands for the goods and services which the development of resources projects would provide. Here it is necessary to do more than merely state that "there is a major flood problem in the West country", or "the level of water quality in the River Trent has reached intolerable proportions", or that "requirements for electric power in the London area will double by 1985". Faced with a growing number of claims on the public purse and with an increasing number of conflicts in the use of particular resources, decision-makers must know *how* serious problems are, not only in terms of their physical magnitude but also in terms of their impact upon human activity and social relationships. They must also have some indication of the willingness of the public to pay for the benefits which resources development projects would provide. Thus, it is essential to have good estimates of the losses that would occur with given magnitudes and frequencies of floods, taking into account various assumptions about human behaviour, with and without the provision of flood control. Similarly, the determination of appropriate policies for water quality improvement requires estimates of the economic and social impact of various levels of water quality, and indications of how much those who are affected would be willing to give up in order to secure an improvement.

Unfortunately, the problem identification and demand estimation phase of the planning and policy-making process is often weak. In many instances, little time or effort are devoted to it, and in some cases it is undertaken almost as an afterthought. Sometimes the data produced are used to *justify* decisions which have already been made rather than to evaluate whether the project involved is the best possible means or whether in fact any project is required at all. Some of the greatest deficiencies in this connection have occurred in water resource planning. In certain instances, several years have been devoted to the planning of dams and diversion structures, with millions of dollars allocated to site investigations and project designs, but only a few months (generally towards the end of the study) and a tiny proportion of the costs of the investigation allocated to studies of the need for the project.

The lack of attention to demand estimates in resources management policy making results in part from the fact that planning in this connection has been largely in the hands of the engineering profession and has involved relatively few social scientists. The training and experiences, as well as the professional interests of the former, are more in the area of supply than of demand (Sewell, 1971). Social scientists for their part, however, have been slow in pointing out this deficiency and in developing satisfactory methodologies for demand estimation. Although some advances have been made in the latter connection in the past few years (Sewell and Bower, 1968), many of the techniques presently in use permit little more than educated guesses about public preferences. In many instances, the estimates are mere extrapolations of past experience. The underlying assumptions therefore are that preference patterns will remain unchanged, that price will have no effect on consumption, and that no innovations will be adopted which will reduce per capita usage. Past experience clearly shows, however, that such assumptions are not valid. People do substitute one form of energy for another and they do engage in new forms of outdoor recreation. Price does tend to affect the demand for goods and services such as domestic water supply (Rees and Rees, 1972) or outdoor recreation. And there is evidence that resource scarcities stimulate the adoption of resource conserving techniques, such as re-cycling and waste water treatment (Kneese and Bower, 1968).

The area of demand estimation is one to which social scientists could make valuable contributions. Not only is research required to develop methodologies but there is a need for skilled practitioners in agencies which undertake demand studies, such as the Department of the Environment and the Water Resources Board.

Identification of Alternative Means and Strategies

There are usually several possible alternative ways of dealing with a given resources management problem or of providing the goods and services which a resource development project would supply. Often the range of choice is quite wide. White has shown, for example, that there are at least seven major alternative ways of dealing with flood problems (White, 1964). Empirical studies have shown, however, that only a few of these possibilities are actually considered by policy-makers concerned with flood problems because of various institutional constraints, professional biases, and other factors (Kates, 1962). Similarly, narrow ranges of choice also seem to characterise decision-making in other fields of resource management, such as the use of arid lands (Saarinen, 1966), the provision of outdoor recreation opportunities (O'Riordan *et al.*, 1970), and the management of atmospheric quality (Bower and Sewell, 1971).

In resources management generally, there seems to be a strong bias towards construction, punitive legislation, and the provision of financial aid even though there may be empirical evidence that other kinds of strategies would be more efficient. Water utilities, for example, appear to concentrate upon reservoir and aqueduct construction as a means for solving water shortages rather than encouraging more efficient use through regulating use or raising the price of water (Hirschleifer *et al.*, 1960).

The typical approach to water quality management has been to fine offenders and in some cases to provide financial assistance for the construction of treatment plants. Little attention has been given to such strategies as the provision of economic incentives (like effluent discharge fees), research or public involvement. Experience in the Genossenschaften in West Germany and more recently in the River Basin Agencies in France suggests that economic incentives may be more effective in controlling pollution than sole reliance in punitive legislation, and the results of experiments in public participation in the United States and France suggest that the latter strategy has merits, not only in identifying the nature of the problem, but also in developing support for the implementation of policies.

The range of choice has also been limited by the tendency to concentrate on only one part of a resources management system. This has been especially so in the search for solutions to the pollution problem. Almost always the focus of attention has been on handling effluents *after* they have been generated: comparatively little effort has been devoted towards the reduction of residuals by altering the production process or the mix of raw materials used in it. Table 12.1 indicates the wide range of possible components of strategies that may be used in dealing with an air quality management problem, and the various points in the management system (Fig. 12.2) to which they might be applied.

Evaluation of Alternative Strategies

Given the nature of the problem to be solved, and a set of alternative strategies, on what basis might a choice be made? In the past, selection has been based largely upon the application of a few simple criteria, such as (a) is the strategy technically possible? (b) is it legally permissible? (c) is it financially viable? Today, however, the task of evaluation is much more demanding. As noted earlier, considerations of overall economic impact, social consequences, ecological impacts, and political effects have to be weighed as well. Table 12.2 sets out a listing of considerations that might be taken into account in evaluating alternative strategies for air quality management. The feasibility of measuring the various parameters, of course, varies considerably, being greatest with the physical aspects and most difficult with those relating to behaviour and institutions.

Considerable progress has been made in recent years in developing techniques of evaluation, and particularly those for estimating economic impacts. As will be pointed out later in this chapter, however, there are still some important weaknesses in present techniques of economic evaluation, and techniques for assessing behavioural, institutional, and ecological dimensions are still at a very early stage of development.

Selection of an Alternative

Based on the information provided by the formal evaluation process described above, as well as various extraneous factors, decision-makers select an alternative which they believe is in the public interest, and which they feel is the best way of dealing with the problem in question. Means are then provided to implement the decision in the form of

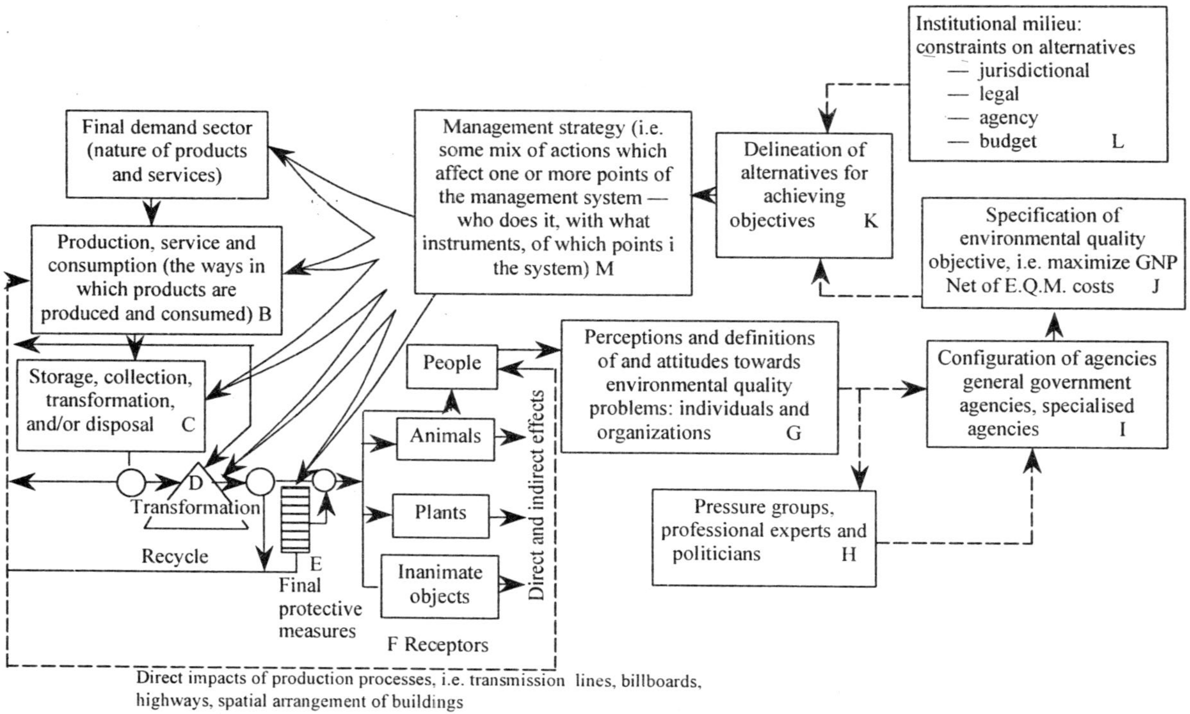

Fig. 12.2: Generalised residuals—environmental quality management system. →, Flow of residuals; --→, flow of information; ⇒, activities (action); O, state of residuals; Δ, environment (atmosphere, water, etc.)

Table 12.1: Possible components of management strategies and possible points of application in the air-quality management system

Possible components of management strategies	*Points of application in the management system*								
	Final demand	*Raw material inputs*	*Production process*	*Handling of residuals after generation*	*Emissions to the environment*	*Environment*	*Protective measures*	*Impacts upon receptors (physical, psychological, economic)*	*Impacts upon perception and attitudes*
Research									
Data collection									
Design of facilities								*	*
Construction of facilities								*	*
Operation of facilities	*							*	*
Regulation									
(a) Land-use zoning		*		*					*
(b) Standards									*
(c) Charges								*	*
(d) Incentives									
(e) Monitoring	*								
(f) Specifying actions	*							*	*
Consider strategies relating to other residuals									
(a) Review strategies									
(b) Veto strategies									
(c) Integrate strategies									
Provision of information									
(a) TV, radio, newspapers									
(b) Support of private groups									

Table 12.2: Elements of indices for the evaluation of management strategies

I. Physical and ecological impacts:
   1. Time and spatial pattern of gaseous residuals generated.
   2. Time and spatial pattern of gaseous residuals discharged.
   3. Time and spatial pattern of ambient air concentrations.
   4. Time and spatial pattern of solid and liquid residuals generated and discharged in the process of handling the gaseous residuals.
   5. Physical impacts upon various physical, natural, and human systems, i.e. distributional effects

II. Economic impacts:
   1. Impacts upon costs of operations of residuals generators over time.
   2. Impact upon damages sustained by receptors over time, where reduced damages comprise the benefits from implementation of the strategy.
   3. Indirect impacts upon income, employment, and their distributions, e.g. trade balance, and international competitive position, interregional distribution of industry.

III. Timing considerations:
   1. Time required to put the strategy into operation.
   2. Time required to obtain first results and/or benefits.

IV. Administrative considerations:
   1. Simplicity considerations.
   2. Costs of administration, e.g. manpower, instrumentation.
   3. Flexibility, e.g. in relation to improving the system of management, to changing the system in response to changed conditions and objectives.

V. Legal considerations:
   1. Constitutional constraints.
   2. Nature and extent of legal precedents.

VI. Political considerations:
   1. Politicians' perceived urgency of the air-quality management problem in relation to other problems of society.
   2. Professionals' perceived urgency of the air-quality problem.
   3. Public's perceived urgency of air-quality problem.
   4. Politicians' perceived impact of the strategy upon various political groups.
   5. Impact upon federal-provincial relations.
   6. Impact upon local-provincial relations.
   7. Degree of coincidence of areal scope of strategy with existing political jurisdictions.

VII. Public responsiveness:
   1. Extent of coincidence of the proposed strategy with notions of the public about such matters as equity, efficiency and adequacy of this strategy to deal with the problem.

legislative enactments, provision of funds and/or administrative readjustments.

Generally this is the final step in the policy-making process. If it solves the problem, the public will be satisfied and the stress which brought it to the decision-maker's attention will be relieved. If it does not, further crises will occur and the demands for more appropriate action will grow (Kasperson, 1969).

Hindsight Reviews

An extremely valuable but generally neglected in the policy-making process is the monitoring of experience in implementing projects and policies with a view to determining the extent to which they succeed in attaining the goals set for them, and the degree to which they result in unpredicted consequences. Studies of agricultural readjustment programmes in Canada have shown, for example, that subsidies to farmers have not succeeded either in improving the lot of the average farmer, or in promoting major changes in the types of farming undertaken (Buckley and Tihanyi, 1967). Reviews of projects sponsored by the World Bank have also indicated that many of them have failed to attain their objectives (King, 1967).

While it is clear that valuable insights could be gained from hindsight reviews, resources planning and management agencies have generally been very reluctant to undertake them. The reasons may be rooted in a fear that the findings of such evaluations might result in criticism of the management agency or its personnel. Politicians may also be reluctant to agree to such evaluations for similar reasons. There is no doubt, however, that they could furnish one of the most useful of all inputs into the policy-making process. It is important of course to ensure that they are undertaken by an independent agency, such as a Royal Commission or a Treasury Board, and that the latter is given the facts it requires for an impartial assessment.

EVALUATION TECHNIQUES

During the past two decades, numerous techniques have been devised for assessing the merits of alternative resource management strategies. Lichfield (1970), Prest and Turvey (1965), Dorfman (1965) and Wildawsky (1966) have furnished excellent reviews of these techniques, noting their theoretical underpinnings, cases to which they have been applied, and their various strengths and weaknesses. Several detailed case studies have also appeared dealing with such problems as airport location (Frost, 1971), hydro-electric power development (Krutilla, 1969), water quality (Davis, 1968), and land conservation (Wibberley, 1959). Handbooks outlining the various techniques and providing guidelines for their application are appearing in rapidly increasing numbers.

An overview of the experience to date in the development and application of various techniques suggests the following four broad conclusions:

(i) Of the various techniques devised so far, benefit-cost analysis appears to have been the most widely-used, the most comprehensive in coverage, and the most severely criticised in its applications.

(ii) There have been several attempts in recent years to broaden the scope of various techniques of analysis by taking into account several goals rather than just one, by attempting to trace impacts beyond first round or direct effects, and by building various alternative constraints specifically into the evaluation. Techniques such as the goals-achievement matrix and engineering-economic analysis have been two of the products of such attempts.

(iii) Much remains to be learned about the ways in which people perceive problems and solutions, and the values they place upon various resources and resource uses and their attitudes as to the locus of responsibility for initiating action. Without this knowledge it is difficult to determine what the public wants or how it will respond to what is provided.

(iv) There is a growing desire to include assessments of environmental impacts in evaluations of resource management policies and programmes, but great uncertainty as to how this can best be accomplished.

Benefit-cost Analysis

Benefit-cost analysis is perhaps the best known and most widely adopted technique of evaluation. Developed mainly in the United States, first by engineers and more recently by economists, it was used initially for the evaluation of water resources development projects, particularly those concerned with navigation or flood control. Its applications are now very wide, embracing policies relating to the management of different types of resources, highway construction, education, mental health and many other problems of public concern (Dofman, 1965). It is used not only by government agencies but also by industry. In the United States, it has become institutionalised in the federal government's procedures for reviewing proposals for public investment in resources management. It is also widely used in Canada, and has been employed in the assessment of major resource development schemes in the U.K. as well.

The popularity of benefit-cost analysis stems partly from the fact that its objectives are fairly easily understood, and partly from the relative ease with which it can be applied to different types of situation. It is especially useful as a technique in situations where (a) the choice is to be made within a single resource context, (b) the benefits and the costs are fairly easily recognised and measured, and (c) the scale is comprehensible (the local area, region, or other basis rather than the nation).

Like any technique of evaluation, benefit-cost analysis is not a panacea. It does not provide answers to all the questions that might be posed in an evaluation of a resources management policy or proposal. It has in fact a number of limitations stemming in part from its conceptual underpinnings, and in part from difficulties in measuring benefits and costs, and from problems of dealing with external effects, time, risk and uncertainty (Prest and Turvey, 1965). In addition, there are the difficulties of taking such considerations as income redistribution, regional economic development, and environmental modification into account.

Cognisant of these problems, and the need to find solutions to them, the U.S. Water Resources Council appointed a special task force to prepare a set of principles and procedures which would improve upon the methods presently in use. The Task Force completed a report in 1969 and this was widely circulated to interested agencies, academics, and other members of the public. A series of public hearings were held and these led to a revision of the proposed methodologies. The revised report (U.S. Water Resources Council, 1972) was also circulated for comments and suggestions and hearings were held in the early spring of this year. The proposals should be of considerable interest to all those concerned with resources management evaluations on both sides of the Atlantic. It is not possible in this chapter to review the proposals in detail but it seems worthwhile discussing a number of the innovations proposed by the Council.

Broadening the Scope of the Evaluation

Traditional benefit-cost analysis has assumed a single goal of public policy, that of increasing national income. The Council recognised, however, that there were several other important objectives of such policy, notably regional economic development, improvement of environmental quality, and improvement of social well-being (such as in income redistribution, protection of life, and national security). These objectives are to be taken into account through the preparation of four separate Accounts, namely: (i) national economic development, (ii) environmental quality, (iii) regional economic development, and (iv) social factors. Lists of beneficial and adverse factors relating to each of these Accounts are to be drawn up and quantified for each proposed plan or policy and its alternative. Illustrations of the types of factors that might be included in the various Accounts, and the manner in which they might be displayed are set out in the Council's report.

The attempt to incorporate objectives in addition to that of national economic development should be applauded, since it recognises a practical aspect of policy formation: the fact that plans and policies generally aim to achieve several goals simultaneously or at least to attain a particular goal subject to one or more constraints. Unfortunately, the Council's proposals in this connection appear to offend the conceptual underpinnings of benefit-cost analysis. The proposals seem to suggest that the locus of evaluation should be shifted from the nation to the region: should this occur, benefit-cost analysis would be robbed of one of its principal means of determining the relative economic merits of proposed plans or projects. Unless a national perspective is maintained, it is argued, there is a danger that funds will be shifted from more economic to less economic activities. To overcome this problem, it has been suggested that a unified national accounting stance be maintained, and that no nationally financed project be considered until it has passed a minimum benefit-cost ratio test which is based solely on national economic efficiency (Ciccetti *et al.*, 1972).

Improving the Measurement of Benefits

The Council recommended three possible approaches for calculating the benefits to be derived from a project: (i) willingness to pay, (ii) change in net income, (iii) costing the most likely alternative. Each one of these approaches has weaknesses as a means of assessing benefits.

Economists have long argued that the value of goods and services indicated by the consumer's willingness to pay for them. While this criterion does show that there is a demand for the goods and services, it is an insufficient measure of the value. One would also need to know what was the cheapest means of providing the goods and services in order to appraise the merits of alternative ways of producing the latter. Similarly, the change in net income may not provide a satisfactory measure of the benefits derived, particularly where subsidies are involved. Only if the latter are subtracted from the income derived is it possible to weigh the benefits of alternative strategies. Finally, the cost of the cheapest alternative is not by itself a satisfactory measure of benefits. It is necessary to know also whether the value society places on the output of the cheapest alternative exceeds the cost of providing it.

Two questions, therefore, need to be posed in appraising the validity of estimates of benefits. First, do the benefits exceed the costs? And second, what is the least-cost means of providing the benefits?

Incorporation Environmental Impacts

The attempt to incorporate environmental impacts specifically into project evaluation has considerable merit. The proposed procedures, however, may not provide a satisfactory indication of the nature and magnitude of these effects. Ideally, the procedures should reflect the opportunity costs of using a resource for one purpose rather than another, such as hydro-power generation rather than sport fishing. The procedures suggested by the Council do not provide for such a comparison.

The procedures appear to be biased towards development rather than preservation. Whereas they call for deleterious effects to be expressed in physical units (such as miles of free-flowing river inundated), positive effects are to be recorded both in terms of physical units (such as the number of additional miles of beaches provided) and in monetary units (such as dollar values of increased swimming and fishing opportunities). This appears to weigh the benefits in favour of development.

The major weakness of the proposed procedures relating to the evaluation of environmental impacts, however, is the failure to require specific statements about such factors as (a) the extent to which a given strategy would lead to an irreversible change in the environment, (b) the importance of keeping options open, and (c) the non-reproducibility of natural environments. Without such statements, it is certain that such considerations will be ignored. And these perhaps provide the major motivation for taking environmental impacts into account !

Interest Rates

The most controversial aspect of benefit-cost analysis in North America is the interest rate selected for discounting benefits and costs. Various economists have suggested that the low rates used by the U.S. federal government have led to gross misallocations of capital, since they have been far below actual costs of borrowing money (Hirschleifer *et al.*, 1960). Fox and Hirfindahl (1964) have shown, for example, that in 1962 if market rates had been used instead of the "administrative rate" of 2.6 per cent, less than 80 per cent of the projects submitted to the U.S. government in that year for funding would have had a benefit-cost ratio in excess of unity.

The Water Resources Council suggests the use of a seven per cent rate of interest for discounting purposes. This is considerably higher than rates used in the past, and no doubt will placate some critics. There will be others, however, who will claim that even this rate is too low, for at least two reasons: first, it is below what the private sector would demand as a return for investment in ventures of comparable risk; and second, it tends to favour development over preservation, and in the case of irreplaceable assets, this does not fully reflect the social cost involved.

Taking Account of Regional Economic Development

It has long been suggested that the impact of resources development projects and policies on regional economic development should be identified and measured as an integral part of the evaluation. There are, however, substantial difficulties in tracing such impacts, and it is not at all certain that the procedures recommended by the Council will overcome these problems. First, although it may be possible to trace the positive effects within a region, it may not be possible to determine whether these are offset by losses elsewhere. Second, it is an open question as to how far resource development, and especially water resource development, stimulates economic growth, and third, it is not certain that investment in water resources projects is more efficient than investment in other means of stimulating such growth. The procedures suggested by the Council would not provide the kind of information required to answer such questions.

Not only should more sophisticated techniques of analysis be used to evaluate the potential contribution of water resources development to economic growth, but the evaluations should be undertaken by an independent body, such as a Department of Economic Development or a Treasury Board.

The Role of Public Participation

The logical extension of broadening the perspective of the evaluation of resources management projects and policies is to determine more accurately what the public wants and how it is likely to react to what is provided. As noted earlier, there may be major gaps between what the planner or policy-maker perceives as important and what the public feels is significant. At present, planners and policy-makers rely mainly upon such means as public opinion polls, the ballot box and the referendum, and public hearings for indications of public views. As the author has shown elsewhere, however, such means do not yield very accurate assessments of such views (Sewell, 1971). Public opinion polls may reflect only the individual's reaction to a question and not his true preference. They provide no information as to strength of preferences or as to how an individual would react if faced with an actual choice. The ballot box has the disadvantage that it usually calls for views upon a collection of issues rather than just one. Like the referendum, it canvasses only those who turn up to vote: sometimes this is as little as 20 per cent of the electorate, and an even smaller proportion of the total population.

The Water Resources Council broke new ground in circulating its proposed methods of evaluation to a wide audience before deciding upon a final set of procedures. It has very little to say, however, about the means by which public views can be obtained in the actual evaluation process. A number of possibilities, however, might be considered, including (i) studies of perceptions and attitudes, undertaken on an *ad hoc* or continuous basis, and (ii) involvement of segments of the public in actual planning and policy-making. A number of experiments in the United States, Canada and France, in both connections appear to have had some success. The experience with respect to the Delaware Estuary Comprehensive Study, in which the views of the public were tapped at various stages of the investigation and fed into the planning process, is instructive (Chevalier and Cartwright, 1971). So also is that of the Susquehanna Basin Study in which the public was directly involved in the planning from the beginning of the study (Borton and Warner, 1970). In both cases, the public's views were fed directly and immediately into the decision-making process.

Among the indirect means of tapping views, studies of perceptions and attitudes offer much promise. This method has already been used in water resources planning in the United States, particularly in connection with flood plain management, and the establishment of air pollution control regulations. Like other methods of assessing public views, studies of perceptions and attitudes have limitations, stemming from problems of soliciting information, the availability of skilled personnel to undertake the studies, and the tendency of views to change over time. Many of these problems, however, can be overcome by skilful organisation and by well-structured and skilfully administered interviews.

Another attractive technique is the game simulation approach in which the actors assume the apparent roles of participants and act out a problem according to certain specified inputs or rules (Sadowski, 1965). It provides the participants with an opportunity not only to isolate the problems which they believe confront those whose role they are playing but also gain a sense of appreciation of the way in which decisions are actually arrived at. Game simulations can be used to furnish reflections of public views on such questions as: what is the best use of a given parcel of land? Should the Fraser River be used for the maintenance of salmon runs or the development of hydro-electric power? What position should British Columbia take on proposals to ship oil from Alaska to the State of Washington along the B.C. coast? Where is the most appropriate location for a new airport?

More specifically, such simulations, if carefully structured, make it possible to

(a) explore each range of alternatives, allowing particularly for the influence of chance/random elements,
(b) explore the role(s) of participants, and especially their perceptions and attitudes and group behaviour,
(c) examine those features of decision-making that are difficult to quantify, such as views about environment quality,
(d) examine those procedures which are conducive to conflict resolution through bargaining.

The technique has been little used to date, but applications to resources management questions by geographers in the U.K. (notably Wellford, 1969), the United States (notably Gould, 1963), and in Canada (notably Wood, 1972), have emphasised its value as a tool for planning and policy-making. Its potential applications, beyond those explored to date, merit serious consideration by planners and policy-makers.

Other Techniques of Evaluation

Besides improvement in benefit-cost analysis, a number of other techniques of evaluation have been development in the past decade or so. These include systems analysis, the goals-achievement matrix, and engineering economic analysis. The development and use of systems analysis in evaluations of resources management projects and policies are discussed elsewhere in the issue by Jeffers and by Chorley. Brief comments on the latter two technique are offered here.

The Goals-achievement Matrix

In a physical resources management decision-making situation, policy-makers try to pursue several objectives simultaneously. Typically too, the attainment of any objective (or set of objectives) is accomplished by a combination of strategies rather than by just one. The problem is further complicated by the fact that differing relative importance is attached to particular goals on the one hand, and to particular kinds of strategy on the other. In addition, the incidence of the benefits and costs of given strategies may vary considerably among different groups in the community. Finally, not all benefits and costs can be expressed in monetary terms. Lichfield (1968) and Hill (1968) have developed an ingenious technique for taking into account multiple objectives, multiple strategies, varying weights, differing social impacts, and effects which are not readily expressed in monetary terms. It is described as the goals-achievement matrix.

For every plan that is proposed a goals-achievement matrix may be drawn up. The set of goals is known and a relative value is established for each goal. The objectives are defined in operational rather than in abstract terms. The consequences of each course of action for each social group are worked out and weights are established for each of the latter. The product of the analysis is conceptualised in Table 12.3.

In the table, α, β, γ, and δ are the descriptions of the goals. Each has a weight 1, 2, 3, ... previously determined. Various social groups, *a, b, c, d* ... are identified as being affected by the course of action, and a relative weight is determined for each group, either for single goals, or for all goals taken together. The costs and benefits of each course of action are assigned the letters A, B, C ... and these may be defined in either monetary or non-monetary units or in terms of qualitative statements.

For certain of the goals, it is possible to draw up a summation of the benefits and costs which is meaningful and useful. This will be the case when all the costs and benefits can be quantified. When this can be done, comparison can readily be made among competing alternative plans and between the pursuit of different objectives. Operationally, comparisons would be made between several matrices similar to that in Table 12.3.

There are a variety of possible uses for the technique, such as decisions relating to the use of the resources of a given river basin, the improvement of water quality, the development of outdoor recreational opportunities, or the rescue of a declining region.

Although the technique has some problems of application—such as those of interaction among objectives, and difficulties where a project serves several sectors—it can be a most useful device for assessing the relative merits of alternative plans. It is particularly valuable where the number of objectives is limited, the number of alternative plans is not large, where the impacts can be quantified in comparable terms, and where weights can be objectively assigned to goals, strategies, and different social groups.

Engineering-Economic Analysis

Engineering-economic analysis represents a very successful blending of the concepts and techniques of the physical sciences with those of the social sciences. Developed initially in the Harvard Water Resources Programme (Maass *et al.*, 1962), it has been refined and progressively expanded elsewhere in the United States, notably by researchers of Resources for the Future, and at Stanford University and the University of North Carolina. Amongst its most successful applications have been the studies of costs of alternative means of attaining specified levels of water quality on the Delaware Estuary (Kneese and Bower, 1968) and on the Potomac River (Davis, 1968). A model, using the same techniques, is now being applied to the analysis of alternative strategies for management of the River Trent. Another is being developed at Resources for the Future to determine the relative merits of applying different kinds of strategies at various points in the production and consumption processes for the improvement of air quality (Russell, 1971).

Engineering-economic analysis holds considerable promise as a technique for evaluation of resources management projects and policies. Its potential will be increased even further once other dimensions can be added to it, such as ecological and social dimensions. Studies in applied ecology by Watt (1968) and others have illustrated the possible uses of the same kinds of techniques in other fields. Doubtless there are many other applications as well.

THE POTENTIAL CONTRIBUTION OF RESEARCH

The foregoing review has indicated that although the perspective in resources management evaluations has broadened considerably in the past decade, and although techniques of measurement are now much more sophisticated, policy-makers still lack the kinds of information they need to make sound decisions. Research, especially in the social sciences, could make an important contribution towards remedying this deficiency. Studies in five areas in particular are urgently required.

(i) The identification of the nature and magnitude of resources problems, and the demands for resources-related goods and services. These include the assessment of natural and man-

Table 12.3: The goals-achievement matrix

Goal description:	α			β			γ			δ		
Relative weight:	2			3			5			4		
Incidence	Relative Weight	Costs	Ben.	Relative weights	Costs	Ben.	Relative weight	Costs	Ben.	Relative weight	Costs	Ben.
Group a	1	A	D	5	E	—	1		N	1	Q	R
Group b	3	H		4	—	R	2		—	2	S	T
Group c	1	L	J	3	—	S	3	M	—	1	V	W
Group d	2	—		2		—	4		—	2	—	—
Group e	1	—	K	1	T	U	5		P	1	—	—
		Σ	Σ					Σ	Σ			

made hazards, and the demands for goods and services derived from water resources, forests, fisheries, mineral deposits, the atmosphere, and agricultural lands.

(ii) Delineation of alternative strategies for dealing with resources problems and for supplying resources related goods and services. In particular, studies are needed of potential alterations in patterns of human behaviour as well as those accomplished through alterations in the physical environment (as in the construction of dams, power plants, or factories).

(iii) Examinations of past performance of particular kinds of strategies such as subsidies in agriculture, flood control works, reforestation, creation of wilderness reserves, and so on.

(iv) Examination of alternative ways of identifying public views, including studies of perceptions and attitudes, experience of direct involvement in the planning and policy-making processes, and the use of simulation games.

(v) The refinement of existing techniques of evaluation and the development of new ones to take into account multiple objectives, multiple strategies, and intangible as well as tangible values.

Table 12.4 provides a summary of certain specific types of studies that would be especially useful in the areas noted above. The listing is intended to be illustrative rather than comprehensive. As a guideline, examples of research undertaken in some countries and with respect to particular resources are noted. The former are drawn largely from North America where much of the previous research effort has been concentrated, and the emphasis is largely upon water resources studies. Much of the pioneering work on the human aspects of resources management research, and particularly that relating to the development of evaluation techniques, has been focused on water problems. The examples, however, do have relevance to research needs in the U.K., and much of what is significant in water management also has parallels in the management of other resources.

Three broad conclusions may be drawn from Table 12.4. Firstly, the range of topics for study is very wide, involving research in both the physical and the social sciences. Much of it, however, requires experience in a specialised area within particular disciplines. The opportunities, as well as the needs, are particularly great for researchers

Table 12.4: Problems of evaluation and related research needs

Problem	*Related research needs*	*Illustrations*
1. Problem identification		
(a) Incidence and impact of natural hazards and man-made hazards.	National and regional assessments, indicating incidence, frequency, impacts, and adjustments adopted.	IGU Man and Environment Commission (1972) Natural Hazards Research Program (1972); McNeill (1971); Jackson (1971)
	Local studies of natural hazards and man-made hazards indicating magnitude, frequency, and adjustments adopted.	
	floods	White (1964); Kates (1962); Burton (1965); Sewell (1965)
	drought	Saarinen (1966); Heathcote (1969)
	snow	Rooney (1967)
	windstorms	Islam (1970); Gentry (1970)
	air pollution	Burton *et al.* (1972)
	water pollution	Cleary (1967)
	weather modification	Hass *et al.* (1972)
	multiple hazards	Hewitt and Burton (1971)
(b) Estimates of demands for resource-related goods and services	National and regional assessments of demands, by sectors	U.S. Water Resources Council (1968) Tinney *et al.* (1967) U.S. O.R.R.C. (1962) RFF (1968) Davis (1958)
	Estimates of demands in local areas	Shaefer *et al.* (1966) Rees and Rees (1972) H.M. Treasury (1972)
(c) Analysis of factors affecting demands	Analysis of influence of various factors, such as:	
2. (a)	Satisfying demands for resources related goods and services, such as:	Hows and Linaweaver (1967): Jackson and
	floods	White (1964)
	air quality	Bower and Sewell (1971)
	water supply	Hirschleifer *et al.* (1960)
	water quality	Kneese and Bower (1968)

Table 12.4:(*Contd.*)

	Problem	*Related research needs*	*Illustrations*
	(b) Identification of factors influencing the choice of strategies	Analyses of various factors which may influence the choice of strategies, such as:	
		the role of perceptions and attitudes	White (1966); Kates (1962); Sewell and Burton (1971)
		the nature of the decision-making process	Kasperson (1969); Sewell and Wood (1971); Lowenthal (1969)
3.	Hindsight evaluation of project performance and policy effectiveness	Analyses of project performance	King (1967); Macinko (1963); Day (1972)
		Analyses of policy effectiveness	Buckley and Tihanyi (1967)
4.	Identifying public views	Identification of views of individuals, interest groups, and leaders	White (1966); Burch *et al.* (1972); Craik (1970)
		Assessment of the effectiveness of various means of identifying public views such as opinion polls, public hearings, referenda, etc.	Mogoluf (1970)
		Assessment of effectiveness of various forms of public involvement in planning and policy-making	Borton and Warner (1970) Chevalier and Cartwright (1971)
5.	Refinement and development of techniques of evaluation	Assessment of the strengths and weaknesses of existing techniques	Lichfield (1970); Prest and Turvey (1965)
		Development of improved means of assessing externalities	R.F.F. (1969)
		Development of improved means of assessing intangibles	Shafer *et al.* (1969); Leopold (1971); Coomber and Biswas (1972)

with sound backgrounds in the conceptual underpinnings of economics, psychology, and ecology; individuals with an understanding of quantitative techniques; and workers with a bent for sophisticated field research. Secondly, much of the most rewarding research will require cooperative efforts from people in a wide variety of disciplines. Fruitful ventures might be anticipated, for example, from geographers, and economists working together on the assessment of national or regional demands for particular resource-related goods and services, or between geographers and various natural scientists in the assessment of natural hazards. In addition, inter-disciplinary approaches involving psychologists, sociologists, political scientists, and geographers seem particularly appropriate to the study of problems such as public participation in policy-making, and in undertaking hindsight reviews of project or policy effectiveness. Third, while some of the research can build upon what is already known, there are certain areas where really pioneering work is required: application of existing concepts or techniques may be either difficult or inappropriate. One such area relates to the evaluation of intangibles—those components of environmental appreciation, entailing either observation or physical exploitation, which are not directly quantifiable, or if quantifiable, cannot be valued by the market mechanism. Another area concerns externalities—the indirect, often unintended effects of resource development. Much of the current public concern about the environment is rooted in these two problems. Unfortunately, present techniques of evaluation do not deal with them satisfactorily. The social returns to successful research efforts in this connection, therefore, will be especially high.

Increasing demands on the public purse, growing conflicts in resource use, and protests about environmental degradation have emphasised the need for improved methods of project and policy evaluation. They have also helped to highlight areas of knowledge which are presently deficient and which tend therefore to impair such evaluations. The research priorities are reasonably clear. The challenge now is to find capable researchers and the financial and institutional support required to put them to work.

REFERENCES

Adams, J.G.V. (1971). London's third airport. *Geogr. J. 137*, 468.

Borton, T.E. and Warner, K.P. (1970). The Susquehanna communication-participation study. U.S. Army Engineering Institute for Water Resources, Alexandria, Va.

Bower, B.T. and Sewell, W.R.D. (1971). *Selecting Strategies for Air Quality Management*, Ottawa: Queen's Printer.

Buckley, H. and Tihanyi, E. (1967). *Canadian Policies for Rural Adjustment*. Economic Council of Canada, Special Study No. 7, Ottawa: Queen's Printer.

Burch, W.R. Jr. Meyersohn, R. and Ferriss, A.L. (1970). Society, personality, and environmental usufruct. In *Society and its Physical Environment, Annals of the American Academy of Political and Social Science 389*, 27.

Burch, W.R. Jr., Cheek, N.H. and Taylor, L. (1972). *Social Behaviour, Natural Resources and the Environment*. New York: Harper and Row.

Burton, I. (1965). Flood damage reduction in Canada. *Geogrl Bull. Ottawa* 7, 165.

Burton, I. *Et al.* (1972). Symposium on the human dimensions of air pollution in the U.K. Background papers. University of Edinburgh.

Canada House of Commons, Hansard, Ottawa. (1958, 1959).

Chevalier, M. and Cartwright, T.J. (1971). Public involvement in planning: the Delaware river case. In *Perceptions and Attitudes in Resources Management* (W.R.D. Sewell and I. Burton, Eds.). Ottawa: Information Canada.

Ciccetti, C.J. *et al.* (1972). Benefits or costs: an assessment of the Water Resources Council's proposed principles and standards. Brief prepared for presentation to Water Resources Council, Washington D.C.

Cleary, E.J. (1967). *The Orsanco Story: Water Quality Management in the Ohio Valley Under an Inter-state Compact*. Baltimore, Md.: Johns Hopkins Press.

Coomber, N.H. and Biswas, A. (1972). Evaluation of environmental intangibles: review of techniques. Deptt. of Environment, Ecological Systems Branch, Ottawa.

Craik, K. (1970). Environmental dispositions of environmental decision-makers in society and its physical environment. *Ann. Am. Acad. Political Social Sci. 389*, 98.

Davis, J. (1958). *Canada's Energy Prospects*. Ottawa: Queen's Printer.

Davis, R.K. (1968). *The Range of Choice in Water Management: A Study of Dissolved Oxygen in the Potomac Estuary*. Baltimore, Md.: Johns Hopkins Press.

Day, C. (1972). Benefit-cost analysis of a multiple purpose reservoir, Deer Creek Watershed, Ontario: a re-assessment. Paper presented to IGU Water Resources Symposium, Victoria, B.C.

Dorfman, R. (1965*a*). Formal (mathematical) models in the design of water resources systems. *Water Resourc. Res. 1*, 329.

Dorfman, R. (Ed.) (1965*b*). *Measuring Benefits of Government Investments*. Washington, D.C.: Brookings Institution.

Fox, I.K. and Hirfindahl, O. (1964). Attainment of efficiency in satisfying demands for water resources. *American Economic Review 54*, 198.

Fraser River Board (1963). *Final Report on Flood Control and Hydro Electric Power in the Fraser River Basin*. Victoria, B.C.: Queen's Printer.

Frost, M.J. (1971). *Values for Money: the Techniques of Benefit-Cost Analysis*. London: Gower Press Ltd.

Gentry, R.C. (1970). Hurricane Debbie modification experiments. *Science*, N.Y. *168*, 473.

Gould, P. (1963). Man against his environment: a game theoretic framework. *Ann. Ass. Am. Geogr. LIII*, 290.

Hass, E., Beggs, K.S. and Bonner, E.J. (1972). Science, technology, and the public: the case of planned weather modifications. In *Behaviour, Natural Resources and the Environment* (W.R. Burch Jr, Cheek, N.H. Jr and Taylor, L., Eds.). New York: Harper and Row.

Heathcote, R.L. (1969). Drought in Australia. *Geogr. Rev. 59*, 175.

Hewitt, K. and Burton, I. (1971). The hazardousness of a place: a regional ecology of damaging events. Research Series No. 6, Department of Geography, University of Toronto.

Hill, M. (1968). A goals-achievement matrix for evaluating alternative plans. *J. Am. Inst. Planners 34*, 19.

Hirschleifer, J., DeHaven, J. and Milliman, J.W. (1960). *Water Supply: Economics, Technology, and Policy*. Chicago: University of Chicago Press.

H.M. Treasury (1972). *Forestry in Great Britain*. London: H.M.S.O.

Howe, C. and Linaweaver, P. (1967). The impact of price on residential water demand. *Water Resour. Res. 3*, 13.

International Geographical Union (1972). IGU Commission on Man and the Environment meeting. Background papers, Calgary, Alberta.

Islam, A. (1970). Human adjustment to cyclone hazards: a case study of Char Jabbar, Natural Hazards Research Working Paper No. 18, Department of Geography, University of Toronto.

Jackson, C. I. (1971). The spatial dimensions of environmental management in Canada. Canadian Department of the Environment Geographical Paper No. 46. Ottawa: Information Canada.

Jackson, C.I. and Bird, P. (1968). Economic charges for water. In *Essays on the Theory and Practice of Pricing* (A. Seldon, Ed.). London: IEA, pp. 3-22.

James, I.C. Jr, Brower, B.T. and Matalas, N.C. (1970). Relative importance of variables in water resources planning. Reprinted from *Water Resources Research* (1969) *5*, 1165.

Kasperson, R. (1969). Environmental stress and the municipal political system. In *The Structure of Political Geography* (R. Kasperson and J. Minghi, Eds.). Chicago: Aldine Press, pp. 481-496.

Kates, R.W. (1962) Hazard and choice perception in flood plain management. Research Paper No. 106, Department of Geography, University of Chicago.

King, J.D. Jr. (1967). *Economic Development Projects and their Appraisal.* Baltimore, Md.: Johns Hopkins Press.

Kneese, A.V. and Bower, B.T. (1968). *Managing Water Quality: Economics, Technology, Institutions.* Baltimore, Md.: Johns Hopkins Press.

Kneese, A.V. and D'Arge, R.C. (1969). Pervasive external costs and the response of society. In *The Analysis and Evaluation of Public Expenditures: The PPB System.* A compendium of papers submitted to the Sub-committee on Economy in Government of the Joint Economic Committee, 91 Congress 1st Session, U.S. Government Printing Office.

Krutilla, J.V. (1969). *The Columbia River Treaty.* Baltimore, Md.: Johns Hopkins Press.

Lawenthal, D. (1969). The West Indies chooses a capital. In *The Structure of Political Geography* (R. Kasperson and J. Minghi, Eds.). Chicago: Aldine Press, pp. 350-365.

Leopold, L.B. (1971). A procedure for evaluating environmental impact. U.S. Geological Survey Circular No. 645. Washington, D.C.

Lichfield, N. (1968). Economics in town planning. *Tn. Plann. Rev. 34*, 5.

Lichfield, N. (1970). Evaluation methodology of urban and regional plans: a review. *Reg. Stud. 4*, 151.

Lime, D., Shafer, E. Jr. Mietz, J., Marans, R. and Driver, B.L. (1972). Behavioural dimensions of outdoor recreation demands. In *Environment and the Social Sciences* (J. Wohlwill, Ed.). Washington D.C.: American Psychological Association, pp. 198-248.

Mass, A. *et al.* (1962). *The Design of Water Resource Systems.* Cambridge, Mass.: Harvard University Press.

Macinko, G. (1963). The Columbia Basin project: expectations, realisations, implications. *Geogrl. Rev. 53*, 185.

MacNeill, J.W. (1971). *Environmental Management.* Ottawa: Information Canada.

Mishan, E.J. (1971). *Cost-Benefit Analysis.* London: George Allen & Unwin.

Mogoluf, M.B. (1970). Citizen participation: a review and commentary on federal policies and practices. Urban Institute, Washington, D.C.

Natural Hazards Research Working Papers (1970). Department of Geography, University of Toronto.

Newland, D. and Newland, N. (1970). *The Bad Trip: The Untold Story of the Spadina Expressway.* Toronto: House of Anasi.

O'Riordan, T. (1971). *Perspectives on Resource Management.* London: Pion Press.

O'Riordan, T. *et al.* (1970). Priorities in outdoor recreation research. In *Resources, Recreation, and Recreation* (H.D. Foster and W.R.D. Sewell, Eds.). Victoria, B.C.: University of Victoria Western Geographical Series No. 3, pp. 146-168.

Prest, A.R. and Turvey, R. (1965). Cost-benefit analysis: a survey. *Econ. J. 75*, 683.

Rees, J. and Rees, R. (1972). Water demand forecasts and planning margins in South-East England. *Reg. Stud. 6*, 37.

Rooney, J.K. (1967). The urban snow hazard in the United States. *Geogl. Rev. 57*, 538.

Russell, C.S. (1971). Models for investigation of industrial response to residuals management actions. *Swed. J. Econ. 73*, 134.

Russo, J.A., Trovern-Trend, K., Ellis, R.H., Koch, R.C., Howe, G.M., Milly, G.H. and Enger, I. (1965). *Operational and Economic Impact of Weather on the Construction Industry in the United States*. Hartford, Conn.: Travellers Research Center, Inc.

Saarinen, T.F. (1966). Perception of the drought hazard of the Great Plains. Research Paper No. 78, Department of Geography, University of Chicago.

Sadowski, W. (1965). *The Theory of Decision-making*. Oxford: Pergamon Press.

Schaefer, J. *et al.* (1966). The water resource: planning its use in N.E. Illinois. N.E. Illinois Planning Commission, Chicago, Illinois.

Schafer, E.L., Hamilton, J.E. and Schmidt, E.A. (1969). Natural landscape preferences: a predictive model. *J. Leisure Res. 1*, 1.

Schramm, G. (1970). Analysing opportunity costs: the South Indian Lake issue. Paper presented to Annual Meeting of the Canadian Institute of Forestry, Winnipeg, Manitoba.

Sewell, W.R.D. (1965). Water management and floods in the Fraser River basin. Research Paper No. 100, Department of Geography, University of Chicago.

Sewell, W.R.D. (1971*a*). Integrating public views in planning and policy-making. In *Perceptions and Attitudes in Resources Management* (W.R.D. Sewell and I. Burton, Eds.). Ottawa: Information Canada, pp. 125-132.

Sewell, W.R.D. (1971*b*). Environmental perceptions and attitudes of engineers and public health officials. *Environment and Behaviour*, *3*, 23-59.

Sewell, W.R.D. and Bower, B.T. (Eds.) (1968). *Forecasting the Demands for Water*. Ottawa: Queen's Printer.

Sewell, W.R.D. and Burton, I. (Eds.) (1971). *Perceptions and Attitudes in Resources Management*. Ottawa: Information Canada.

Sewell, W.R.D. and Roucche, L. (1972). Peak load pricing and urban water demand. Paper presented to IGU Water Resources Symposium, Victoria, B.C.

Sewell, W.R.D. and Wood, C. (1971). Environmental stress and environmental management: the Goldstream River case. Paper presented to Annual Meeting of the Canadian Association of Geographers, Waterloo, Ontario.

Tinney, E.R. *et al.* (1967). *An Initial Study of the Water Resources of the State of Washington*. Pullman, Wash.: Washington State University.

U.S. Outdoor Recreation Resources Commission (1962). *Outdoor Recreation for America*. Washington, D.C.: U.S. Government Printing Office.

U.S. President's Water Resources Council (1962). Policies, standards and procedures in the formulation and review of plans for the development of water and related land resources. *Senate Document No.* 97, *87th Congress,*

2nd Session, 24 May 1972. Washington, D.C.: U.S. Government Printing Office.

U.S. Water Resources Council (1968). *The Nation's Water Resources.* Washington, D.C.: U.S. Government Printing Office.

U.S. Water Resources Council (1972). *Proposed Principles and Standards for Planning Water and Related Land Resources.* Washington, D.C.: U.S. Government Printing Office.

Walford, R. (1969). *Games in Geography.* London: Longman.

Walsh, H.G. and Williams, A. (1969). Current issues in cost-benefit analysis. *CAS Occasional Paper No.* 11. London: H.M.S.O.

Watt, K.E.F. (1968). *Ecology and Resource Management: a Quantitative Approach.* New York: McGraw-Hill.

White, G.F. (1964). Choice of adjustment to floods. Research Paper No. 93, Department of Geography, University of Chicago.

White, G.F. (1966). Formation and role of public attitudes. In *Environmental Quality in a Growing Economy* (H. Jarret, Ed.). Baltimore, Md.: Johns Hopkins Press, pp. 105-127.

Wibberley, G.P. (1959). *Agriculture and Urban Growth.* London: Michael Joseph.

Wildawsky, A. (1966). The political economy of efficiency: cost-benefit analysis, systems analysis and program budgeting. *Publ. Admn. Rev. 26*, 292.

Wood, C. (1972). *Geographical Games.* Victoria, B.C.: Western Geographical Series, Vol. 6.

13

Resource Management and Public Policy: The Changing Role of Geographical Research

J.T. COPPOCK & W.R.D. SEWELL

Whatever definition of their subject geographers adopt, it is unlikely that many would challenge the view that geography is concerned with man's use of the earth's resources. British geographers have investigated many aspects of the use of resources in the United Kingdom, including land, minerals, scenery and water, and a useful bibliography of such work is available[1]; similar investigations have been undertaken in many parts of the world. Until recently, however, the concept of management of such resources has been only implicit in the geographer's approach and, like the planner, he has tended to take the ownership and control of resources for granted. It is interesting to note that only one title among Sir Dudley Stamp's long list of publications contains any reference to management or to managers,[2] though as his major work, *The Land of Britain: Its Use and Misuse*, implies, use presupposes a user, in other words, a resource manager.

This lack of concern with management is understandable, for the traditional training of geographers has encouraged them to focus their attention on the visible expression of use in the landscape, and the very terminology of land-use survey reflects this tradition. Furthermore, data are hard to come by, especially in the United Kingdom, where a belief in the 'sacredness of private property' and a paternalistic attitude on the part of government departments are long-established features, so that decision-makers of all kinds and at all levels show a general

Reprinted with Permission from *Scottish Geographical Magazine,* Vol. 91, No. 1, April, 1975.

unwillingness to reveal the bases of their decision making; indeed, a recent prime minister brushed aside a parliamentary question on the remit and functions of the Cabinet Committee on natural resources with the comment that 'It is not the normal practice to divulge the method of conducting public business'.[3] Even if such difficulties did not arise, geographers have not generally sought to ask questions about the management of resources and have not been equipped by their training to analyse the decisions of individual managers; furthermore, it might be argued that they are concerned, not with such individual decisions, but with statistical tendencies, i.e. what most managers do, and that the visible expression of these decisions is in fact a good guide. Such arguments can hardly be maintained in view of the growing body of knowledge about the differing perception of resources, both by individuals and by groups, and about what D.R. Denman has called 'the honeycomb of estates in land'.[4] Even in the heyday of *laissez faire* individual landowners controlled vast resources; it would hardly have been possible to examine land use in Sutherland in the 1870s without considering the attitudes and policies of the Duke of Sutherland who owned virtually the whole country.[5] It is interesting in this connection to note that historical geographers have probably paid more attention to decision-making than their colleagues studying the contemporary scene. The major difference today is that, while government policies have always affected the decisions of resource managers, the increasing involvement of government in resource use, whether as a manager itself through such agencies as the Forestry Commission, or through the machinery of land-use planning, or through general fiscal and legal measures, implies that it is now impossible for a geographer to evaluate the use of resources without examining official policies and policy measures.

At the same time, there have been shifts in both the challenges which this changing situation offers to geographers and in their responses to these challenges. Governmental agencies are increasingly seeking advice from social scientists on problems arising from the use of resources, though such approaches are more common in North America than they have been in the United Kingdom; nevertheless, the situation here is also likely to change following the government's acceptance of Lord Rothschild's proposals on the funding of government research and development, which envisage a much wider use of contract research.[6] This growing demand has also been matched by a greater willingness on the part of geographers and other social scientists to respond to such approaches than they have perhaps shown in the past. This situation has had some impact on training, particularly at the graduate level, where it has been reflected in the topics selected and in the approaches, concepts and techniques used (though here, too, these trends are more marked in North America).

Levels of Resource Management

One consequence of this growing concern, of particular relevance to geographers, is the need to consider resource management at different scales, of which four can be identified: the individual property or operating unit; the regional or sub-national; the national; and the international. Geographers have an interest in all levels, but have been most active in respect of the last three.

The control of the individual unit of management, be it farm, forest or mine, is the most obvious scale at which resources are managed, though it is increasingly affected by decisions taken at higher levels, which limit the choices available to resource managers or modify their decisions by altering the balance of advantage between various alternatives. This area of decision making has generally been neglected by geographers, though R.L. Millman has emphasised its importance and, single-handed, mapped the estates of rural Scotland.[7] Its importance for geographers has generally been that sample observations for regional or national studies are ideally made at this level, whether by interview or by postal questionnaire. Of course, where geographers must depend on secondary data, as is commonly the case with information derived from censuses, such an analysis will not be possible, and many studies by geographers of the use of resources have necessarily been undertaken with aggregations of individual units, usually by administrative area. Analysis of such data is not impossible, and much statistical ingenuity (and naivety) has been shown in making inferences from aggregated data; but they represent a poor second-best.

At the next level, the term 'regional' issued in a very broad sense to cover any scale above the individual and below the national, and to include functional, morphological and administrative regions. Geographical research into resource management of many kinds is commonly conducted at this scale. The most clearly identifiable examples involve water resources and, perhaps for this reason, these have attracted most attention from geographers; the river basin provides one of the few instances where a natural system and a man-made system coincide, for there is generally some organisation with responsibility for the management of one or more river basins in terms of water supply, pollution, fish conservation and, increasingly, recreation. Another type of regional resource management in Great Britain is represented by the structure plan, which sets guidelines for the individual resource managers in the region, and yet another by the regional plans of executive agencies, such as the Forestry Commission.

The national level of management is concerned chiefly with the policies of government, whether these are explicitly related to resource management, as in such documents as the annual *Review of Agriculture or Forestry Policy*,[8] or implicitly through the management of the economy as a whole, or even incidentally or accidentally, as a by-product of policies in quite different fields. There are also the plans of agencies, such as the British Inland Waterways Board or the Nature Conservancy Council, which have national responsibilities and national strategies for managing specific resources. The recent report of the Select Committee on Scottish Affairs on *Land Resource Use in Scotland* and the evidence presented to it offer a useful insight into the nature and weakness of management at this scale, and H.D. Clout also provides a convenient synthesis.[9]

Lastly, there is growing involvement by geographers in a fourth level of management, the international, which has become of increasing importance with the rise in the number of international agencies, such as FAO and UNESCO. Resource management at this level has been concerned primarily with three kinds of programmes: first, those intended to promote economic and social advances in the developing countries, sponsored both by individual governments, as with the United States' AID programmes, or by agencies of the United Nations, and involving mainly water, energy, forests and agricultural land; secondly, programmes to improve environmental quality or to conserve particular resources, whether undertaken multilaterally, as with fisheries or the dumping of oil at sea, or bilaterally, as with the control of pollution in the Great Lakes; and lastly, programmes to reduce the impact of environmental hazards, such as those sponsored by the various agencies of the United Nations concerned with the relief of disaster. Geographers have made contributions to all three, and it is interesting to note that here, too, the management of water resources, particularly for the generation of hydroelectricity, the prevention of floods, and the management of fisheries, has been particularly important.[10]

Approaches in Geographical Research relating to Resource Management

In addition to descriptive and analytical studies of particular resources and their use, of the kind which have played such a large part in British geographical writing in the past four decades, contributions by geographers in the field of resource management have been mainly of four kinds: (a) the development of abstract models of resource systems; (b) the construction of analytical models of the decision-making process in resource management; (c) case studies of particular policies; and (d) the development and application of techniques of analysis. The balance between these varies greatly, as does the relative importance of contributions from either side of the Atlantic.

Studies of the first kind have been few in number and have been mainly concerned with water management, for example, that by A.G. Wilson, though it should be noted that workers in other disciplines in the United Kingdom have attempted to model the movement of red deer and, more ambitiously, upland economies.[11] The emphasis has largely been on physical parameters and R.J. Chorley has criticised the dependence on negative feedback, characteristic of many ecological models, when a major requirement is for positive feedback, as in control engineering systems, so that account can be taken of changes in policy.[12]

The development of analytic models of decision-making processes in resource management has largely been confined to North America, though several empirically-derived models have been suggested by British geographers.[13] The originators of these models have sought to identify the stages in the decision-making process and the factors which influence each stage, with particular reference to the flow of information. These studies have been broadly of two kinds, those which have sought to identify the factors which influence the choice of a given course of action[14] and those which attempt to determine the roles of different groups in the decision-making process, such as special interest groups or professionals.[15] Such studies begin by proposing a simple model of the process which is then tested in an actual example; the concepts have largely been derived from other social sciences, but they have been refined and sometimes extended by geographers. Once again, the emphasis has been on water-related problems, notably those concerned with drought, flood and pollution, though other kinds of problems, such as air pollution, have also been considered. Several studies are now under way in the United Kingdom, notably at Leeds, where J.W. Birch heads a team investigating the management of land and water resources in Yorkshire and A.V. Kirkby is studying a problem of industrial pollution at Avonmouth. At the national scale, W.R.D. Sewell is investigating water management in Great Britain.

The category of research into resource management which has been best developed in the United Kingdom is that involving case studies. Such studies have been of two kinds: (a) descriptive studies of the ways in which particular resources have been managed and of the policies relating to them; and (b) those which attempt to assess the performance of particular policies. Given the traditional approach to resource use in Great Britain, it is not surprising that investigations of the first kind should have attracted most attention: they have included studies of agriculture, air pollution, amenity, forestry, recreation and water, and have been conducted at both regional and national scales.[16] The second category is much less common, but has included studies of agricultural subsidies, land allocation and preservation and water pricing.[17] A particularly good example is that by C. Day on policies for water management in Ontario.[18]

Investigations in the last category, too, have been most strongly developed in North America. Two principal types of tools and techniques have been used, those concerned with the measurement and evaluation of the costs and benefits of resource development, and those which have sought to identify and measure public preferences, particularly in situations which involve public perceptions and attitudes. The first category draws heavily on work done in economics, especially benefit/cost analysis; general reviews have been provided of such tools in general and of benefit/cost studies in particular.[19] This, too has been a neglected area in British research, though D.N.M. Starkie and D.M. Johnson have used such approaches in the study of aircraft noise.[20] The adaptation and use of tools for identifying and measuring public preferences has been undertaken mainly in the environmental field and such studies have been marked by gradual improvements in, and increasing sophistication of, the methods used, and by an increasing degree of interdisciplinary cooperation, notably between geographers and psychologists, a trend which is illustrated by several studies, by an SSRC-sponsored seminar on environmental perception and by courses at Clark and Colorado.[21]

The Contributions of Geographers

Geographers have thus contributed an increasingly wide range of studies in the management of resources through published papers, books and reports, and in their teaching. Such research has either been a kind which has general application or is related to a particular problem or policy in one specific area.[22] Yet this does not exhaust the contributions of geographers to resource management at regional, national and international levels, for they have been increasingly involved in the work of public agencies and in policy formulation (though these contributions themselves often derive from published work and from a growing appreciation by public officials and other decision-makers that geographers have useful contributions to make in resource management).

Probably the most numerous contributions outside the academic field have been made as members of the committees which advise and make policy in public agencies such as the Countryside Commissions and the Nature Conservancy Council and their predecessors, but geographers have also played a much more direct role as advisers or as members of committees investigating particular aspects of the use of resources.[23] Most prominent in this respect was the late Sir Dudley Stamp, in his roles as Chief Adviser on Rural Land Use to the Ministry of Agriculture, member and vice-chairman of the Scott Committee on Land Utilisation in Rural Areas, member of the Royal Commission on Common Land, chairman of the Natural Resources Advisory Committee, member of the Nature Conservancy and chairman of its England Committee.[24]

Other geographers have acted in similar capacities, at both national and regional levels; for example, H.C. Darby has been a member of the Water Resources Board, J.W. House of the short-lived North Pennine Rural Development Board, and other geographers (including House) of Regional Economic Councils.[25] Geographers, though often not identifiable as such, have played a major part on the staff of government agencies concerned with resources, notably in physical planning, but also in conservation. Of increasing importance, too, is contract research, undertaken by geographers for public agencies, in which plans and strategies have been prepared, tools devised or evaluations undertaken. Such work has been particularly prominent in the study of outdoor recreation, and the Tourism and Recreation Research Unit in Edinburgh has undertaken eight major projects of this kind and has published eleven reports; M.F. Tanner has similarly conducted research for the Sports Council and the Countryside Commission.[26] Geographers have also acted as independent critics of public policy and have contributed to public debates about such policies, both in published work and in submissions to committees of inquiry and the like.[27]

Conclusions

Geographers, particularly in North America and, to a lesser extent, in Australasia, have increasingly been called upon to give advice to public agencies on aspects of resource management. The emphasis so far has been mainly on the management of water resources, whether for human consumption, as a habitat for fish, as a means of transport and as a basis for outdoor recreation, or in respect of the impact of water on other resources, as in flood control, or of other activities on water resources, as with water pollution. This emphasis on water may stem from the nature of the resource itself, as a flow resource in which the unit of operation is large, and because of its obvious links with and dependence on a wide variety of human activities; but other resources are also attracting attention, perhaps because of the growing interest in the 'environment', which embraces but extends far beyond the management of resources.

The contribution of geographers in the United Kingdom has been proportionately smaller than that of their North American colleagues, partly perhaps because of the less important role of public lands, the smaller scale of the country, which makes it easier (though no less wrong) for decision makers to ignore spatial differences, the less severe impact of natural hazards, the much longer period of man's adaptation to his environment and the strength of tradition. Nevertheless, useful progress has been made and there is rapidly expanding interest in some fields, notably outdoor recreation.

It should also be noted that there is a rapid growth of interest in resource management among those in other disciplines. Thus, while agriculturalists and foresters have long had an interest in land at the first level of resource management, the contraction of demand for agricultural advisers and foresters has led them to widen their field of interest to include rural resources generally.

Similarly, the difficulties of finding both students and job opportunities in pure biology have encouraged a parallel trend, and mathematicians, engineers and others are increasingly seeking to apply their skills in the use of resources. While it is clear that the complexity of resource management is such that multidisciplinary approaches are both inevitable and desirable, it is important that geographers should make their interest known publicly; for it is certainly not self-evident to those outside geography, as the absence of a geographer on the Verney Committee shows.[28] The kind of contributions which are being increasingly sought by public officials and policy makers are those which seek to integrate concepts and techniques from a number of disciplines, which use sophisticated techniques of analysis and which can be communicated effectively by research workers to policy-makers. All present a challenge to geographers and, in deciding whether to accept it, they would do well to ponder B.J.L. Berry's dictum that if geographers 'fail to perform in policy-relevant terms, they will cease to be called on to perform at all'.[29]

NOTE

A general view of resource management, not confined to writings by geographers, will be found in T. O'Riordan, *Perspectives on Resource Management*, London, Pion, 1971; for a specifically geographical view, see J.W. Birch, Geography and Resource Management, *Journal of Environmental Management*, Vol. 1, 1973, pp. 3-11.

REFERENCES

1. N. Hilton, An approach to agricultural land classification in Great Britain, in *Land Use and Resources: Studies in Applied Geography*, Special Publication No. 1, Inst. Brit. Geogr. 1968, 127-142; S.H. Beaver, Minerals and Planning, *Geogr. J.* 104, 1944, 166-193; D.L. Linton, The Assessment of scenery as a natural resource, *Scot. Geog. Mag.* 84, 219-238; W.G.V. Balchin, A water use survey, *Geogr. J.* 124, 1958, 476-479; J. House, Geography, decision takers and policy makers, in M. Chisholm and H.B. Rodgers (eds.), *Studies in Human Geography*, London, 1973, 300-305.
2. J. Chibnall, the published work of Sir Dudley Stamp, in *Land Use and Resources, op. cit.*, 71-81.
3. *Parliamentary Debates*, 12th November 1968, Vol. 84.
4. D.R. Denman, The estate in land and the employment of resources, Ch. 7 in *Land Ownership and Resources*, Cambridge, Department of Estate Management, n.d., p. 123.
5. *Returns of Owners of Land*, Party Papers, Vol. 1873.
6. *A Framework for Government Research and Development*, Cmnd.4814, London, H.M.S.O., 1971.
7. R. Millman, The Marches of the Highland Estates, *Scot. Geog. Mag.* 85,

172-181, 86, 186-203, and 88, 126-133, also App. 19, Memorandum by Dr. R. Millman, Select Committee on Scottish Affairs, *Land Resource Use in Scotland*, Vol. 5, House of Commons Paper 511, 1971-72, London, H.M.S.O., 1972, 121-127.

8. *Forestry Policy*, London, H.M.S.O., 1972.
9. Select Committee on Scottish Affairs, *op. cit.*, Report, Minutes of Evidence and Appendices; and H.D. Clout, *Rural Geography: An Introductory Survey*, Oxford, 1972.
10. G.F. White, Contributions of geographical analysis to river basin development, *Geogr. J.* 129, 412-416; W.R.D. Sewell, *The Contribution of Social Science Research to Water Management in Canada*, Ottawa, Queen's Printer, 1968; and G.F. White, Natural hazards research, in R.J. Chorley (ed.), *Directions in Geography*, London, 1973, 193-216.
11. A.G. Wilson, Toward system models for water resource management, *Journ. Environ. Management*, 1, 1973, 65-81; and R.J. Chorley and B.A. Kennedy, *Physical Geography: A Systems Approach*, London, 1971, 298-303.
12. R.J. Chorley, Geography as Human Ecology, Ch. 7 in R.J. Chorley (ed.), *Directions in Geography*, London, 1973, 158-167.
13. For example, J.W. Birch, Farming systems as resource systems, in V. Bonuzzi (ed.), *Agricultural Typology and Land Utilisation*, Verona Center of Agricultural Geography, 1972, 13-20; J. Chorley and B.A. Kennedy, *op. cit.*, p. 341.
14. G.F. White, Choice of use in resource management. *Natural Resources Journal*, 1, 1961, pp. 23-40; and L. Bowden, *Diffusion of the Decision to Irrigate*, U. of Chicago, Dept. Geog. Research Paper No. 97, 1965.
15. R. Kasperson, Environmental stress and the municipal political system, in R. Kasperson and J. Minghi (eds.), *The Structure of Political Geography*, Chicago, 1969, pp. 481-496; J. Wolpert, The decision process in spatial context, *Ann. Ass. Amer. Geogr.*, 54-1964, 537-538; T. O'Riordan, Towards a strategy of public involvement, in W.R.D. Sewell and I. Burton (eds.), *Perceptions and Attitudes in Resources Management*, Ottawa, 1971, 99-110; W.R.D. Sewell and C.J.B. Wood, Environmental decision-making and environmental stress, paper presented at the Annual Meeting of the Canadian Association of Geographers, Waterloo, Ontario, June, 1971; W.R.D. Sewell, Environmental Perceptions and attitudes of engineers and public health officials, *Environment and Behaviour*, 3, 1971, 23-59; M. Barker, *The Structure and Content of Environmental Cognitions*, Unpublished Ph.D. Dissertation, University of Toronto, Department of Geography, University of Toronto, 1972.
16. J.T. Coppock, *An Agricultural Geography of Great Britain*, London, 1971; L. Foster *et al.*, Studies of adjustment to air pollution in the United Kingdom, in a volume edited by Ian Burton, Oxford U.P., forthcoming; J.T. Coppock, The Countryside (Scotland) Act and the geographer, *Scot. Geog. Mag.*, 84, 201-211; J.T. Coppock, Postwar Forestry in Great Britain,

Ch. 4 in R.H. Best and J.T. Coppock, *The Changing Use of Land in Britain*, London, 1962, 99-117; J.A. Patmore, *Land and Leisure*, Newton Abbot, 1970; Keith Smith, *Water in Britain*, London, 1972; A.S. Mather, Red deer land use in the northern highlands, *Scot. Geog. Mag.*, 88, 36-47; See also for a general view, Michael Chisholm (ed.), *Resources for Britain's Future*, Newton Abbot, 1973.

17. I.R. Bowler, unpublished Ph.D. thesis, U. of Liverpool, 1973; R.H. Best and A.G. Champion, Regional conversions of agricultural land to urban use in England and Wales, 1945-67, *Trans. Inst. Brit. Geogr.*, 49, 1970, 15-32; P. Hall *et al. The Containment of Urban England*, London, 1973; D. Thomas, *London's Green Belt*, London, 1970; J. Rees, Water demand forecasts and planning margins in S.E. England, *Regional Studies*, 6, 37-48; J. Rees, Demand for water in S.E. England, *Geogr. J.*, 139, 20-36.
18. J.C. Day, Hindsight evaluation of water management projects in Ontario, in F.M. Leversedge (ed.), *Priorities in Water Management*, U. of Victoria, Western Geographical Series, 1973.
19. W.R.D. Sewell, *et al., Guide to Benefit Cost Analysis*, Ottawa, 1961; and W.R.D. Sewell, Broadening the approach to evaluation in resources management decision-making, *Journ. Environ. Management*, 1, 1973, 33-60.
20. D.N.M. Starkie and D.M. Johnson, Losses of residential amenity: an extended cost model, *Regional Studies*, 7, 173-181.
21. G.F. White, Formation and role of public attitudes, in H. Jarrett (ed.), *Environmental Quality in a Growing Economy*, Baltimore, Md., 1966, 105-127; W.R.D. Sewell and I. Burton (Eds.), *Perceptions and Attitudes in Resources Management*, Ottawa, 1971; B. Goodey, Perception of the environment: a personal overview, Paper presented to the Seminar on Perception of the Environment, Sheffield Center for Environmental Research, 4 July 1972; D. Lowenthal, Research in environmental perception and behaviour: perspectives on current problems, *Environment and Behaviour*, 4, 333-342; T.F. Saarinen, *Perception of the Environment*, Resource Paper no. 5, Washington, D.C., Commission on College Geography, Ass. Amer. Geogr., 1969; R.W. Kates, Human perception of the environment, *Internat. Soc. Sci. J.*, 22, 648-659; T.F. Saarinen and J. Sims, Coping with environmental threat: Great Plains farmers and the sudden storm, *Ann. Ass. Amer. Geogr.*, 59, 677-686; W.R.D. Sewell and B.R. Little, Specialists, laymen and the process of environmental appraisal, *Regional Studies*, 7, 161-171.
22. W.R.D. Sewell, *et. al., Modifying the Weather: A Social Assessment*, U. of Victoria, Western Geographical Series, 9, 1973.
23. J.W. House, *op. cit.*; J.T. Coppock and D.R. Diamond were specialist advisers to the Select Committee on Scottish Affairs, 1971-72, and J.A. Patmore and H.B. Rodgers acted in the same capacity for the Select Committee of the House of Lords on Sport and Leisure.

24. R.O. Buchanan, The man and his world, in Land Use and Resources, *op.cit.*, 8-10.
25. J. House, *op. cit.*
26. B.S. Duffield and M.L. Owen, ed. J.T. Coppock, *Leisure + Countryside = A Geographical Appraisal of Outdoor Recreation in Lanarkshire*, U. of Edinburgh, Tourism and Recreation Research Unit, 1970, and subsequent volumes; and M.F. Tanner, *Water Resources and Recreation*, Sports Council Water Recreation Series, Study 3, London, Sports Council, 1973.
27. For example, J.T. Coppock, Planning for outdoor recreation in the Scottish Countryside, Select Committee of the House of Lords on Sport and Leisure, House of Lords Paper 193, vol. 3, H.M.S.O., 1973, 541-546.
28. Department of the Environment, *Sinews for Survival*, London, H.M.S.O., 1972.
29. B.J.L. Berry, The geography of the United States in the year 2000, *Trans. Inst. Brit. Geogr.*, 51, 22.

SUSTAINABLE RESOURCE DEVELOPMENT

14

World Conservation Strategy, Economic Policies and Sustainable Resource-Use in Developing Countries

CLEM TISDELL

The World Conservation Strategy (WCS) was drawn up in 1980 by the International Union for the Conservation of Nature in consultation with such bodies as the United Nations Environment Programme (UNEP), the Food and Agriculture Organization, and UNESCO, and individuals throughout the world. Its preparation was jointly financed by UNEP and the World Wildlife Federation. Its framers hoped that the document would encourage individual countries to formulate National Conservation Strategies incorporating policies for sustainable development; some countries have embarked on the process of drawing up such strategies. The WCS arose from concern about the rapid and continuing deterioration of the biosphere as a result of the growing human population and the impact of its activities on the environment, especially on living resources.

The strategy is based on the view that unless proper attention is paid to conserving the biosphere and natural ecosystems within it, economic development will be unsustainable. Man depends on living resources for his survival and economic well-being and it is for this reason that serious attention must be given to the deteriorating state of the biosphere. The biosphere contains ecosystems supporting all life, including human life, and damage to it, especially if permanent, can at the very least be expected to reduce economic productivity. The WCS

Reprinted with Permission from *The Environment Professional,* Vol. 7, pp. 102-107.

claims that ecological considerations are not a luxury but a necessity for sound and sustainable economic development.

The view expressed in the WCS document is anthropocentric. Human beings need to manage, arrest or slow down the deterioration of the biosphere for their *own* benefit. While the framers of the strategy may have a reverence for all life (for all species) they believe that most human beings are swayed by their own self-interest and therefore conservation proposals need to appeal to self-interest in order to gain widespread support. Again, the framers of WCS believe that there is little point in campaigning for the utopian conservation goals which policy-makers have no leeway for adopting.

A more realistic approach to influencing policy-makers is required, namely, one which ensures that conservational aspects are taken into account in relation to the options realistically open to the policy-maker. For example, it may have to be accepted that various species and certain natural ecosystems will continue to disappear for some time yet. If this is so, conservationists should provide some guidelines on those species or ecosystems that should be given preference for preservation.

Economic Growth, Environment

WCS states that sustainable economic development requires:

- the maintenance of essential ecological processes and life support systems
- the preservation of genetic diversity
- measures to ensure the sustainable use of species and ecosystems

Agricultural systems, forests, and coastal and freshwater systems are claimed to be the most important life-support systems for human beings and to be under the greatest threat. Economic growth in less developed countries (LDCs) involving the unmitigated exploitation of these systems (such as felling of tropical forests, the removal of mangroves, the felling of forests on steep hill slopes, open-access fishing) may result only in a temporary economic improvement. The long-term economic productivity of the land and the sea may be reduced by such exploitation of nature and may result in an eventual economic and ecological crisis, especially if the country's population rises in the interim (Tisdell and Fairbairn, 1984).

The World Conservation Strategy sees *informed* self-interest as being a powerful force for conservation in LDCs as well as in more developed countries. One of the ways in which LDCs might benefit from conservation is, for instance, through tourism based on conserved natural resources. But unfortunately such tourism sometimes fails to benefit local people who are forced to make a sacrifice for nature conservation. For example, Mishra (1982) suggests that local people in Nepal have been impoverished as a result of the establishment of national parks (Tisdell, 1983).

The way in which any cost of or gains from conservation are distributed cannot be ignored. WCS points out that "local commitment to a protected area can only be assured through provision of local advantage such as increased opportunities for employment and commerce."

Poverty in LDCs

Nevertheless, LDCs may not appropriate all the benefits from their conservation efforts — many of the benefits may spill over to inhabitants of more developed countries without payment being made for them. Furthermore, poverty itself in LDCs is a substantial barrier to conservation. WCS states:

> Much habitat destruction and overexploitation of living resources by individuals, communities and nations in the developing world is a response to relative poverty, caused or exacerbated by a combination of human population growth and inequities within and among nations.... Every country should have a conscious policy to avoid as far as possible the spread of such situations, and eventually to achieve a balance between numbers and environment. At the same time it is essential that the affluent constrain their demands on resources, and preferably reduce them, shifting some of their wealth to assisting the deprived.

Changes in the world economic order such as the removal of trade barriers to goods from developing countries and great development assistance to LDCs may help to improve their economic lot and scope for conservation. Nevertheless, rapid economic transformation of most LDCs is unlikely in the near future, even assuming that widespread change in the world economic order occurs.

Sustainable Resource-Use and Development

Sustainable development and resource-use are seen in the WCS as important and desirable goals. However, "sustainability" is not defined nor is the question debated of whether it is ever desirable to trade off sustainable development for other goals.

One view of sustainability is that the existence of the human race on Earth should be assured for as long as possible (Daly, 1980) and that the economic and other activities of human beings should be so regulated as to make this possible. Daly argues that this is most likely to be achieved if a policy of zero-population growth is combined with one of holding levels of consumption steady, that is, by achieving a steady state economy.

In Daly's view, consumption by those with high levels of income should be reduced. Consumption per capita should not be maximised but brought to a "satisfactory" level for all. Steps should, in his opinion, be taken to ensure greater equality of income and this is likely to require a transfer of purchasing power from more developed countries to less developed ones.

However, in a steady state economy needed to maximise the length of existence of the human race? Much depends on one's theory of what will determine or influence the length of continuing existence of *homo sapiens.* It may be that a variety of patterns of economic activity (not necessarily all steady-state ones) are compatible with maximising the length of existence of the human race but that there is also a set which will reduce its length of existence. In light of Daly's hypothesis, should a nation also attempt to maximise the possible length of its existence? If so, would steady and sustainable levels of economic activity be the optimal way to achieve this? There are certainly many unresolved issues to consider.

There may be circumstances in which it is worthwhile achieving temporary economic growth because no future income has to be sacrificed to obtain it or only a relatively small amount of future income has to be lost for a temporary economic gain. On the other hand, some economic development may be such that a substantial amount of future income has to be given up for a temporary economic gain now. WCS is correct in highlighting possible scenarios of this type. Developing countries may make economic gains now by felling their tropical forests and earning foreign exchange by exporting the products to developed countries, but this may be at the expense of a substantial reduction in the future economic productivity of the land involved in the future.

Sustainability: Another View

In relation to agricultural systems, Conway (1983) has defined sustainability as:

> the ability of a system to maintain productivity in spite of a major disturbance such as that caused by intensive (maintained) stresses or a large perturbation.... Satisfactory methods of measuring sustainability have still to be found. Lack of sustainability may be indicated by declining productivity but, equally, collapse may come suddenly and without warning.

In his view, modern agricultural technologies may at first give high yields when introduced but the associated agricultural systems often prove to be unsustainable. The use of chemical pesticides such as DDT may for example lead to temporary gains, followed by lower yields as resistance builds up. Modern agricultural technologies also require a high degree of management to ensure their productivity. Traditional agricultural systems call for less intensive management and in Conway's view are more likely to be sustainable than "modern" ones. It has been observed for example that high yielding varieties of crops show less tolerance as a rule to extremes in environmental conditions than do traditional varieties, and that traditional systems of mixed cropping are often more resilient and productive than monocultures.

While sustainability may be a virtue, many economists do not consider it to be an overriding goal. Many believe that the optimal social strategy is one which maximizes net present social value. In some cases this can imply that it is optimal to extinguish a species (Clark, 1976) or allow it to become extinct. Furthermore, the optimal agricultural production system is not necessarily one that sustains production. In some cases too, it *may* be optimal to engage in agricultural practices which accelerate erosion or lead to salting of soils (Dumsday *et al.,* 1983).

This is not to say that these practices are always justifiable from an economic point of view. Furthermore, in assessing them one must take account of various sources of "market failure" such as externalities or spillovers. For example, if the accelerated soil erosion reduces the useful life of dams due to more rapid siltation, this should be taken into account. Undoubtedly, there are many environmentally degrading activities that cannot be justified on the basis of economic calculations when interdependencies and social factors are taken into account.

The sustainable use of common-property resources in LDCs is a particular subject for concern. Common-property resources are resources that are shared in common and to which there is common access. The inhabitants of many LDCs have common access, for example, to fishing stocks in coastal waters. When there is common access to such resources, they are liable to be over-exploited. The fishing stock may, for instance, be reduced below the level that gives the maximum sustainable yield (as well as below the level that gives the maximum economic yield). In some cases, as a result of common access, a species may be eliminated due to intensive harvesting even though it is economically optimal to retain the species. LDCs, therefore, face the problem of trying to regulate the economic exploitation of common-property resources.

Restraints in LDCs

Adverse environmental impacts of economic activity in LDCs can have more serious consequences for human welfare than in developed countries. When the adverse environmental effects of economic activity in an area reduce future productivity there, affected communities in more developed countries find it relatively easy for their members to move elsewhere to other economic opportunities. Most developed countries are characterised by a high degree of mobility of labour and capital, and considerable social homogeneity.

On the other hand, most LDCs have low mobility of labour and capital (Todaro, 1981; Gunatilleke, 1973) and considerable social heterogeneity. This means that when an environmental disaster or misfortune strikes a particular area and threatens the livelihood of local people in LDCs, they are less able to move and obtain equal or comparable economic opportunities and social satisfaction elsewhere to those previously enjoyed. Thus their income suffers and they may be thrown into extreme poverty.

A further reason why the assessment of the environmental impacts of projects is likely to be important in LDCs is that when a project has an adverse effect on income or human welfare in a locality, it can be expected that compensating relief from elsewhere in the economy will be limited. Social security systems are poorly developed in LDCs (Nugent and Gillaspy, 1983) and the scope for giving aid from intra-national sources is limited.

The inhabitants of less developed countries are much more dependent for their livelihood on living resources than those of developed countries. The bulk of the population of LDCs is typically employed in agriculture, fishing and forestry and other industries directly dependent on a living resource base (Todaro, 1981). Disturbances to the ecosystems on which these industries depend can have widespread economic consequences. This is an additional reason why any developments in LDCs giving rise to ecological effects need careful assessment.

Resource-Use Policies

Given the importance of the environment (especially the biosphere) to economic activity and human welfare in LDCs, what policies can be adopted to ensure wise resource-use and development in LDCs? Policies can be improved in this regard but one must also remember that the putting into effect of government policies is itself not without cost. Policies have to be devised (this may involve costly research and bargaining) and implemented, and implementation can involve communication, regulation and enforcement costs which can weigh heavily on countries that are already poor.

The cost of policies must be weighed against their likely effectiveness and consequent benefits. A policy that cannot be carried out is of no benefit and indeed may involve considerable cost to the community if government administrators spend their time in devising and debating it. Difficulties, however, are not an adequate excuse for taking no action.

It is important that when public projects are evaluated in LDCs (and the same is also true of private projects that come under public scrutiny) that account is taken of their main environmental impacts. Social cost-benefit analysis should not ignore environmental impacts and ecological spillovers in the assessment of projects in LDCs. In the past, however, major public projects, such as the building of the Kariba Dam, have gone ahead without any prior ecological surveys (James, 1978).

Failure to take account of ecological factors has sometimes occurred for reasons of political expediency, at other times because of failure to realize the potential importance of such variables, and on other occasions because of lack of skilled persons able to carry out evaluation. Lack of skilled evaluators, especially in very small countries (micro-states), can be a significant constraint in project evaluation; this, however, can be overcome to some extent and at a cost by drawing on the worldwide body of professionals in the field.

In foreign aid projects, it is important that environmental dimensions are kept in view. Increasingly, environmental assessments are being made of aid and related projects; for example, United States AID (Agency for International Development) is doing this and so is the World Bank. To the extent that the menu or list of available projects presented to such agencies for possible aid involves presorting by power groups in aid-receiving countries, there may already be some bias against projects that are environmentally sound but less beneficial to these power groups. Yet, it is very difficult to think of practical ways of avoiding such potential biases.

Imported Technologies

Technologies introduced to LDCs from abroad need to be assessed carefully. While some may lead to improved socio-economic and environmental conditions, other technologies may have adverse consequences. Some of the technologies in developed countries (DCs) are inappropriate to the factor composition of LDCs and *may give only temporary (non-sustainable) benefits.*

For example, the use of chemical pesticides in some LDCs has brought a temporary increase in crop yields but has been followed in some cases by increased resistance of pests to the chemicals involved and an increase in the population of non-target pests. Users of a technology may become economically "trapped" into its continuing use even though it would have been best from a collective point of view never to have used the technology at all. This, however, is not to deny the occurrence of circumstances where enlightened use of pesticide technology is preferable to its non-use.

One can take as another example the mechanisation of the traditional fisheries (Yahaya and Wells, 1983). The fishing stock exploited by fishermen in many parts of the world is already overfished both from the point of view of obtaining maximum sustainable yield and from the point of view of obtaining maximum economic yield. The mechanisation of fisheries initially increases the catch, and improved economic gains may be noted at first. However, it eventually leads to a reduction in the fishing stock and a decrease in the total catch if common access to the fisheries is the rule and overfishing is already occurring.

It is possible (indeed, certain, under plausible conditions) that the total catch will eventually be lower than prior to the introduction of the new technology and the cost per unit of the catch higher than before its use. Thus, in the common-access case or in cases where it is not really possible for the government to limit access and exploitation rates or resources, the introduction of new technology can, in the end, have adverse economic and environmental consequences.

In certain cases, introduction of new technology will speed up the rate of extinction of species. Both turtles and dugongs (sea cows), for example, have suffered as a result of the introduction of modern technology (Carr, 1968; Tisdell, 1983): outboard motors make it easier to pursue and capture these animals than was the case with non-mechanised boats. Also, in the case of turtles, mechanisation makes it easier to visit nesting grounds in remote areas and take eggs and adults.

Influencing Factors

Political and economic pressure exists for the introduction of modern technologies into industries harvesting natural resources to which there is common access, despite adverse long-term consequences. Those who obtain the technology first may gain substantially. If the technology is widely available, all will gain *at first.* Any group which does not have the technology may press to maintain its share in the catch or to restore it. Thus, politically, a government may support the introduction of the technology even though collectively its introduction is economically and environmentally damaging in the medium-to-long term. Furthermore, those firms and countries able to sell their technology or equipment embodying the technology have an interest in promoting its adoption. In cases such as this, expressions of individual self-interest may conflict with collective long-term interests in resource-use.

The economic and environmental desirability of introducing a new technology to an LDC often depends on whether use of the technology can be or will be regulated by the government of the LDC. The economic scope for regulating economic activity in LDCs is more limited than in DCs. Consequently technologies that prove to be desirable in DCs may turn out to be unsatisfactory in LDCs because little control over their use can be exercised in LDCs. LDCs need to be selective in their import of foreign technologies.

To the extent that regulation of resource-use in LDCs is possible and socially desirable, governments in LDCs should adopt appropriate regulatory policies. An example would be land-use zoning. Furthermore, educational programmes and extension services can be employed to encourage environmentally-sound methods of production and make individuals aware of changing environmental conditions. Sometimes individuals are slow to perceive or to foresee fundamental changes in ecological and environmental conditions (Tisdell, 1983). Nevertheless, one cannot rely purely on education and communication as the means of encouraging the most socially beneficial use of resources.

Concluding Observations

LDCs do have an interest in the conservation of living resources, at least from the point of view of maintaining production dependent on these resources. This is not to say that LDCs have an interest in conserving or maintaining all of their living resources. Sometimes they find it worthwhile to sacrifice some of these resources for short-term gains.

Again, the prime beneficiaries of nature conservation in LDCs are not always the local people but individuals in DCs and/or the wealthier members of the LDC. This has sometimes led to the view that conservational causes are those of a "rich men's club," and that efforts to promote conservation in LDCs are a scheme primarily to benefit DCs. Nevertheless, all types of conservation in LDCs do not favour the rich nor do they benefit primarily DCs, even though some may. One's view about the desirability of any conservation scheme is liable to be influenced by the way in which its costs and benefits are distributed. Therefore, not only total benefits and costs but also distributional factors should form a part of the assessment of conservational strategies in LDCs.

REFERENCES

Carr, A. (1968). *The Turtle: A National History of Sea Turtles.* Cassell, London.

Clark, C.W. (1976). *Mathematically Bioeconomics*, John Wiley, New York.

Conway, G.R. (1983). Agroecosystem Analysis. ICCET Series E, No. 1. Imperial College, London.

Daly, H. (1980). *Economics, Ecology and Ethics.* Freeman, San Francisco.

Dumsday, R.G., Oram, D.A. and Lumley, S.E. (1983). Economic aspects of the control of dryland salinity. *Proceedings of the Royal Society of Victoria* 95(3):139-145.

Gunatilleke, G. (1973). The urban-rural balance and development: The experience of Sri Lanka. *Marga Quarterly Journal* 2(1):35-68.

James, J. (1978). Growth, technology and the environment in less developed countries: A survey. *World Development* 6:937-965.

Mishra, H.R., (1982). Balancing human needs and conservation in Nepal's Royal Chitwan National Park. *Ambio* 11(5):246-251.

Myers, N. (1979). *The Sinking Ark: A New Look at the Problem of Disappearing Species.* Pergamon Press, Oxford.

Nugent, J.B. and Gillaspy, R.T. (1983). Old age pensions and fertility in rural areas of less developed countries: Some evidence from Mexico. *Economic and Cultural Change* 31(4):809-829.

Tisdell. C.A. (1983). Conserving living resources in Third World countries: Economic and social issues. *International Journal of Environmental Studies* 22:11-24.

Tisdell, C. and Fairbairn, T.I. (1984). Subsistence economies and unsustainable development and trade: Some simple theory. *The Journal of Development Studies* 20(2):227-241.

Todaro, M.P. (1981). *Economic Development in the Third World.* 2nd ed. Longman, London.

World Conservation Strategy (WCS). (1980). The World Conservation Strategy: Living Resource Conservation for Sustainable Development. International Union for the Conservation of Nature. Glands, Switzerland.

Yahaya, J. and Wells, R.J.G. (1983). A case study of three gears in the Tregganu fishery, Malaysia. *The Developing Economies* 20(1):73-99.

15

The Multiple Dimensions of Sustainable Development

MICHAEL REDCLIFT

Sustainable Development

The problem with referring to 'sustainable development' is that, like so many words in the development lexicon, its very strength is its vagueness: sustainable development' means different things to different people.

One point of departure is to define what Barbier (1989) refers to as *sustainable economic development*. This refers to the optimal level of interaction between three systems the biological, the economic and the social — a level which is achieved "through a dynamic and adaptive process of trade-offs" (Barbier, 1989, p. 185). Economists, notably David Pearce, continue to emphasise the trade-off between systems or between present and future needs, as the key issue (Pearce, 1986). In similar terms it is argued that "sustainable economic development involves maximising the net benefits of economic development, subject to maintaining the services and quality of natural resources over time" (Pearce *et al.*, 1987). For economists interested in the environment, then, issues like environmental accounting, which aim to give a numerical value to environmental losses and costs, are essential instruments in seeking to achieve greater sustainability.

Of immediate contrast is what Barbier sees as a much less narrowly defined concept of *sustainable development*. This is expressed in the

Reprinted with Permission from *The Geographical Association*, 1990.

Brundtland Commission's phrase "development which meets the needs of the present without compromising the ability of future generations to meet their own needs" (Brundtland, 1987, p. 43). *Our Common Future* placed the emphasis in sustainable development on human needs rather than the trade-offs between economic and biological systems, an approach which many economists would have difficulty in endorsing. Brundtland mapped a very political agenda, arguing that "sustainable development is a process in which the exploitation of resources, the direction of investments, the orientation of technological development and institutional change are all in harmony, and enhance both current and future potential to meet human needs and aspirations" (Brundtland, 1987, p. 46). The important thing to notice about this approach is that it regards sustainable development as a policy objective, rather than a methodology. It is an over-arching concept, a highly desirable end-point of development aspirations. Such an approach is unapologetically normative, and places both the responsibility for problems, and the political will to overcome them, in the hands of human actors.

An even more 'human-focused' approach is provided by Robert Chambers, in his concept of *sustainable livelihoods*. Chambers served on the Advisory Panel on Food Security, which fed into the Brundtland Commission's final report. He argues that:

> sustainable livelihood security is an integrating concept... livelihood is defined as adequate stocks and flows of food and cash to meet basic needs. Security refers to secure ownership of, and access to, resources and income-earning activities, including reserves and assets to offset risk, ease shocks and meet contingencies. Sustainable refers to the maintenance or enhancement of resource productivity on a long-term basis (Chambers, 1988).

Part of the interest in the discussion of sustainable development is in the way the concept has borrowed from both the natural and social sciences. Chambers' definition, which places the emphasis on poor people coping with stress, is a case in point. Gordon Conway, in a series of very influential papers, argued that "sustainability (is) the ability to maintain productivity, whether of a field, farm or nation, in the face of stress or shock" (Conway and Barbier, 1988, p. 653). Originally, Conway had been thinking primarily in ecological terms about the ability of natural systems to cope with system disturbance, but this led him (through a broader commitment to people rather than things) to seek to define a concept which retained the idea of system disturbance, but added that of human beings as self-conscious actors in the development process. Other writers, such as Bartelmus, an environmental planner, have defined sustainable development more in terms of conserving stocks of what we might term 'natural capital', in contrast to the traditional economic view that resources and the environment were chiefly important as ways of generating income, or flows:

> (sustainable development) is development that maintains a particular level of income by conserving the sources of that income: the stock of produced and national capital (Bartelmus, 1987, p. 12).

This does not exhaust the possibilities for defining 'sustainable development' but it does point to a number of significant areas of both convergence and divergence:

(a) There is little agreement about what needs to be sustained — present or future population levels?

(b) Does this population need to be sustained in terms of its minimum (perceived?) needs, at a particular level of consumption? Or does this level of needs/consumption require changing?

(c) There are different 'levels' at which sustainability is important, e.g. the farm level, the field level and the village level in Conway's agro-ecological analysis, (or the level of the village, region and nation, according to other accounts). These distinctions are important because what is sustainable at one level may not be sustainable at another (and *vice versa*). An example is that of the Santa Cruz area in Eastern Bolivia, where farming systems are 'sustainable' in agro-ecological terms, but the existence of important contraband trafficking, and a buoyant market for coca leaves, the raw material for cocaine, serve to undermine these systems (Redclift, 1986).

(d) Some writers refer to sustaining levels of production, and others to levels of consumption. Again, this is important since it can be argued that what makes development unsustainable at the global level are the patterns of consumption in the rich countries, while most efforts to tackle development problems are essentially production-orientated.

Sustainable development, then, is about meeting human needs, or maintaining economic growth or conserving natural capital, or about all three.

The Absence of Political Economy

It will be clear from what has been written above that there is no consensus about sustainable development, and that differences reflect disciplinary biases, distinctive paradigms and ideological disputes. In my view (Redclift, 1987) there are at least two sets of contradictions which soon become evident when sustainable development is discussed.

Firstly, embedded in much of the 'sustainability' thinking is an important difference of emphasis. Some writers view sustainability as a serious issue because nature is a major constraint on further human progress. They are concerned, basically, with the price paid by the conventional growth model if the warnings we receive from the environment, the 'biospheric imperatives', are ignored. The solution, is either to develop technologies which avoid the most dire environmental consequences of development, or to take measures to assess environmental losses in a more realistic way, thus reducing the danger that they will be overlooked by policy-makers.

Other writers take a rather different view. For them the principal problem is that 'human progress' carries implications for nature itself, and should cause us to re-examine the 'ends' of development, as well as the means. This view is shared by a variety of people: radical ecologists (Gorz, 1980; Bahro, 1982; Ryle, 1988), eco-feminists (Merchant, 1980) and deep ecologists (Devall and Sessions, 1985). For writers of these different ideological persuasions finding technical solutions to environmental problems, including ways of costing environmental losses such as those advocated by Pearce and colleagues, is ultimately self-defeating.

Secondly, considering ' sustainable development' within a North/South framework requires attention to the contradictions imposed by the structural inequalities of the global system (Brundtland, 1987; Redclift, 1987). Green concerns in the North, such as alternatives to work and ways of making work more rewarding, can often be inverted in the South, where the environment is contested not because it is valued in itself, but because its destruction creates value. In the South struggles over the environment are usually about basic needs, strategies to survive, rather than 'lifestyles', and the cost to the individual of pursuing individual self-interest is often carried by the group or collectivity (the basis of the "tragedy of commons" argument). There is no point in appealing, under these circumstances, to idealism or altruism to protect the environment, when the individual and household are forced to behave 'selfishly' in their struggle to survive.

In Chapter Three of *Blueprint for a Green Economy* Pearce *et al.* (1989) argue from a declared interest in environmental quality that environmental improvements are equivalent to economic improvements "if (they) increase social satisfaction or welfare". Their resolve is to demonstrate to economists that there are economic costs in ignoring the environment. This is the first position I outlined above, and the position which is growing in influence within international development agencies, such as the World Bank, the United Nations agencies and the Overseas Development Administration (ODA). It has become, within a short space of time, almost synonymous with environmental management in many people's estimation.

One of the problems with this position is that it works better for developed than for developing countries. As the Tables in Chapter Three of *Blueprint* demonstrate, there is widespread popular concern about the environment in the developed countries, where environmental quality is often placed before economic growth in surveys of public opinion. In their work most neo-classical economists use the "willingness to pay" principle (Pearce *et al.,* 1989, p. 55) as a means of assessing environmental costs and benefits. Pearce argues that the emphasis in environmental policy should be shifted towards this principle to avoid future, anticipated damage to the environment. It is easy to appreciate some of the difficulties when we consider developing countries. In developing countries the creation of value is linked to sacrificing environmental quality rather than improving environmental quality, because the cumulative effects of economic growth on the poor are so often negative. In an area of tropical forest (Choco), currently a Biosphere Reserve on the Colombian coast, which I visited with officials from the Colombian Environmental Agency (INDERENA) in October 1988, men involved in (illegal) forestry operations whom we met, were being paid $10 (US) a cubic metre for cutting hardwoods. The forested area lies adjacent to the Pacific Ocean, and illegal forestry operations meant that people were, literally, risking their lives to cut this wood. This involved taking a small boat into dangerous coastal waters to find suitable forest, and 'catching the tide' by navigating the Pacific Ocean for five hours at a time before returning to the port of

Buenaventura. If one man did not cut the wood others would cut it. The implications of these facts are important for the methods we use to assess environmental costs. In this case the revaluation of tropical forest, to include the environmental costs of unsustainable activities, would do little to prevent forest destruction, although it might highlight the scale of the problem. Colombia's foreign debt enables transnational companies like Carton de Colombia, which bought the hardwoods in the Choco, to pose as national saviours, rather than national vandals. (This corporation was active in sponsoring environmental meetings!). There are also reasons for refusing to overlook the highly unequal context of landholding which forces poor men and women to colonise the tropical forests, and other untitled land. In situations like that of tropical Colombia we need to specify greater equity, or the reduction of poverty, as a primary objective, before the question of environmental poverty can be fully addressed.

Equity considerations, in this context, are not a minor element in total utility, as Pearce *et al.,* suggest (1989, p. 48) but the driving force behind indiscriminate resource degradation. The discussion of sustainable development should not be confined to an assessment of environmental and economic trade-offs, for to do so implies ignoring other essential points of reference, including the regional and national political economy of resource use. It also tacitly endorses a highly ethnocentric, and North-biased, view of the development process. It fails to take seriously the integrity of other cultures, and their view of sustainability.

The Multiple Dimensions of Sustainable Development

To establish an adequate conceptual framework within which to explore the idea of sustainable development we need therefore to identify the multiple dimensions of the concept. There are three dimensions which require our urgent attention: the economic, the political, and the epistemological dimensions.

The Economic Dimension

As we saw in the discussion of environmental accounting, much of the economic argument has been conducted at the level of present and future anticipated demand, assessing the costs in foregone economic growth of closer attention to environmental factors. It was John Stuart

Mill, in his *Principles of Political Economy* (1873), who emphasised the idea that we need to preserve Nature from unfettered growth, if we are to preserve human welfare before diminishing returns begin to set in. With hindsight we can appreciate the full significance of Mill's observations.

This tradition, which we would identify today as part of the alternative, sustainable tradition of thought, was largely opposed to the views of most orthodox economists, who either followed Malthus or, later, Ricardo. The Malthusian tradition emphasised the importance of the ratio of population to natural resources, and has given rise to a 'population ethic', espoused by Neo-Malthusians like Garret Hardin (1968). In contrast, the Ricardian tradition, which has been at the centre of economics this century, took a much more 'optimistic' view of the relationship between economic growth, population and resources. The optimistic Ricardian view was that, following the promethean spirit, human ingenuity and the advances of science were capable of 'putting back' the day of judgment, when population would begin to overtake resources. This optimism was shaken, but not essentially destroyed, by the publication of *Limits to Growth* in the early 1970s (Meadows *et al.,* 1972).

The Political Dimension

The political dimension of sustainability comprises two separate, but related, elements: the weight to be attached to human agency and social structure, respectively, in determining the political processes through which the environment is managed; and the relationship between knowledge and power in popular resistance to dominant world views of the environment and resources. In both cases it is useful to draw on a body of emerging social theory, which has evolved and gained currency while environmentalism has risen to prominence.

The problem of human agency in relation to the environment is well recognised in the literature, especially by geographers (O' Riordan, 1989). It is also a central concern of sociologists, although rarely linked to environmental concerns *per se*. The British sociologist Anthony Giddens has devoted considerable attention to what he describes as a theory of 'structuration', which would enable us to recognise the role of human beings within a broad structural context, in seeking to advance their own, or group, interests. He notes that "...human agents have... as an inherent aspect of what they do, the capacity to understand what they do while they do it" (Giddens, 1984, xxii). It is their knowledge ability as agents which is important. Although Giddens does not apply his ideas specifically to environmental questions, they have clear utility for any consideration of the political and social dimensions of sustainability.

An examination of the way power is contested helps us to explain human agency in the management of the environment, as well as the material basis of environmental conflicts. In this sense it is useful to distinguish between the way human agents dominate nature — what we can term "allocative resources" (Giddens, 1984, p. 373) and the domination of some human agents by others — "authoritative resources" in Giddens' phrase. Environmental management, and conflicts over the environment, are about both processes: the way groups of people dominate each other, as well as the way they seek to dominate Nature. Not surprisingly, the development, or continuation, of more sustainable livelihood strategies carries important implications for the way power is understood between groups of people, as well as for the environment itself. The Green agenda is not simply about the environment *outside* human control; it is about the implications for social relations of bringing the environment *within* human control.

The second question of importance in considering the political dimension of sustainability, is the relationship between knowledge and power, a dimension often overlooked by observers from developed countries when they turn their attention to poorer societies. As we shall see in a moment, the consideration of epistemology in sustainable development carries important implications for our analysis, since it strikes at the cultural roots of quite different traditions of knowledge. It is also important to emphasise, however, that knowledge and power are linked, as Foucault observed in much of his work (Smart, 1985; Sheridan, 1980). We can, following Foucault, distinguish three *fields of resistance* to the universalising effects of modern society, and these fields of resistance are particularly useful in delineating popular responses, by the rural poor in particular, to outside interventions designed to manage the environment in different ways.

The first type of resistance is based on opposition to, or marginalisation from, production relations in rural societies. This is resistance against *exploitation*, in Foucault's terms, and includes attempts by peasants, pastoralists and others to resist new forms of economic domination, which they are unable to control or negotiate with.

The second form of resistance is based on ethnic and gender categories, and seeks to remove the individual from *domination* by more powerful groups, whose ethnic and gender identity has conferred on them a superior political position. In many cases the only strategy open to groups of people whose environmental practices are threatened by outsiders, and whose own knowledge, power and identity is closely linked with these practices, is to seek to distance themselves from 'outsiders' by, for example, reinforcing ethnic boundaries between themselves and others.

Finally, poor rural people frequently resist *subjection* to a world view which they cannot endorse, in much the same way as people in developed countries often confront 'totalising' theories, such as psychoanalysis or Marxism. In developing countries the development professionals frequently have recourse to a body of techniques for intervening in the natural environment, which are largely derived from developed countries' experience: 'environmental managerialism' is one way of expressing these techniques. The refusal to be subordinated to a world view dominated by essentially alien values and assumptions marks what Foucault terms "resistance against subjection". In no way is it implied that resistance can be equated with political struggle, whatever the basis of the resistance itself. Frequently people who are relatively powerless, because their knowledge-systems are devalued, or because they do not wield economic power, resist in ways which look like passivity: they keep their own counsel, they appear respectful towards powerful outsiders, they simply fail to cooperate.

The Epistemological Dimension

Sustainable development is usually discussed without reference to epistemological issues (i.e. those concerned with ways of acquiring knowledge and their integration into conceptual systems). It is assumed that 'our' system of acquiring knowledge in the North, through the application of scientific principles, is a universal epistemology. Anything less than scientific knowledge hardly deserves our attention. Such a view, rooted as it is in ignorance of the way we ourselves think, as well as other cultures' epistemology, is less than fruitful. Goonatilake (1984) reminds us that large-order cognitive maps are not confined to Western science, and that in Asia, for example, systems of religious belief have often had fewer problems in confronting 'scientific' reasoning than has the Judaeo-Christian tradition. The ubiquitousness of Western science, however, has led to traditional knowledge becoming fragmented knowledge in the South today, increasingly divorced from that of the dominant scientific paradigm. This observation echoes contemporary Green thinking, too: in his conversation with Capra, Schumacher noted that "...because of the smallness and patchiness of our knowledge, we have to go in small steps. We have to leave room for non-knowledge..." (Capra, 1988, p. 230).

The philosopher Feyerabend, in his influential book *Farewell to Reason*, has distinguished between two different traditions of thought, which can usefully be compared with 'scientific' and 'traditional' knowledge. The first tradition, which corresponds closely to scientific epistemology, he calls the *abstract* tradition. This enables us "...to formulate statements (which are) subjected to certain rules (of logic, testing and argument) and events affect the statements only in accordance with the rules... it is possible to make scientific statements without having met a single one of the objects described..." (Feyerabend, 1987, p. 294). He gives as examples of this kind of tradition, elementary particle physics, behavioural psychology and molecular biology. In contrast, the kinds of knowledge possessed by small-scale societies, in particular, Feyerabend would label as *historical* traditions. In these epistemological traditions "...the objects already have a language of their own" — the object of enquiry is to understand this language. In the course of time much of the knowledge possessed by people outside mainstream science, especially in developing countries, becomes encoded, in rituals, in religious observations and in the cultural practices of everyday life. In societies which make an easy separation between 'culture' and 'science' such practices can easily be ignored, although they are frequently the key to the way environmental knowledge is used in small-scale rural societies.

Conclusion

This chapter has sought to extend our definition of sustainable development by enlarging the compass of debate, and considering the dimensions of sustainability which usually lie outside the parameters of most Northern environmental policy intervention. As such it represents little more than a small beginning, although there is evidence that more urgency is currently being given to the links between environmental knowledge, political processes and the management of resources (McNeely and Pitt, 1985; IUCN 1990; Norgaard, 1985). We have seen that the environmental discourse being promoted by development agencies today does represent an improvement on the past, but at the same time fails to take adequate account of both international (structural) and cross-cultural factors in sustainable development. By enlarging the discussion it is hoped that we can begin to get at the texture of "actually existing" sustainable practices, and thus to make more qualified decisions about the direction that future policy should take.

REFERENCES

Bahro, R. (1982). *Socialism and Survival*, London: Heretic Books.

Barbier, E. (1989). *Economics, Natural Resource Scarcity and Development*, London: Earthscan.

Bartelmus, P. (1987). *Environment and Development*, London: Allien and Unwin.

Brundtland Commission (1987). (World Commission on Environment and Development) *Our Common Future*, Oxford: University Press.

Capra, F. (1988). *Uncommon Wisdom*, London: Fontana.

Chambers, R. (1988). *Sustainable Rural Livelihoods: A strategy for people, environment and development*, Institute of Development Studies, University of Sussex.

Conway, G. and Barbier, E. (1988). "After the Green Revolution: sustainable and equitable agricultural development", in D. Pearce and M. Redclift (eds.) *Futures*, 20 (6), pp. 651-678.

Devall, B. and Sessions, G. (1985). *Deep Ecology: Living as if Nature Mattered*, Layton, Utah: Peregrine Smith.

Feyerabend, P. (1987). *Farewell to Reason*, New York: Bower.

Giddens, A. (1984). *The Constitution of Society*, Oxford: Polity Press.

Goonatilake, S. (1984). *Aborted Discovery: Science and Creativity in the Third World*, London: Zed Books.

Gorz, A. (1980). *Ecology as Politics*, London: Pluto Press.

Hardin, G. (1968). "The tragedy of the commons", *Science*, 162, pp. 1243-48.

International Union for the Conservation of Nature (IUCN) (1990). *World Conservation Strategy for the 1990s*, (with UNEP and WWF), Gland, Switzerland.

McNeely, J. and Pitt, D. (1985). *Culture and Conservation: the Human Dimension in Environmental Planning*, London: Croom Helm.

Meadows, D.H., Meadows, D.L., Randers, J. and Behrens, W. (1972). *The Limits to Growth*, London: Pan Books.

Merchant, C. (1980). *The Death of Nature: Women, Ecology and the Scientific*

Revolution, New York: Harper and Row.

Mill, J.S. (1873) *Principles of Political Economy*, London:. Parker, Son and Bourn.

Norgaard, R. (1985). "Environmental economics: an evolutionary critique and a plea for pluralism". *Journal of Environmental Economics and Management*, 12 (4).

O'Riordan, T. (1989). "The challenge for environmentalism", in Peel, R. and Thrift, N. (eds.) *New Models in Geography* (Volume one) London: Unwin Hyman.

Pearce, D. (1986). "The sustainable use of natural resources in developing countries", paper delivered to Economic and Social Research Council Workshop on Environmental Economics, University of East Anglia, Norwich.

Pearce, D., Barbier, E. and Markandya, A. (1987). "Sustainable development and cost-benefit analysis", London Environmental Economics Centre, Paper 88-101.

Pearce, D. Markandya, A. and Barbier, E. (1989). *Blueprint for a Green Economy*, London: Earthscan.

Redclift, M.R. (1986). "Sustainability and the market: survival strategies on the Bolivian frontier". *The Journal of Development Studies*, 23, 1, pp. 93-105.

Redclift, M.R. (1987). *Sustainable Development: Exploring the Contradictions*, London: Methuen.

Ryle, M. (1988). *Ecology and Socialism*, London: Century Hutchinson.

Sheridan, A. (1980). *Michel Foucault: The Will to Truth*, London: Tavistock.

Smart, B. (1985). *Michel Foucault*, London: Tavistock/Ellis Horwood.

16

Sustainable Development: Theoretical Construct or Attainable Goal?

DAVID SIMON

Introduction

It is now more than a decade and a half since the Club of Rome's report, *The Limits to Growth* (Meadows *et al.*, 1972) appeared, since The Ecologist magazine produced *A Blueprint for Survival,* and since the late Barbara Ward & René Dubos published their sub-classic book. *Only One Earth,* as *leitmotif* for the 1972 UN Conference on the Human Environment. Although concerned with essentially the same problem of global survival, each of these represented a distinct school of thought and served to fuel often heated debate about the scale of the alleged crisis caused by growth-oriented economic development, the leeway available, and the nature of change required for remedy.

Further evidence of the disastrous effects of the existing world order, characterized by inequitable and environmentally destructive capitalist and state-socialist industrial development, was provided within a year, with the onset of the first oil crisis in 1973 followed by the Sahelian famine. Similar shocks have occurred frequently over the intervening years. And although the Stockholm conference did lead to the establishment of the United Nations Environment Programme, a body which has done some commendable practical and consciousness-raising work, the situation today seems scarcely better than it was in

Reprinted with Permission from *Environmental Conservation,* Vol. 16(1) 1989, pp. 41-48

1972. Indeed, continued population growth in conjunction with the persistence of unsustainable and inequitable economic development is exacerbating conditions in many regions. Certainly, the dawn of a new age in which Man will learn to live with the rest of Nature rather than against it' as envisaged by the editors of *The Ecologist* (1972, p. 10), has yet to arrive.

Nevertheless, some cause for hope, if not unbridled optimism, exists. There are now clear signs that both the nature and seriousness of the global environment-development crisis are being acknowledged in key national and international circles. The recent US and European Community "food mountains" and associated farm crises, chronic industrial pollution in Eastern Europe (Glenny, 1987), the Chernobyl accident, the Third World debt crisis, and the failure of economic growth to keep up with population growth in parts of the Third World (most notably Africa), coupled with the increasing frequency and severity of so-called 'natural' disasters rooted in Humankind's impact on the environment, have all contributed to this. At a more local level, numerous sustainable development projects have been implemented across the Third World, often with noteworthy success. Many progressive international aid agencies and other non-governmental organizations (NGOs) are actively giving a lead in this sphere.

Several encouraging strands can be distinguished in this world-wide reappraisal. Firstly, the news media, and especially television, have been instrumental in alerting the world to the horrors of war and famine (particularly in the Horn of Africa), recurrent floods in southern Asia, poverty and debt in Africa and Latin America, and the mass destruction of tropical rain-forests. Increasingly, the links between apparently unrelated problems are being made much of in news and especially documentary features. Secondly, despite the limitations outlined by Bush (1985), the role of such enterprises as Bob Geldof's "Band Aid" and "Live Aid" in mobilizing public opinion and support, should not be underestimated. Thirdly, many governments in advanced capitalist, state socialist, and Third World, countries alike are coming to realize from hard experience that any development path is ultimately *unsustainable* when achieved at the expense of widespread environmental destruction. Fourthly, *Our Common Future,* the report of the World Commission on Environment and Development (WCED), published in 1987, has spelled out at the highest level the fundamental interrelationships between environment and development, the unsustainability of current practices, and a coherent set of proposals for both short- and long-term action in key spheres.

Ignorance is no longer a valid excuse, and the time left for action is very limited. This paper seeks to advance debate by reviewing current thinking on sustainability, and then raising some pertinent questions about how readily such concepts can be operationalized in the context of the prevailing world order.

The Concept of Sustainable Development

Changing Perceptions

Some traditional economists still do not accept the necessity of sustainability as a precondition for continued survival. They argue that environmental degradation, resource depletion, and even species extinction, may be economically rational and justifiable in terms of utility theory and various project-appraisal techniques (Tisdell, 1988). Far from illustrating the relevance of these approaches, however, such claims demonstrate the *inability* of mainstream economics to come to terms with fundamental social or environmental considerations, which cannot be accounted for merely by adding new variables to, or altering the coefficients or parameters of, an equation. A far broader reconceptualisation is required. Even the steady-state economy advocated during the 1970s by more progressive economists concerned with the limits to growth, seems neither a necessary nor a sufficient condition for ensuring sustainability. As should become clear below, this would depend crucially on the nature of locally specific political, economic, and social processes.

The concept of sustainable development has found growing recent acceptance, to the point where it is now a ubiquitous "buzzword'. Inevitably under such circumstances, it lacks uniform definition and substance. It is these issues which form the focus of this chapter. Furthermore, many supposedly sustainable projects that have been implemented in recent years have turned out to be totally unsustainable for various reasons, including lack of appropriate objectives or scale, or inadequate provision for participation and control by the supposed beneficiaries.

Readers seeking detailed sources on the historical evolution of the concepts of sustainable development are referred to The Ecologist (1972), Meadows *et al.* (1972), Ward & Dubos (1972), and Redclift (1984, 1987). (More detailed coverage of this topic is beyond the scope of the present chapter.) In addition, Tolba (1987) provides a useful, if somewhat repetitive, insight into how sustainable development thinking advanced during the early 1980s. As Executive Director of the United Nations Environment Programme (UNEP), he has been closely involved in promoting the change of perceptions and knowledge. Whereas economic development and environmental conservation were previously viewed as antagonistic, requiring direct trade-offs, bitter experience has increasingly shown that long-term development is sustainable only when it is upheld without causing major environmental destruction. The two are inextricably linked and not inherently contradictory.

A Coherent Approach

Building on the foundations of his earlier book, *Development and the Environmental Crisis* (1984), Michael Redclift's recent contribution, *Sustainable Development: Exploring the Contradictions* (1987), provides probably the most comprehensive and theoretically informed discussion of sustainability to date, despite its almost total concern with rural and agricultural questions at the expense of urban and industrial issues. Deploying illuminating data on the energy inputs to, and efficiency of, various agricultural modes of production, Redclift argues convincingly that, in those respects, many small-scale or indigenous systems are both superior to, and generally more sustainable than, large-scale capital-intensive methods.

Use of a political economy perspective enables him to show how evolution of the current, unsustainable world order has dramatically transformed and internationalized local relations of production, local environments, and people's perceptions and knowledge of them. Nowhere is this more vividly illustrated than in the juxtaposed descriptions of the Valley of Mexico by one of the original *conquistadores* in 1519, and the Mexican Government's Office for Urban Development and Ecology in 1984 (Redclift, 1987,107-13):

> "In the space of four centuries an ecological system built on sustainable agriculture (chinampas and terrace cultivation) had been replaced by one in which labour and land become first separated and then recombined (the hacienda/community) under a new technology (plough and animal traction). The objective, to ensure control over the economic surplus, was achieved at the cost of

destroying the indigenous ecological and cultural systems. Finally, the redistributive changes ushered in by the Mexican Revolution of 1910 provided a means to 'modernization', the ultimate effect of which was to increase social inequality and place the environment in jeopardy. Mexico City became the material representation of a new kind of development, in which in the short-term economic growth and the carrying capacity of the ecological system increased, but which ultimately undermined the long-term stability of the resource base on which the rural population depended."

This quotation embodies many key elements of Redclift's thesis, some of which have already been referred to. He also rightly asserts the necessity of addressing the political and economic forces behind unsustainable practices. Indeed, he cites this as a principal shortcoming of ecocentric philosophies and eco-development approaches, as well as of the World Conservation Strategy (1980), which probably did more than any other document to popularize the concept of sustainability.* Concern with such broad ideals often ignores the poor, who are more concerned with their own short-term survival and livelihoods, and especially their immediate needs and risk reduction, than with conservation. However, even the 'sustainable livelihood thinking', advocated by Chambers (1986) for this very reason, is inadequate, because political economy is just as important as the concerns and priorities of the poor, in determining the scope for attaining sustainable livelihoods (Redclift, 1987, 36). Indeed the first 'contradiction' to be overcome in order to achieve sustainable development, is that comprehensive environmental management must work through the social groups that are being marginalized by the development process (*ibid.*, 80).

For Redclift the second contradiction is that if—as seems clear from world-wide experience—market forces cannot be relied upon to maintain the environment, we need to place far greater reliance on international agreement and planning. Thirdly, he points to the relationship between political struggles over the environment in

---

* The importance of the World Conservation Strategy (WCS) lay partially in its explicit linking of its 3 priorities, namely: (i) maintenance of ecological processes and life-support systems; (ii) sustainable resource utilisation; and (iii) maintenance of genetic diversity, for both directly ecological reasons and the development of agricuture.

developed and the so-called developing countries, which he sees as being very different in character. Fourthly, just as we are finally destroying Nature, scientific developments in biotechnology and related fields mean that we are "producing" Nature for the first time, thereby altering the frontiers of sustainability. Fifthly, the failure of political economic theory to address environmental issues is bound up with its history during the nineteenth century, when biological determinism was being discredited.

In my view, Redclift's third 'contradiction' is exaggerated, because he underestimates the fundamental and global environment-development concerns of an important group of social movements and NGOs based in, or originating from, so-called developed countries—for example Friends of the Earth, Greenpeace, Oxfam, Survival International, and War on Want. Also, the WWFs recent name-change, from World Wildlife Fund to World Wide Fund for Nature, is indicative of its changing concerns, which are increasingly focused on habitats, ecosystems, and the human pressures which impact upon them. This is not to argue that all such organizations have common concerns or strategies. A wide spectrum clearly exists. But toxic discharges into the North Sea, for example, are no less life-threatening than pouring poisons into the South China Sea. Similarly, tropical rain-forest destruction is intimately related to hardwood utilization in Europe and North America. The impact will ultimately be felt everywhere.

Global problems require global solutions, particularly in view of the great contemporary importance of transnational corporations in resource exploitation and world trade. Most encouragingly, many NGOs are accordingly operating internationally, or are establishing international networks of like-minded movements in various parts of the world. Thus, for example, the Asia-Pacific People's Environment Network (APPEN) brings together more than 330 groups in the region under the coordination of Sahabat Alam Malaysia (Friends of the Earth Malaysia), while the Nairobi-based African NGOs' Environmental Network (ANEN), established in 1982, already has 353 member organizations in 37 countries. Moreover, in partnership with such organizations, groups in developed countries can play an invaluable role, given the often dire political and financial constraints facing many Second and Third World activist groups. The road ahead remains daunting, but there have recently been some noteworthy successes.

Redclift's first 'contradiction', regarding marginalized social groups, is surprising in terms of his overall argument. For me, there is no contradiction, because environmental management will ultimately have to operate *not only* through socially marginalized groups *but also* through dominant and intermediate groups—embracing, for example, transnational corporations, governments, and parastatal corporations. Many of these last operate in strategic sectors of the economy, such as petrochemicals, heavy industry, and the provision of public utilities. Consequently, their activities have a major impact on the environment.

These points apart, I have little quarrel with Redclift's main arguments. His historically-based, international political economy conception is certainly superior to that of the World Commission on Environment and Development's report (1987), which goes no further than stressing contemporary interdependence at different scales. But perhaps that is inevitable, considering WCED's connection with the UN system.

Sustainable Development Defined

Before moving on to consider how practical the ideas, implications, and proposals, of Redclift and the WCED are in the current global context, it is as well to clarify what precisely is meant by Sustainable development.

Much of the early work in the field of sustainability derives from agronomy and ecology, where there has been great concern for many decades with animal carrying-capacities, the recoverability of agricultural systems from disturbances, and conservation of game reserves and national parks. Perhaps the best-known recent exposition in this tradition is provided by Conway (1983, 1985), who defines sustainability as:

> '... the ability of a system to maintain productivity in spite of a major disturbance such as that caused by intensive stresses or a large perturbation... Satisfactory methods of measuring sustainability have still to be found, however. Lack of sustainability may be indicated by declining productivity but, equally, collapse may come suddenly and without warning.' (Conway, 1983, cited in Tisdell, 1988, 375).

The limitations of this approach, which have been discussed in detail by Redclift (1987) and Tisdell (1988), centre on the absence of economic or political dimensions, and of any guide to quantification or how to decide about necessary trade-offs. Tisdell, too, omits any consideration of political factors.

Notwithstanding a whole chapter surveying the concept of Sustainable development, the nearest Redclift (1987) himself comes to defining it is in his conclusion:

> "Sustainable development, if it is not to be devoid of analytical content, means more than seeking a compromise between the natural environment and the pursuit of economic growth. It means a definition of development which recognises that the limits to sustainability have structural as well as natural origins." (1987, 199).

This embodies some of the essentials but begs elaboration. The WCED definition is more precise:

> "Sustainable development is development that meets the needs of the present without compromising the ability of future generations to meet their own needs. It contains within it two key concepts:
>
> - the concept of 'needs', in particular the essential needs of the world's poor, to which overriding priority should be given; and
> - the idea of limitations imposed by the state of technology and social organisation on the environment's ability to meet present and future needs."

Thus, the goals of economic and social development must be defined in terms of the sustainability in all countries—developed or developing, market oriented or centrally planned. Even the narrow notion of physical sustainability implies a concern for social equity between generations—a concern that must logically be extended to equity within each generation (WCED, 1987, 43). The basic mechanism envisaged for achieving this amounts to redistribution with Sustainable growth. In other words, redistribution of wealth and resources must occur, but in concert with Sustainable economic growth. The problem here is that the benefits of growth are *not* usually equitably distributed within or between societies; hence considerable political commitment will be required, together with the establishment and enforcement of appropriate mechanisms and procedures. More radical, but probably even less realistic, strategies might demand immediate redistribution *of existing* wealth and resources, irrespective of possible subsequent economic growth.

A third definition of sustainable economic development has recently been provided by Barbier (1987, 103), who characterizes it as follows:

(i) It is indistinguishable from the total development of society and cannot effectively be analysed separately, as 'sustainability' depends on the interaction of economic changes with social, cultural, and ecological, transformations;
(ii) Its quantitative dimension is associated with increases in the material means available to those living, or destined to live, in absolute poverty, so as to provide for adequate physical and social well-being and security against becoming poorer;
(iii) Its qualitative dimension is multifaceted, and is associated with ensuring the long-term ecological, social, and cultural, potential for supporting economic activity and structural change; and
(iv) It is not easily subject to measurement; the quantitative and qualitative dimensions are mutually reinforcing and inseparable, and thus cannot be fully captured by any concept of direct and measurable economic gain."*

Any development process therefore implies continuous, dynamic trade-offs both within and between the relevant overlapping sets of biological and resource, economic and social, systems.

These definitions vary in terms of their degree of detail and the extent to which they explicitly incorporate, internationally, structural as well as natural dimensions, geographical scales of importance, and intertemporal effects. While this is probably the result of the respective Authors' different ideological, theoretical, or epistemological, positions, there is no actual conflict between definitions as such, and together, in my view, they encapsulate the key concepts.

From Theory to Praxis: Recent Proposals

So far so good: however, if theory and praxis are to be meaningfully (and dialectically) linked, we need a definition which is not only

* The paper quoted here was one of four winners of our Foundation's 'Best Paper Prize' in 1987.—Ed.

analytically rigorous but also of practical utility. The remainder of this chapter seeks to explore (if not answer) the related questions of whether and to what extent the definitions cited above can be made operational, what differences in strategy the respective Authors propose, and how compatible "sustainable development" projects in different parts of the world are, to date, with the approach as defined.

Redclift actually stops short of making practical recommendations on strategy beyond an exhortation '... to interrogate our assumptions about both development and the environment, and give political effect to the conclusions we reach...' (1987, 204).

This is certainly a necessary starting-point, but theoretically and empirically informed critique alone is no adequate guide through the harsh complexities of the real world. The varied and often unsuccessful experiences with apparently progressive and sustainable aid projects outlined by the Panos Institute (1987), amplify this growing realization among analysts and practitioners alike. Redclift's valuable conceptual approach is thus likely to need much further work in developing appropriate tools for implementation.

Global Policies for the Future

By contrast, the WCED report (1987), while not theoretically sophisticated, balances a grim and comprehensive account of present ills with guidelines for broad-fronted policy change at both international and national levels. However, a number of crucial institutional problems must be addressed if the proposed changes are to have any prospect of implementation. Government departments are highly fragmented, and constrained by narrow bureaucratic mandates geared to economic growth, so that those responsible for managing the economy are usually separate from, and inadequately coordinated with, those controlling natural resources and environmental protection. Governments have widely failed to require that bodies whose actions degrade the environment act to prevent degradation. And even effective environmental agencies have necessarily focused on cure (reforestation, reclamation, restoration, rehabilitation, etc.) rather than prevention. The ecological aspects of policy must be considered simultaneously with, and as seriously as, economic, trade, energy, agricultural, and other relevant facets: 'The real world of interlocked economic and ecological systems will not change; the policies and institutions concerned must' (WCED, 1987, 9).

All this is as true at the international level as for national governments, yet many international organizations and agencies (both within and outside the UN system) are currently losing support and becoming politically more and more controversial. This is not a good omen, particularly as the controversy has little to do with actual environmental-development policy in most cases.*

In this short chapter there is space only to summarize some of the key WCED recommendations:

(1) *Population and Human Resources:* The problem is not just rapid population-growth, but how this relates to available resources. Poverty alleviation is an important strategy for dealing with the situation, but urgent steps must be taken to limit extreme growth-rates. Multifaceted long-term population policies are needed to address broad demographic goals of strengthening social, cultural, and economic, motivations for family planning, and for providing relevant education, contraceptives, and services. Choice of family size is a major element of self-determination—a basic human right that is, however, frequently denied to women.

(2) *Food Security: Sustaining the potential:* Global cereal production has accelerated faster than population growth, yet hunger and famine are increasing. Highly subsidized agriculture in industrialized countries has created vast surpluses (and additional storage costs) at great expense to the environment; conversely, agriculture in the Third World, especially in the peasant and small-farms sectors, has frequently been neglected in the face of urban and industrial priorities. The 'terms of trade' must be turned in favour of these groups with appropriate incentives and support, while industrial countries' policies must reduce surpluses, lift unfair trade practices, and institute environmentally sound farming. Redistribution through land-reform and integrated rural development is crucial to alleviate poverty and landlessness in the Third World.

(3) *Species and Ecosystems: Resources for development:* Extinctions are occurring at an unprecedented rate, yet conservation of the global gene-pool is vital for ecological reasons as well as agricultural, medical, and biotechnological, development. The first

* The World Bank and, to a lesser extent, the Inter-American Development Bank, are notable exceptions. Attention has focused on the massively environmentally destructive Polonoroeste project in Brazil, transmigration in Indonesia, and Narmada River dams in India, for example.

priority must therefore be to establish the problem as a major economic and resource issue on political agendas. Development *can* proceed without total destruction or extinction of species and ecosystems. A greatly enlarged and enhanced global network of protected areas is necessary to ensure maintenance of genetic and ecological diversity. Species should be regarded as a global resource, governed by an appropriate international convention.

(4) *Energy: Choices for environment and development:* We have not yet found the safe and sustainable energy pathway that is essential for future development. This latter will necessarily be less energy-intensive than hitherto. Nuclear power is only justifiable if current problems regarding its costs, risks, and waste disposal, are solved in concrete and acceptable ways. Top priority should go to research on increased nuclear safety—especially environmentally sound and viable alternatives. Given the fuel-wood crisis in many poor countries, agriculture there must be reorganized to produce wood and other plant fuels on a large scale. Little of this will arise through market forces alone; direct governmental action is necessary, not least because of the major role which most governments have in energy generation, distribution, and consumption.

(5) *Industry: Producing more with less:* A five- to ten-fold increase in manufacturing output will be necessary to raise consumption levels of the poor *countries* to those of the industrialized world by the time population growth-rates taper off. Antipollution and resource-efficient technologies are available and are continually being improved.* Developing countries require information and assistance in utilizing these optimally, to avoid repeating the harsh lessons learnt elsewhere, but for which they have neither knowledge nor resources. Strict global controls over the export and dumping of hazardous substances and wastes are urgently required.

(6) *The Urban Challenge:*The dramatic rate and scale of urbanization in the developing world require the production and

* Here we think of the International Conference on Waste Minimization and Clean Technology which is being organized by Dr Arthur H. Purcell, Director of the Resource Policy Institute. P.O. Box 39185, Washington, DC 20016. USA. It is taking place in the International Conference Centre of Geneva. 15 Rue de Varembé, Geneva, Switzerland, during 29 May to 1 June of this year—*see* the Important Prospect published in our Summer issue of last year [EC 15(2) p. 189], and we are hoping will be followed periodically by others on the same vital themes.—*Ed.*

maintenance of urban shelter, infrastructure, services, and employment far in excess of existing capabilities. Explicit settlement strategies are necessary, incorporating decentralization to local authorities, and involving amendments to taxation, food-pricing, transport, health, industrial and other, policies which might conflict with such strategies. Closer work with the urban poor, 'the true city-builders', is necessary, while site and service schemes have wide potential as a contribution to upgrading their living environments.

(7) *The International Dimension:*—Change is necessary to ensure the sustainability of ecobiomes and component ecosystems on which the global economy depends, and such that partners in economic exchange feel the basis of exchange to be equitable. Three broad areas for action are identified in this context: managing the commons *(à la* Law of the Sea); making connections and clear choices between peace, security, development, and the environment; and institutional/legal change (along the lines already mentioned).

Overall, then, the WCED (1987) sets out a clear policy agenda, although perforce at a general level because of its global focus. More critically, one could argue that this approach also ensures maximum international acceptability and minimum controversy. Country- and institution-specific changes are thereby left for subsequent formulation by the respective bodies. While pragmatic, and in some cases necessary, this exposes the key flaw. As with the Brandt Report (*cf.* Brandt Commission, 1980, 1982) and similar initiatives, this report will almost certainly be paid lip-service in many quarters but be followed by little concrete action. Indeed, early indications suggest precisely that the WCED report's publication received less public attention than did Brandt, and within weeks it had been slipped quietly onto the bureaucratic bookshelves.

Altogether I fear that this well-timed and cogently-argued document may thus prove an expensive exercise which ultimately does little to hasten the shift to more sustainable development policies. Part of the problem is that, notwithstanding the severity of our global crisis, the report suggests no precise or enforceable mechanism for activating its agenda, and for transforming nationalistic, greedy, expedient, and politically unequal, governments into the more benign, altruistic entities, moved by concern for the common good, that would be necessary for initiating the proposed action.

At a more conceptual level, some of the WCED proposals are open to criticism, though this almost certainly has no significant bearing on the report's reception. Perhaps the most glaring problem is the explicit assumption that all developing countries should or must industrialize:

> 'Many essential human needs can be met only through goods and services provided by industry, and the shift to sustainable development must be powered by a continuing flow of wealth from industry' (WCED, 1987, 16).

While in some respects arguably true, this limits the debate to how to industrialize sustainably rather than posing both fundamental and pragmatic questions about whether all countries should, or indeed can, industrialize. The overall path of sustainable development—for example, whether it should embrace industrialization or not—is a matter for individual states to resolve. However, there is much evidence that generalized industrialization is neither feasible nor desirable for many individual Third World countries—for example the Pacific islands' states, and small or thinly-populated countries in the Sahel or other parts of sub-Saharan Africa, particularly if landlocked. The reasons are too well-known to repeat here.

One possible solution—that of establishing regional groupings or common markets to promote industrialization for their combined populations—has been attempted in various contexts, often less than successfully. In terms of sustainability, such strategies would require satisfactory resolution of problems pertaining to international differences in resource endowment, environmental disturbance and destruction, pollution, population distribution and standard of living, energy supply and recycling, ecosystem safeguards, and the like. Given conflicting national loyalties and the generally slow progress made with such multilateral initiatives to date, these questions pose major difficulties. Yet issues of this nature are as crucial as specifically ecological or economic problems. An historically-informed political economy perspective, such as that proposed by Redclift, is particularly well suited to highlight these issues. This brings me back to my earlier criticism of the WCED report lacking a clear theoretical base.

Analytical Tools

The focus of Barbier's paper (1987) is rather more specific, thus complementing the WCED's broad-brush approach. He emphasizes the need to develop appropriate methodologies and techniques for appraising sustainable development projects such as the successful, modestly-scaled, mainly rural, examples which he cites. In many cases these projects have transformed previously unsustainable systems into relatively sustainable ones.

Barbier discusses progress towards, and problems faced in, the incorporation of environmental objectives in four major techniques of economic planning: social cost-benefit analysis, resource accounting, macro-economic policy, and applied project or sectoral research. All have limitations due to a combination of at least two important factors. Firstly, many environmental impacts are difficult to predict, measure, and value, as they are not marketed but have intangible attributes and/or are enjoyed or consumed collectively.

Secondly, many of the tenets of conventional economic analysis, geared as they are to maximizing growth, are directly contradictory to the requirements of sustainable development. Fundamental reorientation of objectives and hence of the techniques themselves is therefore necessary. Sometimes this may not be possible or adequate. For example, social cost-benefit analysis—a technique rooted in neoclassical economics—attempts to incorporate environmental damage as external costs of the project concerned. However, this approach cannot reflect the facts that such impacts are not external to the system as a whole, that they affect other activities and overall sustainability, and that they have distributional inequities.* Much economic planning is 'top down' in nature, and hence unsuited to the grassroots involvement that is necessary for sustainable development.

To be useful in practice, sustainability must apply to all spheres of human activity. It will always be necessary to balance goals within and between the biological-resource, economic and social, systems, as not all objectives can be achieved simultaneously. Economics can assist in the vital task of making such trade-offs explicit. Barbier sees the next stage of research as being towards the development of analytical tools for applying sustainability to various economic-environmental systems.

With all this I have no quarrel. However, conspicuously absent from Barbier's analysis is any concept of political economy as a frame within which macro-economic planning and cost-benefit analysis, etc.,

* Some economists maintain, nevertheless, that improvements to such existing techniques make them euqal to the task (e.g. Nash & Bowers, 1986; also Tisdell, 1988)

should be situated, and that determines many of the key possibilities for, and limitations of, change. Redclift's criticism of Chambers and other proponents of eco development, referred to earlier, applies to Barbier as well. Secondly, my comments regarding the absence of any political mechanism for initiating attitudinal or institutional change in the WCED report, are valid with Barbier too.

Discussion: The Way Forward

The three main recent contributions discussed here are all important, notwithstanding the criticisms made, and complement one another by focusing at the theoretical/analytical, global policy, and economic planning, levels, respectively. By integrating these approaches, we can begin to develop the necessary systematic, coherent, and well-argued, approach embracing both theory and praxis. While sustainable development undoubtedly is, or has to become, an attainable goal, it has hitherto generally remained rather more of a theoretical construct. However, crucial work remains to be done in mobilizing political and institutional action within the short time available to the world as a whole.

Additionally, as Barbier points out, it is at the lowest level, of applying sustainable development to individual economic-environmental systems, that appropriate techniques must be derived. I will conclude by offering two suggestions in this direction, both of them demonstrating the value of political economy analysis even at this practical level. Firstly, it has been repeatedly shown that development projects stand little chance of success unless the local population not only derive tangible and sustained benefits, but are also actively involved in planning and control throughout (*see* Panos Institute, 1987; Sattaur, 1987; also Redclift, 1987, 150-64 for recent examples). This has commonly been termed 'bottom up' development, in contrast to the 'top down' approach of much conventional economic planning around the world (e.g. Stohr & Taylor, 1981). However this, too, has limitations, given the rate and scale of change required. As argued above, many factors and forces beyond the individual village or project, determine the scope for action and the likely outcome. Attitudinal and institutional changes are required to ensure sustainability at all scales, and facilitate the coordinated delivery of appropriate services, inputs, and expertise, for local development initiatives around individual countries. In essence, therefore, a flexible blend of 'bottom up' and 'top down' approaches is required.

My second proposal sets out the critical variables to consider in evaluating the sustainability of particular agro-ecological systems. Conway (1985) discusses four properties of such systems (productivity, stability, sustainability, and equitability) which can serve as performance indicators. Once again, no explicit link to the political-economic macrostructure exists. This is one of the critical dimensions embodied in my scheme.

Concern with sustainability first emerged in agronomy long before receiving its wider contemporary connotations. Central to this concern was prevention of soil erosion and rangeland deterioration resulting from overgrazing—problems which, for example, already exercised colonial agricultural and Nature conservation officials in southern and central Africa in the early decades of this century. Hence was conceived the notion of carrying capacity, namely the maximum number (or biomass) of a particular species which could be supported on a unit tract of land in a given ecosystem without causing environmental degradation.

As with so many other 'scientific' concepts, carrying capacity was later applied to human activities. Nowhere is this more clearly illustrated than with respect to land husbandry of the increasingly overcrowded native reserves that had been created by colonial authorities across southern Africa. The conventional wisdom regarded peasant agriculture there as 'primitive', 'traditional', environmentally destructive, and so forth, with no conception that the system of 'native' reserves and institutionalized migrant labour which underpinned the colonial political economy lay at the heart of the problem, rather than peasant agriculture *per se*. As has been argued elsewhere (Simon, 1985), there are thus important implicit ideological assumptions in using notions of carrying capacity in the human context. The variables proposed here make such assumptions explicit in a scheme in which sustainability is the central focus, linking the physical environment to local human activity and the wider political economy. There are at least six critical considerations:

(1) The mix of arable and grazing land, and the fallow system used;
(2) The species of crops and livestock that are kept, and hence the potential yields;
(3) The productive technology that is used or available;

(4) The nature and source of energy supply, e.g. whether organic or inorganic, animate or inanimate, generated within or outside the farm or ecosystem, and whether recycled or not;
(5) The land-tenure system or coexistent subsystems; and
(6) Social relations of production—e.g. the nature and dynamics of local political systems, such as community and household structures. Relevant issues include who within them controls access to resources, and on what basis—and access to household and non-household labour for productive purposes.

Both (5) and (6) of the above deal with access to land and other productive resources, and related issues of distributional equity. The variables are necessarily general at this stage; but if they can be agreed upon, more detailed work can then be undertaken to determine appropriate procedures and units of measurement. The intention would be to develop an approach that is both comprehensive in terms of the variables which it embraces, and sensitive to locally specific conditions. Mechanistic application of a universal 'package' would therefore not be the key objective, but rather a broad framework or set of procedures by means of which to undertake comparable or even comparative analysis.

Sustainability does not imply that each system should be closed or autarchic. One of the fundamental characteristics of the modern world is the integration of even distant systems through commodity and other flows of different magnitudes, values, and degrees of equality. What sustainability does indeed require is that energy losses from particular agro-ecological systems, for example through food or other exports, are made up from other sources (complementary imports, organic-waste recycling, organic fertilizers, etc.) to within each system's sustainable degree of tolerance (Barbier, 1987). In other words, individual systems must achieve *relative,* though not necessarily *absolute,* sustainability.

One dramatic example will suffice by way of conclusion. As part of the reorientation of thought and practice required, many problems, pests, and even plagues, should be examined for possible sustainable benefits. Few hazards in Africa are feared more by peasants and commercial farmers alike than locust plagues. Vast sums of scarce foreign exchange are expended annually across the continent in locust control operations. Current practice is almost exclusively chemical spraying, invariably using toxic organochlorides or chlorinated hydrocarbons such as Lindane and

Diazinone. While effective in the short term, these sprays affect non-target species, contaminate the land and surface water, and pose severe health risks to spray teams and farmers. Yet many indigenous people regard locusts as a delicacy and an important source of protein. Before the advent of chemical spraying, many farmers collected locusts to feed to livestock. Recent experiments in South Africa have suggested potentially efficient means of capturing locusts *en masse* at the 'hopper' stage, and processing them commercially into successful animal feeds (Braack *et al.*, 1987; Ledger, 1987).

Locust plagues represent enormous energy and nutrient stores. Large-scale harvesting of them would have the potential to sustain many of Africa's vulnerable semi-arid ecobiomes and narrower ecosystems which would otherwise be devastated—by recycling locusts as human food, animal feed, or organic fertilizer, while simultaneously avoiding the foreign exchange outlays and long-term environmental contamination of chemical spraying.

Summary

Awareness of the environmental implications of different development strategies has grown significantly since the early 1970s. Although much destruction is still being wrought, there are at last hopeful signs that some major multilateral development agencies, governments, and NGOs, are beginning to adopt more environmentally sensitive policies.

Recent advances in environmental and development theory have focused on the concept of sustainable development, arguing that the environment must be seen as an integral pan of long-term sustainable development rather than merely as a resource to be exploited or traded for economic development.

This chapter reviews recent contributions to the literature on both conceptual and empirical aspects of this topical debate, stressing particularly the 'Brundtland Commission' report and the work of Michael Redclift. An historically sensitive political perspective is proposed as most appropriate for embracing not only the more traditional ecological and economic aspects but also the crucial political factors underlying uneven development and underdevelopment in the age of an increasingly integrated global economic system. Although we now have a fairly sophisticated theoretical understanding of sustainable development, appropriate methodologies and techniques for translating this into practice are still required. The chapter concludes that a blend of 'top down' and 'bottom up' approaches would give greatest flexibility, and suggests how the assessment of sustainability at the level of individual agro-ecological systems might be advanced.

Acknowledgement

An earlier version of this paper was presented at the Institute of British Geographers' Conference on Environmental Crises in Developing Countries, Royal Holloway and Bedford-New College, University of London, 19-21 December 1987. The editor and an anonymous Referee also provided helpful comments.

REFERENCES

Barbier, E.B. (1987). The concept of sustainable economic development. *Environmental Conservation,* 14(2), pp. 101-10, fig.

Braack, T., Loubser, J. & Braack, M. (1987). The "Argiope Trap'. *African Wildlife,* 41(4), p. 211.

Brandt Commission (1980). *North-South: A Programme for Survival.* Pan Books, London, England, UK: 304 pp.

Brandt Commission (1983). *Common Crisis: North-South Cooperation for World Recovery.* Pan Books, London, England. UK: 192 pp.

Bush, R. (1985). Unnatural disaster: the politics of famine. *Marxism Today,* 29(12), pp. 8-11.

Chambers, R. (1986). *Sustainable Livelihoods: An Opportunity for the World Commission on Environment and Development.* Institute of Development Studies, University of Sussex, Brighton, England, UK: (mimeogr.), cited in Redclift (1987, 36).

Conway, G. (1983). *Agro-ecosystem Analysis.* Imperial College Centre for Environmental Technology, 'Series E, No. 1', Imperial College, London, England, UK: cited in Tisdell (1988 p. 375).

Conway, G. (1985). Agro-ecosystem analysis. *Agricultural Administration,* 20, pp. 31-55.

Ecologist, The (1972). *A Blueprint for Survival.* Penguin, Harmondsworth, England, UK: 130 pp.

Glenny, M. (1987). Living in a socialist smog. *New Scientist.* 24th September, 41-4.

Ledger, J. (1987). The eighth plague returneth: the locusts are coming! *African Wildlife,* 41(4), pp. 197-210.

Meadows, D.H., Meadows, D.L., Randers, J. and Behrens, W.W. (1972). *The Limits to Growth.* Pan Books, London, England, UK: 205 pp.

Nash, C. and Bowers, J. (1986). *Alternative Approaches to the Valuation of*

Environmental Resources. Paper presented at ESRC Environmental Economics Workshop, University of East Anglia, Norwich, England, UK: mimeogr.

Panos Institute (1987). *Towards Sustainable Development.* Panos Institute, London, England, UK: xvi + 224 pp., illustr.

Redclift, M. (1984). *Development and the Environmental Crisis: Red or Green Alternatives?* Methuen, London, England, UK: x + 149pp.

Redclift, M. (1987). *Sustainable Development: Exploring the Contradictions.* Methuen, London, England, UK: x + 221 pp.

Sattaur, O. (1987). Trees for the people. *New Scientist,* 10th September, pp. 58-62.

Simon, D. (1985). Agrarian policy and migration in Zimbabwe and southern Africa: reform or transformation ? *Review of African Political Economy,* 34, pp. 82-9.

Stohr, W.B. & Taylor, D.R.F. (Eds) (1981). *Development from Above or Below? The Dialectics of Regional Planning in Developing Countries.* Wiley, Chichester, England, UK: xii + 488 pp., illustr.

Tisdell, C.A. (1988). Sustainable development: differing perspectives of ecologists and economists, and relevance to LDCs. *World Development,* 16(3), pp. 373-84.

Tolba, M.K.. (1987). *Sustainable Development: Constraints and Opportunities.* Butterworth, London, England, UK: 232 pp.

Ward, B and Dubos, R. (1972). *Only One Earth.* Penguin, Harmondsworth, England, UK: 304 pp.

World Commission on Environment and Development (WCED) (1987). *Our Common Future.* Oxford University Press, Oxford, England, UK: xv + 383 pp.

World Conservation Strategy (1980). *World Conservation Strategy: Living Resource Conservation for Sustainable Development.* IUCN-UNEP-WWF (obtainable from IUCN, Avenue du Mont-Blanc, 1196 Gland, Switzerland: pack of c. 50 unnumbered pp. in stiff paper folder).

17

Environmental and Resource Economics: Its Role in Planning Sustainable Development

CLEM TISDELL

Introduction

With rising public concern about environmental degradation and natural resource depletion, environmental economics and natural resource economics have attained increased prominence in economics and in policy formulation and planning. This is reflected at university level by the widespread introduction of courses in these areas and in government by the rise of new institutions for policy formulation such as the Australian Resources Commission which partly draws on the theory of environmental and resource economics (ERE) in its decision-making. Existing public policy institutions such as the Industries Commission have also been required to pay increasing attention to ERE. Furthermore, ERE has become important at the international and global level. It is increasingly recognised that many environmental and natural resource problems have international ramifications and that several have global impacts. Therefore, the planning of sustainable development is not only a matter for individual nations but also one that has to be addressed by the international community. Aid giving bodies such as AIDAB are giving greater attention to ERE in providing support for developing countries.

Given the likely impact of ERE in policy formulation and widespread community interest in planning for sustainable development, it is important to have an adequate appreciation of ERE and particularly the philosophies which underlie it. Furthermore, economic concepts of sustainable development and their implications for planning need to be considered.

The Nature and Evolution of Environmental and Resource Economics

By the end of the eighteenth century, economists had recognised three factors of production (land, labour and capital) as important determinants of the level of production and the wealth of nations. By the end of the nineteenth century, an additional productive element, entrepreneurship was also recognised. In economics, land refers to all gifts of God or nature not just soil or spatial area. In effect, it covers all natural resources — soil, minerals, fish in the ocean, natural forests, water and so on. Hence, the whole of the natural environment can be considered to fall within the subject area covered by land economics or as it now more commonly called natural resource economics.

Environmental economics is also concerned with the natural environment but not exclusively so. For example, man-made and cultural or social environments may also be a part of the subject matter of environmental economics. Economic discussions of the relationship between humans and their surroundings seem to be the main focus of environmental economics. It was not until early in this century that the possible economic importance of such relationships, particularly those involving externalities or environmental spillovers became to be recognised. Pigou (1932) was the first economist to give prominence to such effects, although many economists continued to regard such effects as being of trivial importance. However, many of the examples given by Pigou did not relate to natural resources, for example, the case of sparks from coal-fired trains increasing the risk of fires on properties near the rail line. Today much more emphasis is placed on the importance of externalities and several important externalities have been recognised in relation to natural resources. These externalities arise from both the use of such resources to produce material goods and from their use as sinks and receptors for waste from industry. For example, the use of water in one place say for irrigation may affect its availability and quality elsewhere and give rise to an unfavourable externality in production. The use of the air to dispose of gases and wastes from combustion of materials used in industry may give rise to acid rains and to global effects such as those attributed to greenhouse gases. In an increasingly interdependent world, there is a need to ensure that greater account is taken of the real social costs of such activities.

Another area of considerable interest in environmental and natural resource economics is the subject of limits to growth. To what extent, if any, do natural resource constraints provide limits to economic growth? It may prove to be impossible to sustain economic production because natural resources are depleted by their use in the production process or because these resources (e.g. air and water) are no longer able to absorb wastes from economic production without imposing severe economic penalties. Economic growth may falter for the same reasons and because of diminishing marginal productivity arising with intensification and extension of natural resource use, a possibility recognised by Ricardo (1817) in extending and clarifying the theory of Malthus (1798). By the early 1970s, three main possible limits to sustaining economic growth were recognised: (1) natural resource depletion; (2) 'pollution' of natural resources; and (3) diminishing marginal productivity with intensification and extension of natural resource use.

It was also recognised that two factors have played a major role in enabling economic growth to be achieved despite natural resource constraints. These are

(1) scientific and technological progress, and
(2) the accumulation of man-made capital.

The central question then becomes one of whether these factors are likely to continue to reduce natural limits to economic growth. Technological optimists argue that technological progress and capital accumulation are likely to be sufficient to overcome resource constraints. In their view achieving economic sustainability is no problem.

Nevertheless, not all technological optimists suggest that we can continue with 'business as usual'. Many accept the view that environmental externalities are important in the modern world and that those contributing to adverse environmental effects should pay the full costs involved in their activities. This is for example highlighted in the polluter-pays principle. The application of such a principle is likely to assist in sustaining economic production and/or economic welfare by ensuring that all costs, including environmental costs, are taken into account by responsible parties.

However, the extension of knowledge is not costless nor is the production of man-made capital. Both may be at the expense of natural resource stocks. To what extent is it desirable to keep adding to human/ man-made capital if this is at the expense of natural capital? This is currently under debate, particularly in relation to the distribution of income between generations.

Environmental and resource economics has many dimensions — growth, equity and allocative efficiency implications. But as it currently stands the sole focus of ERE is on human welfare. It is anthropocentric (*cf.* Cobb, 1990, 110) environments and other creatures have value only in so far as they have value to human beings. In operational economic models, it is usually assumed that the net value of retaining an environment can be measured by the difference between the amount of money those favouring this retention would be willing to pay for this and the amount of money needed to compensate those disadvantaged by this retention. But this assumes that those destroying the environment or nature have a right to do so. In reality much can depend on how property rights are assigned. If property rights run in the opposite direction, those destroying or using the environment will need to be able to compensate those who wish to conserve it. This test may result in a net benefit being assigned to conservation whereas a net disadvantage may be suggested by the first test. On the other hand, both tests could give the same result, depending on the circumstances. But no matter which of these tests are adopted, the approach is purely an anthropocentric one.

It should also be observed that this method cannot be applied in relation to future generations since they are not alive to express their preferences. But present generations can act, up to a point, as guardians of the assumed interests of future generations by for example including bequest values in their own preferences.

Economic Concepts of Sustainable Development

Several economic concepts of sustainable development exist (see Tisdell, 1991, Ch. 11; 1992) but only the most prominent one will be considered here, namely that type of development which sustains intergenerational economic welfare. Tietenberg (1988, 33) states that "the sustainability criteria suggests that at a minimum, future generations should be left no worse off than current generations". The World Commission on Environment and Development (1987, 43) assumed that "sustainable development is development that meets the needs of the present without compromising the ability of future generations to meet their own needs."

Tietenberg's definition seems to suggest that the real income per head of future generations or their standard of living should be not lower than that of present generations. It leaves open the question of whether these should be higher. Certainly those in less developed countries might hope that the incomes or the standards of living of their people would be higher in the future.

The question then arises of how this criteria relates to conservation of natural resources and strategies for economic development. The view may be taken that natural resources are held by current generations on trust for future generations. Depletion of natural resources by current generations can reduce the ability of future generations to meet their needs. Therefore, Pearce *et al.* (1989, 3) suggest as a general principle that "future generations should be compensated for reductions in the endowment of resources brought about by the actions of present generations". They suggest, for example, that an increase in man-made capital, especially an increase in scientific and technological knowledge might be used to compensate future generations. The question then is how adequate is man-made capital as a substitute for natural capital or as compensation for a reduction in natural resource stocks? Furthermore, to what extent is this substitution possible without endangering the ability of future generations to sustain income levels in an equitable manner?

Implications of the Above Concept for the Nature of Economic Development

Given the above concept of sustainability, the onus is on those who wish to use natural resources and reduce natural resource stocks to show that future generations will be adequately compensated for the loss of these stocks. On this view, there would be no objection to a less developed country such as Indonesia logging its rainforest unsustainably if future generations of Indonesians could be compensated by a larger stock of man-made capital. Similarly, there would be no objection to the elimination of a species by present generations if future generations could be compensated from an increased supply of man-made capital.

Those favouring the traditional economic growth approach might argue that in reality such compensation has taken place in the past. Present generations have benefited from the economic growth impulses and sacrifices of previous generations. They may then go on to suggest that this would also be the best strategy for the future.

However, this overlooks the fact that it may no longer be so easy to ensure rising standards of living for future generations (or maintain current income levels) by continuing to substitute man-made capital for natural resource stock. As resource stocks dwindle, the comparative productive value of remaining stocks may rise. Secondly, with greater demands on the natural environment, it is necessary to take more account of the real costs of using natural resources such as air and water for waste-disposal purposes. The use of these for waste-disposal needs increasingly to be priced. Thirdly, it must be recognised that standards of living do not depend on material or marketed goods alone. Unpriced environmental goods may also have economic value and add to the quality of life. Fourthly, we cannot always be sure of the consequences for future generations of depletion of natural resource stocks. In this case Pearce *et al.* (1989) suggests that it behaves us to be cautious and to try to keep economic options open. This may require greater conservation of natural resources, e.g. ecological resources, than otherwise.

Concluding Comment

The economic criteria of sustainability outlined above does not suggest that conservation of natural resources is a virtue in itself. But rather it suggests that from a practical point of view, greater attention to such conservation is necessary compared to the past if the standard of living of future generations is to be at least as high as that of current generations. One could also add that current generations might in addition obtain a rise in their standard of living as a result of more attention being given to the economic value of conserving environmental and natural resources.

However, it should be observed that some individuals believe that conservation of special environments and of natural resources, particularly living resources, is a virtue in itself. These views have for example been expressed by Aldo Leopold (1933, 1966). Mankind is seen as having a stewardship role in relation to nature. This suggests that humanity should accept some constraints on man-centred economic growth or development to maintain or sustain natural living systems. This view seems to be more widely accepted now than in the past.

While economic concepts of sustainable development seem more precise and operational than many of the general concepts which have currency at present, because of uncertainties, conceptual problems and disagreements about appropriate values and ethics, they are not a straightforward means for planning development. They may be too narrow in their focus (Tisdell, 1990 Ch. 3; 1991, Ch. 11; 1992). Nevertheless they raise important philosophical and other issues that might otherwise be overlooked and seem to be leading to the development of techniques which are likely to enhance their operational value.

REFERENCES

Cobb, J.B. (1990). "An index of sustainable economic welfare". *Development*, No. 3/4, pp. 106-111.

Leopold, A. (1933). *Game Management.* New York: Scribner.

Leopold, A. (1966). *A Sand Country Almanac: with other Essays on Conservation from Round River.* New York: Oxford University Press.

Malthus, T.R. (1798). *An Essay on the Principle of Population as it affects the Future Development of Mankind.* London: J. Johnson.

Pearce, D., Markandya, A., and Barbier, E.B. (1989). *Blueprint for a Green Economy.* London: Earthscan Publications.

Pigou, A.C. (1932). *Economics of Welfare*, 3rd edition. London: Macmillan.

Ricardo, D. (1817). *The Principles of Political Economy and Taxation.* London.

Tietenberg, T. (1988). *Environmental and Natural Resource Economics*, 2nd edition. Glenview, Illinois: Scott, Foresman and Company.

Tisdell, C.A. (1990). *Natural Resources, Growth and Development: Economics, Ecology and Resource-Scarcity*, New York, Praeger.

Tisdell, C.A. (1991). *Economics of Environmental Conservation.* Amsterdam and New York: Elsevier Service Publishers.

Tisdell, C.A. (1992). "The nature of sustainability and of sustainable development". *The Middle East Business and Economic Review*, Vol. 4, No. 1, pp. 21-25.

World Commission on Environment and Development (1987). *Our Common Future*, Oxford University Press, New York.

18

Towards a Sustainable Development: An Economic Policy Perspective

ISMAIL SHARIFF

> *In the old world of the Cold War period, We knew what threatened us. In the new world we will have to learn what threatens us.* —*Les Aspine,*
> U.S. Defence Secretary, January 5, 1993.

I

The unfolding of multiplc cconomic political trends in the twilight of the twentieth century points towards a new transformed world economic order, but one whose character has not yet developed sharp definition and vivid perspective. Thus President Clinton commenting in February 1993 on the post-Cold War World, justifiably cautioned that the enemy is the environment and thus uncertain until positive steps are taken. In other words in specific terms it is tantamount to saying that the world faces a wide variety of critical environmental threat: in terms of degradation of soil, water, and marine resources essential to increased food production: widespread health threatening pollution; stratospheric ozone depletion; global climate change; and loss of biodiversity.[1] At the same time, it faces enormous human problems in the form of vicious, persistent poverty and human misery — despite growing affluence for many. In most of the cases, part of the reason lies in the fact that points to the imbalance between the haves of one third of the world countries to two-thirds of the World's have nots. In a way if one tries to understand the reasoning, it is aptly clear that among the multitude of specifics, it is the human being species that has exploited the earth with prodigious success. To begin with some ten thousands years ago with a few million individuals inhabiting the planet earth whereas, as of 1993, the sheer number of human beings has surpassed the five billion mark. Given this trend in the growth of population and even making allowance for the slow growth rate in recent years, the world population from all calculations will double again in forty to fifty years. It is nonetheless true that in the course of the twentieth century alone the global economy has expanded twenty times. Industrialisation has increased by a factor of more than 5 since 1950.[2] The consumption of fossil fuel running almost apace. The economic explosion has depleted stocks of ecological capital faster than the stocks of fuel, forests, soils, fisheries, and waters can be replenished.[3] Such an accelerated growth in both population and economic activity has the potential to increase dramatically the pressure on natural resources to the very determination of the survival of the planet earth. In other words just as population of say bacterial overreach available resources and collapse in their own waste, in the same way our own biological success thus threatens our very existence on this planet. In support of this impending threat we can point out that as of now more than a billion people in the world are malnourished.[4] On top of this if population continues to grow and double as expected, to provide adequate level of nutrition under the best of conditions would require making very productive use of the world's stock of arable land. Yet according to new estimates by the world's leading soil scientists, more than 1.2 billion hectares (one hectare = 2.2 acres) of vegetable land — an area as large as India and China put together — have been significantly degraded since World War II.[5] If such depletion of soil resources continues unabated, expansion of food production on the scale required will be extremely difficult, if not impossible and thus may greatly worsen human misery. In the last decade, in fact, per capita food production has declined in 69 countries.[6]

Another impending threat relates to the use and misuse of fossil fuels. As of now fossil fuels provide 95 per cent of commercial energy used in the world economy, and their use is growing world-wide at the rate of about 20 per cent per decade.[7] Furthermore, scientists convened by the intergovernmental panel of climate change under the auspices of the United Nations Environmental Programmes and the World Meteorological Organisation (UNEPA WMO) concluded that a 60 per cent reduction in carbon dioxide emissions would be necessary to stabilise carbon dioxide concentrations in the atmosphere at current levels. Protecting the earth's climate, therefore may require significant reductions in global fossil fuel use, even as the world economy expands; alternatively, continued expansion of fossil fuel use at current rates will double atmospheric levels well before the middle of the next century and thus increase the risk of significant climate change.[8]

From the above warnings it is obvious that the world is not now headed towards a sustainable future, but rather a variety of potential human and environmental disasters. It is true that for some time there is this realisation that the environmental problems are inseparable from those of the human welfare and from the process of economic development in general. Nonetheless in reality many present forms of development erode the environmental resources on which human livelihood and welfare ultimately depends. With this recognition in 1989 the United Nations established the World Commission on Environment and Development to examine these issues and make recommendations.[9]

In retrospect, the categorical question facing the world is whether we have the potential to find a way that will pave for sustainable development in the years to come. Sustainable development certainly means arresting the depletion of our resources while providing a decent survival means for the foreseeable future. Also in specific terms it means prudent resource management without diminishing the consumption possibilities of future generations. Therefore economic policy for sustainable development is appropriately focused on true income, i.e. that which is available for consumption in the current period without diminishing the value of capital and natural resources.

This in turn boils down to two specific measures every responsible citizen worldwide have to take under consideration, viz. (1) control of population growth and (2) restricting drastically our way of life to conform to the reality of sustainable development. Failure to do so means the total loss of this plant not only for human habitation but also any other breathing and living entities.

II

With regard to the control of population growth, Nafiz Sadiq, Executive Director of the United Nations Population Funds in *The Futurist*[10] outlines the current world population trends and suggests strategies for curbing population growth rate in the future.

It is but certain beyond any shadow of doubt that the trend set into the decades of the 1990s will decide the speed of population growth for much of the 21st century. The world population in the beginning of 1993 stands at 5.45 billion and is increasing by three people every second — about a quarter of a million everyday. Thus at this rate between 90-100 million people roughly equivalent to the population of Eastern Europe or Central America will be added every year during the 1990s.[11] a billion people — a whole additional China over the decade. But the irony is that more than 90 per cent of the global population growth over the next thirty-five years will be in the developing countries of Africa, Asia and Latin America.[12]

The factors behind such an explosion in the rate of growth of population in the developing countries comes down to the following: (1) most women marry at an early age and the percentage of women who marry is high; (2) the very structure of the agrarian society calls for many offsprings; (3) the early consequences of modernisation tend to reduce death rate, while the birth rate remains constant, and (4) the practice of voluntary birth control is limited despite the growing need for family planning.

Most women marry at an early age. Education is not of prime concern to the female, as parents are more interested in grooming them to be good housekeepers and good wives. As such in the rural areas of a typical developing country usually a girl is married by the time she is sixteen. The culture in many of the developing countries deplores and frowns on late marriages and on those who are not married. The parents try to marry their daughters off at an early age to comply with tradition and culture. The result of such early marriages translates into three or four children by the age of twenty. On the other hand, if the girl had gone to school, until she is twenty years of age, she would not have had these three or four children, for she would be older and more mature and possibly more willing to practice birth control.

Another basic reason for the population growth in the developing countries stems from the very fact that around 60 to 70 per cent of the population is engaged in agriculture with less than 2 acres of land per farm, which requires little mechanisation and much manpower. Thus the farmer strives to have many children, especially boys, so he can work his land without having to hire outside help.

Many children also serve another important purpose in the form of old age security. In many of the developing countries there is no social security or any other form of retirement plan available to the people during their golden years, so the only alternative is to have as many children as possible (preferably males) so that when they are no longer productive they can rely on their children for support, an age old practice which has the forceful blessing of tradition and culture, and therefore in the developing countries the question of old age nursing homes does not arise.

Another equally important cause for the population explosion rests with reducing the infant mortality rate with no corresponding reduction in the birth rate over the years. Before 1921 the now so called developing countries population more or less appeared to be relatively stable with a slight upward trend. This was due, mainly, to the high death rates caused by famines, plagues and diseases. As early as 1921 progress in medical technology began to cut the death rate, while the birth rate remained at the same high level. For example on the average the birth rate in these countries was 48/1000, while the death rate was 47/1000.[13] In 1961 the birth rate was still high at 40/1000 while death rate had fallen 22/1000.[14] This represents a sixty per cent cut in the death rates and only a 12 per cent cut in the birth rates. The result is a 2.5 per cent annual increase in the population as of 1961. However, since then due to the realisation on the part of several of the developing countries the rate of population growth has been brought down to about, on the average, 2.2 per cent.[15] But given the large population base in the reproductive age this 2.2 per cent is the key for the rapid population growth in these countries.

To arrest this threat of population explosion, international organisations and many well intentioned individuals have proposed a multitude of ways to cut population growth — particularly by the developing countries. Most of these suggestions either fall short in terms of the logistics involved or in terms of the solutions themselves. Therefore we should subscribe to the view that "the goal is not survival but survival as human beings. The decisions are not technical, reserved to experts, but political and moral, demanding the intelligent participation of all of us. Therefore the outcome of the human drama depends in large part upon whether, in the next decade, we devote our primary energies to multiplying and redistributing the bread or to reducing the number of guests at the table."[16]

The last sentences in the above quotation nicely summarise the fundamental differences between the Malthusian or Neo-Malthusian approach to population problem perspectives presented by many economists. However the views of neo-Malthusian approach to population problems derive primary from the nature of final organisation, rather than such externalities as built-in-limit to earth's capacity to provide human sustenance. Hopefully, a consequence of this approach will translate into increased attention to finding and using social structures or cultural patterns which will prove more effective than our present systems for feeding, educating, healing, pacifying, and uniting mankind. In contrast, the Malthusian highlights population size as a chief, if not dominant cause of present and future woes. Too frequently their programmes for resolving or preventing crisis boil down to attempts to limit or reduce population size, or to fostering a fatalistic resignation that for at least part of the earth's population – usually the poorer part—will inevitably be doomed partly by war,—famine or pestilence.

Irrespective of the ongoing debate between the neo-Malthusian and Malthusian that reducing overall population growth-rate as the only way to preserve a quality population. In other words the spacious but deductive logic of people cause pollution, ergo fewer people equals less population and less demand on the environment suggests the basic need for constructive population policies in the immediate future. One immediate step along these lines can be initiated immediately by the donor countries and other international organisations (World Bank, International Monetary Fund, United Nations Development Programme, etc.) by conditionally associating aid packages to the developing countries towards an implementation of effective population control policies, preferably on a voluntary basis and if not, insisting on adopting the compulsory Chinese model may be with variations or modifications to suit their own tradition, culture and religious orientations.

III

Most recently in an attempt to make the concept of sustainable development more specific, some scientists have given a narrow definition focused on physical aspects of sustainable development. They stress using renewable natural resources in a manner that does not eliminate or degrade them or diminish their renewable usefulness for future generations, while maintaining effectively constant or non-declining stocks of natural resources such as soil, groundwater, and biomass. On the other hand, some economic definitions of sustainable development have also focused on optimal resource management, by concentrating on maximising the net benefits of economic development, subject to maintaining the services of quality of natural resources. Other economic definitions have focused on the broader notion that the "use of resources today should not reduce real incomes in the future."[17] Underlying this notion is the concept that current decisions should not impair the prospect for maintaining or improving future living standards. This implies that our economic systems should be managed so that we live off the dividends of our resources, maintaining and improving the asset base.[18]

All of the foregoing definitions and interpretations of the concept of sustainable development is based on the premise that each society should leave the next generation economically as well off as it is. But this objective preservation of specific natural resources is unlikely to be the efficient means. Resource reservation — if not economically meritorious on current calculations — will reduce the economic value output through time. It may inadvertently lead to curbing research and capital formation and may very well have a perverse effect on future output and welfare.

Thus it is by no means necessary to reduce production today in order to increase production tomorrow. If, instead, current production and consumption is reduced in favour of research and investment, future production will be increased. Higher production today, if it also means more research and investment today, thus will serve the economic interest of future generations better than reservation of resources and lower current production.

On a world-wide basis sustainable development is a more complicated concept than many advocates of the idea acknowledge. In an excellent brief review of the issues associated with the concept of sustainable development, Veeman[19] suggests three interwoven aspects to be considered, viz., a growth component, a distribution component, and an environmental component.

In terms of the growth component it is true that early theories of economic growth placed great emphasis on the accumulation of physical capital and the need for a high marginal rate of savings to finance capital accumulation. Gradually, the emphasis shifted to acknowledge the contribution of human capital formation to the growth process. The recent emphasis on sustainable development has added two more dimensions:[20] the need to give greater weight to the stabilisation of growth over time; to the inter-generational implication of economic growth; and the need to emphasise the role of natural resources in long-term economic growth.

Whereas in terms of the distributional component it is true that economic growth only becomes economic development when the benefits of growth are widely distributed. Research, for example, which promises to lead to significant growth, which will benefit each and everyone not only at the present but also in the future should be encouraged both through political and private funding.

Finally the balance lies with the third component which emphasises the environmental aspect as a basic core concept of sustainable development. Economists along with other physical scientists have a long tradition of tracking environmental issues rather differently than biological scientists. The concept of externalities, property rights, optimum rates of depletion, and option values are only four of the many ideas which economists have developed to help analyse environmental issues in the context of sustainable development. Perhaps the biggest difference between the economists paradigm and that of most biological scientists is that economists do not perceive natural resources as a fixed quantum with a predetermined finite capacity to satisfy the needs of a mankind. Instead, stressed the ingenuity of man — our capacity to adjust over time and our creation of new institutions, for example property rights; technological change, for example, development of fusion energy; and substitution opportunities such as alternative food source, all greatly change the value to society of a particular set of natural resources. In general, economists are more optimistic and positive about the environmental component of sustainable development than most physical and biological scientists.[21]

There is no doubt natural resources are often grouped into renewable or flow resources (fisheries, forests, rangelands, natural populations and so on) for certain analytical purposes, this is a most convenient division. In the case of renewable resources, a number of conservation or management strategies have been suggested, such as maximum sustainable yield (MSY) and optimum stocking rate or carrying capacity, by biological trained scientists. Unfortunately, in practice, it is usually extremely difficult to implement these strategies with any degree of precision.

Hencc there is a world-wide need for mankind to develop appropriate policies and management strategies of renewable resources such as soil, pastures, native forests and native terrestrial and marine animal populations. In many parts of the world, overexploitation is causing irreversible changes. Renewable resources are becoming non- renewable. Appropriate policies and management strategies cannot be developed, nor successfully implemented, from a purely biological perspective.

IV

In conclusion the sustainable development is like motherhood: no reasonable person is opposed to the idea in principle. Yet, in practice, much of modern perception hinges on higher production and higher income. Obviously this very perception may not be akin to the concept of sustainable development.

In a way there are no easy solutions. However, the problem associated with sustainability are not amenable to purely scientific solutions. The economic and social dimensions are critical if meaningful results are to be achieved. Sustainability issues will require educators in all fields of knowledge of the twenty-first century to place greater emphasis than has been the case in the past on social and economic aspects of sustainable development.

NOTES

1. World Resource A Guide to the Global Environment, United Nations Environmental Program, p. 1, Oxford University Press, World Resources 1992-93, New York, 1992.
2. Brown, R. Lester *et al. State of the World* p. 49, W.W. Norton, New York, 1992.
3. WHO and UNEP Global Environment Monitoring System (GEMS), p. 74, Oxford University Press, 1991.
4. (UNDP) United Nations Human Development Report 1992, p. 14, Oxford University Press, 1992, New York.
5. Oldeman, L.R. VanEngelan, V.W.P. and Pulles, J.H.M. "The Extent of Human induced soil degradation", An Explanatory Note, rev. 2nd edition, Table 7, p. 3.
6. UNFAO, World Food and Agriculture Trends 1991. Table 18.1, p. 273.
7. United Nations Statistical Office, Energy Statistics Year Book, 1992, p. 36, United Nations, New York.
8. Houghton, T. and Jenkins, G.J., *Intergovernmental Panel on Climate Changes* pp. xi-xvi, Cambridge University Press, Cambridge, UK 1991.
9. United Nations, Circular #16, p. 17, 1989, New York.
10. Sakik Nafiz "World Population continues to Rise" *The Futurist*, pp. 10-11, March-April, 1991, World Future Society, Maryland 1991.
11. *Ibid.*, p. 13.
12. *Ibid.*, p. 14.
13. Computed from the Population Reference Bureau Report #10, April 1970 p. 23, New York.
14. *Ibid.*, p. 26.
15. Tables computed from World Development Report 1992.
16. Neuhaus, Richard. *In Defence of People*, p. 31, 2nd edition. MacMillan and Co., New York, 1991.

17. Markandya, A. and Dearer, D.W. Natural Environments and the Social Rate of Discount. Project appraisal, vol. 3, no. 1, p. 11, 1988, New York, MacMillan Press.
18. Repetto, Robert, *World Enough and Time*, pp. 15-16, Yale University Press, New Heaven, Connecticut, 1986.
19. Veeman, T.S. "Sustainable Development: its economic meaning and policy implications", p. 37, *Canadian Journal of Agricultural Economics*, Dec. 1989
20. Baties Sandra, "Sustainable Development", *American Journal of Agricultural Economics*, p. 71, 1989.
21. Goelter, H.E. and Weinborg, A.M., "The Age of Substitutability", *Science* 1991, pp. 683-89.

REFERENCES

Baumol, W.J. and Oates, W.E. *The Theory of Environmental Policy*, Englewood Cliffs, N.J.: Prentice Hall, Inc.

Barbier, Edward B., (1989). *Economics, Natural Resources, Scarcity and Development: Conventional and Alternative Views*. Earthscan Publication Ltd.; London.

Barrett, S. (1991a). "The Paradox of International Environmental Agreements", Mimeo, London Business School.

Cline, William R. (1992). *Global Warming: The Economic Stakes*. Washington D.C.: Institute for International Economics.

Cutler, L.N. (1988). *Global Interdependence and the Multinational Firm*. Headline Series No. 239, New York, Foreign Policy Association.

Daley, Herman E., (1990). "Towards Some Operational Principles of Sustainable Development" *Ecological Economics*, Vol. 2.

Goodland, R. and Ledec G., (1987). "Neo-classical Economics and Principles of Sustainable Development" *Ecological Modelling*, Vol. 38.

Hahn, R.W. (1989). "Economic Prescriptions for Environmental Problems: How the patient followed the Doctor's orders", *Journal of Economic Perspectives* 3, No. 2: 95-114.

Hoel, M. (1989). 'Global Environmental Problems: The Effects of Unilateral Actions Taken by One Country', Working Paper No. 11, Department of Economics, University of Oslo.

Mackenzie, J.J. (1991). *Toward a Sustainable Energy Future: The critical role of Rational Energy Pricing*, World Resource Institute, Washington D.C., May.

MacNeill, J. (1989). "Strategies for Sustainable Economic Development," *Scientific American*, Vol. 261, No. 3, September, 1989.

Repetto, R. (1989). "Population, Resources, Environment: An Uncertain Future" *Population Bulletin*, Vol. 42, No. 2.

Titenberg, T., (1988). *Environmental and Natural Resource Economics*, Scott Foresman and Company, Glenview, IL.

World Bank, (1992). World Development Report, 1992, Development and the Environment. Oxford University Press.

19

Ecologically Sustainable Economic Development: Concepts and Model Implications

JEROEN C.J.M. VAN DEN BERGH & PETER NIJKAMP

Introduction

This chapter aims at clarifying the concept of sustainable development from a modelling viewpoint and suggesting central components of it. These components will each be discussed separately, with specific emphasis on the design and use of models for sustainable development.

The concept of sustainable development is — particularly since the publication of the Brundtland report (WCED, 1987) — increasingly gaining popularity in integrated economic-ecological policy analysis and research. This concept reflects a compromise between growth advocates and ecologists. It recognises the goal of survival of the human species, realisation of an acceptable quality of life for each individual in present and future generations, preservation of diversity and quality in the natural environment, and wise management of natural resources and ecosystems.

In order to harmonise the actions of individuals striving for their own goals, in most countries an institutional system of regulations — rights and rules — is coming into being in order to prevent society from turning into an anarchy with unacceptable environmental externalities. No comprehensive regulation via a system of rights and rules exists that is satisfactory for real-world allocation and tuning.

Reprinted with permission from *Studies in Regional Science Journal* of the Japan Section of the RSAI. Vol. 20, No. 2, December 1990. pp.1-23.

The current set of regulations in most countries may have some effect, but is mainly suited to correct for a socially undesired allocation over space or within the same generation. Although attention towards environmental problems is rising, the main concern of decision-makers is still more about static than about dynamic distributional effects of developments. In a dynamic world we are not only facing static allocational and distributional problems, but also intricate problem of allocation of endowments — of any kind — over time.

This allocation over time results from the development within the ecological-economic system. The development of each sub-system has to be viewed in accordance with that of the other one. In conventional economics and ecology each system is usually studied separately from the other one, while both systems are assumed to behave independently of each other. No feedback of one system to the other is generally assumed. Usually one is interested in feasible and optimal time paths for the system as a whole, so that interactions and feedback mechanisms between the sub-systems may matter. One approach is to consider the effects of a certain economic development on developments in the ecological system. Starting from the ecological system, one can search for constraints that should be imposed on economic development paths to fulfil goals of conservation of ecosystems and sustainable yield of renewable resources.

'Sustainable' is a general concept which denotes that the necessary conditions for some phenomenon to take place are permanently satisfied. Therefore the following definition of ecologically sustainable economic development can be posed: the development of economic activities, human preferences and human population, such that an acceptable standard of life for every human being is fulfilled (the phenomenon) and all aspects of this development can be sustained in the long run by natural resource availability, ecosystems and life support systems (the necessary conditions).

'Ecologically sustainable' refers to the continued existence of the environment, which acts as a basis for human welfare as it provides living conditions and environmental amenities, and acts also as productive basis.

The concept of 'acceptable standard of living' calls also for further explanation. Brown *et al.* (1987) state that all humans should, once born, live to adulthood with a quality of life beyond mere biological survival. Tolba (1987) mentions elements that are essential in arriving at such a quality: food self-reliance, health control, clean water and shelter. While these are especially relevant to developing countries, Pearce *et al.* (1988) mention additional attributes that are more relevant to developed countries: real income per capita, education, access to resources, basic freedom and distribution of income. And still more aspects may be relevant: price stability and regional balance.

The natural environment is in our definition classified as resource availability, ecosystems and life support systems. The latter are essential in providing living conditions for the human species. Resources generate flows of materials and services for economic activities. Ecosystems create conditions for economic activities and provide environmental amenities that make a direct contribution to the level of welfare.

Several elements in a sustainable development strategy can be distinguished, referring to non-renewable and renewable resources and pollution levels. Sustainable use is an element that may serve as a starting point to sustainable development. It refers in a narrow sense to renewable resources, in which case it means that the rate of harvesting or extraction of the resource is not higher than the controlled or natural regeneration rate. In a broader sense sustainable use may include also that pollution generation (waste, congestion) is kept below critical levels. These critical levels are determined on the basis of the assimilative capacity of ecosystems. Another element in sustainable development can be the sparingly use of scarce non-renewable resources. Also substitution and extinction are in principle allowed for in sustainable development. Substitution may occur between natural resources used in production or in generating environmental amenities. Also substitution between economic activities is an option, leading to qualitative changes in the economic system. Furthermore, technological innovation may lead to less intensive use of certain resources or to a replacement by others. Or it may induce the substitution of existing activities by new ones, leading also to qualitative changes in the economic system. Of course some ecosystems should be conserved as they provide living conditions or are crucial to the continued existence of larger natural systems.

These elements in a strategy for sustainable development — a global concept — offer meaningful starting points for operationalising sustainable development at a meso level of aggregation. A meso level is useful for implementing sustainable development for the following reasons: interactions and feedback mechanisms are easier traceable than at a global level; environmental decision making can easily be guided by a regional governmental agency; and regions have specific problems or capacities that should be dealt with in their right context and level of detail. Thus the implementation of sustainable development at an operational level calls for a specific choice of spatial scale. A regional scale of analysis for a finite number of generations is relevant, attainable and apt for accuracy. Furthermore, the time scale is important. In general, the time horizon may be determined on the basis of uncertainty and regeneration rates of renewable natural resources involved.

In the following section sustainable development will be placed in a three-dimensional context of time, space and substance so that a distinction of important components can be made. Next, in section 3 these dimensions will be discussed at a lower level of abstraction along with implications for modelling for sustainable development.

Dimensions of Ecologically Sustainable Development

Now we will place sustainable development in a three dimensional context of time, space and 'substance', in order to get a clear view on the many aspects related to it.

Time can be measured on a continuous or discrete (equidistant) scale. The largest time horizon is still finite, but may be approximated by an infinite horizon. Three types of time can be distinguished, viz., sequential, computational and cumulative time. The first one refers to the fact that events and decisions have consequences and are thus extended over time.

The second type of time is connected with both computational algorithms and adjustment processes, and hence with the common feature of stability. The third category concerns the transfer of embodied information with the passage of time, either through activities by man or by way of an autonomous process, or by a combination of both.

The dimension space can be subdivided into geographical parts, each having the capacity and place for containing some unique entity that is either useful or necessary to discern it from its surroundings. This means that two such parts, which are different in terms of place, will not generally be of the same shape. The sum of all these parts is clearly finite in every direction (e.g., a region and the atmosphere).

'Substance' refers to basic units of a system and may include *inter alia* potential energy, a living entity, or a system (an individual, a population, an ecosystem, an economy or economic sector, a region, etc.). A possible distinction of 'substance' is into human actors, non-human actors (living organisms) and the non-living physical environment. The latter class is dominated by processes in space and time of an autonomous intrinsic physical nature, and is influenced by the first two groups (i.e., human and non-human actors). The second class changes in an evolutionary way along a path guided by laws of the system of living organisms and sometimes disturbed by physical events and often by human intervention. The class of human actors evolves strongly both in terms of number and influence on both other classes, making itself increasingly dependent on these. The space characteristics of a certain 'substance' do perhaps not differ much among some individuals (e.g. individuals in a population), but they may do so in other cases (e.g. industries, forests, river, populations, sub-regions in a region). The time characteristics can be very different, for instance, different 'substances' may take part in processes with different flow velocities (some processes are measured in eons, others in microseconds, just to name some extremes).

In economic models man plays a role in different ways. First, human decision making at a micro level can be described by relating individual behavioural characteristics to external data and developments. Often the actors' decisions interface with one another, like for example in the use of a common property resource (e.g., fishery, or soil, air and water in the case of pollution), and sometimes it may be necessary to control for the outcomes of such interactive processes by directing actions through certain policy instruments such that socially determined goals will be realised. This second way of human action is at a different level than the first one and can be described as an optimisation of some social objective, while of course taking into consideration the behaviour of individuals as well as economic and ecological processes and interactions.

In the sequel we will discuss four central components of sustainable development, viz. intergenerational aspects, interregional trade-off, multiple use, and uncertainty and risk. Although more components can be distinguished than we do here, the most important ones will be mentioned here. However, it is very difficult to formulate components that are entirely non-overlapping in terms of elements of sustainability.

The sequential aspect of time and the central role of man as indicated are also reflected in the intergenerational aspects of sustainability. The problem that arises in this specific context is that of intergenerational equity (or welfare distribution). The question of how to compare the distribution of welfare over time has been the subject of much debate in economics and has resulted in several viewpoints regarding the specification of a social objective function and in many different opinions concerning discount rates to be used in some realistic setting, for example in energy policy (Lind, 1982). Also from a theoretical and practical angle various other problems arise, viz. regarding the measurement and comparability of utility that individuals attach to a given social state.

Both computational and cumulative time are related to uncertainty. The computational aspect refers to stability of equilibria of processes. Dependent on the strength of the stability forces pulling the state of the system back to equilibrium, the system in an equilibrium state may exhibit a certain degree of uncertainty without leaving its equilibrium neighbourhood. In this aspect also the question arises how much time it takes to close gaps between present and desired (or equilibrium) values of variables. Since we opted for both a limited space horizon, leading to a distinction into regions, interactions between regions and the trade-off between equity and efficiency should be considered. These problems and arguments for specific choices of a regional subdivision will be treated hereafter under the heading of interregional trade-offs.

The discussion following the introduction of 'substance' denotes the fact that most entities use and are used by other entities for their existence. It is not an exception that one entity makes use of several others, possibly at the same time (e.g., a factory using water for cleaning or cooling purposes and using air, water or soil for discharge of its residuals). Here, an entity may denote bounded organisations ranging from (non-) human individuals and populations to ecosystems and economic systems. It is also possible that an entity provides several services to one or more other entities. The latter is known as multiple use.

Ecologically sustainable economic development should be preceded by the identification of a time path of economic activities that takes account of constraints on the possible time paths of ecosystems' elements, such that the state of the entire interacting economic-ecological system — represented by appropriate states of all elements in both sub-systems — follows a time path that satisfies the optimal balancing of relevant indicators or criteria within given constraints. The optimal balancing follows from the evaluation of the social (intergenerational) objective function for each feasible time path of the systems variables. In a more operational sense this can be performed in a multiobjective framework or by using satisfying levels for relevant indicator variables.

Components of Sustainable Development and Model Implications

In the present section we will discuss in more detail the central components of sustainable development that were indicated in the previous section.

Intergenerational Trade-off

Intergenerational elements include the time horizon, the social welfare function and bequest function, the social rate of discount and relevant restrictions/constraints. Restrictions can be classified as referring to stocks, controls, stock changes and integrals.

The time-horizon in a sustainability analysis is in general long, including the life span of at least two generations, in order to include intergenerational aspects. Uncertainty elements will make an infinite horizon unrealistic to work with. In sustainable development, long-term behaviour — trends and structural changes — are important. Stability issues at both the economic and ecological systems level may then be relevant for outcomes in the long run. Unfortunately, short-term adjustment processes — concerned with departures from equilibrium — long-term trends — assuming equilibrium — and structural change are often not compatible in one modelling framework. Models are either fitted to short-term data and are only adequate for describing short-term processes, or only long-term data are used and most accurately generated (see Ayres, 1978). In an operational context, a choice of the time horizon depends also on the dynamic behaviour of renewable resources that are important to the region considered.

A social welfare function serves as an evaluation criterion for the identification of decisions. In an ideal situation this evaluation would be based on a social welfare ranking of all possible social states. Here we regard a social state in a general way, viz. the distribution of all goods, services and other utility-determining factors, information, and nature in all its aspects ("quality" and "quantity") over time, space and individuals. A social ranking can be arrived at by aggregating individual welfare rankings of social states. In a static context that would imply a choice for a welfare function with as arguments the utilities of all individual members of a generation at a certain point in time. In a dynamic sense, a social welfare function is based on the utilities of all individuals over time. An individual's welfare ranking is usually made explicit by introducing utility functions. For aggregation of rankings it is necessary to assume — in addition to the usual ordinal significance measurability feature — that cardinal significant individual utility functions be constructed. We make here the distinction between comparability of individual ranking in one generation and that in different generations. For both purposes the cardinal significance condition on utility functions is necessary, whilst for intergenerational comparability also the choice of a discount factor has to be considered.

As a result of the above mentioned aggregation procedure we assume the existence of a social welfare function, through which a ranking of alternative social states is possible. One possible choice of such an aggregate welfare function that is justified by different moral systems (viz., Classical Utilitarianism and the Intuist conceptions; Dasgupta and Heal, 1979), is the additive, separable utility function, that can be formulated (respectively for discrete and continuous time dimensions) as:

$$\sum_{i=0}^{L_0} U_0^i + \sum_{t=1}^{T}[[1/\prod_{s=1}^{t}(1+\delta_s)^s \sum_{i=1}^{L_t}[U_t^i(x)]] \qquad \ldots (1)$$

and

$$\int_0^T exp\{-\int_0^t \delta_s ds\} \sum_{i=1}^{L_t} U_t^i(x)dt. \qquad \ldots (2)$$

Here it is assumed that the discount rate δ_t, the number of individuals in the generation at time t (period t) L_t, and the utility function of individual i $U_t^i(\,)$ may change over time. All relevant information on social states is incorporated in $x(t)$ (denoted by x). The time horizon T is regarded as finite. If in the continuous case the time horizon (which might be reached as the time of extinction of the human race on earth) is following a distribution with a probability density function $p(T)$, then (2) may be generalised as:

$$\int_0^\infty \int_0^T exp\{-\int_0^t \delta_s ds\} \sum_{i=1}^{L_t} U_t^i(x)p(T)dtdT. \qquad \ldots (3)$$

If T is large, an infinite value may be used without making a significant error. On the other hand, if T is infinite, the total infinite sum (1) [or integral (2)] may be replaced by a finite one with a bequest function and additional conditions on stock variables. The lump sum term should approximate the expected total discounted utility to T of social states from time T onwards. This approach bears much resemblance to the way decisions are made in reality, as in general no planner is able to work with infinite horizons.

An alternative welfare criteria is the maximum criterion based on the ethical ideas of Rawis (1971). The objective function to be maximised in this case is

$$\min_{t_0[0,t]}[C(t)]. \quad \ldots (4)$$

This criterion takes the intergenerational equity most strong into account, because it concentrates on the welfare of the generation that is worst off. Thus substitution between generations' utilities will not be stimulated by this social welfare function, in so far as it does not make the inequality in the distribution of utility of generations over time smaller. This is a contrast with the utilitarian criterion by which it may be optimal — in terms of the total welfare weighted by a discount factor — that one generation is subjected to bad circumstances in order to make life for succeeding generations better. The underlying idea for the latter is thus that a certain decrease in welfare for one generation can be compensated by an increase for another. The fulfilment of such a programme implies for a society starting with poverty that it will endure poverty over all succeeding generations. This problem cannot be satisfactorily overcome with an intergenerationally extended 'max-min' principle, for example one in which the utility of one generation is made dependent on both its own consumption level and that of the next generation (Dasgupta, 1974). Then (4) is replaced by

$$\min_{i \in N} U[C(i), C(i+1)], \quad \ldots (5)$$

where I denotes the place of a generation in the total sequence of generations, and $N = \{1, 2, \ldots, n\}$, with n the total number of generations living in [O, T]. Even with a further extension of care for future generations, a permanent escape from the initial level of consumption or capital assets is not possible (see Dasgupta, 1974). The initial consumption level is free in the model, i.e. it will be determined as part of the optimal solution. Alternatively an initial consumption level can be added to the model — as in the case of an initial stock value — resulting from past developments. Imposing a sustainable development constraint — requiring that the consumption level may not decrease — will ensure then even more rigidity than the minimax criterion already does.

A bequest function can be added to the welfare criterion in our model for the finite horizon problem, in terms of the utility of the terminal capital stock. This reflects the expected total discounted utility to T of social states from time T onwards, given the stock level at T. A bequest function can be seen as a more flexible generalisation of a finite stock restriction. Other stocks than the capital goods stock can be valued at the date T. Especially in the context of the problems stated in later sections, stocks of pollution and resources may be considered appropriate. They both are important for the welfare that can be attained by generations living after T.

A next intergenerational element is discounting. This cannot be seen separately from the specification of the social welfare function, choice of time horizon and incorporation of risk in the model. Discounting has to originate from the measure of time preference, which can be made explicit through awarding certain shadow prices to reserving present consumption/production possibilities for future opportunities. A possible way of adjusting a valuation is by correcting costs and benefits upward or downward. Alternatively, costs and benefits with possibly varying social rates of time preference may be used (see Gijsbers and Nijkamp, 1988). However varying rates over different investment projects may cause the problem of financial crowding out. Also an explicit consideration of the relation between the social rate of discount and opportunity costs is useful (see Pearce and Nash, 1981). In general the social rate of discount value should at least be as high as the opportunity cost rate. In a second-best world they will in general not be equal to the social time preference rate. Of course it is then important to set boundaries in order to avoid that all technically possible investments are regarded as realistic feasible opportunities. For the assessment of opportunity costs one needs to determine the welfare forgone by not having endowments available for immediate consumption or reinvestment. So opportunities include those for the present as well as the future. Representation of opportunity costs is possible by means of shadow prices of capital. If these can be assessed, they may be used to transform costs and benefits of investments into private sector equivalents. In this way the issues of social rate of time preference and opportunity cost can be separately dealt with in a modelling sense. Finally, it would also be possible to include a premium (positive or negative) for risk.

It is sometimes argued that it is preferable to undertake a 'pure' discounting by using only the social rate of time preference, while all other aspects mentioned above (including possibly also externalities and intangible elements) can be incorporated in other ways. If discounting is purely based on the social rate of time preference, then the question of identifying the optimal rate emerges. A simple solution to this problem is choosing the social rate equal to the market rate of interest. Many discussions can be found in the literature on these topics of efficient allocation of investment funds, varying discount rates, and differing discount rates between social and private investments (see Lind, 1982; and Nijkamp and Rouwendal, 1988). Finally we add that a reduction in the value of the discount rate may induce the same actions or conclusions as a positive savings rate of resource use.

A major advantage of incorporating many aspects under the heading of one discount factor is that it adds to the simplicity of the model structure. Clearly, clarity and simplicity, which in this respect seem to be contrary, are to be traded off against each other here.

Ethical objections against positive discount rates have been expressed from various angles (see Opschoor, 1987). Also it may be argued that, although individuals use positive discount and time preference rates, this situation does not necessarily carry over to a community or generation. However, the risk argument still holds for communities and may imply a positive social rate of discount.

In addition to the functional form of the objective function and the problem of discounting, also the incorporation of intergenerational aspects in state transition equations, including initial and final conditions on states, has to be mentioned. First, when using dynamic equations (e.g., difference equations), the unit of time is important. If one unit corresponds to the time-span of a human generation, clearly the dynamic system is not flexible enough to describe smooth adjustment processes. Of course different processes in reality have different dynamics and feedback loops, which means that actually the distinction of variables into stocks and flows is somewhat artificial. In such cases essentially different flow rates should be used.

Intergenerational aspects can be taken into account by including conditions on initial and final values of state variables in a model. If T for instance is finite, then a condition for acceptable state values at time T can provide a guarantee that generations living after time T

have the endowments and abilities to satisfy their needs to an acceptable standard. Every generation can — on the basis of a moving forward procedure — optimise (2) for some finite time. The conditions on the starting states would then be determined by the preceding generation, while the end-conditions would be set by the present generation and serve as starting conditions on states for the next generation. In this way the optimising problem with an infinite time horizon can stepwise be approximated by means of a combination of subproblems with a finite horizon, which are inter-related by the initial and end state conditions of the respective dynamic equations.

Another way of capturing inter-generational aspects is putting side-conditions on control variables and changes in stock values. For example, consider a renewable resource that is used for economic purposes. Suppose that its dynamic behaviour can be described by the following equation:

$$y = F(y) - h(t), \qquad \ldots (6)$$

in which $y(t) = y$ denotes the total biomass (or population size, or — in case of a non-living resource — another measure of quantity or quality). Now $\partial y/\partial t = y$ is the net change in biomass, resulting from natural growth according to the rate $F(.)$ and from harvesting with a capture rate $h(t)$ the resource is subject to. The well-known notion of sustainable use of a renewable resource in this case would hold if the side condition $\dot{y} = 0$ would be satisfied all the time. Theoretically this is an idea easy to cope with, but for some specific resources no guarantee of y taking on specific values can easily be given. Inserting an inequality condition is much easier to impose, because safety margins may then be accounted for. These can make up for the fact that the exact determination of the dynamic behaviour of a renewable resource and exact information about stock levels is very difficult. Also the uncertain influences on dynamics add to this unprecision; this aspect will be dealt with in the next issue of sustainable development, viz. risk and uncertainty. An example of a safety inequality in the renewable resource example above may be to impose the condition $y \geq e > 0$ or:

$$h(t) \leq F(y) - \in. \qquad \ldots (7)$$

A problem may here arise in pursing such a strategy, as the stock can increase and a possible profit may be lost (e.g., to other — natural — predators). However, in the case of a closed loop (feedback) control, this poses no real difficulty, because the harvesting institution can observe the growth of the resource and react to it in an appropriate way. In reality such closed loop controls are however not always possible (e.g., in fishery). Also one may use as an indicator the ratio of rates of change in the stock (or depletion/growth rate) to the stock level. This may then indicate the variability, or time of complete depletion (if present rates of extraction are continued) of the stock.

Finally, meaningful conditions may also be included from imposing upper or lower bounds on integrals. First, the objective might be changed from maximising an integral function (functional) to the restriction that the same integral function will not attain a value below/above a critical boundary value. Secondly, irrespective of the objective form, an integral restriction may be added to the problem to ensure that for instance income or derived consumption (in money or utility terms) received during some period exceeds some minimum necessary level, or sufficient resources of some kind are available over a given period (i.e., the period over which the integration takes place), or not more than a maximum amount of pollution is emitted during a given period.

In conclusion, intergenerational issues can be dealt with in a modelling framework in many ways. Some of the approaches are overlapping in terms of description or effect, and therefore a combination of complementary approaches in this sense should be aimed for in model building for sustainable development.

Interregional Trade-off

In many cases we lack sufficient insight into the working of natural and economic processes. When also the mutual relationships between these two processes are considered, much additional uncertainty and many complications are introduced. This provides a definite reason for choosing specific natural systems for observation or analysis, especially when their existence seems crucial to human well-being (directly or through economic production activities). For the same reason one may analyse the behaviour of specific economic activities in relation to those parts of the natural environment upon which they act and depend most strongly. Other reasons for setting geographical boundaries on systems under consideration are of a more practical nature, and are related to data and precision of description, the existence of administrative/institutional regimes for regions, etc.

In the context of a discussion on sustainable development, it is noteworthy that in general sustainable development refers to fairly large spatial units (e.g., continents, countries). The spatial demarcation of an area from the viewpoint of sustainable development is far from easy, as a compromise has to be found between functional economic and ecological areas. The choice will be co-determined by data availability: if economic data at different levels are abundant, it seems plausible to let the regional demarcation be determined by ecological coherence, and *vice versa*. In any case, in view of the need for operational policies a meso level of analysis which is also in agreement with administrative possibilities is desirable.

If one aims at modelling an integrated regional economic-ecological system, the first choice concerns the specific regional boundaries. It is related to the objective of the study that the model-builders or regional planners have in mind. It may be based on purely economic grounds, for example, when an analysis is pursued to determine the effects of certain economic activities on the natural environment. It might also originate from the physical or natural system that constitutes the basis of regional activities. In that case the borders of the resources or ecosystems are crucial (which can range for instance from a forest or a river to groundwater). If a region is based solely on either economic or ecological arguments its size may be such that important relationships in the other system cannot be included appropriately in the regional model (see Brouwer, 1987). To combine the two one may try to minimise all kinds of material and money flows, either economic-demographic or physical-ecological. Clearly, for a small region the need to model interregional flows is in general larger.

If one assumes, for modelling purposes, that key variables from outside the region, impacting on variables inside the region, are given (and hence no feedback influence is possible), then one region may be modelled separately, conditional on certain external parameters. If more regions are involved in this way we obtain a so-called top-down approach. This is a member of the family of region-national (or multiregional) models, in which it is assumed that supply and demand are cleared at the national level, so that linkages between regions do not have to be modelled explicitly (see Issaev *et al.*, 1982).

Next, interregional linkages, both economic and ecological have to be considered. Economic-demographic interactions are especially important when transportation costs and mobility of resources are substantial. The flows between regions (e.g., goods, services, money, production factors, people, information, pollutants, groundwater, surface-water, nutrients, animals, etc.) are different in many respects, e.g. in terms of measurement units, rates, travel distances, variation over time, etc. Other characteristic of flows refer to their control (is control possible, and if so, how) and changes in their structure or composition (e.g., pollution transfer involving chemical transformations); some flows are difficult to follow over time (for instance, chemical flows), or pass through living and non-living nature (e.g., nutrient flows). Another distinction is between purely economic, purely ecological and mixed flows, to be defined as moving only in the economic or ecological system or moving between both systems, respectively.

A problem that arises when some regional utility measure is maximised (e.g., regional welfare) is that of spatial spill-overs. For instance, from a national point of view the shadow prices of, e.g. pollution do not rightly reflect scarcity. This will lead in different regions to over-use or under-use of goods and services in production and consumption, and consequently an undesired distribution of pollution. A solution may be obtained by putting national constraints on the behaviour of regional authorities, or by allowing for bargaining between regions (implying problems to be solved through game-theoretic approaches).

In order to deal with the spatial equity problem, one may either set a minimum level for the total regional derived utility by using appropriate indicators (e.g., income per capita, unemployment, public services, pollution, congestion, noise, vegetation and parks per capita).

The combination of sustainable development and the regional scale provides some ideas for the design of models. A national-(multi) regional integrated model provides the right tool for operationalising the above concepts.

Multiple Use

The fact that individuals, populations, natural resources, or parts of (or whole) ecosystems may perform different tasks (or have several functions), provides the possibility for economic actors to use them in several ways at the same time. When such activities do not interfere in both economic and ecological respects, they can be considered independently from each other. The use levels of certain resources that optimise benefits for each activity can then be determined separately and are in combination also optimal from the viewpoint of total benefit. Often however, activities do interfere, e.g. when they are competitive or when problems of project evaluation have to be solved in order to reach political agreement. Besides, one activity may have a (complementary) positive effect on another one, (e.g. when it generates cash-flows that fit in the investment schedule of the other one). Problems of the latter type are all dealt with in the field of capital budgeting (see for an overview Copeland and Weston, 1983).

In general, ecosystems, populations and resources may provide services for both natural and economic activities. An example, which has been the subject of many modelling activities, is a species functioning both as a prey for a natural and a human predator (e.g., the fishery sector). In this case the services provided to the different users are of the same nature. Another example is the well-known problem of the open-access fishery or common-property use of some area or ecosystem. But the services may also be very different, like a forest that provides timber, recreational facilities, a stable flora and fauna, regulation of precipitation and evaporation of water, assimilation, diminishing pollutant levels, etc.

In using or affecting a resource base, economic activities and natural processes may be independent, competitive (in several degrees, like the extreme case of exclusiveness), complementary or commutative. Some of the relations may be one-sided, e.g., when one activity/process influences the possibilities of another activity/process. If a relationship is two-sided or inter-active, it may be symmetric (e.g., in the case of two predator species preying on the same prey species and in common-property use), or it may be asymmetrical (e.g., in a predator-prey relationship).

The modelling of inter-active relations for multiple use situations in the form of mathematical equations will result in dynamic systems, consisting of difference or differential equations, which have usually non-linear behavioural characteristics. This may imply that the structure of the model in terms of its behaviour may change drastically when certain parameters of the model exceed critical values (e.g., when the number and/or place of stable points change). Bifurcation and chaos theory studies such properties of dynamic systems (see Kelsey, 1988). A dynamic system that does not have this property is called structurally stable. While such indirect non-linearities may occur even with single equations in the system having a linear form, synergetic effects of variables influencing the dynamic behaviour of a certain variable will have to be modelled by a (direct) non-linear dynamic equation. Moreover, a non-linear equation may also be needed as it may more adequately describe the effect of one variable on the dynamic behaviour. As the behaviour of non-linear systems can lead to surprises, it is necessary to take care in acting upon them in one or another way. As in most cases the continued existence of such a system will be one of the elements in a sustainable development strategy, study of the characteristics is especially for such strange behaving systems relevant.

When one considers the multiple use of natural systems and resources, one aims at determining the optimal combination of activities and their respective levels of intensity, which determines the respective use levels and together the total effect on the system or resource in use. One way to model this is optimising the total benefit from all considered activities taking into account the dynamics imposed by all activity levels and the constraints arising from both interferences of activities at the economic and ecological level. We will use as an illustration the following model.

Suppose two species, whose biomasses are denoted by respectively x and y, are competing for the same food. If both species can be harvested, then let $h(t)$ and $g(t)$ be the respective rates of harvest at time t, and resulting benefits with rates denoted by $B1[h(t)]$ and $B2[g(t)]$. Assume that the amount of capital necessary for both harvesting activities is identical. This capital is denoted by $K1[h(t)]$ and $K2[g(t)]$, and constrained by total available capital, denoted by $K(t)$ with price $ck(t)$. Capital is assumed to depreciate at a rate proportional to the stock of capital which can be increased through investments. If an investor, expecting a budget flow $W(t)$, wants to determine the flows of investment and harvest rates such that total discounted benefits over a period with horizontal T are optimised, then he should solve the next problem:

$$\max_{I,h,g} \int_0^T exp\{-\delta t\}[B1\{(h(t)\}B2\{g(t)\} - ck(t)]dt$$

$$s.t.\ \dot{x} = rx(1 - x/k) - \alpha xy - h(t),$$

$$\dot{y} = sy(1 - y/l) - \beta xy - g(t),$$

$$\dot{K} = I(t) - dK(t),$$

$$0 \leq I(t) \leq W(t),$$

$$K1[h(t)] + K2[g(t)] \leq K(t),$$
$$h(t), g(t) \geq 0 \text{ and}$$
$$K(0) = K_0, x(0) = x_0, y(0) = yo.$$

For the species dynamics we have used here Gause's model of inter-species competition (see Clark, 1976). Multiple use refers here to the entire ecological system, modelled for the two species case and its environment. The feedback of a change in the environment (e.g., the amount of food or the concentration of animals) to the population changes in both species — as a result of a change in the species levels — is implicitly incorporated in the model via the parameters r, k, s and I. This model brings together features that are separately treated in Clark *et al.* (1979), and Bishop and Samples (1980).

Another approach for dealing with multiple use is to let the allocation of funds to different activities or the destination of a resource to various uses be determined through multi-objective programming. Each activity may add an objective. If a specific use of the resource is essential, a constraint on the remaining uses can be formulated.

Multiple use of a resource can lead to many relationships between the resource and economic activities, as a result of which a complex model may be stated. If moreover non-linear equations are included in the description of multiple use of the resource, solving a kind of optimal combination of use will be difficult or impossible. Sustainable development may include multiple use of a resource, such that all uses follow stable patterns, and the resource-base remains intact. Simulation exercises can provide indications about the right combination of multiple uses regarding stable development of the resource-base and the uses.

Analysing the concept of multiple use offers some ideas for modelling. However, optimising for multiple use situations may lead to difficult problems, while even determination of multiple use that fits in a sustainable development strategy can be difficult.

Risk and Uncertainty

Prologue

In a technical sense one can distinguish between certainty, risk, uncertainty in a strict sense, and surprise. In case of certainty all events caused by other events and human actions are supposed to be completely sure and known. In case of risk, the existence of an event is known, but its occurrence is not certain; however, one can assign a probability to each possible event (or a probability density function to all possible events when they follow a continuous pattern). With uncertainty the possible events are known, but no indication on the probability distribution of their occurrences exists. Finally, a surprise denotes an event that was not expected *ex ante* with any reasonable insight.

Although quantum field theory (in physics) has indicated the unpredictable character of micro-level dynamics in particles, it is not the main cause for uncertainty regarding the behaviour of economic-ecological systems. One cause from which uncertainty arises is the insufficient knowledge about the relationships, interactions between variables in the economic-ecological system, especially concerning process such as changing preferences and development of knowledge and techniques. Another cause pertains to the errors in a model that result from the inability to take all relevant relationships into consideration, as well as from inaccurate or insufficient data. For instance, a frequently used model to describe population dynamics of species is the logistic growth curve in differential form:

$$b = rb(1 - b/k)$$

b denotes the population biomass or number of individuals. This is a so-called lumped parameter model in which no distinction is made between parameters determining net biological growth. For instance the parameter k, often denoted by the term carrying capacity, contains many aspects of the environment which become scarce if the population keeps growing in number and which have thus an adverse effect on population. This model does not accurately describe the dynamics of a real-world population, because too many factors and dynamic processes are left out. This means that we will at best be able to get an impression on how a population may evolve, but the precise outcome will be uncertain. Deciding whether or not to choose such a model often comes down to weighting the accuracy of its descriptions and the tractability of time-paths generated by it. To handle more efficiently incoming information, and thus decreasing uncertainty, one may choose to use models that use step-wise new information. For instance, Bayesian updating uses risk measures that change as information becomes available.

In the context of sustainability it is clear that much risk and uncertainty emerges from structural changes in a system, which are not due to stochastic changes but to integral shifts in behavioural patterns, exogenous impacts or changes in policy institutions. Thus in such cases sustainability cannot be defined as an optimal system's trajectory with a given (stochastic) parameter space, but as a set of sequential optimality regimes governed by sometimes dissipative structures.

In the following sections we will consider the way economic theory has dealt with uncertainty and discuss the implications for models to be used for sustainable development issues.

Economic Aspects of Uncertainty

Risk and uncertainty are conventional topics in decision theory. Approaches to risk analysis are state-preference theory (focusing on the allocation of resources under uncertainty) and (statistical)-parameter-preference approaches (focussing on the allocation of risks). The latter approach has provided the basis for important developments in the theory of finance (e.g., C.A.P.M.; see Copeland and Weston, 1983). Central in the first approach is the concept of contingent consumption claims: goods are defined to have — in addition to the normal features (physical and service attributes, location, date) — also a subscription to states of nature (states of the world). For such goods a special preference theory has been developed: expected utility theory (see von Neumann and Morgenstern, 1944).

Two forms of uncertainty are normally dealt with, viz. market uncertainty and technological (event) uncertainty (see Hirshleifer and Riley, 1979). In the first concept individuals are uncertain about the actions of other economic agents. At the micro-economic level, search processes dominate, while at a macro/meso level market disequilibrium and price dynamics are essential. This form of uncertainty concerns the endogenous variables of the economic system and is institutionally induced. Even uncertainty on the other hand deals with exogenous data, viz. resource endowments and production possibilities. In the case of exhaustible resources, it is linked with, e.g. size and quality of resource reserves, costs of extraction, discovery of new reserves and invention of substitute products.

Decision-makers can take either terminal actions or informational actions. The first action (passive) will allow individuals to adapt to uncertainty, while by means of the second (active) one individuals can overcome uncertainty. Within the class of terminal actions, we can distinguish between the trade, sharing or modification of risk. Informational decision-making starts with the acquisition of an information service followed by Bayesian updating of subjective prior probabilities assigned to states of the world (for statistical decision theory see DeGroot, 1970). Besides, information may also emerge autonomously with the mere passage of time. Then a trade-off between costs of waiting and irreversibility of some development is possible.

Values of informational activities are based upon the expected utility gains from shifting to better choices among the set of terminal actions. A special informational activity relevant to sustainable development is an indirect one, viz., waiting, in order to benefit from the so-called option value (or flexibility value) (see Fisher and Krutilla, 1985). This option value is defined as the gain from being able to learn about future benefits, that would be precluded by some development, if one does not initially develop (preservation). Thus, option value is a conditional value of information and exceeds (or equals) the unconditional value of information.

Inclusion of Uncertainty in Modelling

For a choice of tools to be used for implementing risk into analyses, there is a large body of techniques, models and rules. Techniques as sensitivity analysis and probability analysis (low probability/high impact analysis; Monte-Carlo experiments), or decision theoretic models (e.g., statistical sequential decision models).

Also several practical approaches to the treatment of risk in benefit-cost analysis may be pursued: use risk-free rates of discount and adjust benefits and costs for risk; use risk-free rates and perform sensitivity analysis; for public investments with returns uncorrelated or negatively correlated with the total returns of a set of assets in a portfolio, the strategy can be discounting at the risk-free rate and taking in consideration the fact that the result understates the present value of the project.

Other rules of thumb may be used, like limiting the period of analysis and restricting the space dimensions of the problem under consideration. Comparison of expected values of benefits and costs is possible, or first reducing these with a premium because of risk-aversion of individuals.

Incorporating risk structures in models can be done appropriately in simulation experiments. When probability density functions can be specified, Monte-Carlo experiments are easy to perform. However, in case of long-term structural changes such experiments may be more difficult to undertake. Surprises can be dealt with by assuming all kinds of improbable developments in scenarios for simulations and investigating the effects on the time paths of indicator variables. Analysis of surprises is more in harmony with the search for sustainable development paths under uncertain conditions and may be based, e.g., on forum or expert techniques (e.g., Delphi-methods).

In order to arrive at stronger (i.e., mathematically based) results, other model forms are available. Stochastic dynamic optimal control techniques are suitable, when a change in values of stock variables over time can be described by a process which has a drift and a diffusion component. The major shortcoming in such advanced techniques is the fact that the existence of an optimal solution requires specific mathematical features of functions used in the model. Moreover, in case of a stochastic control problem with more than one state variable moving according to a stochastic process (or with restrictions on state and/or control variables), the determination of an optimal solution for the control variables is in general very difficult and in most cases impossible.

Alternatively, deterministic optimal control solutions may be derived, while the impact of disturbances in the paths of state variables on the value of the objective function can be investigated by means of simulation modelling. It makes much difference whether or not the optimal control path is very sensitive to slight disturbances in the paths of state variables. It is also important to know the character of stationary points and the sensitivity of equilibria. If more equilibria for the dynamic behaviour of the system output exist, it is necessary to know how the system can move from one to another equilibrium and what this implies for the value of the objective function. Also important is the study of the combined effect upon the system's behaviour and performance when multiple states behave in an uncertain way. For example, one can look into the effects of variables reaching very extreme values (in every possible direction) at the same time or for longer periods.

Of course, sensitivity analysis with respect to initial and end conditions on state variables, parameter values in objectives, state transition equations and constraints are meaningful when uncertainty on their specific values exists.

When the time horizon is very long, a control may be used to reach as fast as possible stationary values for he state variables and keep them at those levels thereafter. These stationary values should be determined as the optimal solutions of a transformed problem, viz. the original objective subject to the variables satisfying static equivalents of the dynamic equations during the planning horizon. Moreover, it is then possible to add more constraints on state control variables. In this way the solution to the original problem is approximated by steering the state as fast as possible to the stationary state, which is the solution to an equivalent static problem. Further refinements in this simple algorithm can lead to improvements. Especially when dealing with uncertain behaviour of state variables, one has to consider the probabilities of moving away from an equilibrium, the character of the equilibrium and the effect on the performance criterion of a state moving away from an equilibrium.

It is noteworthy that in many cases optimal control models take for granted a fixed structure. This may be at odds with long-term changes in parameter structures, so that in that case a blend between optimal control theory and catastrophe theory (or chaos theory; see Kelsey, 1988) has to be used. Alternatively, several iterative linearizing parameter-improving optimisation-approximation methods, with either closed loop or open loop control structures, can be found in the literature. Stochastic simulation with a non-linear model and re-estimation of a linear model while iteratively finding better control is an approach to incorporating uncertainty. In these cases the parameters may change over time so as to allow for making small and drastic changes come out in the model structure. The advantage of feedback control structures, necessary for control of stochastic systems, is the fact that the system behaviour under a given (and possibly optimal) control structure can be studied easily — for both deterministic and stochastic systems (see Chow, 1975).

Conclusions

Modelling integrated ecological-economic systems for sustainable development has to be preceded by a thorough reflection on the concepts to be used. In this paper we have tried to treat this in a systematic manner. Important conclusions reached are: models should describe economic and ecological processes in sufficient and balanced detail; a starting point for the model building process may be either the economic activities module or the ecological basis for activities; all relevant information that is available and are accessible should be taken in consideration in this framework; especially regional models are suitable for a detailed description of spatially varying but nevertheless interwoven phenomena; due attention should be paid to intergenerational aspects, interregional aspects, multiple use and uncertainties; the level of detail of the description and the structure of the model should be such that the model (or derived simplified models) can be analysed either analytically or with numerical methods. It is clear that the idea of sustainable development needs further clarification and refinement in a specific empirical context. In addition to a systems-analytic meaning, it has also a policy-analytic meaning. In this regard, models pertaining to sustainable development problems should also incorporate risk strategies for policy actors.

REFERENCES

Bennett, R.J., and Chorley, R.J., (1978). *Environmental Systems*, Methuen & Co., London.

Bishop, R.C., and Samples, K.C., (1980). 'Sport and commercial fishing conflicts: A theoretical analysis, *Journal of Environmental Economics and Management*, vol.7, 220-233.

Braat, L.C., and Lierop, W.F.J. van, (1987). *Economic-Ecological Modelling*, North-Holland.

Brouwer, F.M., (1987). *Integrated Environmental Modelling: Design and Tools*, Dordrecht, Martinus Nijhoff.

Brown, B.J., *et al.*, (1987). Global sustainability: toward definition, *Environmental Management*, vol. 11, 713-719.

Chow, G.C., (1975). *Analysis and Control of Dynamic Economic Systems*, Wiley.

Clark, C.W., Clark, F.H. and Munro, G.R., (1979). The optimal exploitation of renewable resource stocks: Problems of irreversible investment, *Econometrica*, vol. 47, 25-49.

Copeland, T.E., and Weston, J.F. (1984). *Financial theory and Corporate Policy*, Addison-Wesley.

Dasgupta, P.S., (1974). On some alternative criteria for justice between generations, *Journal of Public Economics*, vol. 3, 405-423.

Dasgupta, P.S., and Heal, G.M. (1979). *Economic Theory and Exhaustible Resources*, Cambridge, Cambridge University Press.

DeGroot, M.H., (1970). *Optimal Statistical Decisions*, McGraw-Hill.

Fisher, A.C., and Krutilla, J.V. (1985). Economics of nature preservations, in A.V. Kneese and J.L. Sweeney (eds), *Handbook of Natural Resources and Energy Economics*, vol. 1, North-Holland.

Gijsbers, D., and Nijkamp, P. (1988). Non-uniform social rates of discount in natural resource models: an overview of arguments and consequences. *Journal of Environmental Systems*, vol. 17, 221-236.

Hirschleifer, J., and Riley, J.G. (1979). The analytics of uncertainty and information – an expository survey, *Journal of Economic Literature*, vol. 17, 1375-1421.

Issaev, B., Nijkamp, P. and Snickars F. (eds), (1982). *Multiregional Economic Modelling: Practice and Prospect*, Amsterdam, North-Holland.

Kelsey, D., (1988), The economics of chaos or the chaos of economics, *Oxford Economic Papers*, vol. 40, 1-31.

Lind, R. (ed.), (1982). *Discounting for Time and Risk in Energy Policy*, Baltimore, Johns Hopkins University Press.

Neumann, von J., and Morgenstern, O. (1944). *Theory of Games and Economic Behaviour*, Princeton University Press.

Nijkamp, P., and Rouwendal, J. (1988). Intergenerational discount rates in long-term plan evaluation, *Public Finance/Finances Publiques*, vol. 43, 195-211.

Opschoor, J.B., (1987). *Duurzaamheid en Verandering*, Amsterdam, Inaugural Address, Free University.

Pearce, D.W., Barbier, E. and Markandya, A. (1988). Sustainable development and cost benefit analysis, Canadian Environmental Assessment Research Council Workshop on Integrating Economic and Environmental Assessment, Vancouver.

Pearce, D.W., and Nash, C.A., (1981). *The Social Appraisal of Projects: A Text in Cost-Benefit Analysis*, MacMillan Press.

Tolba, M.K., (1987). *Sustainable Development: Constraints and Opportunities*, London, Butterworths.

The World Commission on Environment and Development (WCED), (1987). *Our Common Future*, Oxford University Press.

TECHNOLOGY AND RESOURCES

20

Technology and Natural Resources: An Ecological Model for Agriculture and Industry

S. SURESH KUMAR

Simple model for economic activity involves two cyclical flows: (1) flow of inputs, the production and its outputs and (2) a counter-flow of money for these inputs and outputs.

The physical flows are matched by monetary flows. These flows help to measure a country's gross natural product. Hence, in principle, GNP could grow as long as there is possibility of increasing inputs. However, the model does not take into account the consequences of resource depletion on the environmental pollution and ecological equilibrium. The economy and its structure or its process is not isolated from the environment. Hence a more suitable model will be that which is open and takes into account energy and matter as stocks. By introducing the possibility of interaction between economy and environment this will direct attention to the pollution problem.

The flow of energy through nature or the economic system is unidirectional, from low to high entropy, whereas the flow of matter is not so restricted. As the matter and energy stocks enter the economy they are in a condition of low entropy. Humans make use of the stock of artifacts as well as matter or energy to satisfy their needs. In a long-term perspective the stocks including human will be returned to the environment and to rebuild stocks supplies will be taken from the environment. However, a significant feature of the model is that there is a limit on the rate of economic growth based on withdrawal of matter and energy from environment as well as dumping of waste.

The economy renders service to the population through the production and distribution of goods and services and nature renders environmental services which provide inputs to the production and metabolic processes as well as waste disposal and recreational opportunities. But, there must always be a balance between economic and environmental services. The optimum size of economy is reached with that stock of artifacts and population for which total service is maximum which is attainable only in a steady state. This is not against science or technology. On the other hand, by increasing the technological efficiency of the production processes, we can improve the environmental condition or at least reduce damage to nature.

An Ever Increasing GNP

The market imperfection that affects the environment is the failure of the pricing system to consider environmental services. The failure to cover important aspects like natural resources position, regenerating capacity and waste-absorbing capacity leads to externalities. There is an ever increasing gap between entrepreneurial and social costs which often arise out of an inappropriate choice design and operation of a technology which contributes to externalities in the form of environmental diseconomies. Entrepreneurs tend to fix price and not take into account these externalities or social costs. There is no provision in the present economic theory to adequately consider them while allotting resources among different activities or for planning of production and consumer system. The argument is that the consumer is not directly paying for these costs. But it is well known that society as a whole pays for the comforts of a few by using the present models, we arrive at a dichotomous situation where a firm is antithetic to society *vis-à-vis* the situation of equilibrium. A firm equates price and marginal private cost for its equilibrium. This implies for a society that marginal costs paid by society for the externalities are greater than the marginal social benefits.

With the present level of awareness among entrepreneurs and managers we cannot expect them to take measures that will redress the situation. External intervention is undoubtedly required perhaps in the form of a tax on pollution so that the costs of ecological disequilibria are borne by the firms.

Decision-makers in enterprises and the government should expand their perception of reality. Appropriate education can create the needed outlook which goes beyond the narrow issues of economic efficiency to a concern for future generation, other species, altruism and common weal.

Agricultural Scene

Among the decision-makers in the agricultural sector, many people are beginning to recognise that modern agriculture is an unsustainable course and is leading eventually to a global catastrophe. It is based on the assumption that the human kind should overpower nature through the use of technology. Though agriculture is practised since time immemorial, it is only recently that it has made rapid progress. Perhaps the development of implements by the 18th century inventor Jethro Tull in England have given farmers in Europe and America and subsequently in other places the power to terminate nature in their quest for higher yields. The influence of these developments on the farm practice was to develop agriculture from a point of low capital intensity and high human inputs towards opposite position. It is true that at the beginning of this process, a small investment generated a large increase in labour productivity, which was reflected in a decline in the prices. This process was fuelled by the increasing use of mechanical power to drive improved agricultural implements. This has done the farmers a great good by improving their productivity. But the capital intensity of power farming introduced inflationary trends. The rapid development of better chemical industry in a post-war period inundated the agricultural market with pesticides and fertilisers. Intensive agricultural practice gradually led to a host of problems arising out of ecological degradation. The negative impacts of modern farm practices are being felt in both the industrialised and Third World countries. Countries are losing their valuable top soil at an ever increasing rate. In the United States alone, the loss is equivalent to one million hectares of farm land every year. Agriculture depending on external inputs like fertilisers and pumped water is gradually becoming uneconomical besides depleting the soil quality and groundwater resources. Pesticide residues are being concentrated in the foods and tend to an extent that the mother's milk has higher level of residues than cow's milk. The increasing population and the consequent pressures on land and resources in the developing nations add a complex dimension to this worsening situation.

Current yields per hectare have declined in many countries despite the use of fertilisers and improved seed, for example, between the 50s and 80s the decrease was around 30 to 40 per cent in some of the African countries where power farming and intensive agriculture was practised. In a majority of situations the reduction in fallow area in dry-land farming reduces productivity since shorter rotation cycles do not provide for restoration of fertility. Soil erosion undermines the inherent fertility of 20 per cent of the world's cropland.

It is, therefore, high time that we pay more attention to a regenerating agricultural system which makes:

1. Maximum use of solar energy by crop rotation,
2. Use of small irrigation schemes,
3. Recycling of minerals through composting, and
4. Pest control based on biological methods and where farming community invest their surplus income locally.

A well-structured system makes high levels of productivity possible even with reduced levels of physical inputs by adopting products which increase the efficiency of the natural process like nutrient cycle and ecological relationships.

Some of the innovative biological technologies employing regenerate agriculture are suitable to conditions in the developing countries. High input practices in agriculture have compelled the farmer to enter consumer society. The land is regarded as a factor of production, the productivity of which is sought to be increased by application of all kinds of technological innovations. No consideration is given to the fact that land is an ecological asset being part of a fragile but complex biological system. Management of agricultural production taking it as similar to a mechanical process is not correct.

Further, the high expenditure on modern sophisticated agricultural technological practices has produced the need for subsidies from the government. It also means that farmers with a weak capital base and low levels of knowledge of the avenues opened by the government suffer a setback. The majority of the small farmers are bypassed by the green revolution.

Abandoning traditional agricultural practices may increase crop yields but it destroys the agricultural resources base by:

1. A loss of top soil,
2. Waterlogging and salinity in irrigated land (almost 10% of the world's total irrigated land is waterlogged and catchment area and micro watershed programmes are in progress to improve the situation),

3. Increased resistance to chemical pesticides and larger application of pesticides leading to soil and water contamination besides increase in the health risk among field workers as well as among consumers due to residues, and
4. Disappearance of scarce and valuable plant societies and a decrease in the nutritional value of agricultural produce due to depletion of trace minerals which are not replaced by the commonly used fertilisers.

This world-wide impact of high input products in agriculture inform us that there is an integral relationship between human stock and land stock so that self-fulfilment should be sought through the ecological rhythms and wide use of environmental service. The regenerating agriculture is oriented to this end.

Over the past several decades many US farmers have been converted to low input products. This process requires a restructuring of the farms. The crop mix is changed to provide for establishing the right type of rotations. Production costs and energy inputs are as much as 40 per cent lower and farmers get a way to product development on a sustainable footing. Since regenerative products are based on the biological structure of the system, crop yields are increased. It is found from scientific studies of production activities on the farm that the biological structure efficiency of the system is very important for high-yield crops. When the economic system and related biological process deficient, massive inputs of fertilisers and pesticides are required which are only short-term means.

A recent workshop on the problems of agriculture in tropical regions describe the potential of these technologies and practices:

1. Promoting underexploited native plant species which can be integrated into cropping systems reducing the need for chemical inputs and enhancing heat tolerance and pest resistance. Development in tissue culture and plant breeding can make a big contribution to developing suitable native varieties and adopting them to unfavourable environment.
2. Integrated agricultural system that takes advantage of the special benefits provided by species of nitrogen fixing plants; and use of Acacia for plantation in deforested landscape.
3. Using natural mineral soil like zeolite mineral to improve soil

properties and extend fertiliser efficiency since these minerals help to maintain nitrogen available in soils and improve the resistance of plants to water stress. They can also be used as decontaminants in fish farming.

4. Reducing the need for commercial nitrogen by inoculating suitable crops with beneficial soil bacteria like Rhyzobic strains that might give better results.
5. Increasing plant capacity to absorb nitrogen by increasing the growth of beneficial micro-organisms like mycrorrhycl phenyl that increase the surface area of the plant roots which assimilate soil nutrients.

Technological software and hardware system development should help sustain soil fertility, reduce fertiliser input and improve plant yield taking advantage of the biological structure efficiency.

A change to regenerative agriculture from high input product is beset with many obstacles. Although it is the individual farmer who must make the decision to switch over, a national government has the considerable opportunity and responsibility to facilitate this change through appropriate policies. For example, land reforms should help farmers to do away with the agricultural practices that deplete soil resources or lead to uneconomic utilisation patterns. The government should also share the cost of the necessary measures and sponsor research to develop the required hardware and software. Regenerative farm products are highly information and management intensive and hence require considerable educational inputs to make the small farmer aware of the possibilities. In order to make the change farmers in developing countries have not only to be protected from the constraints of the present milieu but they have also to acquire the needed skills. Bernard Woods identifies the following four dimensions:

1. Knowledge and intellectual capacity to comprehend all the factors involved,
2. Practical skills to perform the actions required,
3. Topical information about the changing external conditions, and
4. Organisational/institutional environment (social administration) within which the activity is possible.

Relevance of field extension workers to provide education and training is an extensive, inefficient and indifferent management method. We must rely on para-professionals and lower cost forms of communication making full use of mass media and distant learning techniques. We have to review the role of extension workers in the context of a total communication spectra.

Though large investments are made in infrastructure hardware and technology development, little is spent to enable farmers to acquire the skills and institutional capabilities to operate, maintain and improve the development system. We must create a network of centres for research and information of how to create human and institutional capability to disseminate the information to create the advantages at village level for adoption. In short, we must pay attention to build up the element of social administration. Emphasis on technical, physical and financial solutions to problems of devĕlopment has to be complemented by organisational structures and capability at village and local government levels. A local organisation with clear-cut objectives can be a highly effective means for adoption of regenerative agricultural products. Human capacity is the basis of self-sustainable development and this should be brought home to the small farmer. The Survodaya Sramadan Movement in Sri Lanka and 100 Villages Development Programme are good examples. In six years the programme multiplied into 3,000 villages and became one of the largest non-governmental village awakening movements.

The developing countries and poor areas within them have the need to improve their agricultural systems by external inputs and aid. This should be accompanied by a simultaneous renewal from farmers and the supporting system is to be made aware of the merits of ecologically and economically sound regenerative farm practices.

Industrial Scene

The structures and resources of large and medium-size enterprises make them highly visible to policy-makers. It is their interests for which most S&T policy instruments and S&T institutions are designed.

The vast majority of a country's small commercial firms and enterprises live rather on subsistence economies. Though they provide the underpinnings of the economy there is a lack of technological support. These firms also do not know where to search for knowledge and aid since they rely on a few empirical skills that are inherited or learnt in the struggle for survival. There is also a fear of any wrong change since failure often means total collapse. The technical centres also do not know how to establish contact with these firms. The challenge is hence three-fold:

To increase IFP
To improve contribution from small firms
To protect the support systems in nature

It would be possible in many areas of industrial production to effect an efficient combination of decentralised small-scale production and centralised large-scale distribution of output and/or procurement of inputs. The dairy cooperatives in Finland (Valio) and Argentina (Sancor) are examples. In Brazil ethanol production and distribution follows a similar pattern. The opposite case is also feasible particularly where economies of scale are large; large-scale production by a centralised unit could be followed by a decentralised marketing effort. But even here small-scale options should not be overlooked.

Economies of scale measured in terms of decreasing unit costs are offset by external diseconomies. Large plants can operate below their capacity while functioning in a situation of short supply of skilled labour or widespread labour unrest.

It is found from studies that small-scale businesses are more successful in innovation due to the survival instinct. Creative urge makes up for the financial stringency.

It is hence important to provide appropriate financial support for the two key steps in the innovation cycle — development of technology and its commercialisation. Appropriate financial instruments like conditional loans and venture capital are to be evolved. The administration of these financial instruments is best achieved though the agency of non-governmental organisations. One central feature here is the need to promote entrepreneurial behaviour. Experience shows that NGOs are much more efficient than bureaucratic agencies in this role since these work from within the community and train local young people to be community developers. We must encourage do-it-yourself innovation and services. They may not get reflected in a country's GNP growth, nevertheless, they are an important type of activities the encouragement of which will considerably improve the quality of life. Do-it-yourself for home repairs sale in the USA jumped from 20 per cent in 1985 to 60 per cent in 1989 in all spending on repairs. This activity is yet to catch up in the developing nations.

Use of Renewable Resources

The prices of fossil stocks fail to reflect either the inevitability of depletion or the impacts on the environment that result from their exploitation.

A preference for the production of petrochemicals over processing of agricultural outputs with chemicals for dyes, fibres, detergents, elastomers and pharmaceuticals ensures that the old technologies of agro-based chemistry are not reconsidered by the industry. But these can serve as useful ways to reduce investment, decentralise production, increase employment and decrease environment and human risks. Industry could redirect efforts towards increasing the efficiency of those technologies and even to finding new agro-based technologies for producing a variety of additional products.

In this comparison factory costs are not the only relevant factor to be considered. It is important to take associated externalities into account. Increasing the efficiency of rural-based plants can improve techno-economics particularly when all costs are taken into account.

In transfer of technology the role of personal contacts is very important. Usually international technology transfers take place between large enterprises. The same arrangement can help to effect transfer of technology from an already organised enterprise to an entrepreneur who needs help in starting up a small-scale enterprise.

The Brienpatch Group of 450 small businesses in the San Francisco Bay Area (USA), the Mendragon Cooperatives in Guipuzeoa Province (Spain), the 22,000 small entrepreneurs of the State of Maine (USA) can provide the physical and technical basis for an open-door low-cost technology transfer policy. This can be coupled with appropriate financing mechanisms.

Conclusion

In conclusion it can be pointed out that sustainable development is a product of a changed perspective on social and technological development. The view that nature is a perennial source of energy and an indefatigable waste sink has to be overcast. The consequences of resource depletion and environmental policy are to be taken into account within the framework of an ecological model. In agriculture and industry, it would mean an emphasis on regenerative practices, recycling, resource conservation, increased factor of productivity, improved protection to support systems and being in tune with the homeostatic processes in nature.

REFERENCES

Nat. Res. Forum : 4 (1980)

(a) Articles on Renewable Energy in Developing Countries.

(b) Articles on Materials, Energy & Economic Growth.

Nat. Res. Forum : 5 (1981).

(a) Articles on Investment in Developing Countries.

(b) Articles on Energy Perspectives.

Science & Public Policy, Vol. 14, No. 5, 87 (Articles on Nat. Res. Management).

Science & Public Policy, Vol. 16, No. 2, 1989 (Articles on Nat. Res. Management).

21

Technology and Natural Resources

D. PIMENTEL

Most people of the world would acknowledge that we owe much of our improved standard of living to the many technological advances that have been developed over the centuries. Some of these have increased food and fibre production and stabilised their supplies. Others have helped control serious human diseases, thereby significantly improving public health. Improved public health combined with increased food supplies are the major contributors to the rapid population growth (Fig. 21.1).

Never before in the world history have humans so dominated the Earth by their sheer numbers. The world's present population stands at about 5 billion.[38] What is more alarming is the average 1.7 per cent annual growth rate — a rate 1,700 times greater than that of the first two million years humans inhabited the Earth. At this rate about 250,000 people are added to the world each day. Demographers project that the world population will reach 6.1 billion by the year 2000, approach 8.2 billion by 2025.[42] and probably reach at least 12 billion by 2100. Presently there seems to be no generally accepted way to limit this growth.[22]

Growth in the world population has contributed to the increasing food shortages. Although more people are being fed in the world today, more people are malnourished than ever before in this history of humankind.[41] At present nutritionists report that one billion people are malnourished and the problem is growing in severity.[11] During the early

---

Reprinted with Permission from *Resources and world Development*, D.J. McLaren and B.J. Skinner (ed.), John Wiley and Sons Limited, p. 679-695.

1900s most nations were self-sufficient in food. Today the majority of the world's 183 nations are major food importers,[7] underscoring a growing disparity in food resources.[41] This problem has persisted "and in some cases worsened despite an increased pace of development".[11]

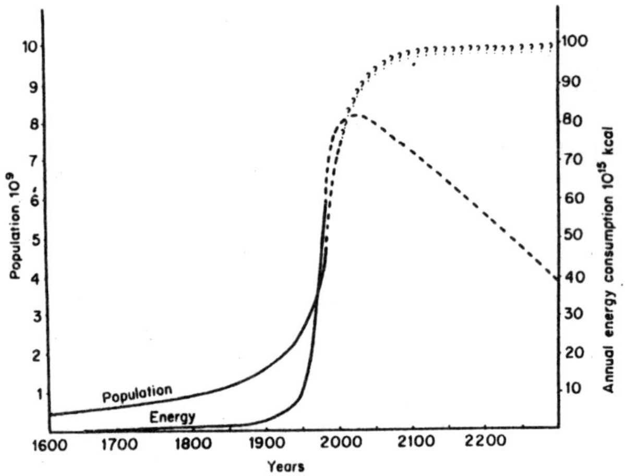

Fig. 21.1: Estimated world population number (——) from 1600 to 1975 and projected numbers (---) (???) to the year 2250. Estimated fossil fuel consumption (——) from 1650 to 1975 and projected (---) to the year 2250.[6, 14]

Worldwide efforts are being made to maintain human food supplies adequate enough to meet the needs of the ever-expanding population. In addition to using more fossil energy for fertilisers and pesticides, more arable land is being brought under cultivation and more water is being used to irrigate crops.

The use of new technologies, especially those powered by fossil energy, has enabled humans to secure better control of their environment. To augment agricultural acreage forests have been cut, land cleared and planted to crops or converted to pasture for livestock. At present most of the highly productive land already has been cleared for crop and livestock production. In most regions only marginal land remains to be used for future production, but this will require high energy inputs.

In this chapter current trends in technology and in the use of land, water, energy and biological resources in the food system are examined.

In addition, opportunities to improve agricultural technologies and resource management to increase food supplies while preserving the quality of the environment will be assessed.

Land Resources

About 97 per cent of all food that humans consume comes from the land, while only about 3 per cent comes from aquatic habitats.[3] Of the 35 per cent or 4.6 billion hectares of the Earth's land area that is used for agricultural production, about 1.5 billion hectares are in crops and about 3.1 hectares are used by grazing livestock.[7]

These lands, though productive, are being degraded by mismanagement. Poor agricultural technologies and practices are responsible for much of the destruction of valuable land resources that already has occurred and continues to take place at an alarming rate[37] (Pimentel *et al.*, unpublished manuscript). For instance, soil degradation by erosion, salinisation from irrigation, and other factors is causing the irretrievable loss of an estimated 6 million hectares of land worldwide each year.[4, 10, 43] In addition, the yearly crop productivity on about 20 million hectares is reduced to almost zero or has negative net economic return because of intense soil degradation.[43] According to FAO[7], the net expansion of total world cropland is about 3.9 million hectares per year. Thus, to compensate for the loses (6 mha) and yearly expansion (3.9 mha) about 10 million hectares of mostly forest land is being converted to cropland each year.

The degradation of agricultural land by erosion and other factors reduces the productivity of the land as measured in kilograms of food. At present, however, degradation is being offset by technologies that rely on increased use of fertilisers, pesticides, and other inputs. These strategies for maintaining and/or increasing production are relying on a presently cheap and abundant supply of fossil fuel, a non-renewable resource. For example, in the U.S. corn production an additional 920 kcal/ha of fossil energy are required to offset the reduction of 1 kg of corn yield (Pimentel *et al.*, unpublished manuscript).

Water Resources

Next to sunlight and the land itself, water is the most vital resource needed to sustain plant growth. Sufficient rainfalls on most arable agricultural land, but periodic droughts continue to limit yields in diverse areas throughout the world. Crops require and transpire massive amounts of water. For example, a corn crop that produces 7,000 kg of grain per hectare will take up and transpire about 4.2 million litres of water per hectare during one growing season.[13] To supply this much water about 10 million litres of rain must fall per hectare, and this must be evenly distributed during the year including the growing season. This amount is equivalent to about 100 cm of rain per year.

Water is a limiting factor such that a reduction in rainfall of only 5 cm at a critical time in the growing season will reduce corn production by about 15 per cent.[8] Decreasing rainfall by 30 cm reduces yields to only about one-fifth of that produced by 100 cm of rainfall.[8] Although other crops such as sorghum and wheat could be substituted for corn because they require less water, these crops produce about one-third less grain than corn per hectare.[47]

When rainfall cannot reliably supply moisture needed for crop production, then irrigation must be employed. Irrigated crop production requires large quantities of water. For example, using irrigation to produce 1 kg of the following food and fibre products requires 1,400 litres for corn, 4,700 for rice, and 17,000 for cotton.[40] In the United States agricultural irrigation presently consumes 81 per cent of the total 360 bld (billion litres per day) that is consumed.[48]

In addition to water use, irrigated crop production is costly in terms of energy. In Nebraska, for example, rain-fed corn production requires about 630 litres/ha of oil equivalents, whereas irrigated corn requires more than three times as much energy.[28] In fact, nearly one-fifth of all energy consumed in U.S. agricultural production is used to pump irrigation water.[44]

Biological Diversity

About 90 per cent of all human food comes from 15 species of cultural plants and 8 species of livestock, all of which originally existed in the wild.[16, 19] Continued agricultural productivity will depend on the presence of most of the natural biota that consist of an estimated 10 million species of plants and animals in the world.[5, 20] We know that humans cannot survive with only presently grown crops and livestock, but exactly what proportion of the natural biota are essential for agricultural production is unknown.

Nonetheless, it is known that natural biota perform many functions essential for agriculture, forestry, and other sectors of the economy.

Some of these include providing genetic diversity vital for successful crop breeding, recycling basic chemical elements within the ecosystem such as carbon and nitrogen, moderating climates, conserving soil and water, and serving as sources of certain wild foods (fish, etc.).[5, 19, 21, 31] In addition, many natural biota help prevent human diseases. Some beneficial organisms destroy human pathogens, some degrade wastes[31], while others remove toxic pollutants from water and soil.

Reducing or exterminating some species groups could seriously disturb the normal functioning of activities that are important to environmental systems. For example, soil quality and agricultural productivity jointly depend upon soil biota, organic matter, and inorganic particles.[2] Each year various soil organisms break down and degrade about 20 tonnes of organic matter per hectare.[1] This degradation is essential for the release of organic nutrients and subsequent recycling for reuse in the ecosystem.[9] Soil biota also help control crop pests and fix atmospheric nitrogen for use by plants.[31] In addition, water percolation is improved by earthworms, insects, and other biota that open holes, loosen the soil, and thereby enhance new soil formation. Because the functions of biota are complex and not fully understood, great care must be taken to prevent new technologies from destroying them.

Energy Resources

Of all resources, the one most responsible for rapid population growth and environmental destruction is fossil energy, used to manipulate and manage ecosystems (Fig. 21.1). Energy-resource use and new energy-dependent technologies have been responsible for raising crop and livestock production yields per hectare. The solar energy reaching a hectare of land during the year in temperate North America averages about 14×10^9 kcal.[39] During a four-month summer growing season in the temperate region nearly 7×10^9 kcal reach an agricultural hectare. Under favourable conditions of moisture and soil nutrients, corn is considered one of the most productive food and fed crops per unit area of land and is used in this discussion to illustrate energy expenditure in crop production.[25] For example, high-yielding corn grown on the good soils of Iowa can produce about 7,000 kg/ha (112 bu/A) or corn grain plus another 7,000 kg/ha of biomass as stover. Converted to heat energy this totals 63×10^6 kcal (heat energy = 4,500 kcal/kg) and represents about 0.5 per cent of the solar energy reaching the hectare during the year or 1 per cent during the growing season.

The efficiency conversion for other crops is much less than that for corn. For example, potatoes with a yield of 40,000 kg/ha have a dry weight of about 8,000 kg/ha. Based on total biomass produced of 12,000 kg/ha and an energy value of 54×10^6 kcal, potatoes have a 0.4 per cent conversion efficiency. Or a wheat crop, yielding 2,700 kg/ha of grain, produces a total of 6,750 kg biomass/ha, which has a heat-energy value of 30×10^6 kcal making the conversion efficiency only 0.2 per cent. Agricultural ecosystems as a whole, including pastures and rangeland, have an average conversion rate of about 0.1 per cent per year, which is similar to that of natural vegetation.[34] In these analyses only the energy in the biomass itself was compared to the solar energy reaching the hectare. Agricultural crop production, however, requires additional energy inputs for tillage, seeds, weeding and harvesting.

In the following analyses several different farming systems and technologies are examined along with their relative efficiencies in producing food-corn energy. Corn produced by hand in Mexico employing swidden or cut/burn agricultural technology requires only a man with an axe, a hoe, and some corn seed (Table 21.1).[36] A total of 1,144 hours of labour is required to produce 1,944 kg/ha. This 1,144 hours represents about 57 per cent of the total labour output for an adult per year. Assuming the individual is from the rural area of a developing country and consumes about 3,000 kcal of food per day, the labour input for a hectare of corn was calculated to be 589,160 kcal.

When the energy for making the axe and hoe and producing the seed is added to the human power input, the total energy input needed to produce corn by hand is about 0.6 million kcal/ha. With a corn yield per hectare of 1,944 kg or 6.9 million kcal, the output/input ratio is 10.7 (Table 21.1).

The energy inputs in tractor-powered agriculture are considerably greater than those of hand-powered agricultural systems (Tables 21.1 and 21.2) and those of animal-powered systems. Typically U.S. corn production relies heavily on machinery for power. The total manpower input is dramatically reduced to only 10 hours compared with 1,144 hours for the hand-powered system such as that in Mexico (Tables 21.1 and 21.2). The input for labour in the U.S. system, which is only 5,260 kcal for the entire growing season, is a minimal input compared with the other inputs (Table 21.2).

But balanced against this low-manpower input is the significant increase in fossil-energy input required to run the machines that replace human labour. In 1983 the energy inputs (mostly fossil fuel) required to produce a hectare of corn averaged about 11.0 million kcal/ha or the equivalent of about 1,136 litres of oil (Table 21.2). Based on a corn yield of about 7,000 kg/ha, or the equivalent of 26.0 million kcal energy, the output/input ratio is 2.34:1. Note that the fossil-energy input in this system represents about 18 per cent of the solar energy captured by the aboveground corn biomass (63×10^6 kcal).

Corn yield is now at about 6,500 kg/ha in the United States (Table 21.2). How high can these yields go? In general it appears that corn yields have tended to reach a plateau since 1970 (Fig. 21.2). Note that the fluctuations in yields have been increasing in amplitude since 1945. This is expected when the production system is stressed by the large inputs of fertilisers and pesticides. The result of such stress is that any limiting factor such as moisture affecting the system is more apt to cause a major decline in yield per hectare.

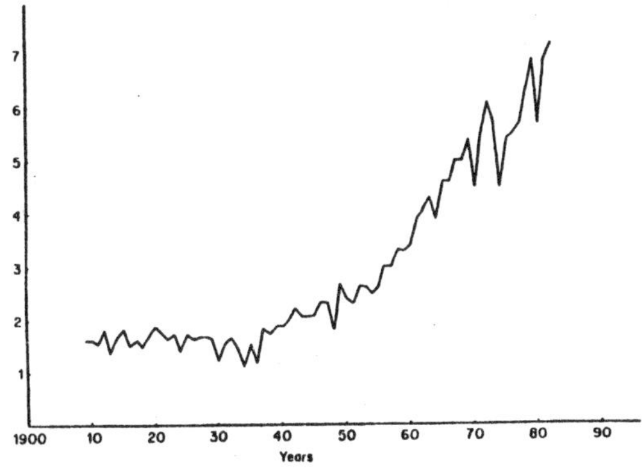

Fig. 21.2: U.S. corn yields from 1909 to the present

Table 21.1: Energy inputs in corn (maize) production in Mexico using only manpower

Item	*Quantity/ha*	*kcal/ha*
Labour	1,144 h[12]	589,160[b]
Axe and hoe	16,570 kcal[a]	16,570[36]
Seeds	10.4 kg[a]	36,608[36]
Total		642,338
Output		
Total yield	1,944 kg[12]	6, 901,200
kcal output/kcal input		10.74

[a] (Estimated)

[b] See text for assumptions for calculating kcal input

This fact emphasises the importance of using an integrated production system to achieve maximum corn yields. The corn variety must be a suitable genotype that will grow best under high fertiliser inputs, effective pest control, ample moisture, suitable temperature levels, and a long growing season.

With a suitable corn hybrid and ideal growing conditions, corn yields may reach 20 t/ha of grain (about 300 bu/acre). For a total biomass of 40 t/ha, this represents 180 million kcal of energy or conversion of about 1.3 per cent of solar energy into corn biomass. This would be about ten times greater than the conversion of solar energy by the hand-powered system described earlier.

The limitation of the approach of increasing one input while holding all others constant has been well illustrated with nitrogen. In Iowa, for example, when no nitrogen was applied the yield was about 2,200 kg/ha. Corn yields continued to increase to 6,900 kg/ha as nitrogen applications rose to about 230 kg/ha. With further applications of nitrogen, corn yields actually declined.[18]

Table 12.2: Energy inputs per hectare for corn production in the United States

Item	*Quantity/ha*	*kcal/ha*
Labour	10 hr	5,250
Machinery	55 kg	1,018,000
Gasoline	401	400,000
Diesel	75 1	855,000
Irrigation	2.25×10^6 kcal	2, 250,000
Electricity	35 kwh	100,000
Nitrogen	152 kg	3, 192,000
Phosphorus	75 kg	473,000
Potassium	96 kg	240,000
Lime	426 kg	134,400
Seeds	21 kg	520,000
Insecticides	3 kg	300,000
Herbicides	8 kg	800,000
Drying	3,300 kg	660,000
Transportation	300 kg	89,000
Total		11, 036,650
Outputs		
Total yield	7,000 kg	26,000,000
kcal output/kcal input		2.34

The unfavourable yields associated with high N application might be offset by increasing the applications of P and K while at the same time increasing the amount of water available to the corn crop. Also desirable would be having a corn hybrid that is tolerant of high fertiliser and herbicide levels.

Improved Technologies and Resource Management

The aim of present and future agricultural production programmes is to maintain and augment crop yields while conserving soil, water, energy and biological resources — all of which have limited supply and availability.

Soil, Nutrients and Alternative Fertilisers

Whenever crops are harvested significant quantities of nutrients that once were in the soil are removed because they have been incorporated into the plant material as it grew. These must be replaced if a high yield is to be achieved in subsequent years. Often a more significant loss occurs from soil erosion by wind and rain (Pimentel and Krummel, unpublished manuscript). Clearly, then, a practical alternative would be to employ soil-conservation practices to reduce nutrient losses.

As a substitute for some or all commercial fertiliser, livestock manure can be used. Manure not only is a source of nutrients that crops need, but in addition it helps to reduce soil erosion and improves soil structure.[24, 50] Although more than 70 per cent of this collected manure is applied to land, it provides agriculture with only about 8 per cent of the needed nitrogen and 20 per cent of the needed phosphorus and potassium.

The amount of nitrogen from manure applied to U.S. lands could be doubled if proper management practices were employed in handling livestock manure (Muck, 1982, personal communication). When manure is left standing most of the nitrogen is lost as ammonium. To prevent this loss, manure should be collected promptly and stored in large tanks or ponds and then immediately covered with the soil when application is made to the land (Muck, 1982, personal communication). Even though distribution of manure requires energy, its use is cheaper than commercial fertiliser.[15, 30]

Before commercial fertilisers were so universally used in corn production, corn often was planted in rotation with a legume crop.[26]

When sweet clover is planted in the fall after the corn is harvested and ploughed under one year later, nearly 170 kg of nitrogen is added per hectare[49] Scott, 1982, personal communication). However, because 2 ha of land must be cultivated to raise 1 ha of corn, this practice became a ploughed when land prices increased. When legume rotations are not feasible, legumes can be planted between corn rows in late July or early August and then this legume planting, considered "green manure", is ploughed under in early spring when the field is being prepared for seeding. Winter vetch and other legumes, for example, planted in this manner yield about 150 kg/ha of nitrogen[17]; Scott, 1982, personal communication). Also, the use of a vetch cover crop protects the soil from wind and water erosion during the winter and has the additional advantage of adding organic matter to the soil.

Substitute Cultural Practices

Relying on a no-till or minimum-till system would reduce the tractor fuel inputs normally required to plough and disc soil by conventional tillage and produce a saving of about 45 litres or 513,630 kcal of fossil fuel per hectare for tractor fuel if a no-till system were adopted. About 60 litres of diesel fuel are used to till 1 ha of soil with a 50-hp tractor, compared with about 15 litres for no-till planting.

On the other hand, with a no-till system herbicide must be increased to control weeds, and insecticides and molluskicides have to be applied to control increased insect and slug problems that often occur in no-till systems.[45] With no-till, pesticide use frequently doubles, thereby making the total energy inputs for no-till greater than those for conventional tillage.

Whether energy inputs are greater or about the same for no-till compared with conventional tillage will depend on the crop and the various practices used, tractor size, type of soil, abundance of pests, and environmental factors. No-till, however, has advantages over conventional tillage because it reduces manpower inputs, decreases soil, erosion, and helps conserve soil moisture.

Alternate Pest Control

Each year the 500,000 tonnes of pesticides applied to U.S. cropland[46] represent an energy expenditure of about 43×10^{12} kcal. A wide variety of alternative pest controls can be used as substitutes for pesticides.[32]

One of these is biological control, which uses parasites and predators to control insects and weeds. If successful, as was the case when the vedalia beetle was introduced into California for control of cottony-cushion scale on citrus, then no further use of insecticides was required for this particular pest.

Many times heavy pesticide use has eliminated or decreased the effectiveness of parasites and predators and other natural controls. The technology, integrated pest management (IPM), aims at making maximum use of natural enemies.[27] In IPM programmes both pest and natural enemy populations are monitored and pesticides are applied only when the pest population will escape natural-enemy control and when economic damage will take place in the crop. The use of natural enemies and other biological controls is ideal from the standpoint of energy. Because parasites are predators obtain their food-fuel directly from the pests, they are in fact solar-powered.

Another successful way to control pests without pesticides is breeding food and fibre crops that have resistance against plant pathogens, pest insects, and weed damage.[32, 33] Most crops now planted in the United States have had some degree of resistance to plant pathogens bred into them. Some major pests controlled by host-plant resistance include cabbage yellows and the Hessian fly pest of wheat.

In addition to the alternatives mentioned, various agronomic or cultural practices in the crop production may be modified to enhance pest control.[32] These include crop rotation, timing of the planting to elude pests, tilling of the soil to destroy weed and insect pests, irrigation-water applications to control growth sequences of crop and pests, plus the judicious use of organic and plastic mulches.[32] All of these techniques have energy and environmental costs, but for certain pests in a particular crop and region they may be highly beneficial in terms of energy and costs.

Water Supplies

Looking to the future and considering the decline of supplies of cheap fossil fuel, hard decisions will be whether land will be irrigated or dryland crops produced. Attention must be focused on the more basic problem of water supply, which collects from precipitation and is held in the vast underground aquifiers. Concern is growing in many quarters about the overuse or "mining" of these vital reserves.[3] Surely conservation of water deserves high-priority attention from all sectors of society.

Many techniques are available for use in conserving water and, not surprisingly, most of these are similar to those for preventing soil erosion. These include using organic mulches as in no-till crop culture, terracing of crops, planting strip crops, and planting crops on the contour. All help retain the water on the land for growing crops.

Livestock Production

Animals used for human food are foodgrains, forages and grasses. Although forage and grasses are unsuitable for human consumption because they cannot be digested, grains surely are excellent human food. In this country about 90 per cent of all grain is fed to livestock which provide meat, milk, and eggs to American consumers[31].

Energetically, anywhere from 7 to 88 kcal of fossil energy are required to produce 1 kcal of animal protein (Table 21.3). This contrasts with the production of protein in soybeans and corn grain that require only 0.7 to 3 kcal of fossil energy to produce 1 kcal of plant protein (Table 21.4). The major reason that animal-protein products are significantly more energy-expensive than plant-protein food is that first the forage and grain feeds have to be grown and then consumed by the animal to produce the desired animal food. In addition, forage and grain have to be fed to the breeding herd to maintain them.

In the United States over 420 million ha of land are cultivated to provide the forage and grains fed to livestock. It is interesting to speculate what could happen if the United States were to switch to a grass-fed livestock system and eliminate the use (and associated energy expenditures) of grains and forage. Estimates are that about 2.8 million tonnes of animal protein could e produced annually or slightly more than half that of the 5.4 million tonnes currently produced[35]. The 2.8 million tonnes of animal protein (meat, eggs, and milk) would provide 40 g protein per day per person. On average, each person in the United States consumes about 32 g of plant protein per day[35]. Thus, the 40 g of animal protein per day from a grass-fed system added to the 32 g of plant protein would total 72 g of protein per person per day. This is greater than the recommended daily allowance (RDA) of about 46-54 g per person per day[23].

Because animal-protein products require significantly larger inputs of energy than plant-protein production (Tables 21.3 and 21.4), some would argue in favour of using grains directly as food so more people would have food. One estimate is that if the 135 million tonnes of

Table 21.3: Energy inputs and returns per hectare for various livestock production systems in the United States[35]

Livestock	*Animal product yield (kg)*	*Yield in protein (kg)*	*Protein as Kcal (10^3)*	*Fossil energy input for production (10^6 Kcal)*	*Kcal fossil energy input/Kcal protein output*	*Labour inpu manhours*
Broilers	2000	186	744	7.3	9.8	7
Eggs	910	104	416	7.4	17.8	19
Pork	490	35	140	6.0	42.9	11
Sheep (grass-fed)	7	0.2	0.8	0.07	87.5	0.2
Dairy	3270	114	457	5.4	11.8	51
Beef	60	6	24	0.6	25.0	2
Dairy (grass-fed)	3260	114	457	3.3	7.2	50
Beef (grass-fed)	54	5	20	0.5	25.0	2
Catfish	2783	384	1536	52.5	34.2	55

Table 21.4: Energy inputs and returns for various food and feed crops produced per hectare in the United States 25 to 36.

Crop	*Crop yield (kg)*	*Yield in protein (kg)*	*Crop yield in food energy (10^6 Kcal)*	*Fossil energy input for production (10^6 Kcal)*	*Kcal food/feed output/Kcal fossil energy input*	*Labour input manhours*
Corn (U.S.)	7, 000	630	24.5	6.9	3.5	12
Wheat (North Dakota)	2, 022	283	6.7	2.5	2.7	6
Oats (Minnesota)	2, 869	423	10.9	2.1	5.1	3
Rice (Arkansas)	4, 742	272	14.0	12.5	1.1	30
Sorghum (Kansas)	1, 840	202	6.0	1.5	4.0	5
Soybean (Illinois)	2, 600	885	10.5	2.3	4.5	8
Beans dry (Michigan)	1, 176	285	4.1	3.1	1.3	19
Peanuts (Georgia)	3, 720	320	15.3	10.9	1.4	19
Apples (East)	41, 546	83	23.3	26.2	0.9	176
Oranges (Florida)	40, 370	404	19.8	11.8	1.7	210
Potato (New York)	34, 468	539	21.1	15.5	1.4	35
Lettuce (California)	31, 595	284	4.1	19.7	0.2	171
Tomato (California)	49, 620	469	9.9	16.6	0.6	165
Cabbage (New York)	53, 000	1, 060	12.7	16.8	0.8	289
Alfalfa (Minnesota)	11, 800 (dry)	1, 845	47.2	3.6	13.1	12
Tame hay (New York)	2, 539 (dry)	160	5.5	0.6	8.6	7
Corn Silage (N.E.U.S.)	9, 400 (dry)	753	29.1	5.2	5.6	15

grain annually cycled through U.S. livestock were fed to humans, 400 million people could be sustained for one year on a vegetarian diet providing about 80 g of plant protein per person per day[35].

Again it should be emphasised that both livestock-based foods and plant food contribute not only calories but also important vitamins and minerals to the human food supply. While animal foods contain fairly high levels of saturated fats and cholesterol, their protein contribution is substantial and of higher quality than that of plant protein.

Livestock production has a major advantage in the food-production system because livestock can be maintained on marginal land that is too poor to grow food crops. This pasture and rangeland can be utilised effectively to produce valuable livestock protein[35], and hopefully in the future this type of animal-production system will be improved by using combinations of livestock types on the same pastures and ranges.

Conclusion

Technologies have enabled humans to use natural resources and improve the standard of living for humanity. More people, for example, are being fed than ever before in history. Unfortunately, at the same time more people than ever before are malnourished.

This suggests two important principles. First, for development it is essential that we have both the technology and resources. Technology without resources is worthless. For example, nations with little or no fresh water and no fossil energy have an almost impossible task for further development. These nations will continue to be dependent on other nations.

Second, resources can be degraded and destroyed — this includes arable land, fresh water, energy, and biota. Topsoils can be eroded, water polluted or ground-water mined, fossil energy mined rapidly, and biological diversity reduced. Thus, even resources that are renewable such as arable land, water, and biota can be degraded through mismanagement so that they are no longer available for development. In fact, the degradation of the world's environment appears to be common[3].

Although some technologies can improve the efficient use of resources, limits for most technologies and resources exist. Thus, these technologies and resources can only support a limited number of humans. World resources and technology can support an abundance of humans, e.g. 10-15 billion humans living at or near poverty, or support approximately one billion humans with a relatively high standard of living.

The decision whether human society lives in poverty or in relative wealth depends on humans themselves. To live with a high standard of living and have a population of about one billion will require that humans control their numbers. It is clear at the extreme limits of population growth — greater than 15 billion — that if humans do not control their numbers, nature will.

Acknowledgements

I thank M. Pimentel for her suggestions in helping to strengthen this manuscript. The preparation of this paper was supported in part by National Science Foundation Grant BSR-8500312.

NOTES

1. Alexander, M., (1977). *Introduction to Soil Microbiology*, 2nd ed. New York: Wiley.
2. Brady, N.C., (1984). *The Nature and Properties of Soils*, 9th ed. New York: Macmillan.
3. CEO, (1980). The Global 2000 Report to the President, *The Technical Report*, vol. II, Washington, DC: U.S. Government Printing Office.
4. Dudal, R., (1981). An evaluation of conservation needs, In *Soil Conservation Problems and Prospects*, ed. R.P.C. Morgan, pp. 3-12, Chichester: John Wiley and Sons.
5. Ehrlich, P.R., and Ehrlich, A.H., (1981). *Extinction: The Causes and Consequences of the Disappearance of Species*. New York: Random House.
6. Environmental Fund, 1979. World population estimates, Washington, DC: The Environmental Fund.
7. FAO, (1982). *1981 Production Yearbook*. Rome: Food and Agricultural Organisation of the United Nations.
8. Finkel, H.J., (1983). Irrigation of cereal crops. In *CRC Handbook of Irrigation Technology*, ed. H.J. Finkel, Vol. II, pp. 159-189, Boca Raton, FL: CRC Press.
9. Golley, F.B. (ed.), (1983). *Tropical Rainforest Ecosystems: Structure and Function*. Amsterdam: Elsevier Scientific.
10. Kovda, V.A., (1983). *Loss of Productive Land due to Salinisation*. Ambio 12, 91, 93.
11. Latham, M.C., (1984). International nutrition and problems and policies. In *World Food Issues*, pp. 55-64, Ithaca, NY: Centre for the Analysis of World Food Issues, International Agriculture.

12. Lewis, O., (1951). *Life in a Mexican Village: Tepoztlan Restudied.* Urbana: University of Illinois Press.
13. Leyton, L., (1983). Crop water use: principles and some considerations for agro-forestry. In *Plant Research and Agroforestry*, ed. P.A. Huxley, pp. 379-400. Nairobi: International Council for Research in Agroforestry.
14. Linden, H.R., (1980). *Importance of Natural Gas in the World Energy Picture.* Paper presented at International Institute for Applied Systems Analysis Conference on Conventional and Unconventional World Natural Gas Resources, Luxembourg, Austria, June 30-July 4.
15. Linton, R.E., (1968). The economics of poultry manure disposal. Cornell Ext. Bull. 1195: 1-23.
16. Mangelsdorf, P.C. (1966). Genetic potentials for increasing yields of food crops and animals. In *Prospects of the World Food Supply.* Washington, DC: National Academy of Sciences.
17. Mitchell, W.H., and Teel, M.R. (1977). *Winter Annual Cover Crops for No-tillage Corn Production.* Agron. J. 69: 569-573.
18. Munson, R.D., and Doll, J.P., (1959). The economics of fertiliser use in crop production. In *Advances in Agronomy XI*, ed. A.G. Normann, pp. 133-169, New York: Academic Press.
19. Myers, N., (1979). *The Sinking Ark.* New York: Pergamon Press.
20. Myers, N., (1983). *A Wealth of Wild Species.* Boulder, CO: Westview Press.
21. Myers, N., (1984). *Genetic resources in jeopardy.* Ambio 13: 171-174.
22. NAS, (1975). *Population and Food: Crucial Issues.* Washington, DC: National Academy of Sciences.
23. NAS, (1980). *Recommended Dietary Allowances*, (9th ed.) National Research Council, Washington, DC: National Academy of Sciences.
24. Neal, O.R., (1939). *Some Concurrent and Residual Effects of Organic Matter Additions on Surface Runoff.* Soil Sc. So. Amer. Proc. 4: 420-425.
25. Pimentel, D. (ed.) (1980). *Handbook of Energy Utilisation in Agriculture.* Boca Raton, FL: CRC Press.
26. Pimentel, D., (1981). *The Food-Land-Fuel Squeeze.* Chem. Tech. 11:214-215.
27. Pimentel, D., (1982). *Perspectives of Integrated Pest Management.* Crop Prot. 1: 5-26.
28. Pimentel, D., and Burgess, M., (1980) Energy inputs in corn production, In *Handbook of Energy Utilisation in Agriculture*, ed. D. Pimentel, pp. 67-84, Boga Raton, FL: CRC Press.
29. Pimentel, D., and Dazhong, W., (1987). Technological changes in energy use in U.S. agricultural production, In *Research Approaches in Agricultural Ecology*, ed. S.R. Giliessman, New York: Springer-Verlag, in press.
30. Pimentel, D., Fast, S., Berardi, G., (1983). *Energy Efficiency Of farming Systems*, Agr. Eco. Env. 9: 359-372.
31. Pimentel, D.; Garnick, E.; Berkowitz, A.; Jacobson, S.; Napolitano, S.; Black, P.; Valdes-Cogliano, S.; Vinzant, B.; Hudes, E.; Littman, S.; (1980). Environmental quality and natural biota, *Bio Science 30*: 750-755.

32. Pimentel, D.; Glenister, C.; Fast, S.; Gallahan, D.; (1982). *Environmental Risks Associated with the Use of Biological and Cultural Pest Controls. Final Report to the National Science Foundation.* Report No. PB-83-168-716. Springfield, VA: National Technical Information Service.
33. Pimentel, D.; Hurd, L.E.; Bellotti, A.C.; Forster, M.J.; Oka, I.N.; Sholes, O.D.; Whitman, R.J.; (1973). Food production and the energy crisis. *Science* 182: 443-449.
34. Pimentel, D.; Nafus, D.; Vergara, W.; Papaj, D.; Jaconetta, L.; Wulfe, M.; Olsvig, L.; French, K.; Loye, M.; Mendoza, E.; (1978). Biological solar energy conversion and U.S. energy policy, *Bio Science 28*: 376-382.
35. Pimentel, D.; Oltenacu, P.A.; Nesheim, M.C.; Krummel, J.; Allen, M.S.; and Chick, S.; (1980). Grass-fed livestock potential: energy and land constraints. *Science 207*: 843-848.
36. Pimentel, D.; and Pimentel, M.; (1979). Food, *Energy and Society*, London: Edward Arnold (Publishers) Ltd.
37. Pimentel, D.; Terhune, E.C.; Dyson-Hudson, R.; Rochereau, S.; Samis, R.; Smith, E.; Denman, D.; Reifschneider, D.; and Shepard, M. (1976). Land degradation: effects on food energy resources. *Science* 194: 149-155.
38. PRB, (1985). *World Population Data Sheet.* Washington, DC: Population Reference Bureau.
39. Reifsnyder, W.E., and Lull, H.W., (1965). *Radiant Energy in Relation to Forests*, Tech. Bull No. 1344, U.S. Deptt. of Agriculture Forest Service.
40. Ritschard, R.L.; Tsao, K.; (1978). *Energy and Water Use in Irrigated Agriculture during Drought Conditions.* US DOE LBL-7866. Berkeley: University of California, Lawrence Berkeley Laboratory.
41. Swaminathan, M.S., (1983). Our greatest challenge — feeding a hungry world. In *Perspectives and Recommendation. Chemistry and World Food Supplies. The New Frontiers, Chemrawn II.* Eds. G. Bixler and L.W. Shemilt, pp. 25-46, Philippines: International Rice Research Institute.
42. UN, (1982). *World Population Trends and Policies, 1981, Monitoring Report.* Vol. 1, Population Trends, New York: United Nations.
43. UNEP, (1980). *Annual Review.* Nairboi, Kenya: United Nations Environment Programme.
44. USDA, (1974). *Energy and U.S. Agriculture: 1974 Data Base.* Vols. I and II. Office of Energy Conservation and Environment, State Energy Conservation Programs, Washington, DC: Federal Energy Administration.
45. USDA, (1975). *Minimum Tillage: A Preliminary Technology Assessment.* Office of Planning and Evaluation, Washington, DC: U.S. Department of Agriculture.
46. USDA, (1981). *Agricultural Statistics 1981.* Washington, DC: U.S. Government Printing Office.
47. USDA, (1984). *Agricultural Statistics*, 1984, Washington, DC: U.S. Government Printing Office.

48. Viessman, W., Jr., and Hammer, M.J., (1985). *Water Supply and Pollution Control*, 4th ed. New York: Harper and Row.
49. Willard, C.J., (1927). *An Experimental Study of Sweet Clover*. Ohio AESR B 405: 1-84.
50. Zwerman, P.J.; Drielsma, A.B.; Jones, G.D.; Klausner, S.D.; Ellis, D.; (1970). Rates of water infiltration resulting from applications of dairy manure. *Proceedings of the Second Cornell Agricultural Waste Management Conference, 1970*, pp. 263-270.

22

Resources Are Not; They Become: An Institutional Theory

THOMAS R. DE GREGORI

In common usage, as well as in traditional mainstream economics, material inputs for production have been thought of as physical resources. Classical economists defined the factors of production in material terms. Land was the "original and indestructible powers of the soil." Resources were "natural" and given. If land and mineral resources are material, then at least in a global sense they are fixed and finite. From an institutionalist perspective, however, following in the tradition of Clarence Ayres and Erich Zimmermann, "resources are not; they become." In the process of becoming, then, they are neither fixed nor finite, and, as we shall demonstrate, the process of becoming is one that is as much ideational as it is material.[1]

The material or physical aspect of resources exists before they become resources. Arguing from "the principle of indestructibility of matter," a view that would have to be modified in light of current physics, Ayres argues that "there is no such thing as a 'new material'." There are, however, new resources. "The history of every material is the same. It is one of novel combinations of existing devices and materials in such a fashion, as to constitute a new device or a new material or both."[2] This creative process of fashioning the material and non-material stuff of our environment in a form usable and serviceable to human beings is determined by science and technology.

Reprinted with Permission from *Journal of Economic Issues*, Vol. XXI, No.3, September 1987, p. 1241-1263

It is the sum total of human knowledge and capability that is the prime resource and the one that defines all others.

Technology and Resource Creation: The Concept

To say that the term "resources" essentially has no meaning apart from a relationship to human beings does *not* mean that all things have a right to exist only to the extent that they serve human beings. We can speak about the living resources of planet Earth. We can argue that we ought to preserve and protect them. Calling them resources and saying that we should act in certain ways, then, means that there can be an operational meaning to the effect that it is in our best interest to preserve as large a genetic heritage as possible. This is an intelligent, sensible argument that many conservationists and environmentalists put forward. We can also argue that other living things have *rights* apart from their service to us.[3] For the sake of consistency in the use of language, we should not use the term "resources" when we are making specific reference to the rights of other creatures.

It is ironic that most mainstream economists have taken a position on resources that is not too different from that of the institutionalists. This was noted by Ayres four decades ago and resulted in some "confusion" for a discipline in which scarcity is the cornerstone.[4] Economists generally maintain that the issue of finite resources is not an interesting question. Reference is made to price changes, substitution, greater efficiency, and discovery. Occasionally, even science and technology are mentioned. Yet, without technology, one cannot indefinitely substitute one resource for another. Substitution alone merely delays reaching finite limits.

Mineral resources is not the only area in which the institutionalist perspective has become orthodoxy. The ideas of science-based agriculture, or of certain technologies as "land augmenting" or that investment creates arable land, make sense in a functional theory of resources, but not in one that assumes land as "natural" or as the non-human, non-manmade factor of production.[5] Direct investment creates arable land in many ways: by increasing crop intensities (more than one crop per season) through irrigation, or by developing crops with shorter growing seasons, or by creating higher yields in a particular crop because of improved seed. The basis for these resources creating investment is the ongoing research in agriculture, which most agricultural economists find to be an investment that has paid extraordinary returns in recent years.

The focus on scientific research as a means of resource creation goes to the very heart of institutional economics. Wesley C. Mitchell stated precisely what should be a fundamental principle of all economics. "Incomparably greatest among human resources is knowledge. It is greatest because it is the mother of other resources."[6] Mitchell's claim is true both as a historical proposition and as an operating principle for policy.

Resources are not things or stuff or materials; they are a set of capabilities. These capabilities use the stuff of the material and non-material universe in a life-sustaining manner. These capabilities define a functional relationship that we call resources. This relationship is what Zimmermann referred to as the "fundamental concept of resources."[7] The relationship implies the prior physical existence of both humans and the material (or non-material) substance. Absent from the relationship, the term "resources" is meaningless. Humans are the active agent, having ideas that they use to transform the environment for human purposes. Resources, then, is a property of things—a property that is a result of human capability.

Logically, one resource—food—had to pre-exist the others. Before hominids, there were proto-hominids, and obviously their survival presumes the use of food resources. Beyond this very basic precondition, ideas precede, not only all other resources (including all other food resources), but also the emergence of homo sapiens. Proto-hominids had ideas and began to use certain objects in their environment, such as stones. This idea and subsequent action established the functional relationship that allows us to call the stones resources. Others saw possibilities of fashioning these stones so that they were more usable. The greater the usability, the greater the resource character of the stones. Tools are, then, used to create still newer and better ones, thus continuing the process of resource enhancement. The stones had not changed, but ideas, skills, and behaviour had, and these literally created the resource.

These new tools allowed for more effective exploitation of the environment. New edible materials became accessible, tubers in rock-hard earth or large animals, and for humans these became food resources. The ability to harvest more food from an area increased the resource character of that land. This process continued through the domestication of plants and animals and on up to the present. It was agriculture that created arable land and not the reverse.

This simple illustration shows the dynamic interactions and reinforcing feedback mechanisms involved in the human generation of ideas and their embodiment in the process of technology and in the creation of resources. Other animals use tools, but both the tools and the resources they create are functionally limited. Humans engage in a dynamic open-ended process called technology. In a recent book of mine, I make an analogy to signals and language. Other animals have closed systems of communication using signs or signals; only humans have the dynamic, open-ended process of language.[8]

Tool-using created resources. It also created homo sapiens; for the use of tools favoured certain members of the proto-hominids who had large areas of the brain controlling the hand that made the tools. This gave a direction to evolutionary processes and established another dynamic feedback relationship because with improved hands and brains one can make better tools.[9]

Tools may have been instrumental in our emergence as homo sapiens; they also made further evolutionary change unnecessary. Until the emergence of technology, living creatures exploited a limited number of resources in an environment. Environmental change wiped out resources and those life forms that could not evolve and adapt. Evolution is the means of adapting to change, and it is the means that allows movement from one environment to another. A successful species is one with the capability of exploiting its environment for continued survival. A failed species may be nothing more than a victim of an environmental change that was too rapid or dramatic to allow for evolutionary change.

With ideas and with the technology in which those ideas are embodied, resource creation can be continuous, and adaptation does not depend upon chance biological change. From a rather limited range of habitat, humans have spread around the globe, inhabiting every conceivable climate and environment. Unique among mammals, we have done this without speciation. The ways in which we use a technology to make an area habitable for humans, to make clothing, shelter, food, and materials, can only be described as resource creation. The very concept of habitability for an area that was previously uninhabited can only have meaning through resource creation.

Historic Concerns about Resources

Concern for the availability of resources is as old as the human endeavour itself. In the quote cited above about knowledge being the mother of other resources, Mitchell adds: "The bulk of man's resources are the result of human ingenuity aided by slowly, patiently, and painfully acquired knowledge and experience."[10] Various stones and pebbles became resources when humans learned to use them to make tools. These same materials ceased to be resources when humans acquired new skills in taking previously worthless earths and smelting them into metals. The new tools allowed humans to exploit more fully their environment and thereby to create still more resources. And so it has been ever since—humans create resources and use them to create still other resources. For all human beings are (virtually by definition) tool users. The very use of tools presupposes both resources to make them and resources to be exploited by them. The use of tools is central to the process of maintaining and sustaining human life. Peoples and cultures achieve levels of population density and styles of life based upon their use of tools, technology, and resources. Rarely, if ever, can a people abandon a technology and its resources and return to an older pattern without loss of life (that is, a lowered population density) and living standard. The ongoing concern for a secure supply of resources is vital to the very life and lifeways of a people. "All forms of life other than human beings deal only with renewable resources," and only humans have found a way to use so-called non-renewable resources.[11] Contrary to the doomsday critics, this is a strength and not a weakness of the human endeavour.

For a significant period in United States history, lack of access to resources was not a primary concern. An abundant natural endowment (as defined by the existing technology) and a seemingly endless frontier contributed to this attitude. By the beginning of the present century, this perspective began to change with the putative closing of the frontier in 1890. In the late 1920s, fear was expressed in official circles that we might be exhausting domestic sources of critical resources.

After Second World War, domestic resource exhaustion was not the only resource concern of the United States. Continued uninterrupted access to foreign sources no longer seemed certain. A series of official commissions and studies testifies to the intensity of these resource concerns. The most famous and important of these studies in the Paley Commission Report (officially entitled *Resources for Freedom*), a comprehensive five-volume report issued in 1952.[12]

The Paley Commission began with the question, "Has the United States of America the material means to sustain its civilisation?"[13] It found that:

> In area after area the same pattern seems discernible: soaring demands, shrinking resources, the consequent pressure towards rising real costs, the risk of wartime shortages, the ultimate threat of an arrest of decline in the standard of living we cherish and hope to help others to attain. If such a threat is to be averted, it will not be by inaction. After successive years of thinking about unemployment, reemployment, full employment, about factory production, inflation and deflation, and hundreds of other matters in the structure of economic life, the United States must now give new and deep considerations to the fundamental upon which all employment, all daily activity, eventually rests: the contents of the earth and its physical environment.[14]

The issues of resource dependency gained a far wider constituency in the 1970s, reaching far beyond official circles. Phraseology featuring the "limits to growth" or an "era of limits" were in popular currency, as sophisticated computer models cranked out conclusions arguing that world-wide resource exhaustion was but decades away. The petroleum crisis also brought to the United States public a vivid sample of the meaning of resource dependency. In the 1960s, there also emerged doomsday and catastrophist theories, which I have attacked in other articles for the failure (fortunately) of their dire prophecies.

By the early 1980s, despite the utter failure of the doomsday prophecies, the proponents of alternate technology came up with newer, presumably more profound, reasons to be opposed to modern technology. Jeremy Rifkin, in his book, *Entropy*, boldly proclaimed "a new world view" in his subtitle.[15] The inexorable law of entropy in thermodynamics requires that matter and energy flow from high to low, from structure to randomness and from heterogeneity to homogeneity. Thus we move from order and complexity to chaos. Since this is a law of the cosmos and of the planet, it is not exactly clear in Rifkin how we could have achieved our current state of complexity and organisation from which descent is inevitable. Similarly, Kirkpatrick Sale argued in *Human Scale* that smallness is an inherent biological virtue.[16] Unfortunately for Sale, he has no solid biological evidence to offer for his thesis. One source that he uses, J.B.S. Haldane's "On Being the Right Size," does speak of the advantages of smallness, but then turns to the advantages of bigness. Evidently, the author of this large book on smallness did not finish the Haldane essay before quoting it.[17]

Someone once joked that Karl Marx had carried classical

economics to its logical absurdity. Much the same can be said of Sale and Rifkin. For the very logical structures that they conjured gave rise to implications the exact opposite of what they advocated. If resources are fixed and finite, then entropy does condemn us to inevitable and ineluctable decline. There is one thing that entropy and scientific and technological inquiry teach us; namely that no process such as recycling or conservation can be one hundred per cent effective. Renewability is, at best, only partially successful. At each turn of the cycle, some bit of order becomes disorder, soil is lost, or a resource is dissipated. Thus, not only are we faced with decline, but also, in the case of Rifkin, we are at a loss to explain how we ever achieved an elevated status from which decline is possible. This decline occurs with constant population; any population growth accelerates the process. Negative population growth delays, but does not prevent, decline.

There is a more respectable and persuasive argument for renewability. In these, the constraints are relaxed, and we have a slightly open system for natural processes to create resources, but at a slow pace. Aquifers are recharged by rain; running water provides sources of energy; soil is created; and new species evolve to replace those that die out. Thus, it is not fixed limits but carrying capacity of a constrained, but open, system that determines sustainability. If we view carrying capacity as purely a "natural" process, then unfortunately, humans transcended these limits at least 10,000 years ago with the development of agriculture. We do not merely harvest the environment, we transform it. In so doing, we have altered the carrying capacity of the environment.

Viewed in these terms, carrying capacity refers not to the environment as it is, but to the environment as it can be. The issue, then, is what technologies are best able to transform the environment for human purposes on a sustainable basis.

This brings us back to the argument of fixed, finite resources. A technology predicated upon fixed, finite resources is one that dooms us to decline. It does this to the extent that it fulfils the assumptions of many of the theorists who advocate it and to the extent that it supplants the technologies that have been deemed to be bad. (This generalisation does not apply to the technologies created by the many dedicated workers who are not operating out of cosmic concerns of grandiose philosophical theories but merely trying to solve practical problems.) However, just as the concept of carrying capacity has a technological component, so does that of resources. Resources are not fixed and finite because they are not natural. They are a product of human ingenuity resulting from the creation of technology and science.

Obviously, at any given time, with a given technology, there is a sense in which resources are fixed and finite. Given these parameters, we can say that some countries are better endowed with resources, be they mineral, soil, or energy, than others. We said "in a sense," for even under the constraint of a given technology, changes in prices can dramatically alter resource availability. In defining the resource endowment of a country, furthermore, it is difficult to distinguish between the rich resources, such as ore deposits, that may even have been found by expatriates, and the arable land resources that was created by investments in applied technology.

The idea of "carrying capacity" has in usage a relatively precise meaning. In a given ecosystem, up to a set number of animals can be pastured or so much water can be drawn from an aquifer with the "natural" regenerative forces allowing for sustainable use. Beyond these limits, an inevitable accelerating decline begins. As such, the concept is useful, cautionary, and scientific. Unfortunately, the term has acquired a more common parlance. We, meaning earth's human inhabitants, must live within our energy budget or within the carrying capacity of the planet. Simply stated, we must live within limits. If these statements are to be accepted as anything other than truisms, then there is the unstated assumption that the resource boundaries established by various policy advocates are fixed by nature. Like other statements of fixed, finite resources, it denies the possibility for technological innovations that alter the boundary conditions.

Technology and Resource Creation: Some Empirical Evidence in Minerals and Food Supply

By the mid-1970s, a series of studies and events appeared to lend scientific support and empirical evidence to the view that resources were being exhausted and that population was outrunning both food supply and resources. Studies such as the Club of Rome-sponsored *The Limits to Growth* used systems analysis and computer models to demonstrate that the mineral resources upon which civilisation is based were being rapidly depleted and that some would be exhausted in a matter of decades unless corrective actions were taken.[18] The rapid rise in food prices in the early 1970s, accompanied by decreasing carryover food stocks and then followed by the oil embargoes and rapid escalation in price, all seemed to confirm the most dire forecasts.

In 1974 and 1975, there was a world conference on population and another on food production. Their conclusions were consistent with the temper of the times. World population had reached 4 billion with ever-increasing numbers being added, so that the dire prophecies of Malthus may have been delayed, but seemed now to be a reality. Famines, as severe as the one that struck the Sahel in Africa, would become frequent and involve more people until it became a permanent global condition. Added to all of this was a rising chorus of concerns about various forms of environmental contamination and destruction. Many argued that the enterprise of being human was about to enter resource bankruptcy unless it was saved by conversion to small-is-beautiful new age ideologies and pursuits. The most frequently cited villain was technology. The irony of these dire forecasts of resource exhaustion was that they came at the end of a period in which the known reserves of most minerals had increased substantially. It is true that population growth rates were increasing during this period. But it was also true that birth rates were falling at record rates of decline and that the cause of global population increase was a dramatic and unprecedented decline in death rates. Despite record rates of population growth, food supply was growing even more rapidly, thereby raising world per capita food consumption. Per capita income was also growing throughout the globe. *The Limits to Growth* study was based on 1970 data and presumably should have reflected the sizeable increases in known mineral reserves that had accompanied the rapid increase in world industrialisation and resource use. From the late 1940s to the late 1960s, reserves of iron ore increased 122.1 per cent, manganese 27 per cent, chromite 675 per cent, copper 179 per cent, and lead 115 per cent.[19]

In the 1960s and 1970s, it was consistently found that the real price of most minerals had been falling throughout this century when measured in either the price of labour or in per cent of total labour and total capital involved in extractive industries.[20] In 1986, the cost of all metal raw material for all uses came to $80 per peson.[21] Similarly, the long-term trends of real food costs and food as a proportion of individual budgets showed a sustained downward movement, even despite the short-term upward movement of the early 1970s. In short, by all measures of scarcity, traditional or non-traditional, virtually all items in the class of economic inputs called land and natural resources were becoming less scarce and not more scarce, as had been predicted by the classical economists and echoed by contemporary catastrophists.

Not all of those who were forecasting a "new era of limits" were blind to the data. It was recognised that technology had rather consistently found new resources as we were seemingly running out of old ones. It was also recognised by some that food production had been growing faster than population and that generally standards of living had been increasing. But as the refrain went, we were living off capital and not income, since we were rapidly drawing down precious stocks of resources that had been slowly accumulated by natural processes. The very accelerated growth in well-being that was conceded was an acceleration in resource depletion that would bring us to limits within which we must learn to live. If such limits are exceeded, an inevitable decline of civilisation will follow.

Others argued that growth since Second World War was historically atypical (which it certainly was in so far as rapidity of change) and that this growth was the result of a fortuitous confluence of favourable events. In agriculture and food supply, for example, there were the "green revolutions" in wheat and rice, there was a run of favourable weather, the price of petroleum for fertiliser and energy was cheap and often falling, and there were still virgin fertile lands to bring under cultivation. These were all one-time conditions, the benefits of which were now realised and were unlikely to be replicated. Similar fortuitous one-time only events were postulated to explain our overall economic fortune. Petroleum had provided an era of cheap energy that explained so much of our well-being, and its presumed imminent depletion presaged the closing of an era. The party, we were told, was over. Thus, while some used bad news to forecast economic catastrophe, others used good news to portend the same outcome. In the literature of the mid-1970s, however, doomsday was forecast; there was an immediacy and an overwhelming sense of urgency for virtually instantaneous change in mental outlook, patterns of behaviour, and economic policy.

The question remains whether or not we did make a historic transition in the 1970s because these one-time fortuitous circumstances were exhausted. As the accompanying table shows, from 1975 to 1985, most known mineral reserves increased, some rather substantially. Even for some that have experienced sizeable decline, the explanatory reason are definitely not resource exhaustion. Tin, which shows the largest decline, has just experienced a virtual collapse of its market. Mines are being closed in Malaysia and Thailand, and Bolivia may exit the market entirely because capacity and production far exceed demand. Given that Brazil is emerging rapidly as a major, if not dominant, producer, it is not at all clear whether the data reflect the full extent of Brazil's known resources.

After Second World War, many were fearful of exhausting high grade iron ore deposits. Since iron is the fourth largest constituent in the earth's crust or 5 per cent of the crust by weight, there was never fear of exhausting it, only that lower grade ores would make the price prohibitive. Because of pelletization and other technological changes and the finding of new reserves, iron ore reserves substantially increased between World War II and the early 1970s. The apparent decline in reserves comes at a time when, at every stage of the process, from ore production to iron and steel, there is considerable excess capacity. More significantly, the relative importance of iron and steel is decreasing with the emergence of ceramics, composites, other metals, and a variety of speciality materials.

Table 22.1: Mineral and Reserves

	Reserves			
Mineral Name	*1975*	*1976*	*1985*	*(% based on year 1975)*
Bauxite	17 B/T	24 B/T	23.2 B/T	+ 36%
Chromium	1.9 B/T	2.9 B/T	7.5 B/T	+ 294%
Cobalt	2.7 M/T	2.9 M/T	9.2 M/T	+240%
Columbium	22 M/P	22 B/P	9.1 B/P	–58%
Copper	450 M/T	506 M/T	525 M/T	+17%
Ilmenite	580 M/T	771 M/T	734 M/T	+26%
Iron Core	259 B/T	255 B/T	206 B/T	–20%
Lead	160 M/T	160 M/T	143 M/T	–10%
Manganese	6 B/T	6 B/T	12 B/T	+100%
Molybdenum	13 B/P	19.1 B/P	25.9 B/P	+99%
Nickel	60 M/T	61 M/T	111 M/T	+85%
Phosphate Rock	18 B/T	20 B/T	34 B/T	+88%
Platinum-Group Metals	561 M/O	560 M/O	1.2 B/O	+114%
Rare-Earth Metals	7.7 M/T	7.7 M/T	48 M/T	+523%
Rutile	13.7 M/T	37 M/T	133.4 M/T	+881%
Tantalum	110 M/P	130 M/P	76 M/P	–30%
Tin	10.2 M/T	10.2 M/T	3 M/T	–70%
Tungsten	3.9 B/P	4 B/P	3.5 M/T	–10%
Vanadium	21.4 B/P	21.4 B/P	36.5 B/P	+70%
Zinc	150 M/T	175 M/T	300 M/T	+100%

B/T = Billions of Tons M/T = Millions of Tons B/P = Billions of Pounds
M/P = Millions of Pounds B/O = Billions of Ounces M/O = Millions of Ounces

Source: For 1975 and 1976—*Commodity Data Summaries*, Bureau of Mines, United States Department of the Interior, 1976 & 1977; for 1986—*Mineral Commodity Summaries*, Bureau of Mines, United States Department of the Interior.

Using price as a measure of scarcity, we find that all categories of commodities, minerals, and various types of agricultural outputs have experienced, with few exceptions, decade-by-decade declines in real prices, so that the mid-1980s real prices for all categories are lower than they were in 1950.[22] The last decade fluctuations were such that the 1984 index of commodity prices in U.S. dollars was lower than in any year since 1976. In real terms, the measured decline was even greater, even allowing for the strong dollar as a measuring stick.[23] From 1980 to 1985, prices of metals decreased 30 per cent, while the overall index of commodities fell 24 per cent. "Moreover, real commodity prices so far in the 1980s have averaged about 16 per cent below the average for the 1970s and in 1985 were about 20 per cent below the average for 1960-1980."[24] Even if we question the faith that some mainstream economists have in price as the sole and absolute measure of scarcity, it is difficult to imagine the mechanism that would allow for these declines in prices in the world of increasing scarcity described by the limits-to-growth theorists. After all, an element of their prophecies that should not be forgotten is the higher real price we would have to pay for everything.

If there is one characteristic that tends to define the world's commodity markets, it is overcapacity and oversupply. World food production in 1985 set a new record, as it has for approximately thirty of the past thirty-five years. The record was both for total and for per capita production. Production in 1986 may be off somewhat, but still the problem in most parts of the world (except for Africa) is low prices and huge, unsold and presumably unsaleable mounds of surpluses of foodstuffs. Even in Africa, some countries such as Zimbabwe are accumulating surpluses of hard-to-sell, coarse grains. Asia, a region we have traditionally identified with poverty, hunger, and famine, is becoming a surplus food producer, even allowing for rising levels of domestic consumption because of rapidly rising incomes.[25] Asia is also the region we generally consider to be at the limits of environmental carrying capacity. Asia, more than almost any other area in the third world, has "created land" by increasing yields in existing areas far more than it has created land by bringing new lands under cultivation. If there is hunger in the world—and so there is, in abundance, even in wealthy countries—it is because of maldistribution of food, not insufficient global production. Hunger has always been with us, but today it is more rare, even though it receives much well-deserved media coverage. Hunger continues to exist today, not for the reasons predicted a decade ago—namely, that we were on an unsustainable consumption binge—but because we have not yet found a way to provide to everyone the capacity to earn sufficient income to obtain what is generally available.[26]

The metals markets are still suffering from overcapacity, even though there have been systematic closings of mines and production facilities in many metals. As this is being written, the real price index for metals (in a basket of currencies) is less than 80 per cent of what it was in 1980.[27] Losses for some traders on the London Metal Exchange have been heavy. "Copper consumption seems set to decline by 2 per cent during this year, while mine production is rising."[28] Ironically, the main hope from the perspective of the producers is that the low prices, having led to reduced exploration, will in time give rise to shortages.[29] Cobalt, which had risen to $50 per pound on the spot market in 1978 (because of political disruptions in Zaire), had fallen to $3.70 in August 1986 before rebounding to $6 per pound with some help from an attempt at cartelisation by Zaire and Zambia.[30] Even the $6 price may be difficult to sustain because world production capacity is about 50 per cent greater than demand.

It is close to a decade and a half since *The Limits to Growth* was published and well over two decades since catastrophic predictions of reaching limits became popular beliefs, yet no empirical evidence has yet emerged to support the thesis. In fact, the preponderance of evidence is pointing in the other direction. Since the surface area of the globe and the concentration of minerals in its crust are fixed (except for possible minuscule geological changes), the primary explanation for the increase in resources and output is technology. Studies such as *The Limits to Growth* were sufficiently specific in their forecasts that the data already available falsify a significant portion of them. Nobody could have accepted any portion of the doomsday literature of the 1960s and 1970s and believed that in the mid-1980s the world would be in surplus in most commodity productions. Yet, though less shrill in tone, the belief in declining resource availability and in the limits to the earth's carrying capacity still predominate in the media. No matter how overwhelmingly the march of time emphatically refutes doomsday forecasts, there remains that lingering belief that good fortune has allowed us to delay the seemingly inevitable. But our luck will not last for ever, and the inevitable will inevitably arrive.

A concept of fixed, finite resources provides the mindset that allows people to refuse to accept evidence of decreasing resource scarcity.

The institutional theory of resource creation provides the necessary framework for correctly understanding the evidence. It is the only theoretical perspective that allowed us to forecast the trends of the post-World War II period. If some mainstream economists in recent years have joined the bandwagon, so much the better. However, it should be clear that, though mainstream economics can explain short-term trends by techniques such as substitution and increasing efficiency, their basic theory of finite resources does not allow for indefinite resource expansion. If some economists are now using the term "resource creation", then we should cheer and remind them of its origin. Similarly, the concept of "land augmentation" is another way of speaking of science and technology creating resources. Touting the institutionalist origins of such significant concepts is not for some purpose of creating intellectual property rights. Its purpose is to show the strength and power of a body of ideas. For whether or not humans have the food and other raw materials to continue the process of civilisation is no small matter. The world has experienced a global revolution in food production, population growth, death rate decline, life expectancy increase, and per capita income increases of unprecedented proportions—all of which was understandable and predicted in institutional theory. If unmet need exists despite overproduction and overcapacity, then the problem is one of creating purchasing power, as institutionalists have long argued.[31] A body of theory with this strength should reasonably be called upon to formulate the policies that will allow the continuation of resource creation and civilisational advance.

Technology and Resource Creation: Arable Land and Mineral Resource Creation

Land as a human resource is created by technology (and science) in the same manner as minerals become resources. The first tools that allowed people to hunt and to harvest the land more intensely increased the resource character of that land. Stone tools that permitted early man to dig out roots from the rock-hard savanna soils made those roots into a human resource, and, with the domestication of plants, some of the wet, insect-invested river bottoms acquired the potential to be agricultural land. Agriculture created arable land.

The history of human migration and settlement is a history of people creating arable land by devising new means and new technologies to produce food. Theodore Schultz has long argued that some of the world's best agricultural land once had poor soil. "The original soils of Western Europe, except for the Po Valley and some parts of England and France, were in general very poor in quality. As farmland, these soils are now highly productive." To Schultz, the inherent qualities of soils do not explain why agriculture is outstanding in some parts of the world and poor in others. He maintains that "a substantial part of the productivity of farmland is man-made by investments in land improvements."[32] N.W. Pirie voices essentially the same idea, that "good farmland is usually created by skilled farming."[33]

There are many ways of creating new land. Bringing uncultivated land into production is only one. Irrigation cannot only bring cultivation to arid lands, it can also frequently add a second or third crop season to the agriculture of a region. Breeding crops with shorter growing seasons, allowing for an extra crop, is yet another way. Research has been, and continues to be, carried out to find or breed crops that are more tolerant of salt or can withstand the stress of acidity from aluminium-toxic soils. Biotechnology and other new breeding techniques give promise that not only will current trends be sustained, but that in the future they may even accelerate.[34]

A hundred-year decline in the real price of food is likely to continue. Clifford Lewis notes that "despite the weakness of data about global food trends, it is clear that global food production has grown at a generally increasing rate since the early decades of the 19th century and has consistently outstripped increases in global population." Lewis' data shows that the real price of wheat (in 1967 dollars) fell from $3.09 in 1890 to $2.10 in 1960 to $1.10 in 1982. There have been "temporary disruptions" in this downward trend, but they have been "when peace has not prevailed."[35]

The frontiers of technological research are as promising for the creation of new material resources as they are for the creation of land. Materials science is emerging as a prime area of research, as new technologies in every area of endeavour have performance demands that require material with specific qualities. Minerals previously little used are becoming vital to technological processes. Our ability to process these minerals is advancing as rapidly as the new materials that we are creating. Silicon chips, fibre optics, and ceramics have turned raw material long in vast abundance into major resources. One of the problems with the metals market is in fact that these new "resources" are substituting for traditional ones, such as copper, decreasing the demand for them. In the case of fibre optics, the new material performs its task better, more efficiently, more reliably, and at a far lower material resource cost.

Even without new and improved technologies for resource utilisation, there are additions to resource reserves because of new finds. The process of resource discovery is also subject to scientific and technological advances. Advances in geology, such as plate tectonics, and in geography give us new understanding of how various ores are formed, sorted, and where they are likely to be found. Remote sensing from satellites has added new dimensions to mapping and discovering minerals, though at times it is easier to be more enthusiastic about the potentials of remote sensing than is yet warranted by the data. Airborne and ground surveys, using a variety of technologies, aid in the search for new material sources.

Contrary to the pessimists, not only is technological change continuing, but the rate of change itself is accelerating.[36] Unchanging technology is resource-using. Changing technology is resource-creating. The history of technology and human societies today testify to these basic conditions. Thus, the growth in resources and the decline in their real price are not fortuitous, or accidental, or temporary, or paradoxical, but fundamental to the process of technological change. Because it is fundamental, it is reasonable to believe that the continued advances in science and technology, which everyone expects to occur, will create the resources necessary to sustain it. Furthermore, if the process is not entirely automatic, we can use our intelligence to structure the process so that we realise the full resource-creating potential of technological change.

The Life Process and the Conditions of Life

In the discourse on institutional economics, particularly in the writings of Veblen and Ayres, reference was made to the life process. Institutional economics was evolutionary economics drawing inspiration from the late nineteenth century post-Darwin period, rather than from the static conceptions of the eighteenth century. It is interesting that many of the current theories on life's origins make these references more appropriate than could be realised at the time. The first life forms "fed" on already existing organic matter, using it in chemical fermentation for life-sustaining energy. Clearly, there was a limited resource, as life was "consuming" organic matter faster than it was being created. Later, procaryotes would evolve photosynthesis, a new energy source that overcame the original resource constraint. Similar to human problem-solving endeavours, the solving of one problem creates new ones. The oxygen that was earlier being given off was creating an ozone layer that was shielding out the ultraviolet light that was creating organic food. To anaerobic procaryotes, moreover, oxygen was a deadly pollutant. Fortunately for us, eucaryotes evolved that were more efficient in energy use and were aerobic.[37]

To the extent that this scenario is correct, then the conditions (that is, the resources) for life as we know it did not exist; they were created by the evolution of life itself. The solution of some problems created others, but still we can understand problem-solving in an expanded energy-opportunity context. At anyone point, "resources" are fixed and finite, and life seems doomed either to exhaust resources or to succumb to its own waste. The process that we are describing is one of emergent evolution. Had there been some kind of intelligence operating in or observing the early procaryotes, it would have proclaimed the limits to growth and the end of life. All logic and reasoning lead to one inevitable conclusion—death. Absolutely nothing in the situation could yield to any inquiry the hope for continuity. It is only after the transformation has occurred that one can begin to understand the process.

The same can be said for hunting and gathering humans. A widely respected thesis is that hunters and gatherers had reached the limits of their potential, creating a food crisis.[38] Where a growing population of hunters and gatherers are pushing the limits of the environment, there is again nothing that an intelligent observer could find in the situation that offered any escape from self-destruction. It is only in retrospect that we can understand the resource creating power of technology.

Having observed these and other processes, we can derive a theory of technological change and of the types of resource creation and other forms of novelty that emerge. This is, of course, part of what evolutionary economics is all about. It is a theory that, at least in outline form, helps us to understand the process and therefore to have an understanding of emerging possibilities. It clearly should make us aware that resources are not fixed and finite, and they definitely are not natural. As long as we do not run out of ideas, then we are not likely to run out of resources.

The assumption of fixed, finite resources has caused many to make catastrophic predictions of resource exhaustion. Fortunately, where these prophesies have been sufficiently specific to be testable, the passage of time and events has falsified them. It has been my argument in several papers that the technologies the prophets offered as resource-conserving in fact would create the problem they claimed to be solving. Living within limits is inherently self-defeating, as the above illustrations demonstrate. Another principle, entropy, has been offered into the argument and guarantees decline.

The life processes and the technological process form an enclave of negative entropy. Energy is taken from a source (that is, the sun) that would be experiencing increasing entropy in any case, and is used to build order and complexity (negative entropy). It is interesting that among the earliest recorded and recovered legends is that of ancient Sumerians and Babylonians about the separation of land from water, order from chaos. This legend celebrates the human achievement of negative entropy and the creation of arable land resources. Throughout the ancient Middle East and on into Greek and Roman culture was the basic proposition that was later expressed as *nihil ex nihilo*—out of nothing comes nothing. Creation out of nothing was impossible. Our idea of resource creation is consistent with that usage. Creation of resources is the creation of order out of chaos, the imposition of our ideas and will upon pre-existing substances.

The dynamic resource-creating power of technology has been central to evolutionary economic thought. It is ironic that mainstream economics has borrowed some modest semblance of this theory, or at least its conclusion, to counter the limits on growth theorists or the catastrophists. We might be wise to follow Ayres' lead and use this opening to raise more fundamental questions. If resources are not fixed but created, then the nature of the scarcity problem changes dramatically. For the technological means involved in the use of resources determines their creation and therefore the extent of the scarcity. The nature of the scarcity is not outside the process (that is, natural), but a condition of it.

Understanding the creative powers of technologies can be infectious to other areas of economic thought. Of the many definitions of capital, technology has to be a key component if we are to comprehend the dynamics of economic change. The other factor, labour, is increasingly addressed, not as a raw unit of measure of other things, but as human capital. Knowledge and skills, the very essence of technology and resource creation, are receiving attention for their critical role in the development process. Even entrepreneurship is about someone allegedly having a better idea.

Technology and Resource Creation: A Liberating Idea

Technology as ideas and as the creator of resources is not only correct, it is also liberating. It provides a conceptual basis for understanding the fact that the resource base of civilisation has expanded, not contracted, with use. It gives us the kind of operational understanding necessary to frame the policies to sustain this resource-creating process. It provides a reasonable basis for optimism that the human endeavour can continue and can expand. It is, finally, the key component of a structure that challenges traditional ways of thought about the economy and opens new possibilities for creative inquiry and dialogue.

A little over two centuries ago, Adam Smith had a series of liberating ideas. The very title of his magnum opus, *An Inquiry into the Nature of Causes of the Wealth of Nations*, argues for the liberating idea that all nations can prosper and that nations need not impoverish their neighbour in order to succeed. He defined wealth as the annual produce of a nation, not merely of its sovereign. And he defined a relationship through markets by which those who participated in economic activity were supposed to be beneficiaries of it. Smith was inquiring into the causes of wealth in his economy, yet in reality he was in the first ferment of an industrial transformation that was to give concrete meaning to his liberal idea.

The idea of scarcity, which some conceive to be the fundamental organising principal of economics, is a static concept and is counter to the liberating potential of Smith's ideas. To the extent that some see scarcity as based upon the principles of nature, then we are back to the concept of fixed, finite resources. The theory of technology as resource creating is dynamic. It removes scarcity as an organising principle of economic inquiry. While it may be true that we do not have infinite resources from which to choose and to allocate, neither are we dealing with fixed resources. They are finite but unbounded. The very economic/technological processes that use "scarce" resources are also creating them; as we have argued, this historic process of allocating, and using, has created far more than it has used. If we define efficiency according to scarcity then we are dealing with a closed system. If we define efficiency according to the technology of resource creation, then we are describing and creating the conditions for an open-ended process.

The resource-creating power of technology is a never-ending problem solving process. It is a process by which people make choices and have even greater opportunities to make choices. By implication, the idea that problem solving continues indefinitely means that there will always be problems around to be solved. The critics of modern technology have confused using resources with using them up and see the existence of resource problems as an argument against modern technology. The simple fact is that without technology, there are no resources and therefore no resource problems. But the resource problems of human existence will only be terminated with the ending of the human endeavour itself. So-called alternate technologies that are resource conserving but not resource creating engender more problems than they solve.[39]

The biggest resource problems that technology creates are the hypothetical ones. The empirical argument that begins "if present trends continue" can inevitably demonstrate a future crisis if technology is held constant.[40] To counter that technology has historically made resources more available does not necessarily address the specifics of future resources needs and opportunities. Very simply, we can learn much from the historic process of technology that allows us to predict many aspects of the future course of events, as well as to plan and take action to make those events more favourable to the human enterprise.

Since we have described the process as one of emergent evolution, then, there are emergent possibilities that we cannot predict. Further, if the thesis is held true that we create the conditions of our existence, it is equally true that we can destroy the conditions of our existence. This has always been the case; it is only in modern times that it has been dramatically obvious. Of course we can do it in many ways. The one most frequently noted is to destroy ourselves with nuclear weapons. Out of fear of the unknown future, we can also do it by failing to carry forward resource-creating technology that is the basis for the sustainability of human civilisation. It is our destiny to choose our future, not to choose is itself a choice as the existentialists have told us. What Albert Camus said about the individual is true for humankind: the most important choice we face is whether or not to commit suicide. Camus meant this as an affirmation, "as a lucid invitation to live and to create, in the very midst of the desert."[41] Similarly, we can understand technology transfer and economic development as a collective affirmation of the worth of life and the life process.

Technology, resource creation and emergent evolution engender not a world of unknown future but of emerging possibilities. Our destiny is not in being but in becoming. We as humans have turned adversaries into allies. What greater threat was there to primate life and habitat than fire? Yet fire was controlled and turned into a tool for converting ores into metals (that is, making clay into pottery and other dirts into ores) and for making the cold climates fit for human life. Ergot, a plant disease that threatens human life, is now used as a cure for migraines. Poisons from plants have been turned into life-saving or supporting drugs. The list is endless, and so is the future potential of humankind. Those who would turn us aside out of some fictitious fear of resource exhaustion would protect us from the dangers of the unknown but would also deny us its possibilities. The liberating idea of technology and resource creation is the human potential that is there, if we are aware of it and if we frame our policies accordingly. We will exhaust resource if we exhaust creative imagination. Technology as ideas and resource creation means that Descartes was more correct that he could possibly imagine when he said *cogito ergo sum*, that is, I think therefore I am. We think therefore we are and, more importantly, can be.

NOTES

1. Quote from Erich Zimmermann, *World Resources and Industries* (New York: Harper & Bros, 1951) p. 15.
2. C.E. Ayres, *The Theory of Economic Progress* (Chapel Hill, N.C.: The University of North Carolina Press, 1943), p. 113.
3. One can find instances throughout human history of conservation and the protection of other species. Far more prevalent has been the wanton destruction of the environment and other life forms. As I argue in my book. *A Theory of Technology*, modern science and technology have created the understanding and conditions that have fostered the current wildlife and conservationist movements. Thomas R. De Gregori, *A Theory of Technology Continuity and Change in Human Development* (Ames, Iowa: Iowa State University Press, 1985).
4. Ayres, *The Theory of Economic Progress*, p. 113.
5. Theodore Schultz, *Transforming Traditional Agriculture* (New Haven, Conn.: Yale University Press, 1964), is seen by many as the seminal work on science-based agriculture that generated a vast amount of empirical, theoretical, and applied work in world agriculture.
6. Wesley C. Mitchell, "Conservation, Liberty and Economics," in *The Foundations of Conservation Education* (New York: National Wildlife Federation, 1941), p.1.
7. Zimmermann, *World Resources and Industries*, p. 129.
8. De Gregori, *A Theory of Technology*, pp. 9-13.
9. *Ibid*., p. 12. The thesis used here is derived primarily from the work of Sherwood Washburn.

10. Mitchell, "Conservation, Liberty, and Economics," quoted in p.1, Zimmermann, *World Resources and Industries*, p. 9. See also Robert C. Cowen, "Minerals: Breaking the Import Habit, Part 2: Knowledge, the Essential Raw Material," in *The Christian Science Monitor*, 12 January 1982, pp. 12-13.
11. Isaac Asimov, *A Choice of Catastrophes: The Disasters that Threaten Our World* (New York: Simon and Schuster, 1979), p. 291. Asimov notes that the word *metal* comes from the Greek, "to reach for," (p. 294), which is what humans do with metals and other resources; they reach for a better way of life.
12. *Resources for Freedom*. Communication from the President of United States. Transmitting the Report of the President's Materials Policy Commission, June 1952, Washington D.C.: U.S. Government Printing Office, 1952. Five volumes, Doc. 527, 82nd Congress, 2nd Session.
13. *Ibid.*, Vol. 1, *Foundations for Growth and Security*, p. 1.
14. *Ibid.* As in Dickens' *A Tale of Two Cities*, "It was the best of times, it was the worst of times ... in short, the period was so far like the present period."
15. Jeremy Rifkin, *Entropy: A New World View* (New York: Viking, 1980).
16. Kirkpatrick Sale, *Human Scale* (New York: Coward. McCann and Geoghigan), 1980.
17. J.B.S. Haldane, "On Being the Right Size." In J.B.S. Haldane, *Possible Worlds* (New York: Harper & Row), 1928.
18. Donella H. Meadows *et. al.*, *The Limits to Growth: A Report for the Club of Rome's Project on the Predicament of Mankind* (New York: Universe Books), 1974.
19. DeGregori, *A Theory of Technology*, p. 61. Data are derived from J.S. Carman, *Obstacles to Mineral Development* (New York: Pergamon Press), 1979. Detailed data on population growth and food supply can be found in DeGregori, *A Theory of Technology*, Chap. 9, pp. 114-22 and p. 49.
20. H.J. Barnett and C. Morse, *Scarcity and Growth: The Economic of Natural Resource Availability* (Baltimore: Johns Hopkins University Press for Resources for the Future, 1963), and William Nordhaus, "Resources as a Constraint on Growth," *American Economic Review* 64 (May 1974): 22-26.
21. Max Singer, "How Dependent is the U.S. on Strategic Minerals?" *The Wall Street Journal*, 14 August 1986.
22. *World Development Report 1986* (New York: Oxford University Press for the World Bank, 1986), p. 7.
23. *World Economic Outlook*, April 1986, Washington, D.C.: International Monetary Fund 1986, pp. 139-45.
24. *Ibid.*, pp. 139 and 141.
25. Leonard A. Pauleno, *Food in the Third World: Past Trends and Projection to 2000* (Washington, D.C.: International Food Policy Research Institute) Research Report 52, June 1986, pp. 41-42. Late projections for some food crops, such as wheat, hold the possibility that 1985/1986 may also set the records. Andrew Gowers, "World Harvest Record Forecast," *Financial*

Times (London), 10 December 1986. And *World Agricultural Supply and Demand Estimates*, (WASDE-200), United States Department of Agriculture, Economic Research Service, Foreign Agricultural Service, 10 December 1986.

26. See Nicholas Eberstadt and Clifford M. Lewis, "How Many Are Hungry? *The Atlantic*, May 1986, pp: 34-38, for an analysis of current greater food availability. See also Irma Adelman, "A Poverty-Focused Approach to Development," in *Development Strategies Reconsidered*, ed. John P. Lewis and Valeriana Kallab (New Brunswick, N.J.: Transaction Books, 1986), pp. 52-53, for data showing that the proportion of the world's population living below the poverty level fell from 39.8 per cent to 22.4 per cent between 1950 and 1980, even though inequality was increasing.
27. *Financial Times* (London), 4 November 1986.
28. *The Economic* (London), 4 October 1986, p. 75.
29. *Ibid.*
30. *Financial Times* (London), 20 November 1986.
31. See for example Louis Uchitelle, "A Worldwide Glut Crisis," *The New York Times*, 17 December 1986.
32. Theodore W. Schultz, Lectures in Agricultural Economics, Washington, D.C.: Economic Services Bicentennial Lecture Series Committee, 1917, pp. 16-17.
33. N.W. Pirie, "The World Food Supply: Physical Limitations," in *Reading From Futures: A Collection of Articles From the Journal Futures*, ed. R. Jones (Guilford Surrey, England: Westbury House, 1981), p. 305.
34. DeGregori, *A Theory of Technology*, Chap. 10.
35. C. Lewis, "Global Food Security: A Manageable Problem," *Development Digest*, 21 (July 1983): 106-121, at pp. 106, 107. See also Per Pinstrup-Anderson and Peter B.R. Hazell, "The Impact of the Green Revolution and Prospects for the Future," *Food Reviews International* 1(1985): 1-25, and Frederick H. Buttel, Martin Kenney and Jack Klopperburg, Jr., "From Green Revolution to Biorevolution: Some Observations in the Third World," *Economic Development and Cultural Change* 34 (October 1985): 31-55.
36. John H. Lienhard, "Some Ideas About Growth and Quality in Technology," *Technological Forecasting and Social Change* 27 (1985): 265-81.
37. DeGregori, *A Theory of Technology*, pp. 3-9. These conclusions are drawn from many authors and reflect no individual inquiry by me.
38. Mark Nathan Cohen, *The Food Crisis in Prehistory: Overpopulation and the Origins of Agriculture*, New Haven, Conn.: Yale University Press, 1977.
39. On the rather limited gains from "appropriate" technologies, see R.S. Eckaus. "Appropriate Technology: The Movement Has Only a Few Clothes On." *Issues in Science and Technology* 3 (Winter 1987): 62-71.
40. In fact, it can be argued using data from work such as that of Lienhard, that historically, trends are more sustainable than the particular

technologies driving them. For example, for any major endeavour today, such as computation or information transfer, it is clear that the trends over the last forty years were absurd or scientifically impossible and not sustainable under the known technologies of the time. That today we have such capabilities, or even greater capabilities, is the result of emergent possibilities of new technologies. Just since the completion of this article, developments on superconductivity have occurred that promise to greatly increase the resource character of barium, yttrium, and possibly lanthanum. Most of the material composites having superconductivity are ceramics, which are relatively cheap. Increasing efficiency in the transmission and use of electricity, will also increase the resource character of the "stuffs" used to create electricity. All these factors will contribute to a continuing expansion in resources and a downward movement in real prices—and as problems of application are overcome, we will find new uses and unexpected possibilities for development.

41. Albert Camus, *The Myth of Sisyphus and Other Essays* (New York: Vintage Books), 1953, p. v.

23

Application of Aerial Photo Interpretation to Resource Studies

K.K. RAMPAL

Aerial Photo: An aerial photo is a record of the earth's surface at the instant of camera exposure taken by an aerial camera mounted in an aircraft flying at a certain height above the surface of the earth (Fig. 23.1). The photo is called vertical or oblique (See Fig. 23.2) depending upon the inclination of the camera axis. If this axis is vertical (within ±3°) we call it vertical photography. If the angle between the vertical direction and the camera axis is more than 45° and the horizon appears in photo, we call it 'high oblique photo', otherwise it is called 'low oblique photo'. Both vertical and oblique photos can be used for the purpose of the photo interpretation.

The most important part of the aerial photo is the 'scale' of the photo and is given by the ratio of the focal length of the camera and the height of the camera above the terrain. Thus, if a photo is taken with a camera of focal length 150 mm and the height of the camera above the terrain (called flying height) is 3000 metres, the scale of the photo is:

$$\text{Scale} = \frac{150 \text{ mm}}{3000 \text{ m}} = \frac{150 \text{ mm}}{3000 \times 1000 \text{ mm}} = \frac{1}{20{,}000}$$

The information content of an aerial photo is inversely proportional to the scale; larger the scale smaller is the area covered on the ground and, hence, lesser is the information content. However, the resolution, that is, the smallest distance or size of the object that can be identified by human eye, is directly proportional to the scale. Larger the scale more clearly the object can be identified for the purpose of photo interpretation work.

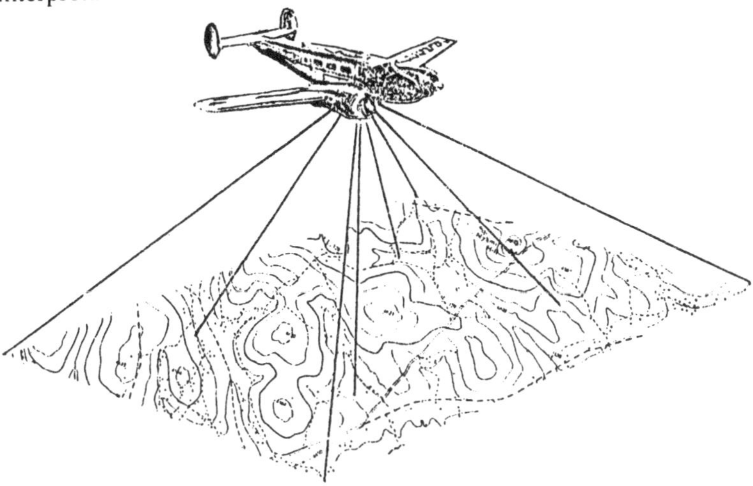

Fig. 23.1: Aerial Photo is a record of the earth's surface at the instant of Camera exposure.

Fig. 23.2: An oblique aerial photo. Notice the convergence of parallel roads.

Aerial photo are generally available in two sizes, i.e., 9″ × 9″ and 6″ × 6″. This, however, is linked to the focal length of the camera. The photo format is described in respect of the angle subtended by the photo diagonal at the centre of the camera. Thus, if the photo size is 220 mm × 220 mm and the focal length of the camera is 150 mm the total angle subtended by the diagonal namely 110 × √2 mm at the centre of the lens is 90°. The photos are called 'Normal' angle, or 'Wide angle' or 'Superwide' angle depending upon whether the angle is 60°, 90° or 120°. The wide angle aerial photography has found much more use these days on account of certain facilities.

An aerial photo differs from a map due to certain inherent defects. The scale of a map is constant whereas the scale of an aerial photo differs from point to point. Unless it is taken with perfect vertical camera axis and of perfectly flat terrain the scale always varies. The variation of scale in an aerial photo is due what are called geometric deformations. The two major deformations are due to tilt of the photo and the variation of ground height. For the purpose of photo interpretation these deformation can be of certain advantages.

A pair of overlapping photos with 60 per cent overlap in the forward direction can be used to see the third dimension under a stereoscope (Fig. 23.3). Thus, the ground and other surface objects appear in their true height form. Similarly, a tilted photo not only covers more ground but can bring out certain perspectivity of the view for better interpretation.

In order to see a three-dimensional view of the ground a pair of overlapping aerial photos are placed below the stereoscope side by side. A stereoscope consists of two plane mirrors mounted on two supports which reflect the light on two eyes of the observer through two lenses fitted with two right angle prisms. This allows the left photo to be seen by left eye and right photo by right eye of the observer. In order to see the height of an object, its image is identified on the left photo and then the corresponding image on the right photo and then both the eyes see these two images as one. This may require adjustment of spacing between the two photos. At the beginning, an observer may see the images but after a little while the two images fuse into one bringing the third dimension, namely, the height into view. The stereoscopic depth, namely, seeing the third dimension depends upon the inter-ocular distance of the observer (the distance between the centres of the two eyes, the scale of the photo, the photo base. The shadows help to create this depth vision.

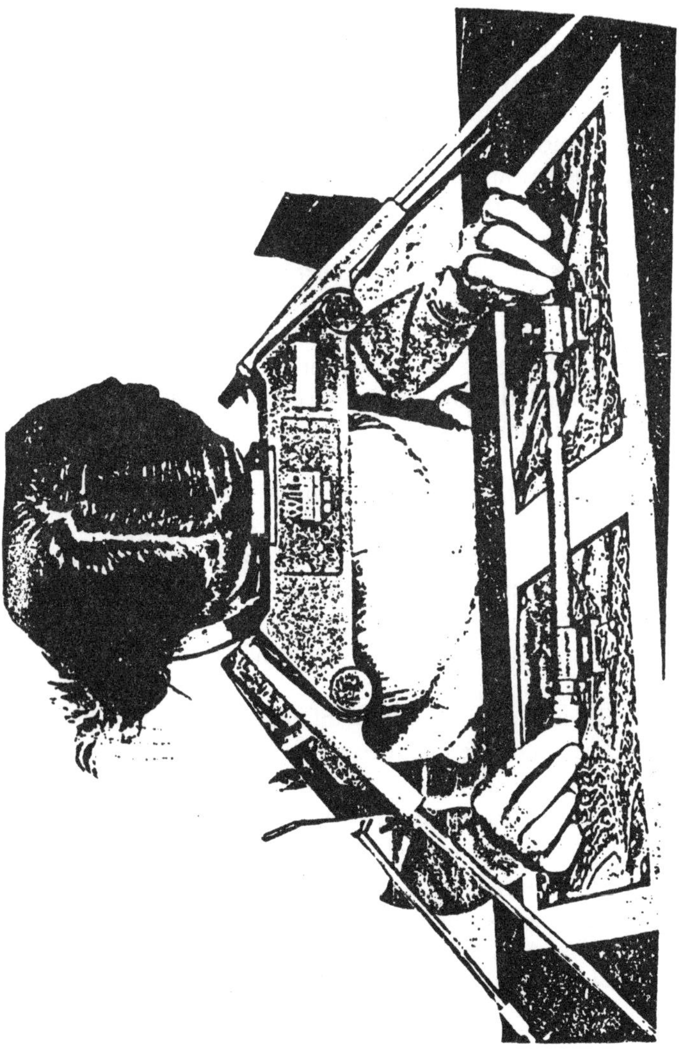

Fig. 23.3 A pair of aerial photos seen under a stereoscope and parallax bar for measurement of heights of terrain points.

Image Interpretation

Introduction

The remote-sensed imagery is recorded on CCTs (Computer Compatible Tapes) and on film. The interpretation can, therefore, be done quantitatively. The qualitative (non-digital) method is a man-photo system whereas the quantitative (Digital information) is a computer photo system. The man-photo system is based on human experience as a result of converging evidence obtained from several factors such as pattern recognition and elementary image interpretation techniques of tone, texture, size, shape, shadow, association, site and resolution considerations. On the other hand, computer-photo system is based on statistical analysis and other digital techniques such as auto-pattern recognition, multivariate analysis, discriminant function analysis and clustering analysis techniques whereas the man-photo system is limited to 3-dimensions the computer-photo system can be extended to n-dimensions.

Three-Dimensional Image Interpretation (Qualitative) Method

The basic requirement here is a set of overlapping imagery and a stereoscope to obtain a three-dimensional view of the terrain. Information about the object is then collected based on the following interpretation keys and other converging evidence:—

(i) *Tone*: Ground objects of different colour reflect the incident radiation differently depending upon the incident wavelength, physical and chemical constituents of the objects. The imagery as recorded in remote sensing is in different shades or tones. For example, ploughed and cultivated lands record differently from fallow fields. Tone is expressed qualitatively as light, medium and dark. In SLAR imagery, for example, the shadows cast by non-return of the microwaves appear darker than these parts where greater reflection takes place. These parts appear of lighter tone. Similarly, in thermal imagery objects at higher temperature are recorded of lighter tone compared to objects at lower temperature which appear of medium to darker tone. Similarly, top soil appears as of dark tone compared to soil containing quartz sand. The coniferous trees appear in lighter tone compared to broad leave tree clumps.

Table 23.1 gives the tonal ranges for different terrain factors such as topography, geology, vegetation, etc. for the reflectance characteristics and different tones as recorded in radar imagery.

(ii) *Texture*: Texture is an expression of roughness or smoothness as exhibited by the imagery. It is the rate of change of tonal values. Mathematically, it is given as $\frac{dD}{dx}$ and can be measured numerically by the use of micro-densitometer. Changes of density 'D' in going from point 'A' of the imagery to point 'B' (Fig. 23.4) as measured by the micro-densitometer divided by the distance gives the texture values numerically. Texture is dependent upon (a) photographic tone, (b) shape, (c) size and (d) pattern and scale of the imagery. Any slight variation of these can change the texture. Texture can qualitatively be expressed as course, medium and fine.

(iii) *Association*: The relation of a particular feature to its surroundings is an important key to interpretation. Sometimes a single feature by itself may not be distinctive enough to permit its identification. For example, sink holes appears as dark spots on as imagery whereas the surface or immediate subsurface soil consists of lime stones. Thus, the appearance of sink holes is always associated with surface limestone formation. Another example is that of kettle holes which appear as depressions on photos due to terminal moraines and glacial terrain.

(iv) *Shape*: Some ground features have typical shapes due to the structure or topography. For example, air fields and football stadium can be easily interpreted because of their finite ground shapes and geometry whereas volcanic covers sand, river terraces, cliffs, gullies can be identified because of their characteristics shape controlled by geology and topography.

(v) *Size*: The size of an image also helps for its identification whether it is relative or absolute. Sometimes the measurements of height (as by using parallax bar) also gives clues to the nature of the object. For example, measurement of height of different clumps of trees gives an idea of the

Table 23.1: Terrain Factors and Representative Tonal Ranges

	Factor	*Reflection Characteristic*	*Tonal Range*
1. *Topographic*			
(a)	Flat Surface	Specular Reflection if Surface is smooth: no return	Dark Tone
(b)	Sloping surface facing antenna/ camera	Relatively low return due to orientation effects	Medium to light tones
(c)	Sloping surface facing away from antenna or camera	Relatively low return due to orientation effects	Medium to dark tones
(d)	High relief	No return from shadow areas	Dark tones
2. *Geologic*			
(a)	Rough Surface	Diffused Reflection, medium to high return	Medium to light tones
(b)	Smooth surface	Specular reflection if surface is flat: no return reflection influenced by topographic factors	Dark tone, lighter tones produced by orientation effects
(c)	Natural corner reflectors produced by in bed rock by weathering	Maximum reflection, high return	Very light tones
3. *Vegetation*			
(a)	Trees	Diffuse Reflection	Light tones
(b)	Woods & Forests	High returns	Light tones
(c)	Bush	Higher returns with increasing dense of occurrence	Light tones in number in sub-humid areas medium to dark tone in arid areas environments
(d)	Natural Grass	Diffuse Reflection, medium to low returns, dry spares vegetation produces less scatter than lush rich-vegetation	Medium tones in humid to sub-humid areas. Dark tones in arid environment
(e)	Broad leaf crops with high moisture content	Diffuse Reflection high returns	Light tones
	Small leaf crops	Diffuse Reflection medium returns	Medium tones

different species, similarly the measurement of dip and strike of rocks formation help in identifying sedimentary formation. Similarly, the measurement of width of roads helps in discriminating roads of different categories, i.e., national, state, local etc. Size, of course, is dependent upon the scale of imagery.

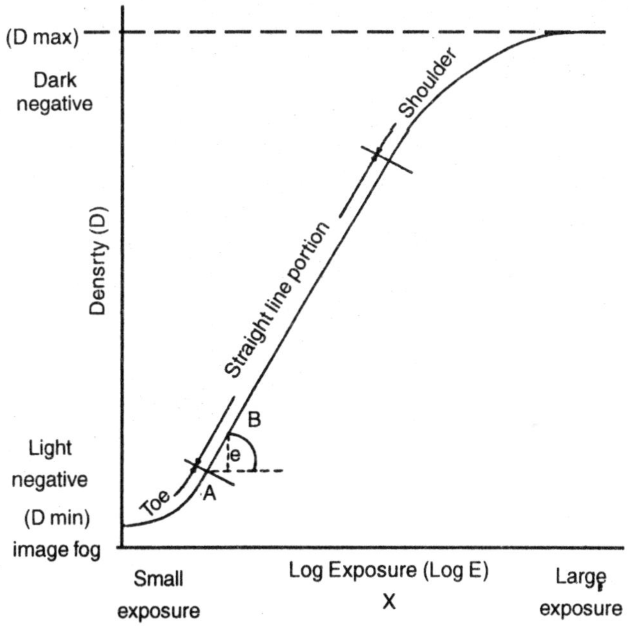

Fig. 23.4: Plot of Density 'D' versus log of exposure time in seconds. Density is the inverse of Transparency.

(vi) *Shadows*: Shadows cast by objects are sometimes important clues to their identification and interpretation. For example, shadow of a suspension bridge can easily be discriminated from that of cantilever bridge. Similarly, circular shadows are indicative of coniferous trees. Tall buildings and chimneys, and towers etc. can be easily identified for their characteristic shadows. Shadows, on the other hand, can sometimes render interpretation difficult, i.e., dark slope shadows covering important detail.

(vii) *Site Factor or Topographic Location*: Relative elevation or specific location of objects can be helpful to identify certain features. For example, sudden appearance or disappearance of vegetation is a good clue to the underlying soil type or drainage conditions.

(viii) *Pattern*: Pattern is the orderly spatial arrangement of geological, topographic or vegetation features. This spatial arrangement may be two-dimensional (plan view) or 3-dimensional (space).

Geological pattern may be linear or curved. Linear patterns are formed of a very large number of continuous or discontinuous short ticks which when viewed by eye appear to be continuous lines. Examples of linear geological pattern are faults, fractures, joints, dykes, bedding planes, anticlines, etc. (Fig. 23.5). Examples of curved features are plunging anticlines and folds (Fig. 23.6).

Lineament or lineations may be short, medium or long running for several hundred kilometres. These are very important expressions of the lithologic characters of the underlying rocks and the attitude of the rock bodies, spacing of planes of bedding and other structural weaknesses, and the control extended by their over the surface features.

Vegetation pattern may be of the 'Block' type or 'Alignment' type. The 'Alignment' type may be further subdivided into the Linear, Parallel and 'Curved' type. Example of Block type are the timber trees in Montana, U.S.A. due to extensive outcrop of rocks of uniform character, i.e., presence of unaltered quartz monozonite.Alignments are due to narrow rockbands or faults. Since faults retain moisture, vegetation is aligned along the fault lines.

Examples of topographic pattern are the typical drainage patterns (controlled and uncontrolled type). The uncontrolled type are those which are purely governed by topography, that is the slope whereas the controlled type are those which are governed by the underlying geological formations.

The well known drainage patterns are: (i) Dendritic, (ii) Trellis, (iii) Annular, (iv) Radial, (v) Rectangular, (vi) Parallel Type, (vii) Braided, (viii) Anastomatic, (ix) Asymmetrical, and (x) Collinear.

Fig. 23.5: Example of a linear fault traversing the whole and central part of the photo. As a result of faulting the left part is at a higher level.

Drainage patterns take an important place amongst the various interpretation elements, used as criteria for identification of geological and geomorphological phenomena. Factors to be considered are amongst other the density which is measure for the erodibility of the rocks; the amount of geological control on the drainage pattern and the integration and homogeneity of the pattern.

In alluvial terrains the anastomatic pattern (Fig. 23.7) of meandering streams, cut-off meanders, oxbow lakes and interlocking channels is the most common. The Yazoo pattern (Fig. 23.7) occurs if the natural levees of the trunk river force the tributaries to flow parallel to the main stream before debouching. The dichotomic pattern (Fig. 23.7) of radiating (centrifugal) drainage channels occurs in alluvial fans. Some channels may have a blind end because the water largely percolates into the coarse fan material. Other streams may then originate as springs in the lower part of the fan. Some deltas have a similar pattern. The braided pattern (Fig. 23.7) develops where excessive sedimentation occurs, e.g. due to a sudden decrease in gradient of the river which then is able to carry on its load. The sediments then force the river emerge from the mountains and enter the alluvial plain. The recticular pattern (Fig. 23.7) is a system of interconnected stream channels formed in coastal lowlands when tidal currents occur. Special drainage types are amongst other the deranged, phantom and internal lacunate patterns etc.

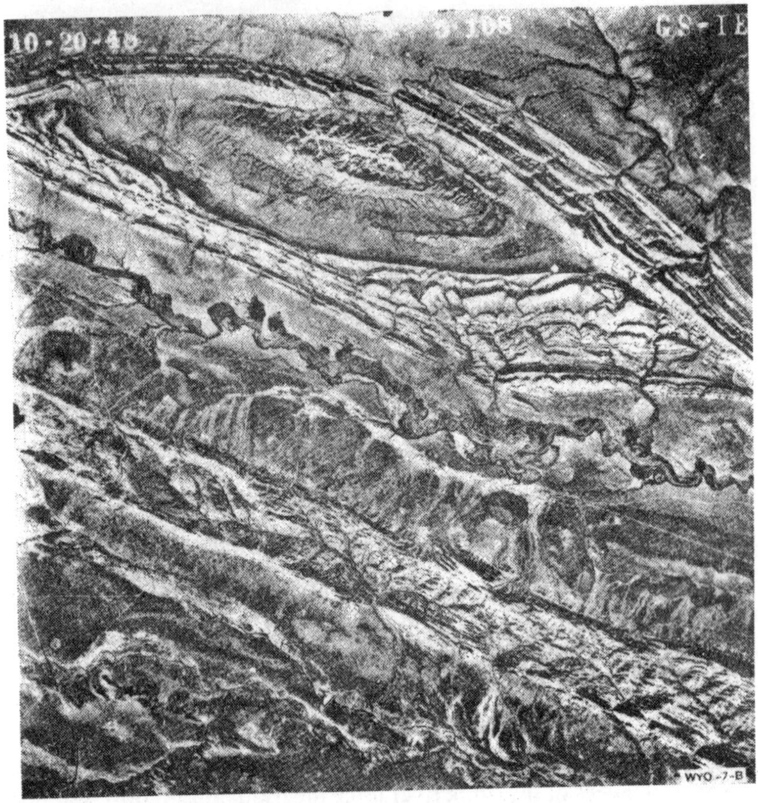

Fig. 23.6 Photo Scale 1 : 23,600. Area : Wyomihs, U.S.A.
Feature Illustrated : A small area of Jurassic rocks is exposed in the centre of this elongated dome that is largely outward dipping Cretaceous beds composed of shale and some sandstone. The beds are tightly folded along the southeast plunging anticline axis. The lowlands around the dome are underlain by cody shale that is largely concealed by alluvium and terrace deposits.

If in erosional terrain the influence of geological structure on drainage is negligible, the following main patterns are found. The dendritic (arborescent) pattern (Fig. 23.7), resembling the stem and the branches of a tree, is the most common. The parallel pattern (Fig. 23.7) composed of more or less parallel channels is developed if the influence of the general slop of the terrain is more pronounced. Sub-dendritic and sub-parallel patterns (Fig. 23.7) are transitional forms, where geological structure may have slightly influenced the trunk rivers. A radial pattern (Fig. 23.7) is also not usually directly influenced by structure. It is either centrifugal (Volcanic cone: dome) or centripetal (depression).

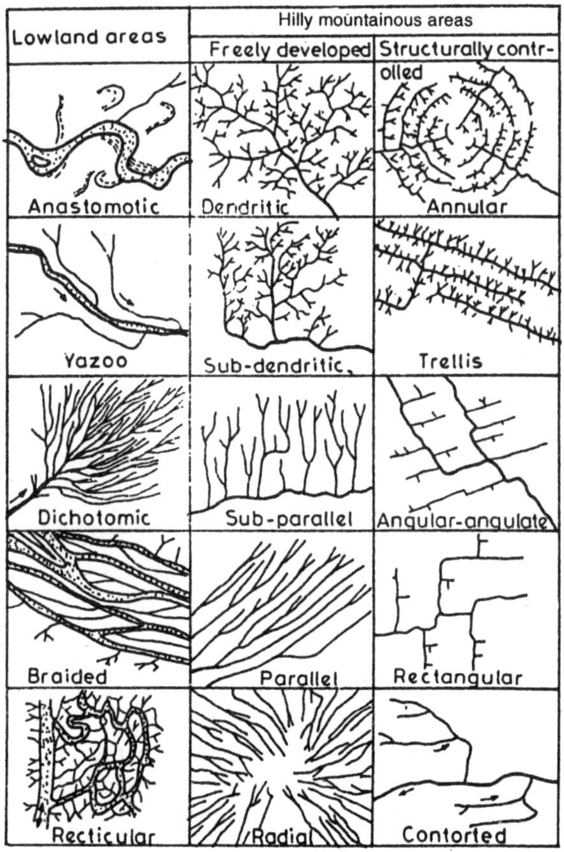

Fig. 23.7: Main drainage patterns — lowland, structurally controlled and freely developed.

The influence of structure begins when beds of different resistance are exposed by erosion. An annular pattern (Fig. 23.7), then, will result in case of a dome structure. It is composed of circular or ellipsoidal, subsequent drainage element located in the less resistant rocks, which debouch in the pre-existing and consequent, radial streams. The trellis pattern (Fig. 23.7) is characterised by long, rather straight main rivers, many of which are parallel. The tributaries are short. This type originates if in sedimentaries straight strikeness and parallel main faults occur. The angulate and rectangular patterns (Fig. 23.7) are characterised by many sharp angular bends of the streams which are due to faults or joints. Special types of patterns in erosional landscapes are pinnate, collinear, swallow hole, contorted, barbed patterns etc. Internal drainage patterns may occur in areas of important infiltration.

Other geomorphological indications are numerous. The watershed pattern is, e.g., a phenomenon to be considered in conjunction with drainage pattern. It is especially useful in areas where little resistant beds of gentle to moderate dips occur. The dip slopes, then, are largely eroded, but the U or V-shaped divides may still indicate the direction of dip and the general strike.

The dissection of the area (coarse-medium-fine) and the size, steepness and shape of a slope may also yield important information. The form and development of slopes depend as far as lithology is concerned on the resistance of the rocks against surficial run-off and against mechanical or chemical weathering. Factors influencing run-off effects are cohesion plasticity and permeability. The effect of mechanical weathering is governed by the massivity (fractures etc.) of the rocks, the grain size and the homogeneity of the grains (size, colour, etc.). The rate of chemical weathering is influenced by the solubility of the rocks and minerals, the susceptibility of these minerals to certain chemical processes etc. Resistant to surficial run-off are, e.g. most igneous rocks and sandstones. Non-resistant in this respect are clays, sands and shales (weak cohesion or great plasticity). Limestone is particularly influenced by chemical processes.

Another group of interpretation elements in the cross-sections of valleys and other erosional features, usually, of small scale. The shape of gullies (Fig. 23.8) is largely governed by the material in which they are formed. Their characteristics, thus, have some value for the determination of the kind of material occurring, provided that the other factors influencing their forms such as climate, vegetation and stage of development are comparable. The erodibility of a soil is influenced by two factors, viz., the mechanical friction between the grains and the physical/chemical cohesion. Medium to coarse sands and gravels have considerable resistance due to the high internal friction inherent to their grain size, whereas clays derive their strength from the cohesion. The material between 2 and 200 m (fine sands and silt), is according to Lueder, easily erodible. The height of the slope is another important factor in this relation. If it is less than the critical height of the material occurring, a vertical slope will be maintained, whereas mass movements (sliding, slumping, etc.) will create a characteristic and more gentle slope profile as soon as the critical height is exceeded. The critical height ranges from 0 metres for dry sand and max. 1 metre for moist sand to max. 10 metres for material with a certain silt or clay content. Extremely high values are found in loess and volcanic tuffs (100 metres).

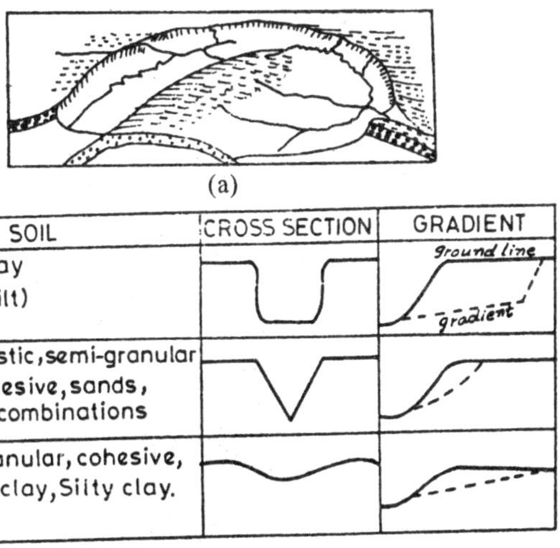

(b) (c)

Fig. 23.8: (a) A characteristic erosional patterns.
(b) Cross-sectional view of erosional pattern.
(c) Profile of erosion

The following three characteristic types of cross-section exist. In non-cohesive porous material (sands, gravels), a V-shaped profile (See Fig. 23.8b) with a low vertical cliff at the upper end of the slope is characteristic few branches occur. In cohesive, rather impervious material shales, clay the cross-section is characterised by its width and its smooth forms. Many branches occur, cross-sections of gullies occurring in intermediate material (sandy shale etc.) have a moderate width and smooth vertical sides (U-shaped). Intricate pattern occur. The longitudinal profile of the gullies may also have some value for the estimation of the kinds of material occurring. Rather steep and short longitudinal profiles normally occur in non-cohesive porous material, whereas long and gently sloping valleys, with a almost unnoticeable valley-heads are characteristic for cohesive material of low porosity. The easily erodable material of intermediate grain size has normally a moderate gradient with abrupt and steep valley head. The characteristic longitudinal profiles and cross-sections are indicated in Figure 23.8c. Fig. 23.9 shows a plot of resistance to erosion versus the size of the eroded particles.

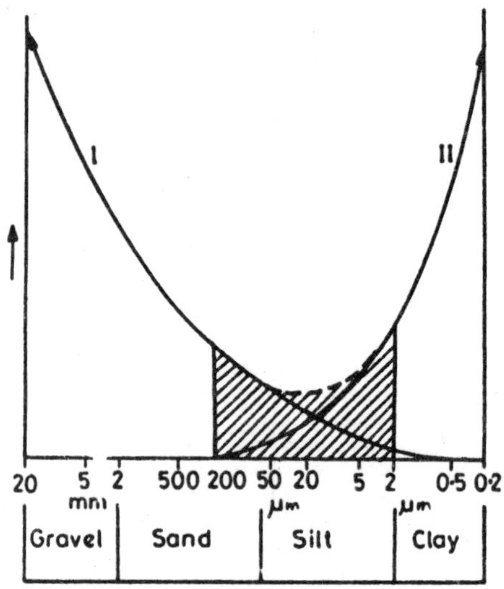

Fig. 23.9: A plot of resistance to erosion versus size of the eroded particle.

Grey Tone Criteria

The photographic grey tone is more limited an interpretation element that the above-mentioned group of landform (relief) elements. Definite conclusions usually are only arrived at in conjunction with other criteria. It should be borne in mind that only the tonal differences are important and not the absolute total values. The latter depends largely on the sensitivity range of the film emulsion used and upon the processing of the film. Tonal differences of geological origin are, of course, rather rare in areas covered by a uniform vegetation (tropical rain forest). The grey tone creterium is most valuable for geological purposes in non-vegetated areas. Part of the tonal variations then are due to the different rock or soil colour and another part is the result of differences are often particularly striking in semi-arid countries. Capillarity largely influences the saturation and descation of the ground and thus is important in this field.

The *Patterns* of tonal features also may offer a clue, e.g. to reveal a creek system, joint pattern, etc. A comparison of densitometer measurements of the photographic image with reflectivity data of rocks or soils collected in the field, may be useful as an aid in improving the interpretability of an area.

Optimum use of the grey tone criterium requires sufficiently large tonal differences. It is not uncommon, however, that certain features having a low grey tone contrast are particularly important as interpretation criteria, whereas the high tonal contrasts are due to factors of non-geological interest (e.g. shadows). Electronic dodging by reducing those high contrasts, then may add considerably to the interpretability of the photos.

Associated Phenomena as Criteria

Vegetation and landuse features are the most important amongst the associated phenomena, which make up the third group of interpretation criteria, special tree/vegetation types may regionally be characteristic for a certain rock type or inversely, may not occur under certain lighological conditions. Zoning of the vegetation frequently indicates clearly the strike direction in areas of sedimentary or metamorphic rocks. Such vegetative indications in photogeology may either be due to the physical or the chemical characteristics of the soils or result from difference in soil humidity or permeability. Faults and fractures are often well visible from the air due to vegetation features and humidity conditions (See Fig. 23.10).

Apart from specific species, the vegetative cover, as a whole may offer a clue, by way of its characteristics density, height size and regularity.

An example of this phenomenon is, e.g. the much higher, though similar vegetation occurring in Surinam on Dolerite dykes than on the surrounding granites, Micro-vegetation sometimes is of special importance in arctic and semi-arid regions. Careful distinction should be made, however, between patterns of geological importance and others related to factors like human activity and topographic exposure to rain, wind or sun.

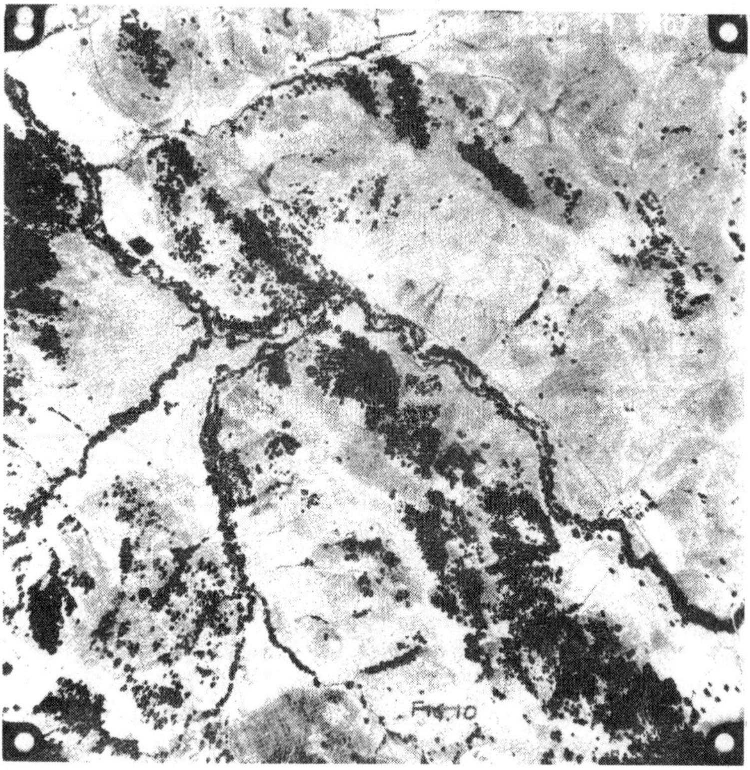

Fig. 23.10: Vegetation pattern. The vegetation occurs chiefly along streams or low lying areas indicative of moisture holding soil and characteristic rock type.

Vegetation on the other hand may also obscure a great amount of geological details, particularly if it forms a dense cover. A homogeneous cover is less disturbing than an irregular, dotted one and particularly less than the intricate pattern produced by intense land use. It is for this reason that photogeology of intensely cultivated areas in N.W. Europe is sometimes more difficult than jungle covered areas, particularly those where sedimentary rocks occur. Many geological details can often be traced with remarkable details underneath.a jungle of rather uniform height.

Evaluation of Various Criteria

The various interpretation criteria mentioned above, can be applied to the three types of geological/geomorphological photo-interpretation: structural, lithological and dynamical interpretation.

Structural interpretation is particularly important where sedimentaries occur (oil-exploration). The understanding of the geological structure is usually arrived at during the process of delineation of boundaries and it thus precedes the lithological interpretation. Dip and strike observations are a main concern and are dealt with in more detail. Other indications for the structure are in the first place outcrop patterns. The actual outcrops of exposed rock only play a role of importance in non-vegetated countries, provided that the scale of photography is sufficiently large. Next in importance ranks the drainage pattern. Annular and trellis patterns frequently occur, with subsequent rivers located in the less resistant beds and particularly if the dips moderate or steep. The length of tributaries sometimes is an indication for the dip direction as usually the longer ones are found on dip slopes, whereas the shorter ones occur on the face slope of the beds. Exceptions to this rule may, however, occur if the beds are steeply dipping. Dendritic patterns indicate the occurrence of horizontal beds or possibly very weak beds of any dip. Faults can often be detected from the air on the strength of horizontal displacement of the bedding, drag, scarps, drainage features, etc. Unconformities also can be pointed out when discordances of dip and strike, abrupt contact between different formations etc., occur. Care must be taken, however, not to be misled by cross bedding, or faulting.

Structural interpretation of metamorphic areas is much less revealing and usually confined to incomplete scattered features, the interconnection of which is difficult or not at all possible. Foliation and cleavage are common in these kinds of rocks. Contact zones, veins and plugs, are structural elements to be mapped in igneous areas. Cleavage can sometimes be observed. A particularly interesting aspect in igneous (and in some sedimentary) rocks is the mapping and interpretation of joint patterns. Two aspects can be considered, viz. the frequency distribution of joint directions (azimuth) or the regional distribution (delineation) of certain patterns of joint density characteristics.

The dynamic interpretation is quite a different aspect of photo-interpretation. The changes occurring in the landscape, due to various processes (river work, coastal processes, mass movements, etc.) then is stressed. This approach is particularly important for certain geomorphological studies and if rather rapid changes are concerned. It is advantageous to have two or more photo coverages from different years, or otherwise a reliable map and a set of photos from another period. Quantitative evaluation of the changes then will result from comparative studies. The dynamic approach is still possible, however, if only one photo-coverage exists. A number of subsequent positions of coastlines, natural levees of rivers etc. are often visible from the air and thus the trend of development can be studied.

Extrapolation of the observed changes, into the past or into the future is feasible. Extrapolation into the future is of particular interest for engineering purposes.

In practice the various aspects of interpretation are used in combination although the accent is not always on the same aspect. Direct evidence is sometimes obtained, but more important are usually the conclusions drawn by deduction from indirect evidence. In mineral exploration, e.g. can are deposits related to faults or veins and also gossan, often be easily detected from the air. Mineralisation slumping is another direct indication. If ore deposits in the contact zone surrounding an intrusive body or hydrothermal deposits are covered, direct indications are usually lacking and it will then only be possible to point out areas where the chances for mineral accumulation are best. Lateritic ores and placer deposits are detected mainly on the strength of their morphological appearance.

Resolution

The capacity to differentiate two very closely situated objects is defined as resolution. Among other things the incident wavelengths is one of the most important criteria for resolution. The shorter the wavelength the greater the resolution. High resolution gives better object discrimination and hence more information about the object. Thus an imagery with high resolution be of great use in identifying ground features of small extent such as small fractures. joint buildings and nature of trees etc.

Spectral Response

The fact that imagery in different wavebands is available in remote sensing can considerably enhance the art of visual interpretation compared to Black and White photography. The response of objects to different wavelengths being different, the examination of the different waveband imagery can help pick up the particular object. For example, if we were to differentiate between surface water bodies and vegetation a comparison of the four waveband imageries in band 4, 5, 6 and 7 will immediately show the presence of water bodies distinctly in band 7. This is because water has strong absorption for infrared waves, the band 7 imagery will clearly show water bodies distinct and prominent than forest or vegetation areas (on the positive transparencies they will appear darker).

The nature of multispectral imagery help interpret and collect more information is respect of the following fields in the manner indicated below:

Application of Aerial Photo Interpretation

Aerial photos have been used for several applications. Using the principles of visual photo interpretation information about the earth's surface feature can be obtained. Some of the areas where aerial photos have been extensively used are in the areas of:

(a) Topographical mapping
(b) Geology
(c) Soil mapping
(d) Forestry
(e) Terrain Evaluation
(f) Land use/Land cover mapping
(g) Agriculture
(h) Water Resources
(i) Environmental Studies/Flood Damage Studies

Topographical Mapping

The basis of topographical mapping using aerial photographs is the common overlap between two successive photos in the forward and lateral direction. The forward direction is the direction of the aircraft flight and the minimum forward overlap required is 60 per cent. The lateral overlap, at right angles to the forward direction can vary from 25 to 30 per cent.

The overlapping photos are placed in the so-called stereo projectors in such a manner that the model of the ground is recreated and the observer sees the three-dimensional view of the ground. For this it is necessary to create geometrical conditions between the two photos in the stereo projector in such a way that the inclination between the two successive photo is exactly the same as at the time of taking pictures by the aerial camera. This is best illustrated by Fig. 23.11. It is possible to draw not only the planimetry but also the contours at desired scale and interval by suitable selection of ground control points. These ground control points appear on the aerial photos. The biggest advantage of aerial mapping lies in cost and efficiency. Whereas a very large number of such control points are required for mapping by traditional ground survey methods, such a plane tabling, a much less density of control points is required by aerial methods. The time required by photo

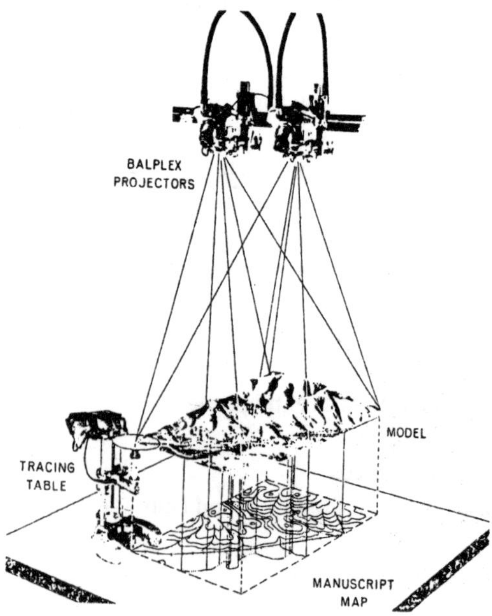

Fig. 23.11: Creation of a three-dimensional model in a stereo projector by a pair of overlapping aerial photos.

mapping is also much less compared to ground methods. At present, the accuracy achieved is much and the aerial mapping has almost become a universal technique of mapping.

Geology

The geological mapping involves both surface and sub-surface mapping for mineral and other geophysical exploration. An aerial photo gives an excellent birds eyeview, a so called 'synoptic' view of the terrain from a given height. Higher the elevation from where the photo has been taken greater is the synoptic view. In case of geological surface features it is sometimes very difficult to recognise it from the ground. For example a fault of width of a few metres may not be recognised while standing on the ground but if seen from a height the fault will appear very clearly on the photo. This is due to what is called the lineament effect. Human eye can some how recognise features if they extend over a long distance even though the width of the feature is beyond the resolution of the eye. Using the principles of photo interpretation and by the help of so called 'Key' it is possible to do geological work for the following:

(i) *Structural mapping*: such as for Faults, Folds, Dykes, Joints, Dip and Strike. Using the method of 'Parallax Bar' it is possible not only to determine the direction but also the slope and hence the dip and strike of formations. Similarly displacements due to big faults, folds, with anticling and synclines, fold axis etc. can be easily identified on the aerial photos. The classical joints and dykes, volcanic cones etc. are also very easily recognised because of their characteristic shapes. Some of these are illustrated in Fig. 23.12.

(ii) *Rock Types*: The three major rock types, namely igneous, sedimentary and metamorphic rocks can be identified with the help of drainage pattern and other characteristic features like erosion pattern. Sand stone and limestone rocks show very poorly developed drainage pattern and typical Karst phenomenon of sink holes (See Fig. 23.13). These holes appear as dark round features on the aerial photos. Granite rocks appear as massive rounded dome like structures with typical drainage pattern and absence of vegetation or vegetation

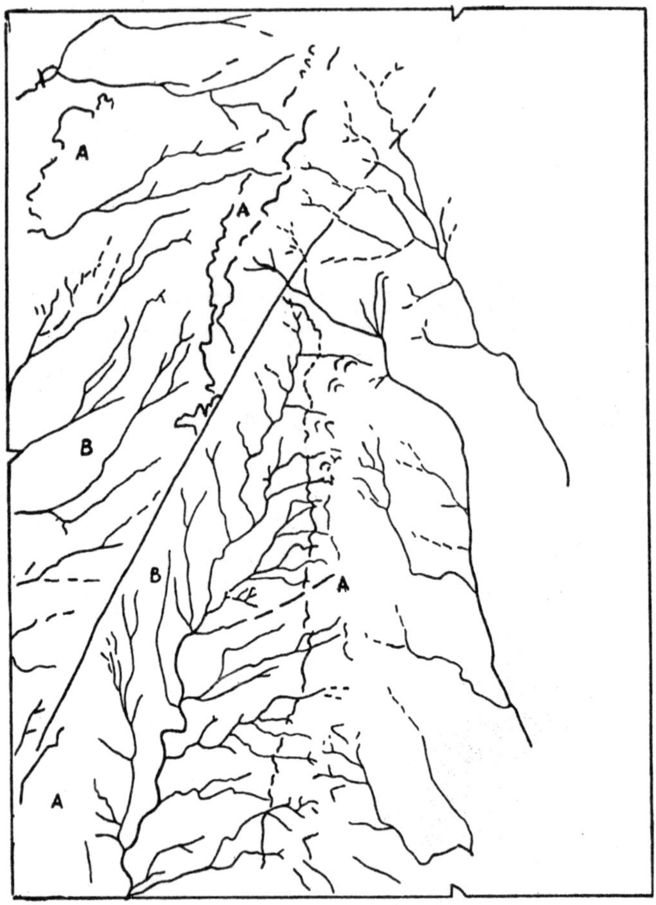

Fig. 23.12: Gently Dipping Sedimentary (Overlay), Rocks Offset by near Vertical Fault (Utah), Scale 1: 20,000.

Line separating areas of contrasting photographic tone is trace of fault. The straightness of the fault trace indicates that the fault has approximately a vertical dip. Note vertical offset of dark toned shale bed *A* and difference in erosional character of topography on off sides of fault at *B*. Faint trace of fault in alluvium at *C* is locally marked by differences in drainage on opposite sides of the fault. Light toned sandstone interbeds, *D*, cap local areas and exhibit senated margins as a result of closely spaced joints. Fine textured drainage is typical of the poorly resistant shale and thin sandstone interbeds.

appearing in areas of joints. Volcanic rocks appear with radial drainage pattern and typical lava flow and volcanic vents. (See Figs. 23.14 to 23.16). The metaphoric rocks have a banded structure which can sometimes be identified on the aerial photos. In general interpretation of metamorphic rocks is much more difficult compared to sedimentary (Fig. 23.17) and igneous rocks.

Fig. 23.13: The slightly dissected eastern edge of the Southern High Plains is dotted with shallow Sink holes (Karst Phenomenon) which appear as dark circular holes on the upper part of the aerial photo. The underlying indurated bed rock is limestone and sandstone. These rocks are largely concealed.

Fig. 23.14 Sakura-Jino Volcano. The photo shows a wealth of interesting detail and should be studied carefully. The main volcano is a triple cone with two, probably younger, craters of almost equal size and a smaller (probably older) one wedged in between them. The larger ones, with craters, may have developed from adventive craters. On photo 980 — a longer lava flow has built up a peninsula by invading the sea. Cultivated land and settlements were probably destroyed here. The wrinkled surface of the flow suggest ropy lava of a viscous type. Higher up the slope a collapsed lava tube is seen, surrounded by a cracked-up area strikingly resembling the creracing of a cascading glacier and being due to the slow downward movement during refrigeration. Domes, plugs and spatter cones are seen and a blow holes, probably a gas vent surrounded by mineral deposits (light tone). Older lavas are partly

(*Cont.*)

covered by vegetation.
Upper part of the volcano is covered with fresh ash (light tone). On 979-80 an adventure cone is breached by a lava flow, on to which another, somewhat younger flow has spilled over in a cascade branching off the main flow. This flow has a slightly darker tone than the older one. Several small vents are seen (not cone forming). Surface of flows again strongly resembles that of glaciers. The difference is only in tone (and substance). The small stream along the edge of the flow has been faced to alter its coarse as the old valley was invaded and now forms a young incision. Note the strange wall-like rim of the flow. The flow has built up a peninsula in the shape of a bird's foot delta. The older flow levels abruptly in a steep escarpment. The phenomena described point to the presence of viscous lava. Note pattern of cultivation (innumerable small plots) which is explained by the extreme density of settlements along the coast and the presence of fertile volcanic soils.

Soil Mapping

It is well known that soils are derived from rocks and that soils are in general surface features and hence cannot be directly mapped the same way as in forestry, geology or topographic mappings. A photo will serve to prepare a Base Map on which ground information can be inserted and a correlation between the type of soil and corresponding tone and texture on the aerial photo be identified. Using this the experienced soil scientist can use aerial photos to his benefit. In addition viewing the photos under a stereoscope gives him additional 3D view. Other factors which help in soil type mapping are the soil moisture content, soil texture, surface roughness, the presence of iron oxide and the organic matter content.

The unpredictability and indirectness of relationship between individual landscape elements and soils has led to an emphasis on the use of so called 'Physiographic Systems' in photo interpretation. Such a physiographic system is defined as specific set of physiographic conditions which can be inferred by the use of 'Converging evidence' produced by different individual landscape elements on the photos. These physiographic systems may be related more specifically to conditions created by stratigraphy, block faulting, ground water and surface water hydrology, geomorphology, erosion and weathering processes, wind action or sedimentology, but more generally they are

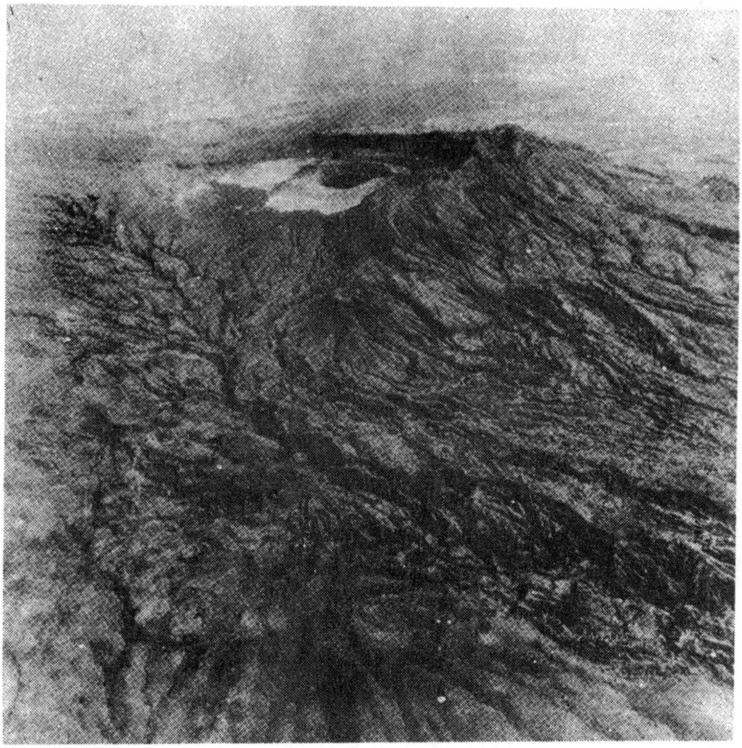

Fig. 23.15: Excellent volcanic crater and cone containing Deriba Lake (Africa). Extensive Erosion by streams.

related to combinations of these conditions and processes. An example of this is the physiographic system of Bhabar and Tarai below the foothills of the Himalayas, which is not only a hydrological system but has also aspects related to sedimentology and soils. Another well known example is the physiographic system produced by block faulting processes north of Dehra Dun which has both geological and sedimentological aspects, but which is also influenced by resulting erosion, weathering and seepage processes. The third example is the system produced by gently dipping Gondwana sandstones overlaying Gondawana shales. In all these situations these physiographic systems are expressed on the aerial photos in not just one but in combinations of almost all the individual photo-interpretation elements.

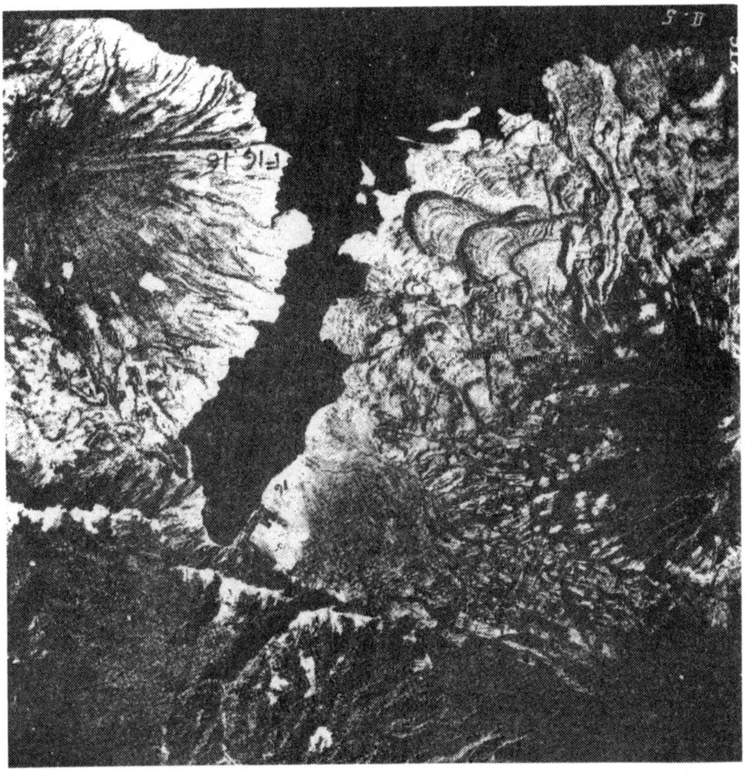

Fig. 23.16: Active Lava Slopes (Japan).

A model of the process and conditions governing certain physiographic system and their resulting soil patterns can generally be presented in the forms of a detailed cross-section. A model like this is established during detailed studies in sample areas. After it is fully understood, its influence on soil patterns studied and its different expressions on the photographs established, the model can be applied to the other parts of the survey area for which the sample is representative. The validity of this extrapolation of knowledge is then checked by some rapid traverses in the rest of the area. These traverses may take the form of a field check and a "predicted soil map" based on the physiographic model drawn up in the sample area. If the predicted soil patterns along these traverses prove to be correct we may conclude that the model is applicable. If not, either the model as a working hypothesis was not correct or the sample area was not truly representative. In the latter case we may have to select new sample areas and change our first interpretation.

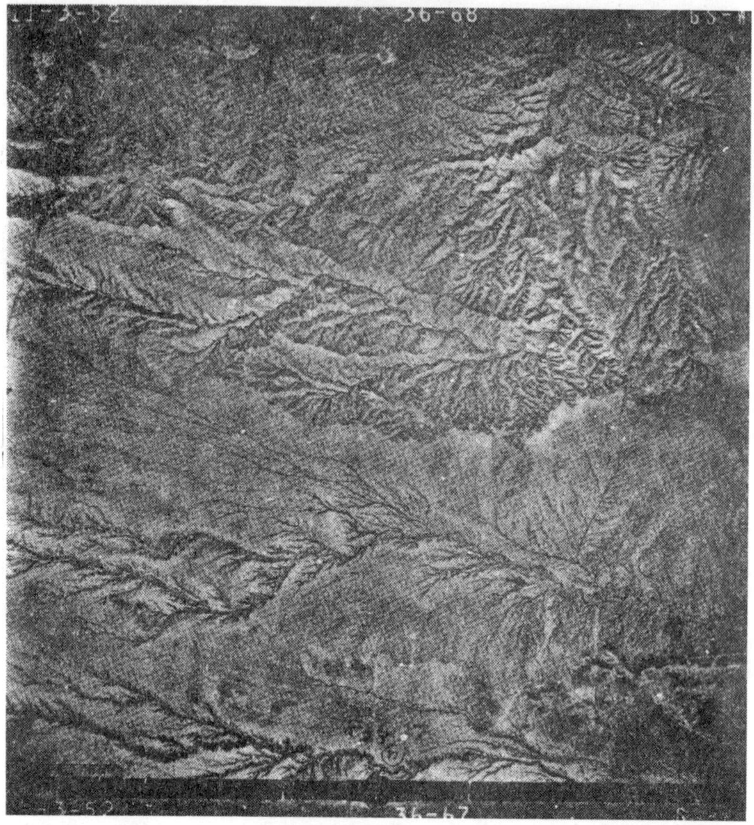

Fig. 23.17: Shale in Semiarid Climate Area (Utah). Scale: 1 : 20,000

Fine-textured drainage is typical of shale and other fine-grained classic rock types. Relief is commonly subdued and divide areas gently rounded. Note that rounding of some divide areas may not be conspicuous because of vertical exaggeration of the stereoscopic model. For example, the relief at *B* is only 70 ft. The fine textured drainage and erosional topography suggest plastic soils. The numerous angular crenulations in minor tributaries probably reflect closely spaced joints. Their light-toned bands *A* are expressions of bedding.

Forestry

The main application of photo interpretation to Forestry involves (a) preparation of a Base Map, (b) Identification of Tree species, (c) Quantitative measurements about the density of trees in a given area, height of trees and crown shapes and volumes. The principles of photo interpretation as explained earlier such as shape, size, pattern, shadow, tone and texture are applied for (a) and (b) mentioned above.

Individual tree species have their characteristic shape and size. With some ground knowledge and experience it is possible to identify these on the air photos. Shadows of trees help to know their shape in profile. Changes of tone and texture also help in identification of species. Tree also give a peculiar pattern depending upon underground moisture condition. Trees along a straight line may be due to underground water channel. Trees also occur in clumps. Knowledge about tree height can easily be obtained using a simple parallax bar with viewing under stereoscope. Physiographic conditions also help in identification of tree types. For example, Sal trees generally grow a low hills upto 1000 metres and pine trees upto 2000 metres or more of terrain heights above sea level.

Terrain Evaluation

The study of terrain is essential and a prerequisite for proper planning and utilisation of land resources. The purpose could be a short term military requirement for certain localised zones a long term peace time need like development and exploitation of mineral resources, availability of construction material, exploration for ground water etc. The aim of terrain study is to gather maximum and systematic information on various aspects of the ground so that proper evaluation of this information can be done to meet the requirements of different users. A system of classification of terrain is, therefore, necessary where a given area can be subdivided into basic units. The question becomes more important for an inaccessible area where the only available tool is the aerial photo and the concept of 'known to the unknown' will hold good. In fact the aerial photos, when seen under a stereoscope, bring the 'Ground' to the laboratory.

The two important units in terrain classification are Pattern and Facet. A Facet is the fundamental unit in the classification. It is desirable as a piece of ground possessing uniform physical properties for all practical purposes. It is classified on the basis of surface configurations, nature of surficial deposits, surface and subsurface water region, land use and its associations with other terrain units. A landscape pattern is an area or areas of regularly occurring pattern of topography and surficial deposits including soils. The landscape pattern is recognised on the basis of geologic set up, climate and topography. The following information is recorded for each terrain unit:

Terrain Unit		Type of Information Card
Pattern	:	Pattern Card, Pattern description, Climate
Facet	:	Facet Card, Ground Description, Surficial deposit and soils, Land use, Vegetation, Soil Properties and Classification Engineering Resources and Water Supply.

The detailed method of Terrain study is as follows:

Area of Study

1. *Library Work*: Collection of basic material and background information
2. *Laboratory Exercises*: Scanning of air-photos, checking of quality, scale etc., study of maps and delineation of major units, preliminary list of landscape patterns and facets.
3. *Ground Reconnaissance*: Initial Field Traverses.
4. *Study of Aerial Photos*: Delineation of facets and planning of fieldwork.
5. *Detailed Fieldwork*: Checking of photo-characteristics, recording terrain data, collecting soils samples field tests for moisture content and soil strengths. *Final List of Pattern and Facets.*
6. *Laboratory Tests:* Soil tests, rock identification etc.
7. *Completion of Reports*: Confirmatory Reccee, if required. Finalisation of report, typing of cards and preparation of maps. Main Report, Appendices (Pattern, Facets and information cards, Facet maps).

The process of photo-interpretation can be divided into steps like observations and measurements, logical reasoning and influence. The equipment required is simple and constitutes pocket stereoscope for quick scanning in the field, mirror stereoscope for detailed work, parallax bar for height measurement and sketch master to transfer the interpreted data to the base map. In the case of terrain studies presenting in progress the details are directly transferred to existing topsheets.

The recognition elements used for photo interpretation aids to describe different terrain units are:

(a) Position in landscape and association with other terrain units.
(b) Morphology, surface configuration and micro relief.
(c) Drainage pattern, texture and density internal and external drainage.
(d) Erosional features and gully sections.
(e) Landuse and cultural features.
(f) Vegetation.
(g) Tonal variation and special photo textures and pattern, if any.

(f) Land Use/Land Cover

The term land use refers to the human activity associated with a specific piece of land whereas the term land cover related to the type of feature present on the surface of the earth. The United States Geological Survey has devised a classification scheme at different levels for Land Use/ Land Cover system for use with aerial photos. Example of Level I and Level II are:

Level I	*Level II*
1. Urban or Built up Land	11. Residential
	12. Commercial and Services
	13. Industrial
	14. Transportation, Communication and Utilities
	15. Industrial and Commercial Complexes
	16. Mixed Urban
	17. Other Urban

Similarly under urban or built-up land levels I, II, III are:

Level I	*Level II*	*Level III*
Urban or Built up land	11. Residential	111. Single Family
	12. Commercial	112. Multi Family
	13. Industrial	113. Group Quarters
	14. ,,	114. Residential Hotels
	15. ,,	
	16. ,,	
	17. ,,	

All these land use/land cover types can easily be delineated on aerial photos seen under stereoscopic vision. The resolution or the smallest distance that can be identified depends upon the scale. The larger the scale of photos greater is the clarity and resolution. In fact for land use/land cover work photos on large scale such as 1:10,000 to 1:5,000 are recommended. Colour photos enhance the features much more and hence give much more information. Shadows play an important role in identifying multistoreyed houses and tall structures. Ground verification follows the photo interpretation map.

Agriculture

The three major areas in which photo interpretation can help in the discipline of agriculture are: (i) Crop condition assessment, (ii) Crop type classification, (iii) Crop yield estimation. Crop type is characterised by characteristic pattern and texture on an aerial photo whereas crop condition, i.e. healthy or diseased are identified by virtue of tonal and grey level changes. The crop can be damaged due to several causes such as insects, moisture excesses, iron deficiency, nitrogen deficiency, soil salinity and air pollution. The crop yield can easily be determined by determining the area under cultivation for a particular variety.

The photo interpretation steps involved in agricultural studies relate to determination of drainage pattern and analysis, erosion pattern and analysis, photo tones, textures and vegetative feature and their pattern.

Water Resources

The application of photo interpretation techniques to water resources involve two types (a) mapping surface water bodies and (ii) subsurface or ground water potential. The first part is simple as surface water bodies like streams, rivers, lakes, etc. can be easily identified on the aerial photos. Water bodies appear darker in tone compared to rest of the features because of the simple fact most of the sunlight that enters a clear water body is absorbed within about two metres of the surface. The degree of absorption depends upon the incident wavelength. This infrared light in the region of 1 to 2 micrometer wavelengths is absorbed within a length of a metre for the surface.

The ground water location on the other hand is not so simple as this is a sub-surface feature. The indicators of ground water are the topography and vegetations, namely presence of springs and wells and other seepages. Present photo interpretation techniques cannot be applied for estimation or determination of ground water depth. The other features of the interpretation techniques are the delineation of watershed and its assessment for reservoir selection and snow cover mapping which help in determination of water available from snow melt. The underground on buried stream can also be mapped for vegetation patterns on the surface along their streams and which also help in locating possible ground water zones.

Environmental Studies

Under the heading the areas of study are (i) Water pollution and (ii) Deforestation and denudation and (iii) Industrial pollution water pollution is caused by organic waste from domestic sewage and industrial wastes, production of excessive algae and water weeds and sediments brought down by rivers etc. These pollution can often be seen on aerial photos and delineated due to different tones and textures. For example, pure water appears with light grey and polluted water with darker tone. Deposits of oil on water also show darker tone. Use of aerial photos for flood damage can also be done by taking aerial photos before and after floods. Areas prone to successive flooding can be marked and preventive measures can be adopted.

REFERENCES

Aerial Photographs in Geologic Interpretation & Mapping published by US Geological Survey, Washington D.C. Professional Paper #373.

Aerial Photographic Interpretation, by D.R. Lueder, Mc Graw Hill, N.Y., U.S.A., 1959.

Interpretation of Aerial Photographs by T.E. Avery, 4th Edition, Burgen Pub.

Co., Minnesota, USA, 1985.

Manual of Photographic Interpretation published by American Society of Photogrammetry & Remote Sensing, Falls Church, Virginia, U.S.A.

Proceedings of Second International Symposium on Photo Interpretation, Paris, France, 1966.

Photo Geology Part I & II, Text Book on Photo Interpretation, Vol. VII, ITC Publication, Enschede, The Netherlands, 1962.

Remote Sensing in Civil Engineering edited by T.J.M. Kennie & M.C. Mathews, Survey University Press, U.K., 1985.

Remote Sensing & Image Interpretation by Thomas M. Lillesand & Ralph W., Kiefer John Wiley & Sons, 2nd edition, 1989.

Selected Aerial Photographs of Geological Features by USGS, Professional Paper, 590.

Logical Thoughts on Psychology of Photo Interpretation ITC Publication 41, Enschede, The Netherlands, 1967.

24

Role of Geographic Information System in Natural Resources Management

V.K. SRIVASTAVA

Economic development of any country depends on proper management and utilisation of its natural resources. Therefore basic resources such as agriculture, forest, water, soil and mineral resources should be inventoried speedily, developed and utilised judiciously with consideration to eco-system for accelerating regional development. But the utilisation of the resources are in general interdependent, i.e. use of one resource may influence other resources. For example, use of water for irrigation may profoundly influence growth of agricultural resources. Lack of proper drainage in a region may result in water logging and excessive salinity of soil. Therefore for proper management of the natural resources an integrated approach has to be adopted by considering all aspects which control growth, production and utilisation of the resources in a geographical region.

As a first step, such study involves collection of data about the manner and form in which they are distributed over a region and which is to be used as data base for further analysis and interpretation. Collection of such spatially referenced data is of course as old as cartography and every atlas has wide varieties of such data from various sources. However, one faces difficulties in evaluating these wide varieties of maps/data within certain time limit. Also, eyes become confused and mind tends to boggle when more than two or three sets of maps/data are visually analysed by an analyst.

But, with the advent of computer and its application in map/data handling and evaluation, this limitation has been overcome to a large extent. This total process or system of efficient handling, processing and evaluation of spatial data/map data of a geographic region by the computers and finally, dissemination of results to user is designated as Geographic Information System (GIS). The output is generally in the form of maps or reports. However, a GIS is not a simple computer system for making maps, although it can create maps at different scales, in different projections with different colours. In addition GIS identifies links between various kinds of spatial data sets with geographic information about a particular feature on a map and computes new informations about map features from stored data (Burrough, 1986). The data base of GIS can be further augmented and updated by entering new data without writing fresh programme.

So, a GIS is a unique system which facilitates the storage and intelligent use of geographic data with the applications of high speed computing system and sophisticated softwares. When the data base pertains to natural resources, this forms the Geographic Information System of Natural Resources.

Natural Resources data comprise informations regarding land use/ land cover, water resources, soil type, geology, vegetation type, forestry and agriculture as shown in Fig. 24.1. Such data are either in tabular form or in graphical form. The tabular data which are in reference to graphical entities are called attribute data. For example the positions of stretch of a river is given by set of latitude and longitude coordinates while attributes of the river such as discharge, depth, slope, chemical composition etc. form a set of descriptors.

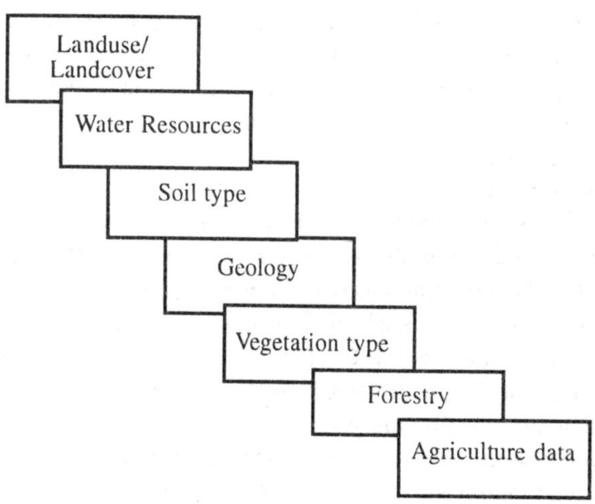

Fig. 24.1: Basic data elements of natural resources

Sub-elements of natural resources data sets are not shown here which are mainly dependent on region and type of resources under study. Therefore, one has to device his own sets of data elements and structure appropriate to his study. Flow diagram in Fig. 24.2, shows *Geographic Information System* as applicable in Natural Resources study. Geographical Information System in general comprises of four operational steps (see Fig. 24.3), viz., Data Encoding, Data Management, Data Manipulation and Data Presentation and are described briefly as below:

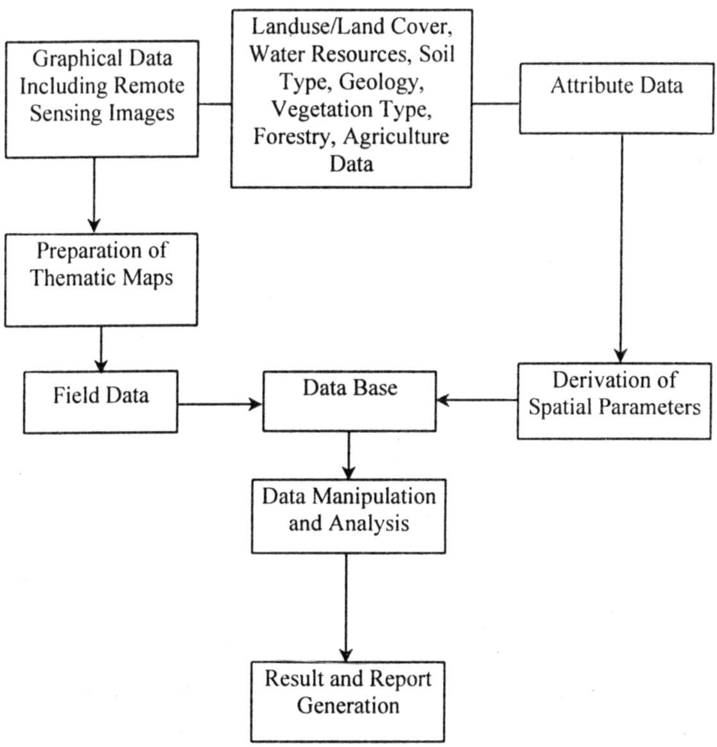

Fig. 24.2: Flow diagram showing geographic information system for natural resources management

Data Encoding: This step involves with the digitisation of spatial data either into units of polygons or grids which may corresponds to features such as fields, geographical boundaries, land cover type etc. Boundaries of polygons comprise sets of line/arc and lines/arcs are represented by very short segment of straight lines which can be represented by an ordered sequence of points defining the line segment (Marble and Pauquet, 1983). This is, what is called vector format.

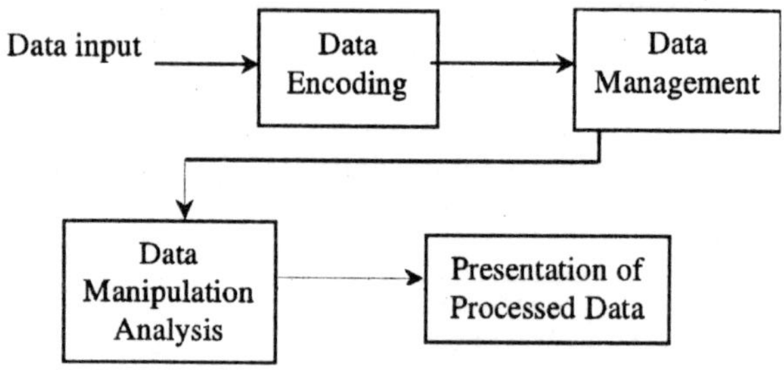

Fig. 24.3: Basic components of a geographic information system

In other approach, graphical data are converted into computer readable format by scanning the same with the help of either optical scanner or scanning densitometer.

This records spatial data in narrow strips across the data surface, thus producing raster format.

The raster format includes grids or cells or matrix data structure, and are more compatible with modern input/output computer hardware.

However, both these formats are convertible into each other by developing a set of transformation equations (Mayer, 1984). The set of equations which converts the vector format of the geographic system into the raster format of image is

$$S = f_1(x,y)$$

and $P = f_2(x,y)$,

where S = scan line

P = element number within scan line

x = horizontal coordinates of the geographic information system map projection

y = vertical coordinates of the geographic information system map projection.

Similarly the set of equations which converts the raster image data set into the vector format of the geographic information system is,

$$x = f_3(S,P)$$
$$y = f_4(S,P)$$

These equations are represented by the polynomial functions derived by least square analysis of control points that can be visually identified on an image/map.

Data Management: This step involves with the storing of digital data sets in convenient form for quick retrieval. This requires that the data is to be organised into some type of structure rather than unrelated data files.

Data Manipulation and Analysis: This includes retrieval of stored data for manipulation, analysis, integration and modelling using suitable GIS software package. Such GIS packages have been developed by various user agencies to handle their own data sets.

Data Presentation: At this final stage of GIS, the evaluated results are produced in the form of reports, maps and graphic output for the use of decision makers. This may be in the form of floppy, computer compatible tape or in printer output.

A very popular GIS software is Arc-Info package which has been developed by Environmental System Research Institute (ESRI), CA, USA. This GIS software package is being widely used in India for handling of Land Resources Based data in vector format.

Now once a theme oriented GIS is created it becomes easier to study the process of management and development of resources by (i) indicating how changes and improvements in the existing situation can be achieved; (ii) considering what effects can be expected as a consequence of the changes envisaged.

Importance of GIS further increases with the availability of Digitised Survey Data/Topsheets/Land use maps which could be directly taken as inputs to GIS. Also periodic imaging of earth surface in digital mode through Remote Sensing technique provides another kind of raster digital data sets which can be taken as input to monitor temporal changes in the status of natural resources.

In conclusion handling of natural resources data through Geographic Information System provides informations regarding growth, distribution and production of the resources for overall management and utilisation in an area.

The utility of GIS is further enhanced with the availability of real time remote sensing images of the earth's surface for augmenting and updating of data base and thereby providing updated informations to analyst.

REFERENCES

Burrough, P.A., 1986, Principles of Geographical Information System for Land Resources Assessment, Clarendon Press, Oxford.

Marble, D.F. and Peaquet, D.J., 1983, Geographic Information System and Remote Sensing, In Colwall, R.N. (ed.) *Manual of Remote Sensing*, American Society of Photogrammetry, Falls Church, Virginia, pp. 923-58.

Mayer, W.L. 1982; Integration of remotely sensed data into geographic information; In Richason, Jn B.F.(ed.) Proc. PECORA VII Symposium, *Remote Sensing : An Input to Geographic Information System in the 1980s*, American Society of Photogrammetry : Falls Church, Virginia, pp. 3-14.

25

Remote Sensing and GIS for Resource Management in India

R.B. SINGH

Introduction

Space informatics have great benefit for humankind. The present age is called the "Information Age" or "Space Age" that is supported with electronics such as computers, optical-electronics such as laser, and communication technology such as internet, etc. The generation of geoinformatics data is the foundation upon which a sound resource monitoring is based. Availability of authentic and reliable geosystem data also helps in processing the utilization pattern, future needs and resource management strategy. The science of geoinformatics is a multi-disciplinary subject for extracting reliable georeferenced data of geosystem and the environment. This covers the data acquisition, processing, and representation of geospatial data. Under geoinformatics, the techniques relating to surveying, geodesy, photogrammetry, remote sensing, cartography, GIS and GPS, are being combined for solving local, regional, national and global problems. Geoinformatics monitor the spatial/location of objects and characteristics of natural or geosystem features and aerial coverage of the earth. The emerging advance technologies in remote sensing, i.e. Very High Resolution Satellite images. Synthetic Aperture Radar (SAR), Airborne Remote Sensing and GPS, are providing great opportunities to monitor and manage geosystem in a sustainable manner (Singh and Murai, 1998; Singh, 1998).

Resource management task of a region is performed either manually by a map overlay method or with computer technology using numerical spatial data sets or geo-based files. The manual approach is performed by overlaying transparent maps in order to visually merge the set of information for producing output map. Limits of this method are the reduced number of maps that can be possibly overlaid simultaneously for visual analysis and the difficulties to obtain or produce transparent maps at a common scale. The computer assisted approach requires information in digital form. Interrelation of resource features (attributes or factors) is performed through numerical transformations. The development of modern data-gathering techniques and computer assisted cartography give new impetus of data storage and exchange. Subsequently, the combined use of Geographic Information System (GIS), and Digital Image Processing provide better prospects of resource and environmental monitoring and forecasting over wider areas within limited time-span (Bae Yu and Yong Ku, 1998). It would be easy to develop predictive model capabilities in order to achieve effective public policy in years to come.

State of Space Technology — Remote Sensing

Remote sensing is a multi-disciplinary activity which deals with the inventory, monitoring, predicting and assessment of environmental resources through the analysis of data obtained by observations from a remote platform. Remote Sensing is the science of deriving information about an object from measurements made at a distance from the object without actually coming in contact with it. When the sources of energy is not the sensing system nor the target but external sources such as Sun, then Remote Sensing System is called Passive. It detects the solar energy reflected from the target. When the surface of energy is the target, the Remote Sensing System is then called Passive as it detects the energy emitted from the target. When the energy is produced by the remote sensing system itself, then it is called active and it senses the energy reflected from the target (Table 25.1).

Different Steps in Remote Sensing

On the basis of various processes involved in remote sensing activities (NRSA, Department of Space, 1996), the different steps are the following:

1. Origin of electromagnetic energy (sun, transmitter carried by the sensor).
2. Transmission of energy from the source to the surface of the earth and its interaction with the intervening atmosphere.
3. Interaction of energy with the earth surface (reflection/absorption/transmission) or self-emission.
4. Transmission of the reflected/emitted energy to the remote sensor placed on suitable platform.
5. Detection of the energy by the sensor converting into photographic image or electrical output.
6. Transmission/recording of the sensor output.
7. Preprocessing of the data for generation of data products.
8. Collection of Ground Truth and other collateral information.
9. Data processing and interpretation.

Table 25.1. Components of Remote Sensing

Component		*Related Processes*
The Energy	—	Electromagnetic energy.
Sources of Energy	—	The remote sensing system itself.
		The target More frequently the Sun.
Transmission Path	—	Atmosphere.
The Target	—	Earth surface features emit and reflect energy towards the sensing system.
The Remote Sensing System	—	Sensing Instruments.

Historical Development of Remote Sensing

With launching of operational remote sensing satellites IRS-1A (1988) and 1B (1991) and setting up of various information systems, about 350 national/regional level remote sensing application projects have been conducted in India. The successful launch of second generation and indigenously built IRS-1C satellite on 28th December, 1995 has provided tremendous opportunities for applying space informatics in areas of disaster monitoring and natural resources management (Singh, 1991, 1994 and 1995). Browse data for PAN and LISS-III are being generated for users. The IRS-1C marks a major milestone in the India's satellite remote sensing programme by contributing to National Natural Resources Management System with better resolution, coverage and revisit in order to provide invaluable data on environmental resources.

The IRS-1C surveys the whole earth's surface in just 24 days.

The IRS-1C satellite has three types of advanced imaging sensors. The Panchromatic Camera (PAN) provides very high spatial resolution data of 5.8 m and a ground swath of 70 km. The PAN camera can be steered to ñ 26 degrees which in turn increases revisit capability to 5 days. Linear Imaging and Self-Scanning (LISS-III) Sensor provides multispectral data collected in four bands. The Wide Field Sensor (WiFS) collects data in two spectral bands. All the three cameras are operating in real time over Indian ground station visibility circle two or three times a day (NRSA, 1996). The satellites IRS-1C and IRS-1D have the best spatial resolution of space based remote sensing data. The demand for satellite data was going up by 15 to 20 per cent a year and with IRS-1C it would be possible to meet 90 per cent of the requirement from the own satellite. With the recent launch of IRS-1D using our own launch vehicles, PSLV, India has established capability to place 1200 kg. class satellites in polar sun-synchronous orbit. India INSAT system is one of the largest constellation of domestic communication satellites in the world (Singh, 1998).

Global Positioning System for Resource Survey and Field Work

GPS, the Global Positioning System, is all-weather radio navigation system developed by US military in which individual receivers process data beamed down from satellites. It provides three-dimensional positions and velocities on a 24-hour-per-day basis all around the world. The space segment consists of 24 satellites having a circular orbit and an orbital period of 12 hours. The satellites carry an atomic frequency standard to generate a stable signal. They transmit at the frequencies L1=1575.42 MHz and L2=1227.6 MHz. These carriers are modulated with two codes generally referred to as the coarse/acquisition (C/A) code and the precision (P) code. The ground receivers receive these transmitted signals to compute the position on the earth based on the satellite position. Most of the navigation systems use input from just one receiver. The accuracy in such cases depends on whether the P-code or C/A-code is observed and the level of selective availability (SA). SA represents the measures that the military uses to degrade the quality of the signals transmitted by the satellites, thereby reducing the positional capability of civilian receivers. Commonly used standalone navigation solutions have an accuracy of about 100m (Nagarajan, 1999).

To obtain high accuracy, use of differential GPS is necessary, in which at least two receivers measure carrier phases simultaneously. The carrier-phase measurement technique can be explained as a comparison of the incoming satellite transmission with stable oscillator of the receiver. The carrier phase observations recorded at individual stations are combined at other stations to form double- and/or triple-difference carrier phase observables and these differences essentially are free of satellite clock errors. Thus, relative three-dimensional positions can be obtained with high accuracy. Kinematic GPS is a differential GPS, designed to receive transmitting signal continuously in running mode. In this case, one receiver is fixed at known benchmark and other receiver (called rover) is used to take observation in running mode. The components of the GPS include the following:

1. Identification of ground measure points
   Free horizon (above 15°)
   Position points away of others transmitters influence (200M)
   Position points away from reflection surfaces (Multipath)
   Time between different stations
2. Satellites visibility and measure period choice
   Measure window for 4 satellites simultaneously
   Same time for satellite visibility and ground measurement
3. Network Conception
   Satellite visibility for each measure window
   Moving time available between each measure period and vehicle
   Available number of receiver

GIS for Spatial and Resource Modelling

GIS technologies are of great importance to solve environmental problems in the world to promote geoinformation systems and decision support systems and to share information and expertise about the utilization of remote sensing and GIS for environmentally sound and sustainable development. GIS for sustainable development meets the objectives of Agenda 21 of the Earth Summit in 1992. This considers high resolution satellite data as well as low resolution satellite data in a multitemporal dataset to support regional, national and local projects for sustainable development. Space informatics promote the latest information about products and systems in the field of space technology, image processing, GIS, computer mapping and GPS, etc. Other potential development includes very high resolution satellite images with the ground resolutions in MSS, using SAR inferometry in DEM, latest development in airborne remote sensing with laser scanner and three-line scanner, and mobile mapping system, etc. (Murai, 1996).

Space informatics require effective networking which is an essential element to bridge the gap between the users, end-users and data providers. The volume presents a holistic perspective in the above context. It is important that sharing digitized GIS data as well as socioeconomic and statistical data is a key issue to promote remote sensing and GIS for sustainable development. Space informatics, therefore, call for the establishment of a national human communication network in developing countries. The strategy needed to implement space informatics on a framework which considers people first, information second, processes third and tools last. It is essential to highlight that the human role in the environment and sustainable development is significant. Environmental practices and stresses can be best understood by analysing remotely-sensed data with socio-economic and cultural data. Therefore, space informatics will become a key science for decision support of sustainable development and management of environmental resources.

Role of GIS Based Data Bases in Development of Resource Information System

There is a need for disaster process understanding by developing multi-dimensional and integrated geoinformatic data base establishment at micro-levels in order to understand complex atmosphere-geosphere-biosphere interaction. This includes identification of key data bases like geographical, glacial, meteorological, anthropogenic, land uses and socio-cultural. Application of geoinformatics becomes essential for the study of complex parameters which comes into play in the overall hydrological cycle. This is further used for monitoring and predicting natural hazards, i.e. landslides, soil erosion and floods. The hydrological hazards like floods are the result of complex interaction between various natural systems which modify topographic gradients and anthropogenic activities in a watershed. Geoinformatics can be used as decision support system for identifying and integrating natural disaster management for sustainable development (Murai, 1996; Singh and Murai, 1998).

The Ministry of Environment and Forests has started six regional offices to facilitate environmental management plans for new projects and to improve the monitoring of their implementation. These stations are coming up at Chandigarh, Shillong, Calcutta, Lucknow, Bangalore, and Bhopal and are headed either by a chief conservator of forests or by senior scientists. These locations were selected as areas having either a concentration of industries or extensive forests. This administrative decentralization is a part of a series of new measures designed to ensure that environmental responsibility is built into all future project planning. However, the entire western industrial belt is not covered. For use of Indian Satellite IRS-IA data, the Department of Space has started Regional Remote Sensing Research Centres at Bangalore, Dehradun, Nagpur, Kharagpur and Jodhpur.

Natural Resources Data Management Systems (NRDMS)

The Department of Science and Technology launched a comprehensive programme in 1982 on the development of multi-disciplinary Natural Resources Data Management Systems (NRDMS) by setting up computerized data bases at micro-levels, taking the district as the unit. Natural resources are a great asset for any economy or region. An integrated approach to the utilization, monitoring, conservation, and management of natural resources along with protection and preservation of the environment is essential. The main objective of the NRDMS is to integrate the natural resources and socio-economic data bases in order to facilitate monitoring exercises by providing information on different spatial units — village, block, and district. Conventional land-based and remotely sensed data are integrated so as to develop comprehensive data bases in a particular area that can be used for micro-level planning. The system involves two distinct tasks: (i) development of interface technology to link satellite remote sensing to conventional district data base and (ii) adoption of a grid-based geo-coded integrated data system for macro and micro-level analysis as well as planning.

National Natural Resources Management System (NNRMS)

The Planning Commission of the Government of India set up the National Natural Resources Management System (NNRMS) in 1983 in order to achieve optimum utilization of natural resources through a proper and systematic inventory of resource availability. The Department of Space has been identified as the nodal agency for establishing NNRMS in the country. Taking into account the recommendations and suggestions by the task forces, six standing committees have been set up to cover the following sectors: (i) Agriculture and soils, (ii) Bio-resources and the Environment, (iii) Geology and Mineral Resources, (iv) Ocean Resources, (v) Water Resources and (vi) Remote Sensing Technology and Training Sectors. The various ongoing projects include crop acreage and production estimation, soil moisture estimation using ERS-I, SAR, marine fisheries, coastal zone mapping, brackish water aquaculture, water-land mapping, grasslands of the Banni area in Kachchha, watershed prioritisation, environmental impact studies for the Narmada and Tehri projects, land use/land cover mapping for agro-climatic regional planning, drought monitoring, flooded area mapping and damage assessment, wasteland mapping and snow-melt run-off forecasting. Recently NNRMS has approved the projects begun with the initiative of the Ministry of the Environment and Forests for Natural Resources Audit as part of UNCED's Agenda-21 recommendations.

National (Natural) Resources Information System (NRIS)

Since a comprehensive system is essential for policy-makers to ensure the optimum utilization of natural resources, development of a NRIS has been conceived as a major component under NNRMS. The information system would provide updated and systematic information on natural resources related to land, water, forest, minerals, soils, and oceans etc. which are, in turn, being integrated with the socio-economic data. A computer system based on a Geographical Information System (GIS) is being developed with capabilities for data integration and easy retrieval. The NRIS has advanced capability and is proposed as an integrated information system with linkages with the other existing systems. Such an integrated information system of spatial (maps) and non-spatial (socio-economic) data at the districts, states and country level, provide an efficient and powerful tool for resource managers and policy-makers.

Integrated Mission for Sustainable Development

The Integrated Mission for Sustainable Development is a new initiative by the Department of Space, Government of India for generating thematic maps covering arid and semi-arid regions in India, in 157 districts on a 1,50,000 scale. These districts cover 45 per cent of India's geographical area perennially affected by drought and floods and are located in hilly and tribal areas. Using data from Indian Remote Sensing Satellites, the methodology of the study involves the generation of thematic maps showing current land use/land cover, types of wastelands, forest cover/types, surface water resources, drainage patterns, potential groundwater zones, landforms (geomorphology), geology (rock types, structural features, mineral occurrence), soil types etc.

Monitoring and Mitigation of Flood Hazard

In India 40 million ha of geographical area is vulnerable to floods. According to Central Water Commission estimates, the average flood damage in India is Rs. 9,375.6 million during 1955-90. As frequency and intensity of floods have increased, the area liable to flood has also doubled from 20 million ha in 1971 to 40 million ha (59 million ha as per remote sensing estimation) at present. The major flood affected tract lies between the Gandak and the Tista. Hydrological system as a linking element between mountains and plains is very sensitive to unsustainable and unadapted anthropogenic activities in the highlands as well as in the lowlands. There is no doubt that the Himalaya has undergone a most dynamic change in land use due to the rapid increase in the population. Subsequently natural disasters cause great deal of harm and damage every year and it has generally increased over the last decade (Messerli and Ives, 1997; Singh and Haigh, 1995).

The occurrence of extreme events such as landslides and other types of mass-wasting are becoming a common feature in Indian Himalaya. It is very difficult to say that the hazards are mainly produced by natural fragility of the region or the biotic degradation and land use practices are more significant for the disaster process. Any change in physical configuration of a watershed directly affects its environmental sustainability downstream. The combination of type and causal processes is the basic condition for the classification of hazard risks and critical zones in a watershed. The degree of criticality is determined by the magnitude, frequency and type of hazard/risk. Most of the risk zones are confined to the slopes with less vegetative cover and densely populated regions. Few important characteristics are high steep slopes, rapid bio-climatic gradient, avalanches, lithologically weak structure, high population density, irrigated and terrace agriculture, tourism based economy and construction activities. Some snow and glacier related hazards being severe are considered moderate because they occur away from human habitation. Human induced hazards are prominent around construction activities. Construction causes erratic run-off making the area locally prone to mass wasting (Gardner, Pandey and Singh, 1997). Such processes are significant for causing flood disasters in highlands.

Satellite remote sensing is very effective in mapping flood affected areas. Multiple satellite data from IRS, landsat and ERS provides very useful information on the flood situation. Microwave data can provide information on flood inundated areas even under clouds which is not possible with optical data. In India microwave data from ERS-1 SAR is operationally used along with optical data from IRS-1A/1B/1C for flood management. Frequent occurrence of flash floods is reported in the state of Sikkim due to rupture of moraine-dammed lakes using IRS data. Rapid retreat of glaciers can lead to the formation of terminal moraines which obstruct the glacial melt run-off and forms a lake. After reaching a certain level, water can spill over and break the barrier, sometimes resulting in a catastrophic flood. The latter can also get triggered due to a surging glacier or avalanches. Remote sensing provides useful information about such glacial lakes and valleys prone to flash floods. Space technology is also being used for issuing of flood warning through collected data from data collection platforms (Singh, 1996).

Flood management is more appropriate than flood control. Thus for its management, the important management areas are wastelands, water storage, embankments and the construction of small scale integrated projects, to be given priority. Another effective method is the collaboration of states for Integrated Watershed Management for effective use of water. Flood control measures include channel flow regulation and intensity reduction by various measures. This problem should be considered as an integral part of National Forest and Water Policy. Flood mapping has been operational in India and management plans are drawn up for each flood risk zone, so as to arrest extensive damages consequent to floods.

Resource Monitoring of Drought Prone Areas

A major chunk of agricultural land more than sixty per cent, in India is rained and therefore is subjected to vagaries of monsoon. During the drought years, there is not only shortage in foodgrain production, but also its impact is felt due to scarcity of fodder and drinking water supply. Reduction in water in the reservoirs and rivers leads to decline in power generation and a chain of events thereafter. Drought indicates water scarcity. Drought occurs due to below-average precipitation or water available above or below ground. Frequent drought can lead to aridity and desertification. The impact of drought is governed by moisture deficiency, dry spell duration and affected areal size. There are nine major droughts that the country suffered since 1972 (Table 25.2). The largest and severe drought of the century occurred in 1987. It is also true that the more severe a drought, the larger the areal coverage. The drought-prone region accounts for about 20 per cent of the area and 12 per cent population of India. Over 70 million people and 18 million ha of cropped area spread over 7 states were in the grip of drought in 1992. The drought management strategy involves short and long term plan for stabilising the economy and restoring environmental conditions. In recent years drought mitigation is closely linked with weather forecasting and ground water management. Geographic Information System (GIS) is an automatic method to evaluate the potential of an area for ground water recharge in crystalline hard rocks covered by granite and gneiss assemblage. The method ranks the potential of an area on the basis of recharge favourability scores by using statistical relation among factors that are assumed to be related to ground water recharge (Singh, 1997). GIS coverage programme stores all the data needed to decide the site as to its suitability for recharge.

Mapping Agricultural Crops and Land Use

Large Area Crop Acreage Estimation for several major crops (wheat, rice, groundnut, sorghum, cotton and oil seeds) and integration with yield relationships for making production estimates has been undertaken. It is supplemented by development and demonstration of remote sensing based yield models for wheat and rice and a crop assessment system for wheat; mapping saline/alkaline soils of entire country on 1:250,000 scale and for selected districts on 1:50,000 scale; inventory and mapping of land use/land cover, using high resolution data, for the whole country (Level II) at 1:250,000 scale and of culturable wastelands of specific areas at 1:50,000 scale; identification, classification and monitoring of drought at district level for drought prone Districts and at taluka level for Karnataka State. Projects have been undertaken at ISRO/NRSA along with Department of Agriculture and Cooperation, Ministry of Agriculture, Government of India and Central Water Commission and India Meteorological Department and in active collaboration with various State government departments on:

(i) monitoring and early warning of droughts, and
(ii) drought management through integrated land and water resources studies.

Under the drought monitoring and early warning project, vegetation index map, which is based on the concept that vegetation vigour is an indicator of drought, have been prepared, using NOAA-AVHRR data. The composite vegetation index map are compared with ground parameters to establish interrelationship and the results obtained so far show a great promise. Based on the analysis of both Vegetation Index Map and Greenness Map as well vegetation index statistics, the drought assessment bulletin from National Agricultural Drought Assessment Management System (NADAMS) are regularly sent to concerned personnel at Centre/State Govt. Organisations/Institutions.

Disaster Mitigation and Management

Disaster mitigation requires input from remote sensing, meteorology, conventional data, vegetation index, and surface water index, in order to prepare short and long term integrated plan for mitigation (Rao, 1996) (Table 25.2). Drought management is a challenging task and it requires effort and suitable planning to combat it. For this purpose the desert areas are to be mapped by using NOAA/AVHRR in dry season and post-rainy season. A botanical method by using mycorrhizal fungi is being used for afforestation as they are beneficial for soil micro-organisms. Three steps are necessary for drought management: (a) short duration crops/mixed cropping, (b) water conservation/water harvesting, and (c) improved methods of irrigations.

For drought monitoring and mitigation, a few innovative programmes (Singh, 1996) undertaken are (1) Cloud seeding programme, (2) Automation of weather data collection, (3) Ground water exploration using NME based hydroscope, (4) Assessment and monitoring system, (5) Utilisation of remote sensing, (6) Improved technique of medium range weather forecasting, (7) Evapotranspiration observations, (8) Monsoon Activity Centre, and (9) Soil moisture observations.

Table 25.2: Drought mitigation plan using space technology

Remote Sensing Inputs	*Conventional Data*	*Integrated Drought Management Plan Short/Long Term*
* Geomorphological for Ground Water Targeting	* Use of Existing Bore Wells * Meteorological Information	* Ground Water Targeting * Minor Irrigation Plans
* Surface Water Bodies	* Cropping Pattern	* Ground Water Recharge Point
* Land-use Patterns	* Population Pattern	* Watershed Development
* Drainage Patterns	* Administrative Zones	* Optimum Cropping Pattern
* Vegetation Index	* Irrigation Pattern	* Optimum Fodder Development
* Waste Lands	* Evapotranspiration	* Optimum Water Management (Surface + Ground) etc.
* Soil Mapping	* Ground Geographical Survey etc.	*

Conclusions

GIS mapping of hazardous areas and potentially hazardous zones are most important as they pose hazard risk to human population particularly to poor and threat to environmental resources and development. Disaster monitoring and mitigation plan should be implemented as the efforts or policies to mitigate the adverse impacts of the disaster. This can be done by preparing a detailed mitigation plan based on the three broad aspects: (1) Maximal risk reduction based on standards, (2) Optimal risk reduction based on limitations, and (3) Saving lives rather than property. Remote Sensing is playing a significant role in this context. A standard has to be set forth to compute the intensity and risk of the disaster that affects an area. The maximum risk that can be done by a disaster has to be assessed in a quantitative as well as qualitative form. Further, the optimum carrying capacity of region has to be assessed or calculated and limitations should be made for the activities that may lead to the disaster. Certain guidelines or rules and regulations or policies should be framed that should be strictly adhered to in its implementation. Several other preventive measures should be devised that can effectively check the disaster. The most notable among them should be the active public participation in mitigating the disaster. For formulating an Environmental Impact Assessment (EIA) plan, emphasis should be given to both structural and non-structural measures. The development of weather stations network all over the country particularly in the disaster prone region to monitor the climatic variation and use of numerical and statistical methods with computer aided precision maps for prediction should be used. As population explosion and its massive concentration poses serious challenges to disaster prevention strategies in critical Indian regions, they require careful short and long term monitoring, comprehensive disaster preparedness and prevention efforts.

In respect of integrated studies of land and water for combating floods and drought on a long term basis, remote sensing techniques are used for quick generation of thematic maps on soil, land use, ground water potential, surface water bodies, potential zones for ground water exploitation and artificial recharge of the same. This will help in preparing a comprehensive plan of action for rain water harvesting, soil and water conservation, grass land development. The drought impact and severity is being assessed using the GIS capabilities to combine and segregate spatial units to satisfy complex conditions and to assign different weightages to input parameters. Considering and studying the input parameters like NDVI, soil, land use, etc. the agricultural drought is characterised, based on its impacts on agricultural area in each district, major crops affected and socio-economic factors like agricultural population. Geographical Information System (GIS) offers such capabilities as they integrate multi-sector, multi-level and multi-period data base. Subsequently, GIS can be used as decision support system identifying and integrating monitoring and predicting natural hazards, which are the major environment risks in developing countries. Integrated Watershed Management Plans that consequently result could help reduce the disastrous impacts of disasters that continuously threaten us.

REFERENCES

Bae Yu, K. and Yong Ku, C. (1998). 'The Integration of Remotely Sensed Data into GIS", In Singh, R.B and Murai, S. (eds.) *Space Informatics for Sustainable Development*, Oxford & IBH Pub., New Delhi.

Murai, S. (1996). "Advanced Technologies in Geoinformatics", Proceedings of International Seminar on Space Informatics for Sustainable Development, UNCRD, Nagoya.

National Remote Sensing Agency (NRSA). (1996). IRS-1C Sensors: Interface. 7:1-8, Hyderabad.

Nagarajan, B. (1999). "GPS for Large Scale Surveying", GIS @ Development, Jan-Feb.

Rao, U.R. (1996). "Remote Sensing for Sustainable Development", *Science and Culture*, Vol. 62, Nos. 1-2, pp. 40-51.

Singh, R.B.(ed.) (1991). Environmental Monitoring: Application of Remote Sensing and GIS, GIC, Hong Kong and EMS, Delhi.

Singh, R.B. (1994). Space Technology for Disaster Monitoring and Mitigation in India, INCEDE, University of Tokyo.

Singh, R.B. (1995). *Global Environmental Change: Perspectives of Remote Sensing and GIS*, Oxford & IBH Pub., New Delhi.

Singh, R.B. (ed.) (1996). *Research in Geography*, Vol. 1, *Disaster and Environment: Monitoring and Forecasting*, Vol. 2, *Land Use Changes and Sustainable Development*, APH Pub., New Delhi.

Singh, R.B. (ed.)(1996). *Disasters, Environment and Development*, Oxford & IBH Pub., New Delhi.

Singh, R.B. (1997). "Water Resources Monitoring for Environmental Sustainability under Increasing Uncertainty in the Himalayan Region". Proceedings of Rabat Symposium SI, IAHS Publication No. 240.

Singh, R.B. (1997). "Monitoring Tropical Geosystem, Underground Topography and Potential Water Resources for Sustainable Development Using Geoinformatics — Indian Case Study", Proceedings of the 12th International Congress of Speleology, Volume 1, Switzerland.

Singh, R.B. (ed.) (1998). *Ecological Techniques and Approaches to Vulnerable Environment: Hydrosphere-Geosphere Interaction*, Oxford & IBH Pub., New Delhi.

Singh R.B. (1998). "Earth Science Data and Information Technology Network Development in India", In Singh, R.B and Murai, S. (eds.) *Space Informatics for Sustainable Development*, Oxford & IBH Pub., New Delhi.

Singh, R.B. and Murai, S.(eds.) (1998). *Space Informatics for Sustainable Development*, Oxford & IBH Pub., New Delhi.

INDEX